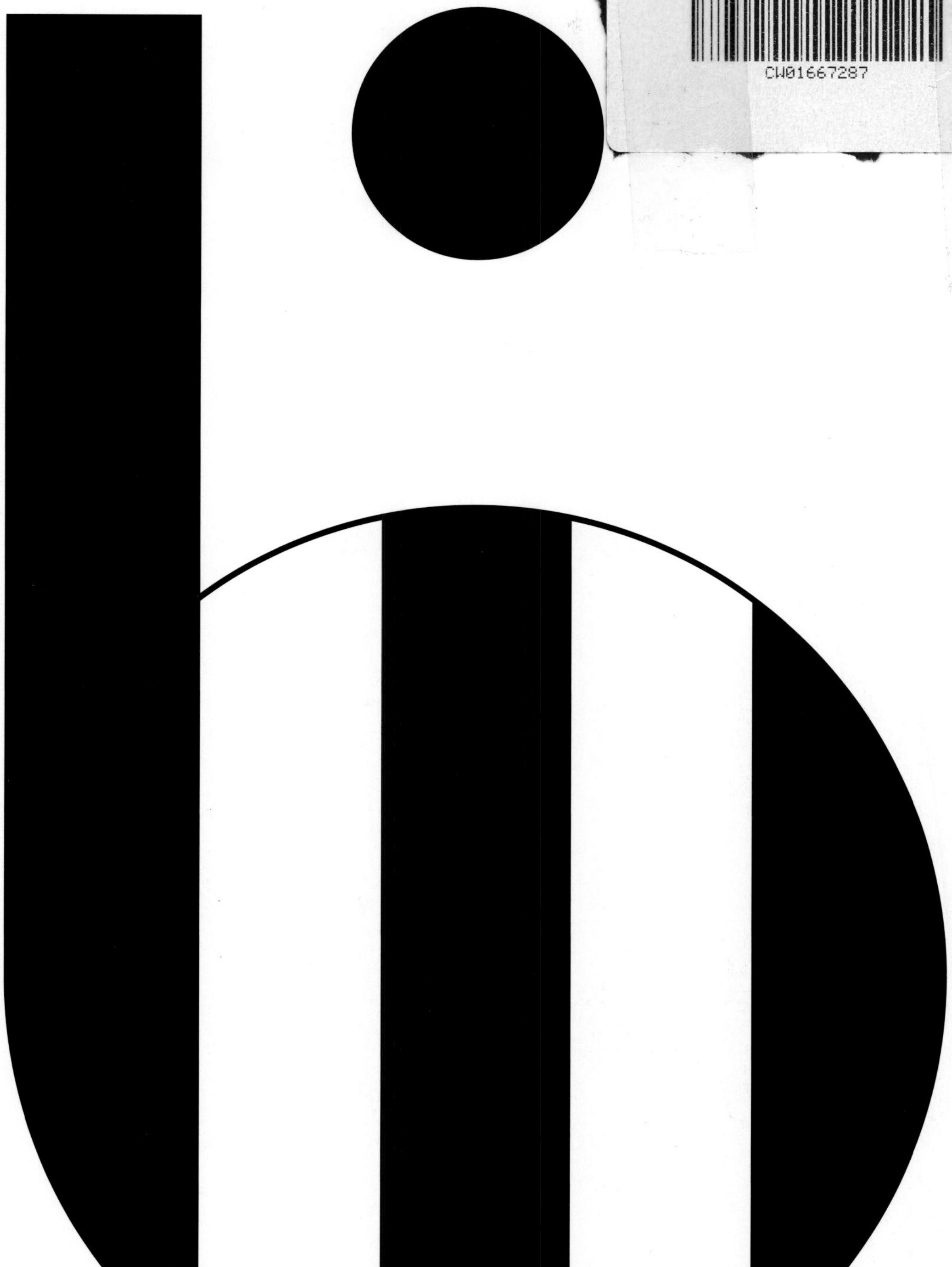

bauhaus

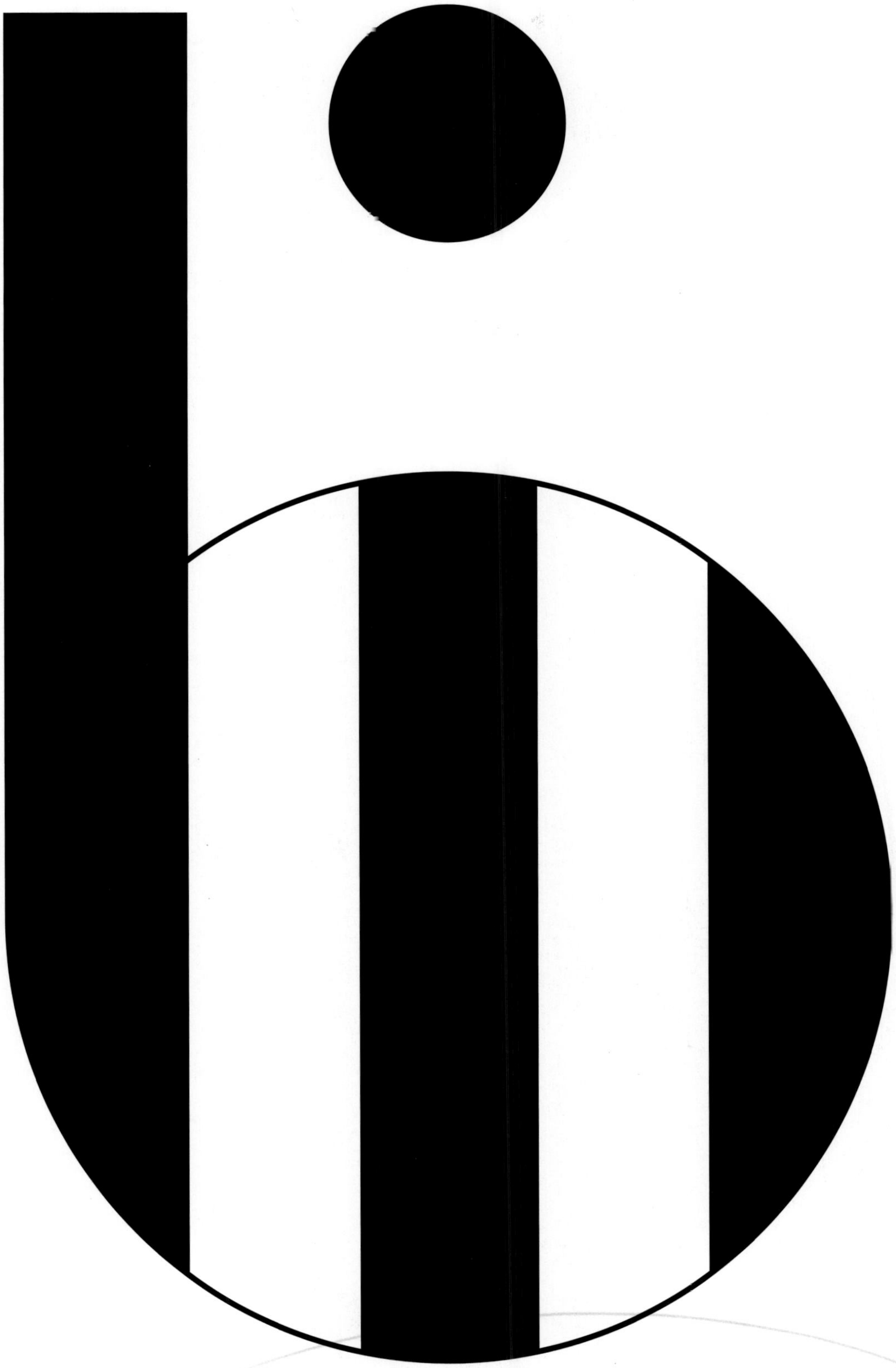

bauhaus

imaginista

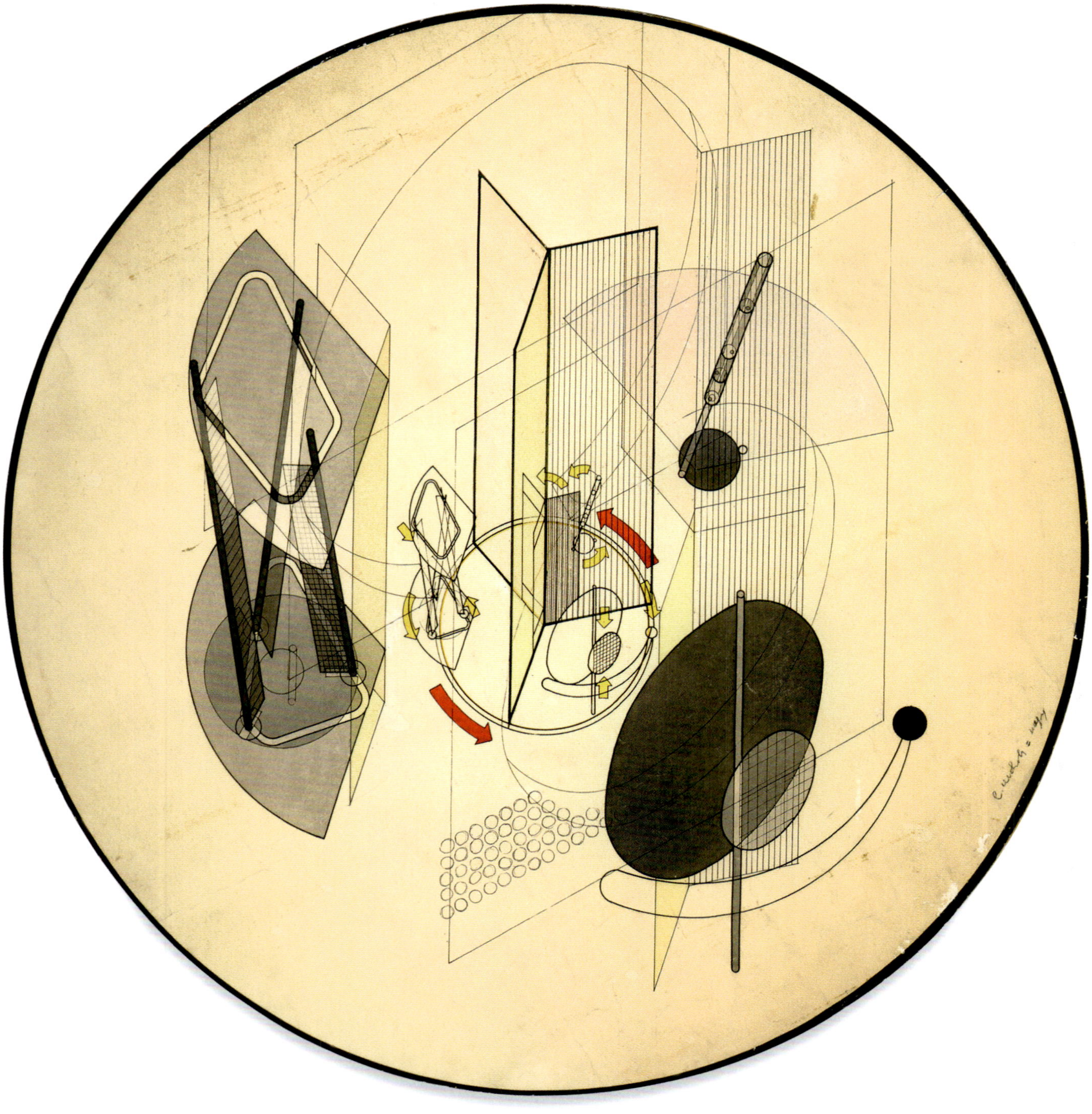

bauhaus imaginista

A School in the World

Edited by
Marion von Osten
and Grant Watson

Thames & Hudson

With 206 illustrations

Contents

9. *Forewords*

12. Marion von Osten and Grant Watson
bauhaus imaginista

Chapter 1 Corresponding With

16. Marion von Osten and Grant Watson
Introduction

26. Magdalena Droste
Walter Gropius's Bauhaus Manifesto

36. Partha Mitter
Teaching Art at Santiniketan and Weimar: Some Unexpected Meeting Points

44. Anshuman Dasgupta
The Intimate and the Contingent: Art and Craft in the Pedagogy of Santiniketan

53. The Otolith Group
Living in an O Horizon

56. Helena Čapková
Framing Renshichirō Kawakita's Transcultural Legacy and His Pedagogy

66. Yoshimasa Kaneko
On the Reception of Johannes Itten's Art Education in Japan

68. Hiromitsu Umemiya
Manual for Teaching Thinking through Construction (1934): An Introduction

71. Luca Frei
Model for a Pedagogical Vehicle

Chapter 2 Learning From

80. Marion von Osten and Grant Watson
Introduction

92. Fabienne Eggelhöfer
Paul Klee's Pictures of Architectural Tapestries

106. Susanne Leeb
Books on World Art from the 1920s: On the Ambivalence of a Discursive Awakening

112. Kader Attia
Colonial Melancholia

118. Mohamed Melehi
The Bauhaus as a Catalyst

128. Virginia Gardner Troy
The Andean Textile Paradigm at the Bauhaus

132. Elissa Auther
The Appropriation of the Ancient Past in Modern Fibre Art

142. Elvira Espejo
Watch and Learn: Local Instructions from My Community

146. Ailton Krenak and Bené Fonteles
The Bauhaus and Indigenous Cultural Production

149. Paulo Tavares
Des-Habitat

Chapter 3
Moving Away

160. Marion von Osten and Grant Watson
Introduction

174. Hilde Heynen
Anticipating the Future: Three Lines of Development

182. Beatriz Colomina and Mark Wigley
Designing Life

188. Daniel Talesnik
The Red Itinerary

194. Thomas Flierl
The CIAM Protest: From Moscow to the Patris II (1932)

202. Zoe Zhang
Modern Craft and Art (1932): An Introduction

206. Eduard Kögel
Useful Tradition? Walter Gropius meets China (or I. M. Pei)

212. Suchitra Balasubrahmanyan
Designing Life in India

224. Regina Bittner
Design for Need: Sudhakar Nadkarni's Milk Kiosk

228. Zvi Efrat
Arieh Sharon's Nigerian Campus Project: Ife University (1960–85)

● 235. Wendelien van Oldenborgh
Housing with Shadows and Mirrors: Notes towards a Work

Chapter 4
Still Undead

244. Marion von Osten and Grant Watson
Introduction

256. Melissa Venator
Kurt Schwerdtfeger's Reflektorische Lichtspiele (Reflecting Light Plays, 1922)

260. Christian Hiller
bauhaus past forward

268. Tom Holert
From Giving to Unforgiving Light: Remarks on the Kaleidoscopic and the Stroboscopic

276. Adrian Rifkin
Untimely lessons, or how we could no longer learn from the Bauhaus

278. Gavin Butt
Polytechnics and Punks: The 1970s After-life of the Bauhaus

● 283. László Moholy-Nagy
Sketch for a Score for a Mechanized Eccentric

288. Notes
296. Contributors
300. bauhaus imaginista: The Project
302. Acknowledgments
303. Picture Credits
305. Index

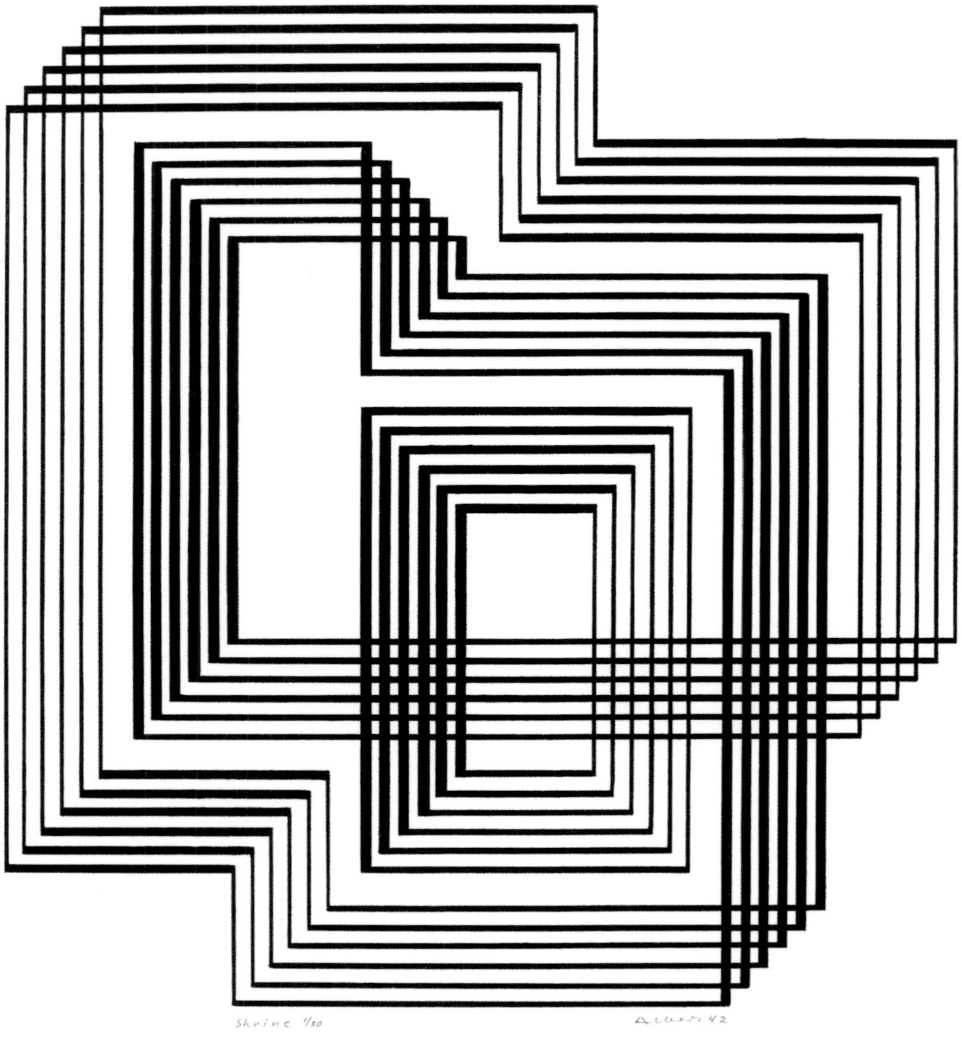
Shrine 1/30
Albers 42

Forewords

From the outset, 'bauhaus imaginista' grasps the Bauhaus as part of a modern era that drew its impulses and ideas from transcultural exchanges and encounters. Consequently, the international research and exhibition project does not portray the international impact of the Bauhaus a century after its founding as a narrative of the transfer of ideas from Germany into the world, nor does it take the iconic Bauhaus as its starting point. Instead, it begins with four areas of research, lines of inquiry with which to explore the legacy of the Bauhaus from the perspective of today's challenges.

In 'Corresponding With', a parallel is drawn between the Bauhaus Manifesto of Walter Gropius and art and design schools that were founded in Asia around the same time as the Bauhaus, and which likewise became hubs for social change. 'Learning From' begins with Paul Klee's drawing of a North African carpet and explores learning processes, appropriations and resulting syntheses of objects, ranging from pre-modern craft to modern design. Marcel Breuer's collage *ein bauhaus-film* updates design history in an unknown future and, in 'Moving Away', forms the focus of research into a modern approach that sees design as a tool for improving everyday life. Last but not least, 'Still Undead' turns postmodern critique of modern Bauhaus architecture upside down, with a revival of Kurt Schwerdtfeger's *Reflektorische Farblichtspiele* (Reflecting Colour-Light-Play) serving as an impulse for emancipatory pop and subcultures.

Our existence today, like that of the Bauhauslers, is a global one. It thrives on exchange and encounters, but also on the conflicts and upheavals that a world brought into motion elicits, and that once again influence the zeitgeist. 'bauhaus imaginista' envisions this controversial search for cultural articulations under the circumstances of the ongoing separation of cultural artefacts and ideas from their local contexts and their relocation and transformation in new constellations. In this sense, the different and far-flung iterations of the Bauhaus become resources that help us understand and shape the problematic twenty-first century. With this shared interest, the Bauhaus Kooperation Berlin Dessau Weimar, the Goethe-Institut and the Haus der Kulturen der Welt (HKW) decided to join forces. Having begun in 2016, 'bauhaus imaginista' will be realized in eight locations on four continents through exhibitions, symposiums, archive tours and accompanying publications in the scope of the Bauhaus Centenary 2019, in addition to being shown in the framework of '100 Years of Now' at the HKW.

We would like to thank the Goethe-Institut in Shanghai, Peking, New Delhi, Lagos, Moscow, New York, Rabat, São Paulo and Tokyo, as well as the independent art room Le Cube, Rabat; the China Design Museum, Hangzhou; the National Museum of Modern Art, Kyoto; the Garage Museum of Contemporary Art, Moscow; SESC, São Paulo; Nottingham Contemporary, Nottingham; and Zentrum Paul Klee, Bern, for their help and cooperation. 'bauhaus imaginista' was generously supported by the Federal Government Commissioner for Culture and the Media, the German Federal Cultural Foundation and the Federal Foreign Office. We would also like to congratulate the curators Marion von Osten and Grant Watson, who developed 'bauhaus imaginista' with a team of international researchers, artists and designers, on their challenging concept and the successful realization of the project.

Claudia Perren, Director, Bauhaus Kooperation
Bernd Scherer, Director, Haus der Kulturen der Welt (HKW)
Johannes Ebert, General Secretary, Goethe-Institut

The statement 'Art is not a luxury, but a necessity' is attributed to the painter Lyonel Feininger, who in 1919 was the first Bauhaus Master appointed by Walter Gropius to teach at the newly founded Staatliches Bauhaus in Weimar. Today we look back in wonder at all those artists who, a century ago, brought courage and radicalism, a strong social conscience and a wealth of creative energy to their search for a new design vocabulary. Art, design, fashion and architecture opened up to modernism, while industrial production processes were combined with creativity in craft and design. Of course, the Bauhauslers drew their inspiration not only from local or national traditions, but also from Europe and further afield. Years later, many of them were forced to change their perspective: the global dissemination of the Bauhaus idea owes a great deal to the history of repression, persecution and forced migration that sent many Bauhauslers into exile when the National Socialists closed the Bauhaus in 1933.

The project 'bauhaus imaginista' endeavours in various ways to explore how the design ideas and universal art concepts of the Bauhaus influenced daily life in and outside Germany. In doing so, it looks to the past and examines how the ideas of the Bauhaus were adopted and further developed in other cultures and societies; which modern movements in other countries gave impetus to the Bauhaus; and where the Bauhaus sparked conflict. It also looks at 2019, and at how the ideas, forms and techniques of the Bauhaus are being perceived and reflected in other parts of the world.

This catalogue, edited by Marion von Osten and Grant Watson, invites the reader to learn more about this discourse and to rediscover the seemingly familiar. It takes the reader on a journey through a hundred years in which the Bauhaus's central idea of uniting the arts and crafts, together with, as Feininger said, the perception of art not as a luxury but as a necessity, grew to be hugely influential and left indelible traces across the world. I wish every reader an enjoyable and inspiring reading experience.

Prof. Monika Grütters, Federal Government Commissioner for Culture and the Media, Germany

When Walter Gropius founded the Bauhaus a hundred years ago, he said: 'The Bauhaus is not a style, system, dogma [or] canon.' This is still true today. The idea that the Bauhaus could eradicate social disparities and contribute to an understanding between peoples has lost none of its relevance.

The exhibition 'bauhaus imaginista' looks at the current forms of the Bauhaus, and has collaborated with institutions worldwide to achieve this, with fascinating results. The ideas of the Bauhaus were interpreted, explored and further developed all over the world. As such, 'bauhaus imaginista' demonstrates the international nature of this legacy. Last but not least, it also shows how National Socialism played a part in the closure of the Bauhaus in 1933, leading to its further development elsewhere.

The Bauhaus was more than an art school, combining education, design, modern craft and photography. Much of what appears familiar to us today began at the school as innovative and quasi-revolutionary experiments. The Bauhaus movement also adopted a social stance, which centred on change and progress for the good of mankind – a social force of Bauhaus culture that is still active today.

A collaborative project of this kind, which successfully crosses geographical and political boundaries, raises the hope that we can prevent a resurgence of the nation-state mentality. Only by moving beyond traditional structures of thought and committing to open dialogue can we move forward and build bridges, rather than create rifts, between peoples.

I would especially like to thank the project's curators, Marion von Osten and Grant Watson, the participating branches of the Goethe-Institut, the independent art room Le Cube in Rabat, the China Design Museum in Hangzhou, the National Museum of Modern Art in Kyoto, the Garage Museum of Contemporary Art in Moscow, SESC in São Paulo, the Haus der Kulturen der Welt in Berlin, Nottingham Contemporary in Nottingham and the Zentrum Paul Klee in Bern for their cooperation and dedication.

I wish all artists every success for the future.

Michelle Müntefering, Minister of State at the Federal Foreign Office, Germany

'Art [that] contains no future potentialities', wrote the painter and later Bauhaus teacher Wassily Kandinsky in 1912, '… is a castrated art. It is transitory; it dies morally the moment the atmosphere that nourishes it alters.'

The atmosphere would alter, very quickly and brutally. The epoch-defining upheaval that led to the horrors of the First World War explains the radicalism with which the Bauhauslers rediscovered their artistic 'future potentialities' and turned them into reality in the 1920s. What arose partly from necessity, partly from a prophetic ardour, was a programmatic urgency to reshape society from scratch, embracing all facets of modern life. The effects of this upheaval were felt not only in Germany but also throughout the world, as the international project 'bauhaus imaginista' clearly demonstrates. After all, the visionary ideas of the modern era that are still with us today did not emerge exclusively from the Bauhaus to migrate around the globe; they came from all points of the compass to Weimar, Dessau and Berlin.

'bauhaus imaginista' has tracked down the many, often unknown artistic impulses worldwide for which the Bauhaus served as a catalyst. Travelling across four continents, it has assembled diverse positions on (pre-)modern design vocabularies, progressive educational approaches and further developments in everyday life triggered by migration movements. In doing so, it has shed light on a complex network of relationships that extends from Johannes Itten's influence on design education in Japan to the Bauhauslers' exploration of indigenous methods of production, thus providing new insights into the global interdependencies of modernism.

A look back in history also entails examining the Bauhaus's current relevance. The 'Still Undead' part of the project reflects specifically on the future potential of the Bauhaus and examines the extent to which this may be updated in the contemporary artistic discourse. The title 'Still Undead' can be interpreted in two ways: by being remembered in a ritualized way, has the Bauhaus long-since been relegated to the ossified realm of the undead? Or are the ideas and methods of a hundred years ago still influential today, perhaps precisely because of the multifaceted international connections?

The German Federal Cultural Foundation would like to thank the curators Marion von Osten and Grant Watson and their team for their shrewd realization of this highly complex project. We would also like to thank the contributing artists and all other international partners, who have shown that although based in Weimar, Dessau and Berlin, the Bauhaus was represented throughout the western and non-western world.

Hortensia Völckers, Executive Board/Artistic Director
Alexander Farenholtz, Executive Board/Administrative Director
German Federal Cultural Foundation

bauhaus imaginista

Marion von Osten and Grant Watson

Today, in the twenty-first century, the question still remains of how to reimagine the relationship between the arts and society. The need to radicalize art and design as a part of this question ran through the twentieth century, and when thinking of the Bauhaus, a history of radical pedagogy immediately appears. The ethos of this school, established in 1919 in the immediate aftermath of the First World War, reflected a younger generation who wished to reject a nationalistic, militaristic and authoritarian past. They believed that by reshaping their material environment through the reformation of art, craft, design and architecture, it would also be possible to imagine a new society.

The Bauhaus, in all its different phases from 1919 to 1933, was a school *by* practitioners *for* practitioners. The vision that Walter Gropius (the school's first director, 1919–28) had for the Bauhaus constituted a break with the classical art training of the past, including its distinction between the fine and applied arts. Countering the specialization of the manual and technical fields, he believed that experimental and artistic knowledge could intervene into the conditions of production, from artisanal craft to the machine. For Gropius, access to education did not mean studying for another academic qualification but rather the principle of apprenticeship, of formal and material studies, and of the workshop and laboratory as spaces to establish a new mode of design research. Under the Bauhaus's second director, Hannes Meyer (1928–30), a more poly-technical understanding of education was realized, featuring architecture and societal research, before in its last phase the Bauhaus took the form of a master class under the directorship of the architect Ludwig Mies van der Rohe (1930–33). In 1933 the Bauhaus was closed by the National Socialists and the school was forcibly dispersed through migration and flight.

From its inception, the Bauhaus was internationally oriented. Students and teachers travelled from Croatia, Hungary, Japan, Palestine, Russia, Switzerland, the United States and elsewhere to Weimar and later Dessau and Berlin to become part of the school. Young people from all over the world were particularly drawn to the Bauhaus because of its cosmopolitan, avant-garde perspective and hands-on curriculum. This was reflected in the way in which the school received and interpreted diverse influences, ranging from British Arts and Crafts, reform pedagogy and Eastern spirituality to Constructivism and popular culture, machine production and the key role it played in the *neues bauen* (New Building) movement. Art and design at the Bauhaus also frequently contained an implicit transcultural element, gleaned through exposure to non-western[1] cultures, from books and museum collections and research travel, and through interaction with foreign students and visiting lecturers.

This book provides the rare opportunity to explore a history of transcultural exchange in the twentieth century through the specific lens of the Bauhaus and its reception in different geographies and time periods. As part of the large-scale project bauhaus imaginista, which marks the school's centenary, the focus here is on the experimental, open-ended character of modernism, as well as its inherent cosmopolitanism. As the curators of the project and editors of this book, we understand the global circulation of the Bauhaus not in terms of impact, but rather through its participation in international networks prior to 1933, and how this was mirrored in the school's afterlife.

In the examples published in this book, we see how the Bauhaus circulated and lived on through its transmission by students and masters, through personal encounters, and through the study, interpretation, appropriation and rejection of its curriculum. Within this process, we see how Bauhaus concepts fragment as they come into contact with local struggles, but also how a diverse appropriation of the Bauhaus can shine a light on the school's own internal complexity, its essential hybridity. Throughout the book, we argue that the Bauhaus has played a key role as beneficiary, interlocutor and point of reference in the work of changing ideas into material forms and of reimaging the relationship between art and society.

bauhaus imaginista is divided into four chapters. Each begins with a focal object selected from the Bauhaus. What these four objects have in common is their propositional character and their material ephemerality. They consist of a copy of the 1919 Bauhaus Manifesto by Walter Gropius, the 1927 drawing *Teppich* (Carpet) by Paul Klee, the collage *ein bauhaus-film* by Marcel Breuer from 1926 and *Reflektorische Farblichtspiele* (Reflecting Colour-Light-Play) by Kurt Schwerdtfeger from 1922. Our curatorial approach has been to decipher these objects in relation to their own historical context, but also for what they suggest in the way of a future genealogy of Bauhaus forms, practices and concepts.

Chapter 1, 'Corresponding With', departs from the Bauhaus Manifesto to explore early twentieth-century art and design pedagogy at the Bauhaus and at two other connected schools: Kala Bhavan, established in 1919 by Rabindranath Tagore in India, and Seikatsu Kōsei Kenkyūsho (Research Institute of Life Construction) founded by Renschichirō Kawakita in Japan in 1931. These three avant-garde institutions participated in cosmopolitan networks and navigated the tensions between nationalism and internationalism in their respective societies. Chapter 2, 'Learning From', takes Klee's drawing of a Berber kilim to reflect on the modernist appropriation of art from outside the European mainstream. It includes the revival of craft knowledge in post-independence Morocco at the School of Fine Arts in Casablanca, the influence of pre-Columbian textiles on Bauhaus émigrés to the United States, and such figures as the architect Lina Bo Bardi, who embraced the Bauhaus as well as the popular to redefine Brazilian modernism. Chapter 3, 'Moving Away', takes the evolution of the chair in Breuer's collage to trace how Bauhaus design is transformed by societal and geopolitical change. From the modernization of the USSR to post-independence India, there is pressure for architecture and design to adapt. Former directors Meyer and Gropius had to update Bauhaus modernism, while courses at the Ulm School of Design and at the National Institute of Design (NID) in Ahmedabad both take and leave Bauhaus ideas. Chapter 4, 'Still Undead', uncovers a history of light and sound experiments, starting with Schwerdtfeger's 'reflecting light plays'. Subsequently developed by László Moholy-Nagy at the New Bauhaus (later named Institute of Design, IIT) in Chicago, at the Massachusetts Institute of Technology (MIT) by his colleague György Kepes, and at Leeds College of Art in the United Kingdom, such experiments transgress the boundaries of academia and enter the world of popular culture through electronic music and strobe lighting.

The project as a whole could only be realized by working intensively with a group of international collaborators, including artists, designers, architects, activists, historians, cultural theorists, anthropologists and others – principally from Brazil, China, Germany, India, Japan, Morocco, Russia, the United Kingdom and the United States.[2] We are extremely grateful for their generosity and for their willingness to share their ideas with us. We would also like to acknowledge the support we received from institutions in the aforementioned countries; from our core partners, the Bauhaus Kooperation Berlin Dessau Weimar, the Goethe-Institut and the Haus der Kulturen der Welt (HKW); and from Thames & Hudson.

Finally, as part of the first large-scale project of its kind – one that does not take national and western perceptions of the Bauhaus as its guide, but rather attempts to undo this episteme from the perspectives of Africa, Asia and the Americas – we propose this book as a point of departure. While we aim to be rigorous, the result is not comprehensive, and the contributions gathered together here reflect not only the wealth and breadth of new knowledge about the cosmopolitan Bauhaus, but also the potential to germinate future study, reflection and imagination.

Chapter 1

Corresponding With

► Lyonel Feininger, *Kathedrale* (Cathedral), 1919, cover of the manifesto and programme of the Bauhaus, April 1919, reproduction of woodblock print on paper, 31.9 × 19.6 cm

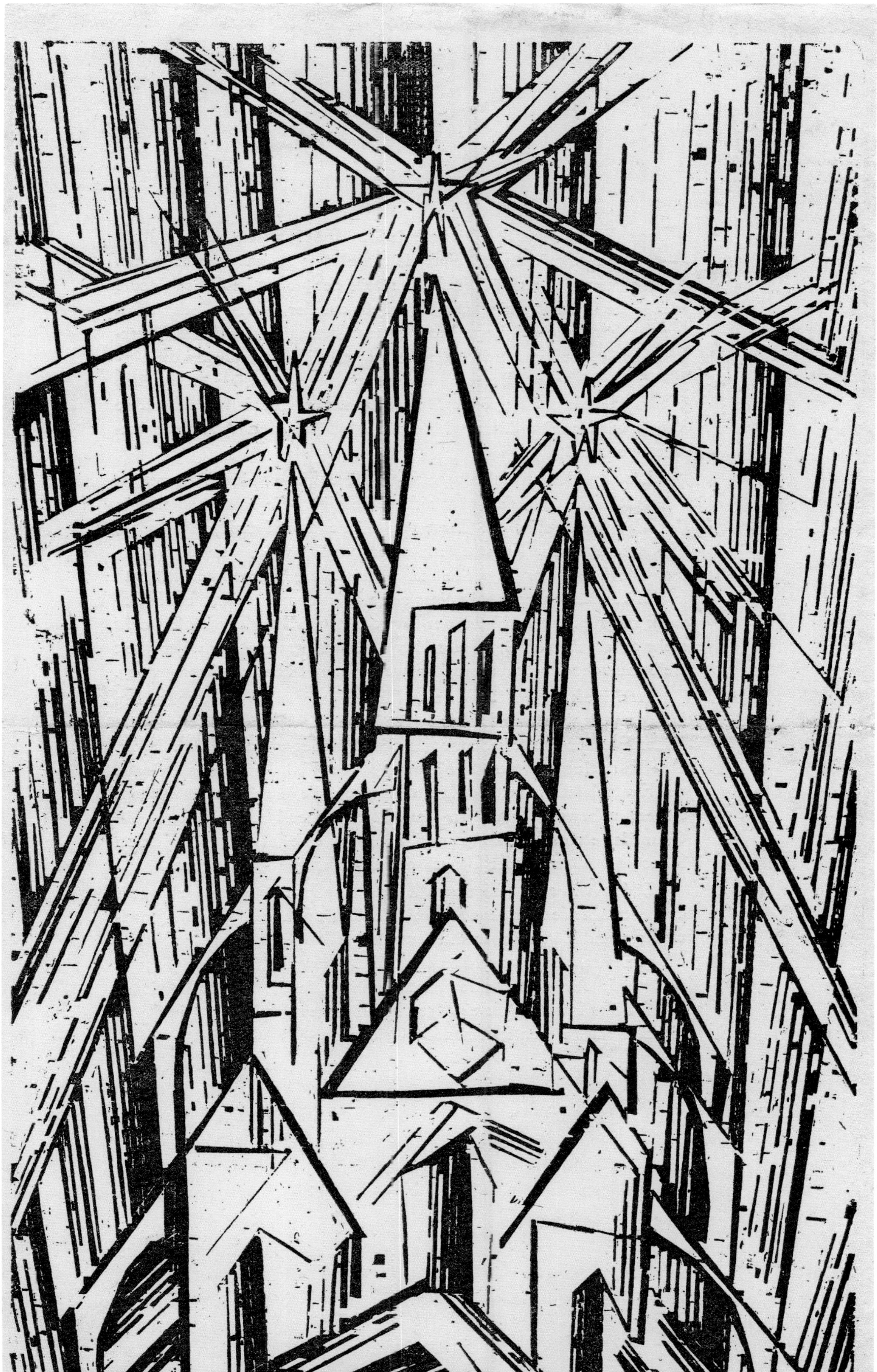

'Corresponding With' starts from a manifesto produced by Walter Gropius in 1919 to establish the Bauhaus school.[1] With an Expressionist woodcut of a cathedral by Lyonel Feininger on the facing page, it calls for a 'guild of craftsmen' to create 'the future'. The Bauhaus Manifesto looks backwards and forwards, invoking the medieval guilds to construct, as if by hand, a utopia. In this sense, the Manifesto is of its time, drawing on a movement in culture that understood the symbolic and material value of craft, which contained within it the possibility to redress the alienation and destruction of nineteenth-century industrial capitalism. Here, out of the chaos of war, social breakdown and economic recession, there is a turn towards educational reform. The cathedral motif, embedded within an architectonic constellation of light, also points to the spiritual currents that would infuse the early Bauhaus. The school was at the confluence of ideas concerning alternative communities and individual well-being. In the early years, these included an interest in folk art, anthroposophy, twelve-tone music, synaesthesia, yoga and occultism. An emphasis on material experimentation was reflected in the preliminary course, and the emphasis on craft took root in the Bauhaus's newly established workshops.

As Magdalena Droste notes in her text, from the start the Bauhaus turned away from nationalism and towards cosmopolitanism and internationalism, a course of action that would finally put the school in conflict with the rise of Nazism. The school also corresponded with contemporaneous educational initiatives in other parts of the world, including Kala Bhavan (Institute of Fine Arts) in Santiniketan, India, and the Seikatsu Kōsei Kenkyūsho (Research Institute of Life Construction) in Tokyo, Japan – in some instances literally, through texts, but also through direct encounters between people and works of art. The Bauhaus opened in April 1919, and in that same year the Indian poet Rabindranath Tagore opened the Kala Bhavan art school as part of Santiniketan, an already existing utopian community, on a piece of land to the north of Calcutta (today Kolkata) in West Bengal. Born out of the poet's own childhood antipathy to academic teaching, and the need to decolonize and renew Indian culture, then under British rule, this school represented an extraordinary experiment, which created a type of rural modernism not bound or defined by western industrial modernization.

Like the early Bauhaus, Kala Bhavan drew on resources from the past, as well as on the British Arts and Crafts movement. It looked to ancient Indian forest schools (*tapovan*), India's craft traditions, the cave paintings of Ellora, but also to Javanese batik and Japanese brush-stroke technique, as well as the continental European avant-garde, in order to synthesize a distinctive aesthetic language. In 1922 the Austrian art historian Stella Kramrisch, who taught classes at Kala Bhavan, wrote a letter to Johannes Itten in which she pursued the possibility of a Bauhaus exhibition in India, prompted by Tagore's own trips to Europe and in particular Germany, which he had visited a year earlier. This exchange of correspondence led to the first international Bauhaus show, held at the Indian Society of Oriental Art in Calcutta in December 1922.[2]

Another Bauhaus-related exhibition, in Tokyo in 1931, brought Bauhaus education to the fore. While the Calcutta show had displayed works by 'Bengal School' artists[3] on a wall opposite a folio of prints by Bauhaus masters, the Tokyo exhibition, organized by the architect Renshichirō Kawakita along with recent Bauhaus graduate Takehiko Mizutani, featured an integrated environment that included elements of the Bauhaus preliminary course and the curriculum for a new school. This exhibition effectively launched the education experiment mentioned above, the Research Institute of Life Construction, founded by Kawakita in 1931, which later became the School of New Architecture and Design (Shin Kenchiku Kōgei Gakuin). This school continues to have a significant influence on design education in Japan today. In its early days, like the Bauhaus Weimar, the Tokyo school pursued an Expressionistic style, but combined it with Japanese paper art as well as new industrial forms of production. In this context, Kawakita published (with Katsuo Takei) a book on *kōsei* education, *Kōsei Kyōiku Taikei* (Manual for Teaching Thinking through Construction), in 1934. The Japanese word *kōsei* can have many interpretations, depending on the context: design, structure, composition, organization, building or education. Kawakita used it in its broadest sense and thus transformed experimental Bauhaus principles into a new, modern Japanese educational theory. Although Kawakita's school was launched without an initial manifesto, his texts in the magazine *I See All* and his comprehensive book on art education, as well as illustrations by the students, set out his principles of 'creative/constructive education'.

Reflecting his dislike of regimentation, Tagore famously proclaimed there would be 'no curriculum' for Kala Bhavan. But through documents that include his own writings, as well as those of leading artists and teachers from the school, we can see the organic formation of ideas that would become an established set of teaching practices. By looking at these texts and instructional drawings made during the early years of the last century, we can read the Bauhaus Manifesto as a comparative document – as an attempt, in dialogue with contemporaneous movements worldwide, to reshape society through educational aesthetics. As part of the Manifesto, Gropius included the 'Programm des Staatlichen Bauhauses in Weimar' (Programme of the Weimar State Bauhaus). In it, there is a detailed outline of media and classes, a concrete plan to materialize the Manifesto's utopian vision. Perhaps it is this capacity to align idealism and practicality, to hold open the space for experimental practice and research with a social application, true of all three schools mentioned here, that makes them still relevant today, particularly in relation to building new institutions.

Marion von Osten and Grant Watson

Bauhaus Manifesto, April 1919, print on paper, 31.9 × 19.6 cm

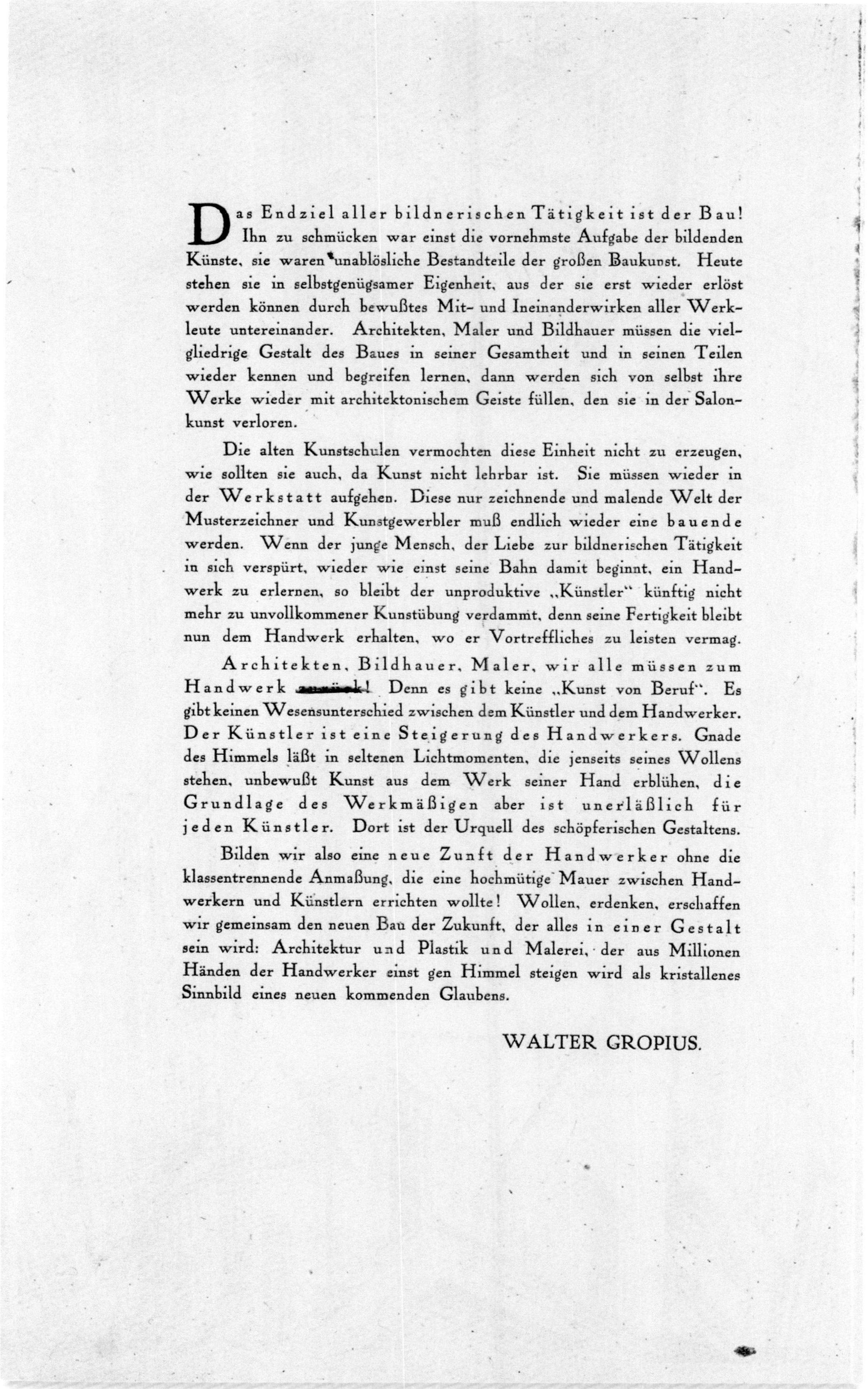

Das Endziel aller bildnerischen Tätigkeit ist der Bau! Ihn zu schmücken war einst die vornehmste Aufgabe der bildenden Künste, sie waren unablösliche Bestandteile der großen Baukunst. Heute stehen sie in selbstgenügsamer Eigenheit, aus der sie erst wieder erlöst werden können durch bewußtes Mit- und Ineinanderwirken aller Werkleute untereinander. Architekten, Maler und Bildhauer müssen die vielgliedrige Gestalt des Baues in seiner Gesamtheit und in seinen Teilen wieder kennen und begreifen lernen, dann werden sich von selbst ihre Werke wieder mit architektonischem Geiste füllen, den sie in der Salonkunst verloren.

Die alten Kunstschulen vermochten diese Einheit nicht zu erzeugen, wie sollten sie auch, da Kunst nicht lehrbar ist. Sie müssen wieder in der Werkstatt aufgehen. Diese nur zeichnende und malende Welt der Musterzeichner und Kunstgewerbler muß endlich wieder eine bauende werden. Wenn der junge Mensch, der Liebe zur bildnerischen Tätigkeit in sich verspürt, wieder wie einst seine Bahn damit beginnt, ein Handwerk zu erlernen, so bleibt der unproduktive „Künstler" künftig nicht mehr zu unvollkommener Kunstübung verdammt, denn seine Fertigkeit bleibt nun dem Handwerk erhalten, wo er Vortreffliches zu leisten vermag.

Architekten, Bildhauer, Maler, wir alle müssen zum Handwerk [redacted]! Denn es gibt keine „Kunst von Beruf". Es gibt keinen Wesensunterschied zwischen dem Künstler und dem Handwerker. Der Künstler ist eine Steigerung des Handwerkers. Gnade des Himmels läßt in seltenen Lichtmomenten, die jenseits seines Wollens stehen, unbewußt Kunst aus dem Werk seiner Hand erblühen, die Grundlage des Werkmäßigen aber ist unerläßlich für jeden Künstler. Dort ist der Urquell des schöpferischen Gestaltens.

Bilden wir also eine neue Zunft der Handwerker ohne die klassentrennende Anmaßung, die eine hochmütige Mauer zwischen Handwerkern und Künstlern errichten wollte! Wollen, erdenken, erschaffen wir gemeinsam den neuen Bau der Zukunft, der alles in einer Gestalt sein wird: Architektur und Plastik und Malerei, der aus Millionen Händen der Handwerker einst gen Himmel steigen wird als kristallenes Sinnbild eines neuen kommenden Glaubens.

WALTER GROPIUS.

Unknown photographer, Mural Workshop with works by Josef Maltan and Alfred Arndt, Bauhaus Weimar, 1923, gelatin silver print, 18 × 24 cm

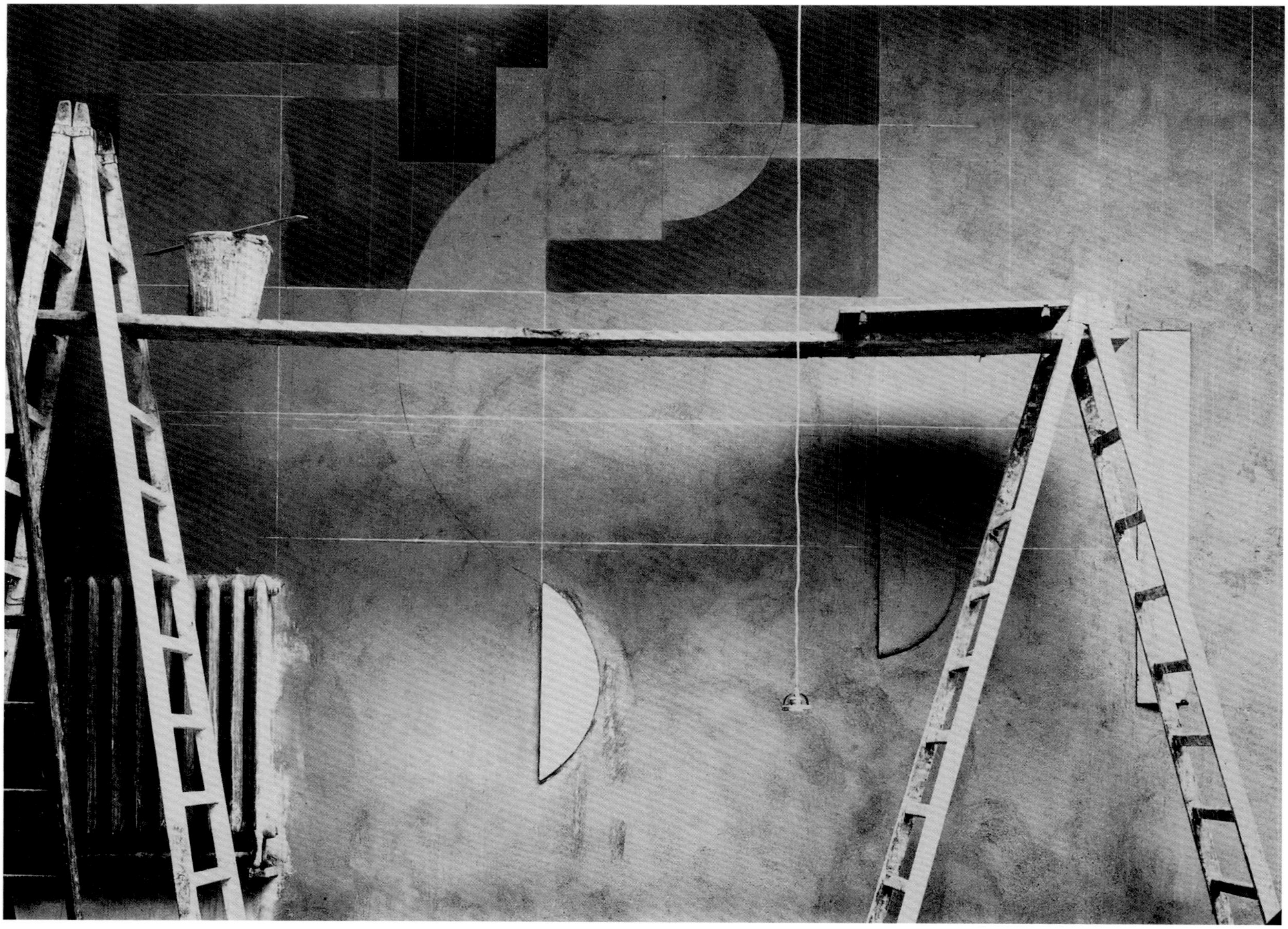

Nandalal Bose, *Instructions for Mural Painting*, n.d. [1929/30], fresco on cement wall, *c.* 80 × 100 cm, Kala Bhavan, Santiniketan, India

Kala Bhavan campus, Santiniketan, India, 2017

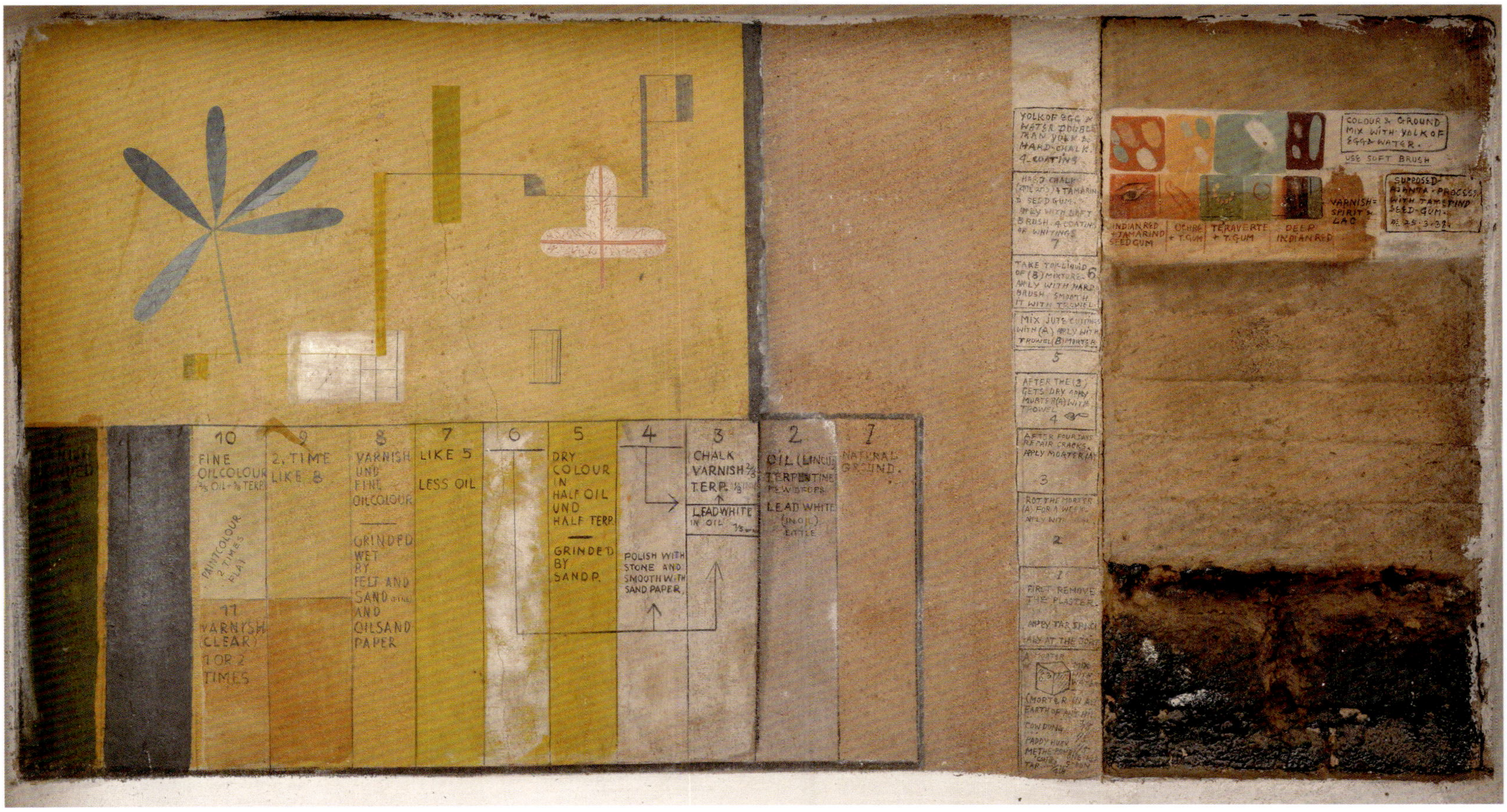

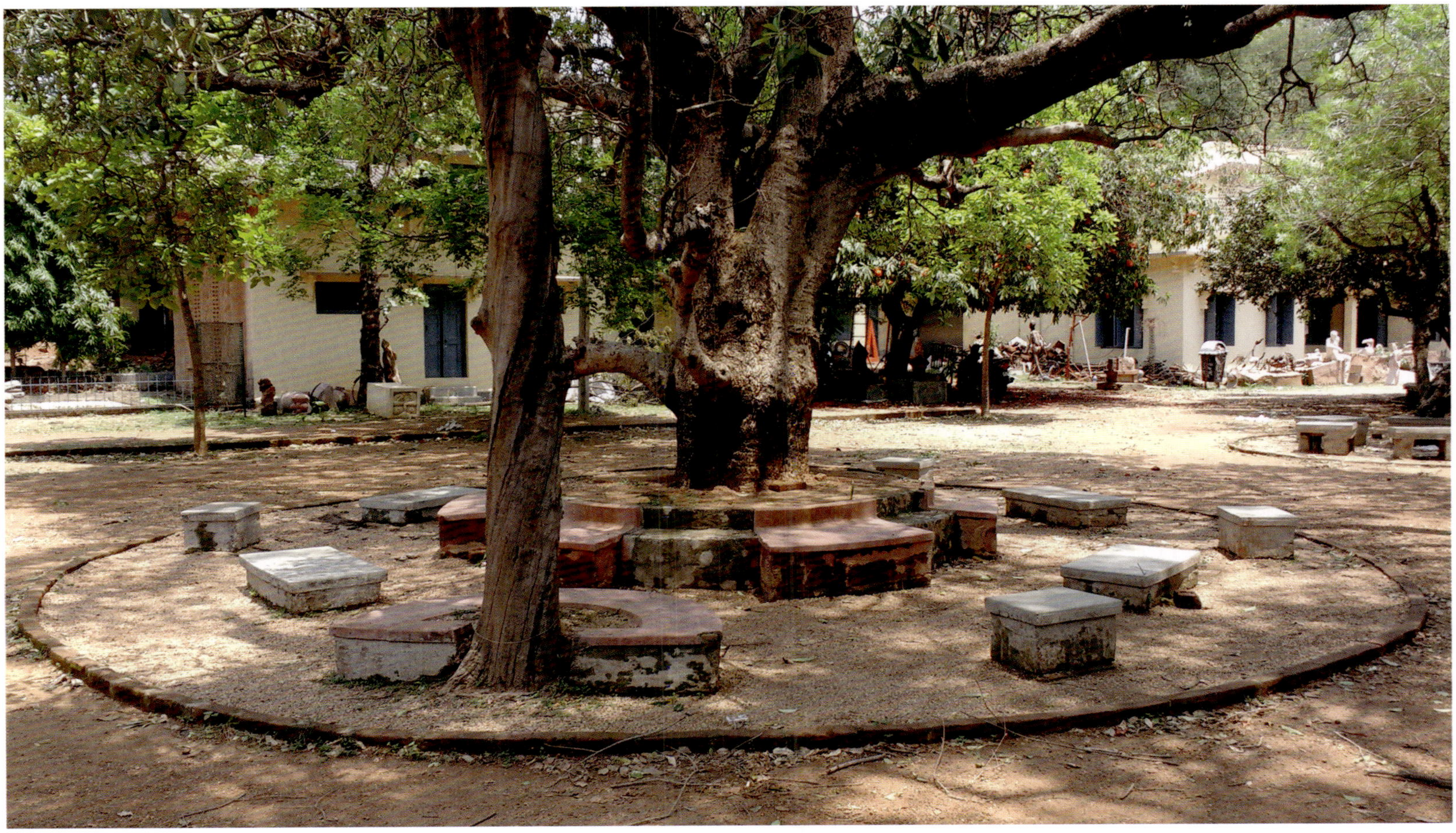

Postcard sent to Krishna Reddy, 1944, watercolour on paper, *c.* 14 × 8.9 cm

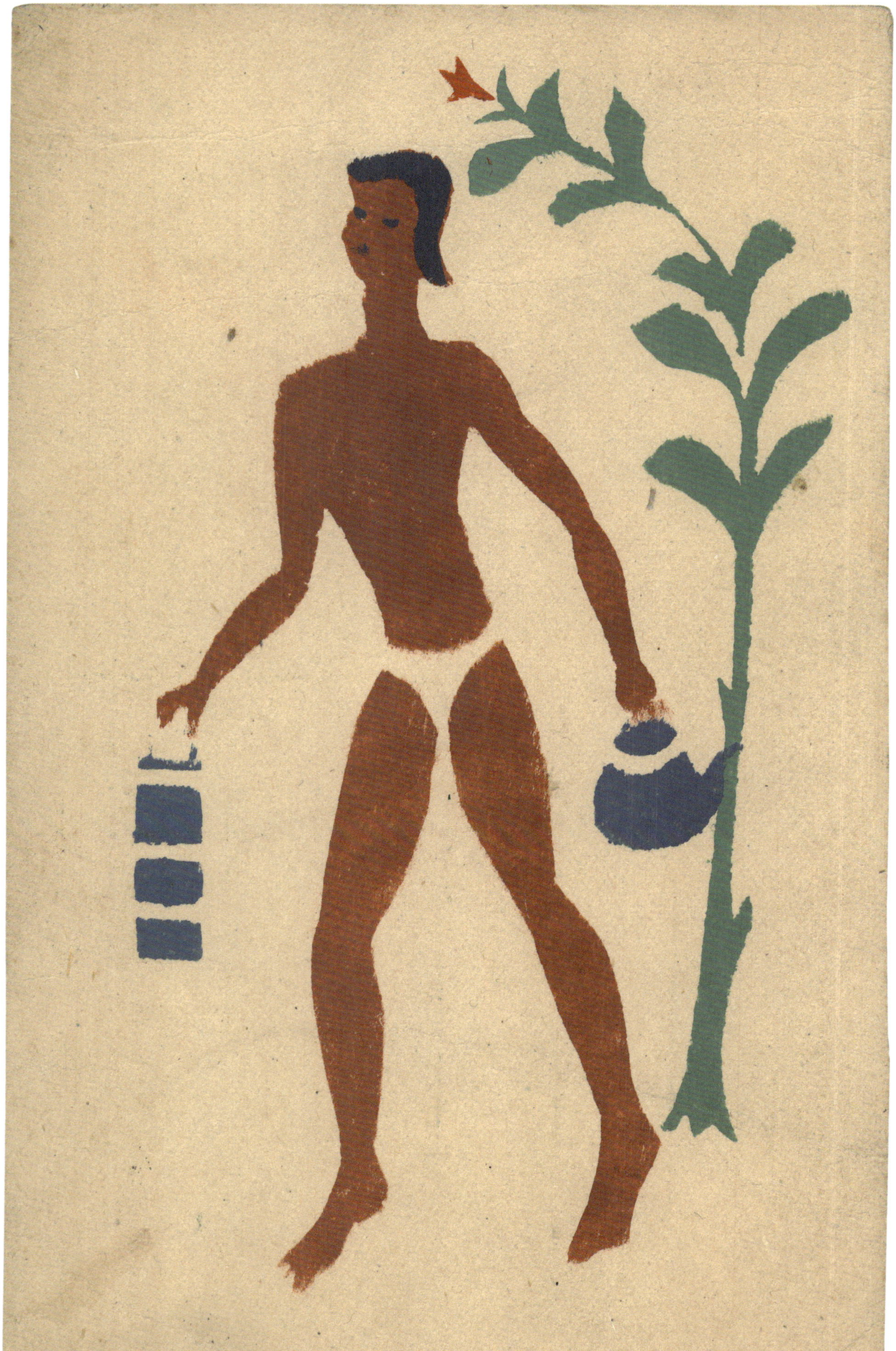

Takehiko Mizutani, *Studie zum Simultankontrast (Unterricht Josef Albers)* (Study on Simultaneous Contrast (Class of Josef Albers))
1927, gouache on cardboard, 80.4 × 55 cm

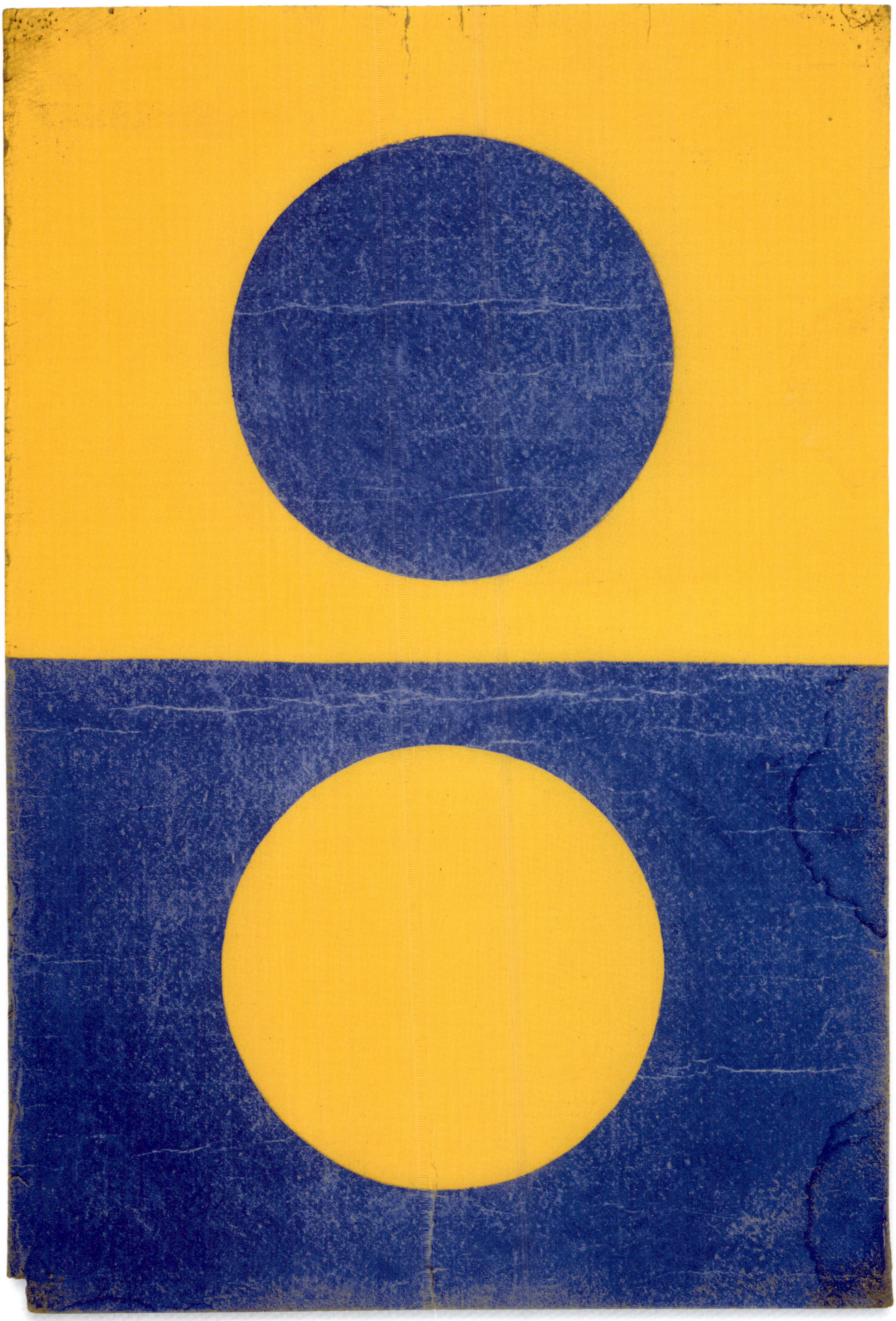

Lena Bergner, studies from the Paul Klee course at the Bauhaus, 1927–28, litho print, 29.2 × 20.5 cm

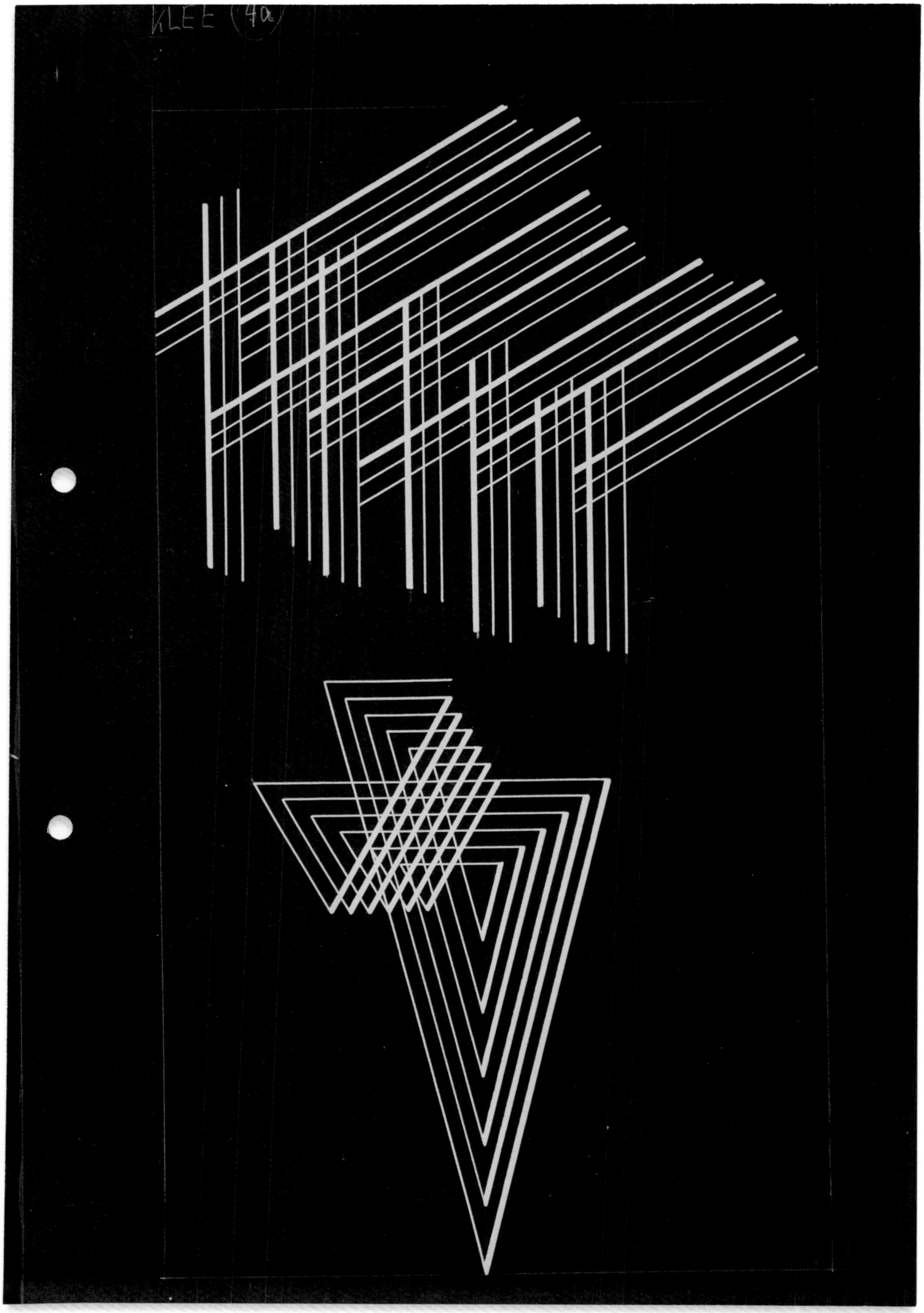

Iwao Yamawaki, Tamae Ōno and Michiko Yamawaki in Berlin, *c.* 1932, gelatin silver print, original size unknown

Renshichirō Kawakita and Katsuo Takei, *Kōsei Kyōiku Taikei* (Manual for Teaching Thinking through Construction), Tokyo: Gakko Bijutsu Kyokai Shuppan-bu, 1934, pp. 414–15

▶ Pages 24–25: Renshichirō Kawakita teaching his *kōsei* course, Wakayama, Japan, 1932, in *Kenchiku Kōgei I See All* (Architecture Design I See All), March 1933, p. 36

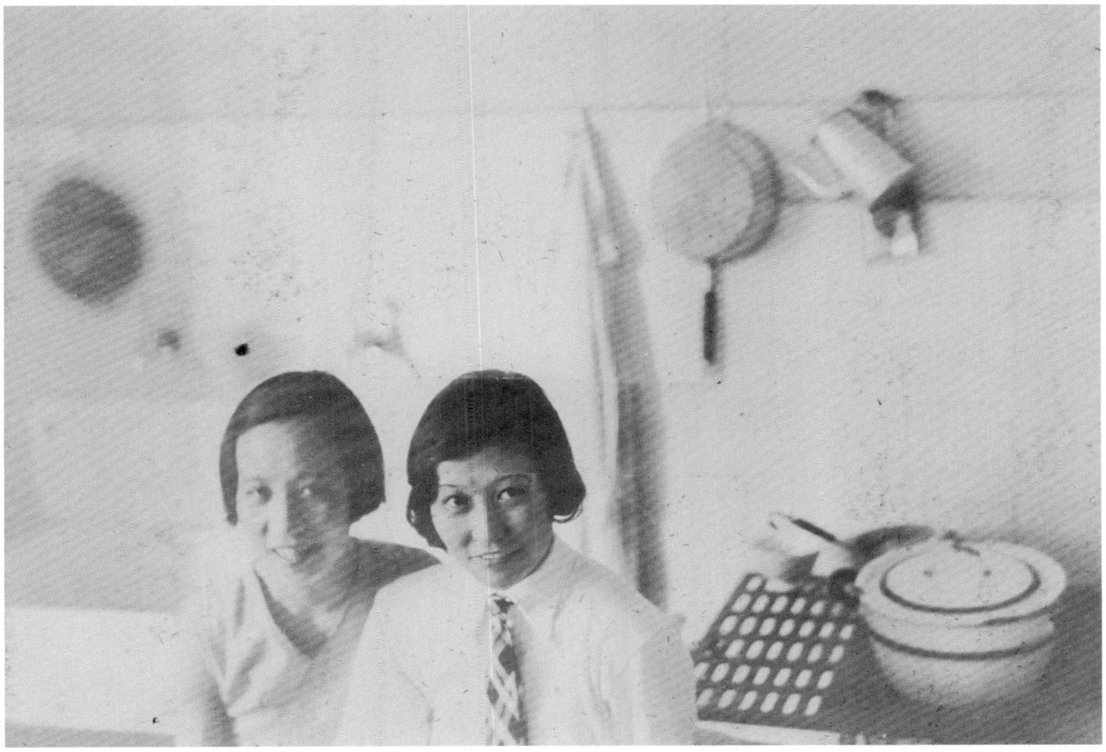

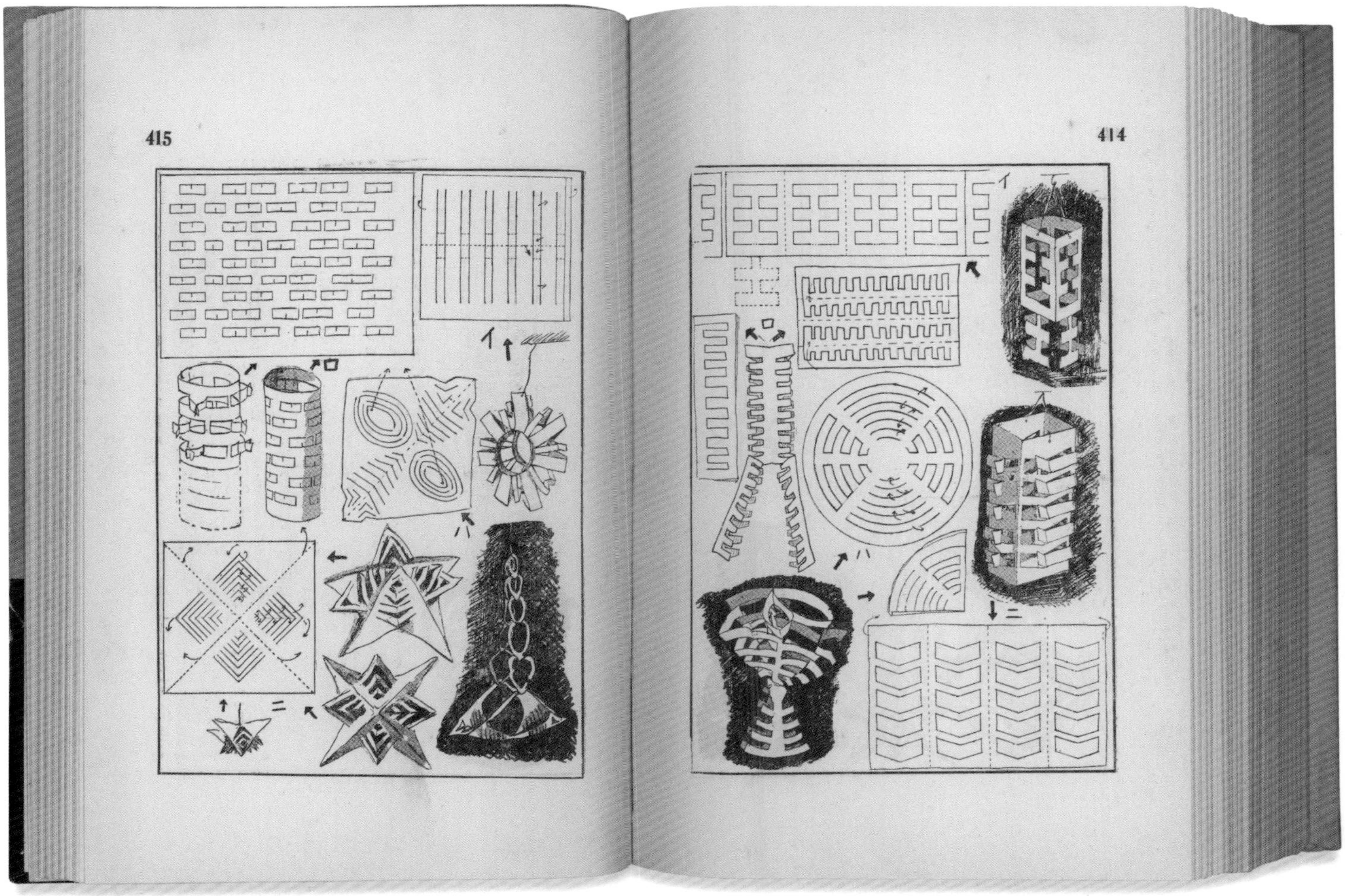

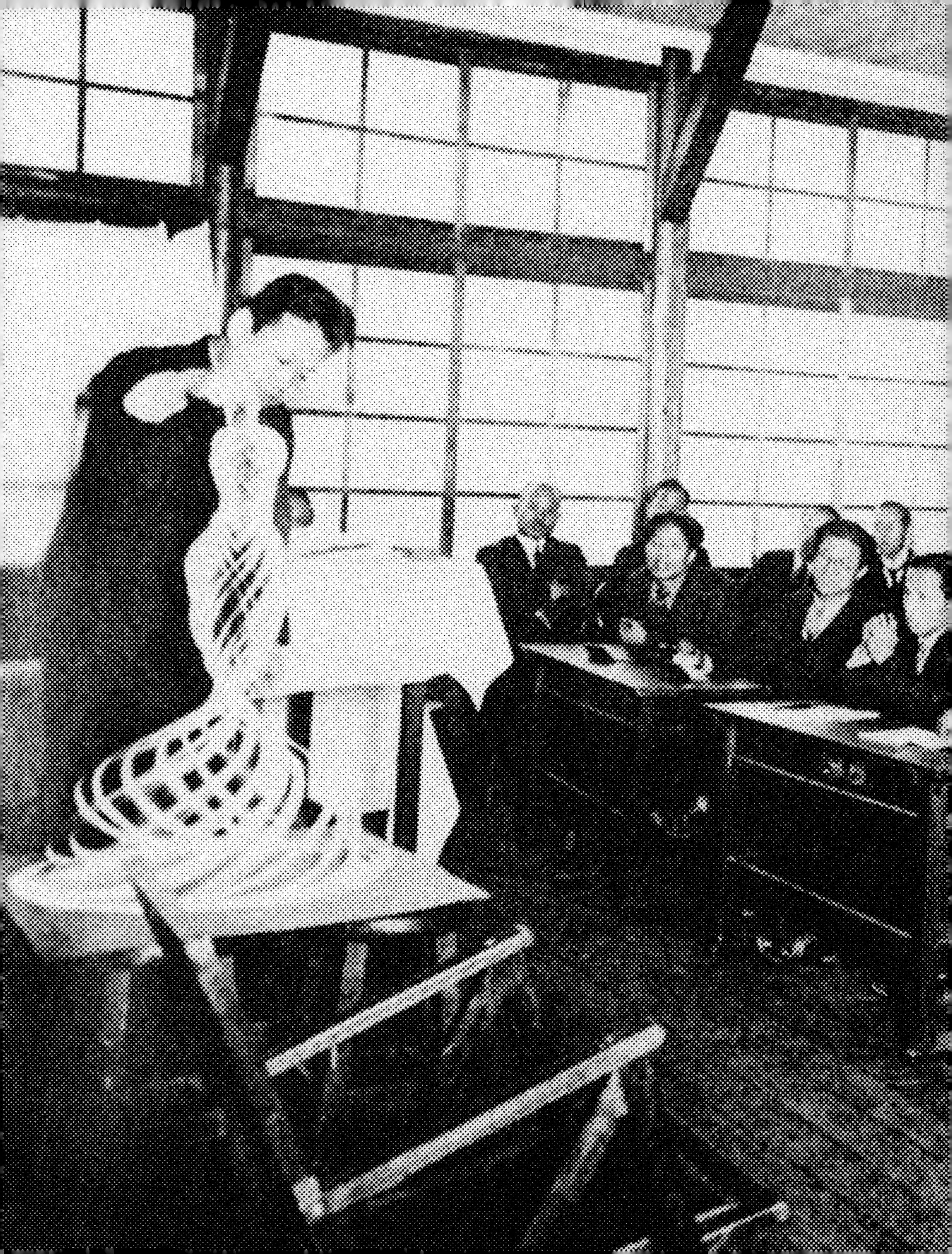

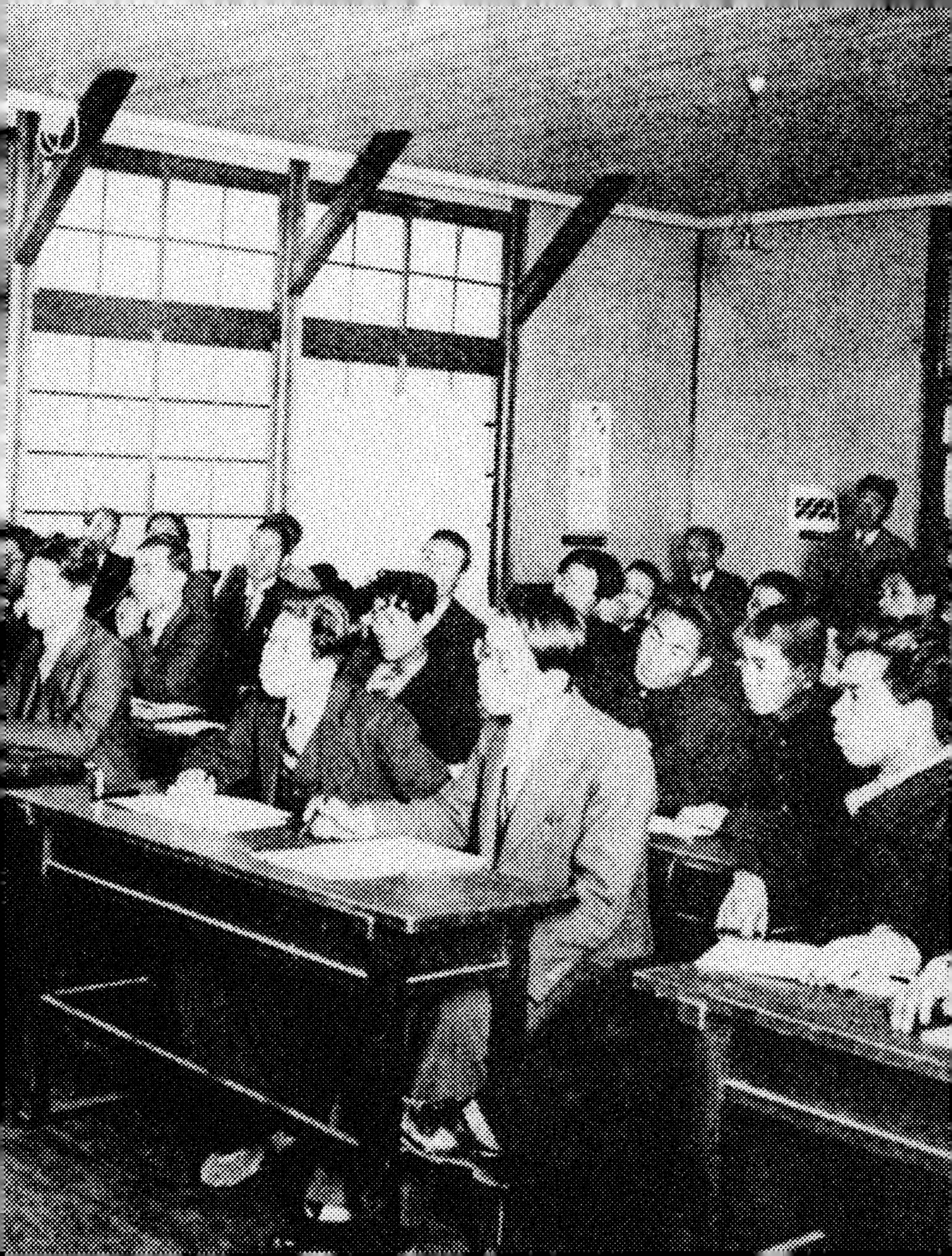

Walter Gropius's Bauhaus Manifesto

Magdalena Droste

In November 1918, the architect Walter Gropius returned to Berlin from combat during the First World War and became active in the politically restless city, where leftist and rightist forces were becoming increasingly radical. One of his first acts was to co-found the Arbeitsrat für Kunst, a union of young artists, who discussed how their art could contribute to shaping the future.[1]

Not long afterwards, in April 1919, and following skilful negotiations, Gropius was appointed director of a newly founded art school in Weimar. He called the school 'Bauhaus' – officially, the Staatliches Bauhaus in Weimar (Weimar State Bauhaus).[2] What made this particular school different was that it was formed from two existing institutions: a traditional academy and a school of arts and crafts. These two types of school, dedicated to fine art and applied art respectively, were brought together under the umbrella of architecture. Gropius believed that only a school such as this was appropriate for the times.

In the same month as his appointment, Gropius formulated the 'Programm des Staatlichen Bauhauses in Weimar' (Programme of the Weimar State Bauhaus),[3] together with a separate declaration of principle that Gropius elsewhere called the 'manifesto'.[4] At the time, this four-page prospectus was sent out unsolicited or upon request to draw attention to the newly founded school and to attract students.

The prospectus, which today is referred to simply as the Bauhaus Manifesto, begins with the manifesto proper, which has no headline and commences with an emphatic declaration: 'The ultimate goal of all art is the building!' It calls for a return to craft, and regards 'the new building of the future' as a 'symbol of a new belief to come'. The crafts are stylized as a redemption. Artists and craftsmen were to collaborate as a work group of the future to design new buildings. The name 'Bauhaus', invented by Gropius, was publicized for the first time in the Manifesto. The aptly chosen label quickly became a synonym for the new and the collective – the first of many unique features that soon distinguished the school from others.

The structure of the study course is described in the programme part of the Manifesto: workshops form the core of the school, and several years of training are outlined. The teachers are not professors but 'masters', and the students are called 'apprentices' or 'journeymen', thus adopting for the school the names used in craft guild training at the time.

Umfang der Lehre (Curriculum), back page of the manifesto and programme of the Bauhaus, April 1919, print on paper, 31.9 × 19.6 cm

Umfang der Lehre.

Die Lehre im Bauhaus umfaßt alle praktischen und wissenschaftlichen Gebiete des bildnerischen Schaffens.

A. Baukunst,
B. Malerei,
C. Bildhauerei

einschließlich aller handwerklichen Zweiggebiete.

Die Studierenden werden sowol handwerklich (1) wie zeichnerisch-malerisch (2) und wissenschaftlich-theoretisch (3) ausgebildet.

1. Die handwerkliche Ausbildung — sei es in eigenen allmählich zu ergänzenden, oder fremden durch Lehrvertrag verpflichteten Werkstätten — erstreckt sich auf:
   a) Bildhauer, Steinmetzen, Stukkatöre, Holzbildhauer, Keramiker, Gipsgießer,
   b) Schmiede, Schlosser, Gießer, her,
   c) Tischler,
   d) Dekorationsmaler, Glasmaler, Mosaiker, Emallöre,
   e) Radierer, Holzschneider, Lithographen, Kunstdrucker, Ziselöre,
   f) Weber.

Die handwerkliche Ausbildung bildet das Fundament der Lehre im Bauhause. Jeder Studierende soll ein Handwerk erlernen.

2. Die zeichnerische und malerische Ausbildung erstreckt sich auf:
   a) Freies Skizzieren aus dem Gedächtnis und der Fantasie,
   b) Zeichnen und Malen nach Köpfen, Akten und Tieren,
   c) Zeichnen und Malen von Landschaften, Figuren, Pflanzen und Stilleben,
   d) Komponieren,
   e) Ausführen von Wandbildern, Tafelbildern und Bilderschreinen,
   f) Entwerfen von Ornamenten,
   g) Schriftzeichnen,
   h) Konstruktions- und Projektionszeichnen,
   i) Entwerfen von Außen-, Garten- und Innenarchitekturen,
   k) Entwerfen von Möbeln und Gebrauchsgegenständen.
3. Die wissenschaftlich-theoretische Ausbildung erstreckt sich auf:
   a) Kunstgeschichte — nicht im Sinne von Stilgeschichte vorgetragen, sondern zur lebendigen Erkenntnis historischer Arbeitsweisen und Techniken,
   b) Materialkunde,
   c) Anatomie — am lebenden Modell,
   d) physikalische und chemische Farbenlehre,
   e) rationelles Malverfahren,
   f) Grundbegriffe von Buchführung, Vertragsabschlüssen, Verdingungen,
   g) allgemein interessante Einzelvorträge aus allen Gebieten der Kunst und Wissenschaft.

Einteilung der Lehre.

Die Ausbildung ist in drei Lehrgänge eingeteilt:

I. Lehrgang für Lehrlinge,
II. „ „ Gesellen,
III. „ „ Jungmeister.

Die Einzelausbildung bleibt dem Ermessen der einzelnen Meister im Rahmen des allgemeinen Programms und des in jedem Semester neu aufzustellenden Arbeitsverteilungsplanes überlassen.

Um den Studierenden eine möglichst vielseitige, umfassende technische und künstlerische Ausbildung zuteil werden zu lassen, wird der Arbeitsverteilungsplan zeitlich so eingeteilt, daß jeder angehende Architekt, Maler oder Bildhauer auch an einem Teil der anderen Lehrgänge teilnehmen kann.

Aufnahme.

Aufgenommen wird jede unbescholtene Person ohne Rücksicht auf Alter und Geschlecht, deren Vorbildung vom Meisterrat des Bauhauses als ausreichend erachtet wird, und soweit es der Raum zuläßt. Das Lehrgeld beträgt jährlich 180 Mark (es soll mit steigendem Verdienst des Bauhauses allmählich ganz verschwinden). Außerdem ist eine einmalige Aufnahmegebühr von 20 Mark zu zahlen. Ausländer zahlen den doppelten Betrag. Anfragen sind an das Sekretariat des Staatlichen Bauhauses in Weimar zu richten.

APRIL 1919.

Die Leitung des
Staatlichen Bauhauses in Weimar:
Walter Gropius.

The cover of the Manifesto was created by the painter Lyonel Feininger, whom Gropius knew from the Arbeitsrat für Kunst, and whom he appointed the Bauhaus's first master. Feininger's cover consists of a woodcut of a Gothic cathedral, which has often been interpreted in programmatic terms, with the three stars above the spire symbolizing the arts of sculpture, architecture and painting working together on the 'grand building'. The woodcut lent the newly established school an identity that conveyed Feininger's Expressionistic style – the most modern form of expression in 1919. A short while later, Gropius spoke of the 'cathedral of the future'.[5]

In many respects the Manifesto is Janus-faced, with the text and image pointing to both the past and the future. The cathedral on the cover stands for the past, for the church masons' guild of the Middle Ages.[6] It was believed that the craftsmen and artists of that time were united to create the 'grand building', a notion that had arisen during the German Romantic period. Around 1919, Gothicism and Romanticism merged to become components of a concept of modernization pointing to the future. The idea of the future was an important message conveyed by the Manifesto, with the text and image symbolizing the dawn of a new culture.

Its idealistically formulated goals and recourses to the Gothic and Romantic periods firmly anchor the Manifesto in German cultural traditions and in the contemporary situation of the country's defeat in the First World War. Gropius's response to the present was open to the future and accompanied by a rejection of all forms of nationalism. In the following years, he made the school international, as can be seen in the selection of masters: Feininger was German-American, Johannes Itten and Paul Klee were from Switzerland, Wassily Kandinsky was Russian, and László Moholy-Nagy hailed from Hungary. A third of the students had a foreign background.

India

It was this openness to the world that in 1922 made it possible for 250 works by Bauhaus masters and two female students to be sent to Calcutta (present-day Kolkata) in India.[7] This was facilitated by the Viennese art historian Stella Kramrisch, who had arrived in Calcutta via London to teach at the Kala Bhavan art school, founded in 1919. She had written to Master Itten, whom she possibly knew from Vienna, where in 1917 Itten had delivered a lecture, 'On Composition', in the art-historical seminar attended by Kramrisch.[8] When the exhibition of Bauhaus works was presented in December 1922, 'India' had already been a frequent topic of discussion at the Bauhaus. Indeed, the keywords that Gropius had written down for his first speech to the students were 'Building! Designing! Gothic – India!'[9]

For Gropius, the Indian temples were collective works by artists and craftsmen. Itten was looking for a different India, seeking to lend his art a higher meaning, one imbued with spirituality, and in 1921 he focused on Rabindranath Tagore, who had received the Nobel Prize in Literature in 1913 and whose sixtieth birthday was celebrated in Weimar in January 1921 (see opposite). Both cultures, German and Indian, viewed each other in a selective manner. The Indian art school wanted to understand the potentials of abstract art and was especially interested in the works of the painters Klee, Kandinsky and Itten. Imagined India and real India encountered each other repeatedly from 1919 onwards. Today, the 1922 exhibition in Calcutta is considered a crossing point between two reform-oriented art schools in the international transfer of modernism.

Japan

At first sight, the crossing points between the Bauhaus and Japan are less distinct. No strong sense of Japan can be detected at the Weimar Bauhaus itself. The oft-cited 'Japanese' adaptations via the architecture of Frank Lloyd Wright and the De Stijl architects did not attain a semantic value of their own.[10] In the Japanese discourse of modernism, the Bauhaus came into view only in 1924,[11] with Itten playing a role in this context as well. The Japanese architect Nakata Teinosuke had written about his visit to the Bauhaus in 1924, and this marked the start of the Bauhaus's reception in Japan. A few years later, in 1931, the Japanese architect Renshichirō Kawakita founded an art school in the spirit of the Bauhaus and appointed the first Japanese Bauhaus student, Takehiko Mizutani.[12] Practices of the preliminary courses held by Itten and Josef Albers were also adopted. Mizutani had been a Bauhaus student from 1927 to 1929. At the time, his fellow student Edmund Collein created a collage showing Mizutani holding an enlarged glass circle in front of his body (see page 34). Its pattern is as enigmatic as the student, who is met with a 'foreign gaze'.

The couple Iwao and Michiko Yamawaki came to the Bauhaus in Dessau shortly afterwards. Iwao Yamawaki appropriated the technique of collage and in 1932 created the collage *Der Schlag gegen das Bauhaus* (The Attack on the Bauhaus), which is today regarded as an illustration and denouncement of the forced closing of the Bauhaus in Dessau. Alienation and adaptation appear as a fluid process here in the microcosm of the Bauhaus. During their travels through Germany and Europe, the couple shot numerous photographs that can today be read as testimonies to the Japanese appropriation of modernism.[13] They sought to blend their Japanese tradition with Bauhaus modernism, and are today considered its most significant ambassadors in Japan.[14] They also went on to teach at Kawakita's Japanese institution.

Programme for a celebration in honour of Rabindranath Tagore's sixtieth birthday at Deutsches Nationaltheater, Weimar, 29 May 1921

► Pages 30–31: Johannes Itten, *Porträt Tagore* (Portrait of Tagore), 1921, pencil on paper, 17.5 × 22 cm

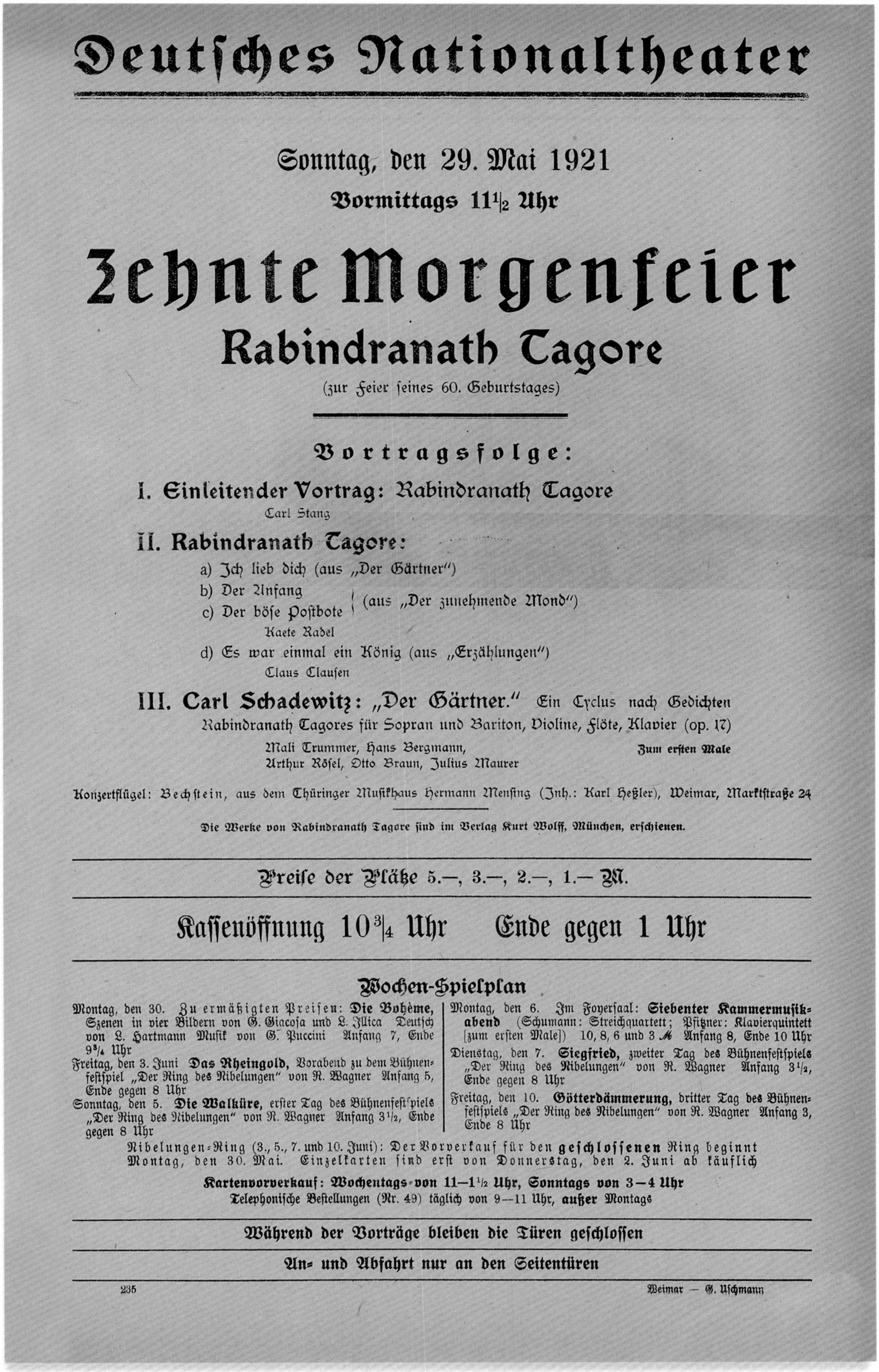

Deutsches Nationaltheater

Sonntag, den 29. Mai 1921

Vormittags 11½ Uhr

Zehnte Morgenfeier

Rabindranath Tagore

(zur Feier seines 60. Geburtstages)

Vortragsfolge:

I. Einleitender Vortrag: Rabindranath Tagore
Carl Stang

II. Rabindranath Tagore:
a) Ich lieb dich (aus „Der Gärtner")
b) Der Anfang
c) Der böse Postbote } (aus „Der zunehmende Mond")
Kaete Radel
d) Es war einmal ein König (aus „Erzählungen")
Claus Clausen

III. Carl Schadewitz: „Der Gärtner." Ein Cyclus nach Gedichten Rabindranath Tagores für Sopran und Bariton, Violine, Flöte, Klavier (op. 17)
Mali Trummer, Hans Bergmann, Arthur Rösel, Otto Braun, Julius Maurer — **Zum ersten Male**

Konzertflügel: Bechstein, aus dem Thüringer Musikhaus Hermann Mensing (Inh.: Karl Heßler), Weimar, Marktstraße 24

Die Werke von Rabindranath Tagore sind im Verlag Kurt Wolff, München, erschienen.

Preise der Plätze 5.—, 3.—, 2.—, 1.— M.

Kassenöffnung 10¾ Uhr   Ende gegen 1 Uhr

Wochen-Spielplan

Montag, den 30. Zu ermäßigten Preisen: **Die Bohème,** Szenen in vier Bildern von G. Giacosa und L. Illica Deutsch von L. Hartmann Musik von G. Puccini Anfang 7, Ende 9¾ Uhr

Freitag, den 3. Juni **Das Rheingold,** Vorabend zu dem Bühnenfestspiel „Der Ring des Nibelungen" von R. Wagner Anfang 5, Ende gegen 8 Uhr

Sonntag, den 5. **Die Walküre,** erster Tag des Bühnenfestspiels „Der Ring des Nibelungen" von R. Wagner Anfang 3½, Ende gegen 8 Uhr

Montag, den 6. Im Foyersaal: **Siebenter Kammermusikabend** (Schumann: Streichquartett; Pfitzner: Klavierquintett [zum ersten Male]) 10, 8, 6 und 3 M Anfang 8, Ende 10 Uhr

Dienstag, den 7. **Siegfried,** zweiter Tag des Bühnenfestspiels „Der Ring des Nibelungen" von R. Wagner Anfang 3½, Ende gegen 8 Uhr

Freitag, den 10. **Götterdämmerung,** dritter Tag des Bühnenfestspiels „Der Ring des Nibelungen" von R. Wagner Anfang 3, Ende 8 Uhr

Nibelungen-Ring (3., 5., 7. und 10. Juni): Der Vorverkauf für den **geschlossenen** Ring beginnt Montag, den 30. Mai. Einzelkarten sind erst von Donnerstag, den 2. Juni ab käuflich

Kartenvorverkauf: Wochentags von 11–1½ Uhr, Sonntags von 3–4 Uhr
Telephonische Bestellungen (Nr. 49) täglich von 9—11 Uhr, **außer** Montags

Während der Vorträge bleiben die Türen geschlossen

An- und Abfahrt nur an den Seitentüren

235   Weimar — G. Uschmann

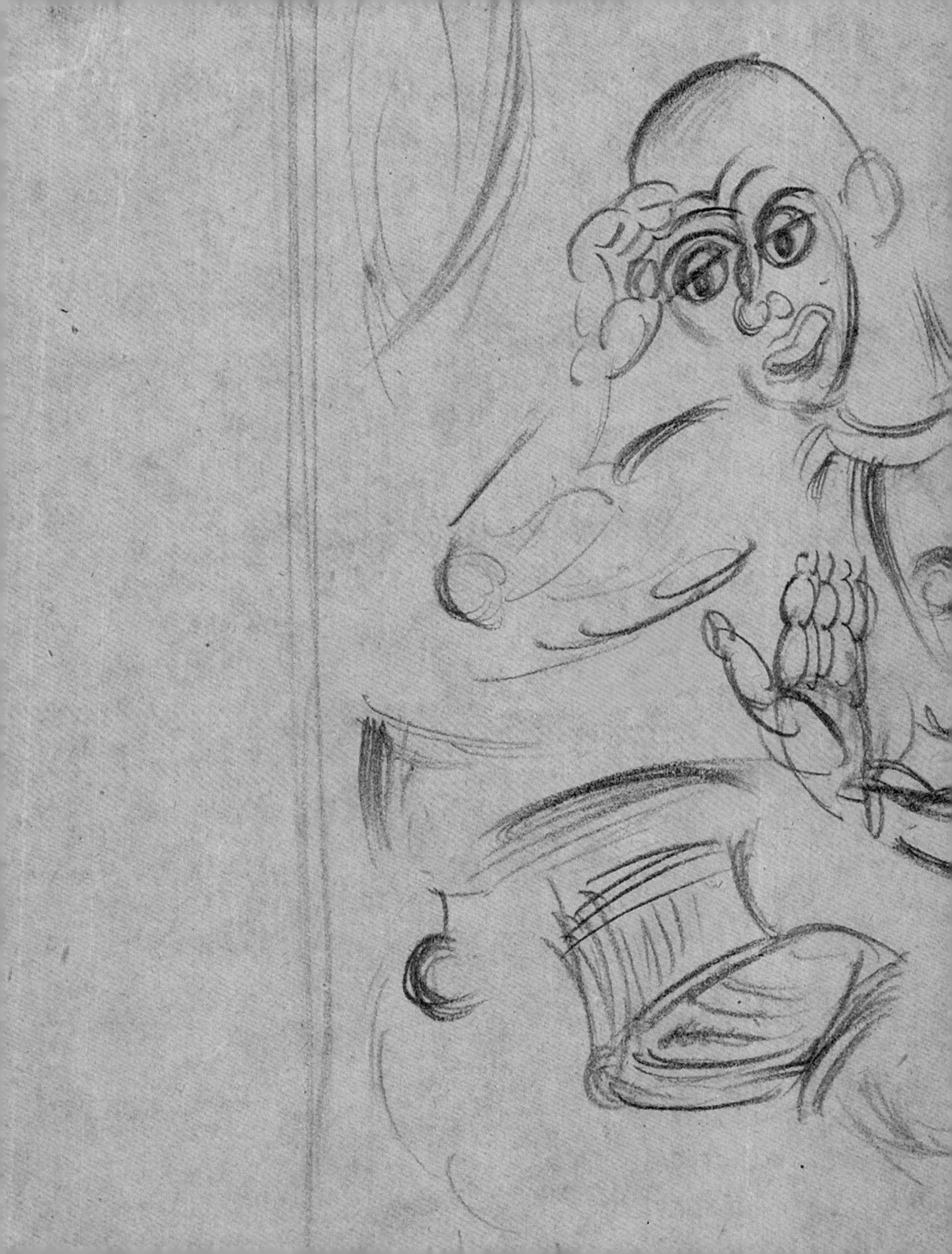

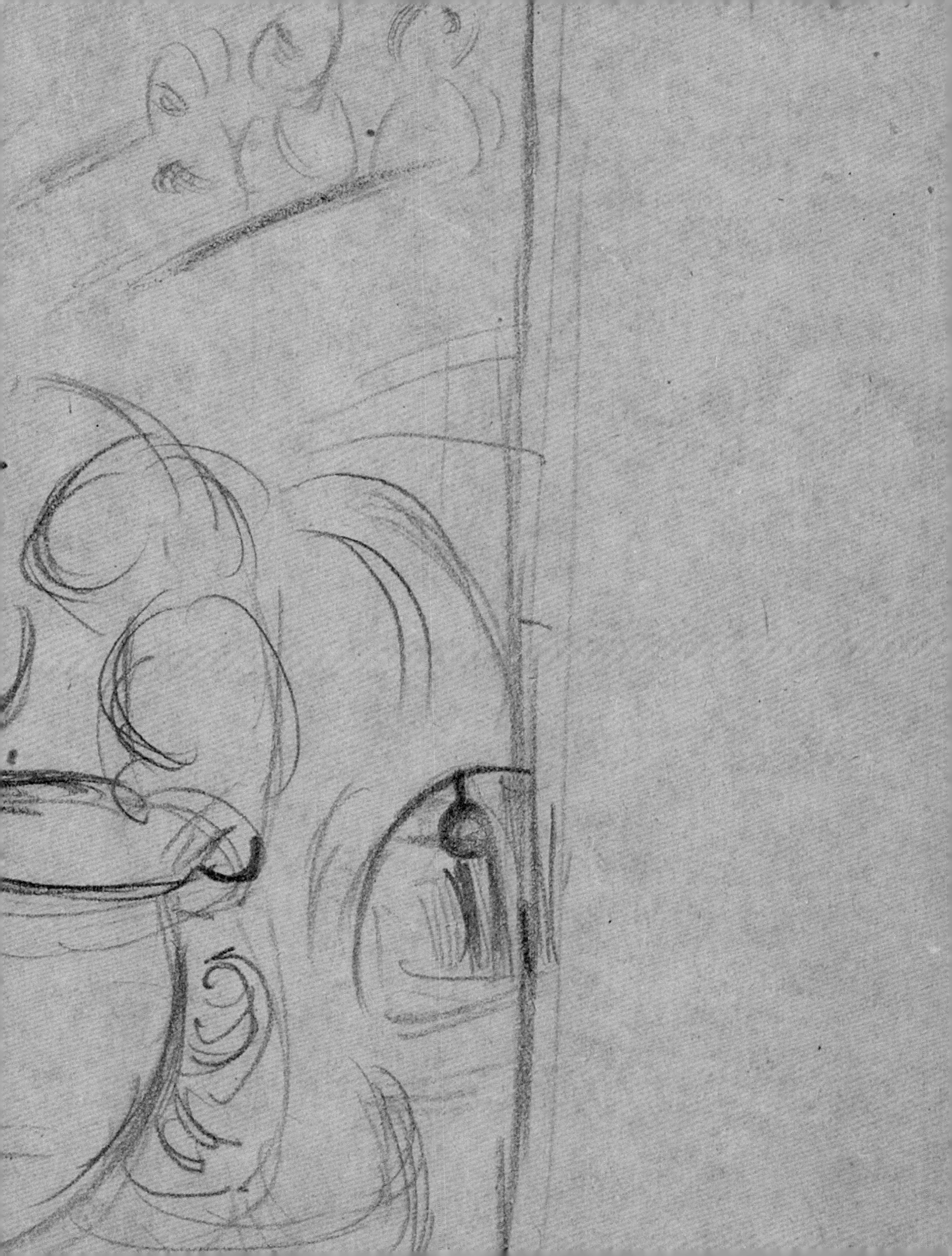

Lyonel Feininger, list of artworks for an exhibition at the Indian Society of Oriental Art in Calcutta (Kolkata), India, 1922, manuscript

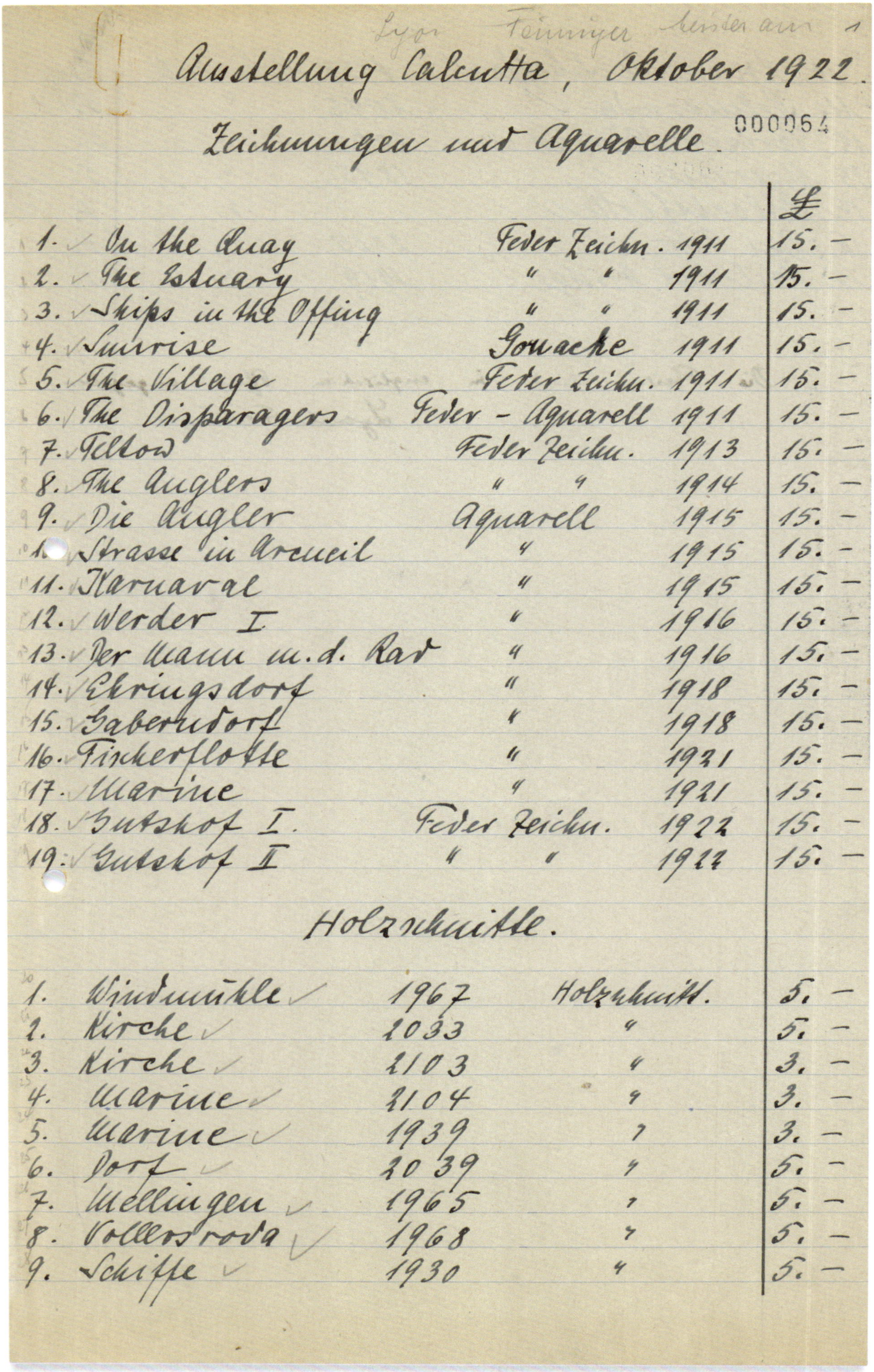

Ausstellung Calcutta, Oktober 1922.

000064

Zeichnungen und Aquarelle.

				£
1.	On the Quay	Feder Zeichn.	1911	15.–
2.	The Estuary	" "	1911	15.–
3.	Ships in the Offing	" "	1911	15.–
4.	Sunrise	Gouache	1911	15.–
5.	The Village	Feder Zeichn.	1911	15.–
6.	The Disparagers	Feder – Aquarell	1911	15.–
7.	Tellow	Feder Zeichn.	1913	15.–
8.	The Anglers	" "	1914	15.–
9.	Die Angler	Aquarell	1915	15.–
10.	Strasse in Arcueil	"	1915	15.–
11.	Karnaval	"	1915	15.–
12.	Werder I	"	1916	15.–
13.	Der Mann m.d. Rad	"	1916	15.–
14.	Ehringsdorf	"	1918	15.–
15.	Gaberndorf	"	1918	15.–
16.	Fischerflotte	"	1921	15.–
17.	Marine	"	1921	15.–
18.	Gutshof I.	Feder Zeichn.	1922	15.–
19.	Gutshof II	" "	1922	15.–

Holzschnitte.

1.	Windmühle	1967	Holzschnitt.	5.–
2.	Kirche	2033	"	5.–
3.	Kirche	2103	"	3.–
4.	Marine	2104	"	3.–
5.	Marine	1939	"	3.–
6.	Dorf	2039	"	5.–
7.	Mellingen	1965	"	5.–
8.	Vollersroda	1968	"	5.–
9.	Schiffe	1930	"	5.–

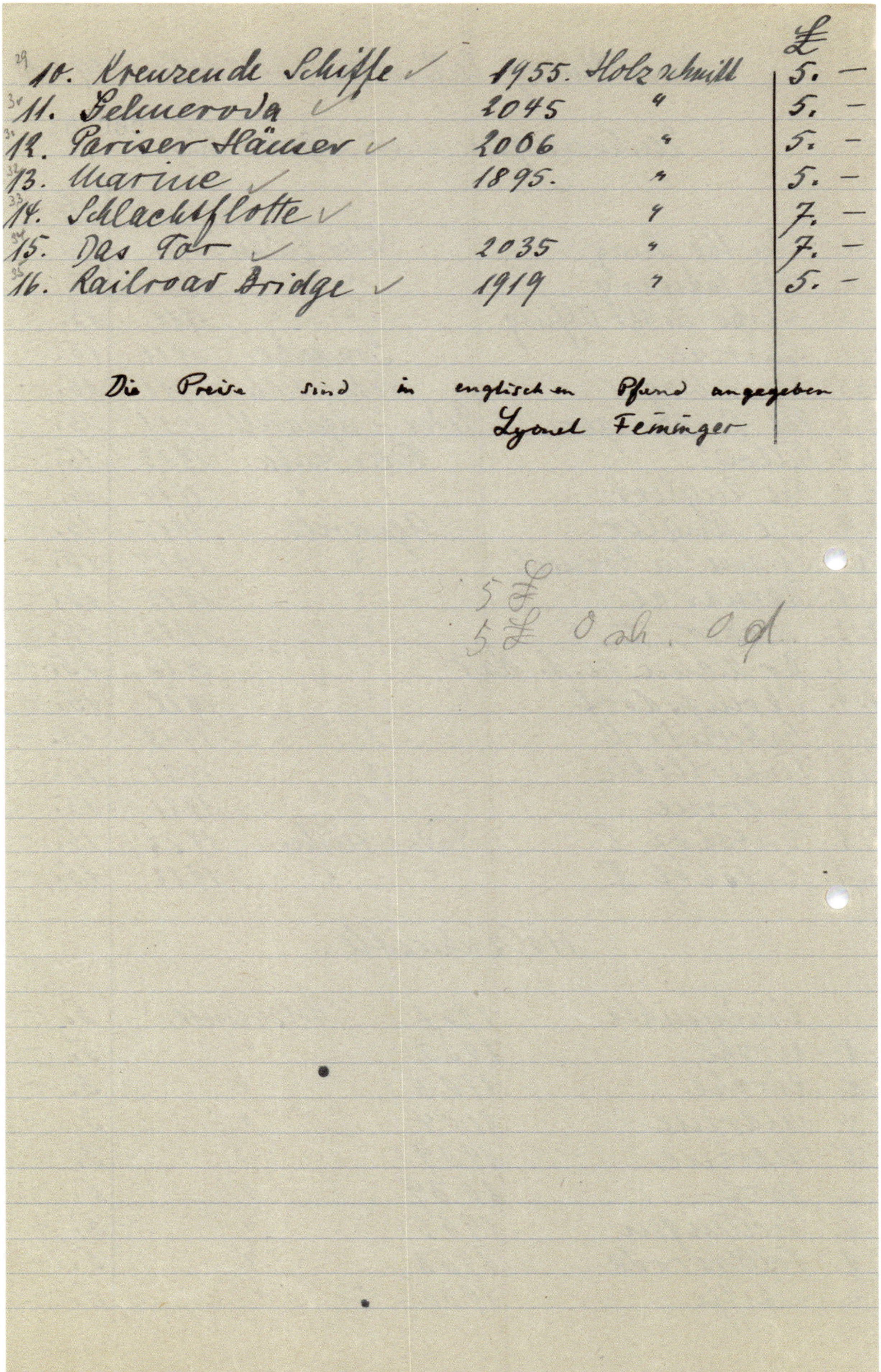

29	10. Kreuzende Schiffe ✓	1955.	Holzschnitt	£ 5.–
30	11. Gelmeroda ✓	2045	"	5.–
31	12. Pariser Häuser ✓	2006	"	5.–
32	13. Marine ✓	1895.	"	5.–
33	14. Schlachtflotte ✓		"	7.–
34	15. Das Tor ✓	2035	"	7.–
35	16. Railroad Bridge ✓	1919	"	5.–

Die Preise sind in englischen Pfund angegeben

Lyonel Feininger

5£
5£ 0 sh. 0 d.

Edmund Collein, *Photoplastik, Japanese Student at Bauhaus Holding Circle of Shadows*, 1928, gelatin silver print, 7.9 × 5.7 cm

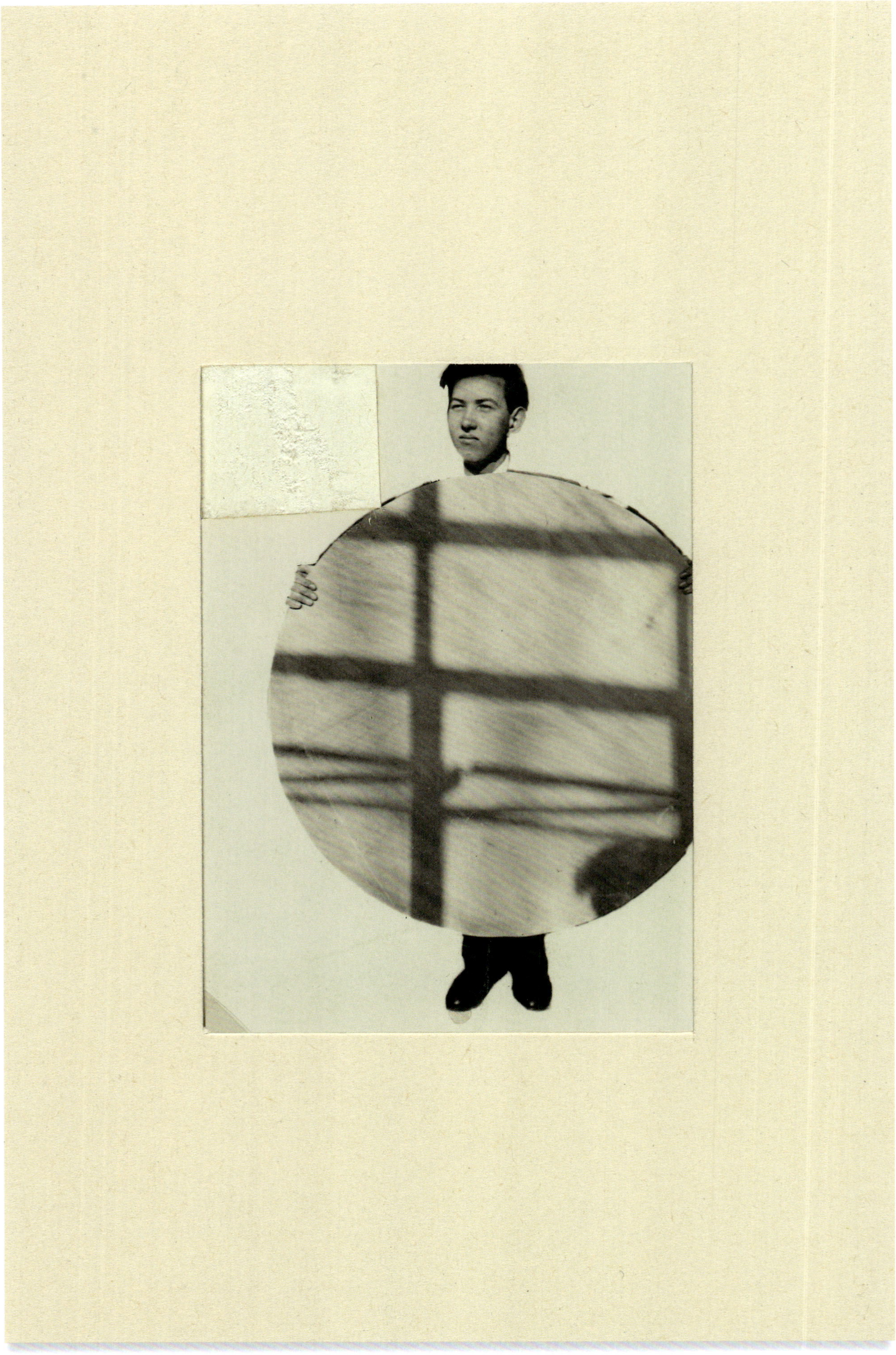

László Moholy-Nagy, *Von Material zu Architektur* (From Material to Architecture), Bauhausbücher 14, Munich: Albert Langen Verlag, 1929, p. 32

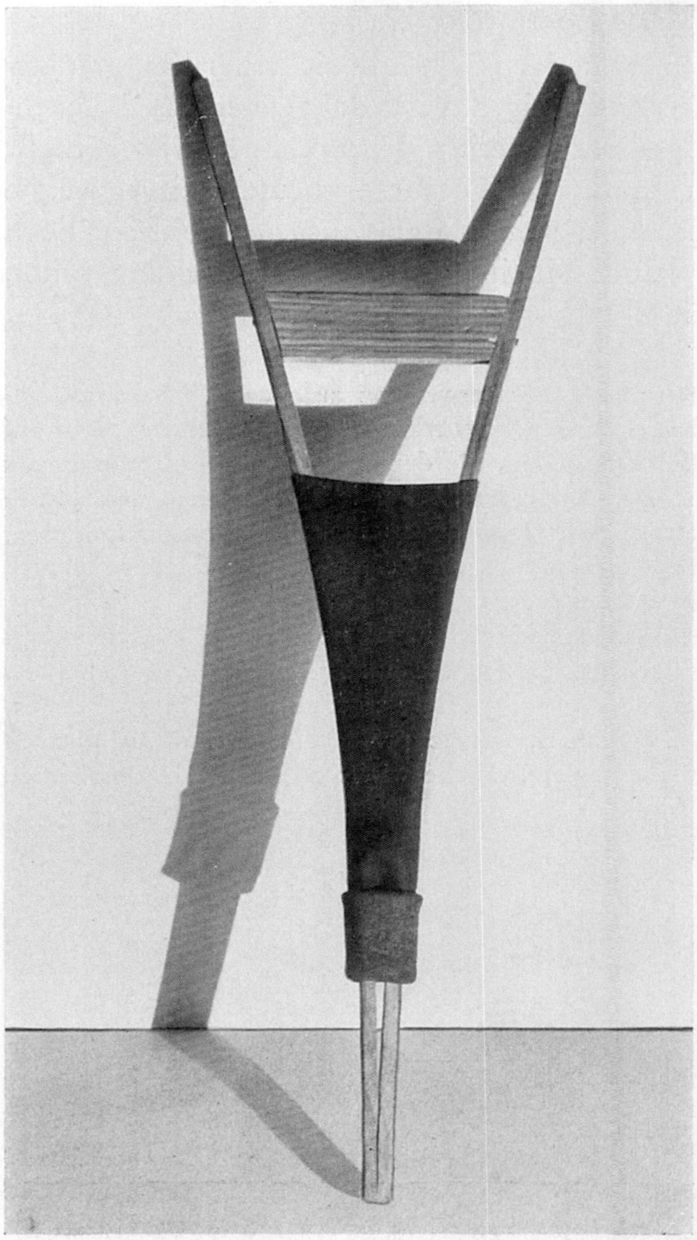

foto: clasen / dessau

abb. 13 mizutani (bauhaus, 2. semester 1927)
durch zwei gebogene holzstäbe federnde konstruktion mitgummibespannung fürdruckwerte.
(man trommelt auf der bespannung.)

es war interessant, bei diesen übungen die verschiedenen sinnes-kulturen zu beobachten. die japaner z. b. haben zweifellos eine aktivere beziehung zu den tastwerten als die europäer. das äußerte sich auch bei den tastübungen mit zugebundenen augen. gegenüber seinen kameraden, die die materialien meist streichelnd zu erfassen suchten, tanzte mizutani förmlich mit den fingern daran. das streichelnde abtasten war für ihn nicht ausreichend.

32

Teaching Art at Santiniketan and Weimar: Some Unexpected Meeting Points

Partha Mitter

The communication revolution that followed European expansion worldwide created a global community of like-minded individuals who transformed art education, especially in the early twentieth century. The Bauhaus is of course renowned. However, as I argue in this essay, such a phenomenon was not confined to the West. Two pedagogic institutions – the Bauhaus and Santiniketan – founded in 1919 challenged the project of urban industrial modernity that had caused the breakup of integrated rural communities (*Gemeinschaft*) and the alienation of individuals in society (*Gesellschaft*).[1] The great Indian poet Rabindranath Tagore (1861–1941) and Walter Gropius probably never met, but there was an unexpected meeting of minds here.

Tagore created a form of anti-colonial resistance that centred on a radical approach to the environment. As early as 1909, during the early phase of Indian nationalism, his influential essay 'The Hermitage' rejected the urban industrial society propagated by colonial rule in favour of a rural India that had existed since time immemorial.[2] Tagore's holistic conception of a 'hermitage' university, inspired by ancient Indian thought, nourished emotion and intellect in contrast to the sterile vocation-centred colonial education system. Tagore emphasized the unity of life, the inner life of the individual and a harmonious community.

The Bauhaus embodied two distinct but recognizable strands of thought. The better-known, as propagated from 1923 by László Moholy-Nagy, is the celebration of industrial design based on the integration of science and technology with the arts. Gropius is also best known for championing radical modernist architecture and design. Yet, when we turn to his text, 'The Theory and Organization of the Bauhaus', we discover the reflections of a different Gropius – a Platonist critic of mechanized work and an advocate of the German *Werkbund* ideal of communal art. He insists on 'the essential oneness of all things and their appearances [that] endows creative effort with a fundamental inner meaning...[one perceives] every form as the embodiment of an idea, every piece of work as a manifestation of our innermost selves. Only work which is the product of inner compulsion can have spiritual meaning'.[3] This aspect dominated the pre-1923 Weimar era with the support of like-minded artists and teachers Johannes Itten, Wassily Kandinsky, Paul Klee and Oskar Schlemmer, who espoused a form of critical modernity that drew inspiration from eastern 'spirituality' instead of a commitment to the machine age. Their interest led to a major exhibition of Bauhaus artists in Calcutta (present Kolkata) in 1922.[4]

VISVA-BHARATI NEWS

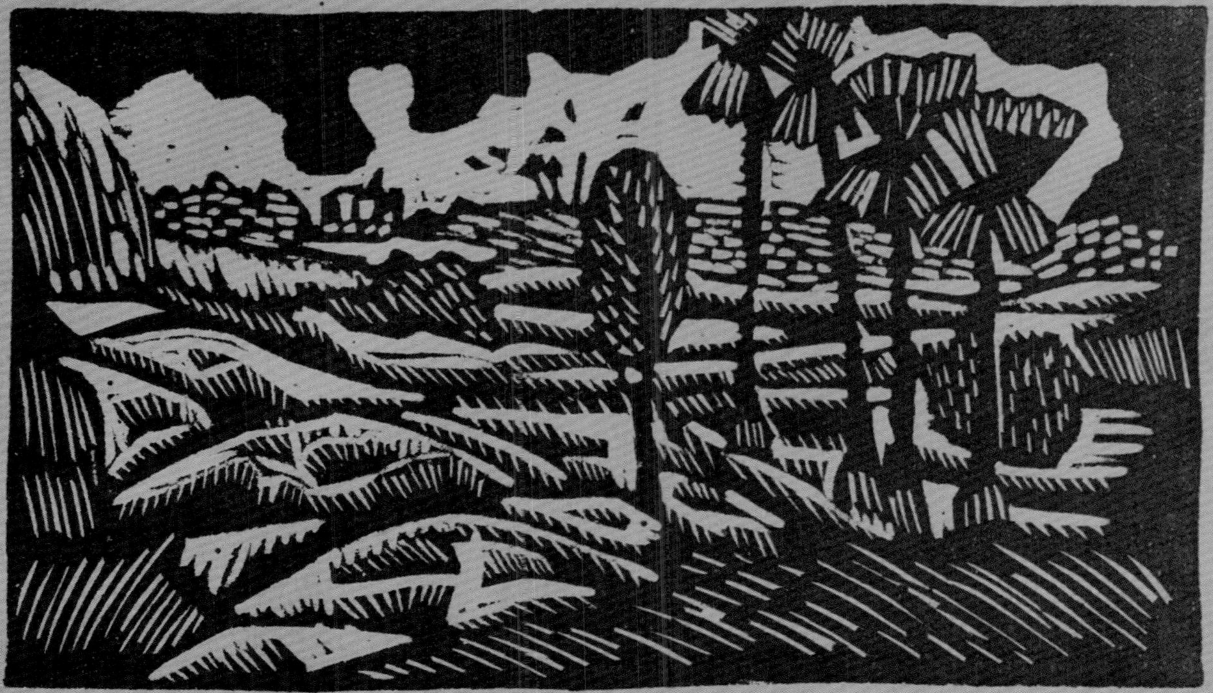

By Nandalal Bose

Volume I. July, 1932 Number One

FOREWORD

From a secluded shelter of a few students and educators the Santiniketan school has grown into an Educational Colony of varied departments of activity attracting scholars from far and wide and maintaining a civic life intimately linked up with the wellbeing of villages beyond its confine. The ideal of complete education that lies at the heart of our Institution has taken shape in classes for academic as well as applied knowledge, extending its zone from a wide range of artistic and scholarly activities to practical work in agriculture, dairy, tannery, weaving, as well as in medicine and sanitation. Due to this rapid growth along diverse paths of self-expression it has now become increasingly difficult for members of our Institution to take a wide view of the Visva-bharati as a whole outside their own immediate spheres of work which in order to be fruitful must be informed by the pervading spirit of an inner creative purpose. For friends who visit us for a short time there is a similar danger of emphasizing upon isolated items of work or forming a vague idea of our *Ashrama* life by a hurried attempt to deal at once with all its functions.

I welcome, therefore, the publication of this News Sheet which will fulfil a longfelt need if it can adequately acquaint us with details of work carried on in the different departments of our Institution presenting them in their natural co-ordination in an endeavour to realize the complete personality of Man.

SANTINIKETAN,

June 26, 1932.

Rabindranath Tagore

Tagore showed little interest in the Bauhaus reform of industrial design that became a hallmark of the German institution. The roots of his radical educational ideals lay in his childhood. Largely taught at home, he spoke movingly in his memoirs of the oppressive atmosphere of his primary school that stifled a child's imagination. Later on, he never ceased to insist on the importance of unfettered creativity and freedom of expression in a child. During his visit to Europe in 1921, he sought confirmation of his ideas in the educational reformer Franz Cižek's class for children that encouraged free creativity.[5]

These various strands in Tagore's thought came to fruition when he set up his experimental teaching institution, the Visva-Bharati (Indian universe) at Santiniketan in rural Bengal in 1921, two years after the Kala Bhavan was founded. Santiniketan developed an integrated and holistic system of education from the primary school stage to the university level, in which art played a humane role. The Kala Bhavan (or art school) as part of its educational complex would nurture budding artists, producing in time some remarkable figures. As his ideas began to crystallize, Tagore chose the artist Nandalal Bose (1882–1966) to give flesh to his radical art education programme. Under the leadership of Tagore's nephew Abanindranath Tagore (1871–1951), Nandalal and his cohort had created the first nationalist art movement in India around 1905. A quiet man of strong moral fibre and iron resolve, Nandalal was prepared to renounce the urban comforts of Calcutta in order to realize Tagore's vision. Santiniketan was founded during the nationwide Gandhian Non-Cooperation movement. A spiritual disciple of both Tagore and Mahatma Gandhi, Nandalal drew upon Tagore's radical environmentalism, Gandhi's critique of western capitalism, the nationalist valorization of village India, as well as an anti-urban romantic primitivism. Students would live in a natural environment and learn in a close-knit community, rather than pursue the prevalent colonial syllabus merely for obtaining a job in the imperial bureaucracy. In 1925, in order to encourage student–teacher bonding, Nandalal arranged for them to work next to each other in a studio, with students having the freedom to pursue their own particular interests. In 1928–29, he assigned to each student a personal instructor, aiming to revive pre-colonial apprenticeship under a master.[6]

Nandalal was deeply imbued with the poet's vision of free creativity but he also invested it with a firm discipline and a clear programme. How did this come about? At the turn of the last century, a group of radical thinkers from Asia (and Europe) had formulated Pan-Asianism, a regional avant-garde discourse that questioned western hegemony, and its artistic expression, academic naturalism.[7] The Japanese ideologue Okakura Tenshin spent the early years of the century with the Tagores, developing some of his Pan-Asian ideas in Calcutta, evolving three cardinal artistic principles – nature, tradition, creativity – as a selective response to westernization, principles that formed the basis of Nandalal's curriculum. Less acknowledged but ironically equally important were the lessons learnt by Nandalal at the colonial art school in Calcutta. Even though he had been part of the nationalist rebellion against academic art, he retained a respect for basic colonial art school training, especially geometry and strong structure as the foundations of drawing.

These creative tensions between complete freedom and strict discipline under a strong leader worked to the advantage of Kala Bhavan. Conscious of the need for an underlying armature in a painting, Nandalal was never comfortable with the *morotai* wash technique of Abanindranath. He was even prepared to accept scientific anatomy, which had been anathema to the orientalists. However, as a concession to them, he devised schematic 'stick' figures to mimic naturalist poses rather than use nude models, at the same time introducing vigorous life studies of animals.[8] By the 1930s, however, Nandalal was forced to introduce a more conventional curriculum, including Renaissance art principles and free life drawing, after his failure to ensure competent levels of art training. His growing openness to western art owed partly to the influential Austrian art historian Stella Kramrisch's sojourn at Santiniketan (1920–23). These various influences that lay at the heart of Nandalal's attempts at a synthesis of East and West provided the foundations of modernism at Santiniketan. Its finest flowering can be seen in the work of the painter Benodebehari Mukherjee (Mukhopadhyay) and the sculptor Ramkinkar Baij.[9]

Nandalal Bose, *Untitled (Temple on Hill Top)*, 1960, ink on rice paper, 30.2 × 45.4 cm

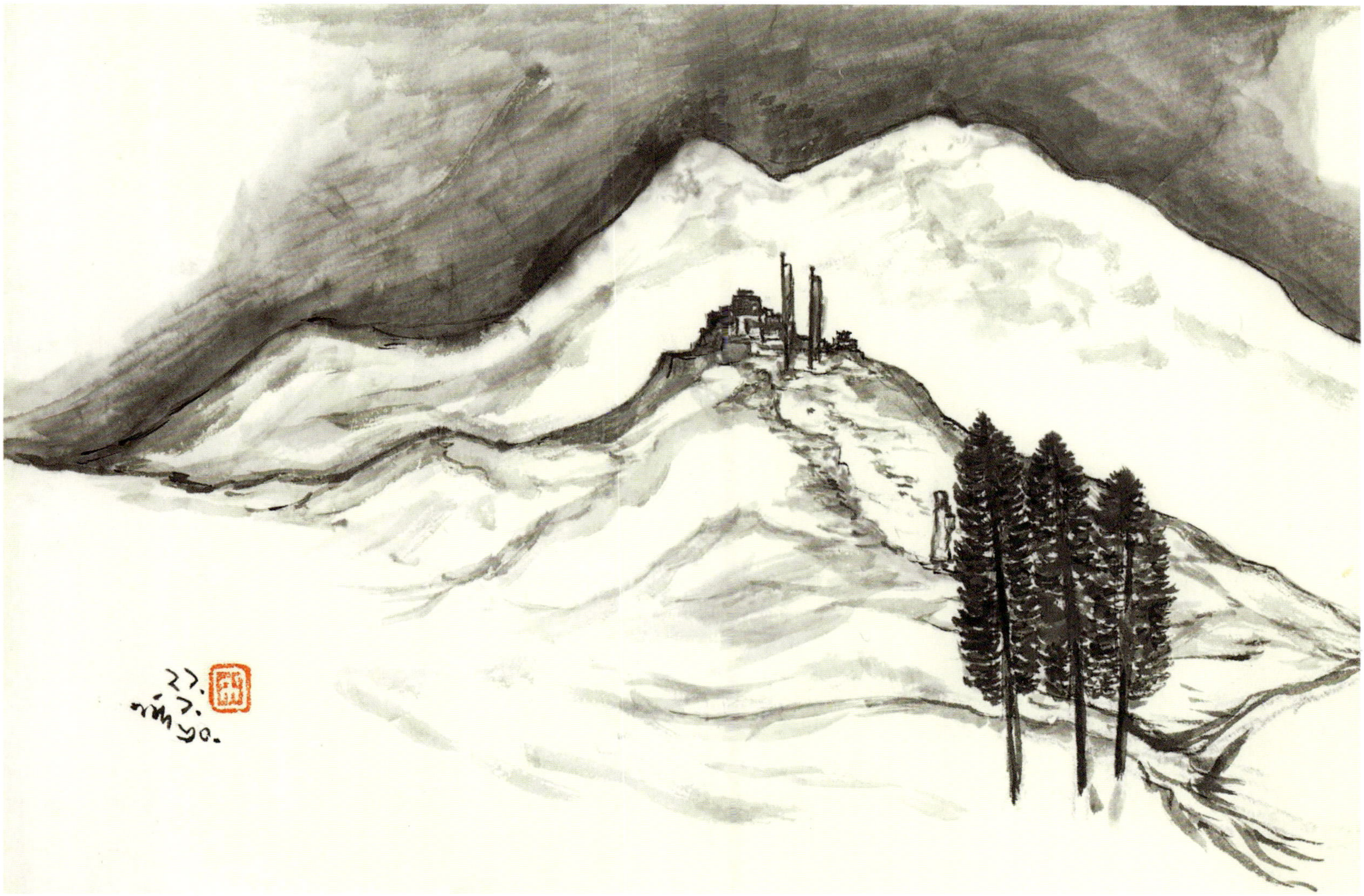

Nandalal Bose, *Untitled (Santal Woman Welcomes Her Father-in-Law)*, 1954, watercolor and ink on paper, 19.7 × 16.5 cm

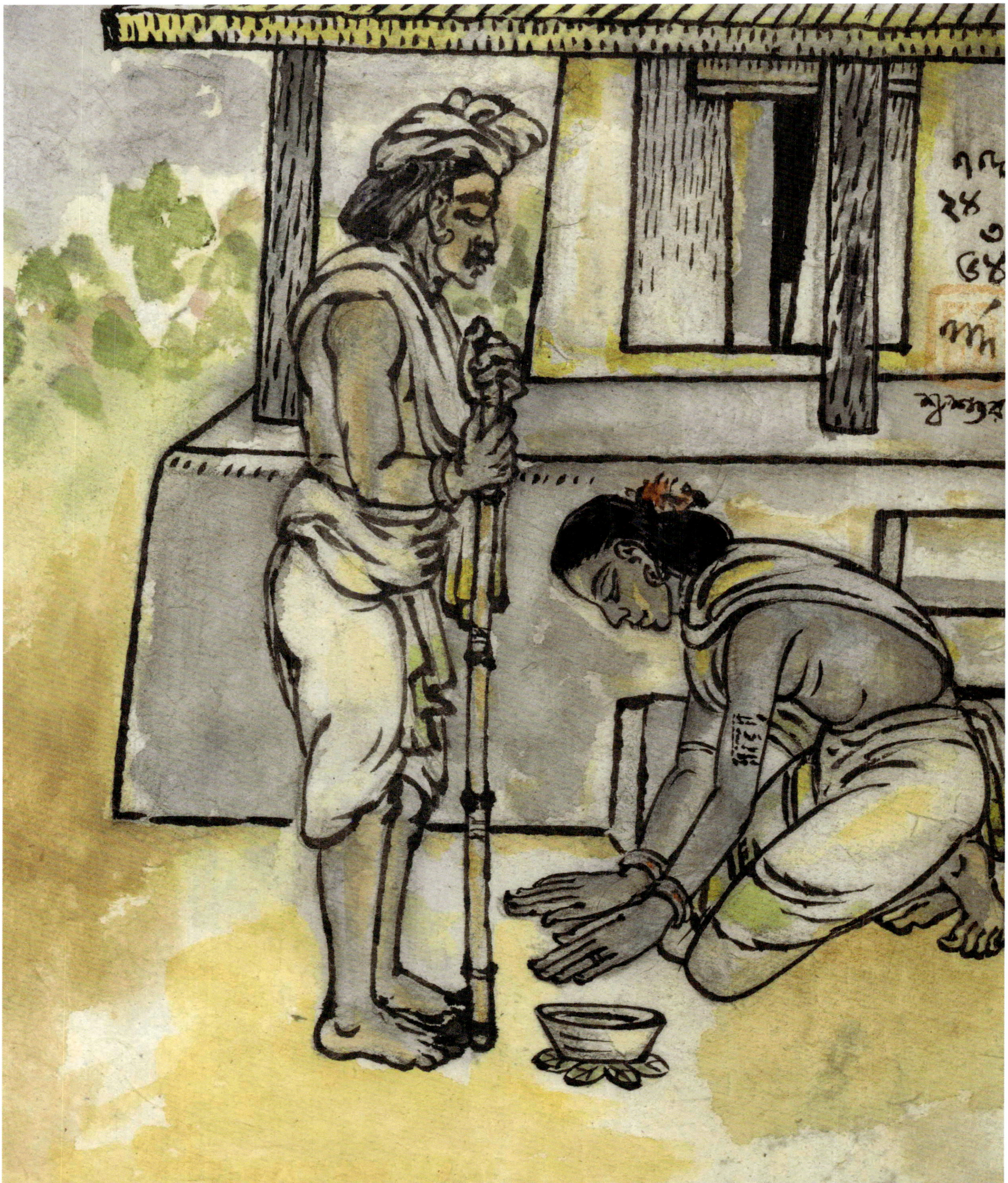

A striking aspect of Santiniketan's radical environmentalism was the experiment with outdoor murals that could withstand the elements. As a student, Nandalal had made copies of the ancient Buddhist caves at Ajanta and Bagh, held by nationalists to be the sine qua non of nation-building. Nandalal's experience of Ajanta strengthened his resolve to make monumental mural painting rather than miniature watercolours the cornerstone of his teaching. A decisive influence of his early outdoor experiments was Patrick Geddes, the noted British urban planner, who was visiting Santiniketan at the time. Geddes advised him to use charcoal as a durable medium for the foundational drawing; he also urged students to decorate the exteriors of buildings with paintings in order to make them an integral part of the environment. This appealed to Nandalal's own ideal of making painting relevant to everyday life.[10]

The foremost pupil of Nandalal, Benodebehari Mukherjee (1904–1980), carried forward his achievements in mural painting. Romantic primitivism in Santiniketan – exemplified by a new perception of peasants, craftsmen, the tribal peoples, and an interest in rural regions untouched by urban colonialism as the true uncorrupted India – reached its apogee in Benodebehari, whose murals offer us some of the most strikingly original visions of subaltern India. In contrast to Nandalal's use of a horizontal format for the murals, Benodebehari developed a 'multiple focus' approach derived from diverse traditions including Japanese scrolls, a style that enabled him to create flowing monumental images of the human pageant in his murals of Indian saints. He appreciated traditional Indian art but he also believed in the need to progress. The tension between geometry and representation, he stated, underpinned all successful art; it is this tension that he found present in both ancient Indian and European modernist art. These lines may be taken as Benodebehari's credo for the murals.[11]

These two examples of Santiniketan and the Bauhaus teach us about different cultural solutions to common global problems. The specific response to the crisis of colonialism/capitalism in the twentieth century in different regions highlights certain 'structural affinities' within what I call the global 'virtual cosmopolis'. The colonial world order spread hegemonic languages – English, French and Spanish – through the medium of print culture. The 'virtual cosmopolitan' on the periphery was able to engage with the ideas originating in the centre on the level of the imagination and generate new ideas of modernity, without recourse to direct contact with the metropolis. This dialogic process also applied to the West, where artists, for instance, learned about non-western art through reproductions in books and journals. One notices this in the western reaction to the profound crisis of industrial society. For example, German artists and critics, including Bauhaus teachers and students, saw in the crisis of twentieth-century art the breakdown of the social order; Indian thinkers, such as Rabindranath Tagore, on the other hand, held colonial urbanity responsible for destroying not only Indian art but also Indian communal life. These diverse ideas came together in the exhibition of Bauhaus teachers and students in Calcutta in 1922. A holistic approach and a sense of community represented by the *Werkbund* ideal in Gropius's manifesto for the Bauhaus (1919) found remarkable parallels in Tagore's experimental Kala Bhavan art school. To end on a note of reiteration: the origins of these ideas, be it in post-Versailles Germany or in colonial India, were indigenous. They were creative responses to the structural crisis of the industrial world.[12]

Benodebehari Mukherjee, *Life of Medieval Saints*, 1946, mural, Hindi Bhavan, Santiniketan, India

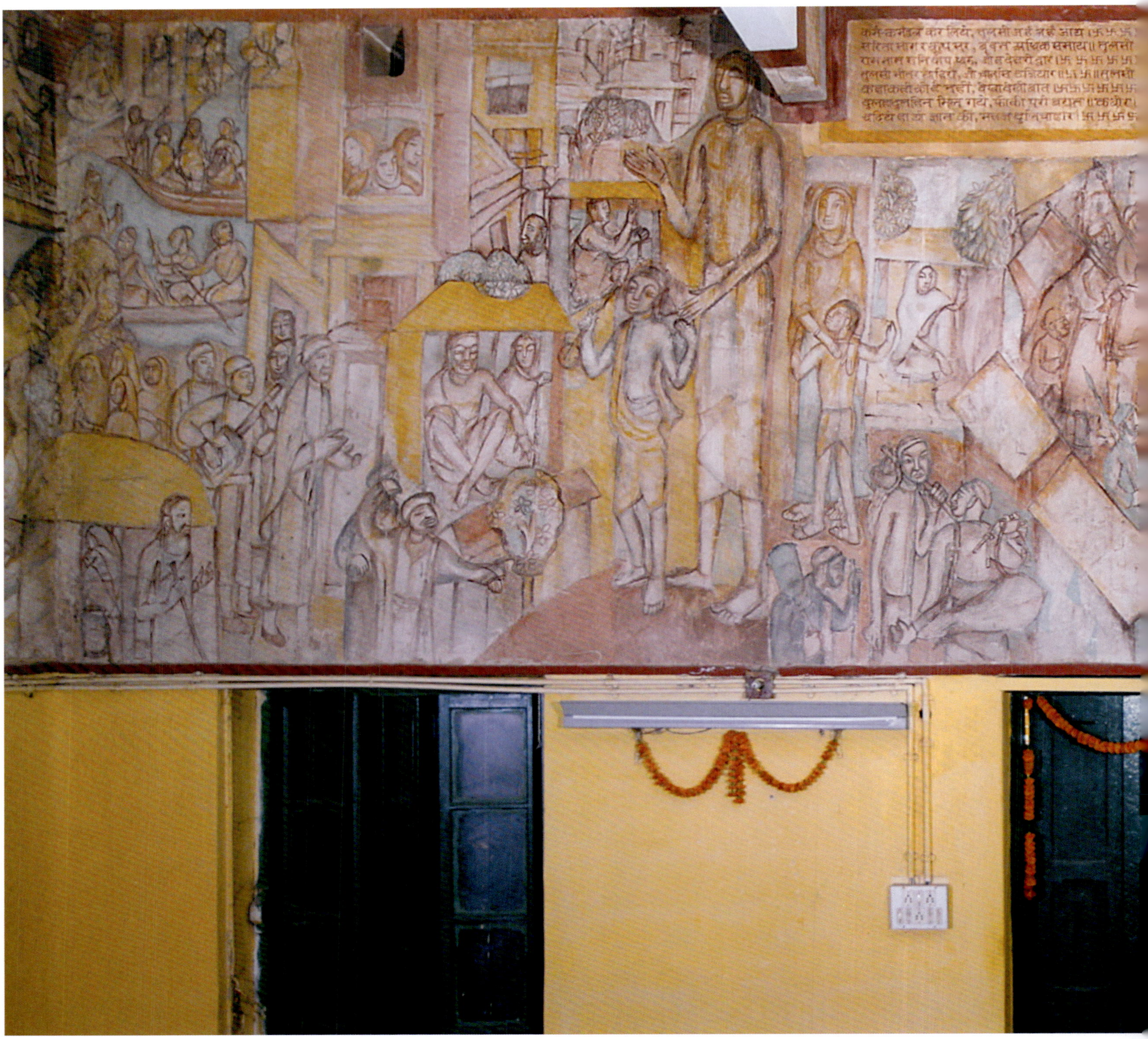

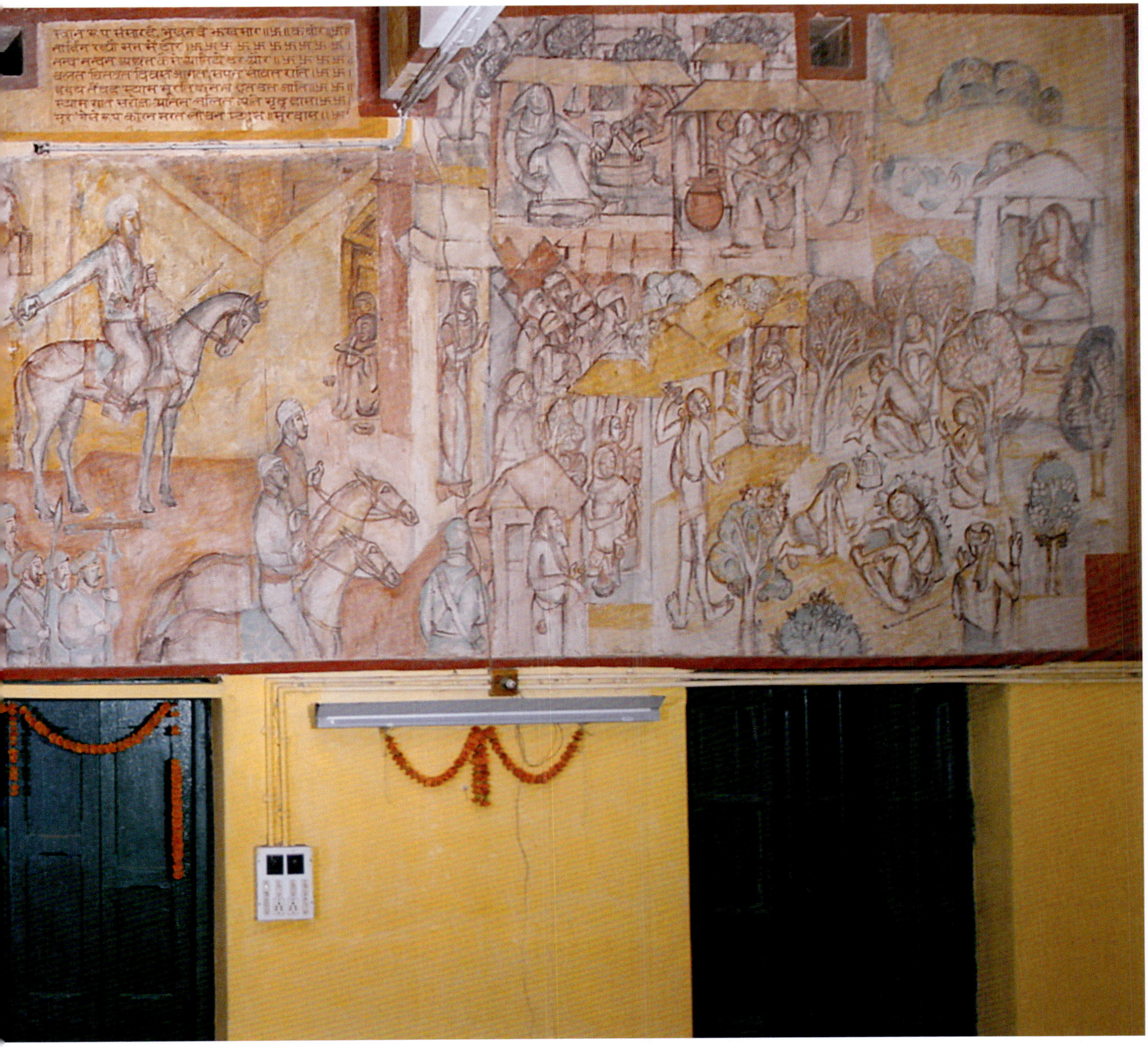

The Intimate and the Contingent: Art and Craft in the Pedagogy of Santiniketan

Kala Bhavan, the art school established by Rabindranath Tagore in 1919, was founded on the premises that art and craft traditions could share a platform and that it was possible to embrace a new idea of community unbound by territorial nationalism.

This approach resonated through the educational practices of Kala Bhavan and also registered in the everyday experiences of the artists, and it was reflected philosophically in the daily flow of the school and wider environment of Santiniketan. It was also evident in the efforts made towards the building of an archive – a repository of sensibilities – an inventory of corresponding images. The mode of address during the early years of the school was both with and away from object-creation in the conventional sense of art and craft production.

Anshuman Dasgupta

1. Nandalal Bose, *Fishing Line Maker, Surul*, 1946, postcard, 14 × 8.9 cm

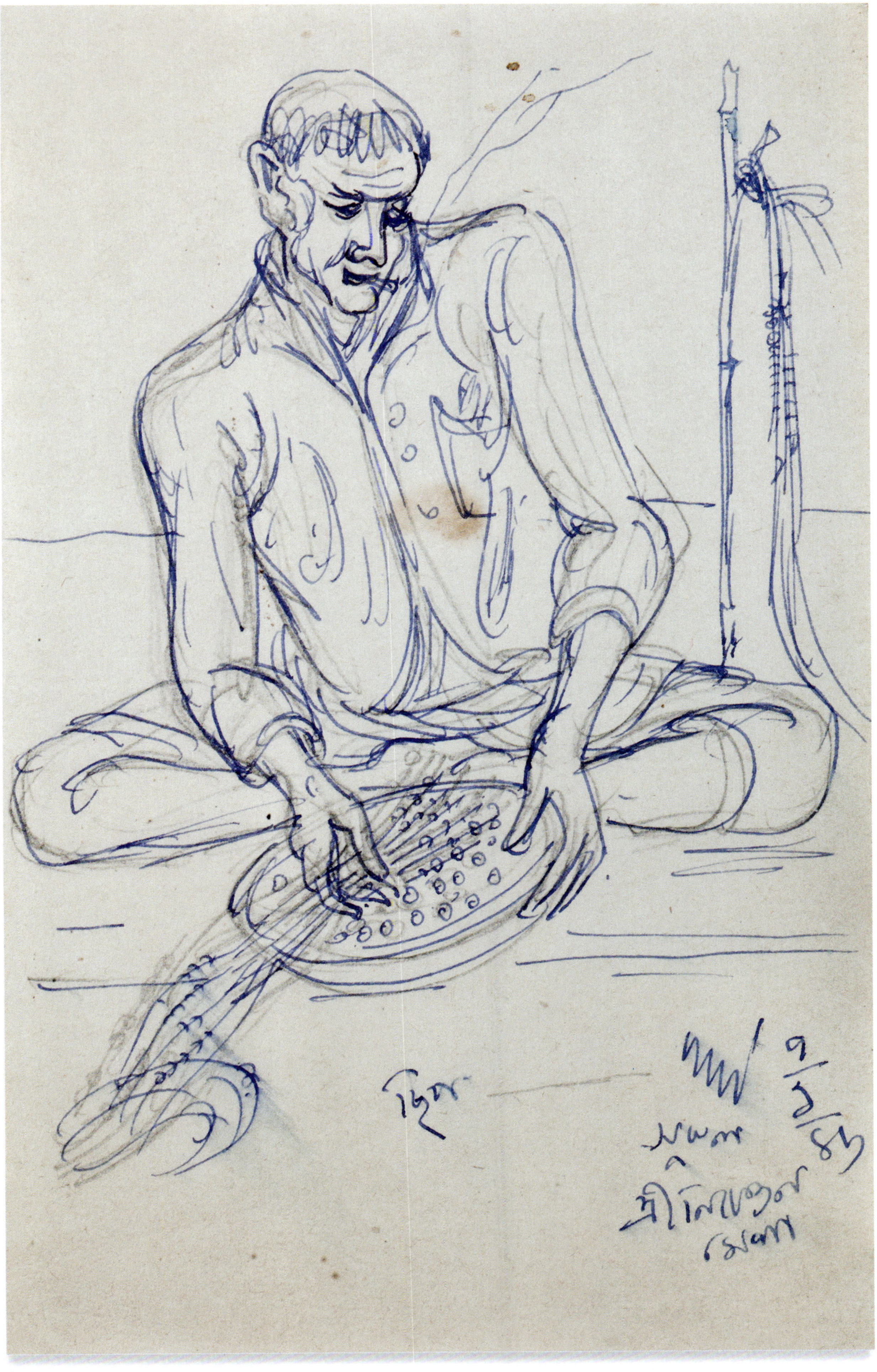

1

Nandalal Bose was invited by Tagore to lead the new art school. His consciousness of the craft traditions of India came to fruition in his folk-style posters and pavilion design, which were commissioned by Mahatma Gandhi for the sessions of the Indian National Congress at Faizpur and Haripura in 1937 and 1938 respectively.

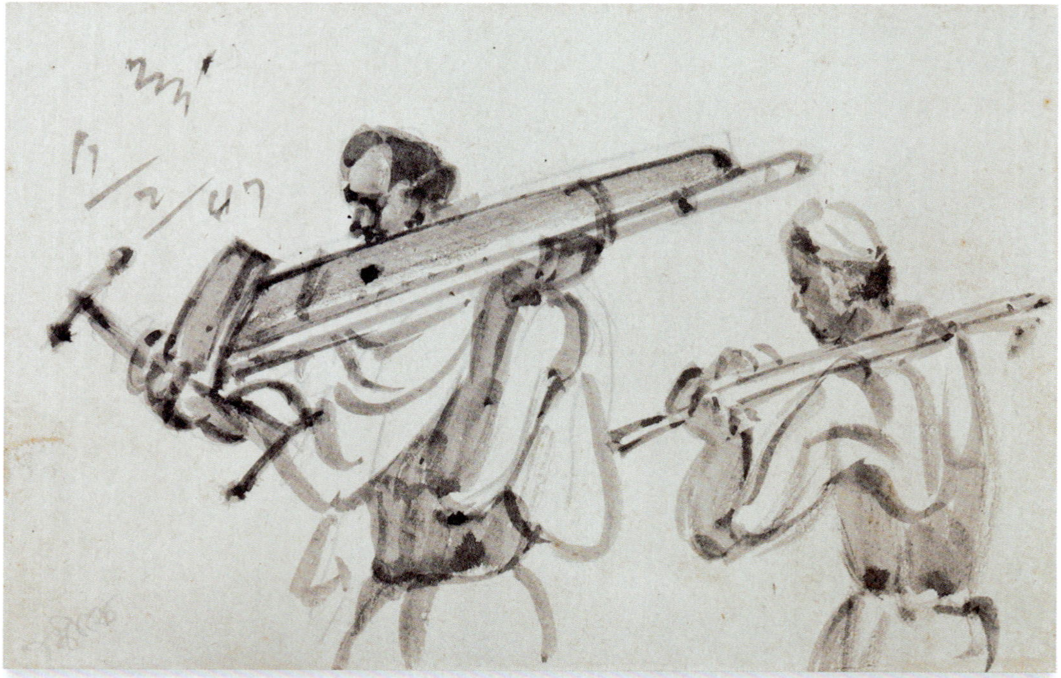

2

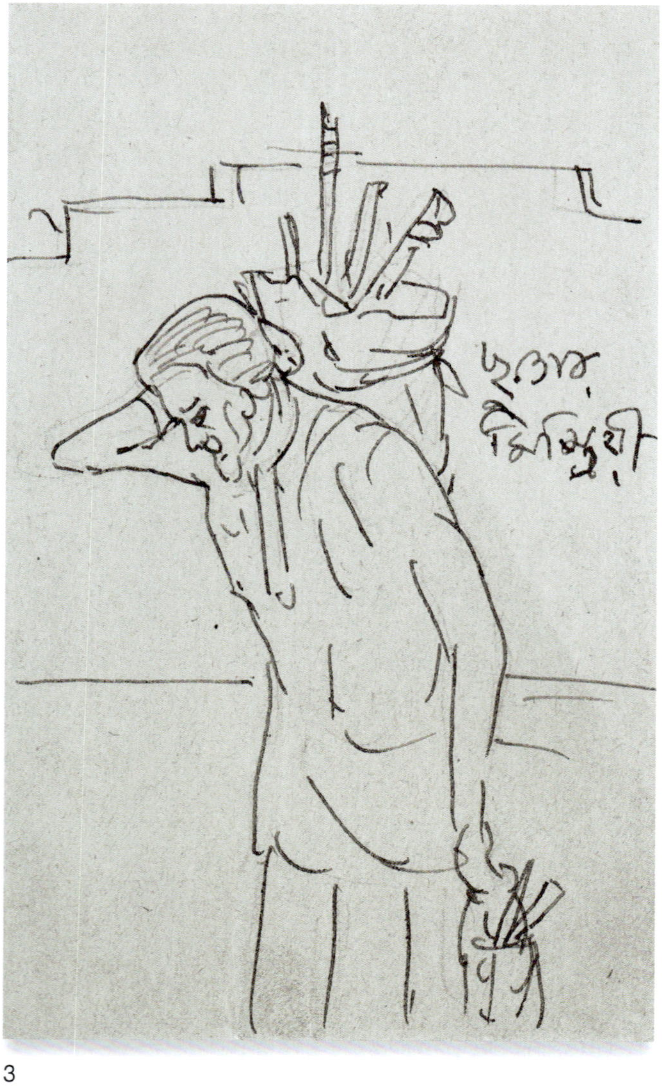

3

The illustrated postcards Bose sent from the Congress were explorations of the life-world in which the 'artist-craftsman' played a crucial role. It was as if the labour intensiveness of the craft world had met its counterpart in the 'creativity' of art.

To put artists and craftsmen on the same platform was Nandalal's vision and that influenced his pedagogy...

Benodebehari Mukhopadhyay (Mukherjee),
Adhunik Shilpashiksha (Modern Art Education), 1972

2. Nandalal Bose, *Carpenters*, 1947, ink and brush on paper, 8.9 × 14 cm
3. Nandalal Bose, *Carpenter*, n.d. [c. 1936], postcard, 14 × 8.9 cm

Santiniketan's pedagogy involved the study of the rhythms of everyday life and live natural phenomena, and their translation into art.

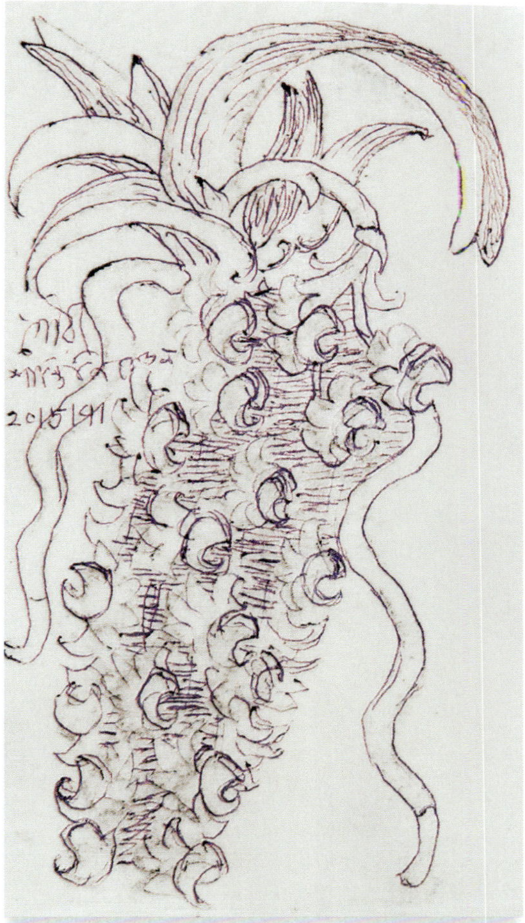

4

This translation was comprised of the different states of transformation of a design idea derived from nature – the journey from an imitative copy to a stylized design element – waiting to become part of some handicraft or useful daily object (such as a stool, bedcover or table mat).

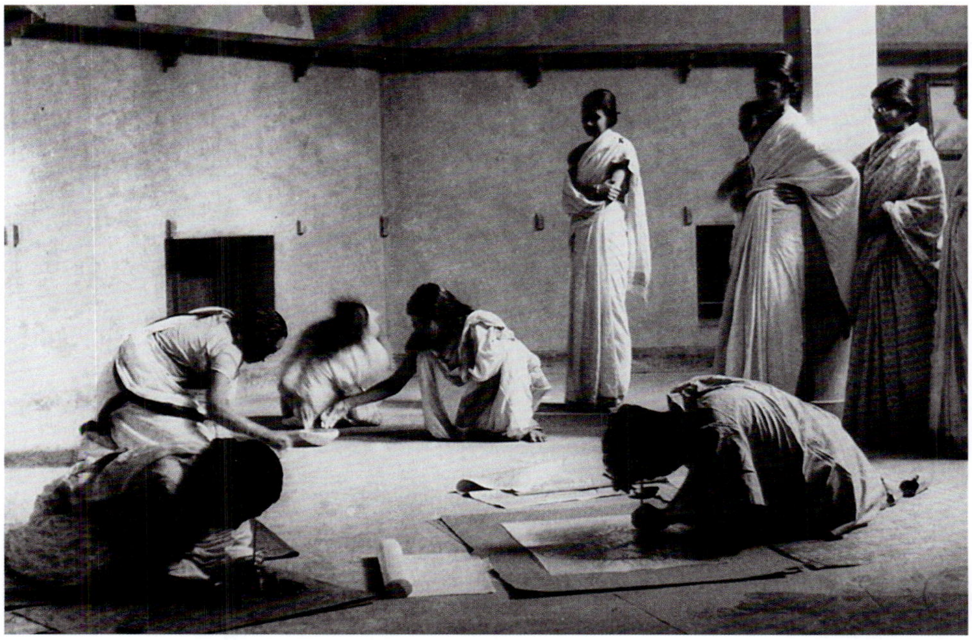

5

'Craft in everyday life' was the objective on which the educational paradigm of Santiniketan was based. Everyday life involved the practice and celebration of many existing and invented rituals and festivals, in a unique and inclusive hybridization of tradition. This gave rise to many individual creative practices engaging with necessities and devising inventions.

4. Gauri Bhanja, *Studies from Nature*, n.d. [*c.* early 1940s]
5. Gauri Bhanja's classroom

Significant in this process was a large number of women artists from the community, who directed the design scene in Santiniketan. Artists such as Gauri Bhanja and Jamuna Sen (both Nandalal's daughters) were an important part of the teaching team at Kala Bhavan.

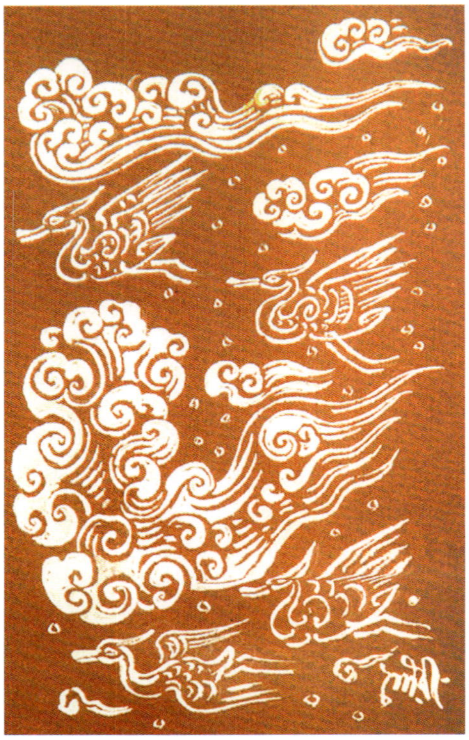

6

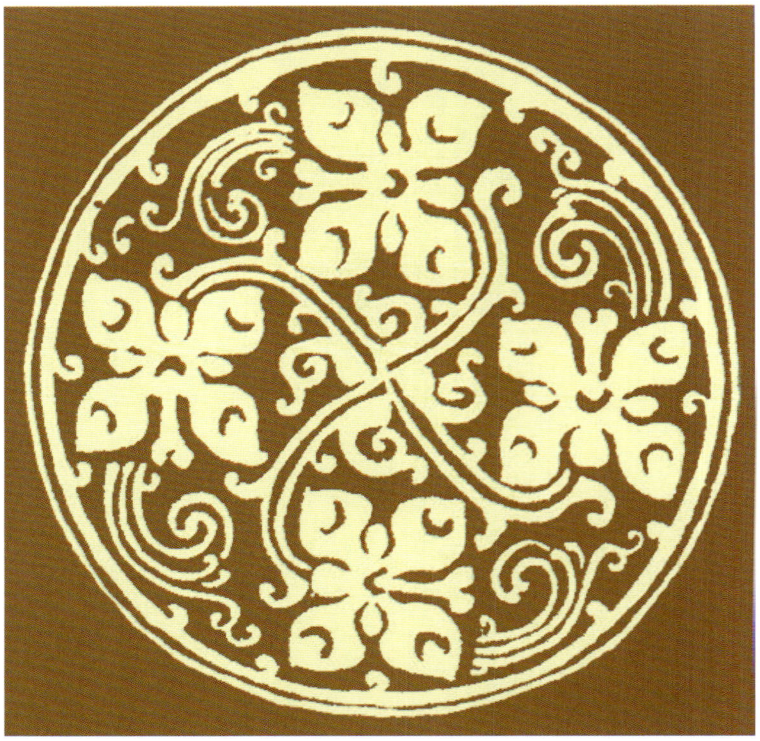

7

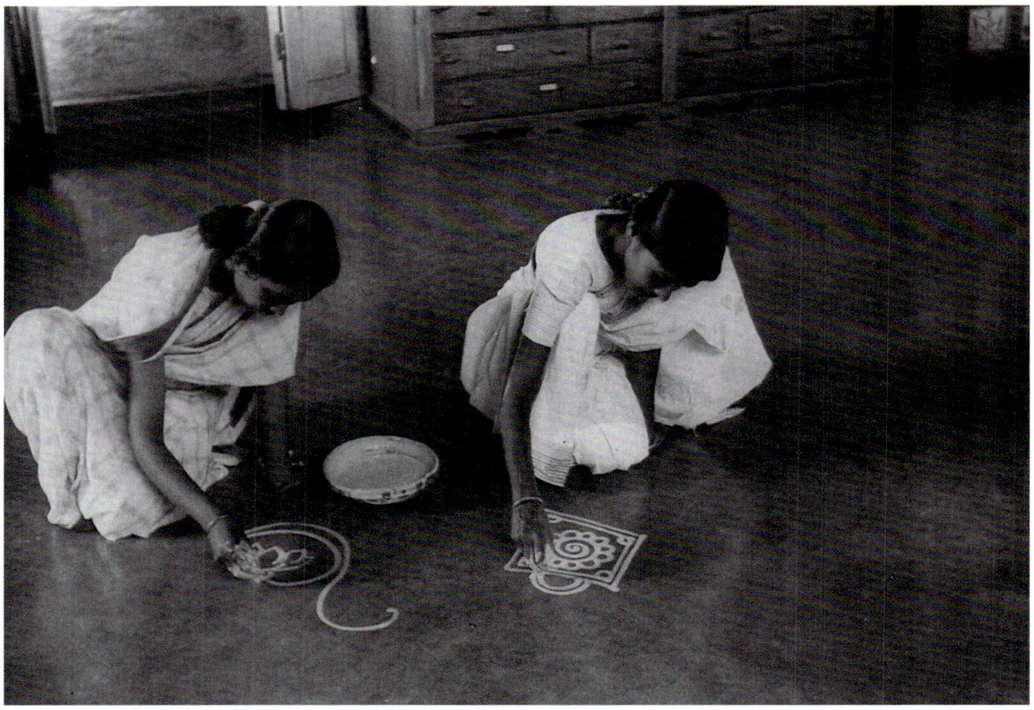

8

6. Gauri Bhanja, design on board for batik, derived from Indonesia, *c.* 1940s
7. Gauri Bhanja, design for *alpana* (flat design on coloured ground), n.d. [*c.* 1930s]
8. Two girls creating *alpana* (ritual decoration) on the floor, Kala Bhavan, Santiniketan, India, 1930s

Along with his commitment to anti-colonial resistance, Nandalal built an important archive at Kala Bhavan that registered the production of craft works to be assimilated into the world of 'art' and used as an educational resource for the school.

He sent back postcards featuring drawings and instructions to his colleagues from the different places in India where he travelled – a method picked up by some of his contemporaries. Sometimes objects and the sketches made of them come face to face, as can be seen here in figs 9 and 10 from the original collection of Prabhatmohan Bandopadhyay. Bandopadhyay was an artist who, like Nandalal, was also active in the anti-colonial cultural movement.

In the line of craft's relation to art is the furniture making of Santiniketan from this period. Tagore's son, Rathindranath learnt woodcraft in Japan and applied this knowledge to his practice on returning to India. Low-height furniture became the Santiniketan signature after his designs. The 1930s mise en scène of Santiniketan was gradually absorbing the architecture of alternative constructional and aesthetic principles, via the idea of a bridge between art and craft.

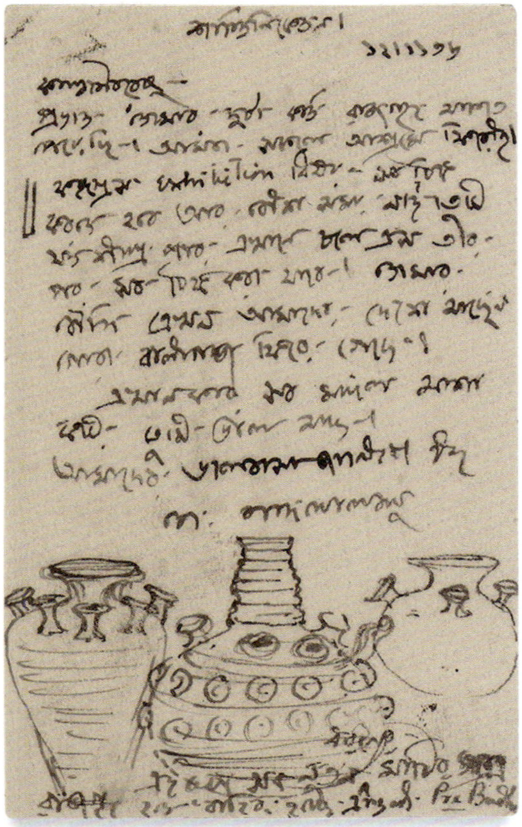

9

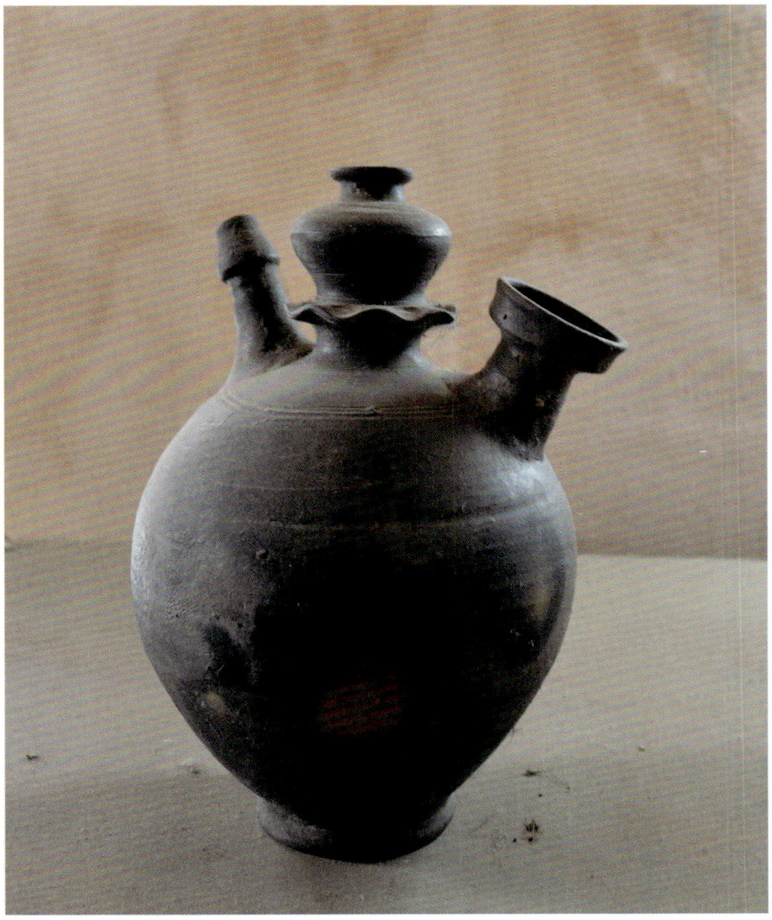

10

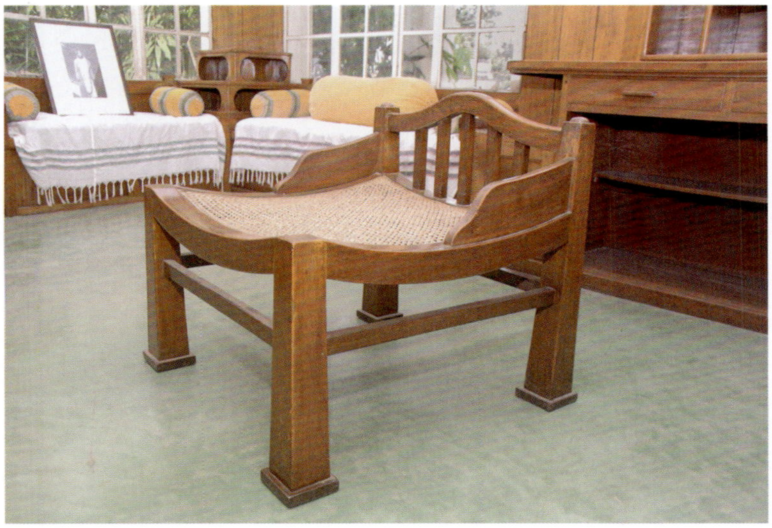

11

9. Postcard from Nandalal Bose to Prabhatmohan Bandopadhyay suggesting the creation of paintings for the Haripura and Faizpur sessions of the Indian National Congress, *c.* 1935–36
10. Glazed terracotta pitcher with multiple spouts, corresponding to the drawings on the postcard in fig. 9, Subir Bandopadhyay collection by inheritance, collection period *c.* 1935–36
11. Furniture designed by Rathindranath Tagore on display in Protima Devi's studio, period range *c.* 1930s–40s

Mural was one medium in which art and craft came to a resolution. As the new buildings of Patha Bhavan, China Bhavan, Hindi Bhavan and the Havell Hall of Kala Bhavan were completed in the 1920s and 1930s, the new agenda of mural making created a site for experimentation and demonstration of a pedagogy.

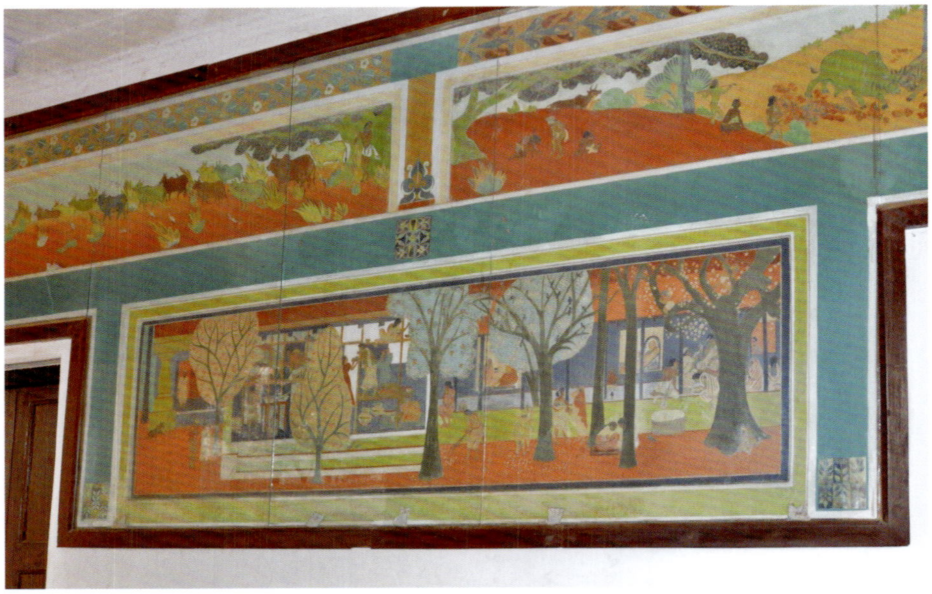

12

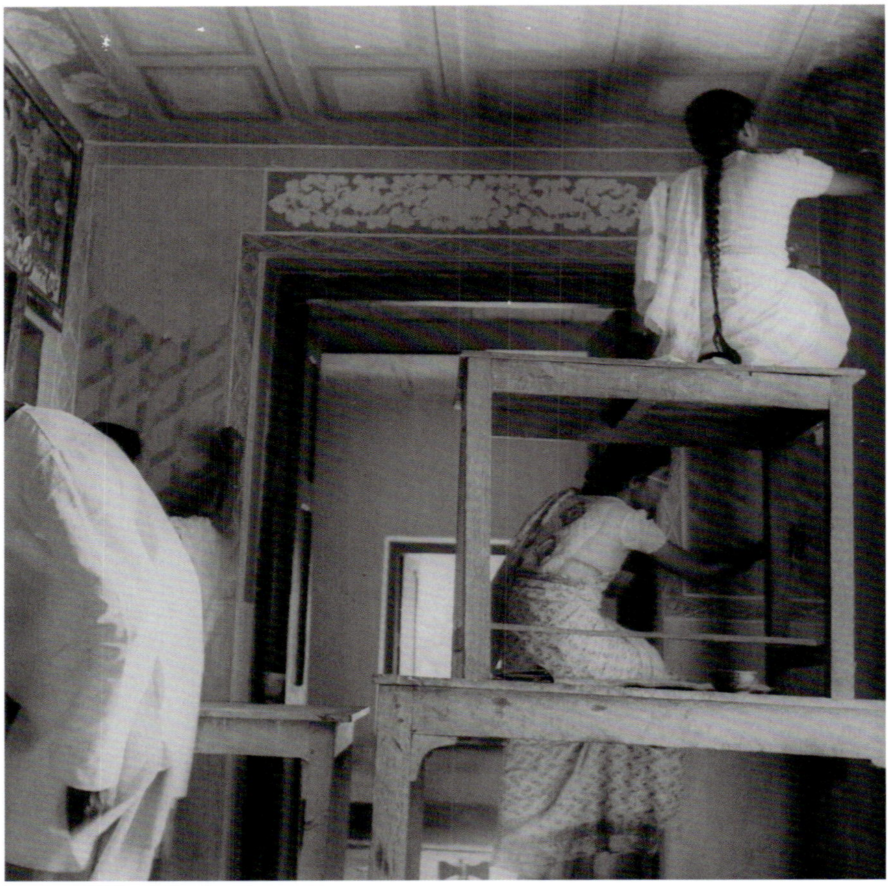

13

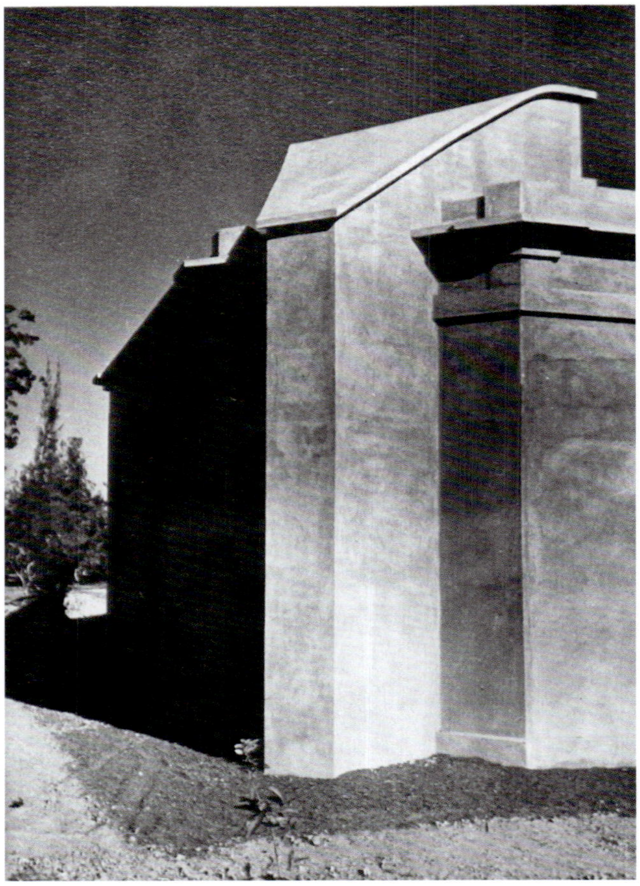

14

12. Nandalal Bose, *Untitled*, *c*. 1930s, mural, Patha Bhavan, Santiniketan, India
13. Students working on a mural, *c*. 1930s
14. Havell Hall, late 1920s

The pedagogy of the art school at Santiniketan was centred on Nandalal's ideas of nature and tradition, his concept of individual talent and the aesthetic currents derived from Tagore and Ananda Coomaraswamy. However, the artist Benodebehari Mukhopadhyay (Mukherjee) had an equal part in shaping its timbre and distinctiveness. He brought a transnational approach to his teaching at the school and made learning vital and accessible for students.

Some examples of these approaches are to be seen in Nandalal's illustrations to Tagore's poems in *Sahaj Path* (1936, fig. 15), his *Drishti O Srishti* (Vision and Creation, 1999, fig. 17) and on Benodebehari's page in *Adhunik Shilpashiksha* (fig. 16).

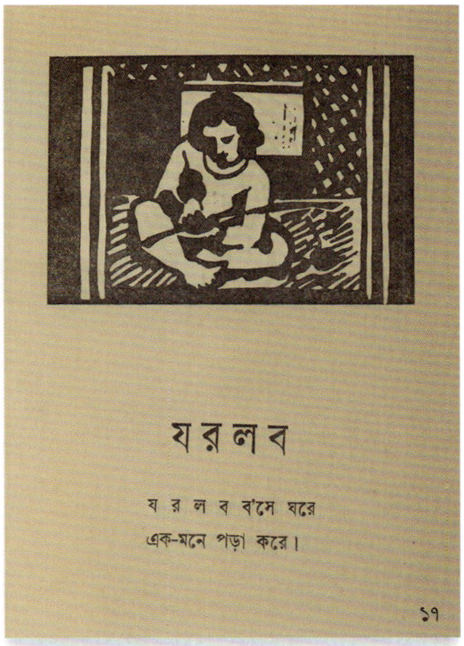

15

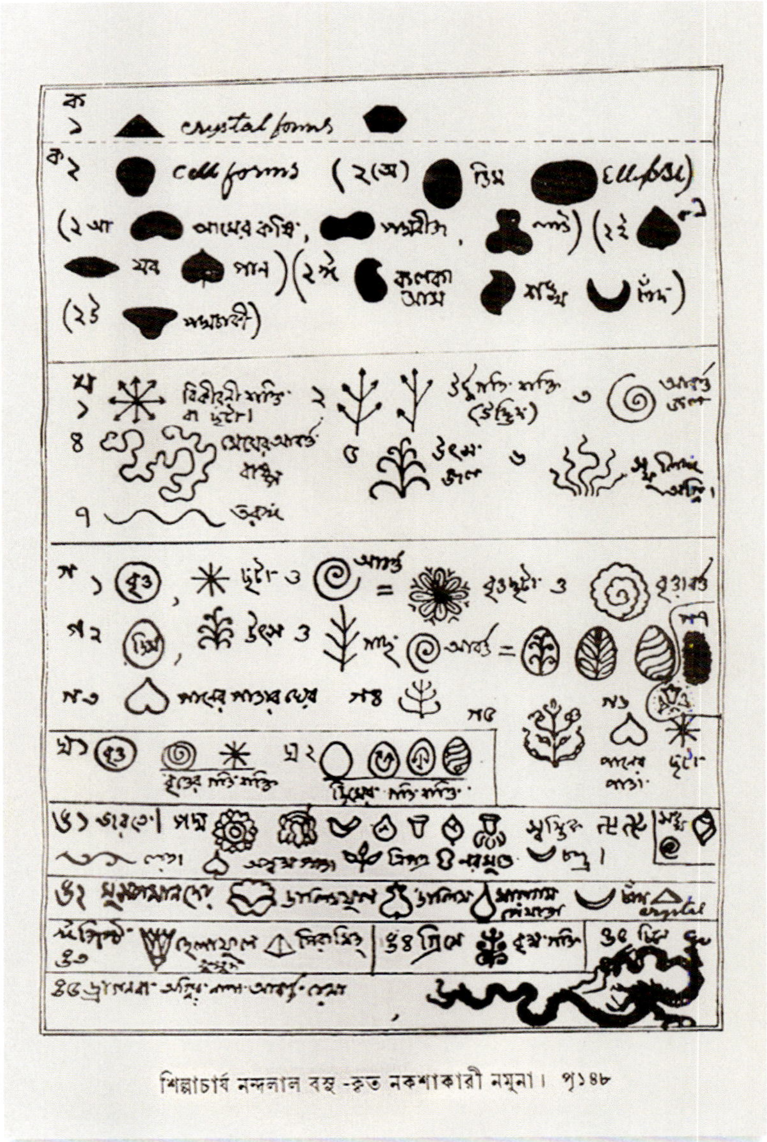

16

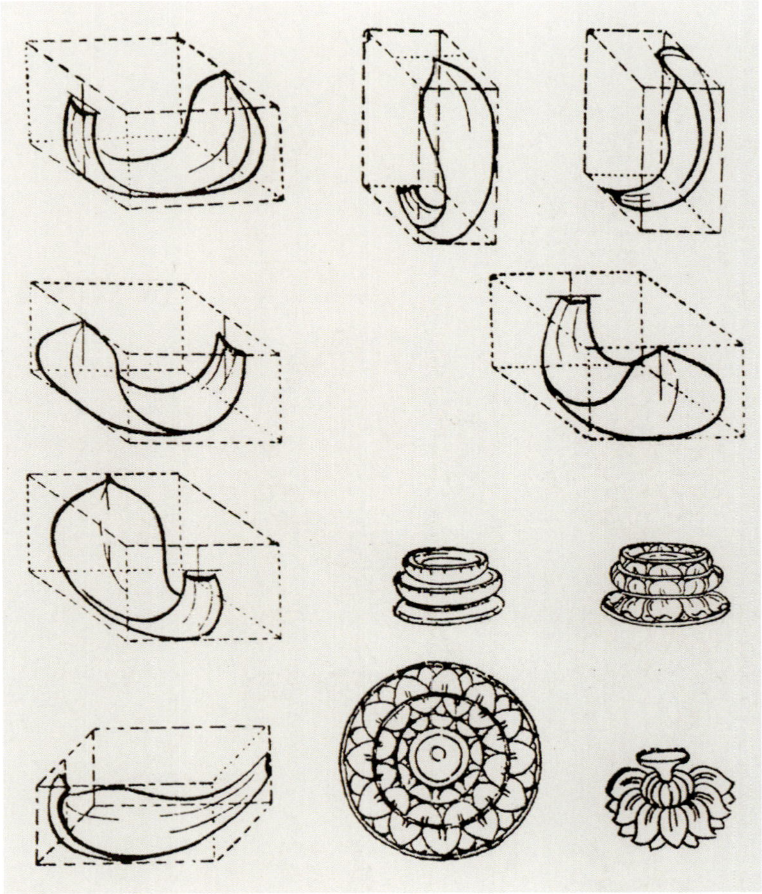

17

15. *Sahaj Path*, Bengali-language primer written by Rabindranath Tagore and illustrated by Nandalal Bose, 2nd edition, 1936
16. From Benodebehari Mukhopadhyay (Mukherjee), *Adhunik Silpa Siksha* (Modern Art Education), Calcutta: Visva-Bharati Pub., 1972
17. From Nandalal Bose, *Drishti O Srishti* (Vision and Creation), Calcutta: Visva-Bharati Pub., 1999

It is not difficult to observe the similarity between the pedagogy of the Bauhaus and Kala Bhavan. The main difference was in their analysis of the significance of modern civilization.

Benodebehari Mukhopadhyay (Mukherjee), *Adhunik Shilpashiksha* (1972)

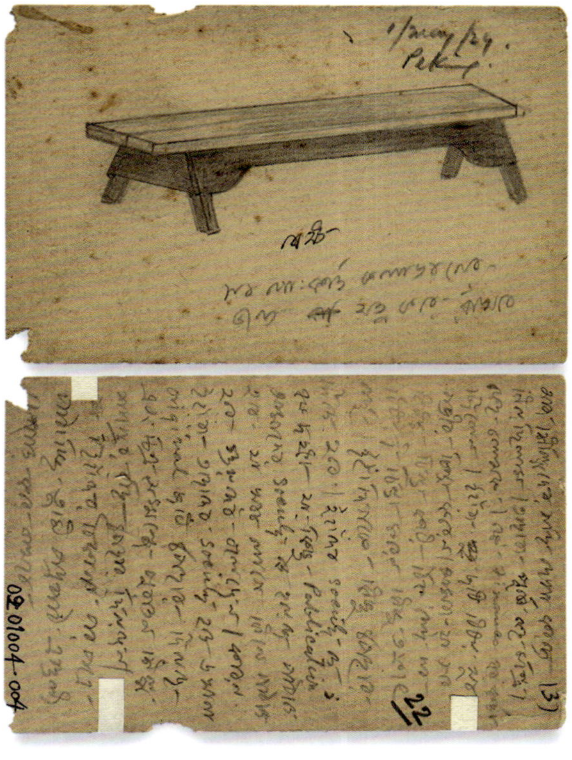

18

Some more examples of Nandalal's postcards (figs 18 and 19) show that these were very often instructive and, in addition to his regular and direct contact with students, constituted an important part of his teaching practice.

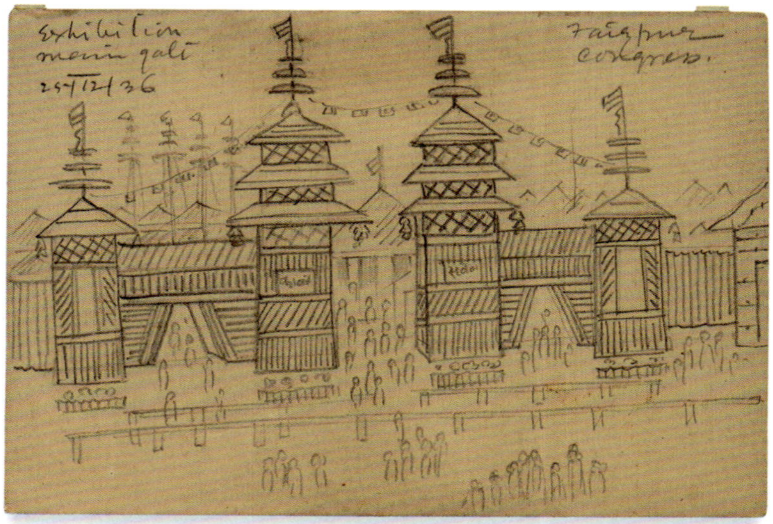

19

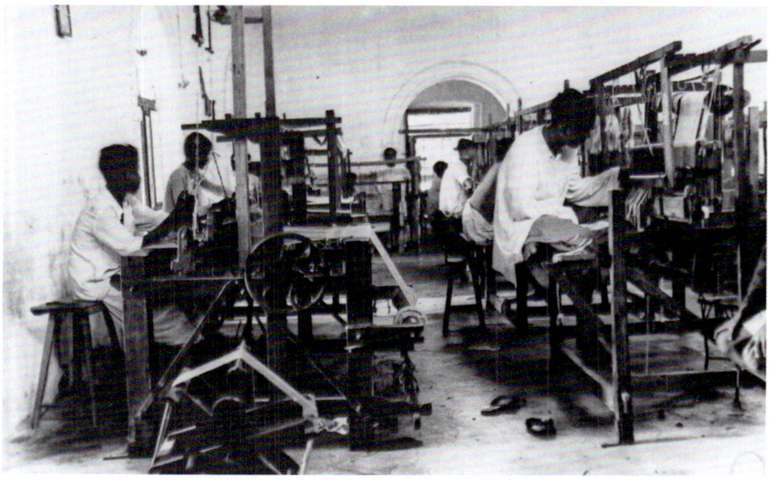

20

By the 1930s, Santiniketan was also gearing up to accept the machine, at least in its counterpart institution Sriniketan, a centre established to regenerate the local economy, where execution mattered as much as creativity. This factor introduced a new, contingent man–machine relationship into the intimate everyday aesthetic practices associated with Kala Bhavan.

18. Nandalal Bose, postcard from China with a study of a low bench, which he wanted his colleagues to take note of for its usefulness and reproducibility, 1927, 14 × 8.9 cm
19. Nandalal Bose, Faizpur Congress, entry doors, 1936, pencil on paper, postcard, 8.9 × 14 cm
20. The modernized looms in Sriniketan, India, *c.* 1930s

The Otolith Group

Living in an O Horizon

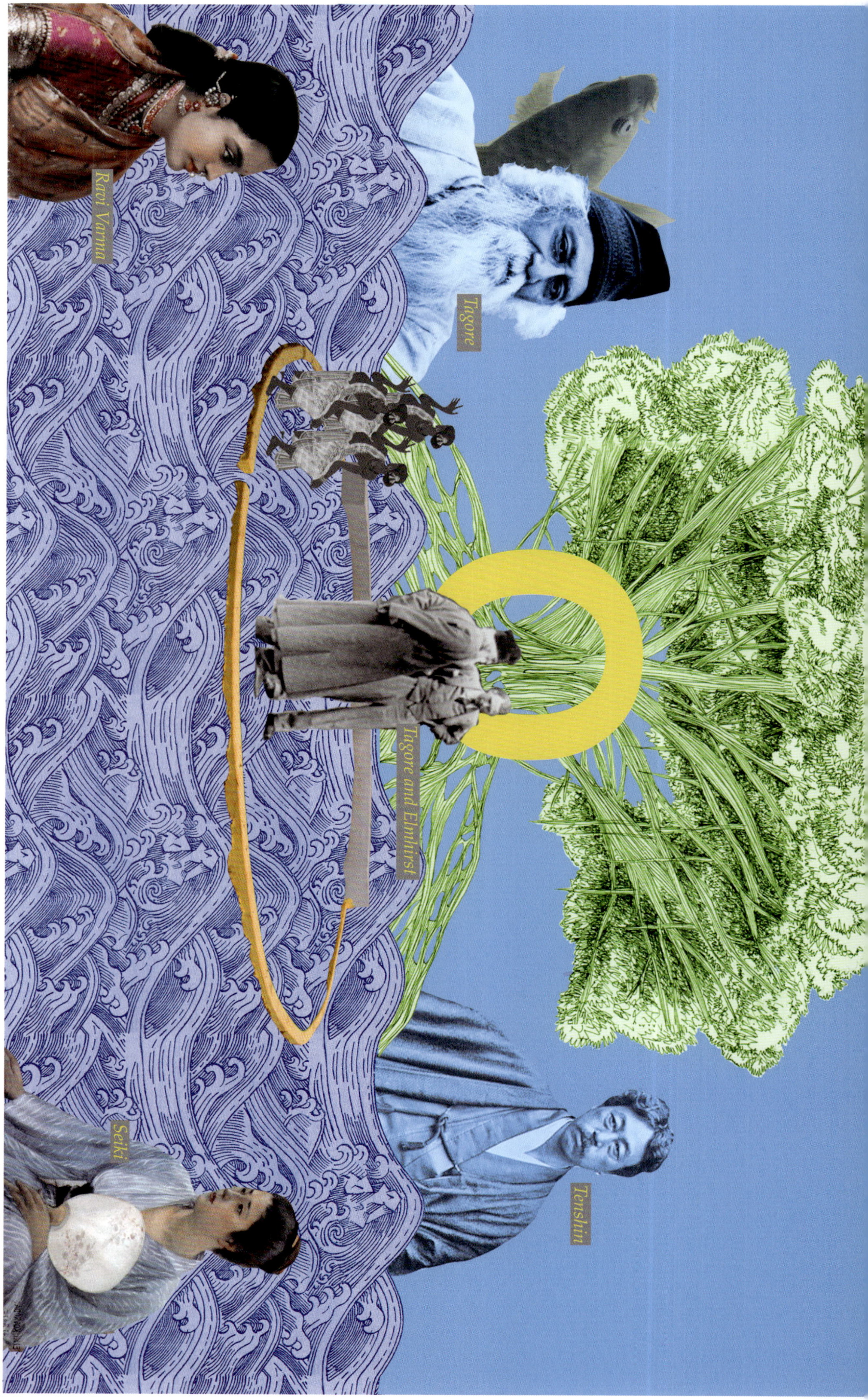
Ravi Varma
Tagore
Tagore and Elmhirst
Seiki
Tenshin

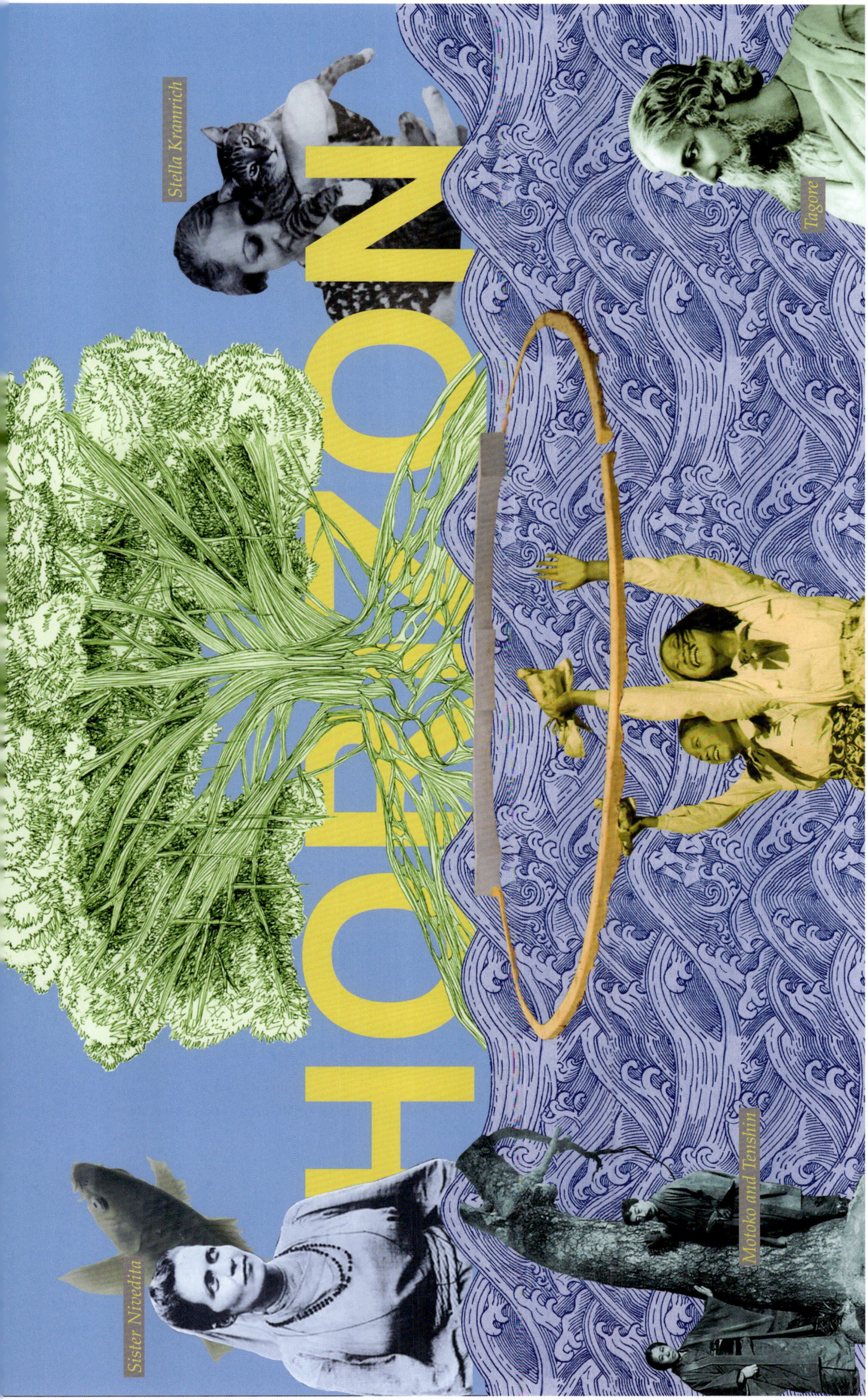
HORIZON
Stella Kramrich
Tagore
Sister Nivedita
Motoko and Tenshin

Framing Renshichirō Kawakita's Transcultural Legacy and His Pedagogy

Helena Čapková

Art writing in Japan mapped very closely the complex histories and often contradictory ideas of the Bauhaus during the 1920s and 1930s. This interest and curiosity is demonstrated in the writings of Sadanosuke Nakada (1888–1970) and Takehiko Mizutani (1907–1969), who studied at the Bauhaus Dessau from April 1927 to April 1929. In his influential article 'The State Bauhaus' printed in *Mizue* art journal, Nakada quoted Walter Gropius, who advocated the merging of art and technology – the 'synthetic art' at the Bauhaus.[1]

This synthetic approach was characteristic of the energetic activities of architect, Renshichirō Kawakita (1902–1975) and his pedagogy, which adhered to the original Bauhaus models of teaching art and design while remaining synthetic in nature. This agglomeration reflects Kawakita's longstanding interest in certain ideas developed by primarily Eurasian and European avant-gardes, whose practices he followed closely through extensive reading and translation. Although he never left Japan, Kawakita appeared on the radar of the international avant-garde in 1930 when he received fourth prize for his proposal for a theatre in Kharkov, Ukraine in an international competition that was widely followed by the architecture press.[2]

The ideas Kawakita absorbed were subsequently transferred to a Japanese readership by means of translation. He lectured extensively and associated himself with like-minded designers, with whom he opened an experimental research institute, a platform for reflection upon contemporary issues in design teaching. In 1932, Kawakita established a private school in Tokyo entitled Shin Kenchiku Kōgei Gakuin (School of New Architecture and Design), where he developed a curriculum based on the model of the Bauhaus's preliminary course and invited teachers with Bauhaus experience. The key printed matter which carried Bauhaus ideas and principles to the public was the magazine *Kenchiku Kōgei I See All* (Architecture Design I See All) published in fifty volumes from 1931 to 1936. The book *Kōsei Kyōiku Taikei* (Manual for Teaching Thinking through Construction) by Kawakita and Katsuo Takei, published in 1934, was designed to introduce new methodology and teaching materials to wider audiences, specifically art teachers active in elementary schools. Further, Kawakita did not limit his activities to his Tokyo-based institute and travelled widely, giving lectures for professionals and manufacturers all over Japan.[3]

Cover of *Kenchiku Kōgei I See All* (Architecture Design I See All), No. 12, 1935

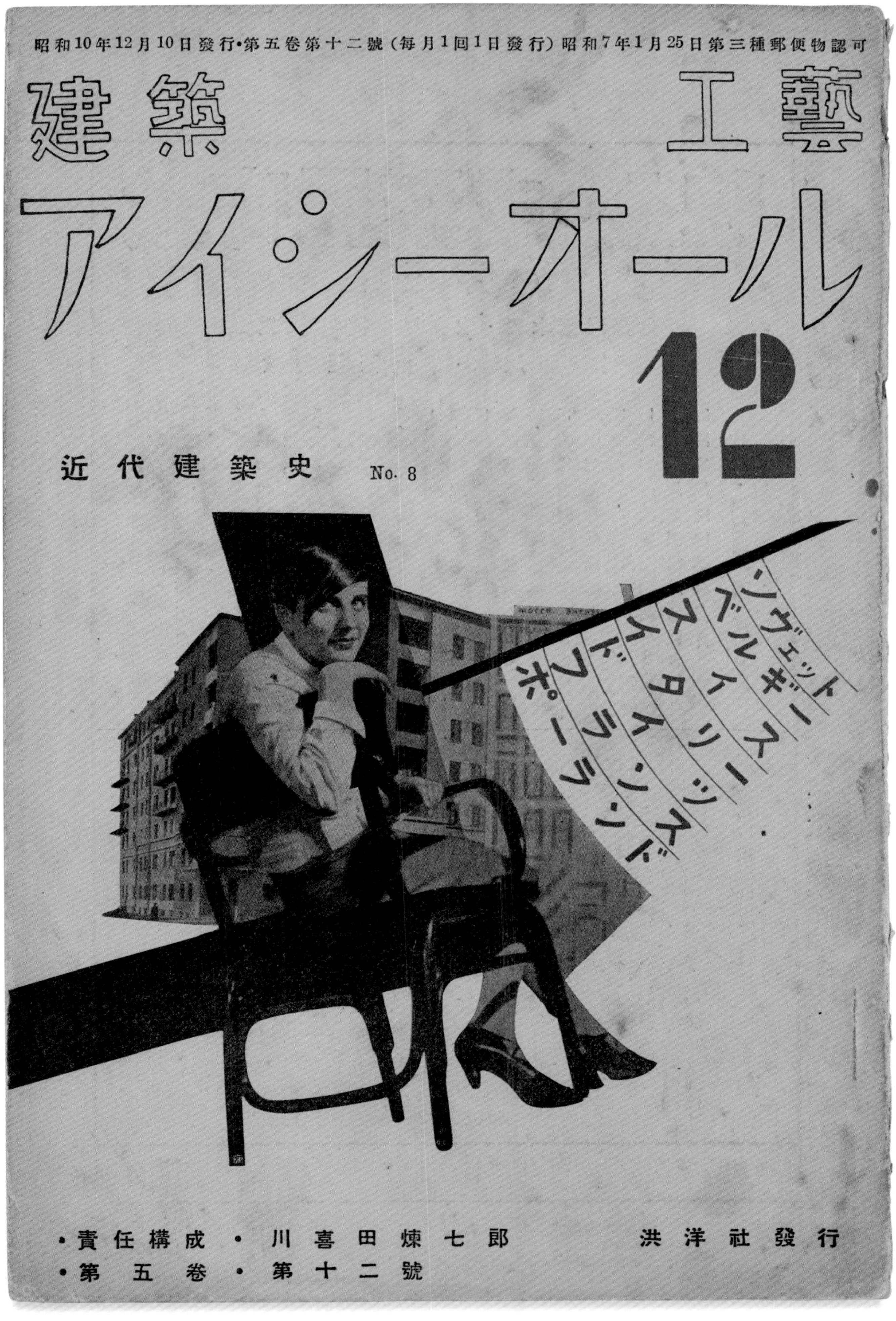

Cover of *Kenchiku Kōgei I See All* (Architecture Design I See All), No. 2, 1935

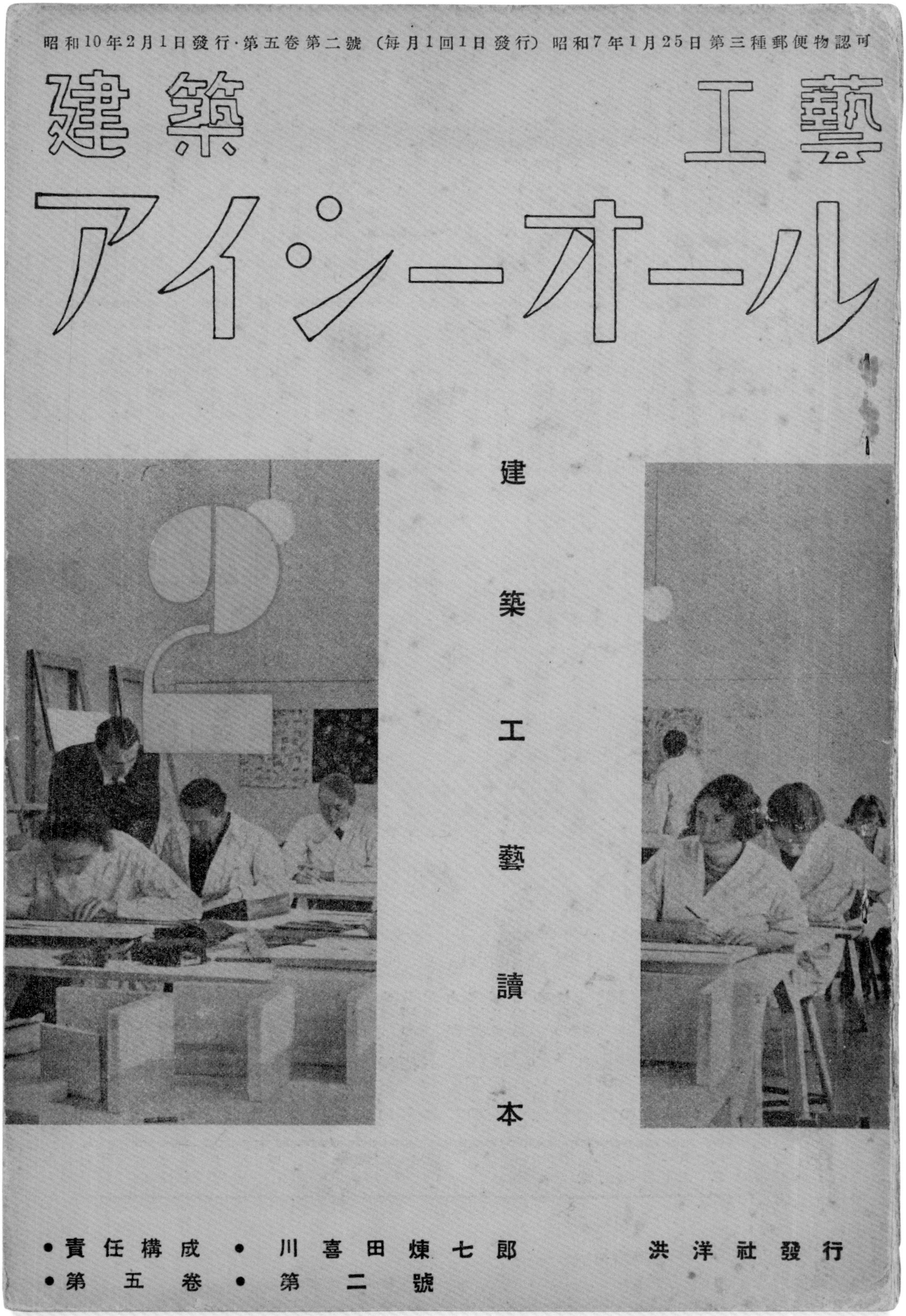

Among the founding members of the research institute was Mizutani, an architect and designer who spent a couple of formative years at the Bauhaus Dessau and was the first from the group of Japanese Bauhaus students to experience the entire Bauhaus curriculum. In 1931 Mizutani wrote about *kōsei* (construction) and identified it as the keyword and the fundamental element of education.[4] This had an enormous impact on Kawakita's activities as well as on other progressive educators who formed the new wave of Japanese art and design education in the later years.[5]

For example, Michiko and Iwao Yamawaki studied at the Bauhaus Dessau in the 1930s and became closely associated with Kawakita and teachers at his school upon their return home in 1932. Kawakita invited both of them to teach in his school. In 1934 new courses were added to its curriculum; Michiko became the head of the weaving course and her colleague Shizuko Kageyama became the head of western fashion design. Both courses, in the newly formed Centre for Weaving and Fashion Design, were advertised in the contemporary women's magazine *Fujin gahō.* Michiko taught a three-hour class once a week and the course lasted three and a half months. For this purpose, Michiko designed a small loom, which became known as the Michiko *teoriki* (Michiko's loom). From 1934 Michiko again used the portable loom when she started teaching textile design at the Jiyū Gakuen. Michiko soon became an award-winning textile designer and weaver, but stopped her artistic career entirely, for domestic reasons, just a few years before the outbreak of the Second World War. Iwao Yamawaki's photographic documentation of the Bauhaus is widely known and collected. When he returned to Japan, he carried with him a portfolio of forty-seven photographs taken during his studies and about a thousand negatives. In Japan he taught photography for half a year at the School of New Architecture and Design. He exhibited some of his photographs at Michiko's solo show at the Shiseidō gallery in 1933. However, dissatisfied with the lack of criticality in the photographic scene, he eventually quit photography completely. Despite halting their respective artistic careers, the Yamawakis were involved in pedagogy intermittently all their lives and lectured widely about their experiences.[6]

Iwao Yamawaki, 'About the Tendency of Tubular Furniture in Germany',
in *Kokusai Kenchiku* (International Architecure), March 1932

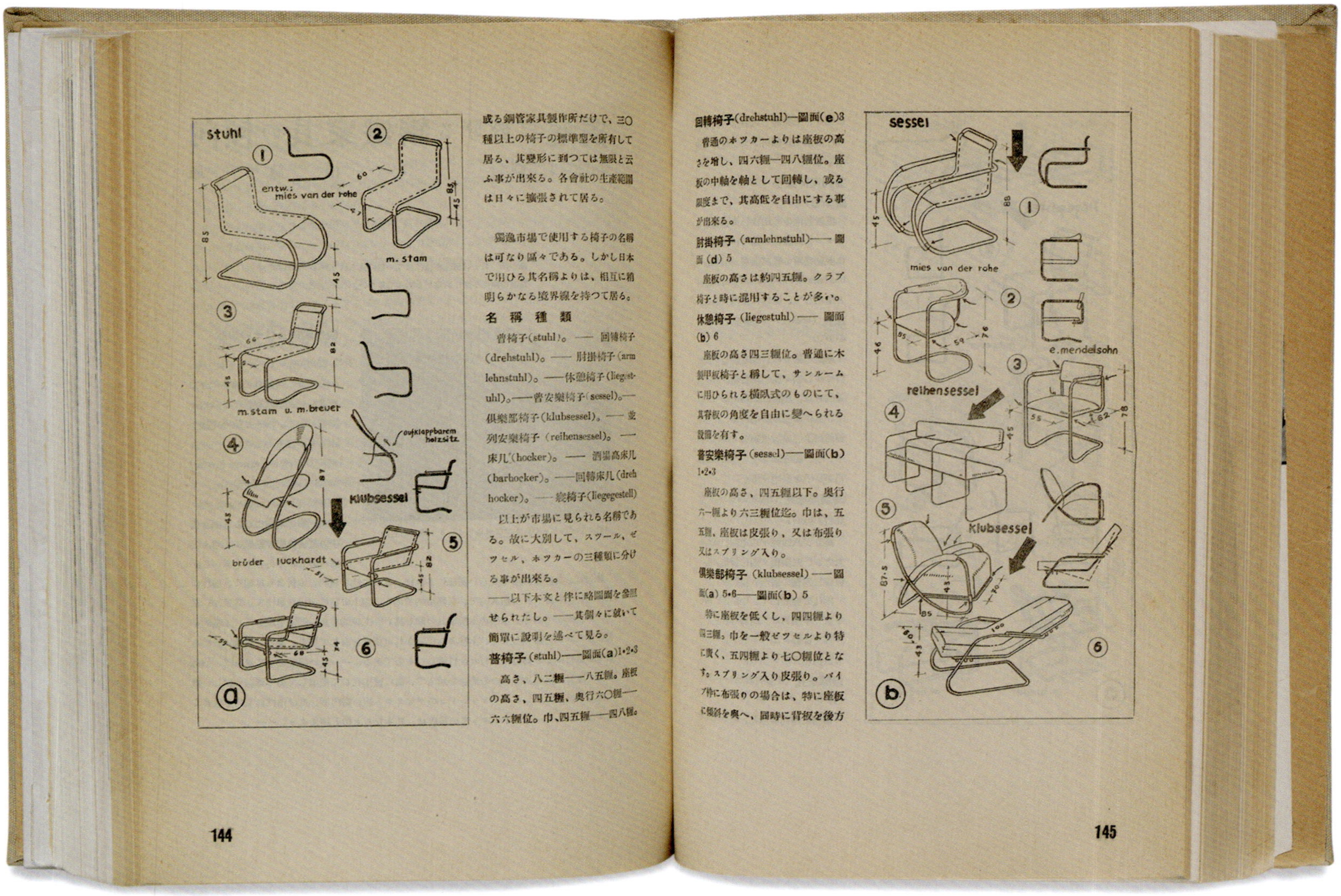

或る鋼管家具製作所だけで、三〇種以上の椅子の標準型を所有して居る、其變形に到つては無限と云ふ事が出來る。各會社の生產範圍は日々に擴張されて居る。

獨逸市場で使用する椅子の名稱は可なり區々である。しかし日本で用ひる其名稱よりは、相互に稍明らかなる境界線を持つて居る。

名　稱　種　類

普椅子(stuhl)。—— 回轉椅子(drehstuhl)。—— 肘掛椅子(armlehnstuhl)。——休憩椅子(liegestuhl)。——普安樂椅子(sessel)。——俱樂部椅子(klubsessel)。—— 並列安樂椅子(reihensessel)。—— 床几(hocker)。—— 酒場高床几(barhocker)。——回轉床几(drehhocker)。——寢椅子(liegegestell)

以上が市場に見られる名稱である。故に大別して、スツール、ゼツセル、ホツカーの三種類に分ける事が出來る。

——以下本文と伴に略圖面を參照せられたし。——其個々に就いて簡單に說明を述べて見る。

普椅子(stuhl)——圖面(a)1•2•3

高さ、八二糎——八五糎。座板の高さ、四五糎、奥行六〇糎——六六糎位。巾、四五糎——四八糎。

144

回轉椅子(drehstuhl)—圖面(e)3

普通のホツカーよりは座板の高さを增し、四六糎—四八糎位。座板の中軸を軸として回轉し、或る限度まで、其高低を自由にする事が出來る。

肘掛椅子 (armlehnstuhl)—— 圖面(d) 5

座板の高さは約四五糎。クラブ椅子と時に混用することが多い。

休憩椅子 (liegestuhl) —— 圖面(b) 6

座板の高さ四三糎位。普通に木製甲板椅子と稱して、サンルームに用ひられる橫臥式のものにて、其背板の角度を自由に變へられる設備を有す。

普安樂椅子 (sessel)——圖面(b) 1•2•3

座板の高さ、四五糎以下。奥行六一糎より六三糎位迄。巾は、五五糎、座板は皮張り，又は布張り又はスプリング入り。

俱樂部椅子 (klubsessel) ——圖面(a) 5•6——圖面(b) 5

特に座板を低くし，四四糎より四三糎，巾を一般ゼツセルより特に廣く、五四糎より七〇糎位となす。スプリング入り皮張り。パイプ枠に布張りの場合は、特に座板に傾斜を與へ、同時に背板を後方

145

'Kōsei Kyōiku Sakuhin-ten' (Exhibition of Study Works of Education about Construction), Wakayama, Japan, 1934

▶ Pages 62–63: Iwao and Michiko Yamawaki, *Bauhaus und Bauhäusler, dessau – berlin*, 1931–33, page from scrapbook

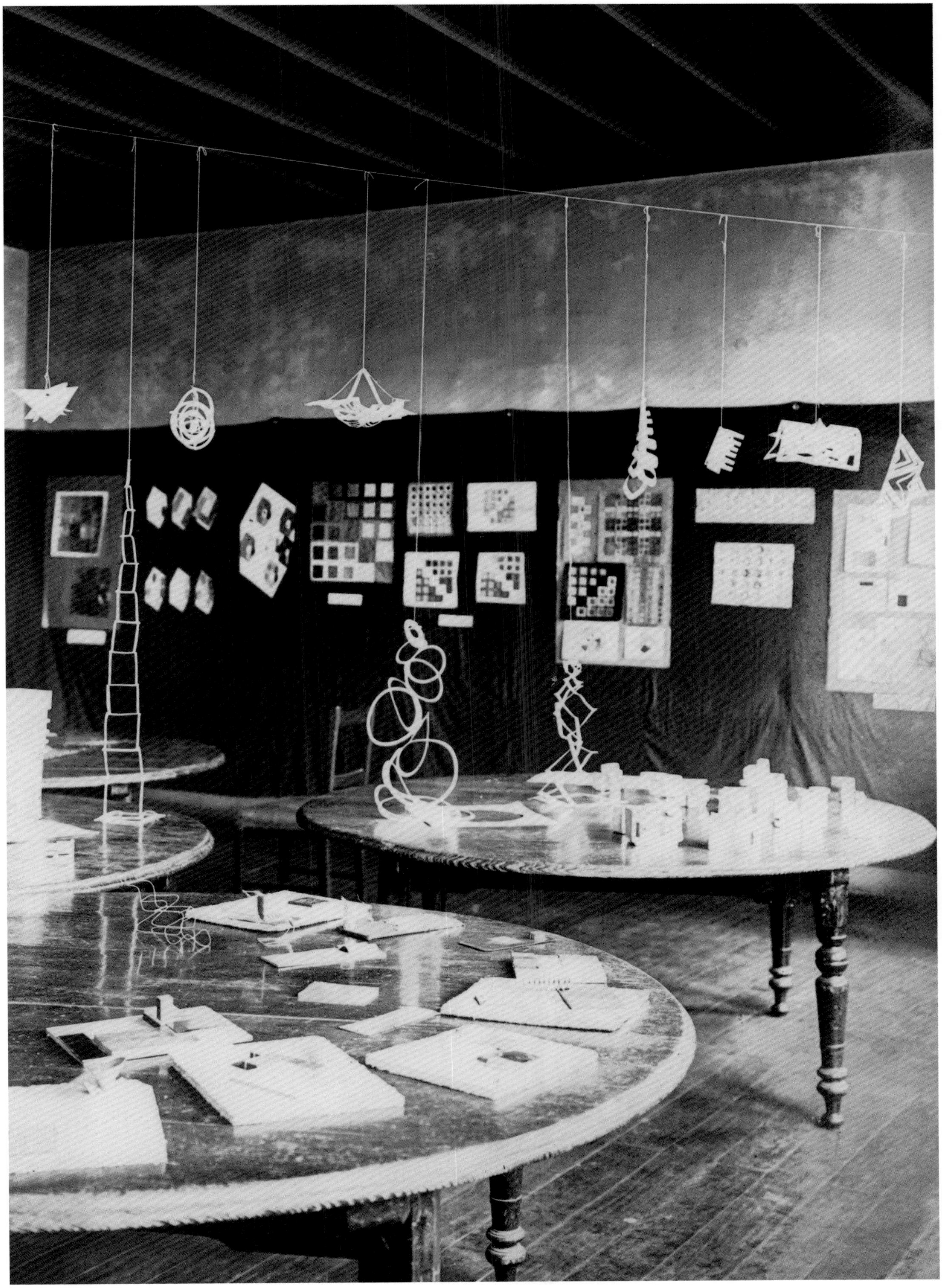

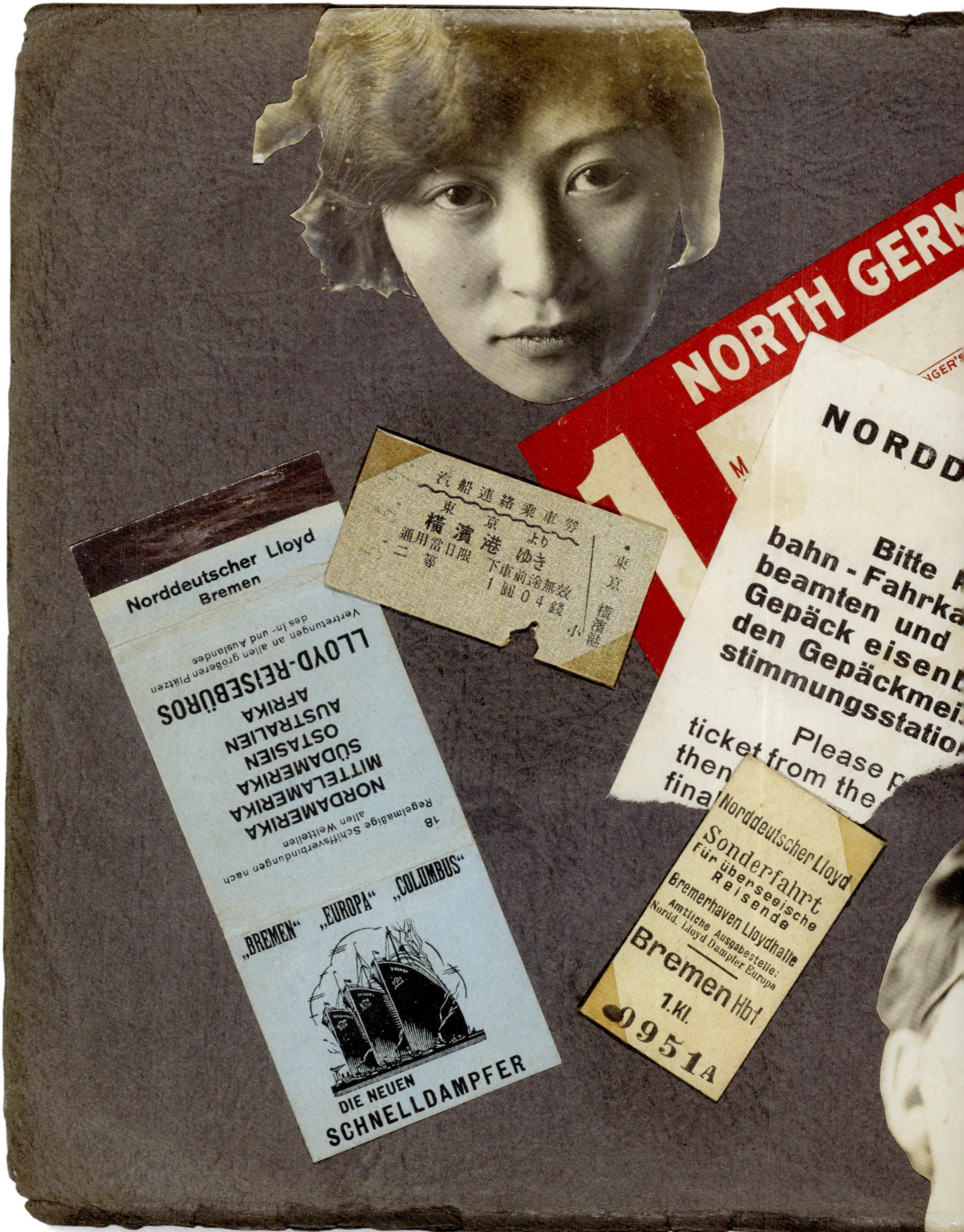
NORTH GERM
NORDD
Bitte
bahn - Fahrka
beamten und
Gepäck eisen
den Gepäckmei
stimmungsstation
Please
ticket from the
then
fina
Norddeutscher Lloyd
Bremen
LLOYD-REISEBÜROS
Vertretungen an allen größeren Plätzen des In- und Auslandes
AFRIKA
AUSTRALIEN
OSTASIEN
SÜDAMERIKA
MITTELAMERIKA
NORDAMERIKA
Regelmäßige Schiffsverbindungen nach allen Weltteilen
18
„BREMEN" „EUROPA" „COLUMBUS"
DIE NEUEN
SCHNELLDAMPFER
東京より
横濱港ゆき
1圓04錢
Norddeutscher Lloyd
Sonderfahrt
Für überseeische Reisende
Bremerhaven Lloydhalle
Amtliche Ausgabestelle: Nordd. Lloyd Dampfer Europa
Bremen Hbf
1. Kl.
09514

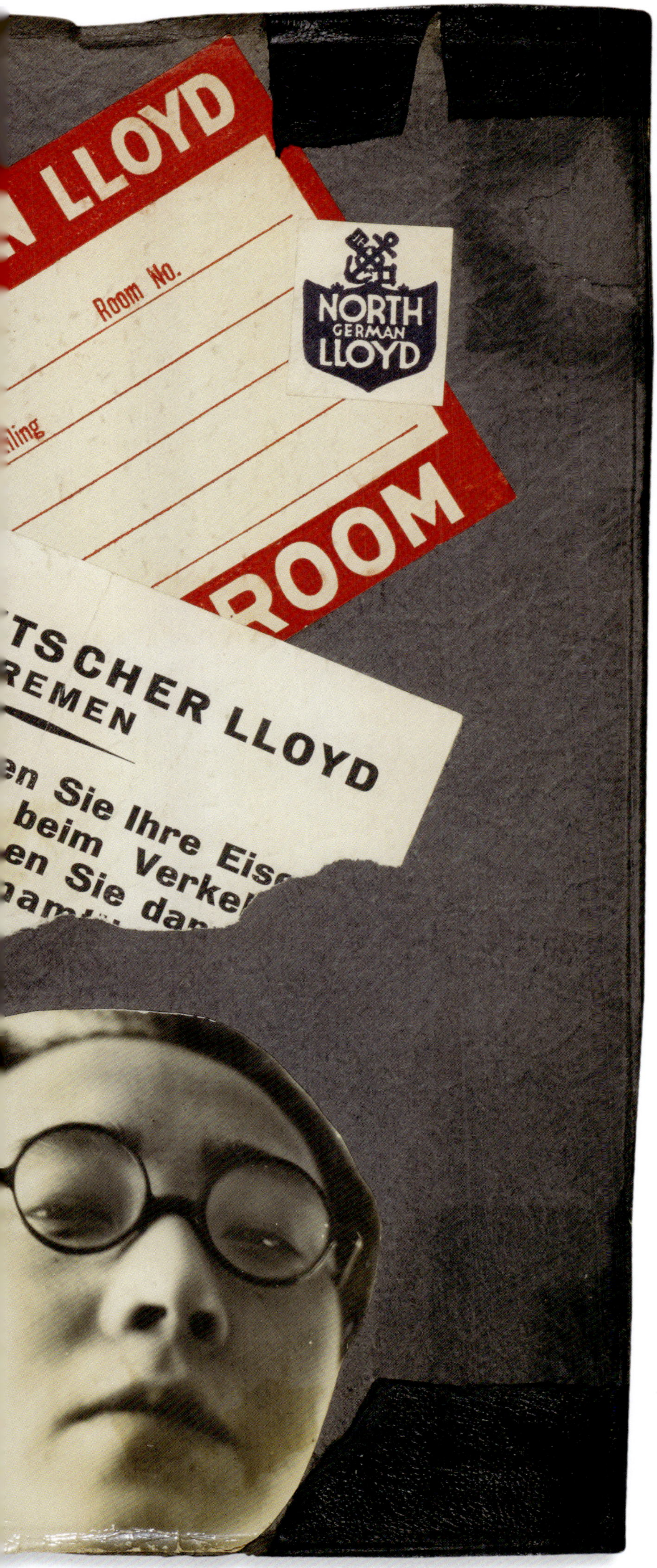
LLOYD
Room No.
NORTH GERMAN LLOYD
ROOM
TSCHER LLOYD
REMEN
en Sie Ihre Eis
beim Verke
en Sie da

Kawakita's interpretation of modern art and design education reflected a diversified interest in the international modernist design teaching that latently carried within it practices derived from craft and architecture, but also spiritual and oriental art practices melded together into an appealing and progressive methodology. This intense dynamic between the spiritual and the scientific manifested in, for example, the struggle over the meaning of the term *spannung*[7] between Kawakita and the Seinen Kenchiku-ka Club (Young Architects' Club) in 1933 and 1934. Kawakita's definition presented in *Manual for Teaching Thinking through Construction* was considered broad and misleading and supported the opinion of the club that the book is too 'mystical and spiritualistic' for education.[8]

In the 1930s the area of Japanese design itself was going through transformation and became officially regarded as a symbol of modern Japanese identity.[9] This process manifested in development of good Japanese design that was supervised by the Ministry of Trade and Industry and Kōgei Shidōsho (Design Research Institute); a group of foreign experts was even invited to Japan to supervise proper development. This was the case for acclaimed architect Bruno Taut, who stayed in Japan from 1933 to 1936. As nationalism intensified throughout Japan, modern design was suspected to be associated with the international socialist movement, which also contributed to the shift in Kawakita's activities. The experimental school closed in 1936, and in his 1942 book, *Kōsaku Gijutsu Taikei* (A General Guide to Industrial Techniques), Kawakita focused on applying *kōsei* education in an industrial context that catered to a militarized society.[10]

The transnational exchange in design and design education was muted during the Second World War, but was carried beyond the war by many progressive designers, such as some excellent students from the School of New Architecture and Design: fashion designer Yōko Kuwasawa (1910–1977) and graphic designer Yūsaku Kamekura (1915–1997). When the American occupation of Japan ended in 1952 and with the emergence of special procurement needs during the Korean War, industrial production increased. In 1958 the Ministry of Education first included 'design work' in the new Course of Study for the school art curriculum, reflecting the contemporary design boom and general recognition of design as an important professional field. The Good Design Selection System, initiated in 1957, also had a role in activating the discussion of design, and the G-mark was designed by Kamekura. His iconic poster designs for the 1964 Olympic Games in Tokyo marked the peak of the design boom of previous years.

A new Bauhaus impulse arrived in Japan with the global Bauhaus revival in 1950s, which was embodied by Gropius (then Harvard-based), who toured Japan and Australia in 1954, funded by the Rockefeller Foundation's programme to champion cultural exchange between the 'East' and the 'West'. Gropius was hosted by many of his Bauhaus contacts, including the Yamawakis, and visited Yōko Kuwasawa's Kuwasawa Design School, which she opened in the same year. On this occasion, Gropius evaluated the school positively, congratulating Kuwasawa as follows: 'Here I have found genuine Bauhaus spirit, the desirable trend I am looking for: the transitional, creative bridge between the East and the West. Great success to you!'[11]

The refracted history of the Bauhaus has significant anchoring in the political sphere: while the pre-war Bauhaus resonated with progressive, left-leaning, queer or eccentric personalities, such as Kawakita, in the post-war era the Bauhaus came to be identified with a solid, mainstream modernist narrative that became associated with the US and Gropius. As such it resonated with a different spectrum of designers that catered to the large, 'western-oriented' Japanese audiences. Yet, the queer/non-conformist aspect of the Bauhaus has not disappeared entirely; indeed it has carried on to the present day in the Japanese design scene as a part of art and design education.

Organization chart of the Bauhaus, in Renshichiro Kawakita (ed.), *Kenchiku Shincho* (New Wave of Architecture), Special Issue: Bauhaus, Vol. 10, No. 11, Tokyo: Koyo-sha, 1929, p. 5

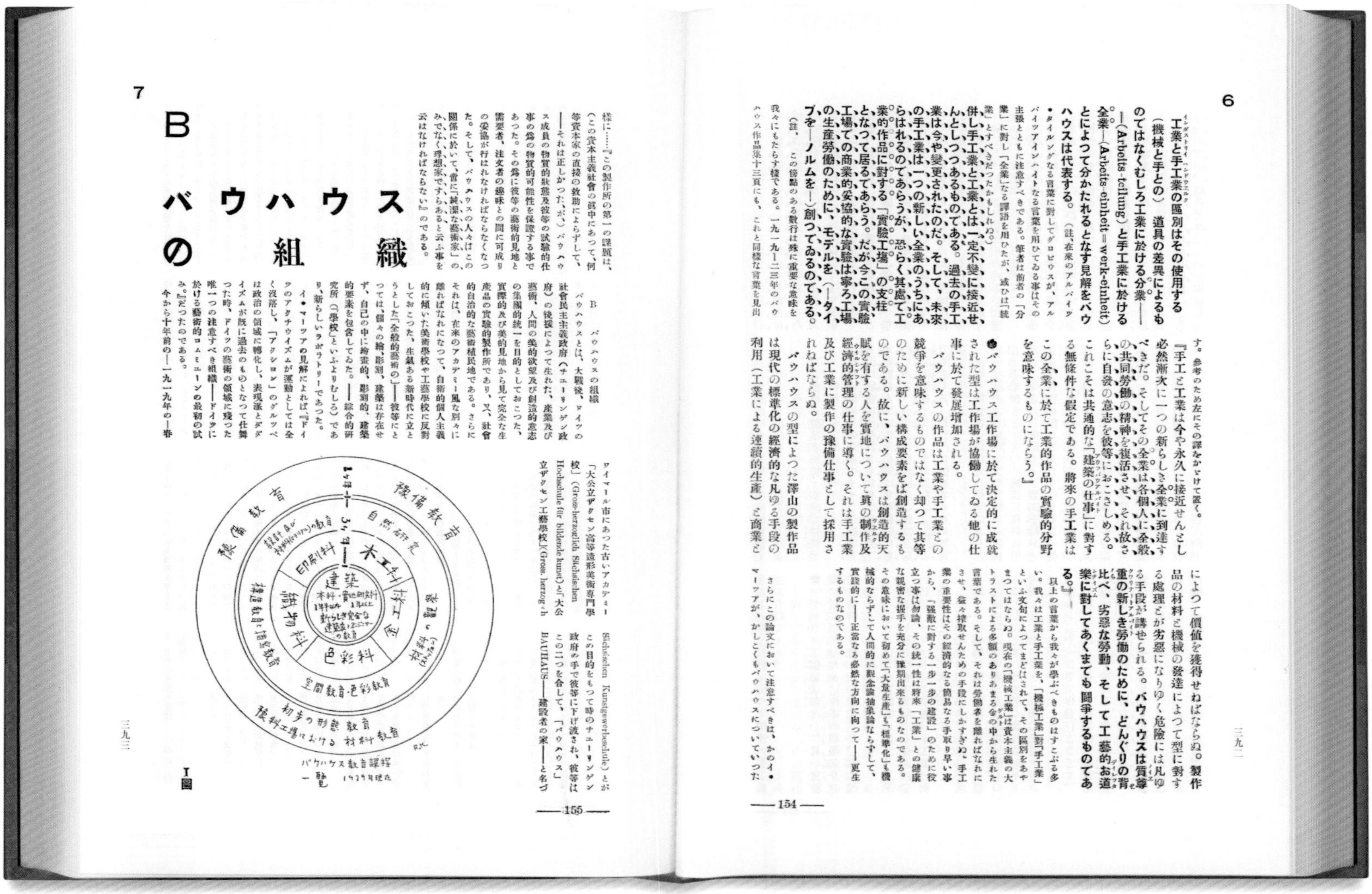

7

B

バウハウスの組織

6

—155—

—154—

On the Reception of Johannes Itten's Art Education in Japan

Yoshimasa Kaneko

Significant educational interaction between Johannes Itten and the Japanese took place mostly during the time he ran the Itten-Schule (Itten School) in Berlin, in particular between 1931 and 1933. At the Itten School, Shōnan Mizukoshi gave lessons on Japanese ink drawing *sumi-e* (*Nanga* style) in 1931,[1] and Yumeji Takehisa also gave lectures on *sumi-e* in 1933.[2] For Itten, this was a period when his interest in Asia, most particularly in Japan, peaked through his encounters with Japanese painters. In fact, the 1932/33 prospectus of the Itten School provided an additional reference to the 'Pinselzeichnen nach chinesisch-japanischer Art' (Brush Drawing according to Chinese-Japanese Methods). But above all, the interaction was with Mitsuko Yamamuro and Kazuko Imai (married name Sasagawa), Jiyū Gakuen school students, who studied at the Itten School under Itten in 1932 and played a key role in the reception of Itten's art education in Japan.[3]

Immediately following their return to Japan in November 1932, the Jiyū Gakuen Arts and Crafts Institute (Laboratory) was established, and there Yamamuro and Imai were key to its development. They conveyed Itten's basic education (morning gymnastics and singing, brush drawing with *sumi*-ink, light and dark studies, form studies, analysis of masterpieces, study of lines, study of colors, study of materials and a monthly assignment) to Jiyū Gakuen and its Institute. At the same time, they introduced the educational methods of the Itten School in a monthly magazine, *Fujin-no-Tomo* (Women's Friend), as well as through exhibitions held at Jiyū Gakuen. Interestingly Yamamuro and Imai learned the significance of Japanese *sumi*-ink drawing from Itten.

Furthermore, Yamamuro and Imai presented a detailed report on Itten's educational methods to Renshichirō Kawakita at a round table discussion held at the New Architecture and Industrial Arts Research Institute in Ginza on 11 December 1932.[4] When Japanese Bauhäuslers Takehiko Mizutani, Iwao and Michiko Yamawaki, and Tamae Ōno studied at the Bauhaus, Itten was no longer Bauhaus-Meister. As such, Yamamuro and Imai became an invaluable firsthand source of Itten's art education. Kawakita was the president of the aforementioned New Architecture and Industrial Arts Research Institute and its Training School in Ginza (later renamed Shin Kenchiku Kōgei Gakuin (School of New Architecture and Design)), where he provided training sessions, introducing the art education of the Bauhaus. The School produced well-known artists such as Yūsaku Kamekura (graphic designer) and Sōfū Teshigahara (Japanese flower arrangement artist). *Kōsei Kyōiku Taikei* (Manual for Teaching Thinking through Construction, 1934), which Kawakita co-authored with Katsuo Takei, has become a significant book that sheds some light on art education at the Bauhaus. The book also contains the work that Yamamuro created at the Itten School, making it clear that Yamamuro and Imai had made contributions to the publication of *Kōsei Kyōiku Taikei*.[5] In addition, Kawakita and Takei point out the common aspects they could see in the Japanese *sumi*-ink drawing rendering and the light and dark studies as they describe the said studies in the book.[6]

Later, Itten gave a keynote address at the 1958 FEA-Congress in Basel, during which an exhibition of works created by students following Itten's educational methods was presented. At Itten's request, Jiyū Gakuen school sent its students' works of art to him for the exhibition, which were displayed with praise from Itten.[7] In a letter to Yamamuro that same year (dated 22 December 1958), Itten wrote about the progress of his study in Zen by reading a book on the subject.

Eva Plaut, who had studied at the Itten School with Yamamuro and Imai, came to Japan in 1935. And then she gave seminars based on Itten's educational methods in Tokyo.[8] Hiroshi Ōchi focused on Itten's teaching methods he had learned from Plaut and put them together into sixty-six panels for his graduate research. He also co-authored *Shin-Seikatsu-Bi-no-Houkou* (The Direction of New Beauty in Life) in 1944 with Genichirō Ushiyama, who also took Plaut's seminar. Some of Itten's educational methods can be found in this book. In 1954, Ōchi met Itten in Zurich, and later he translated Itten's *Kunst der Farbe* (The Art of Colour) into Japanese together with Matashirō Tezuka, who also translated *Mein Vorkurs am Bauhaus* (Design and Form: The Basic Course at the Bauhaus). These two translations helped to promote Itten's educational methods widely in the world of art education in Japan.

Upon his meeting with Itten, Tezuka mentioned in writing how amazed he was by the profound insights Itten offered into Japanese art. A handful of other people in Japan also had the chance to meet Itten. The founder of the Tamagawa Gakuen school, Kuniyoshi Obara, who promoted 'Zenjin Education' (well-balanced, all-around education), met Itten in Berlin in 1931. There he observed a lecture which Mizukoshi was giving on the art of Japanese *sumi*-ink drawing. After listening to Itten's thoughts on the subject, Obara was reminded anew of the educational values of Japanese *sumi*-ink drawing.[9] Also in 1958, Shūzō Takiguchi, a leading Japanese art critic, met Itten in Zurich. According to Takiguchi, Itten talked about the significance of character building and growth as human beings in professional art education, for which one would have to develop the ability to concentrate. Itten continued to tell him how the spirituality of Japanese Zen was helpful in order to achieve this goal.[10]

As described above, Itten's educational methods in art were accepted in Japan through a variety of encounters and the continued interaction that he had with Japanese people. In these exchanges, we are all the while reminded of the significance of personal growth through art education as well as the educational benefits of the spirituality of Japanese *sumi*-ink drawing and Zen.

Manual for Teaching Thinking through Construction (1934): An Introduction

Hiromitsu Umemiya

The book *Kōsei Kyōiku Taikei* (Manual for Teaching Thinking through Construction) by Renshichirō Kawakita and Katsuo Takei, published in 1934 (9th year of Showa Era), was designed to introduce new methodologies and teaching materials to art teachers in elementary schools. This new approach to the teaching of art, the emphasis of which was on the construction or composition of elements (i.e. materials, colours and forms), followed upon the preceding movement in art education, *jiyūga* (free drawing).

Liberated art production aimed at nurturing the individual personality and creativity of children by letting them paint and draw freely, without telling them what to conceive. By contrast, *Kōsei Kyōiku Taikei* focused on acquiring fundamental skills necessary for creative production by cultivating the ability to grasp the material specificities, structures and connections among various objects present in everyday life. Rather than individuality, the specific concern of the book was an emphasis on the development of a fundamental, general set of skills.

The book was written in the context of the contemporary impact of the Bauhaus preliminary course in Japan. Although one of the authors, the architect Kawakita, followed Bauhaus ideas very closely through reading numerous publications, he started the new design education only after 1931 when instructed in detail by Takehiko Mizutani, an actual student of the Bauhaus who had participated in the preliminary course. This new education was initially conceived for professionals dealing with architecture and furniture design, but very early on a group of elementary school teachers joined and studied this method enthusiastically. Kawakita's collaborator and the co-author of the book, Katsuo Takei, was inexhaustibly active in teaching and disseminating *Kōsei Kyōiku Taikei.* Many illustrations in the book are in fact works by his students with whom he experimented in his workplace.

In the interwar period, *Kōsei Kyōiku Taikei* was never adopted as part of the regular curriculum of school education. However, after the war, some elements of it became reflected in the regular curriculum of art education. One of the reasons for this was that teachers who experienced the approach of *Kōsei Kyōiku Taikei* in the interwar period suddenly became leaders in art education after the war. In this period, the importance of design was recognized in relation to post-war Japan's reconstruction and development, and thus art education was supported as part of this trend.

In this way, the impact of the Bauhaus preliminary course in Japan became widespread among many people who may not have known about the original Bauhaus and its interwar history. This book illustrates the beginning of the process of adopting and accommodating Bauhaus ideas into Japanese art education.

Renshichirō Kawakita and Katsuo Takei, *Kōsei Kyōiku Taikei*
(Manual for Teaching Thinking through Construction),
Tokyo: Gakko Bijutsu Kyokai Shuppan-bu, 1934, pp. 398–99

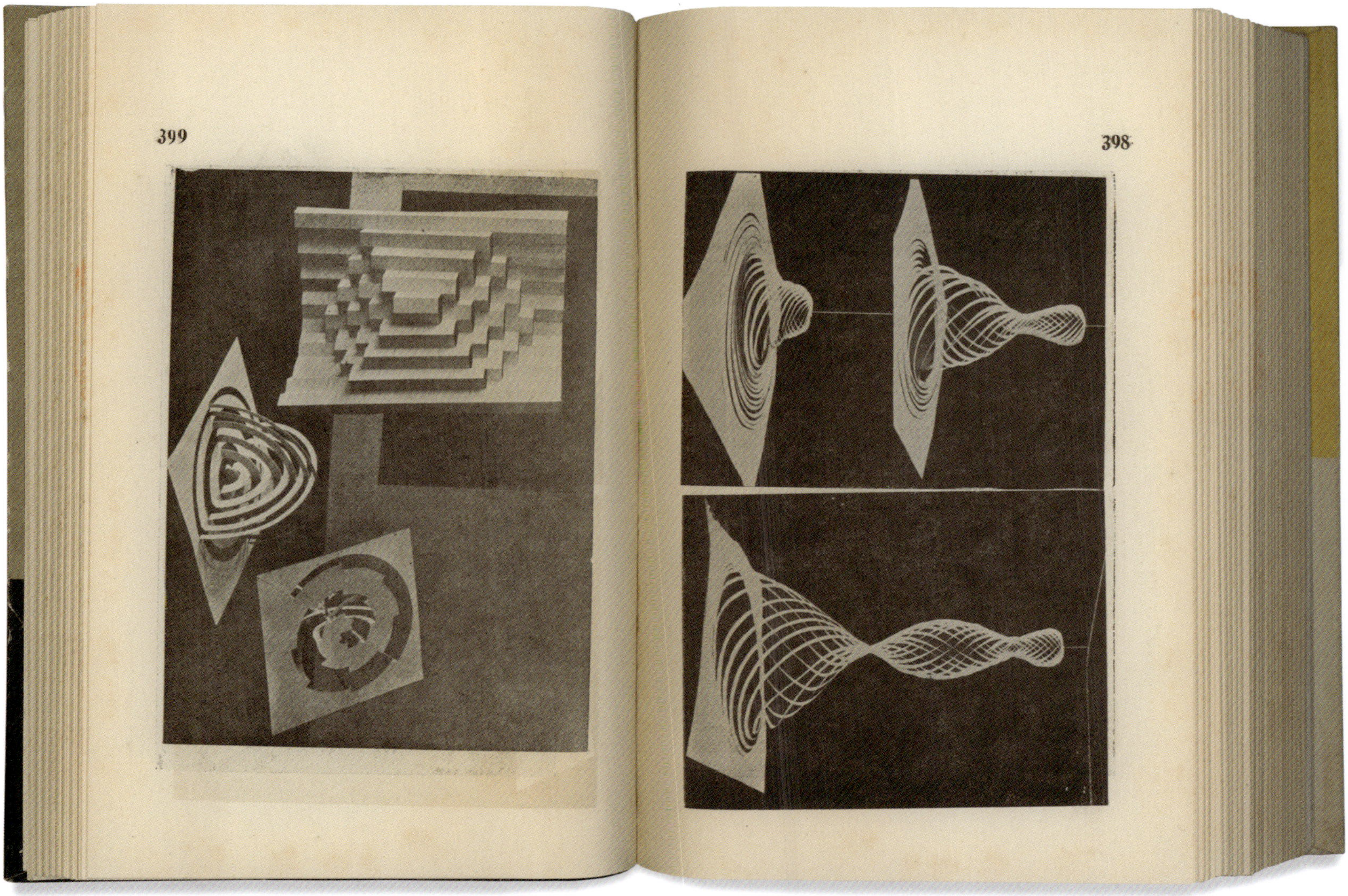

Renshichirō Kawakita and Katsuo Takei, *Kōsei Kyōiku Taikei*
(Manual for Teaching Thinking through Construction),
Tokyo: Gakko Bijutsu Kyokai Shuppan-bu, 1934, pp. 400–01

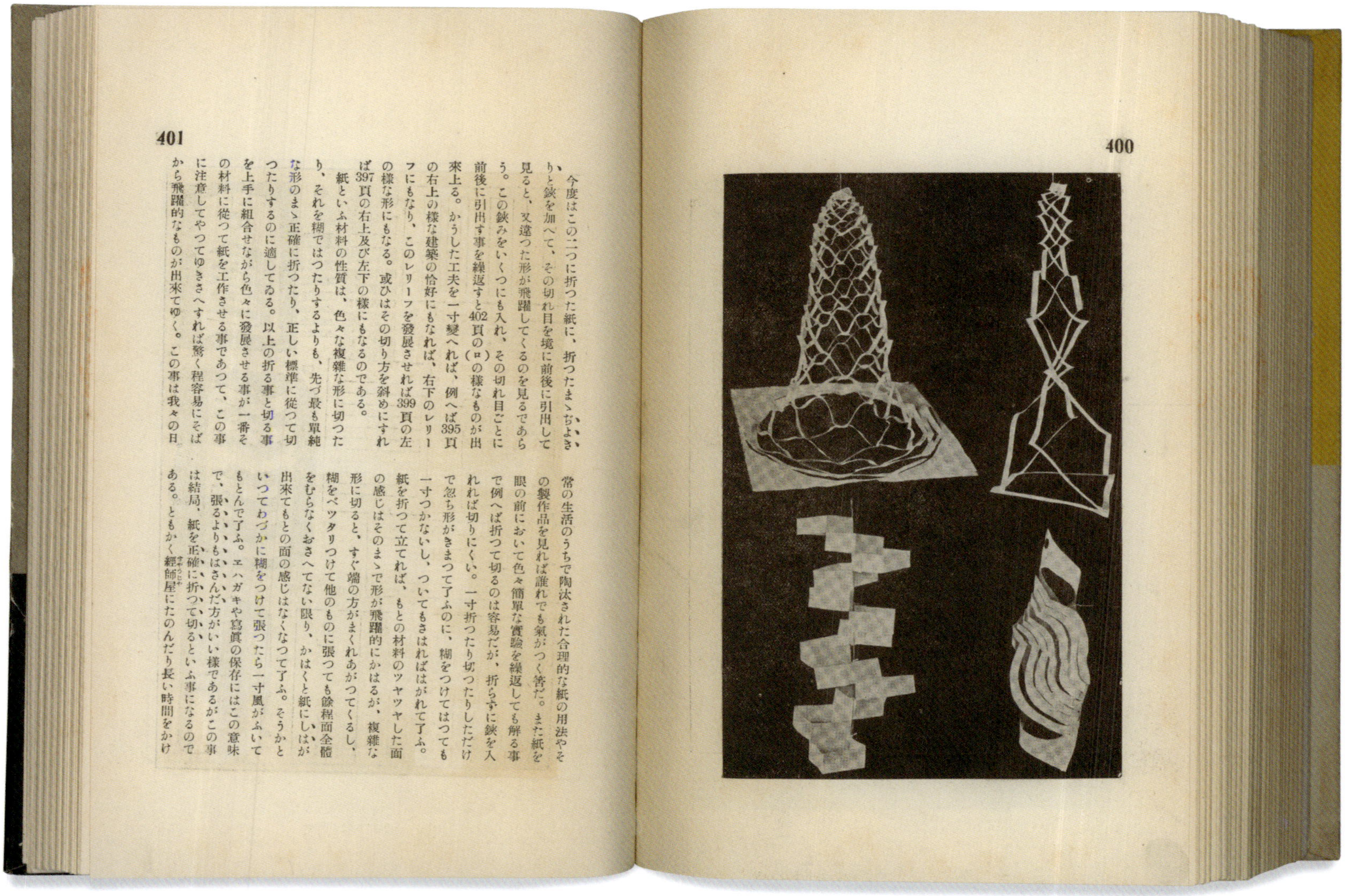

401

今度はこの二つに折つた紙に、折つたまゝちよきりと鋏を加へて、その切れ目を境に前後に引出して見ると、又違つた形が飛躍してくるのを見るであらう。この鋏みをいくつにも入れ、その切れ目ごとに前後に引出す事を繰返すと402頁の(ロ)の様なものが出來上る。かうした工夫を一寸變へれば、例へば395頁の右上の様な建築の恰好にもなれば、右下のレリーフにもなり、このレリーフを發展させれば399頁の左の様な形にもなる。或ひはその切り方を斜めにすれば397頁の右上及び左下の様にもなるのである。

紙といふ材料の性質は、色々な複雑な形に切つたり、それを糊ではつたりするよりも、先づ最も單純な形のまゝ正確に折つたり、正しい標準に從つて切つたりするのに適してゐる。以上の折る事と切る事を上手に組合せながら色々に發展させる事が一番その材料に從つて紙を工作させる事であつて、この事に注意してやつてゆきさへすれば驚く程容易にそばから飛躍的なものが出來てゆく。この事は我々の日常の生活のうちで陶汰された合理的な紙の用法やその製作品を見れば誰れでも氣がつく筈だ。また紙を眼の前において色々簡單な實驗を繰返しても解る事で例へば折つて切るのは容易だが、折らずに鋏を入れれば切りにくい。一寸折つたり切つたりしただけで忽ち形がきまつて了ふのに、糊をつけてはつても一寸つかないし、ついてもさはればはがれて了ふ。紙を折つて立てれば、もとの材料のツヤツヤした面の感じはそのまゝで形が飛躍的にかはるが、複雑な形に切ると、すぐ端の方がまくれあがつてくるし、糊をベツタリつけて他のものに張つても餘程面全體をむらなくおさへてない限り、かはくと紙にしいが出來てもとの面の感じはなくなつて了ふ。そうかといつてわづかに糊をつけて張つたら一寸風がふいてもとんで了ふ。エハガキや寫眞の保存にはこの意味で、張るよりもはさんだ方がいい様であるがこの事は結局、紙を正確に折つて切るといふ事になるのである。ともかく經師屋にたのんだり長い時間をかけ

400

Luca Frei

Model for a Pedagogical Vehicle

The installation, which is visual and tactile, includes elements of handicraft, architecture and printmaking and can be approached at many levels. It originates from a personal reading of four photographs documenting the 'Seikatsu Kōsei Exhibition' at Bunka Gakuin (School of Culture) in Tokyo, organized by Renshichirō Kawakita in 1931 to introduce Bauhaus ideas and pedagogy to Japan.

The display structure refers in part to the set designs of Jikken Kōbō (Experimental Workshop, 1951–57) a group who are emblematic of the reception of the Bauhaus in post-war Japan. In this sense the installation as a whole can be seen as an attempt to reconnect these two distinctive understandings and approaches to Bauhausian pedagogy and philosophy before and after the Second World War.

► Pages 73, 75: Luca Frei, *Design for Pillows*, 2017, gouache, pencil and collage on foam core, 70 × 100 × 3 cm

►►► Page 77: Luca Frei, *Model for a Pedagogical Vehicle*, 2017, wood, textile, gouache, dimensions variable

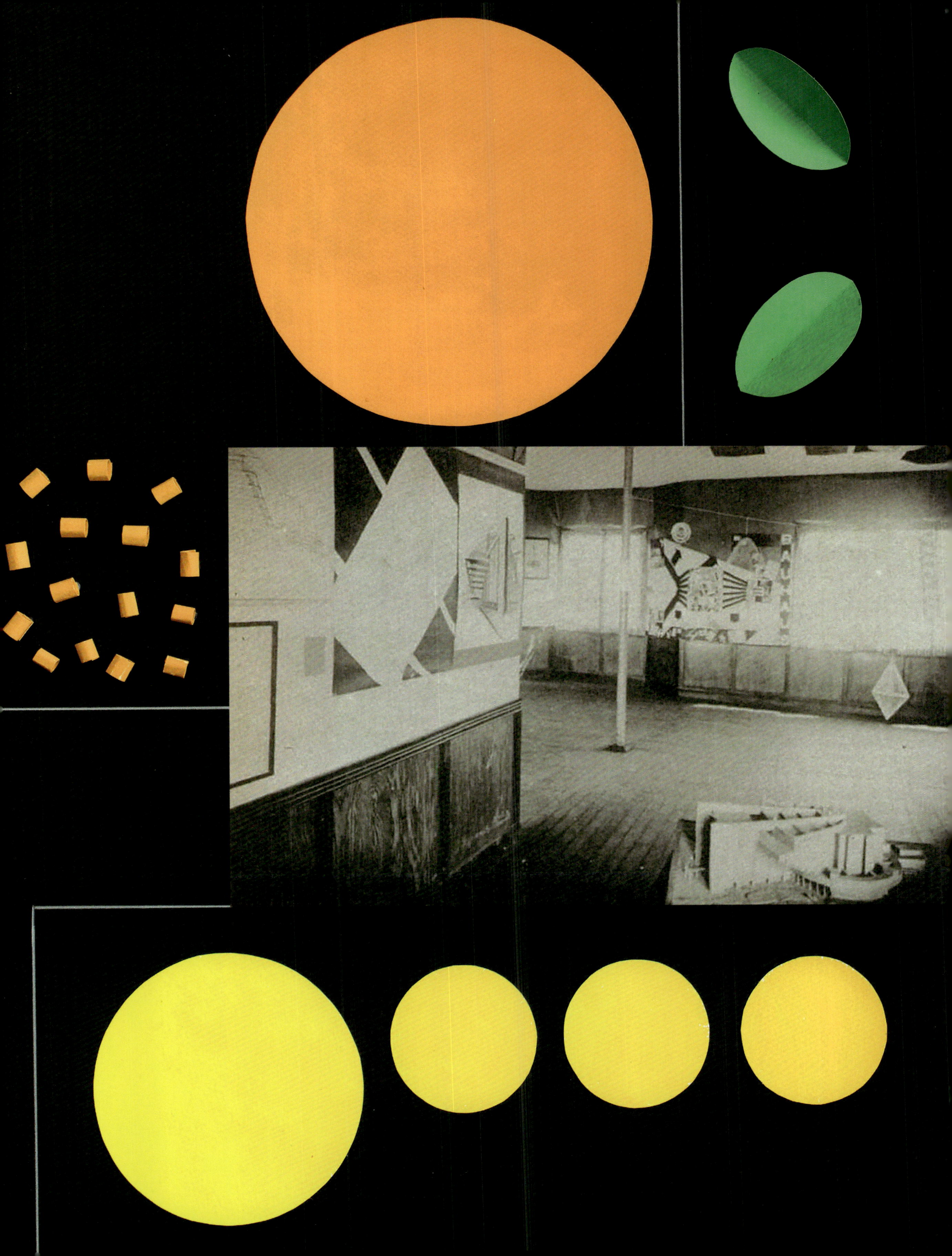

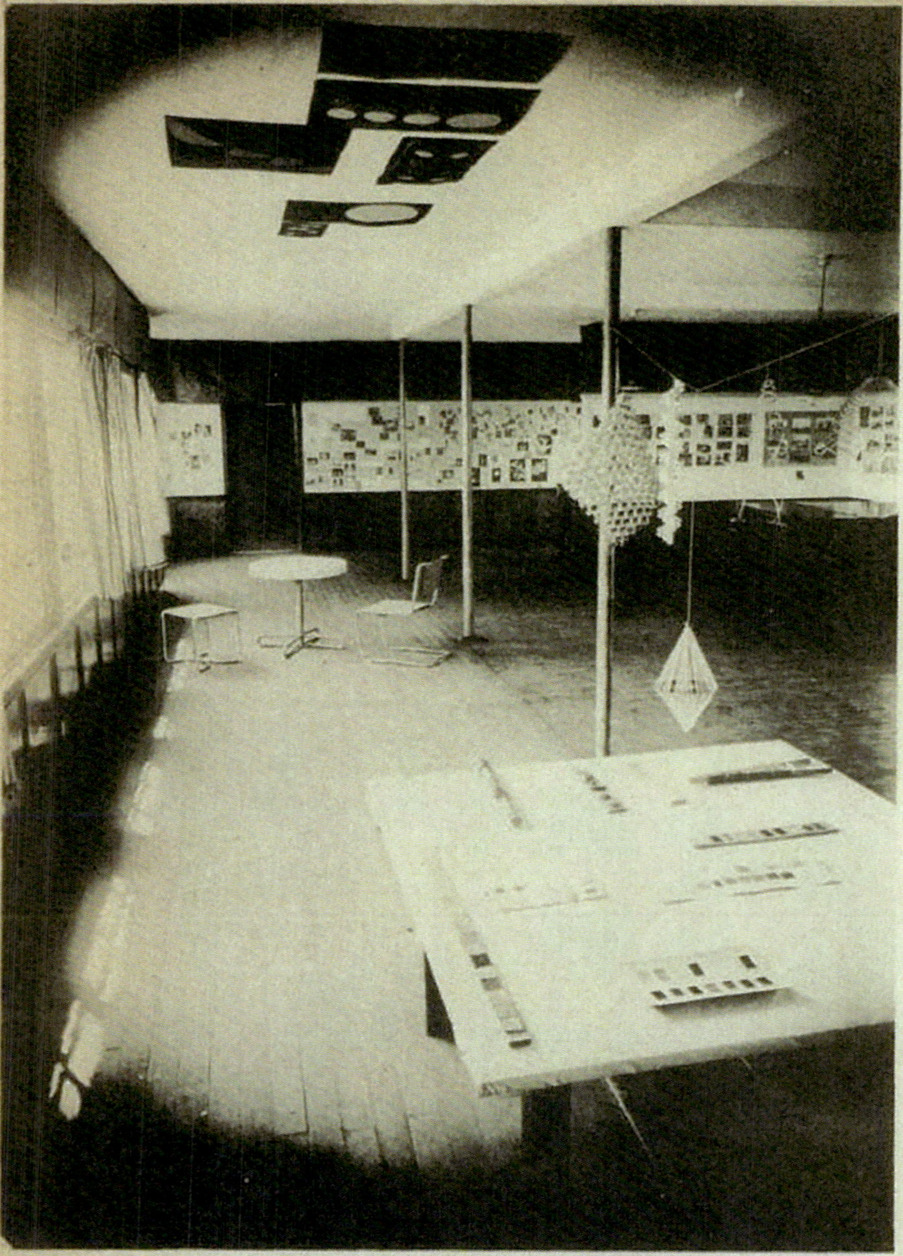

生活構成展覽會　2

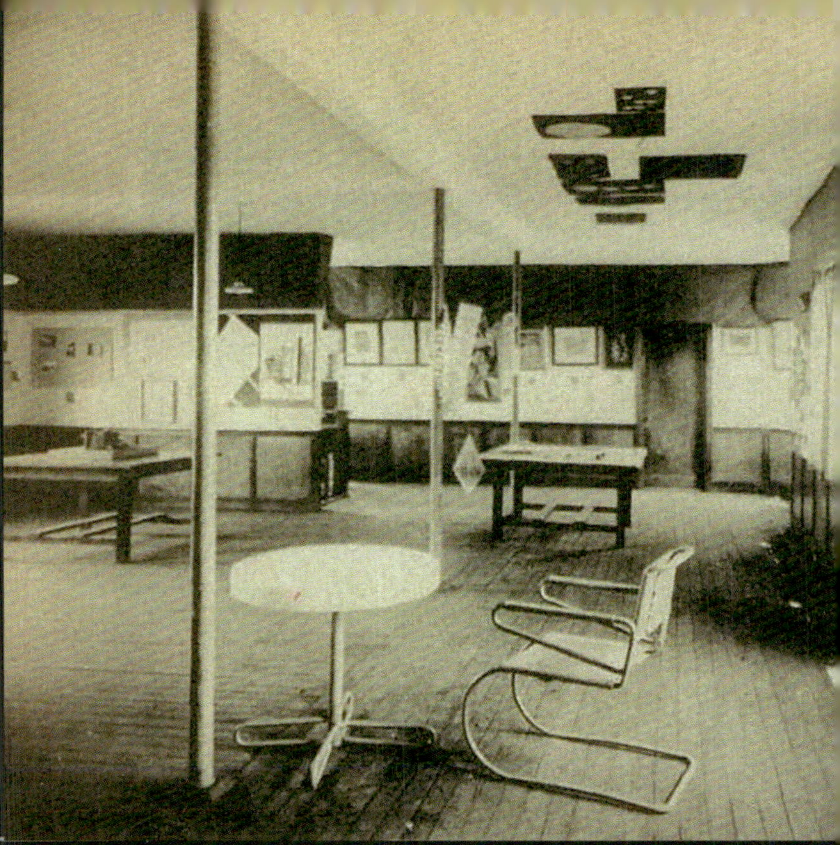

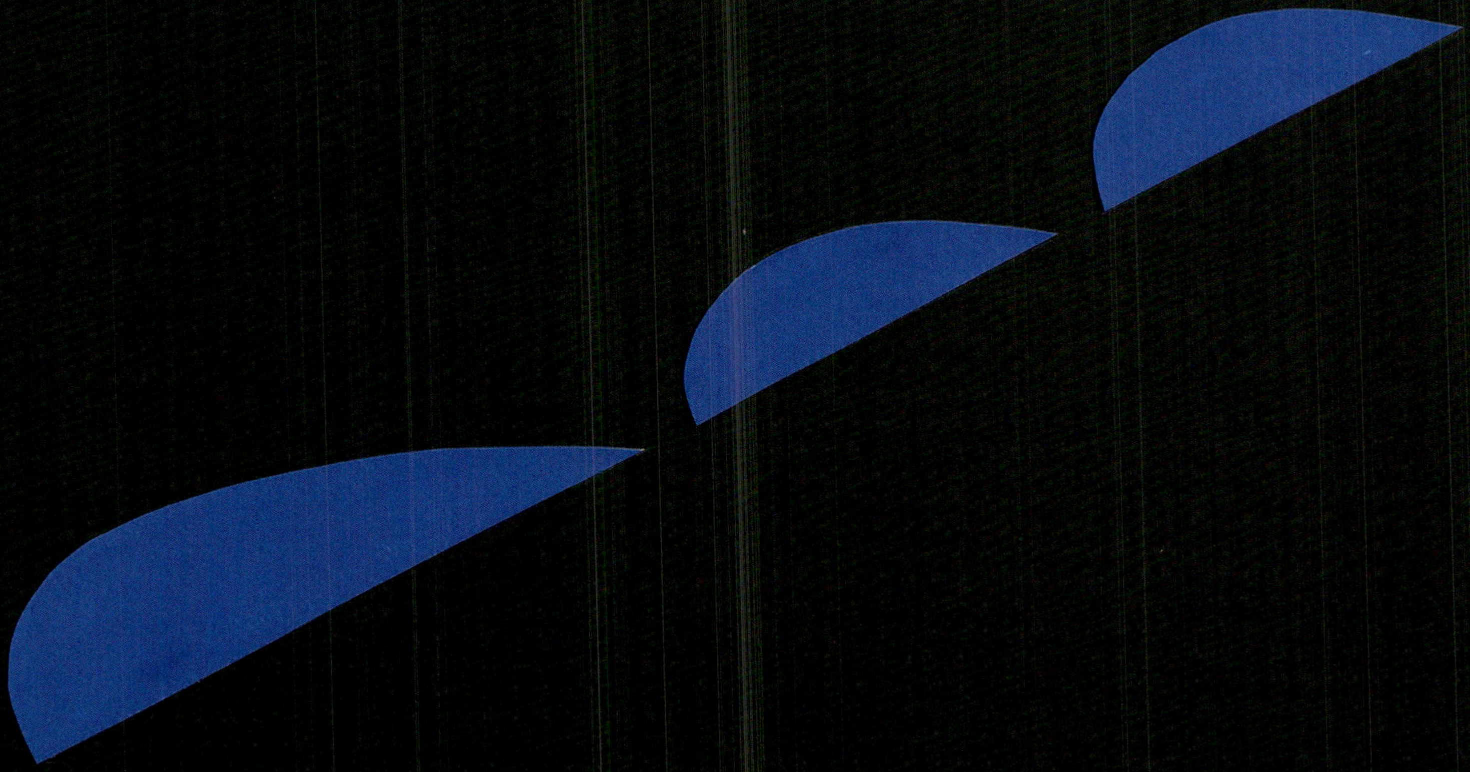

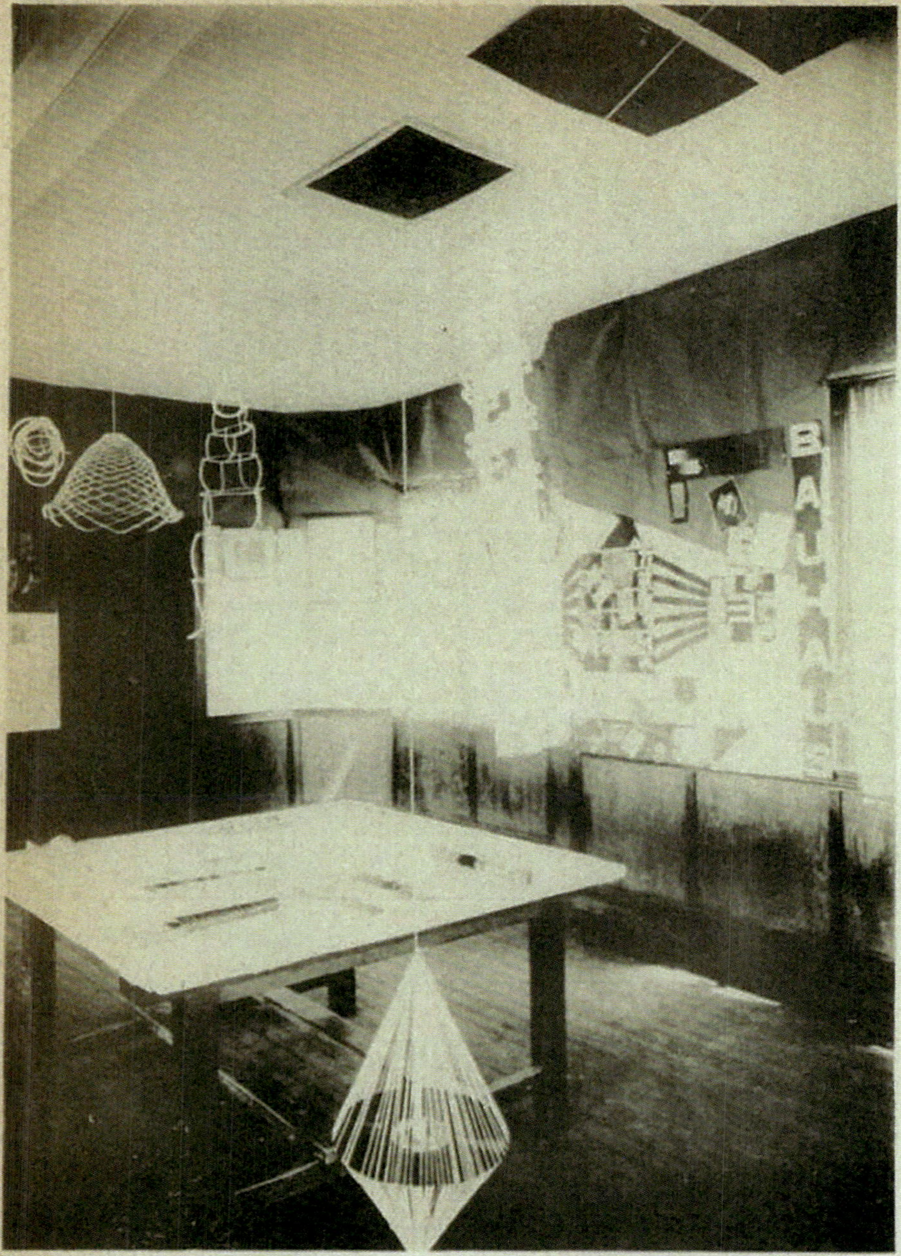

3 「生活構成」展覽會 全 3

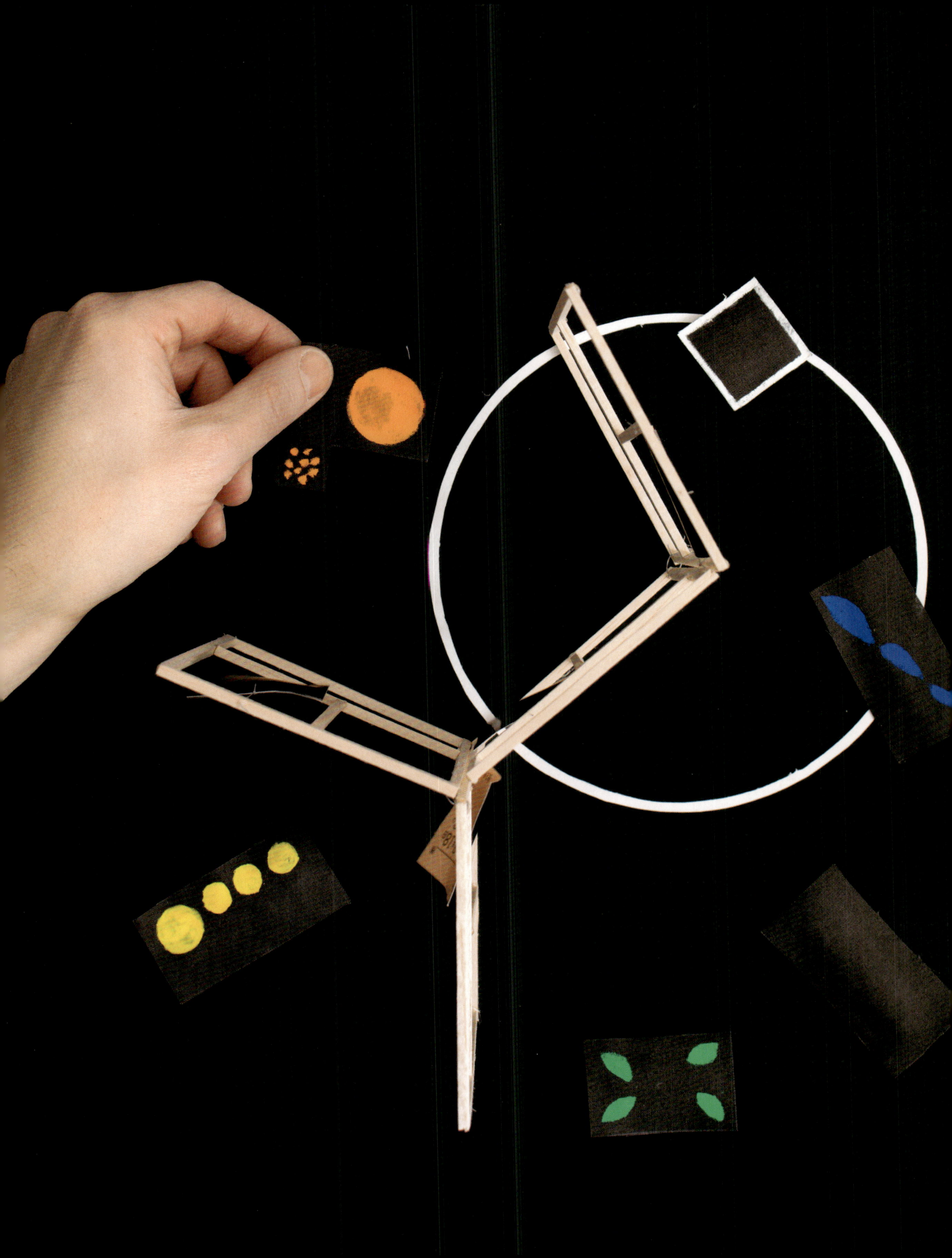

Chapter 2

Learning From

► Paul Klee, *Teppich* (Carpet), *1927, 48*, pen on paper on cardboard, 23 × 30 cm

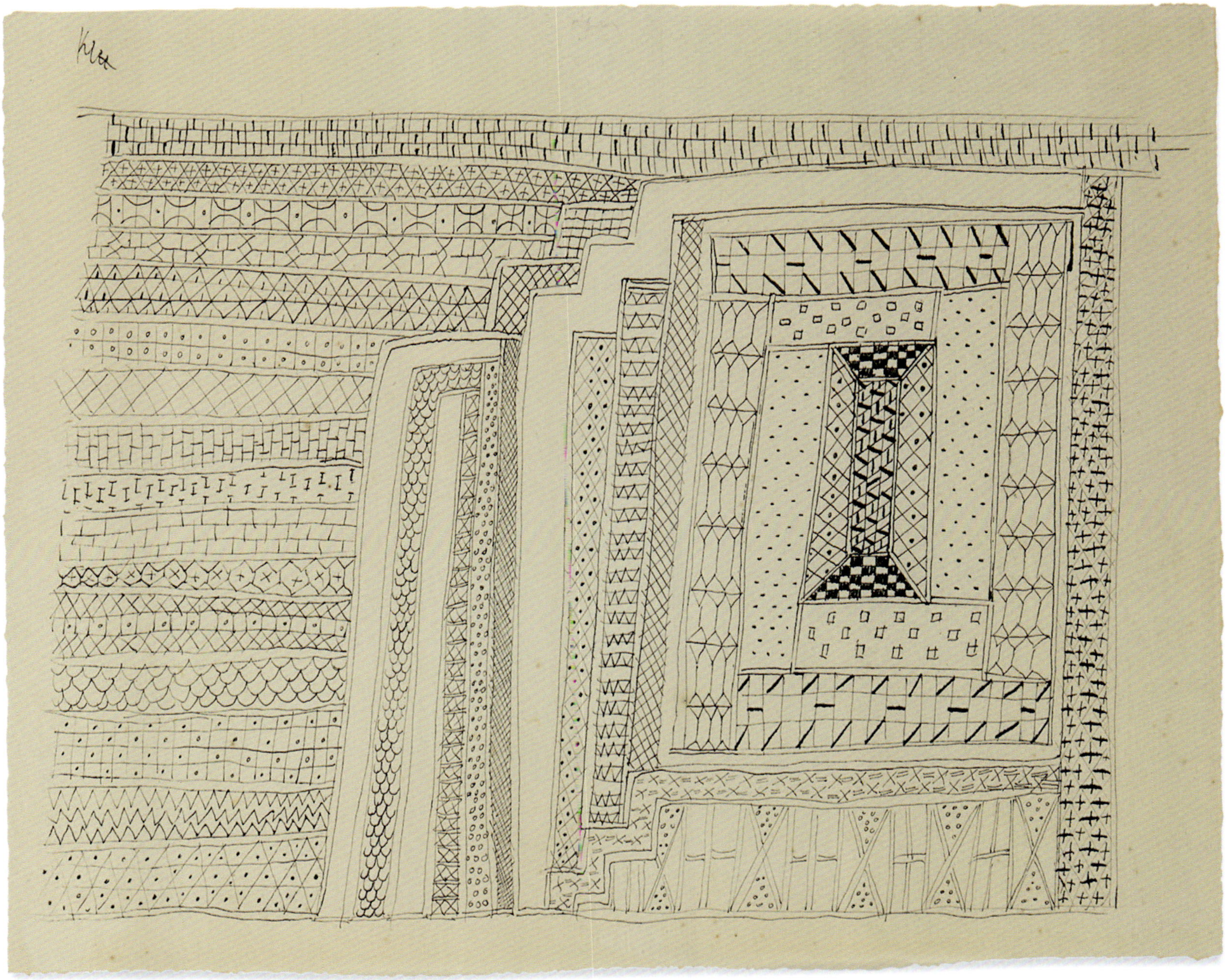
Klee

In 1927 Paul Klee created the small ink drawing *Teppich* (Carpet), which draws on the geometric composition of a North African carpet. This work links Klee's early interest in textiles and ornaments with the exploration of an abstract visual language. It also speaks to a lesser-known Bauhaus approach, in which masters and students actively studied premodern forms and techniques to innovate modern designs for use in a new democratic society. Information about non-European cultures came early at the Bauhaus, including in the school's Weimar library, which comprised photographic compendia of 'world culture' published after the First World War that were regarded as expanding and opening up national vocabularies. Knowledge was also transmitted through the collections of artefacts held by the ethnographic museums in Berlin, Hamburg, Vienna and Munich, as well as in the private collections to which members of the Bauhaus had access. A broader overview of that period might locate Klee's drawing within a modernist tendency to study objects and practices from outside the western canon – seeking a rupture with European classicism through such diverse sources as Indian temple architecture, Andean textiles and European folk traditions.

After the school was shut down in 1933, many Bauhaus members imperilled under National Socialism fled Germany. For some in exile, this opened up a possible encounter with what was once mediated through books and museum collections. Hannes Meyer, the second Bauhaus director, and the weaver Lena Bergner were living in Mexico from 1947 to 1949, where they began to include the social-revolutionary ideas prevalent in the country, but also the needs of indigenous populations, in publications and school projects. Bauhaus émigrés Josef and Anni Albers and Marguerite Wildenhain travelled to Central and South America to observe, document and collect the work of pre-Columbian as well as contemporary indigenous cultures. This knowledge was brought back into teaching situations such as at Black Mountain College in North Carolina, where it informed aesthetic and technical developments but was also used to challenge art/craft hierarchies. Anni Albers, her fellow weavers and their students, including a younger generation of 'fibre artists', turned to the woven traditions of ancient Peru not just for their technical innovation, but also because they believed its culture afforded textiles a social relevance that was denied their own art in the US and in Europe. Albers published her own book *On Weaving* (1965), which echoes the books on world culture found in the Bauhaus library. It comprehensively documents weaving techniques from around the world, and arguably creates a discourse around textiles as artistic research.

The turn towards vernacular traditions becomes more affirmatively political in the postcolonial context of Morocco in the 1960s, where, in a movement to decolonize culture, local crafts were recuperated from their subordinate position within colonial categories, introduced through the French Beaux-Arts division of fine and applied arts. Moroccan jewelry, textiles, ceramic tiles and murals on the ceilings of mosques were all revisited for what they could teach the contemporary artist and designer. In an attempt at decolonizing cultural production, their study was integrated into the curriculum at the School of Fine Arts in Casablanca. Significantly, the rediscovery of craft's symbolic, social and practical value was also cross-referenced with Bauhaus pedagogy and its synthesis of the arts, instead of their separation, by a group of post-independence artists including Mohamed Melehi, whose reflections are included later in this chapter.

In Brazil, a new design school called the Instituto de Arte Contemporânea (IAC), established by Lina Bo Bardi, Pietro Maria Bardi and Jacob Ruchti, and attached to the Museu de Arte de São Paulo (MASP, São Paulo Museum of Art), also claimed Bauhaus credentials through its curriculum and teachers. Prizes given to Max Bill and Walter Gropius at the São Paulo Biennial in 1951 and 1953 also suggest respect for the Bauhaus, but there were antagonisms too. In Brazil, a resistance to hegemonic European modernism and the need to produce a specifically Brazilian aesthetic vocabulary led Bo Bardi to embrace the full force of Brazilian popular culture – its technical innovations, its economy of means, beauty and use value – in publications, exhibitions and collections. This can be seen particularly in her move to north-eastern Brazil. As Ailton Krenak and Bené Fonteles write, cultural appropriations termed 'anthropophogy' in Brazil can be read as part of a long tradition evident already in the 1920s, with artists such as Tarsila do Amaral turning towards depictions of indigenous iconography to define Brazilian modernism as a new national style.

But what does it mean to extract cultural materials from their original context and inscribe them within new regimes of meaning, whether this is done by the nineteenth-century ethnographic museum, the avant-garde artist, the mid-century teaching collection or in contemporary art? Arguments contained within this chapter suggest an ambivalent response to this question. On the one hand, this move can give force to a critique of high-art traditions and introduce perspectives beyond the western episteme. On the other, as we see through the texts published here, in these moves a powerful dislocation of meaning occurs when materials are taken from the collective and spiritual body of groups who simultaneously experience the destruction of their culture and environment, even today.

Marion von Osten and Grant Watson

Checkerboard tunic from Argentina, Peru or Bolivia, Inca, 16th century, camelid fibre, 87 × 76.5 cm

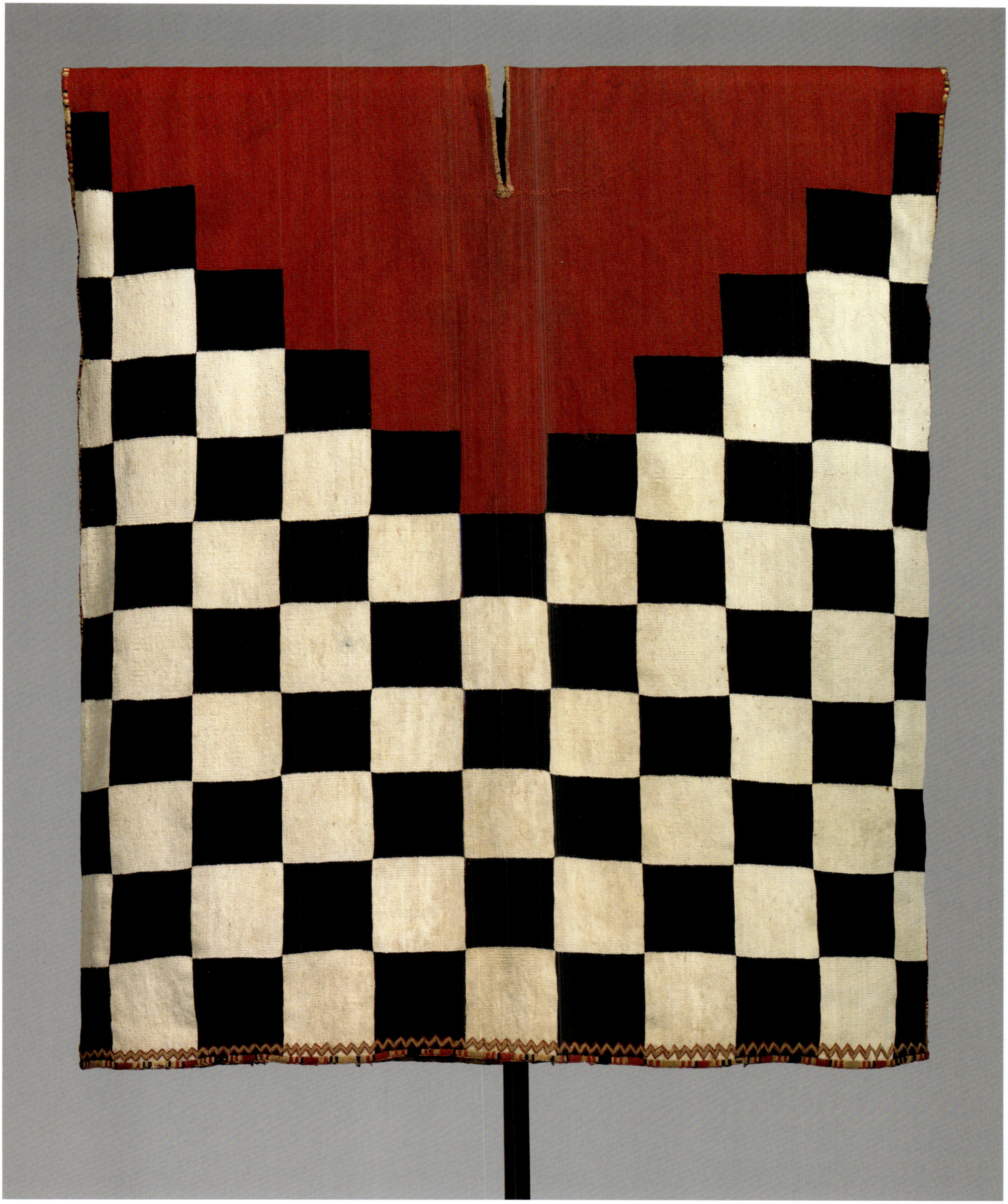

Josef Albers, *Detail of Loggia Wall*, 1967, brick, 2.5 × 21 m overall,
College of Science, Rochester Institute of Technology, New York

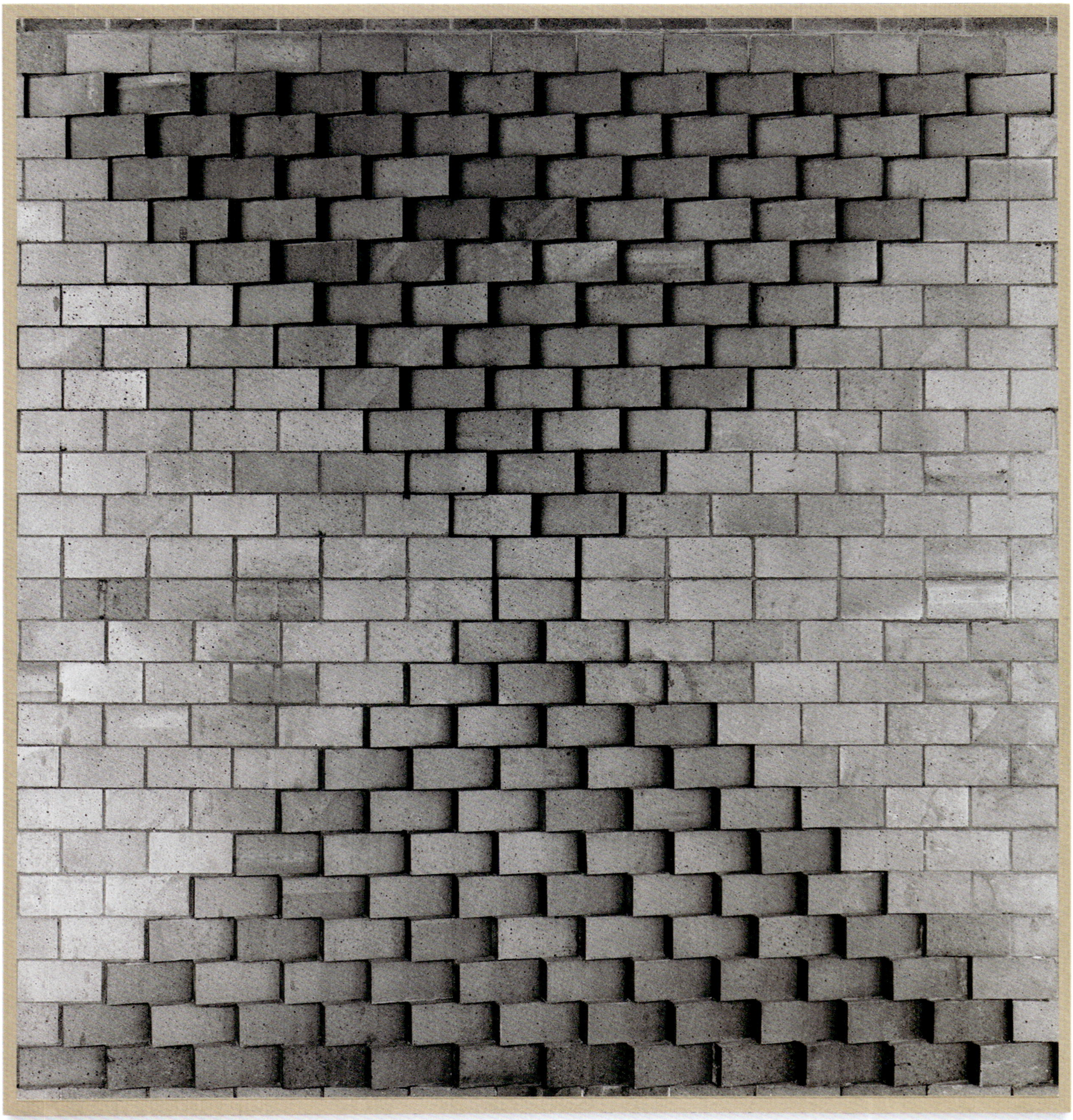

Lena Bergner, *Untitled (Draft of a Hand-Loom)*,
n.d., ink, coloured pencil on paper, 29.5 × 21 cm

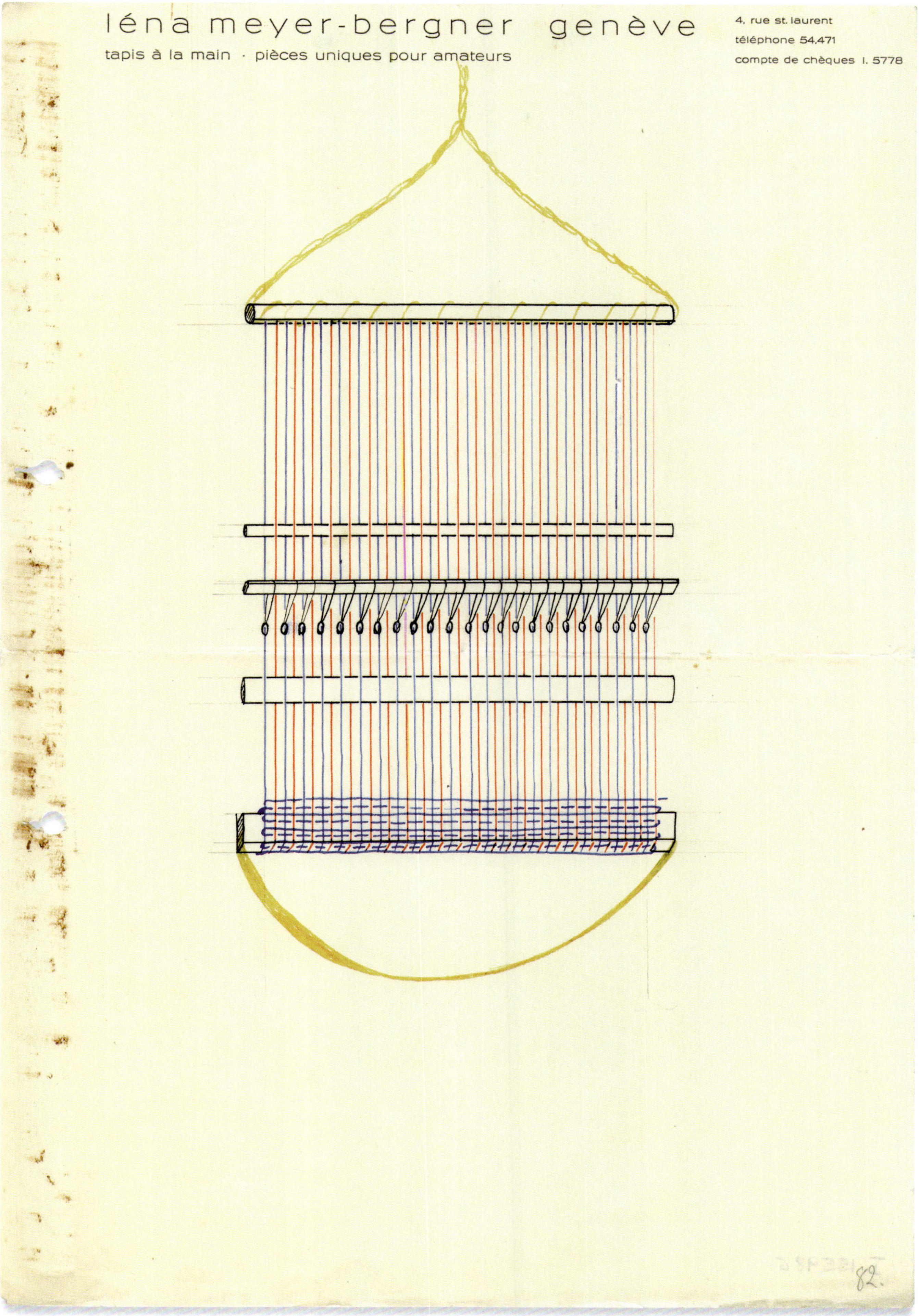

Hannes Meyer (ed.), *TGP Mexico, el taller de gráfica popular, doce años de obra artística colectiva* (The Workshop for Popular Graphic Art: A Record of Twelve Years of Collective Work), La Estampa Mexicana: Mexico City, 1949, p. 93, illustrations by Leopoldo Méndez

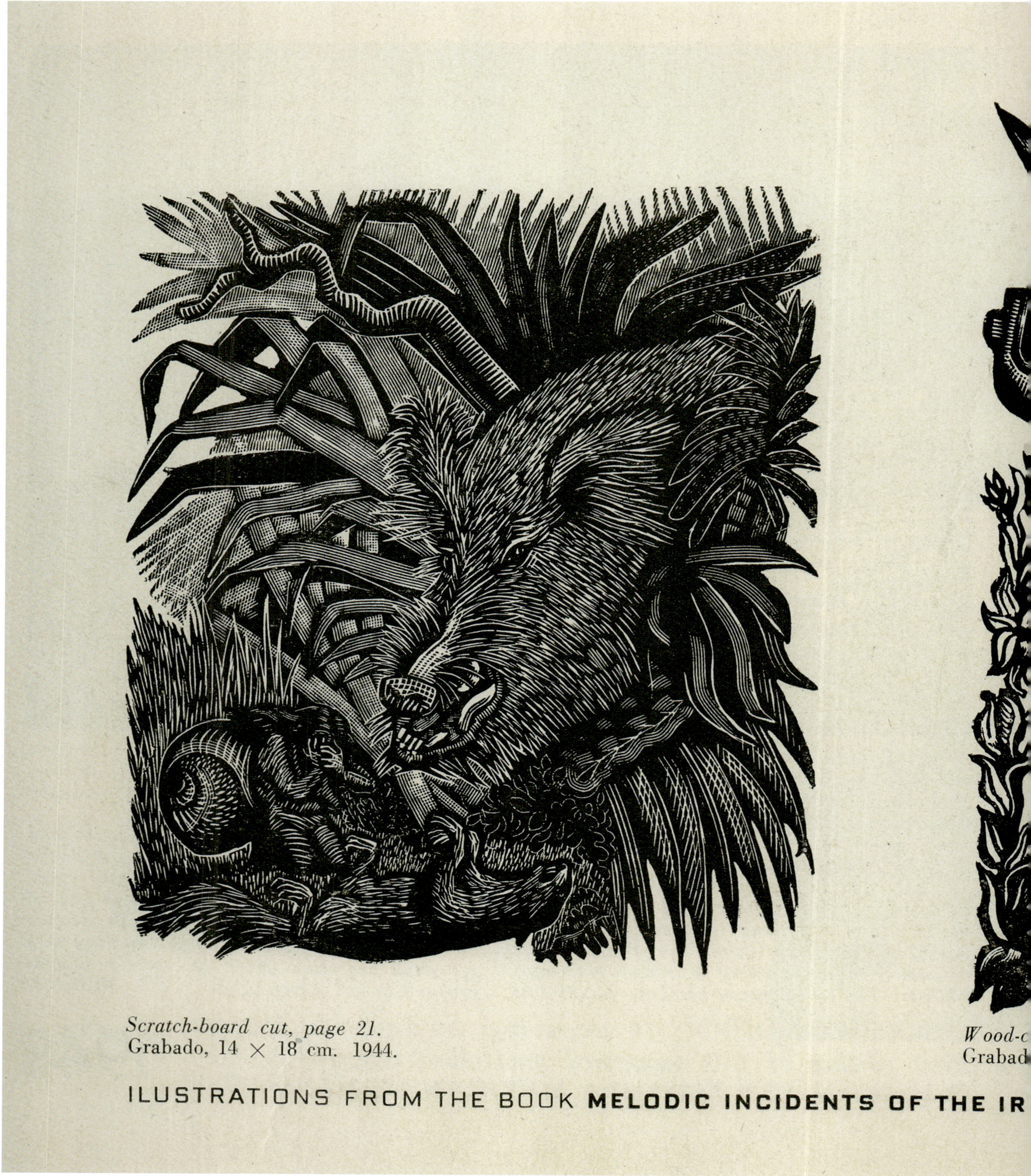
Scratch-board cut, page 21.
Grabado, 14 × 18 cm. 1944.

ILUSTRATIONS FROM THE BOOK **MELODIC INCIDENTS OF THE IR**

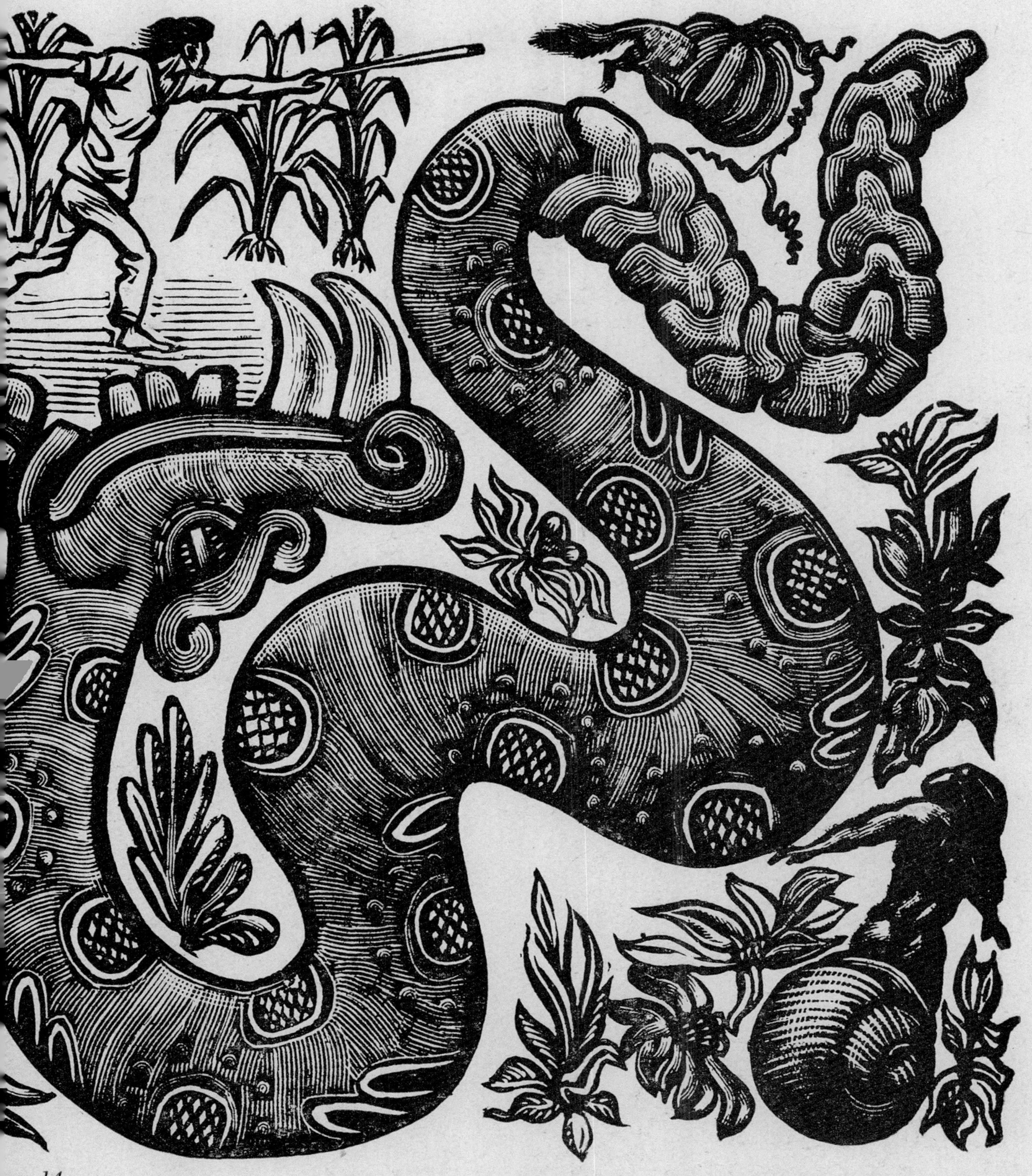

ge 14.
× 14 cm. 1944.

IONAL WORLD, BY JUAN DE LA CABADA

93

Leopoldo Méndez

Richard Chalfen, film-makers Johnny Nelson and Alta Kahn while shooting *Navajo Film Themselves*, 1966, photographs

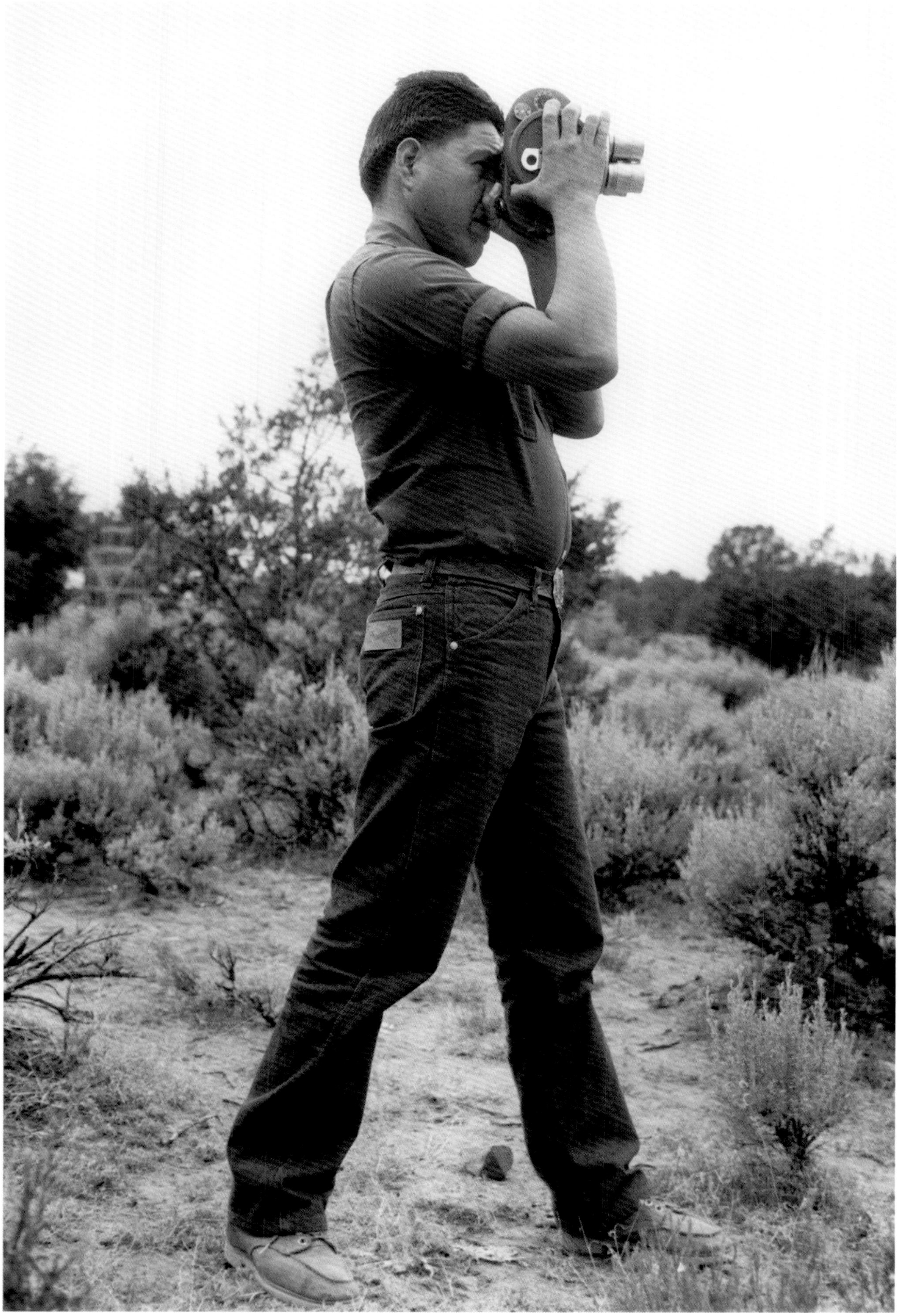

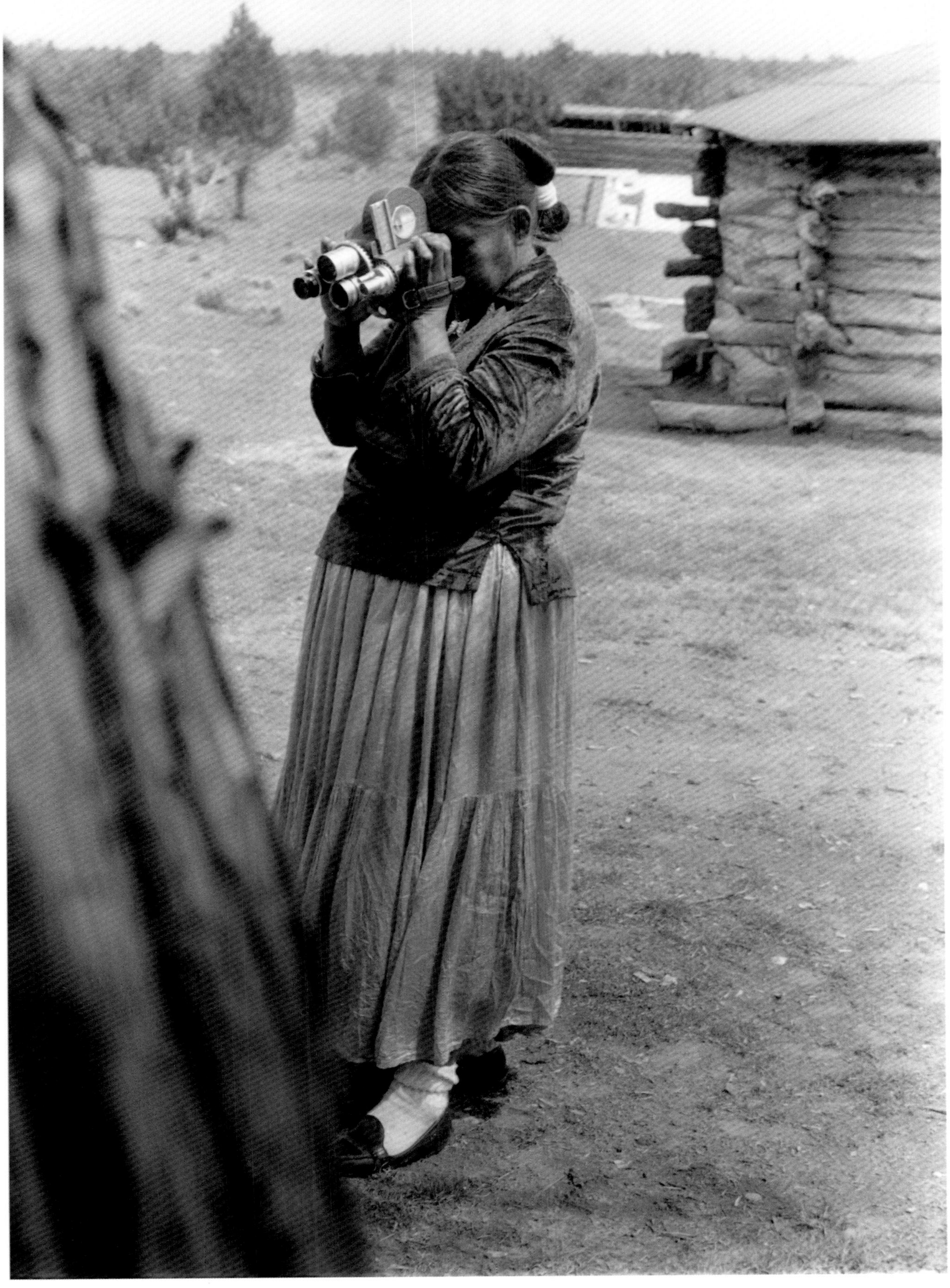

Marguerite Wildenhain, pamphlet for exhibition at the Santa Rosa Junior College Art Gallery, California, 17 March – 11 April 1975

View of the exhibition 'Civilização do Nordeste' at the Museum of Modern Art (MAM), Salvador, Brazil, 1963

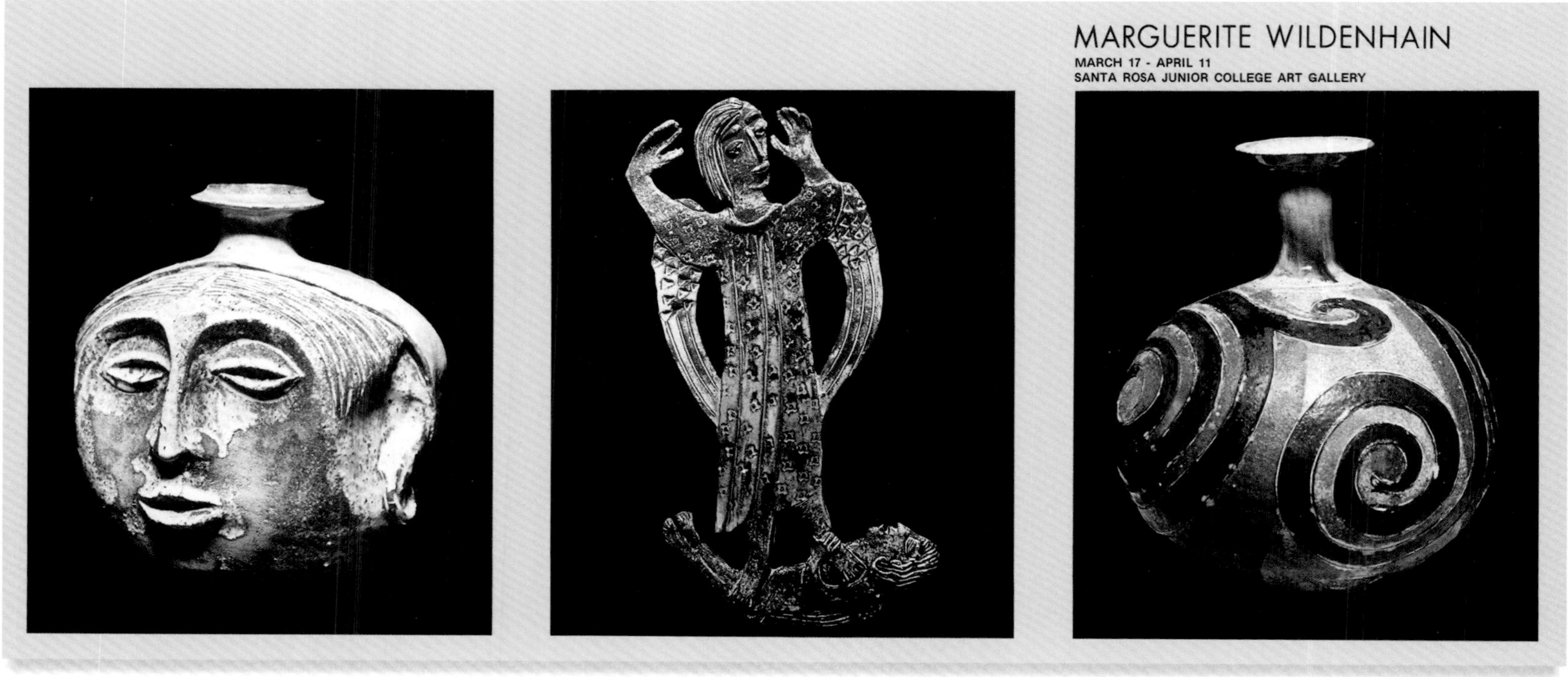

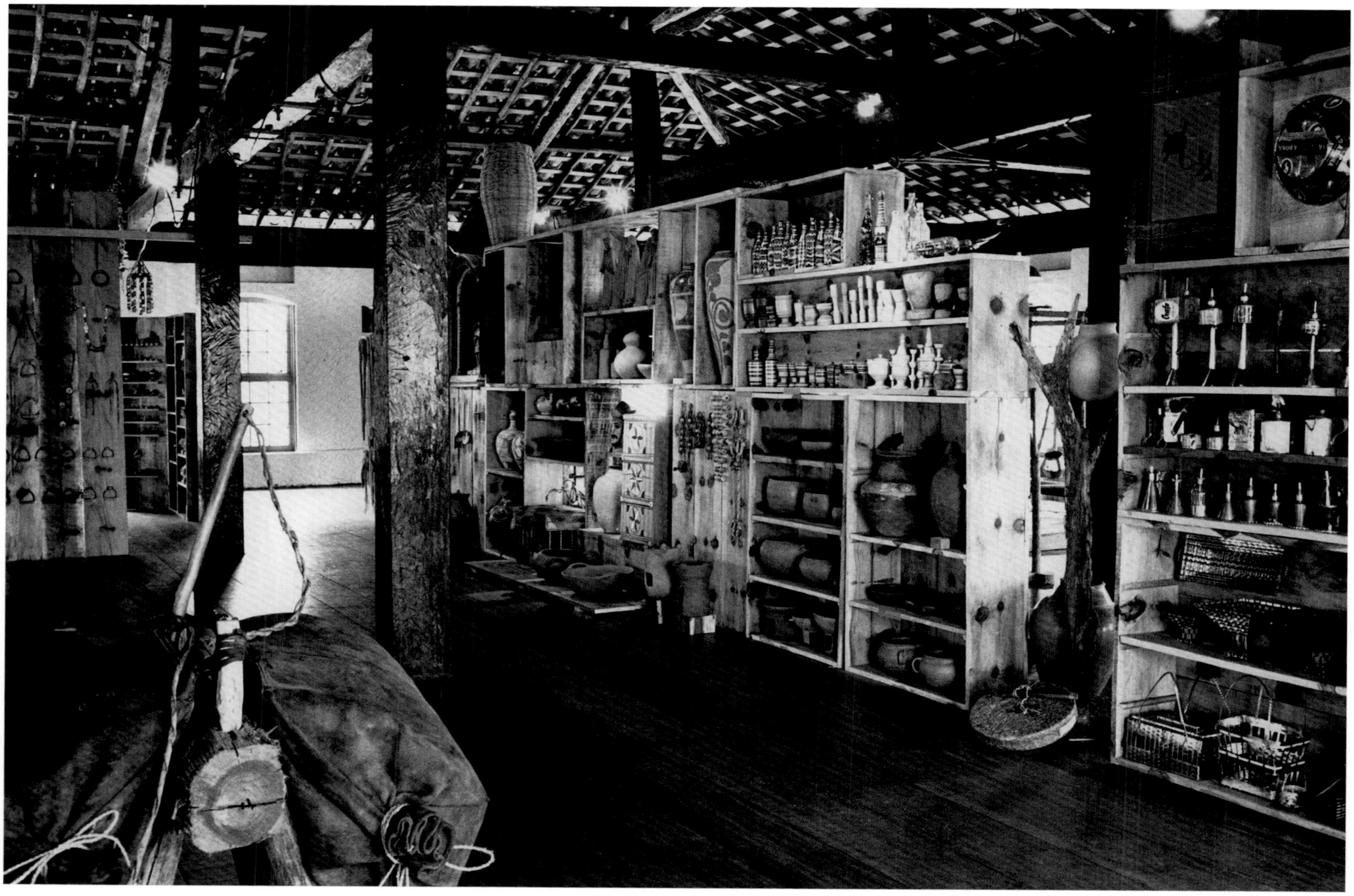

Rogério Duarte, film poster, *Deus e o Diabo na Terra do Sol*, 1964, directed by Glauber Rocha

▶ Pages 90–91: Toni Maraini teaching her art-history class at the École des Beaux-Arts de Casablanca, taken from a pedagogical brochure produced by the school, 1962–65

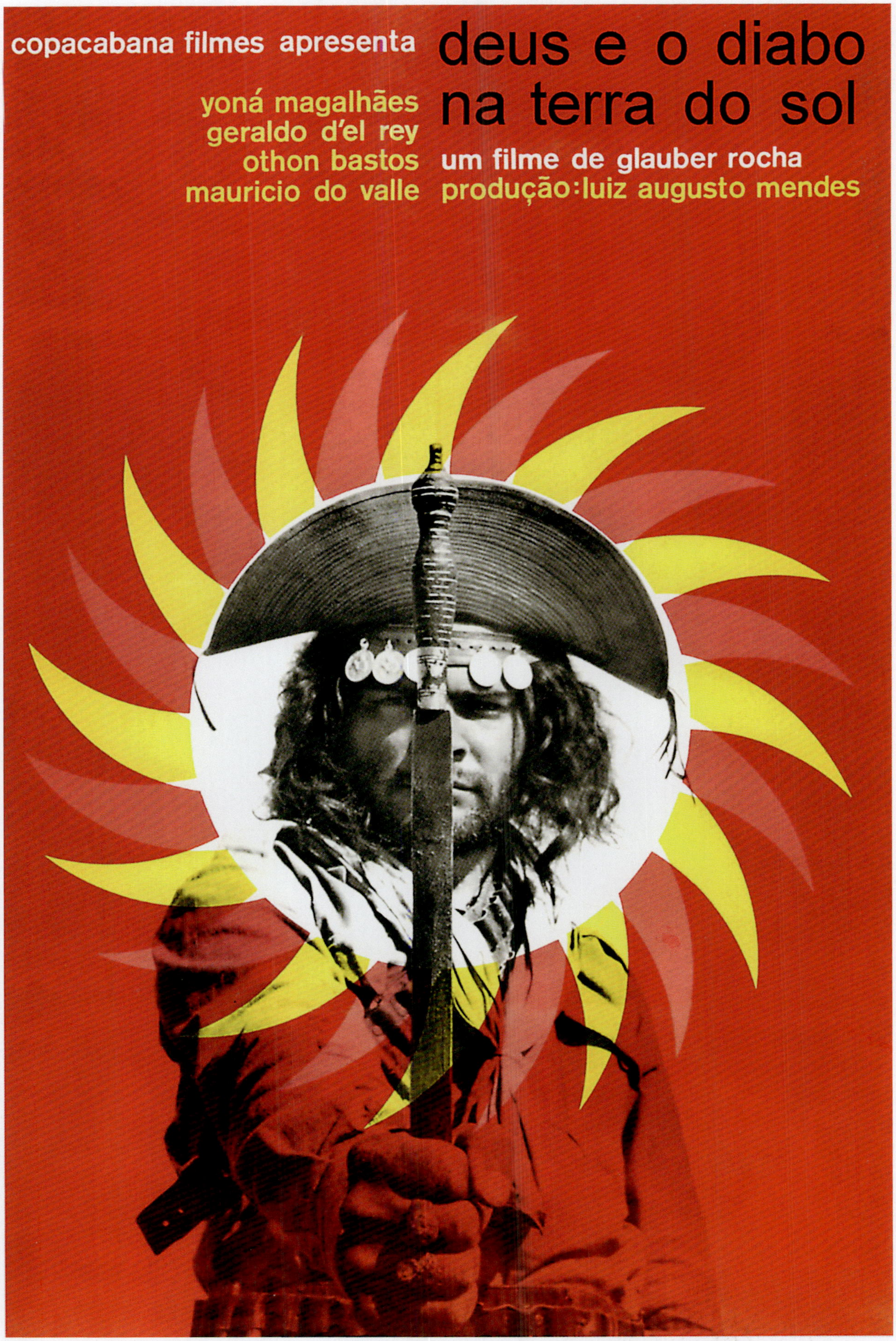

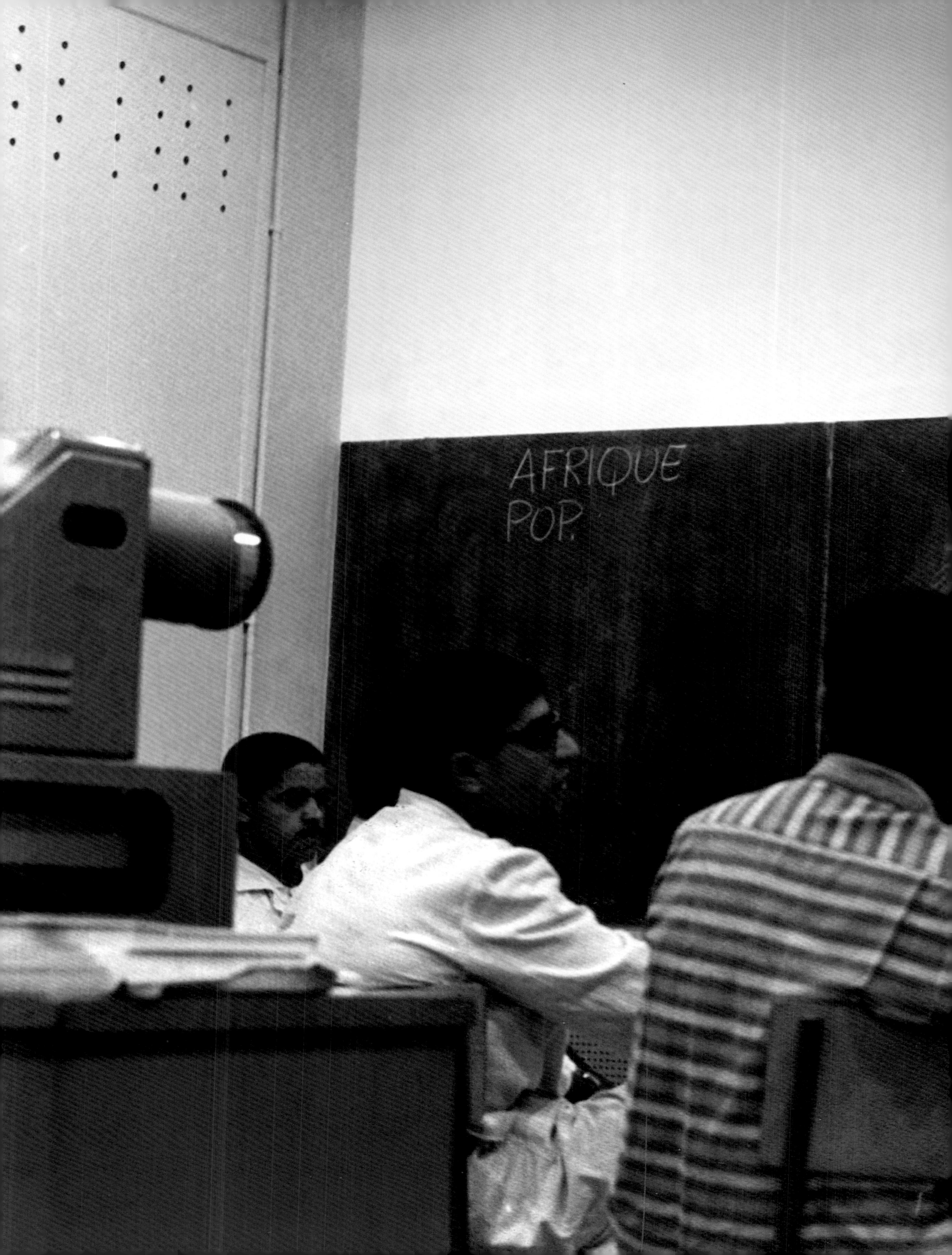
AFRIQUE
POP.

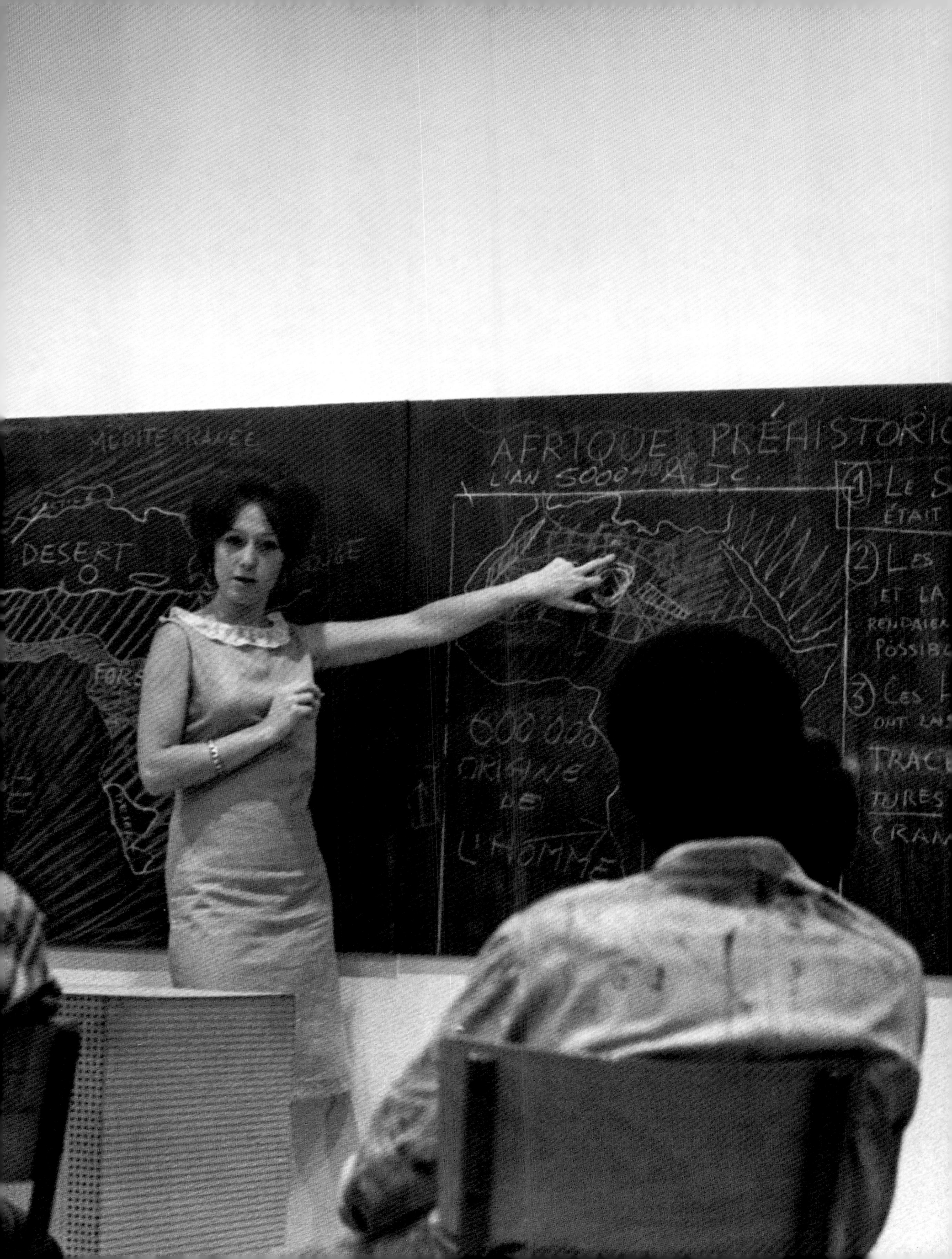
MÉDITERRANÉE
DESERT
AFRIQUE PRÉHISTORI
L'AN 5000 A.J.C.
ÉTAIT
POSSIBL
ORIGINE
DE
L'HOMME
TRACE
TURES

Paul Klee's Pictures of Architectural Tapestries

Fabienne Eggelhöfer

In 1927 Paul Klee created a series of 'carefully executed, decorative pen drawings', as Jürgen Glaesemer described the architectural formations included in depictions of an imaginary city called 'Beride'.[1] Did Glaesemer find these drawings decorative because they indeed reveal a certain proximity to weavings? We know that Klee's relationship to decorativeness was ambivalent. As with many of his contemporaries, he searched for so-called pure, abstract forms that already existed in the ornamental, while at the same time seeking to distance himself from the notions of femininity and decorativeness that were often associated with his art.[2] Several of his works, including the first two drawings of the Beride depictions, do resemble textile designs in a certain way (see *Beride, 1927, 41* and *Beride (Wasserstadt)* (Beride (Water Town)), *1927, 51*). Klee's Beride compositions consist of a warp structure covering the entire sheet built up like a woven pattern. They are based on a drawn construction made up of horizontal lines as well as vertical and diagonal strokes connected by powerful black accents. This combination of recurring strokes and small black rectangles is strongly reminiscent of textile designs on paper as they were made by the weavers at the Bauhaus (see the work sheet by Gertrud Arndt, *c.* 1925). The merging of artwork and textile design was most likely the reason why *Beride, 1927, 41* was reproduced in the Bauhaus advertising brochure from 1929.[3] The drawing *Teppich* (Carpet), *1927, 48* (page 78) blends in with the various types of patterns in this group of works, for it triggers associations with the art of both weaving and architecture, as is also the case with the Beride drawings. And it is in line with Klee's predominant concern of creating lively artworks, since no pattern is repeated and the structure of the surface is constantly interrupted and made rhythmic in different ways by new elements.

Paul Klee, *Beride (Wasserstadt)* (Beride (Water Town)), *1927, 51*, pen on paper on cardboard, paper 16.3 × 22.1 cm, cardboard 16.7 × 22.4 cm

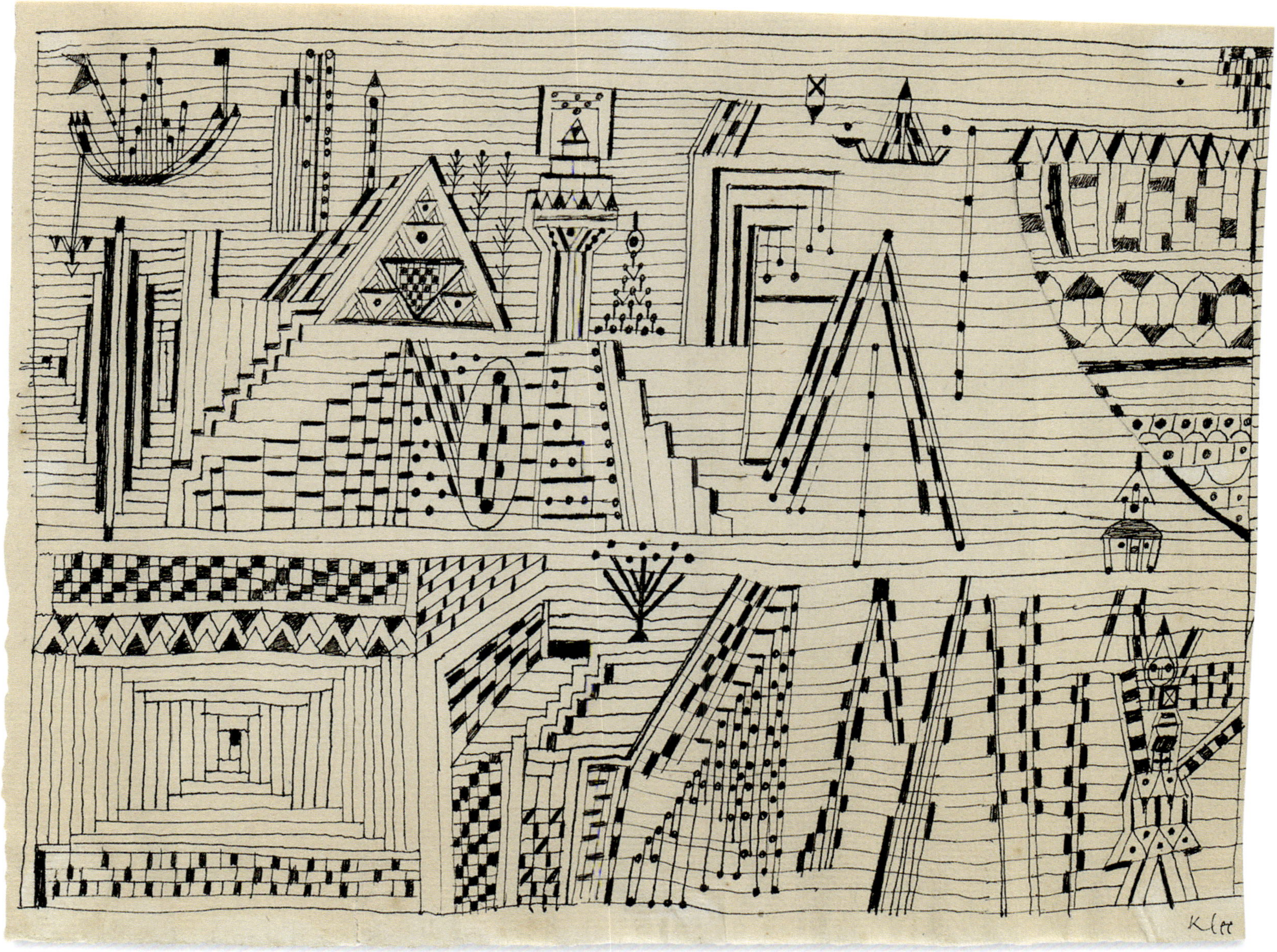

Paul Klee, *Beride, 1927, 41*, pen on paper on cardboard, 17.1 × 30.5 cm

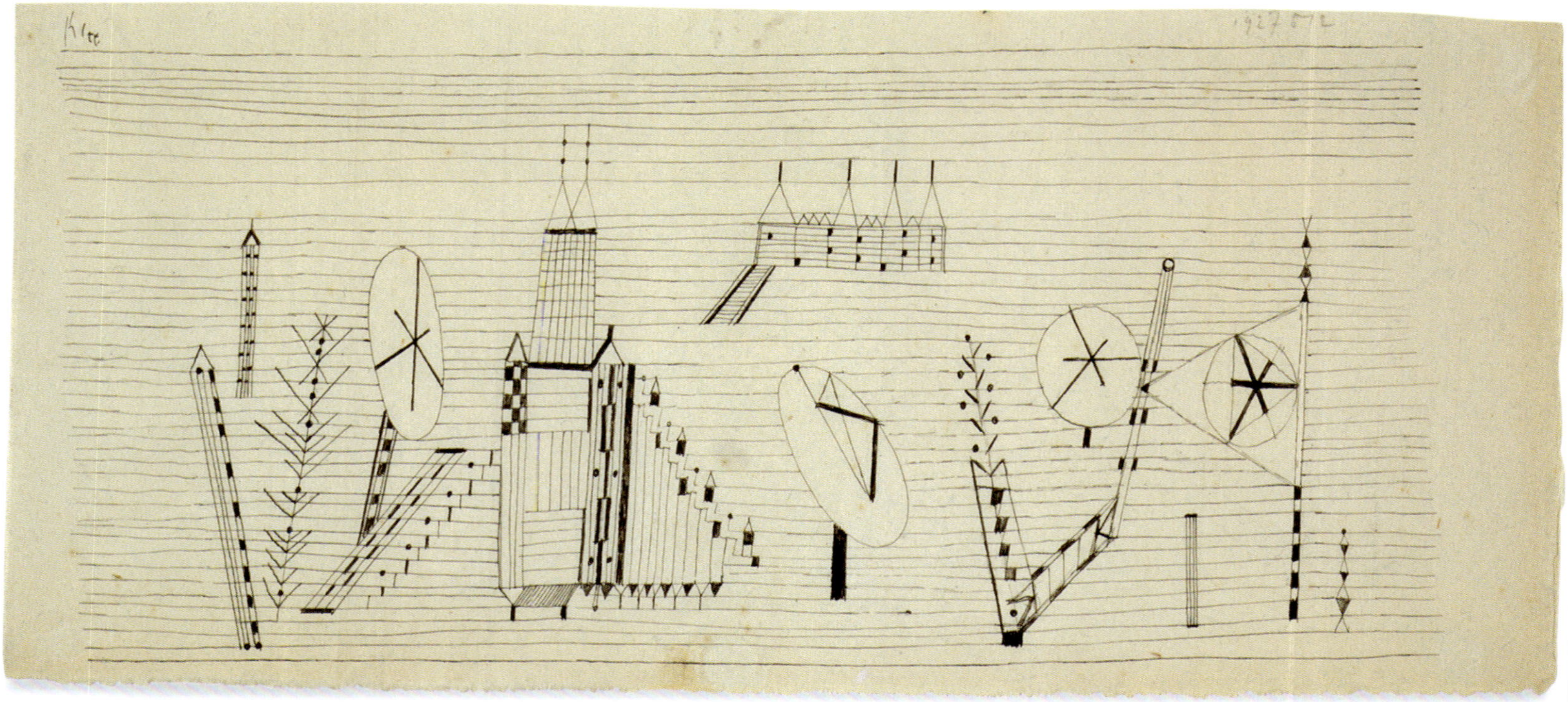

Lena Bergner, *Detail of a Medieval Knotted Carpet from the Orient*, *c.* 1927–28, 20.9 × 29.8 cm

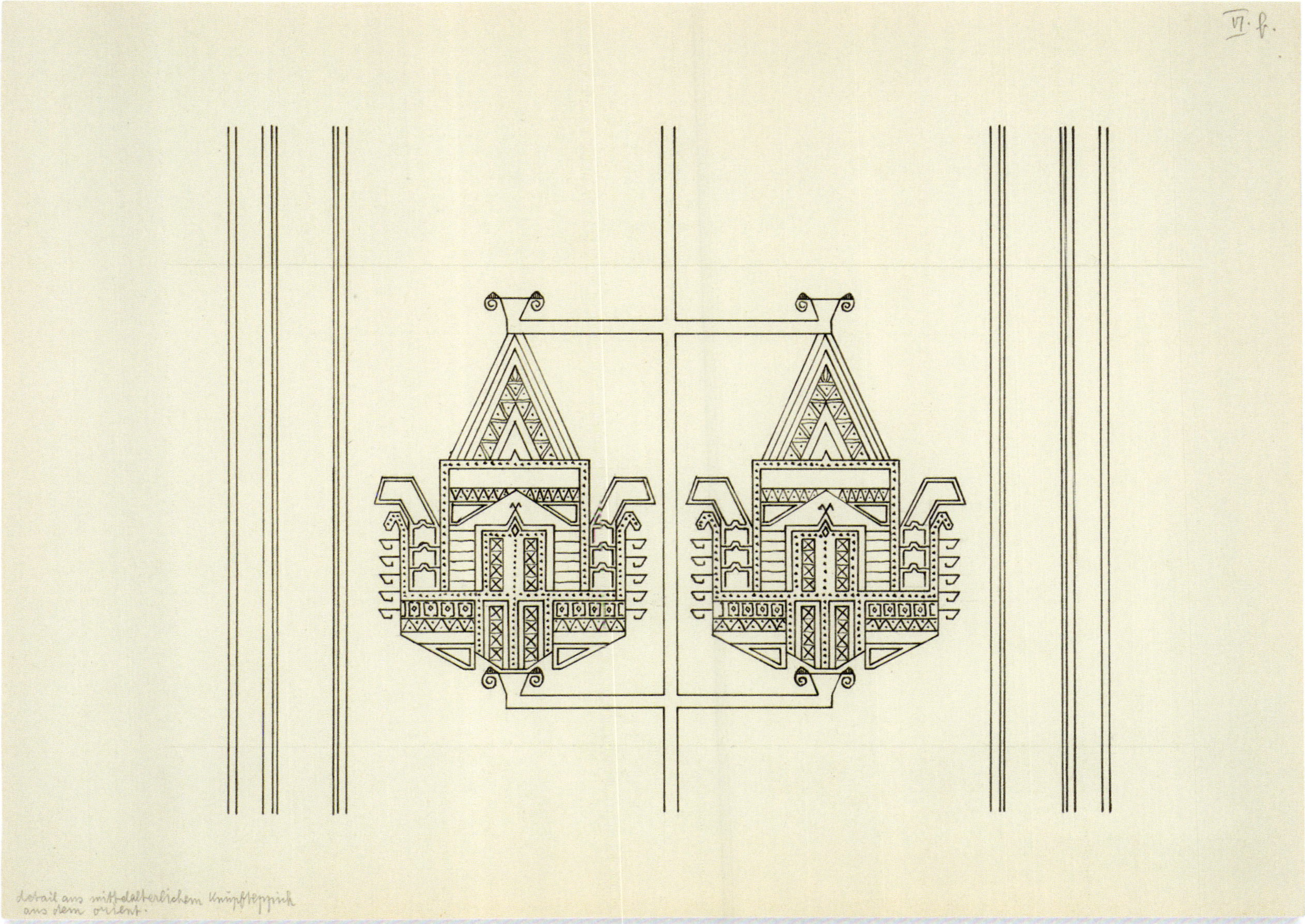

Gertrud Arndt, worksheet, *c.* 1925, mixed media on paper, 22.3 × 41.2 cm

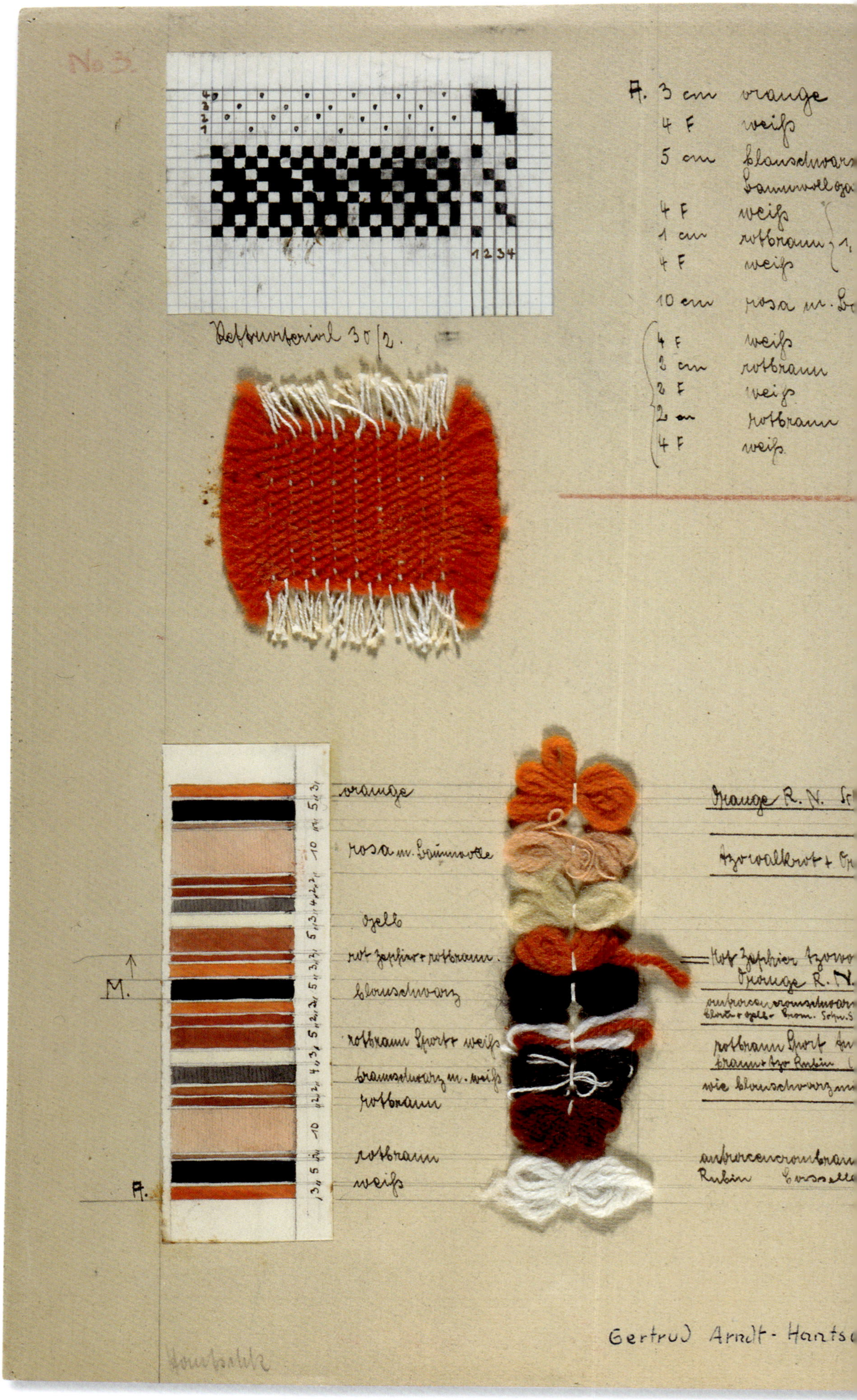

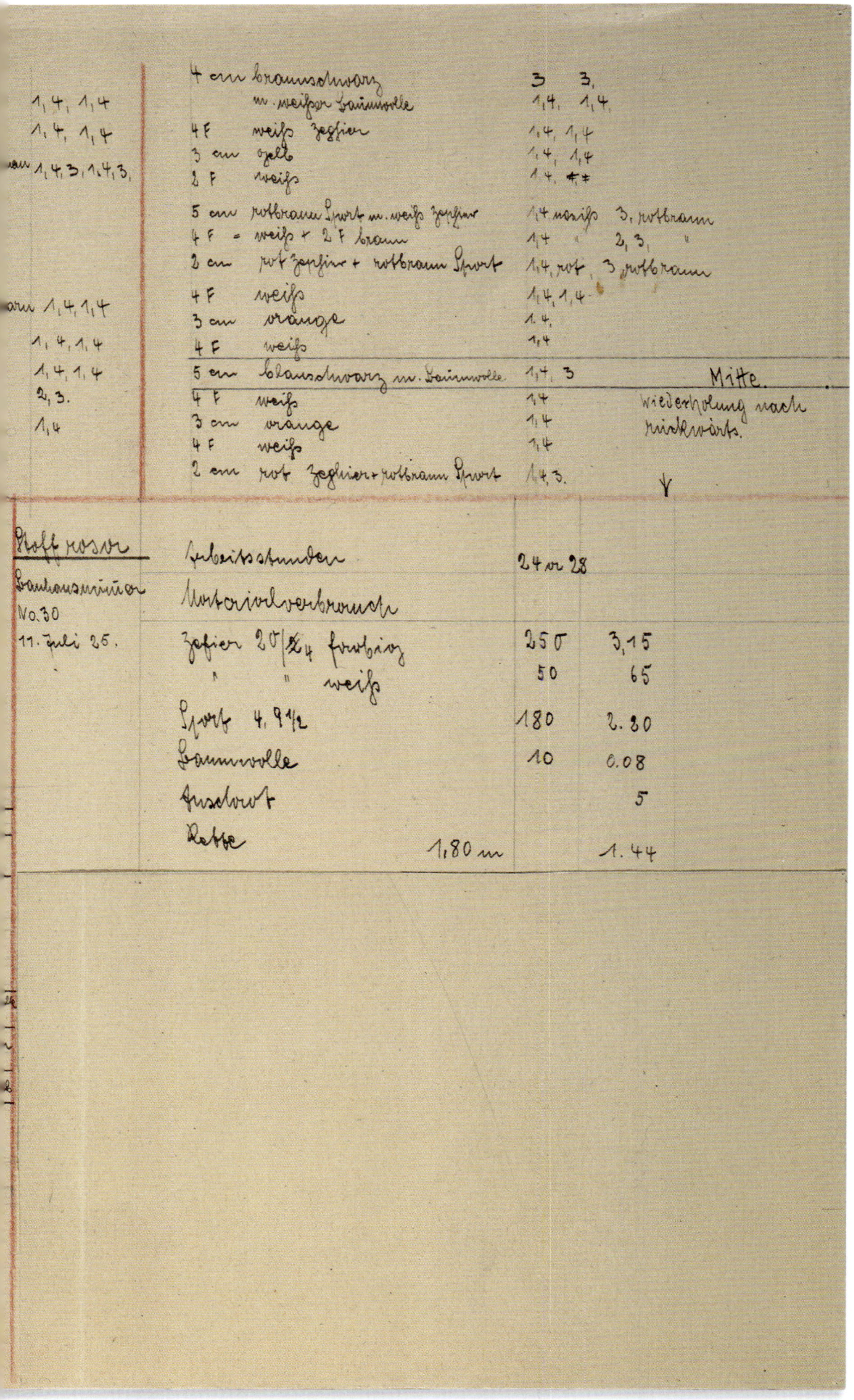

	4 cm braunschwarz	3 3,	
1,4, 1,4	m. weißer Baumwolle	1,4, 1,4,	
1,4, 1,4	4 F weiß Zephir	1,4, 1,4	
	3 cm gelb	1,4, 1,4	
...au 1,4,3,1,4,3,	2 F weiß	1,4, ~~4~~	
	5 cm rotbraun Sport m. weiß Zephir	1,4 weiß 3, rotbraun	
	4 F = weiß + 2 F braun	1,4 " 2,3, "	
	2 cm rot Zephir + rotbraun Sport	1,4, rot, 3, rotbraun	
...aun 1,4,1,4	4 F weiß	1,4,1,4	
	3 cm orange	1.4,	
1,4,1,4	4 F weiß	1,4	
1,4,1,4	5 cm blauschwarz m. Baumwolle	1,4, 3	Mitte.
2,3.	4 F weiß	1,4	Wiederholung nach
1,4	3 cm orange	1,4	rückwärts.
	4 F weiß	1,4	
	2 cm rot Zephir + rotbraun Sport	1,4,3.	↓

Stoff rosa	Arbeitsstunden	24 od. 28	
Bauhausmuster No. 30 11. Juli 25.	Materialverbrauch		
	Zefier 20/2×4 farbig	250	3,15
	" " weiß	50	65
	Sport 4. 9½	180	2.30
	Baumwolle	10	0.08
	[illegible]		5
	Kette 1,80 m		1.44

The fact that Klee created compositions with a 'textile character' precisely in 1927 must be seen in connection with his teaching activities at the Bauhaus. After the departure of Georg Muche, who had headed the weaving workshop until then, Klee offered an additional course from the summer semester of 1927 onwards, which he called 'design course weaving workshop' in the lesson plan of his pocket calendar.[4] It is possible that he had already been temporarily in charge of the weaving workshop in the summer semester of 1923, as a statement by Gunta Stölzl suggests.[5] According to art historian Jenny Anger, Klee was closely associated with the weaving workshop between 1923 and 1927,[6] where he continued to teach the design course until he left the institution in the spring of 1931. As can be gathered from his pocket calendar, he not only taught the theory of forms, which was mandatory for all students, but also gave classes to the female students of the weaving workshop for several semesters.[7] Klee taught universal composition principles such as the mirroring, rotation, shifting, repetition and superimposition of elements, as well as different ways of structuring surfaces. The collection of Lena Bergner[8] includes several pen drawings depicting carpet patterns, among them a detail of a medieval knotted carpet 'from the Orient', making it evident that Klee's female students also dealt with oriental artefacts.

Klee's works have often been described as going back to North African woven artefacts, such as the kilim carpet or the *bakhnoug*, a Tunisian textile used as a woman's shawl.[9] Klee did in fact make use of universal, abstract design principles or schematized and simplified depictions of animals, humans and plants, which he discovered in numerous archaic artworks. We cannot say for sure whether Klee studied carpets and fabrics during his trip to Tunisia in April 1914, since he gave no account of it. What is more, even before his trip he had created abstract watercolours whose titles referred to woven works (*Teppich* (Carpet)*, 1914, 19*). Instead of textile souvenirs, the artist brought back watercolours depicting fantastical urban architectures that decorated the walls of coffeehouses in Tunisia.[10] Even if Klee himself stylized his stay in Tunisia as an experience of awakening in regard to colour, he seems to have been equally impressed by the architecture of Tunisian towns, for he subsequently succeeded in creating a synthesis between urban architecture and pictorial architecture in his art.[11] The impressions gained in Tunisia and his engagement with Cubism helped him overcome illusionistic, perspectival representation and treat the picture as a surface. The emphasis on the surface was an important achievement that also played a pivotal role in his theoretical teachings at the weaving workshop. The study of archaic artefacts was equally key in his attempt to depart from the western image tradition. Klee made no specific comments on the art of certain peoples or tribes, but several books and periodicals that inspired him to invent archaic symbols and geometric patterns can be found in his library.[12] And there was also a significant number of ethnological publications in the library of the Bauhaus, including the Propyläen volume *Die Kunst der Naturvölker und der Vorzeit* (The Art of Indigenous Peoples and of Prehistory) by Eckart von Sydow, featuring houses decorated with geometric patterns along with fabric patterns that may have inspired Klee to create works such as *Teppich (Carpet), 1927, 48*.[13]

Paul Klee, *Teppich* (Carpet), *1914, 19*, watercolour on paper on cardboard, 16.8 × 9 cm

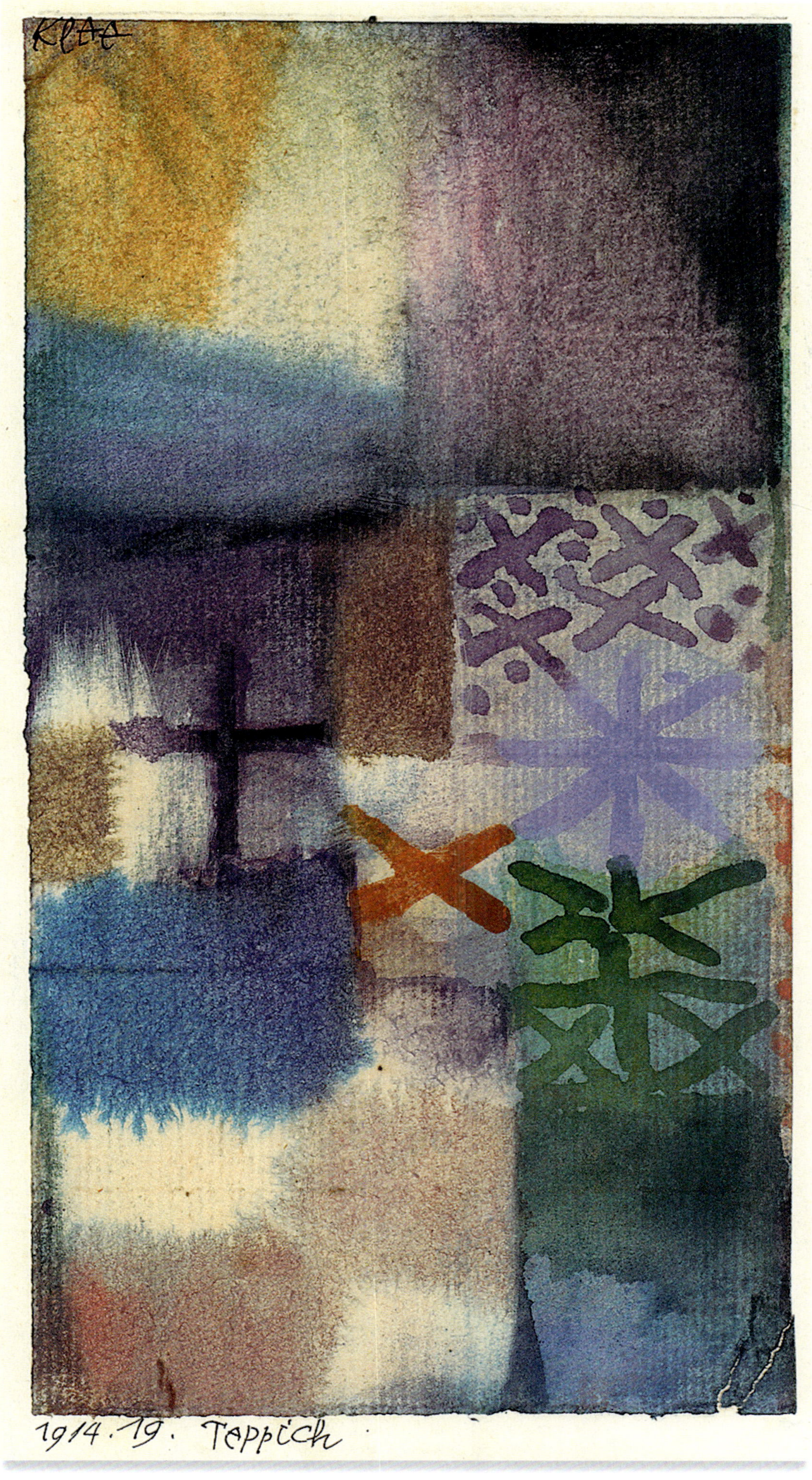

Anonymous, *Untitled (Fantasy Architecture with Three-gated Propylons)*, brought back from Tunisia by Paul Klee in 1914, watercolour and shell gold on paper, 31 × 42.1 cm

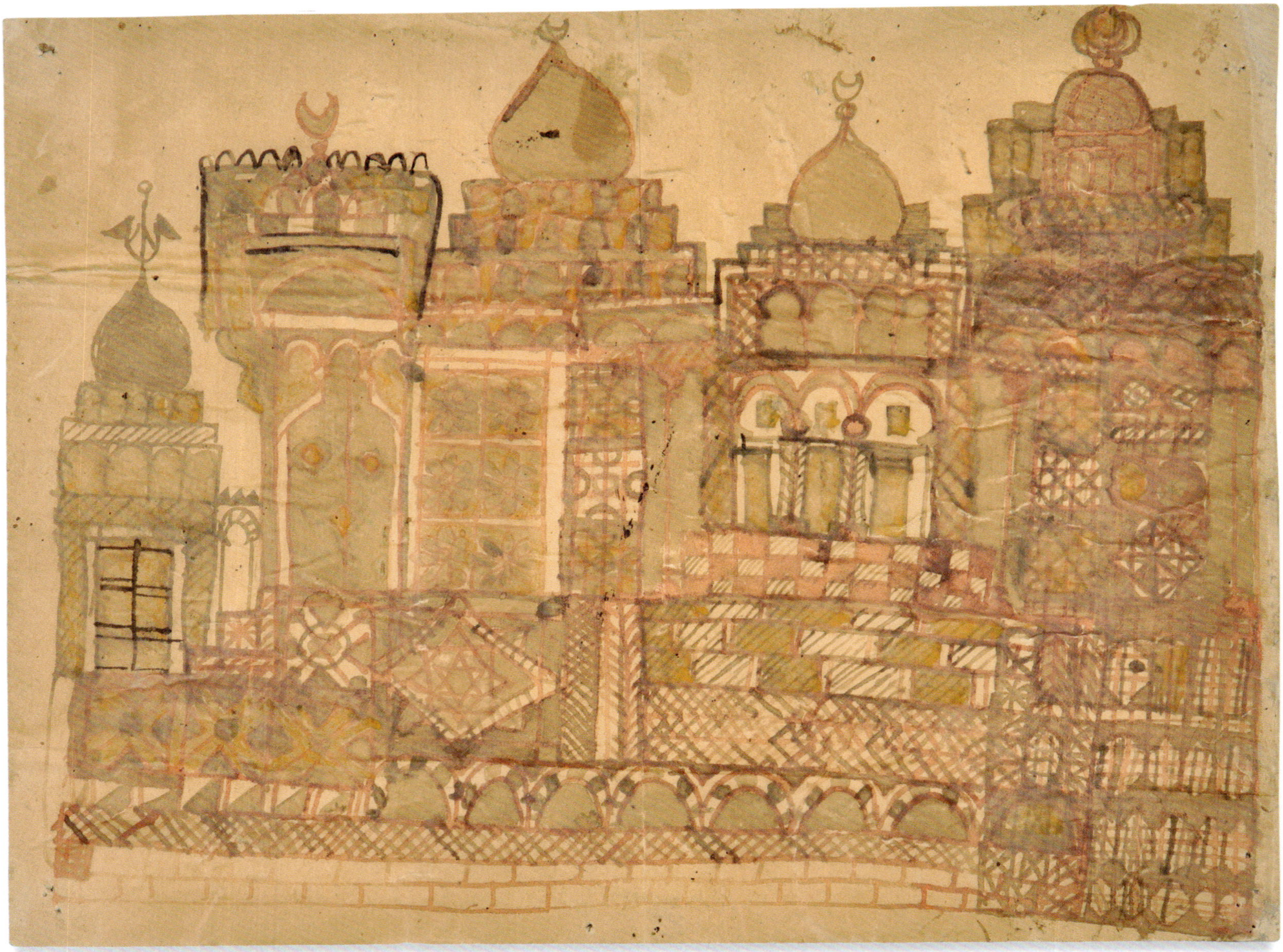

Postcard sent by Paul Klee to Louise Frick
(Tunisia, minaret of the Grand Mosque), 12 April 1914

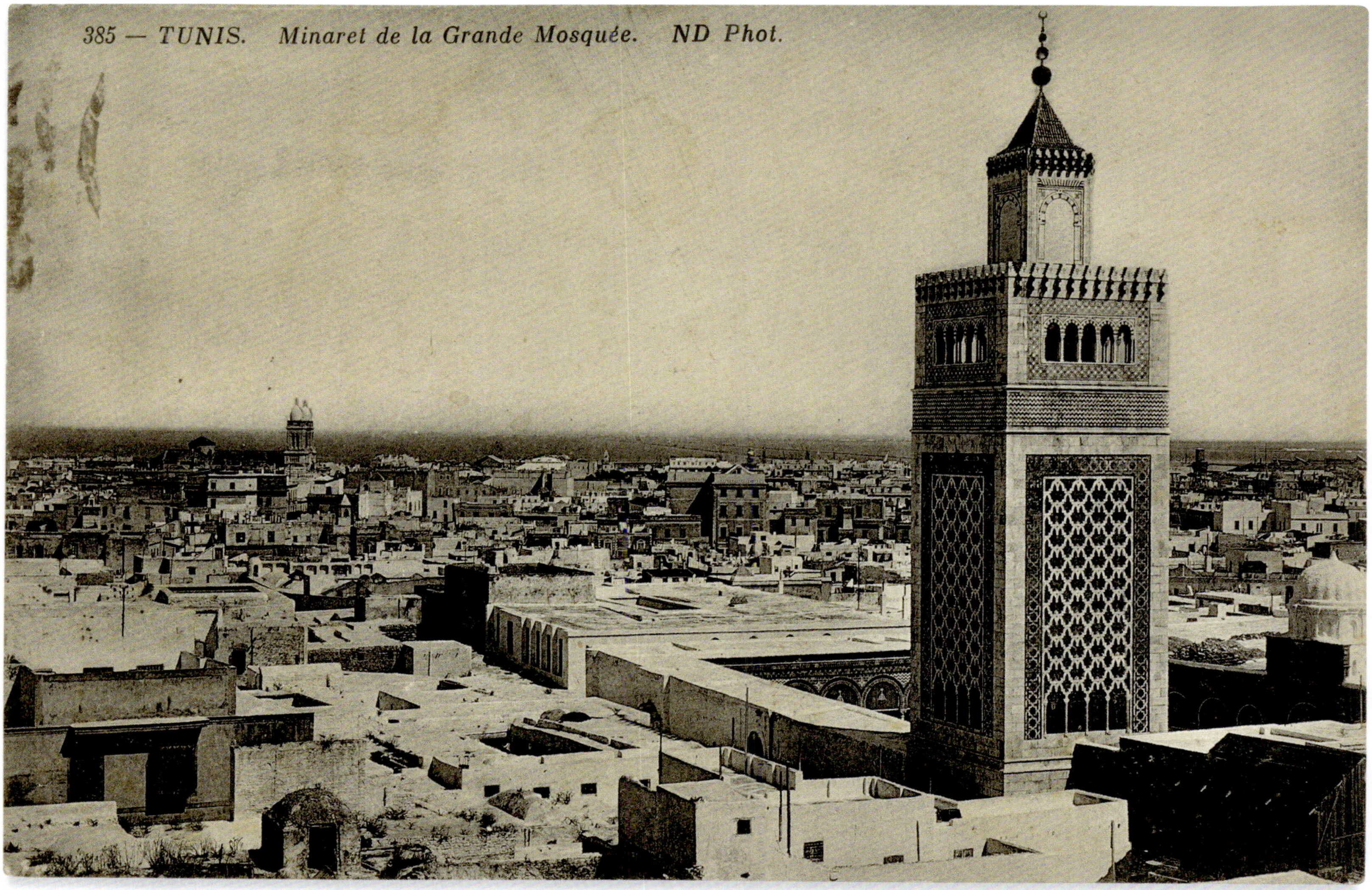

It has been repeatedly suggested that Klee's watercolours or rectangular pictures from the Bauhaus period served as models for the carpet designs of the weavers. It can certainly be said that all those works are based on the combination of colour fields created according to the universal composition principles taught by Klee: mirroring, rotation, shifting, repetition or superimposition (cf. Klee's teaching note *Bildnerische Gestaltungslehre: I.3 Specielle Ordnung* (Theory of Pictorial Configuration: I.3 Special Order), BG I.3/93, with Lena Bergner, clean copy from Klee's *Unterricht, I. Allgemeiner Teil, I.4 Gliederung* (Teachings, I. General Part, I.4 Structure), 1927–28). Klee's classes in the weaving workshop were oriented towards the composition of the surface, much like the mandatory theory of forms. Therefore, the theoretical lessons for the weavers did not substantially differ from the theory of form. Klee wrote the *Beiträge zur bildnerischen Formlehre* (Contributions to the Pictorial Theory of Form) as well as the dated lecture notes of *I.2 Principiellen Ordnung* (I.2 Principle Order) and *II.21 Mechanik* (II.21 Mechanics) in Weimar, while a considerable part of the second major chapter of his teaching material, *II. Planimetrische Gestaltung* (II. Planimetric Configuration) was written in Dessau.[14]

Based on the transcripts of Otti Berger, Helene Nonné-Schmidt, Stölzl, Bergner and Gertrud Arndt (née Hantschk), who all studied at the weaving workshop, the main focus of Klee's design classes for the weaving workshop can be reconstructed.[15] Following a brief introduction to the *Principielle* (Principle) and *Specielle Ordnung* (Special Order) of pictorial elements – dot, line and surface – and the pictorial means – line, chiaroscuro, colour – Klee in the chapter *I.4 Gliederung* (I.4 Structure) elaborated the different ways in which a surface can be structured. He mainly placed importance on a rhythmic and lively segmentation that he achieved through the synthesis of regular and irregular divisions of the surface, or, in Klee's words, a combination of 'dividual' and 'individual' segmentation. The repetitive, invariable rhythm can easily be attributed to an organic, individual whole. It supports the essence of the whole without determining it.[16] A lively rhythmization of the picture surface is something he also put into practice in his own art at the time (*Monument im Fruchtland* (Monument in the Fertile Country), *1929, 41*). In this watercolour, Klee worked with the impressions of his trip to Egypt in 1928, especially the way in which the landscape was structured by fields in the Nile Delta. The planimetrical composition showing various ways of constructing geometric forms on the surface was the next main topic of his lessons.[17] The geometric forms were to be created organically as well, so that the results would display a certain liveliness. In addition to the transcripts, the chiaroscuro and colour studies of the students have also survived.

Klee's classes in the weaving workshop were exclusively theoretical. There are no indications in his teaching notes that address the practical implementation of his theory. The haptic or material features of threads or fabrics were never a topic. From the winter semester of 1925–26 onwards, Gunta Stölzl was responsible for the practical implementation. Klee's strictly geometric design classes seemed to have supported the weavers in their attempt to overcome the tradition of the narrative picture carpet.[18] Stölzl demanded that the fabric must be entirely surface and 'always have an effect as a surface'. That does not exclude 'that static, dynamic, sculptural, functional, constructive, and spatial elements lie in its field, insofar as they belong to their compositional means and are subjected to the law of the surface'. She continues: 'Today, we do not weave flowers and fruits, figurative scenes and architectural perspectives, just as little as we deal with an ornamental effect.'[19] The process of weaving gained significance under Stölzl's direction. Drafts were no longer simply implemented and thus reproduced as carpets as had been the case beforehand; instead, they served as starting points that could be altered during the process of weaving. In this manner, she put into practice one of Klee's central concerns, namely, that the process determines the result.

To develop his abstract pictorial language and his teachings at the Bauhaus, Klee drew from the most varied sources that he came upon in everyday life, during his travels or in books. The study of the non-European design of buildings and fabrics, the fantasy architecture of the watercolours he brought back from Tunisia or the weavers' textile patterns designed on paper formed the foundation of works such as *Teppich* (Carpet), *1927, 48*. Klee translated the insights and impressions he gained into his own image language in which he created rhythmic liveliness with elementary means.

Paul Klee, *Bildnerische Gestaltungslehre: I.3 Specielle Ordnung* (Theory of Pictorial Configuration: I.3 Special Order), n.d., pencil and coloured pencil on paper, 33 × 21 cm

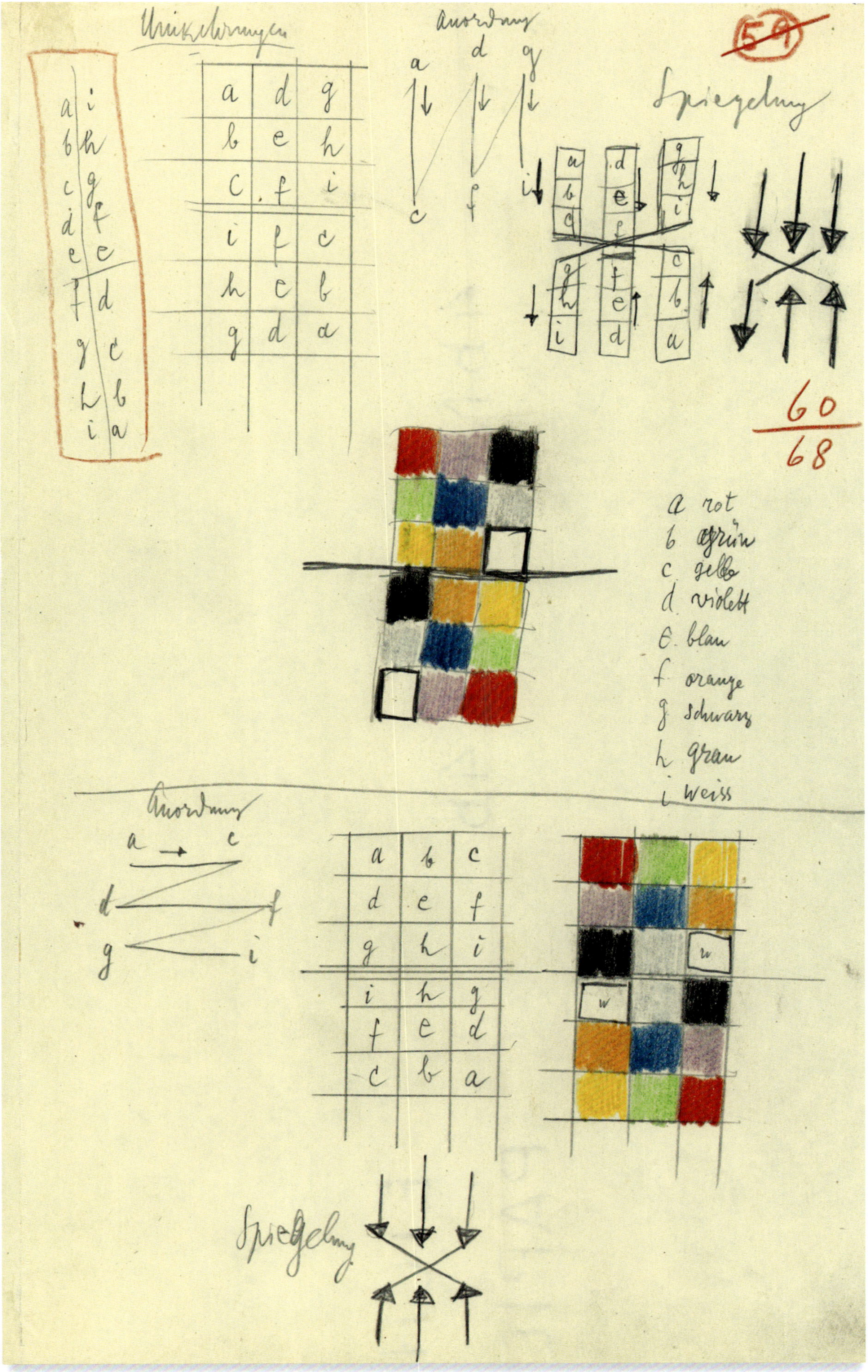

Lena Bergner, *Reinschrift von Paul Klees Unterricht, I. Allgemeiner Teil, I.4 Gliederung* (Clean Copy of Paul Klee's Teaching, I. General Part, I.4 Structure), 1927–28, 29.7 × 21.1 cm

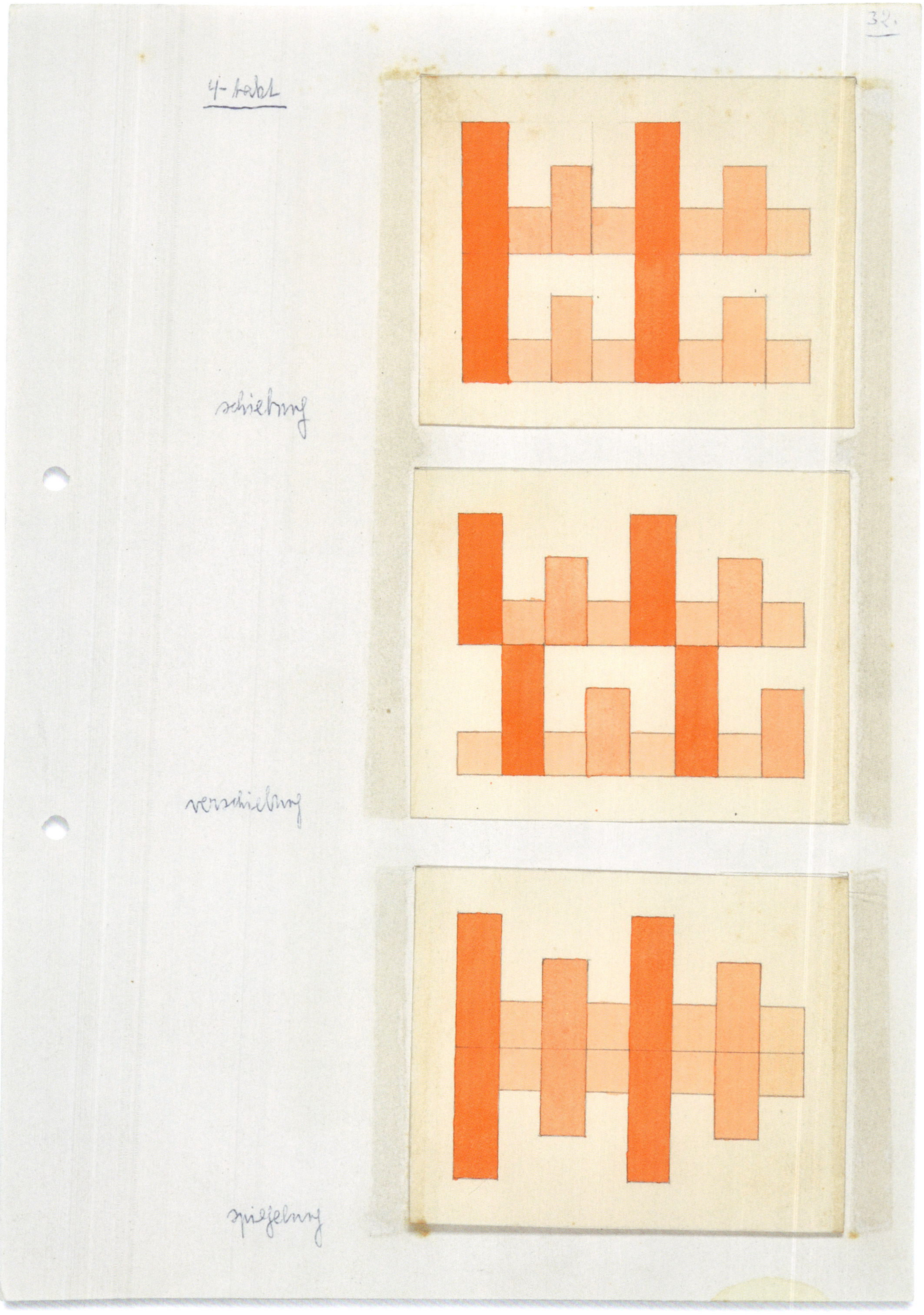

Paul Klee, *Monument im Fruchtland* (Monument in the Fertile Country), *1929, 41*, watercolour and pencil on paper on cardboard, 45.7 × 30.8 cm

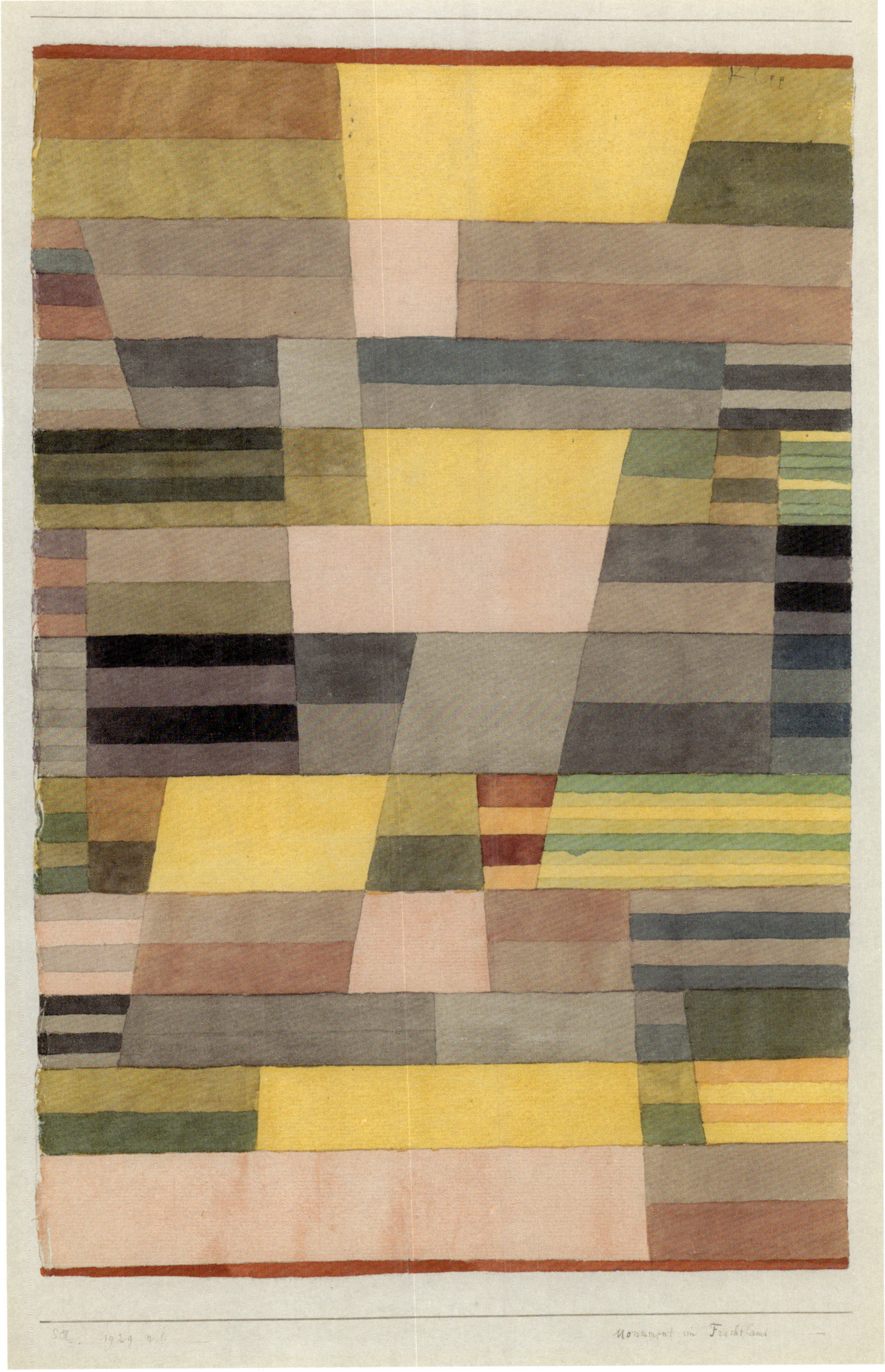

Books on World Art from the 1920s: On the Ambivalence of a Discursive Awakening

Susanne Leeb

Around 1900, the first compendia and guides on so-called world art were published, for example, Karl Woermann's *Geschichte der Kunst aller Zeiten und Völker* (Art History of All Times and Peoples, 1900). But by the 1920s, the German-speaking world saw an explosion of publications on non-European art forms, many of which were swiftly included in the Bauhaus library that had been established in 1919.[1] Among these publications were the twenty-volume series *Orbis Pictus/Weltkunst-Bücherei* (Orbis Pictus/World Art Library, 1920–35), edited by Paul Westheim,[2] and *Kulturen der Erde. Material zur Kultur- und Kunstgeschichte aller Völker*[3] (Cultures of the World: Material on the Cultural and Art History of Peoples, 1919–23), also comprising twenty volumes, which was edited by the social-revolutionary Ernst Fuhrmann, who wrote most of the introductory texts himself.[4] The title *Orbis Pictus* already reveals the programme of this sort of series: spanning the entire 'earth cycle', it bears the name of the first children's textbook richly illustrated with woodcuts, *Orbis sensualium pictus* by the humanist Johann Amos Comenius, which sought to educate through a combination of texts and illustrations and was originally published in 1658. Conceived as textbooks and picture books, these series – even if the introductory texts of the volumes explain the meaning of the respective artefacts – show under which conditions non-European art was received. Serving not least as a source of inspiration and to critique the canon of European high art and abolish the separation between fine art and arts and crafts, nevertheless this interest was not about personal exchange or contact whose 'transnationalism' at the time surmounted 'the geographical, cultural and "racist" boundaries of the colonial world order'.[5] Instead, the world represented in these series was that of the traditional ethnological museum,[6] whose collections were for the most part compiled in the wake of colonialism.

Ernst Fuhrmann, *Reich der Inka* (The Inca Empire), Vol. 1 of *Kulturen der Erde. Material zur Kultur- und Kunstgeschichte aller Völker* (Cultures of the World: Material on the Cultural and Art History of Peoples), Hagen i.W. and Darmstadt: Folkwang-Verlag, 1922

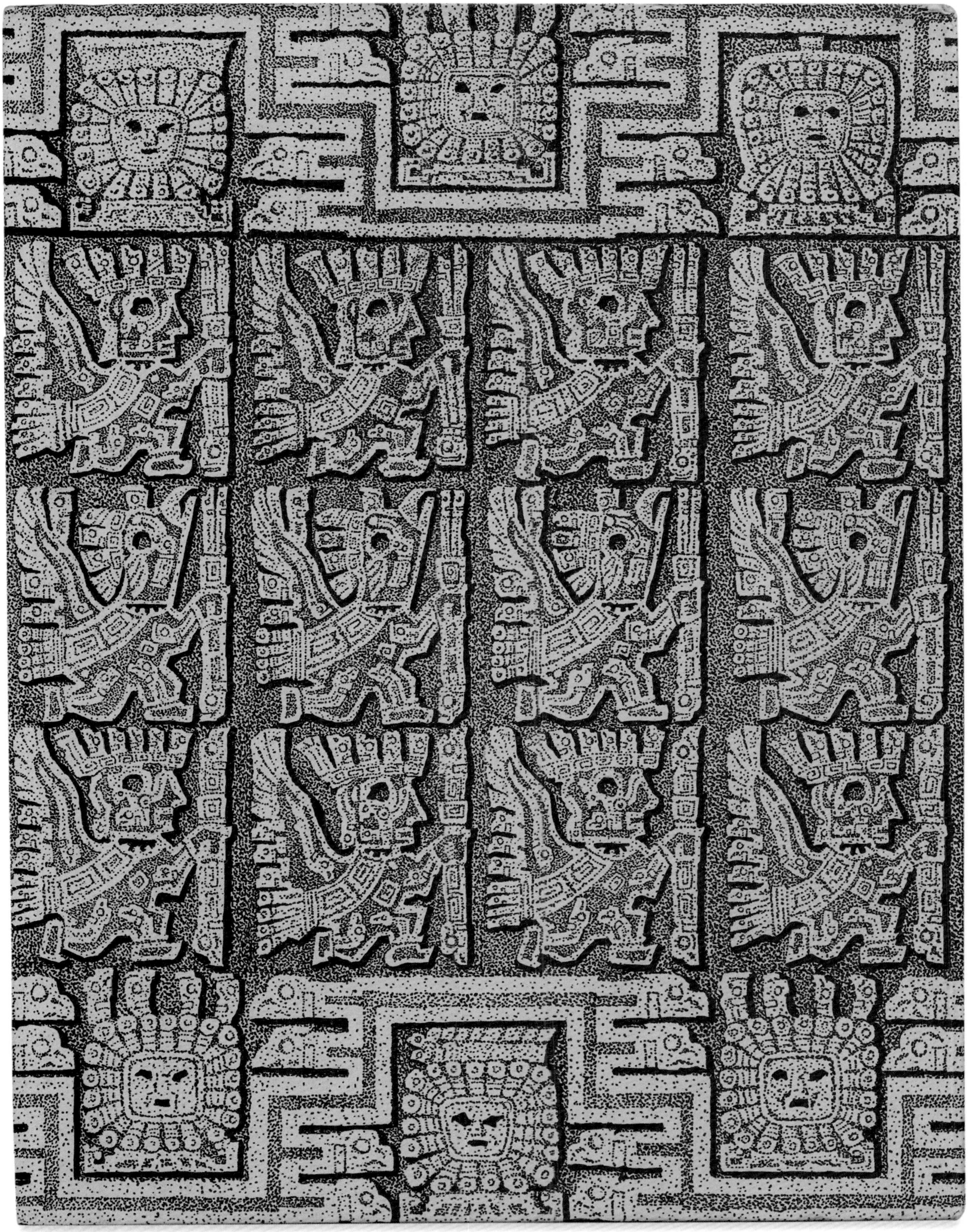

Ernst Fuhrmann, *Peru II*, Vol. 2 of *Kulturen der Erde. Material zur Kultur- und Kunstgeschichte aller Völker* (Cultures of the World: Material on the Cultural and Art History of Peoples), Hagen i.W. and Darmstadt: Folkwang-Verlag, 1922

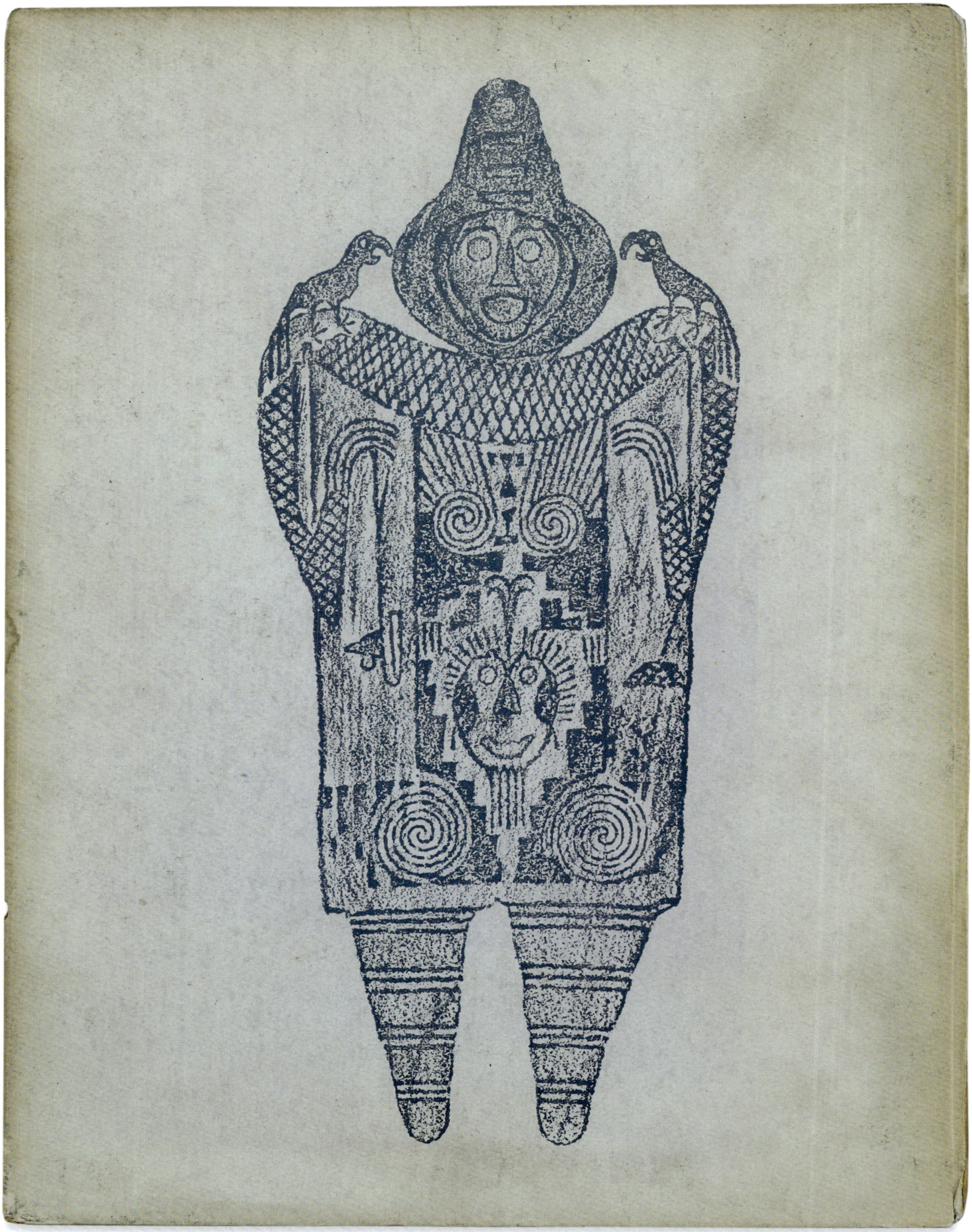

Thus, this extremely wide opening of art history simultaneously implied the inscription of the objects in concepts of art, not least based on specific institutional framings, the material conditions of reproduction and historical-philosophical narratives. The frequent diagnosis of the decay of non-European societies, both contemporary and ancient, which was represented through their art, followed a biologistic model of history that assumed that societies pass through a cycle of rise, flowering and decay, with this history never being a specific one but always human history. 'In the Near East, humanity completed the first epoch of its history in the course of 4,000 years.'[7] So reads the first sentence of Otto Weber's introduction to *Die Kunst der Hethiter* (Hittite Art, *Orbis Pictus*, Vol. 9). And Carl Einstein, who later radically revised his position, wrote in the same series on *Afrikanische Plastik* (African Sculpture, *Orbis Pictus*, Vol. 7) – albeit assigning responsibility to colonialism: 'The old tradition disintegrated under colonialism.... It appears as if African artisanship were in the last phase of decay.'[8] For others, such as the art historian Wilhelm Hausenstein, who first argued along socialist lines, then in an increasingly cultural-pessimistic way and finally in the 1950s from a religious perspective, these arts implied a collectivist, archetypically democratic model in the name of which he countered the modern division of labour and the principle of individualism in *Bild und Gemeinschaft. Entwurf einer Soziologie der Kunst* (Image and Community: Outline of a Sociology of Art, 1920). Two years later, in *Barbaren und Klassiker. Ein Buch von der Bildernei exotischer Völker* (Barbarians and Classics: A Book on the Imagery of Exotic Peoples, 1922), he then contrasted an Oswald Spengler-style diagnosis of the tragic exhaustion of Europe with the vitality of exotic masks.

Classical/anti-classical was one of the most widespread distinctions made by those who sought to free themselves from a narrative that saw the origin of all cultures in classical Greece via the reception of non-European art.[9] This anti-classical orientation could go in two political directions, which here I can only roughly outline: those who aimed at a socialist relativization of their own culture and called for an anti-national communal thinking in the sense of a people's culture (one example being the art historian Oskar Beyer in *Welt-Kunst. Von der Umwertung der Kunstgeschichte* (World Art: On the Revaluation of Art History, 1923)), and those arguing against Greece in favour of a *völkisch* blood community or a Nordic spirit, as was the case with the art historian Josef Strzygowski, who arrived at a National Socialist art history.

Alongside these classifications in cultural-historical narratives, the objects were radically transformed foremost by their inclusion in museums – which always also implied a change in ownership – and by inventory photography. Photographed against a neutral background, the once mostly ritual objects were transformed into sculptures. With the fundamental fact of new ownership relations, this also resulted in a new commodification and the formation of art-historical expertise.[10] In analogy to Karl Marx's concept of the fetish, Sylvester Okwunodu Ogbechie remarked that '[t]his dispensation renders the real producers of African artworks invisible'.[11] The effects of such a de- and recontextualization were, according to Ogbechie, isolation, monumentalization, individualization, formalization, the identification of 'masterpieces' and, not least, the normalization of these new object categories via their dissemination through photography. This is revealed in the above-mentioned shift of the objects to new categorizations, whereby viewing such arts as mere ornaments is also part of this shift. In their respective societies of origin, these so-called ornaments were and are complex forms of coding on or out of different materials. Through a European practice of reproduction, they were separated from a material support (bodies in the case of tattoos, devices, houses, ritual objects, etc.), from social usage, and transferred to two-dimensionality, thus becoming, like in Owen Jones's *Grammar of Ornament* (London, 1856), the visual material of a 'global' pattern book. Thus these 'ornaments' were used as decorations for book covers, as can be seen in the series *Kulturen der Erde*. A short while later, in the 1930s, Carl Einstein was already criticizing this method of formalization: 'This isolating of artistic activities effected an historically insufficient, merely aesthetic point of view that diminished history to a kind of mechanics of forms and styles.'[12] He instead demanded a complex, cultural-historical contemplation of these objects.

In the broadest sense, epistemological and material conditions codetermined a certain mode of reception: a preference for form/style over materiality, objectness over social context, aesthetics over historicity. The question of whether the modern medium of photography that was so central for the Bauhaus could possess a facture of its own was debated at the end of the 1920s, especially with regard to textiles and the category of the haptic under the influence of New Objectivity, to which Ernst Fuhrmann, the editor of *Kulturen der Erde*, also belonged as a plant photographer.[13]

Hence, the aim of propagating the arts of all cultures with these books was an ambivalent affair, to say the least, since they were simultaneously inscribed with the new valorization, expansion, and in the function of criticizing European high art in the epistemological framings that are until today institutionally cemented in ethnological, archaeological and art museums, among others. The books circulating at the time were to relativize these borders to a certain degree, especially since they prompted the interest in delving into the arts and artefacts of other societies in the first place. But their own framings were in turn disrupted only through protests against this form of culturalization, through migration or transnational collaborations – a project already politically proclaimed in the wake of anti- and decolonialization movements – and, as shown by demands for restitution and a radical restructuring of ethnological museums, all the way to the massive critique of the Humboldt-Forum in Berlin, one that is yet to be completed.[14]

Ernst Fuhrmann, *Mexiko III* (Mexico III), Vol. 13 of *Kulturen der Erde. Material zur Kultur- und Kunstgeschichte aller Völker* (Cultures of the World: Material on the Cultural and Art History of Peoples), Hagen i.W. and Darmstadt: Folkwang-Verlag, 1922

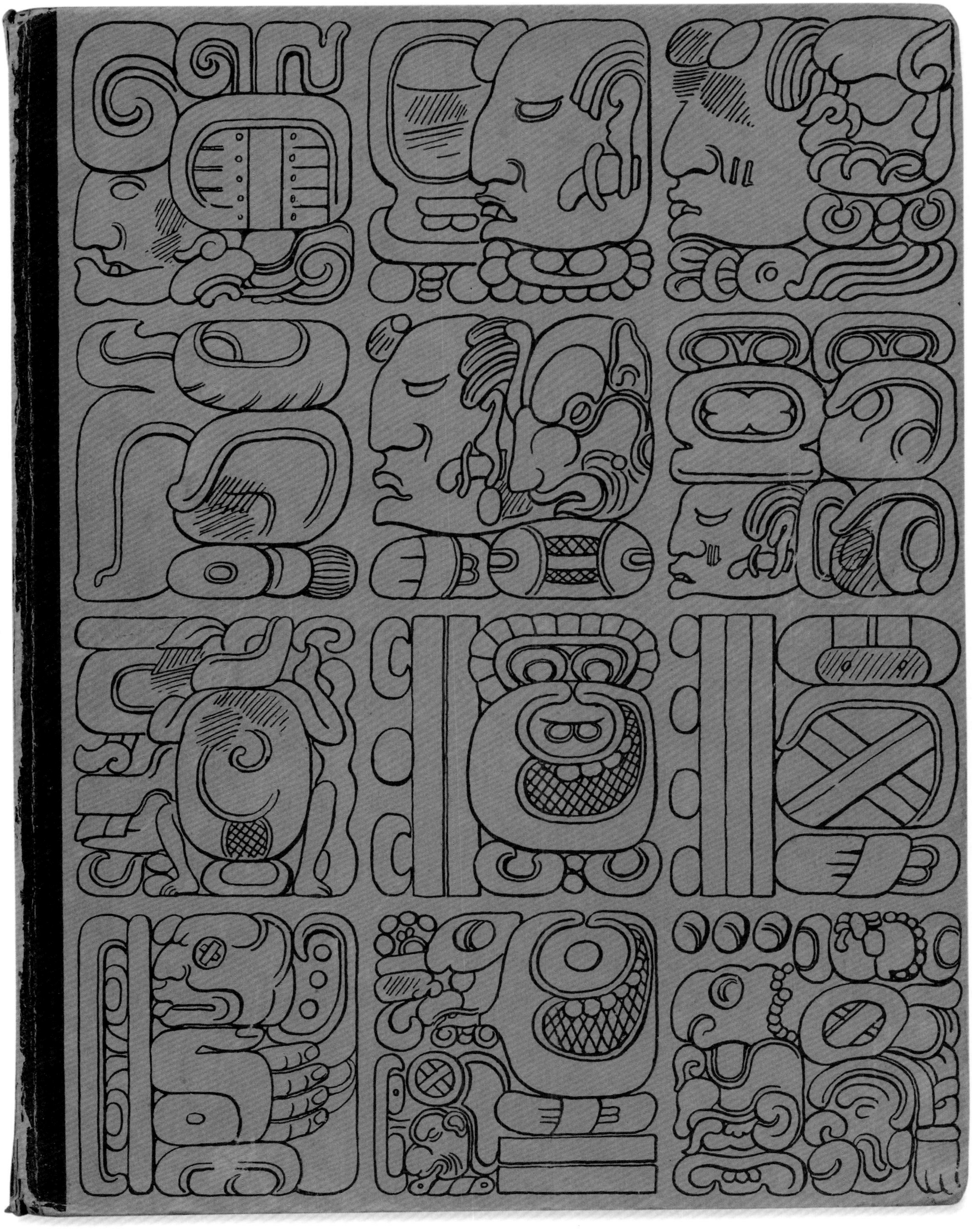

Colonial Melancholia

Kader Attia

One of the biggest misunderstandings regarding the impact of colonization on colonized societies is to think that, because it has been developed within a modern agenda from capitalism to universalism, traditions have first been erased. To think in such a way promotes this misunderstanding and produces the opposite effect that this statement is supposed to defend. That is wrong, because we have never been traditional or modern; a continuum would be more adequate to simply acknowledge mankind's evolution from nature to culture.

Following years of field research and observing my surrounding environment, I have developed a perception of failures or accidents, which I defined first as early signs of re-appropriation. Signs of cultural cannibalism, which occupied societies from Algeria to Brazil, have visually but silently developed as forms of mimesis of their invaders and rulers within their own cultures. The contact with significant elements of western modernities, such as manufactured items, from weapons to technological devices, has generated reactions rather than imposed influences on passive native subjects.

It is what the Lebanese philosopher Tarek El-Ariss has called 'trials' in his book *Trials of Arab Modernity* (2013); clearly because the reaction, which results from contact with western modernity, is not passive but active – from a resistance to an absorption. Western modernity, from its technological promise to its political one – the age of reason from German and French philosophy (Kant and Descartes) – has also been welcomed by secular societies in the non-western world, in North Africa and the Middle East. But less known is that when Al Tatawi the traveller, sent by the Sultan Mohamed Ali from Cairo to Paris in the late 1820s, was describing a certain enjoyment in the city's modernity, he did not know that Algiers would be attacked with cannons and taken in 1830…

Below and pages 115–17: Kader Attia, research material, Berber jewelry including coins from the colonial power

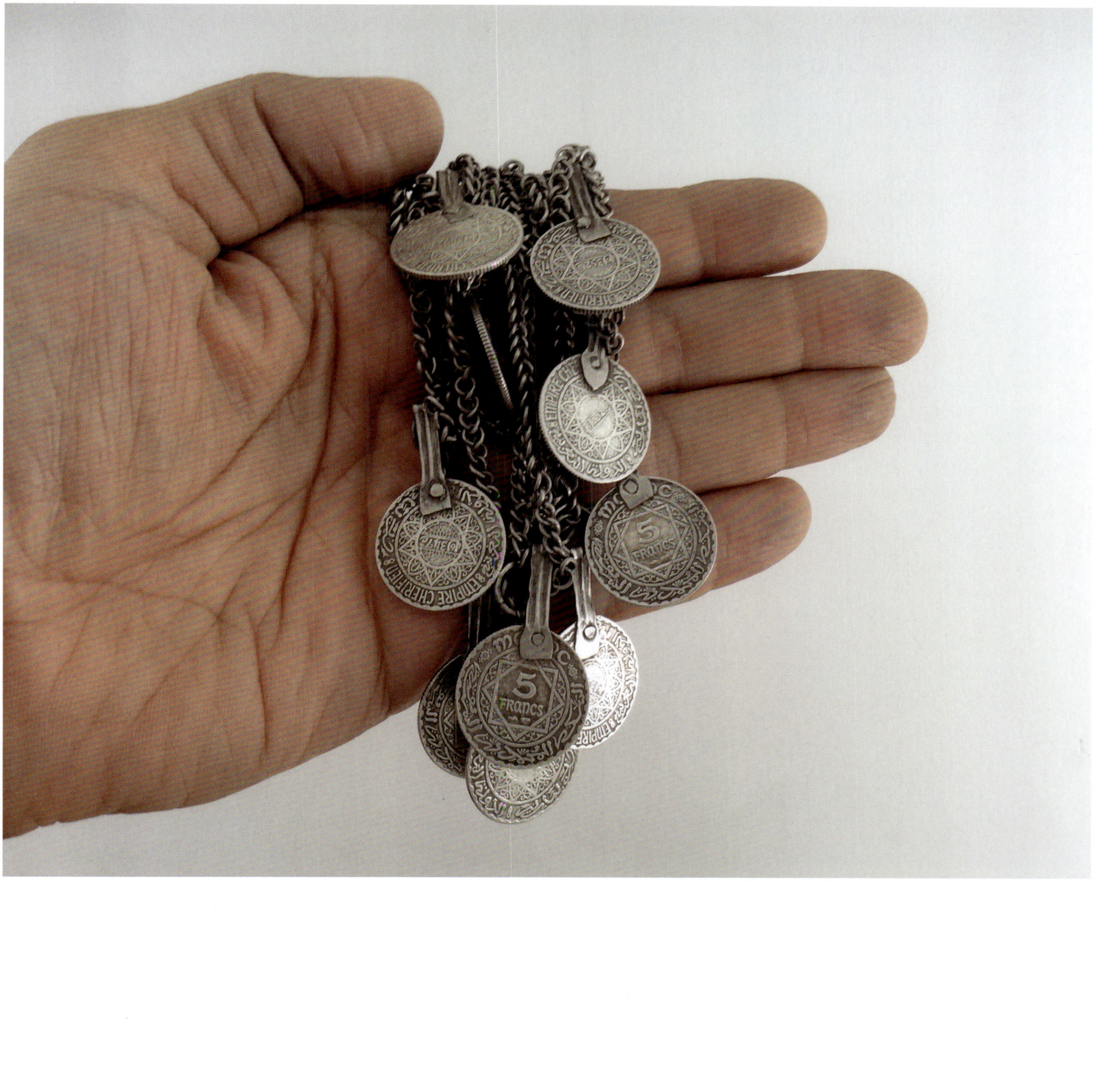

From the Napoleonic Egypt campaign in the final years of the eighteenth century, which was militarily and artistically ruled, to the attack on Algiers, almost thirty years passed. And between the takeover of Algiers and the colonial expansion, which accelerated from 1848 with Napoleon III, North Africa was no longer delusional about the French occupation; on the contrary, the guerrilla resistance started a parallel war against the occupiers. This parallel war was the basis for more reactions and 'trials' in the sense of El-Ariss's theory, or, in Brazil – far away from Africa in space and time – what Brazilian poet Oswald de Andrade wrote about in his 1928 manifesto 'Cultural Anthropophagi'.

These reactions, these trials, are modernities inside the non-western societies: modernity deliberately taken as such by people from the individual to the group. They are new concepts as well as new political orientations shifting to new forms of resistance. Here is an example: wherever people have been colonized, they have produced artefacts using regular, old local material, but always with a deliberate absorption of high symbols of power, such as coins showing representations of the Queen of Spain, or England, or of the Emperor Napoleon, or the allegory of the Republic, or German or Belgian currencies. This transformation has synthesized both the shift within a society, which is not what it used to be anymore, and a message for equality: we cannot only mimic the occupiers, we can transform them.

This form of re-appropriation has been for me more than a re-enactment; it contains signs of a deep desire for repair. Not only the earliest signs of reorientation (not a re-orientalism) towards freedom, which a century later will finally lead to independence.

This transformation – including a western, modern, manufactured object – is actually an absorption of a ready-made, which is a counter ready-made or what Marcel Duchamp would have called *un ready made aidé* (a helped ready-made).

The way all repaired objects, especially artefacts from a non-western colonized society, result not only from fixing but also from a process of re-appropriation of an anonymous person's freedom, who is in charge of the repairing, leaves open the question of whether this ready-made used in the process of repair is forever an incarnation of such: a ready-made or the contrary…

Inside the loop that defines this oxymoron – because repair is also the injury, and injury is inseparable from any repair – we should underline the counter ready-made function, the signifier of which is the counter-object of desire. The anti-Lacanian object of desire that Lacan has explained as lost forever.

The repair includes a counter ready-made as much as the ready-made is an incarnation of the Lacanian object of desire. The object that we all want to possess but never get, because its role is to draw one towards it to be enjoyed.

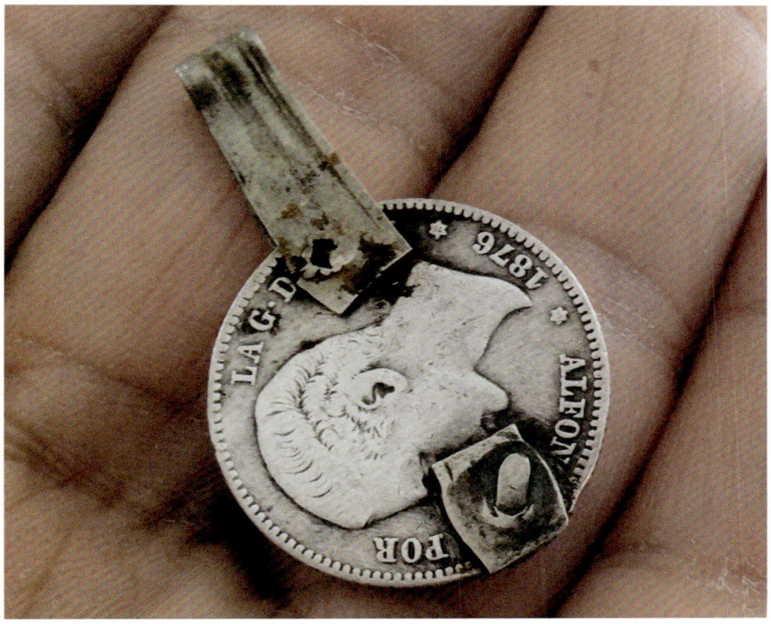
1876
ALFON
POR

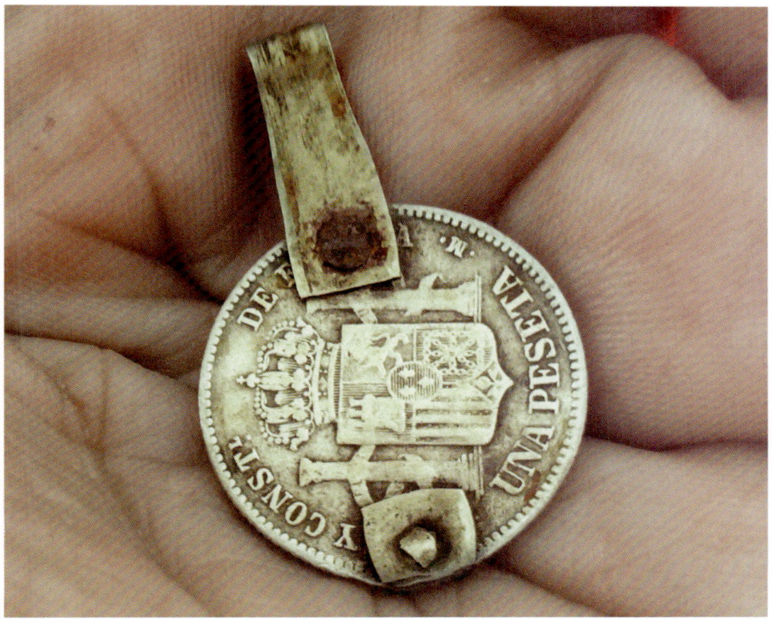
UNA PESETA
Y CONST.

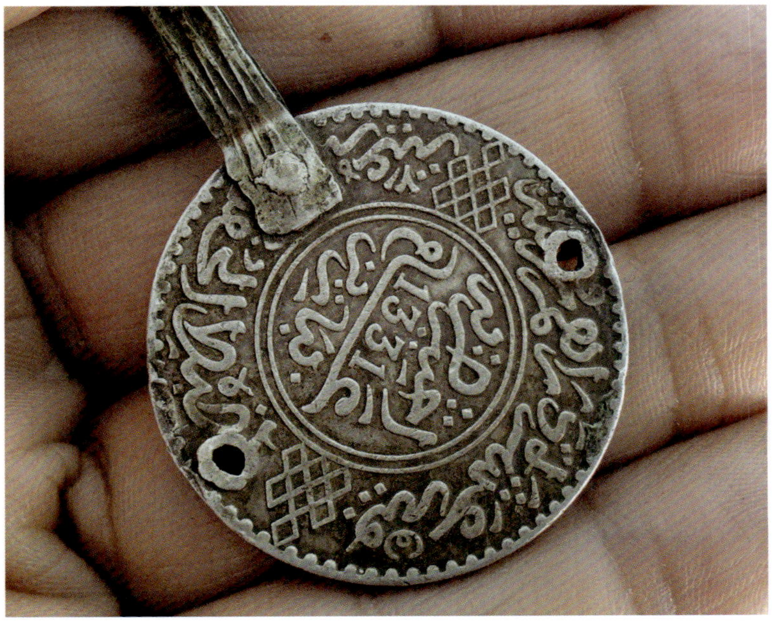

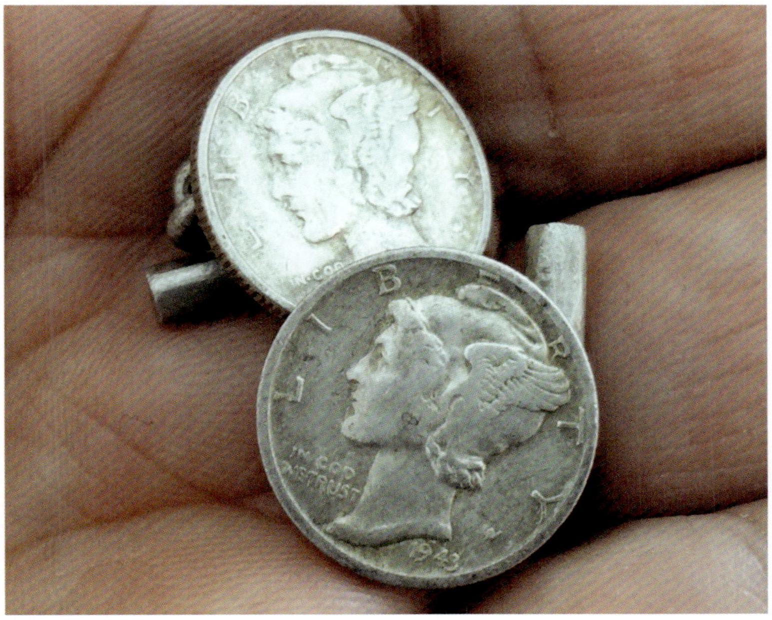

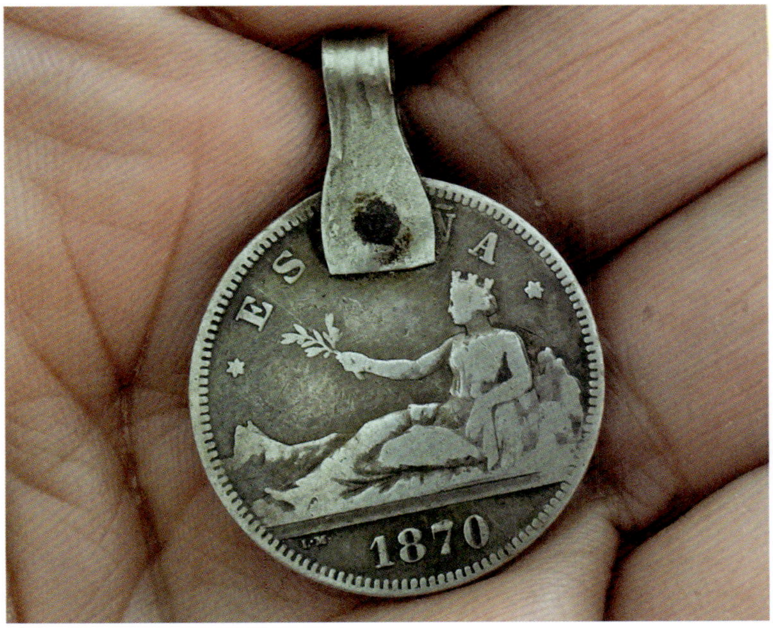
1870

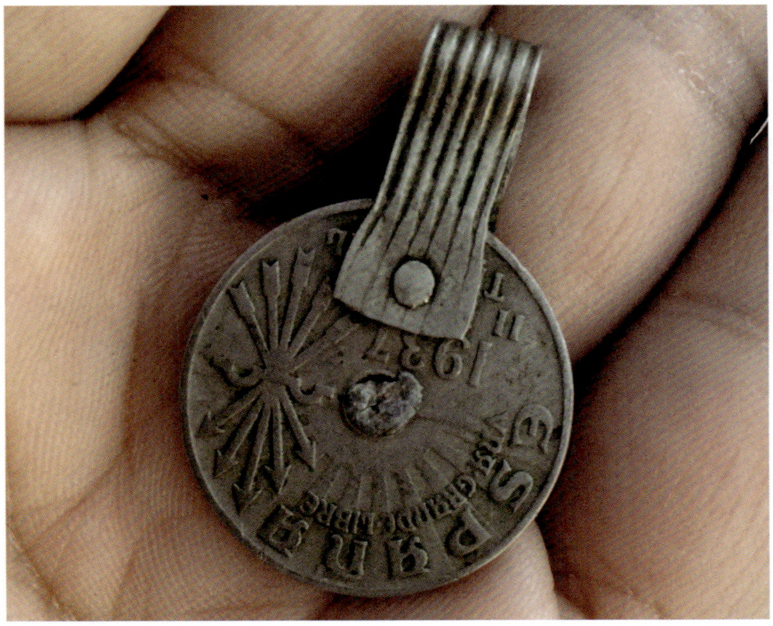

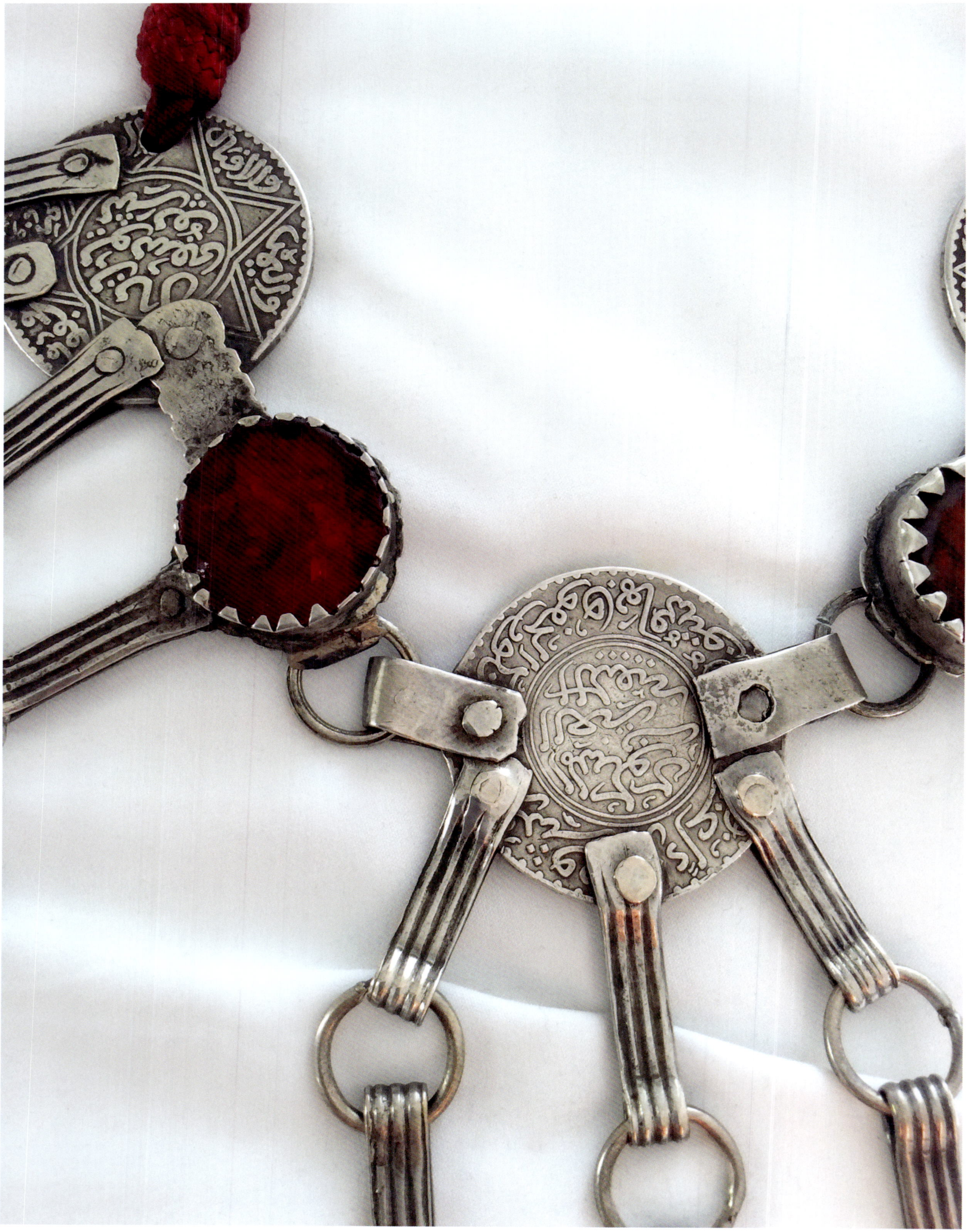

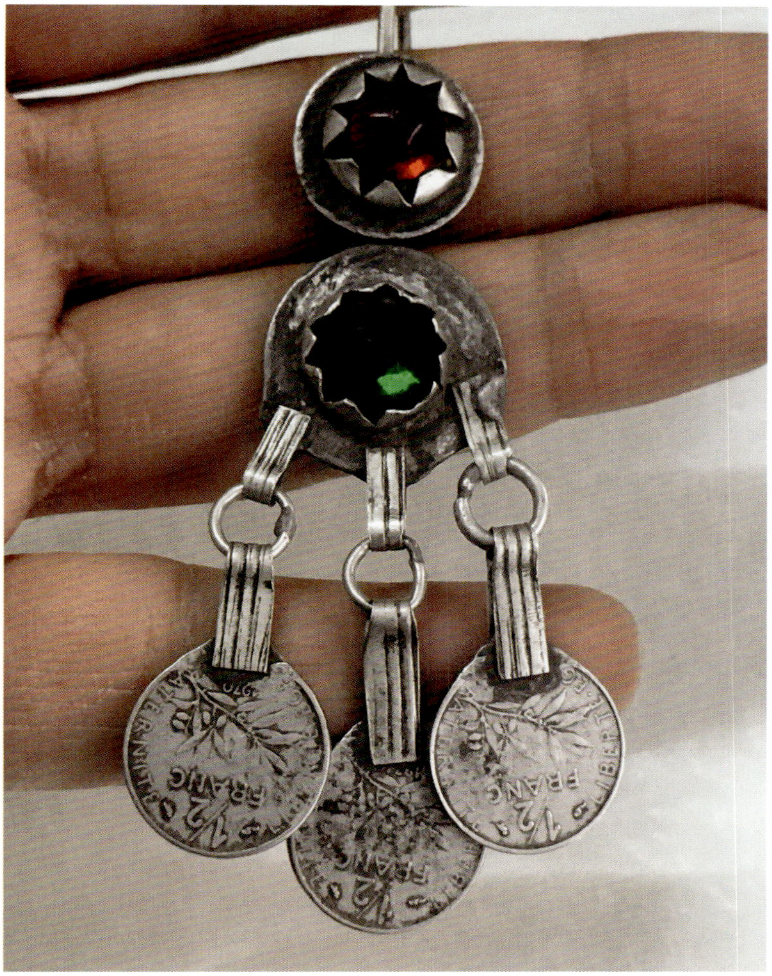
1/2 FRANC
1/2 FRANC
1/2 FRANC

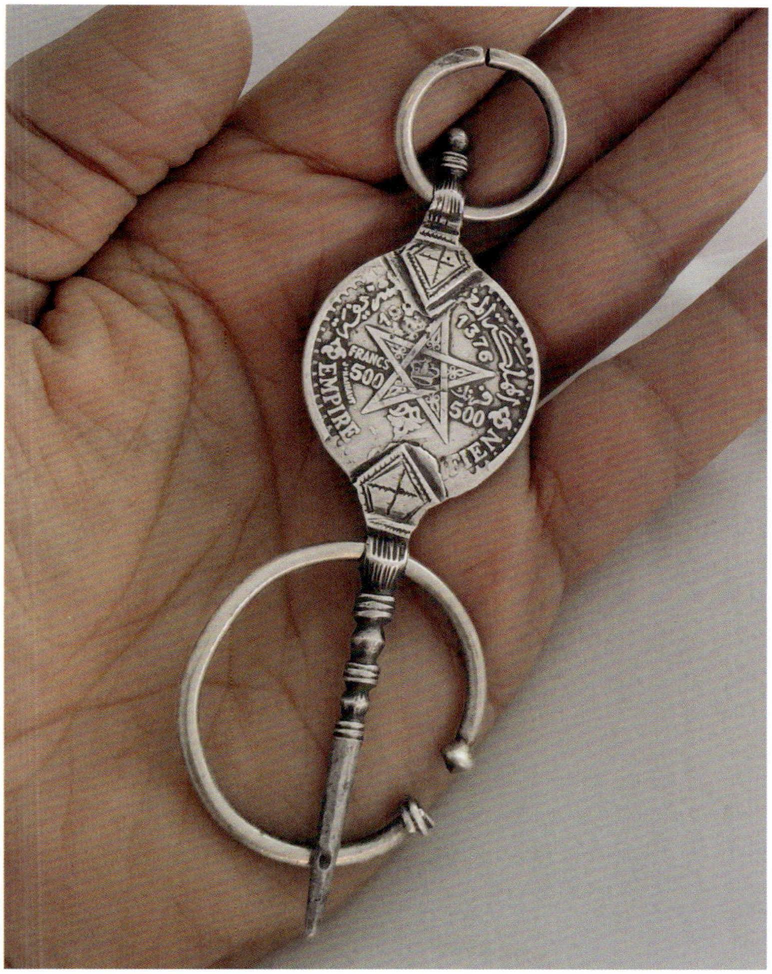
1370
FRANCS
500
EMPIRE
500

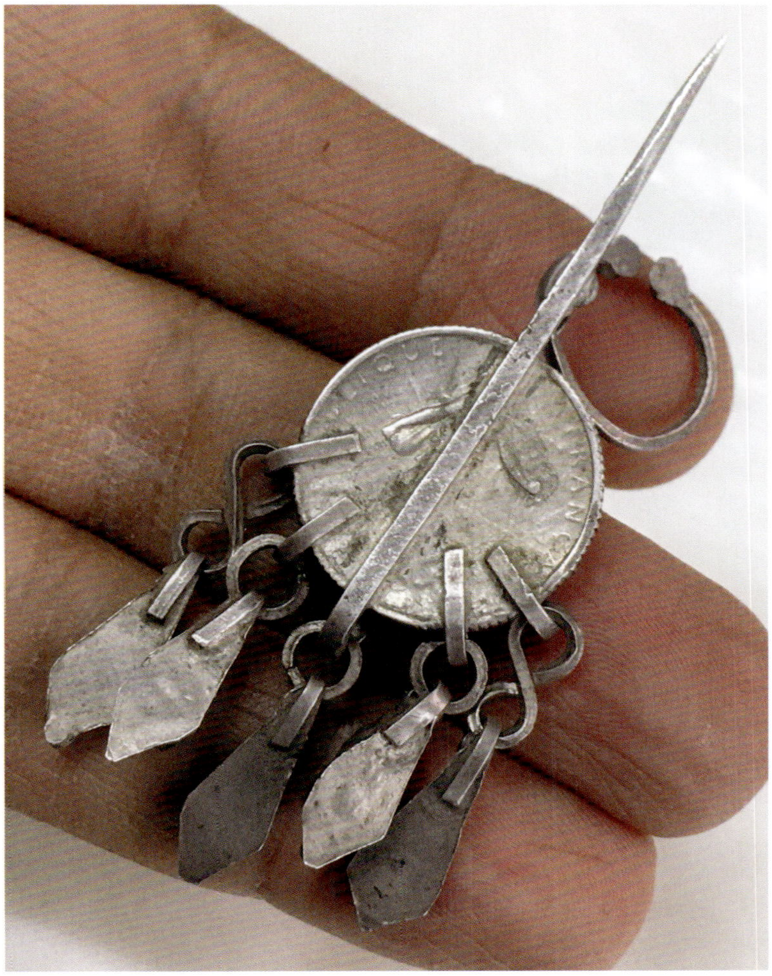

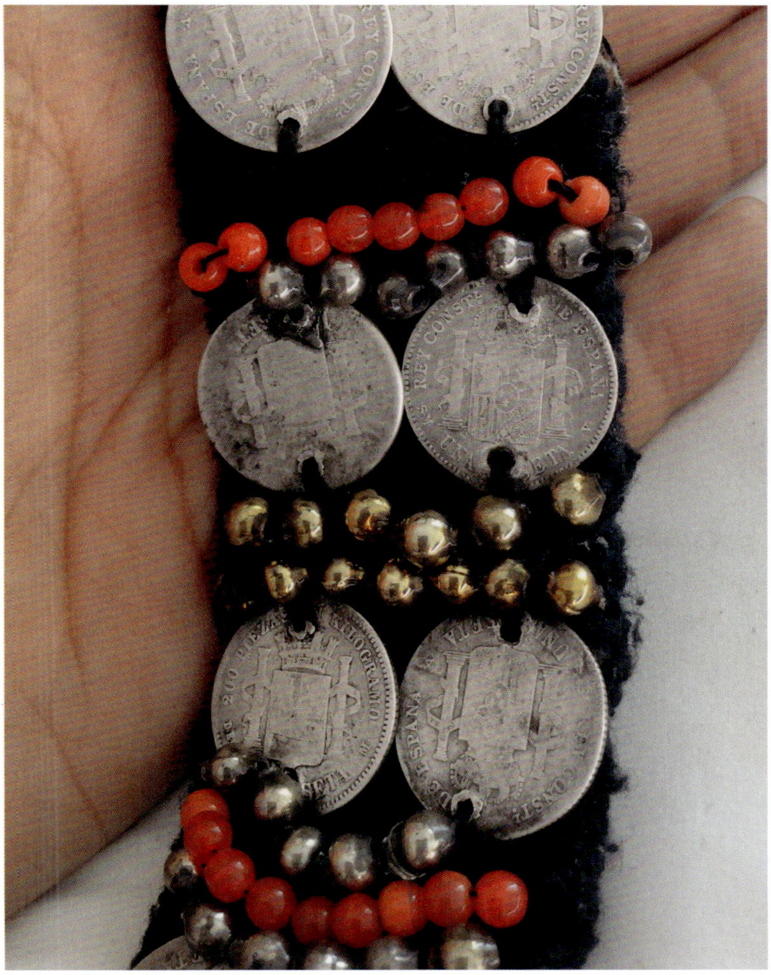

The Bauhaus as a Catalyst

Mohamed Melehi

In 1966, ten years after Morocco's independence, the School of Fine Arts in Casablanca became the breeding ground for artistic and ethnographic research, where a group of teachers drew up a new form of pedagogy based on studios and art-history courses that employed modern research methods, a far cry from the decrepit academic dogma that had been in place before. We were a group that formed in 1965, determined to change the teaching and curriculum that dated from the colonial period; the group members were Farid Belkahia (head of the School of Fine Arts), Toni Maraini (professor of Art History), Bert Flint (professor of Anthropology), Mohamed Chabâa (professor of Graphic Arts) and myself, Mohamed Melehi (professor of Painting and Photography). We then started investigative fieldwork in forms and symbols contained within works mainly produced in rural areas, in order to demonstrate that modernism does not always flow directly from a historical period or evolution.[1]

The School of Fine Arts, since its inception in 1953, had been based on a western-style system of teaching that was modelled on the curriculum of French art schools. We felt instead that Morocco, having been blessed with its own ethnic iconographic heritage, deserved to be the source for artistic practices. The discovery of silver jewelry in South Morocco and of vernacular paintings on the ceilings of mosques in the Atlas Mountains made a considerable impact on us.[2] It was necessary to replace classical methodologies, in order to correct or redirect the common vision, through the introduction of a teaching methodology that was coherent with the multifarious subtleties of Moroccan culture. One of these teaching methods was the introduction of a new classroom experience, namely, the replacement of plaster casts and memento mori objects in a still life with rural rugs from the mainly Arabic region of Haouz in Marrakesh, and with silver jewelry from Souss in the Tamazight language region, which were then photographed and enlarged as teaching material for students to research and study. This new departure was reinforced by the introduction of a course in Arabic calligraphy and another in architectural drawing, held within the department of decorative arts.[3]

Cover of *Maghreb Art*, No. 1, 1965, published by the École des Beaux-Arts de Casablanca, graphic design by Mohamed Melehi

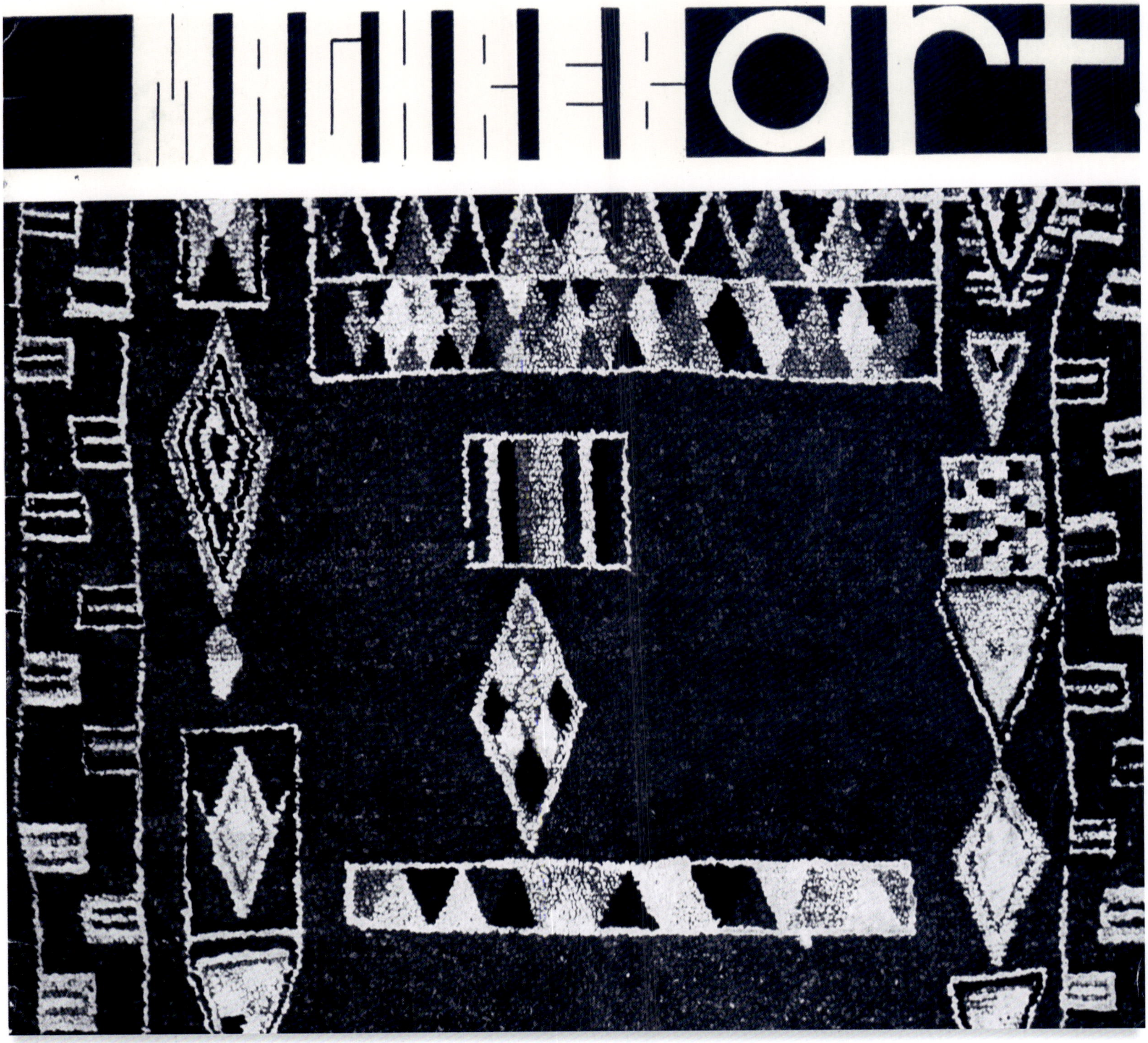

Cover of *Maghreb Art*, No. 2 (dedicated to popular art), 1966, published by the École des Beaux-Arts de Casablanca, graphic design by Mohamed Melehi

Title page of *Maghreb Art*, No. 2, 1966, graphic design by Mohamed Melehi

Cover of *Maghreb Art*, No. 3, 1969, published by the École des Beaux-Arts de Casablanca, graphic design by Mohamed Melehi

Page 5 of *Maghreb Art*, No. 3, 1969, graphic made by students to accompany the article 'Note on the Experience of Painting and Decoration Workshops Run by Painters Chebaa [Chabâa] and Melehi at the École des Beaux-Arts de Casablanca'

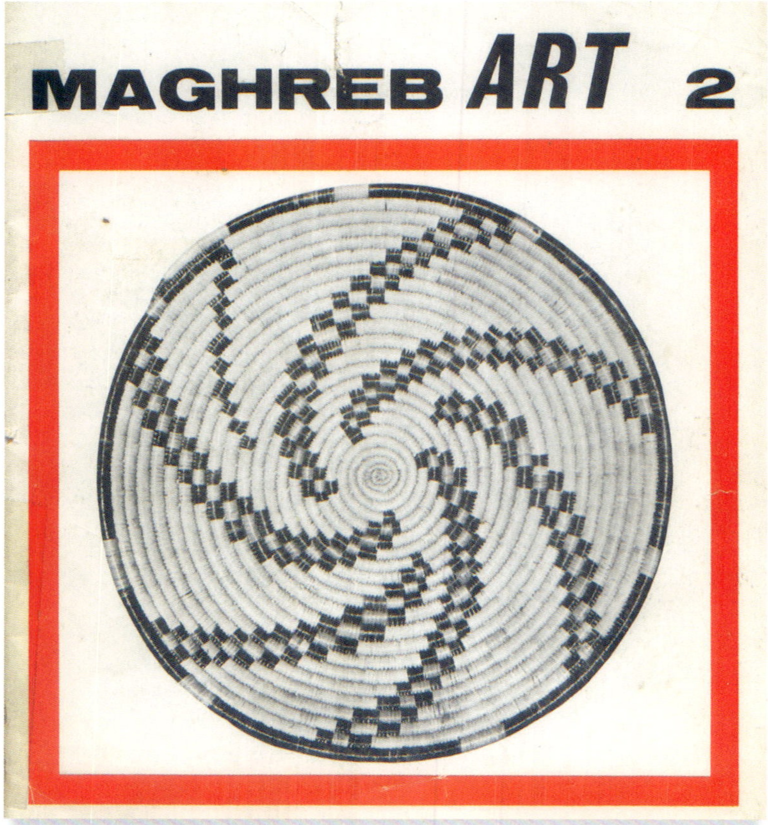

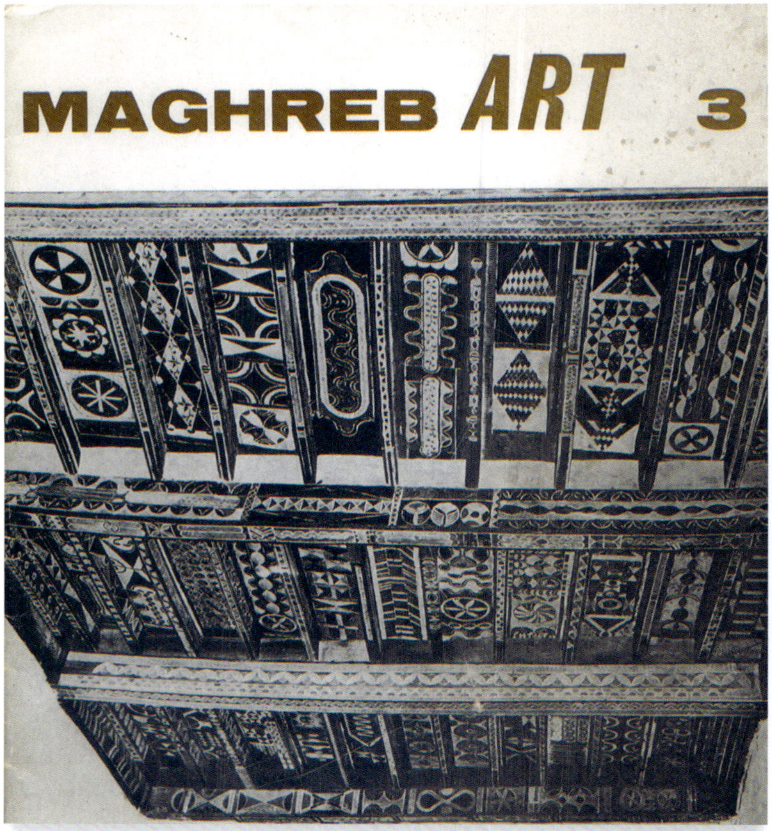

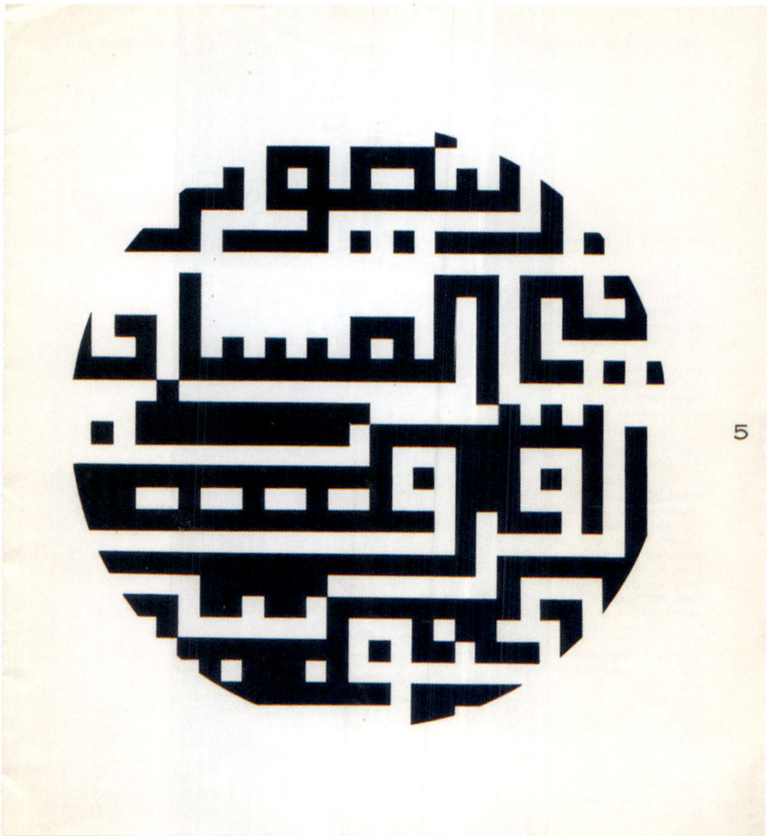

Page 14 of *Maghreb Art*, No. 2, 1966, published by the École des Beaux-Arts de Casablanca, photograph of carpet illustrating the article 'Some Considerations on Traditional Folk Art in Morocco' by Toni Maraini, photograph by Mohamed Melehi

14

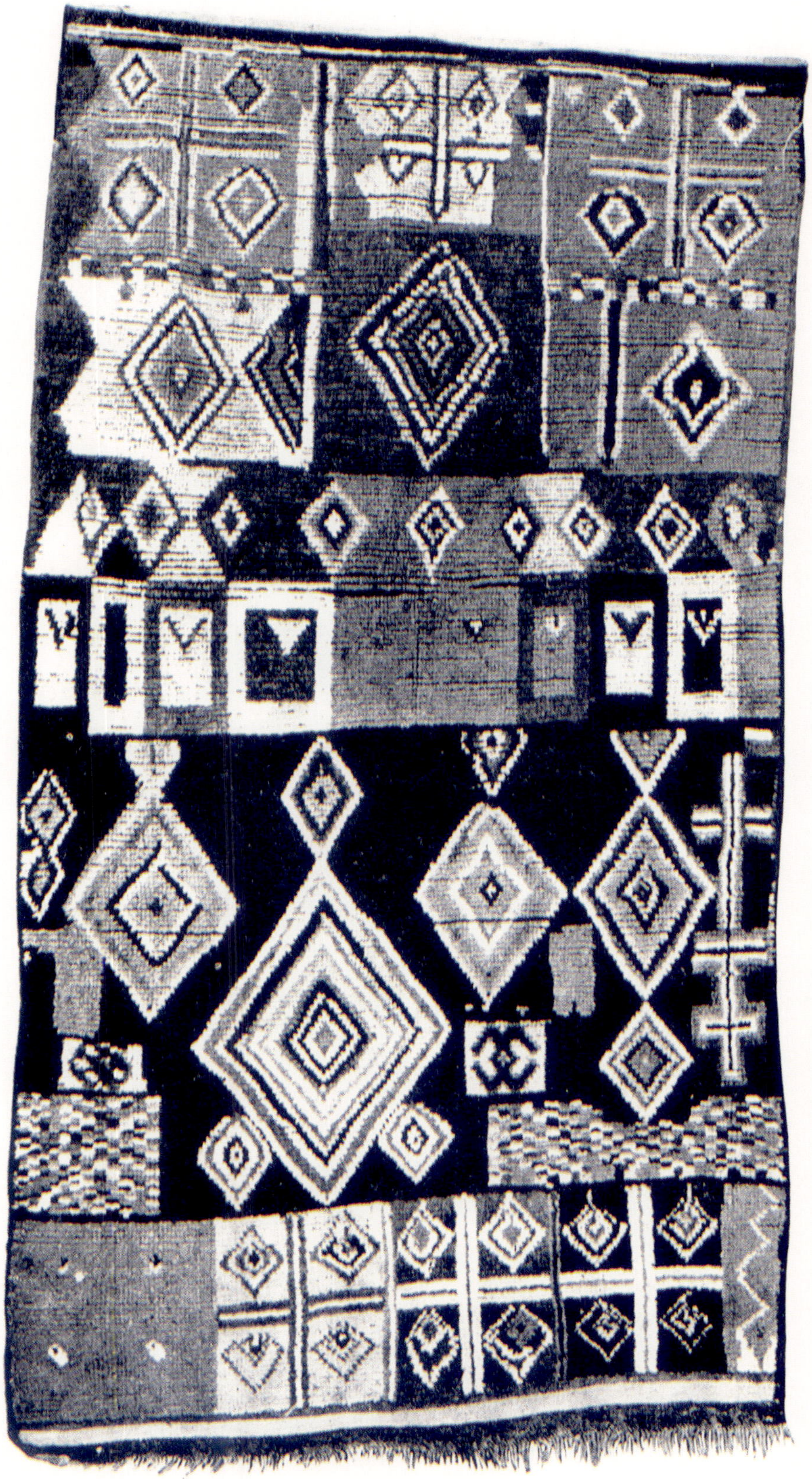

2

With the school, the aim was not to conduct a study into the Bauhaus – which as the best example of its type revolutionized art movements and was the forerunner of the contemporary application of art to everyday life – but to explore its contribution to the clarification of our perspective and to our thinking on the reciprocal relationship between our indigenous Moroccan artistic legacy and the broader scope of art history. The Bauhaus sustained us during our journey and helped us open our eyes to our own iconographic heritage. We cannot end our discussion here without naming just a few of the great pillars of the Bauhaus: László Moholy-Nagy, Herbert Bayer, Paul Klee and his contact with North Africa through his time spent in Tunisia, Wassily Kandinsky, the bare minimalism in the techniques and compositions of Josef Albers, and the architecture of Ludwig Mies van der Rohe or Walter Gropius. The Bauhaus approach helped us to create a bridge between a western movement and our vision of modern art in Morocco, in spite of the absence of a strong tradition of European classical figurative art. Moroccan artists had studied different periods of art history, but the Bauhaus was exceptional in allowing us to reconcile our own artistic tradition to higher decorative art forms.

Page 32 of *Maghreb Art*, No. 3, 1969, published by the École des Beaux-Arts de Casablanca, photograph of fibula illustrating the article 'Note on the Experience of Painting and Decoration Workshops Run by Painters Chebaa [Chabâa] and Melehi at the École des Beaux-Arts de Casablanca', photograph by Mohamed Melehi

32

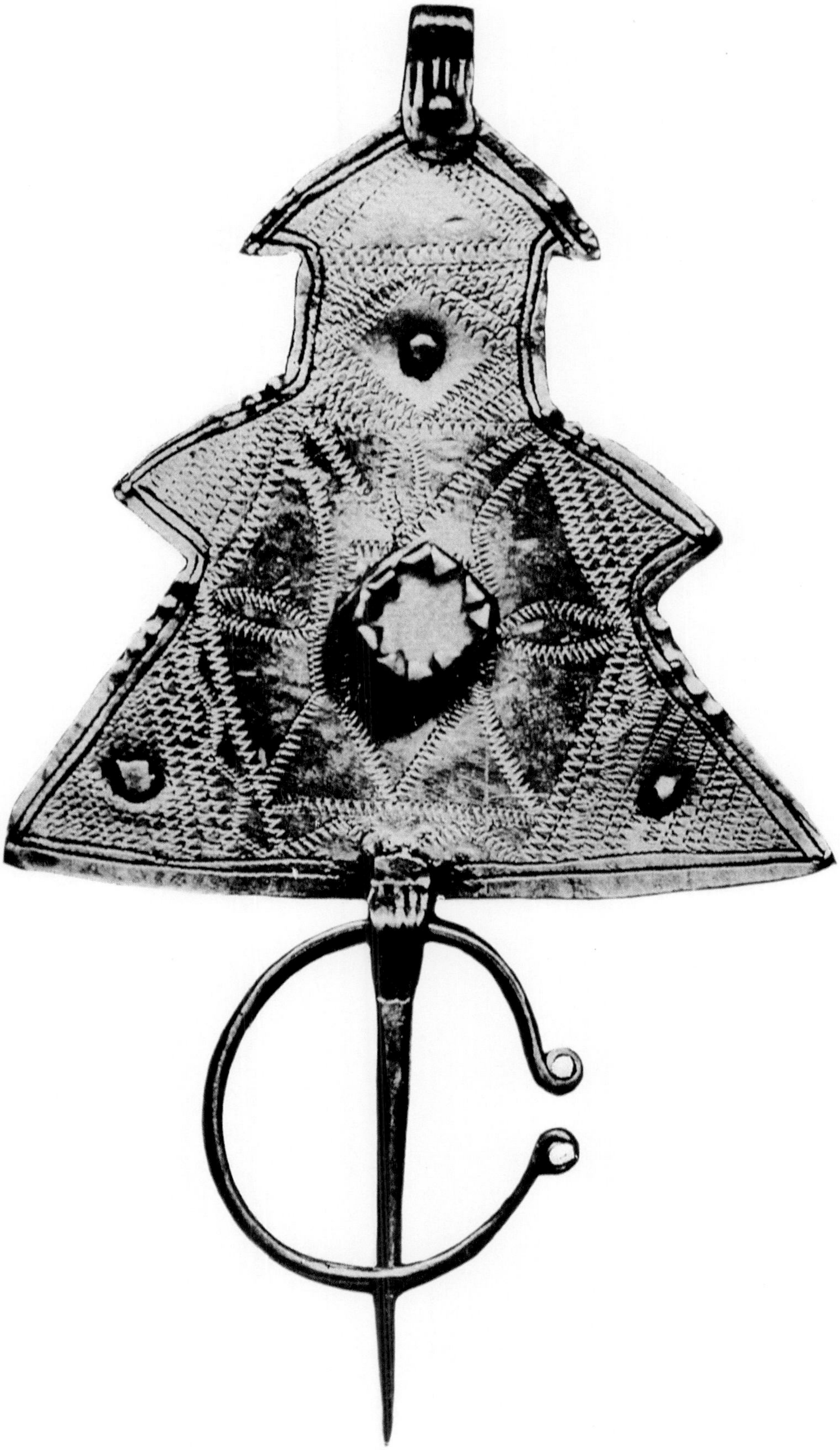

Page 33 of *Maghreb Art*, No. 3, 1969, published by the École des Beaux-Arts de Casablanca, graphic made by students to accompany the article 'Note on the Experience of Painting and Decoration Workshops Run by Painters Chebaa [Chabâa] and Melehi at the École des Beaux-Arts de Casablanca'

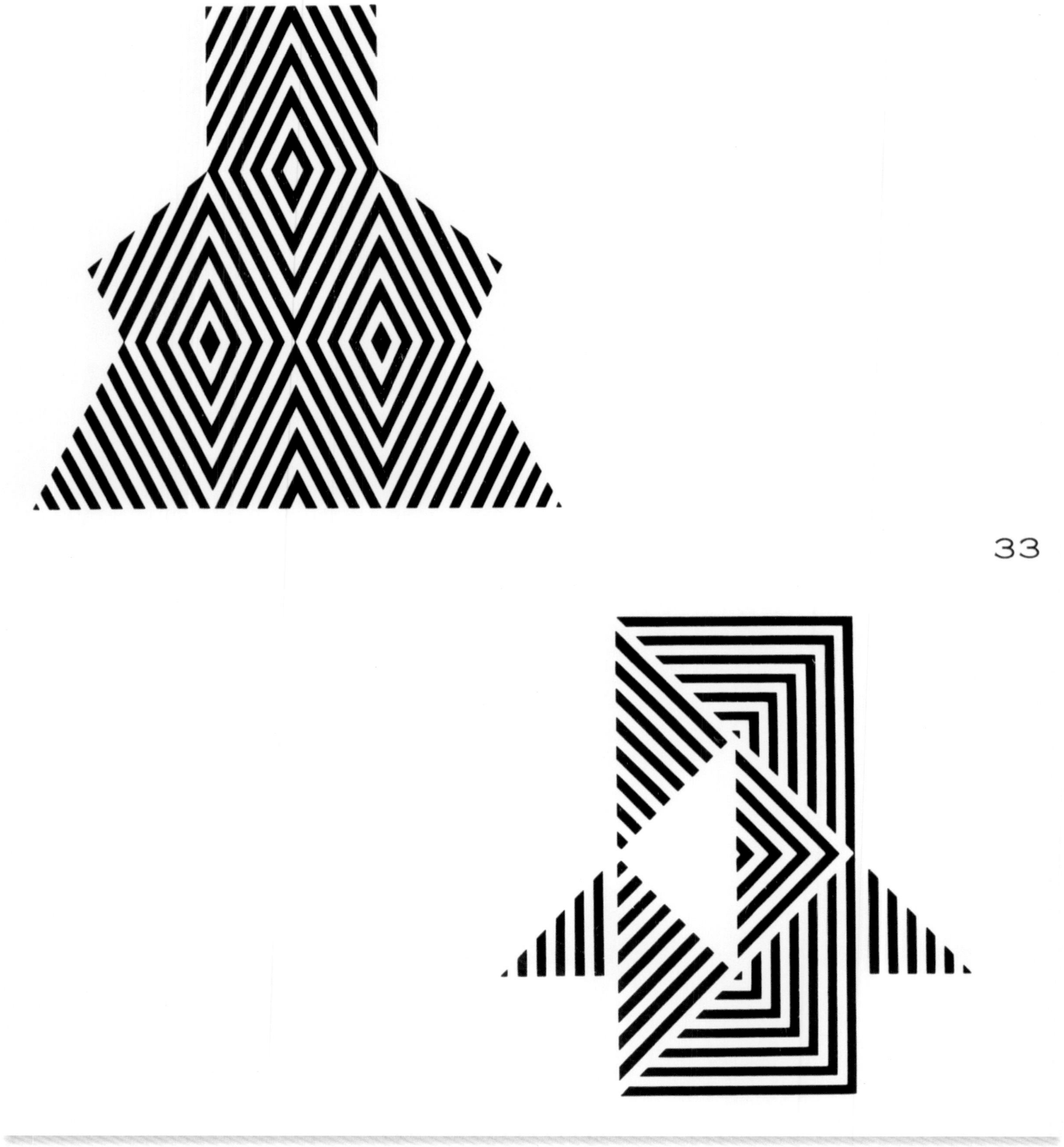

Poster advertising an exhibition of the work of Farid Belkahia, Mohamed Chabâa and Mohamed Melehi, Théâtre National Mohamed V, Rabat, 1965, design by Mohamed Melehi

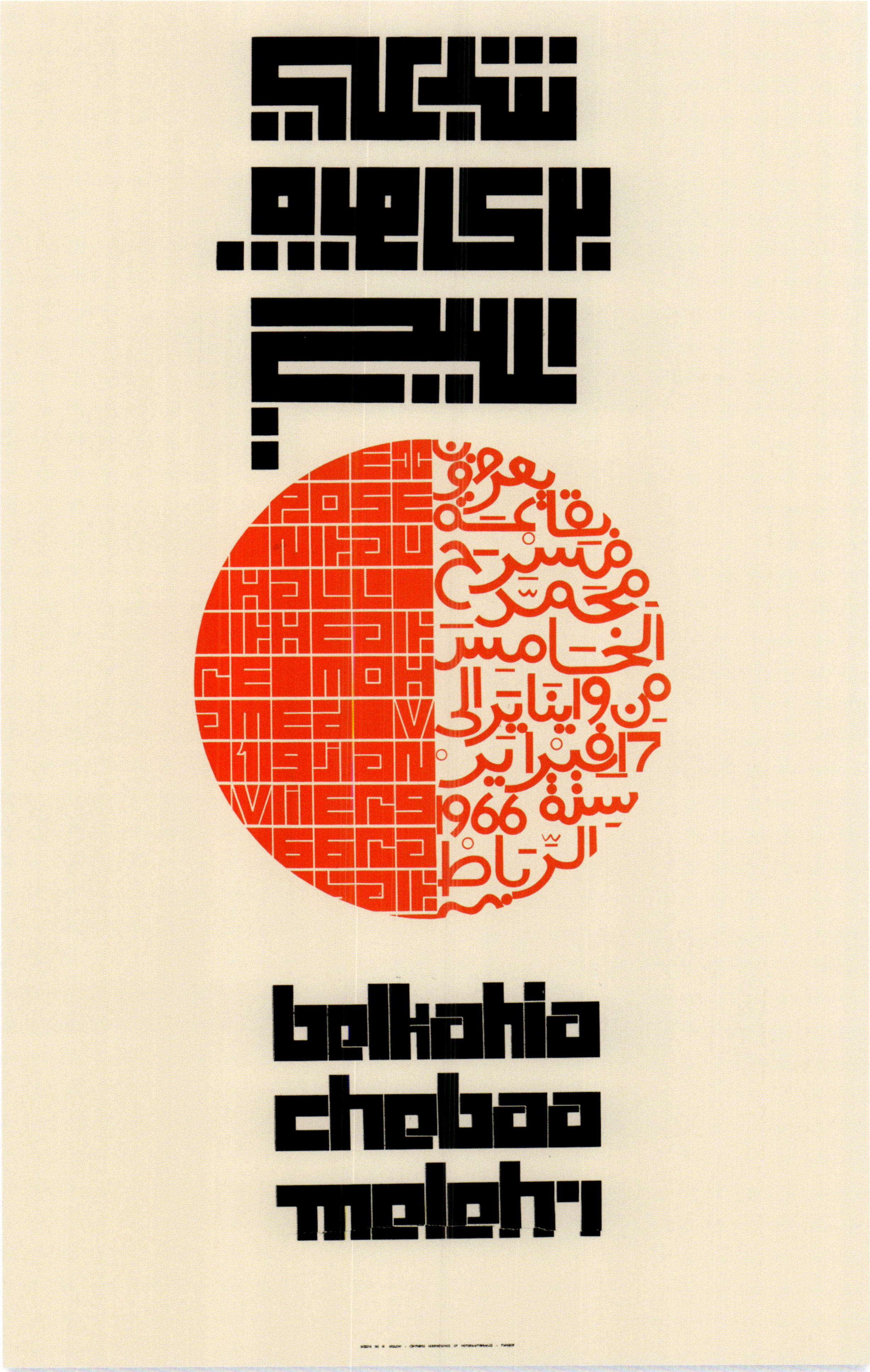

Graphics made by students of the École des Beaux-Arts de Casablanca to accompany the article 'Note on the Experience of Painting and Decoration Workshops Run by Painters Chebaa [Chabâa] and Melehi at the École des Beaux-Arts de Casablanca', in *Maghreb Art*, No. 3, 1969, published by the École des Beaux-Arts de Casablanca, p. 44

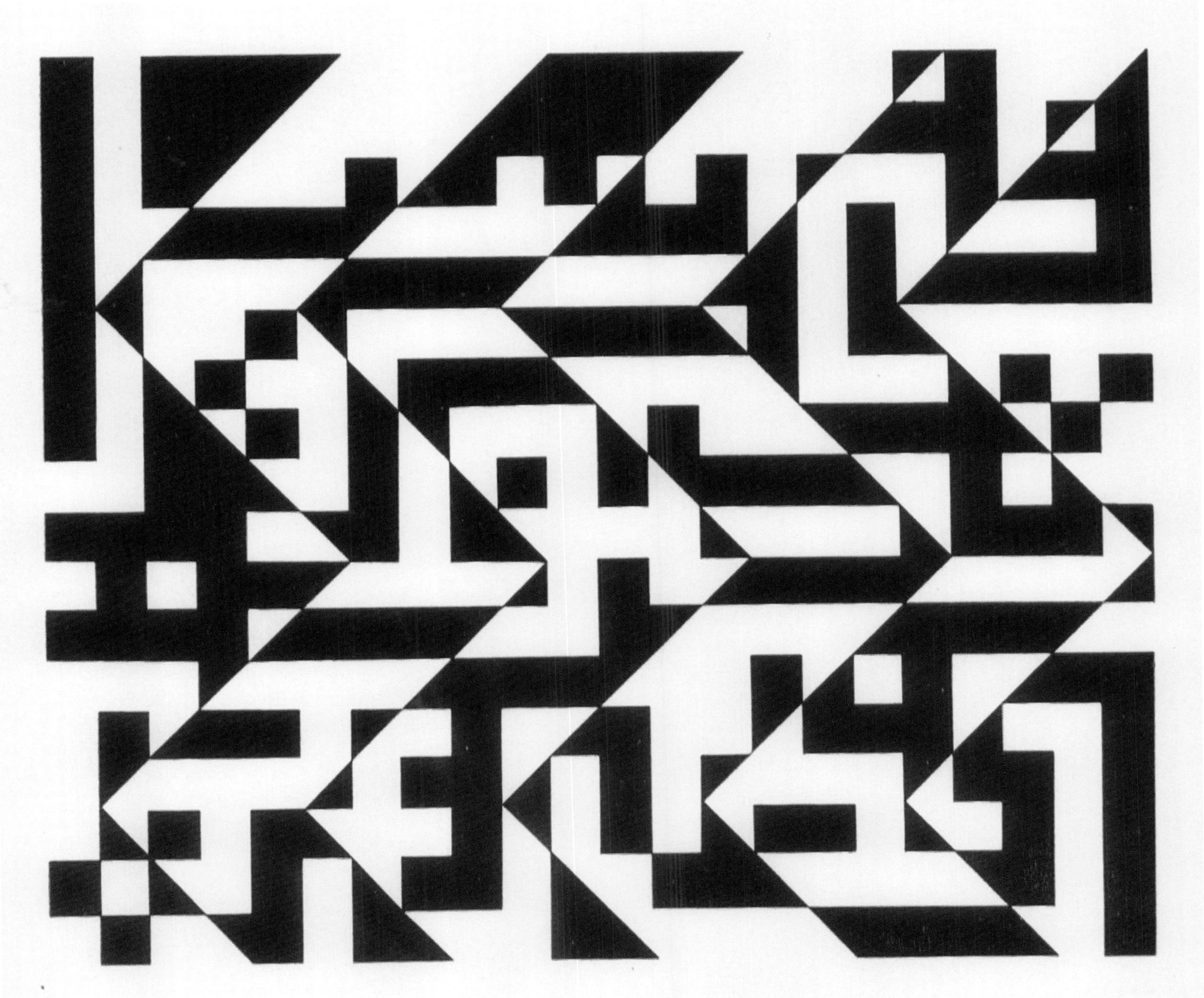

The Andean Textile Paradigm at the Bauhaus

Virginia Gardner Troy

[...] Anni Albers – artist, teacher, writer, and collector – held a unique position as an intermediary between the ancient past and the modern machine age by applying the lessons she learned from the visual and structural language of Andean textiles to the needs and sensibilities of her time. Albers was among many artists and writers working during the first decades of the twentieth century who studied the material culture of non-European societies. The western interest in so-called 'primitive' art and the discourse of primitivism during this period was complex and far-reaching, involving, in part, the supposition that 'primitive' art – the handmade art produced by small-scale pre-industrialized cultures – was both useful and artistically designed according to fundamental social and spiritual beliefs.[1] This was in contrast to the perceived uselessness and poor design of much European art, especially decorative art.

[...] At the same time in Germany, the Berlin Museum für Völkerkunde was undertaking an intensive acquisition program of non-European art, particularly Andean textiles, thanks to extensive archaeological work conducted by German scholars and collectors working in Peru, whose collections ultimately ended up in the Berlin museum. For example, by 1907 the Andean art collection at the Berlin Museum für Völkerkunde was enormous; the textile collection alone exceeded 7500 pieces, by far the largest collection of Andean textiles in Europe at the time.[2] Collectors were fascinated by the technical complexity and abstract pictorial imagery of these textiles created on simple hand looms by a sophisticated culture that did not use conventional western writing systems but instead employed symbols to communicate their ideas.[3] This direct communication of use and design resonated fully with Bauhaus ideals; the abstract visual language and incredible technical mastery of Andean woven textiles were qualities that many modern artists admired and adapted, Albers chief among them.

[...] Members of the Bauhaus Weaving Workshop engaged in primitivist discourses particularly focused on Andean textile techniques and forms. At first, members of the workshop valued and borrowed the geometrically abstract motifs of Andean textiles. When attitudes toward production and technology changed at the Bauhaus, they began to look at and apply increasingly complex Andean weaving structures and forms to their work. Indeed, the Weaving Workshop was a place where numerous formal and production theories were instigated and demonstrated, partly due to its members' increasingly sophisticated knowledge of Andean fiber art.

Unknown photographer, Weaving Workshop at Bauhaus Dessau, *c.* 1927, gelatin silver print, 9 × 6.4 cm

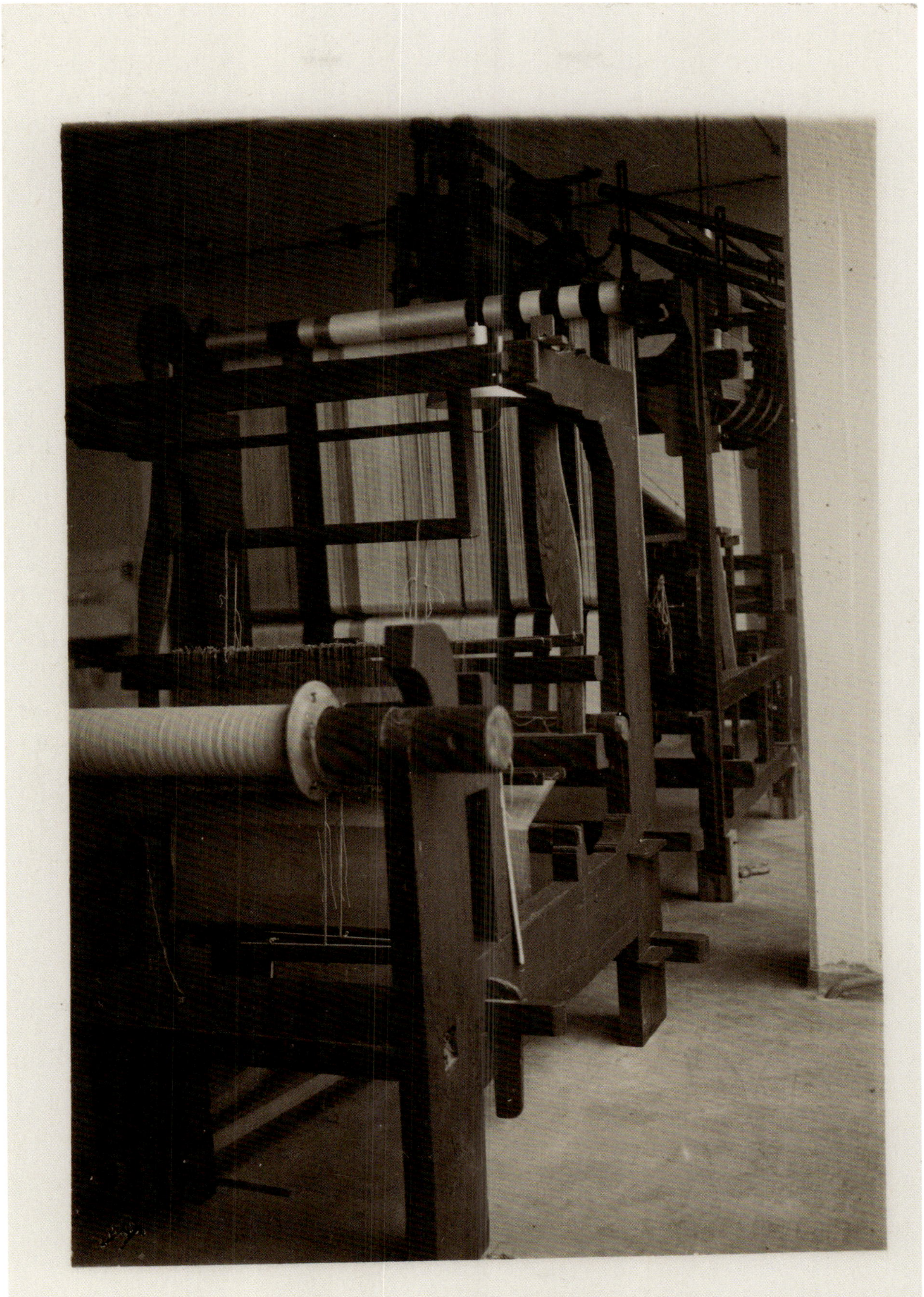

The first major stage of the Bauhaus Weaving Workshop, from 1919 to roughly 1923, is often referred to as the Expressionist phase of the Bauhaus. It corresponds with Johannes Itten's tenure, and was a period when the Bauhaus as a whole was attempting to build up supplies and staff during a time of economic hardship. Itten's background in art education reform reinforced the emphasis on hand-made processes and experimentation. Albers recalled that 'in the early years there was a dabbling in a kind of romantic handicraft.'[4]

[...] When Itten's tenure ended in 1923 as the pull of International Constructivism strengthened, [Walter] Gropius was at the same time under pressure by state authorities to provide tangible results of the school's progress in the form of the exhibition and model home which the Bauhaus produced in 1923. It was clear to many members of the Bauhaus that in order to rebuild for the future, students needed to be trained to work in accord with the machine rather than in opposition to it. Handwork came to be regarded as a first step in the production process, rather than an end in itself. These developments were strengthened by the influence of De Stijl and Russian Constructivism, two international movements that encouraged the unity of art and industry. These changes inspired a more sophisticated interest by members of the Weaving Workshop in weaving materials and their natural properties, natural dyes, and geometric patterning as they began to investigate how this knowledge could be applied to industry. During this period members of the workshop had access to an increasing amount of source material on Andean textiles, and this information clearly informed their work. For this reason, it appears that the weavers looked closely at Andean tunics from the Wari and Tiwanaku societies of the Middle Horizon period (500–900 ce), and other Andean textiles that exhibited complex color and shape patterning.

During the Dessau Bauhaus period (1925–1932) members of the Weaving Workshop, particularly Albers, explored complex color and shape patterning in conjunction with complex weaving structures such as multi-layered weaves. There was an increased emphasis on machine-like precision and experimentation with synthetic fibers. These emphases were partly due to the growing technical proficiency of the members of the workshops, as well as to their analysis of new Andean textile models. This was also the period during which [Paul] Klee taught courses exclusively to members of the Weaving Workshop, including Albers. It was Albers who most successfully synthesized Klee's lessons with what she was learning from studying actual weaving examples, Andean textiles among them. More than any other ancient example, Andean textiles served as useful counterpoints to Klee's design theories and practices.

From the later Dessau Bauhaus period, under the direction of architect Hannes Meyer, and from 1930 until the Bauhaus permanently closed in 1933, under the direction of Ludwig Mies van der Rohe, the Weaving Workshop was a place where art was almost exclusively produced according to social needs, due in large part to the school's anti-pictorial and anti-art stance. Anni Albers received her Bauhaus diploma in February of 1930, but she continued her contact with the Weaving Workshop, serving as acting director of the workshop in 1931. Probably due to Albers, the Andean textile model provided the weavers with actual physical information that they needed in order to translate their ideas regarding production, construction, and utilitarianism into the domain of weaving. Interestingly, this was also a period when the handwoven product was highly valued at the Bauhaus, no longer as an individual Expressionist statement but as an example for production. For this reason, because of the emphasis placed on maintaining the relationship between process and product, the Andean textile paradigm was valued.

This text is comprised of excerpts, selected by the author, from *Anni Albers and Ancient American Textiles: From Bauhaus to Black Mountain*, Burlington: Ashgate, 2002

Anni Albers, *Black-White-Gray*, 1927, cotton and silk double weave, 147.9 × 121.3 cm

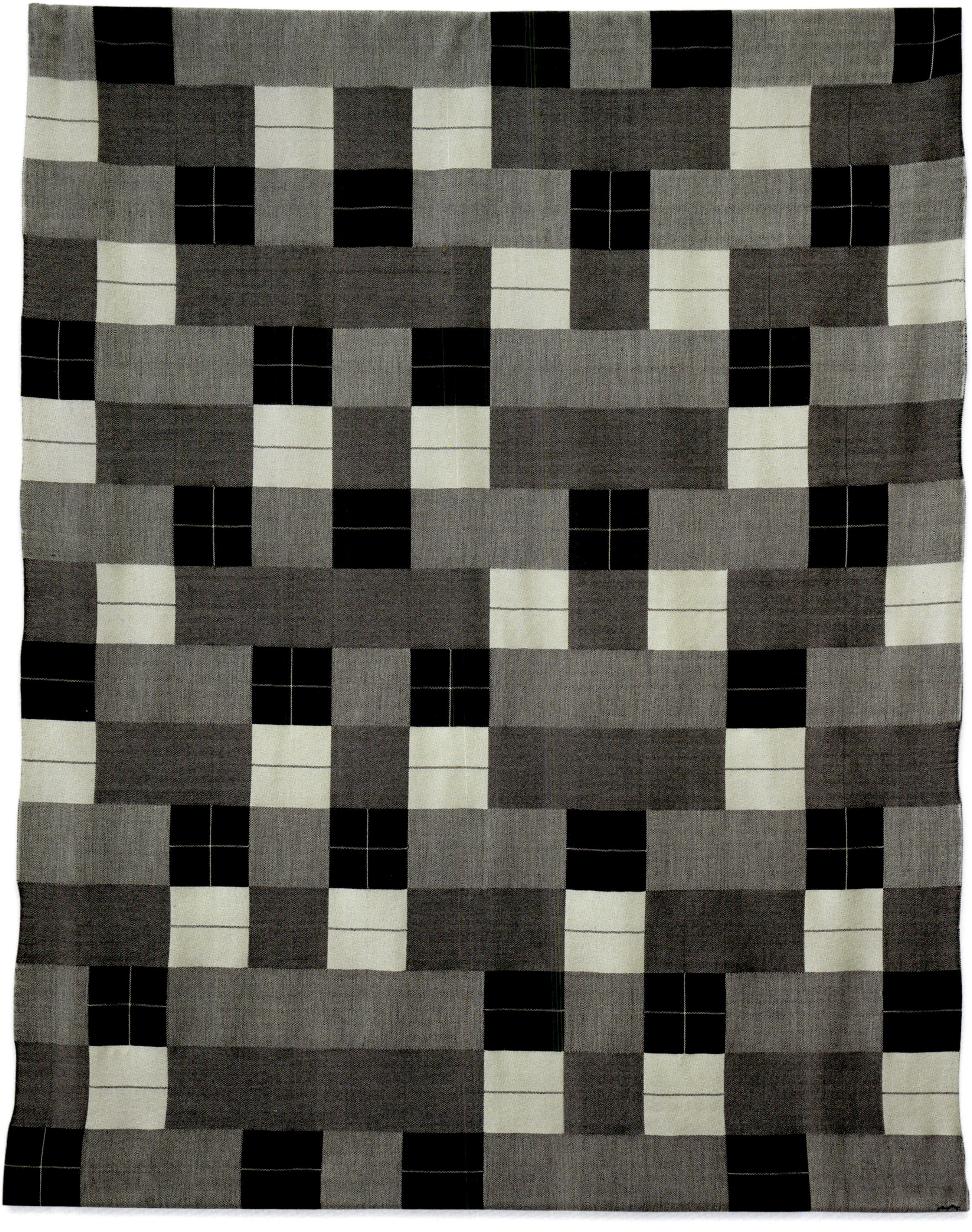

The Appropriation of the Ancient Past in Modern Fibre Art

Elissa Auther

Ancient and indigenous textile cultures of the Americas, Andean weaving included, played a critical role in the development of the work of a generation of fibre artists who came of age in the late 1950s and 1960s and formed the core of what would be called the Fibre Art Movement. Artists such as Sheila Hicks, Alice Kagawa Parrott, Lenore Tawney, Ed Rossbach, Ruth Asawa, Claire Zeisler and Kay Sekimachi, to name just a few of the pioneers of the field, openly professed an admiration for traditions ranging from Navajo weaving, to the use of the backstrap loom in Mexico and Central America, to the ancient weaving techniques of Peru. They studied such textiles in museum collections and anthropological publications, encountered indigenous weavers through travel, acquired material for teaching and study purposes and, in unique ways, replicated, appropriated, translated, incorporated or otherwise drew inspiration from ancient and living textile traditions in the Americas for their own work.

One way to make sense of this abiding interest on the part of a younger generation of US-based artists working in fibre is to view it as a feature transmitted through Anni Albers and other Bauhauslers, and thus representative of the spread of the Bauhaus's influence beyond the school's gates. Sheila Hicks is a good example of a young artist in Albers's immediate orbit in the mid-1950s, who developed a rich relationship with Andean weaving and other textile techniques that continues to inflect her work to this day. Yet the evidence suggests that Hicks's interest in Andean textiles was already in a nascent form by the time she was introduced to Albers while a student at Yale.

Sheila Hicks, *The Principal Wife Goes On*, 1969,
linen, silk, wool and synthetic fibres, dimensions variable

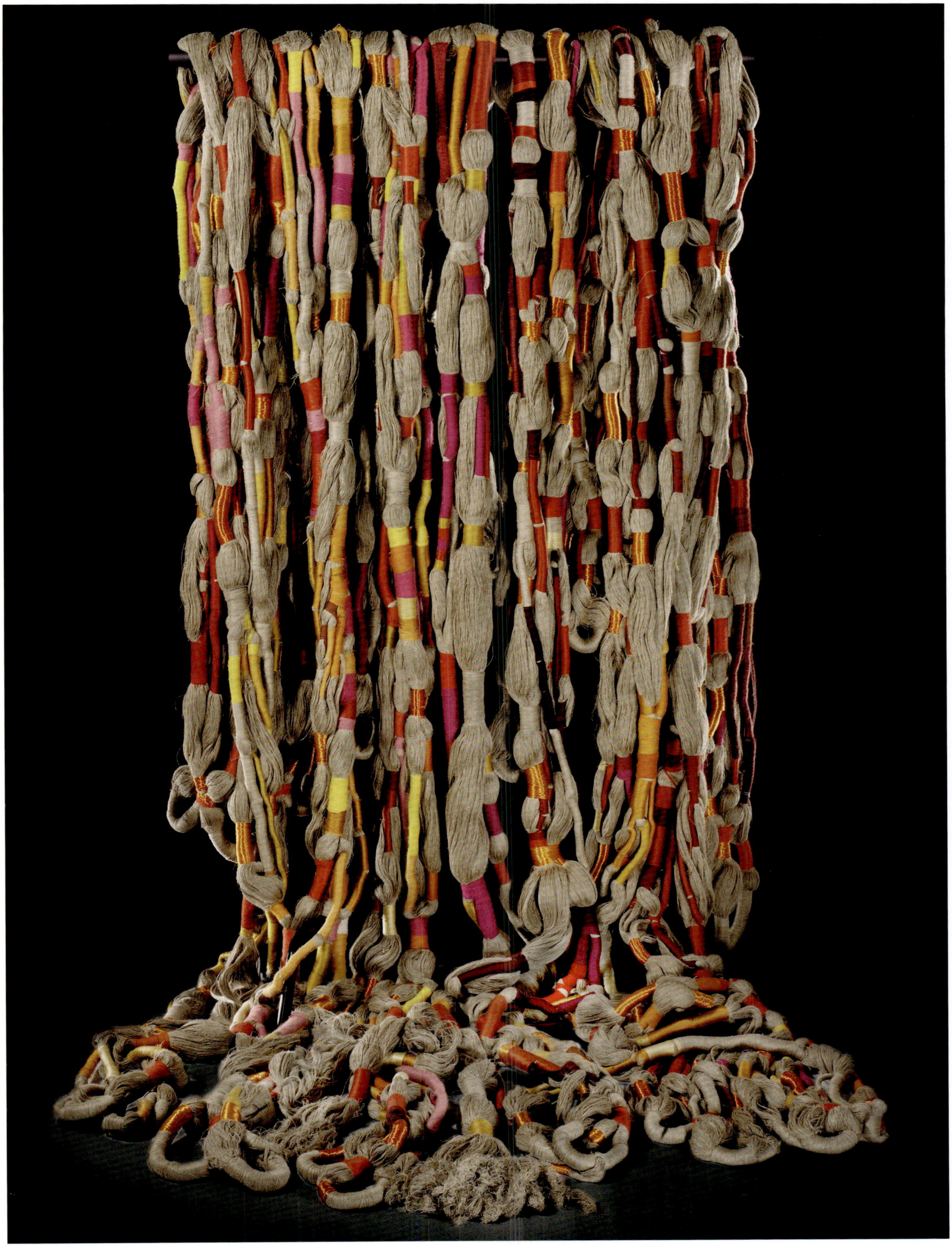

Hicks found a teacher and mentor in the archaeologist Junius Bird, the world-renowned scholar of Andean textiles who was Curator of South American Archaeology at the American Museum of Natural History. Although a painting major at Yale, Hicks would write her undergraduate thesis on Andean textiles with Bird as an advisor. Hicks was first introduced to Andean weaving as an undergraduate at Yale University in a course on Latin American art taught by the historian of pre-Columbian art George Kubler. As she recalls:

> When I was at Yale studying painting with Josef Albers and pre-Columbian civilizations with George Kubler, the content, and particularly the structures of pre-Columbian textiles really fascinated me.... It was even more intriguing than the Bauhaus program![1]

In the same passage, Hicks cites the French ethnologist Raoul d'Harcourt's seminal study published in 1934, *Les textiles anciens du Pérou et leur techniques* (The Ancient Textiles of Peru and Their Techniques), as an important influence: 'This book by d'Harcourt encouraged me to try my hand very freely at intertwining my threads, giving me permission, as it were, to follow in the footsteps of those artisans to explore my own games and the creation of a universal language.'[2] Hicks took Kubler's course in 1954, and it was around this time that Josef Albers introduced her to Anni, who aided her in her early experiments on the loom.

Hicks continued her exploration of Andean weaving on research trips between 1957 and 1959, which allowed her to travel throughout South America and expand her knowledge of weaving traditions and techniques. After moving to Mexico in 1959 upon the completion of her MFA, she continued to develop her practice as a weaver. The influence of Andean textile culture appears in her work from this period and beyond in numerous ways. For instance, her four selvage works made with a single thread, such as *Blue Letter* or *Ancient Writing*, reference the ingenuity of Andean technique alongside her interest in Mayan glyphs as a writing system.[3] Hicks's work also makes indirect reference to the Peruvian burial or mummy bundle, the funerary practice in which the deceased is placed in a basket and wrapped in multiple layers of textiles tied with sashes. The bundle form as well as the technique of wrapping have appeared in her work throughout her career. More generally, the cords, tassels and stacked additive components that make up such works as *The Evolving Tapestry* or *The Principal Wife* are also connected to her appreciation for fringe and other non-woven finishing techniques typical of Andean textiles, as well as the ruins of Meso-American and pre-Columbian architecture.[4] Hicks's interest in Andean weaving also extended to her design work. One of the most relevant examples for the purposes of this essay is the woven yardage she produced for a suit she made (and wore) based on the checkerboard or square pattern typical of Incan tunics and illustrated in d'Harcourt's study.

Sheila Hicks, *White Letter*, 1962, hand-spun wool, 118.1 × 96.5 cm

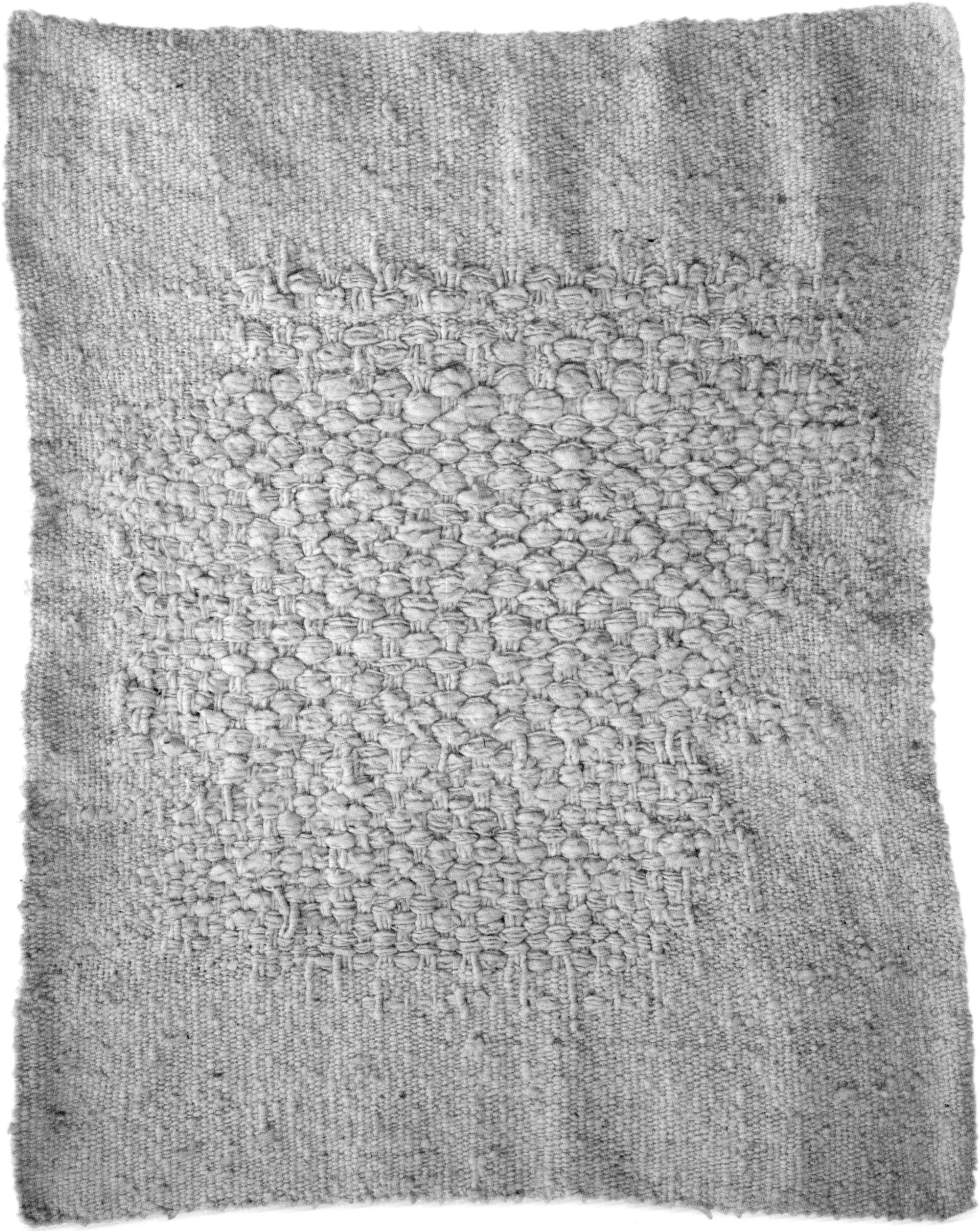

Lenore Tawney, *Orinoco*, 1967, linen, 328 × 57 × 10 cm

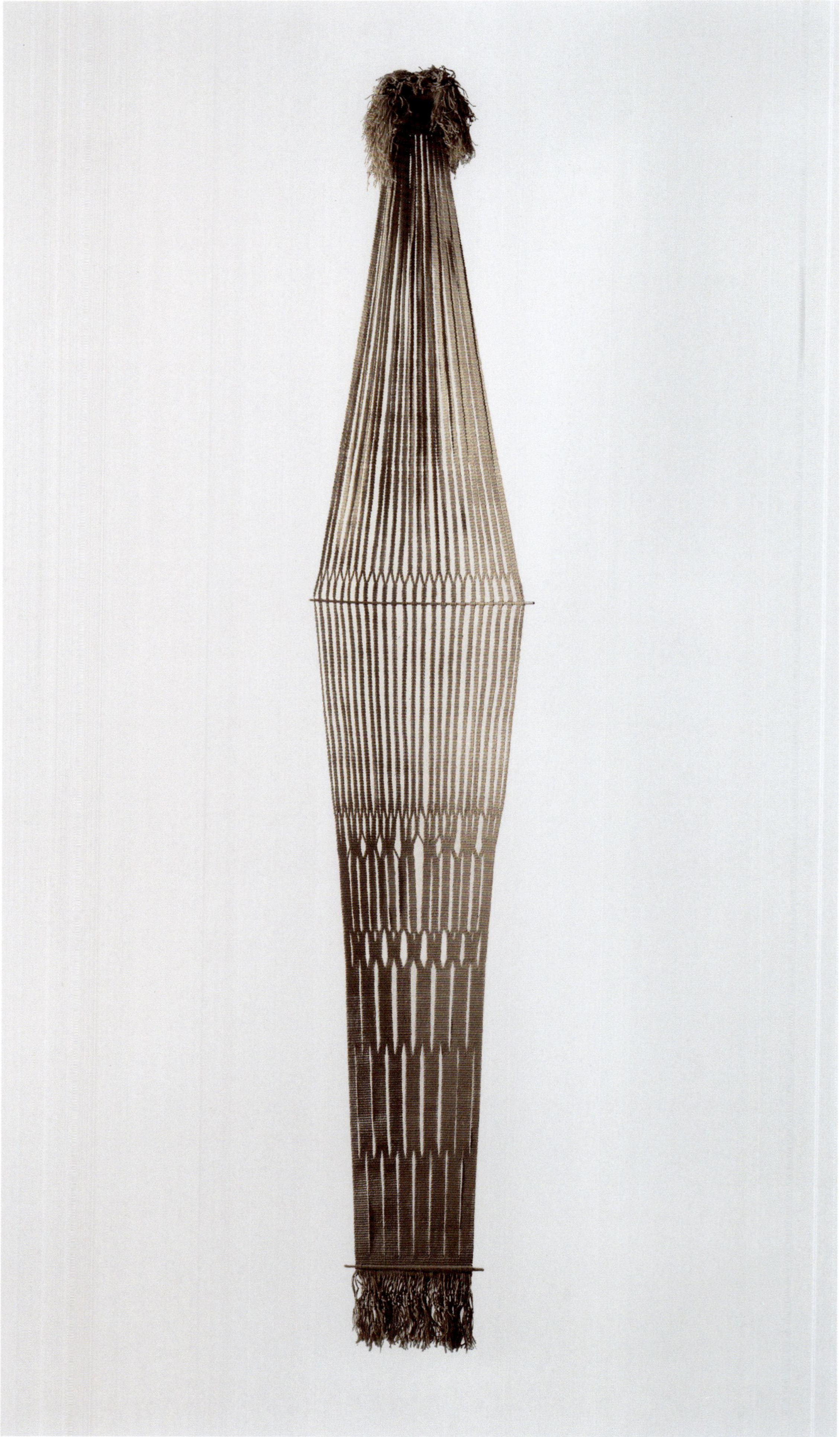

Lenore Tawney, who studied under two Bauhaus émigrés – Moholy-Nagy at the Institute of Design in Chicago in 1946 and, subsequently, the weaver Marli Ehrman – turned to Andean weaving techniques in the creation of her breakthrough, sculpted, free-hanging Woven Forms, such as *Orinoco* (1967). Art historian Rebecca Klassen has addressed the way that the artist's references to a nationality or culture appear frequently in the titles of her work and/or were often 'based on her associations with a chosen technique', as in the double weave used in the panel titled *Peruvian* from 1962.[5] 'Peruvian'-ness was also extended to include the knots and fringes that begin and terminate the Woven Forms and many other works. This connection was noted by curator Paul J. Smith in his catalogue essay for the exhibition 'Woven Forms' at the Museum of Contemporary Craft, New York, in 1963;[6] it also appears in Jack Lenor Larsen's remarks about Tawney's work in *Beyond Craft: The Art Fabric*, where he replaces 'Peruvian' with the term 'pre-Columbian'. 'From her study of pre-Columbian art,' he wrote, 'Tawney felt that finish might be the most detailed, most labored part. One typical result was the knotted top knots.'[7]

Tawney's melding of cultural references extended to the incorporation of found material into her work that gave her weaving a generalized 'non-western' or 'ethnographic' look. For instance, on a trip to Peru in 1965 she acquired beads that were used in *Shield IV* (1966), although she referred to them as 'pre-Columbian'. Other works from the same series – all with the title *Shield*, which conjures ancient and/or tribal associations – incorporated shells, feathers, whelk egg cases and porcupine needles. Tawney's trip to Peru was one of many that included encounters with indigenous peoples, art forms and world views different from her own that fuelled her process. In another essay by Larsen regarding Tawney and artistic inspiration, he remarked that, 'Travel, to her, means perspective, and a reorientation of values necessary as an antidote to some of the culturally deadening aspects of American life.'[8] This is reflected in Tawney's own writing, in which she expresses a longing for an alternative way of being in the world in concert with broader countercultural desires for a reconnection to nature and associated with indigenous cultures wherein creative practice is seamlessly integrated into life. The artist's integration of beads or natural materials into her weaving, among other aspects of her practice, allowed her to annex Andean weaving and Native American aesthetics to her work, linking it cross-culturally and trans-historically with indigenous textile traditions. Hicks also understood textiles as a universal language, but in the sense that fibre allowed her to work across media, from painting to sculpture to architecture.

Andean weaving, as well as other textile traditions of the Americas, offered a range of resources to artists of the Fibre Art Movement. To name the most obvious, the Andean textile provided a model of ingenuity that was touted as unsurpassed in the history of textiles, facilitated weavers in a quest to expand their knowledge of technique, and – by virtue of being distanced in time and place – valorized the medium of fibre, offering the modern artist a connection to an ancient past in which textiles were presumed to hold a place of cultural centrality. These elements, which reflect and intertwine aesthetic regard and admiration for textile traditions of the Americas and more problematic forms of psychic identification with the ancient and/or indigenous weaver, highlight the appropriation of the ancient past as instrumental to modernism's allegiance to the present.

Below and opposite: Lenore Tawney, *Peruvian*, *c.* 1962–63, linen (double weave), 218 × 46 cm

►► Pages 140–41: Lenore Tawney, *Shield II*, 1963, natural linen, Chinese golden pheasant feathers, porcupine quills, 45.7 × 61 × 1.3 cm

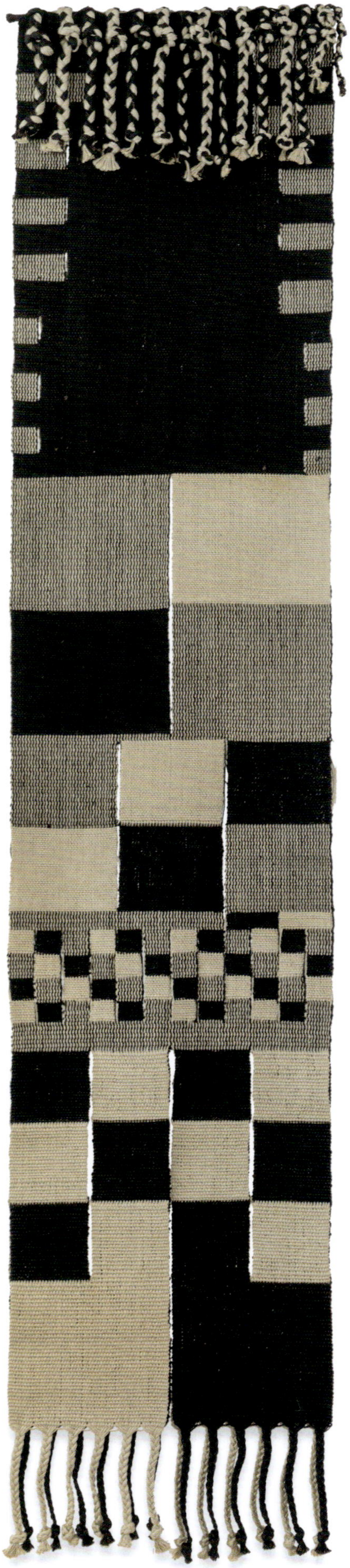

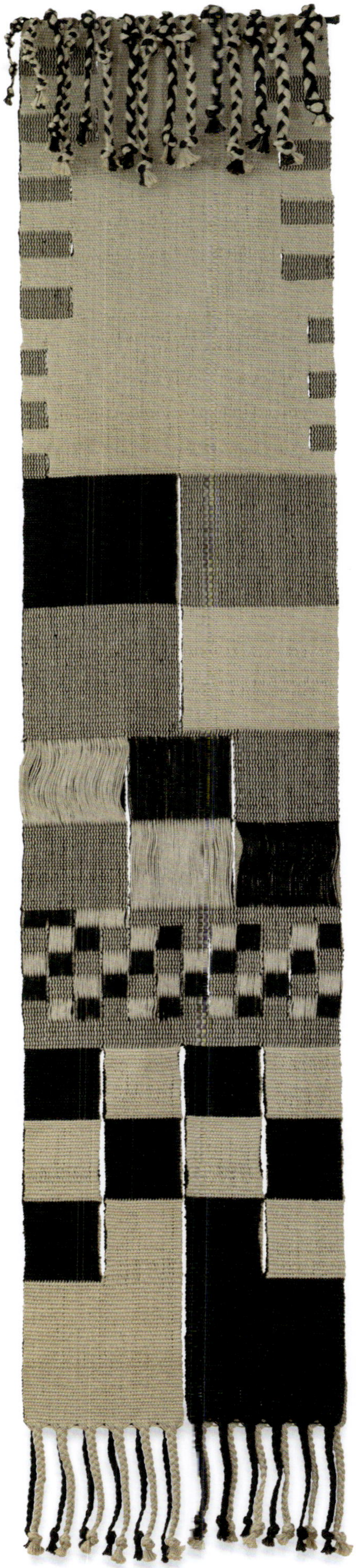

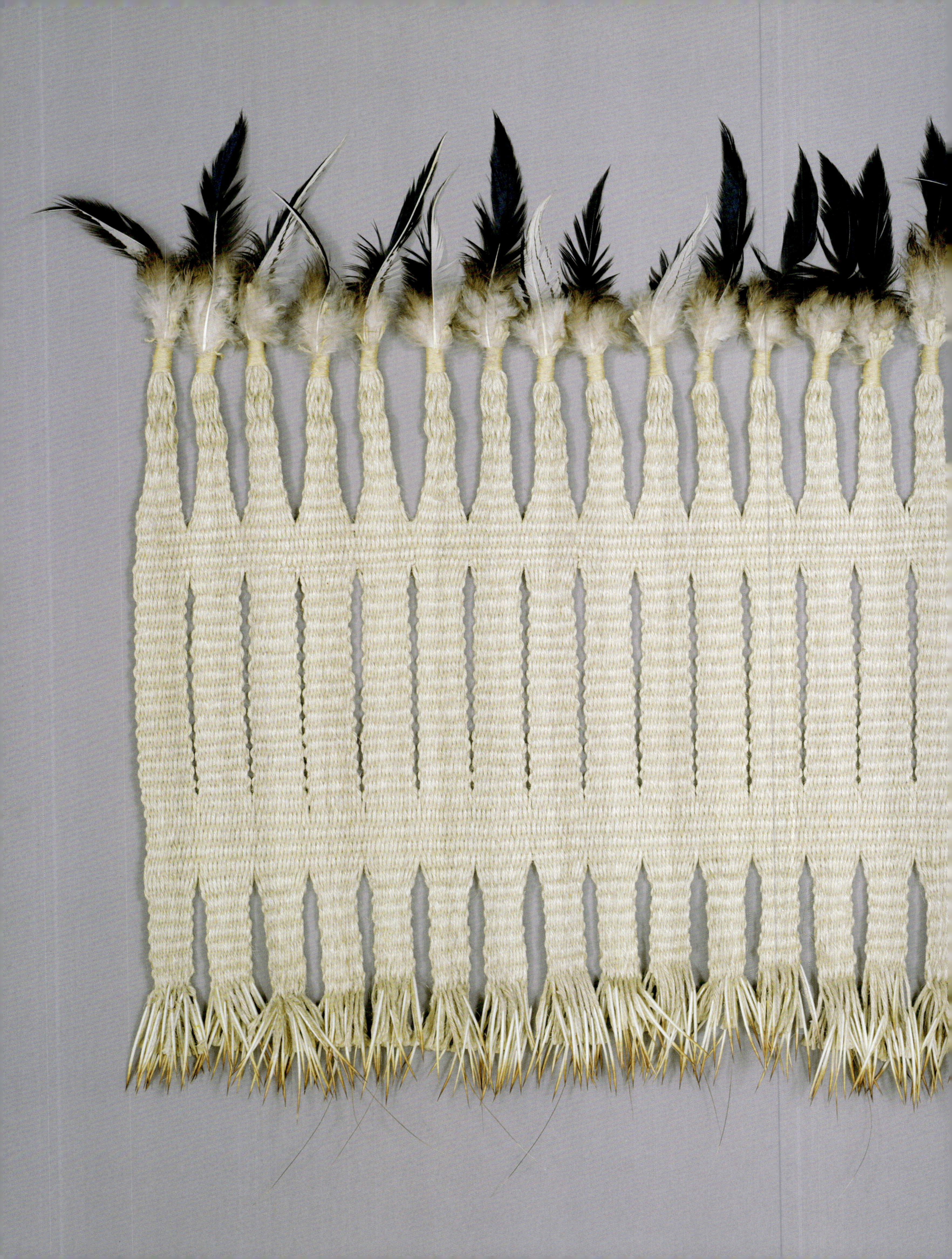

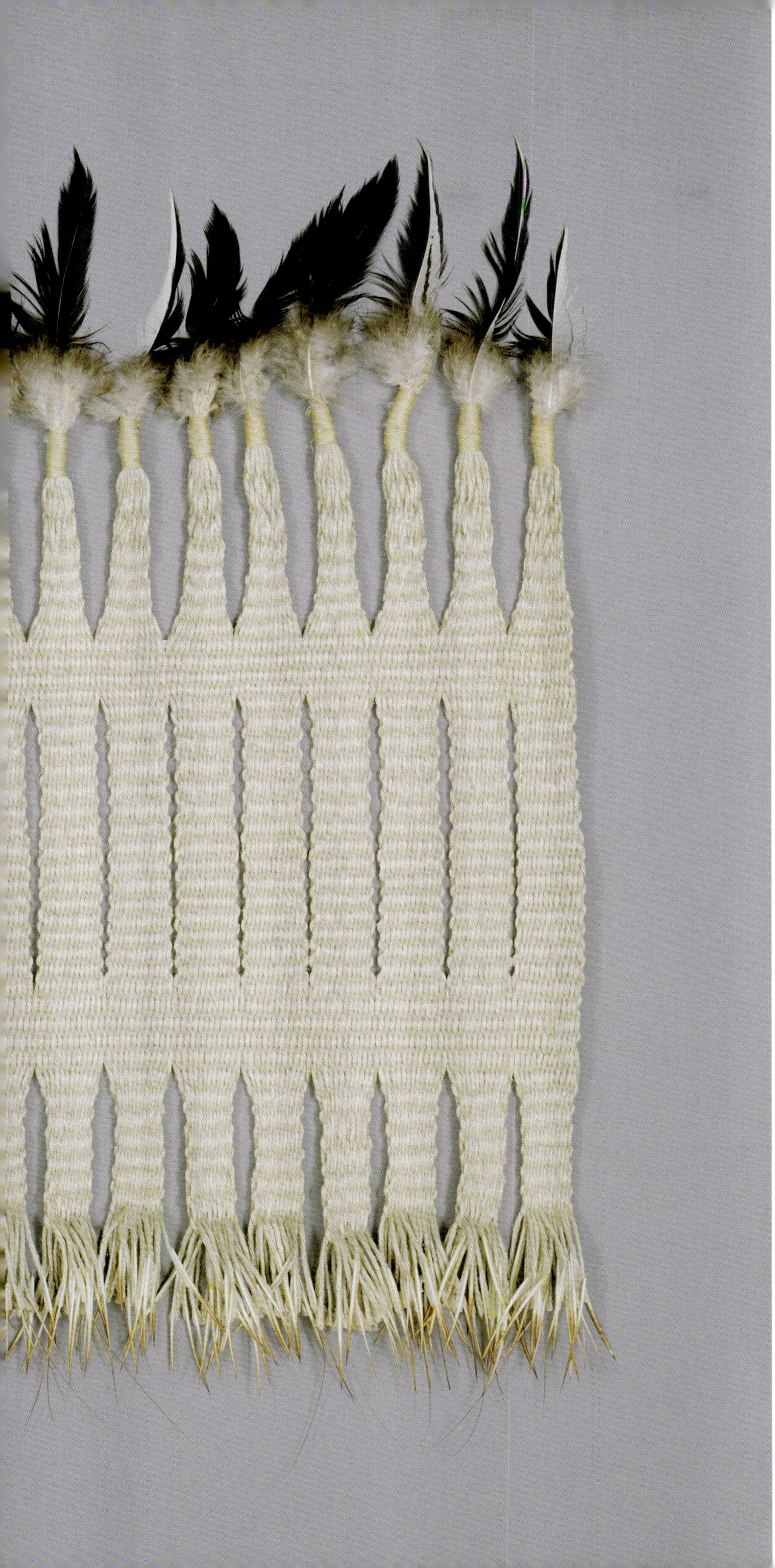

Watch and Learn: Local Instructions from My Community

Elvira Espejo

It is now the time to thank my people, the grandmothers and grandfathers who have maintained the documentary memory of the planning of colour as identity and millenary culture, passing the information from generation to generation. Thanks to such documentary memory we can now share this experience.

The current text explores the planning of colour found in the weaving pirn[1] of the female weavers as a visual document of all the palettes and possible colour combinations that predominate in textile art, an identity and culture that might involve thousands of styles depending on the period, region and community.

In rural communities, far from the places where paper is widely available, the quality and complexity of the distribution of structures, techniques and textile designs generate a range of colour combinations in specific parts of a garment that determine its use and style. The combination that makes a piece of garment unique is what we work on with the female weavers from the community. And here we encounter some communication problems, among them with the way western information is received, and whether we use the same tools for explanation – such as drawings on paper or lines on a blackboard – in order to create a standard of colour according to the demands imposed by the commercialization of the items. From here emerges the need to recuperate a documentary memory of the weavers' communication of their specific ability, with the colour range that is planned in the weaving pirn – the *musa waraña*, as it is said in Aymara. This transmission of information within the communities is ignored because of the educational approach of the teachers themselves, who only speak about what they learned at university and don't take into account local knowledge or documents that could contribute to a reflection – from the environment, from the past towards the present. They also neglect to establish international, national or local comparisons, differences that could help us understand unique styles found in a specific community, family or even a person.

A selection of *musa warañas* against a background of balls of yarn. In Andean weaving, *musa warañas* are models of the colour combinations to be used in a particular garment.

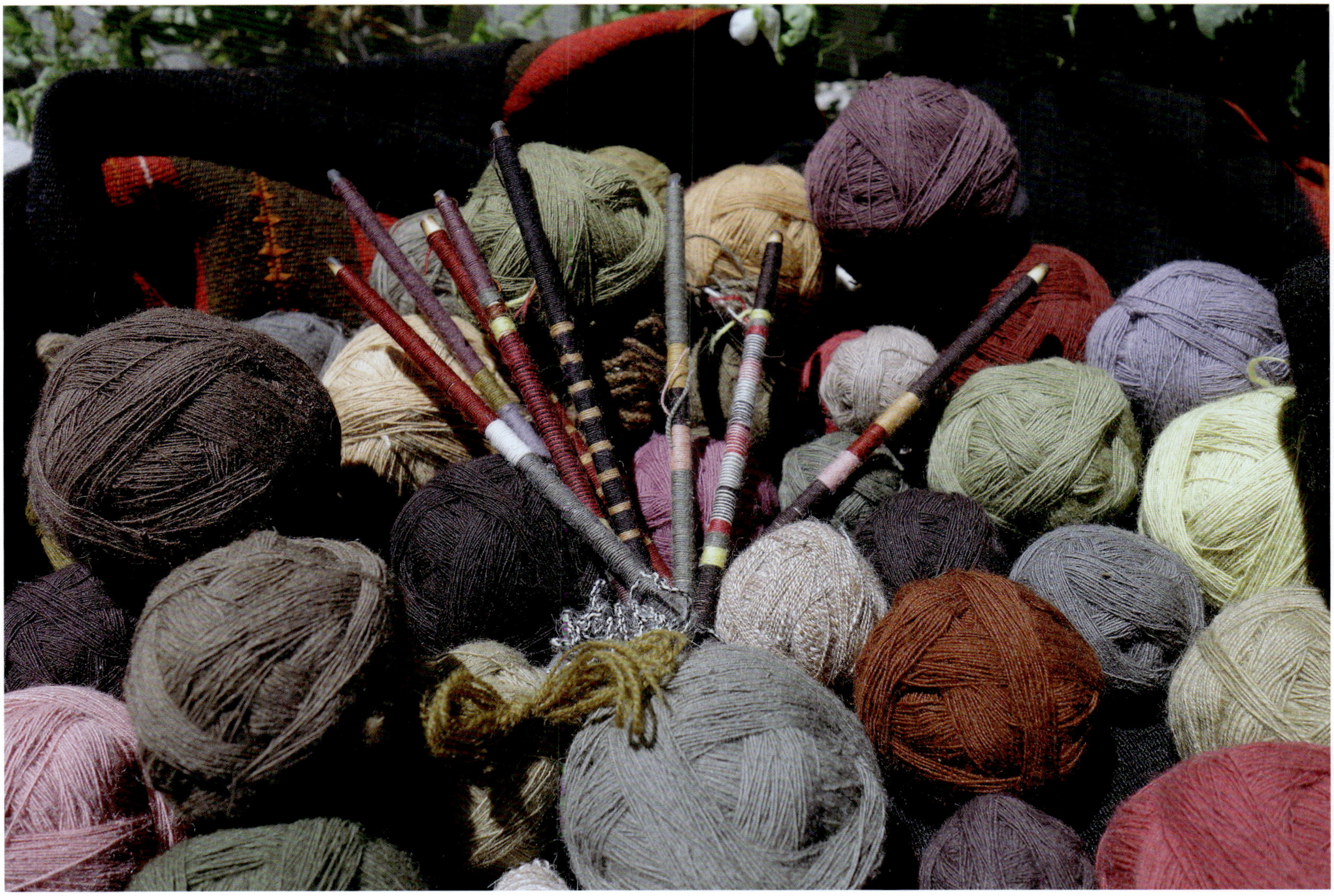

Musaña is an Aymara verb that means 'to combine'. *Waraña* means 'to throw', 'to flow from one side to the other'. Bringing together both words, the *musa waraña* fulfils the function of planning colour in order to transfer this information from one generation to another according to the taste of a family or person. These instruments, which have been ignored in recent decades, are where the female weavers communicated their colour planning; they are instruments that transmit information. In order to learn about these objects, I had to walk together with the weavers for months to different communities. One of those days we met an elderly weaver, Doña Lucía Mamani, who offered us information about the *musa waraña*. At the beginning of the conversation she didn't trust us because the conversation was too directed and too precisely about colour. During the conversation I had to tell her about the colour ranges that the international market demanded according to the season, accessory and fashion conjunctures. Understanding, she undid her bundle of yarn where she kept two *musa warañas* containing the colour range of her family, which she said she had inherited from her mother, who gave them to her when she turned fifteen, and therefore reached maturity. To aid in her learning all the processes that made up the necessary textile expertise, they gave her the following instruments: one was a blanket (*awayu*), a garment for women, and the other was a poncho, a garment for men. With these two instruments for colour composition, she could increase the diversity according to the style of the community, but also, as a future daughter-in-law within another community, she could receive other colour ranges according to the family that she would then be part of, and she would therefore have other possibilities for using the two-colour ranges and the chance to develop her own versions using the two different sources.

As colour planning models, the *musa warañas* are of utmost importance before the weaving of the garment, as there are many options that can be explored within a stick braided with coloured threads, according to the range that would please whoever wanted to work on her own garment, such as the *awayu* blanket. There is also an issue of structures, be they simple or complex: the simple ones are often braided with a few colours in a uniform manner, while the complex ones can be braided with additional colours and include instructions with knots similar to the *quipus*,[2] where the knots are divided in tens, twenties, thirties and so on, depending on the garment that will be developed and the format that is required. What is interesting about this information is that it leads us to discover that there are many ways of understanding the colour range, and that we mustn't remain within the dominant language and its understanding of art through the perception of an environment of light and shade. Instead of imposing that perspective, we must accompany the developments of science and technology which are specific to the communities themselves.

Examples of simple *musa warañas* (top) and more complex models (bottom).

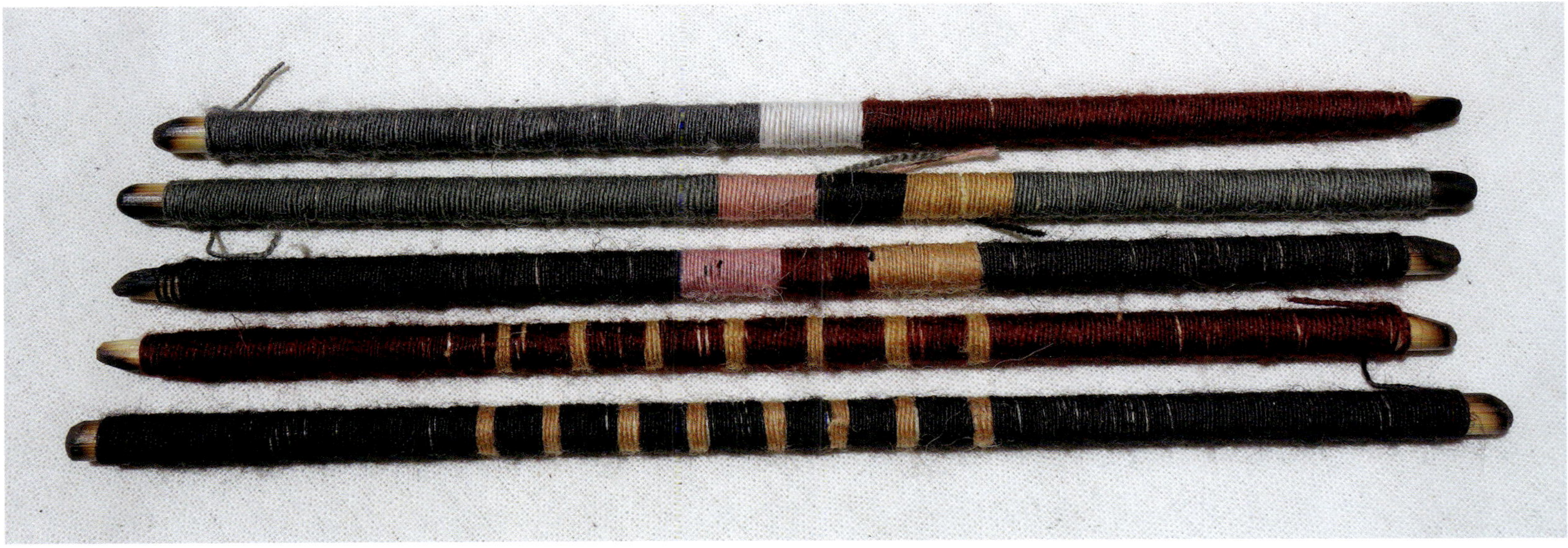

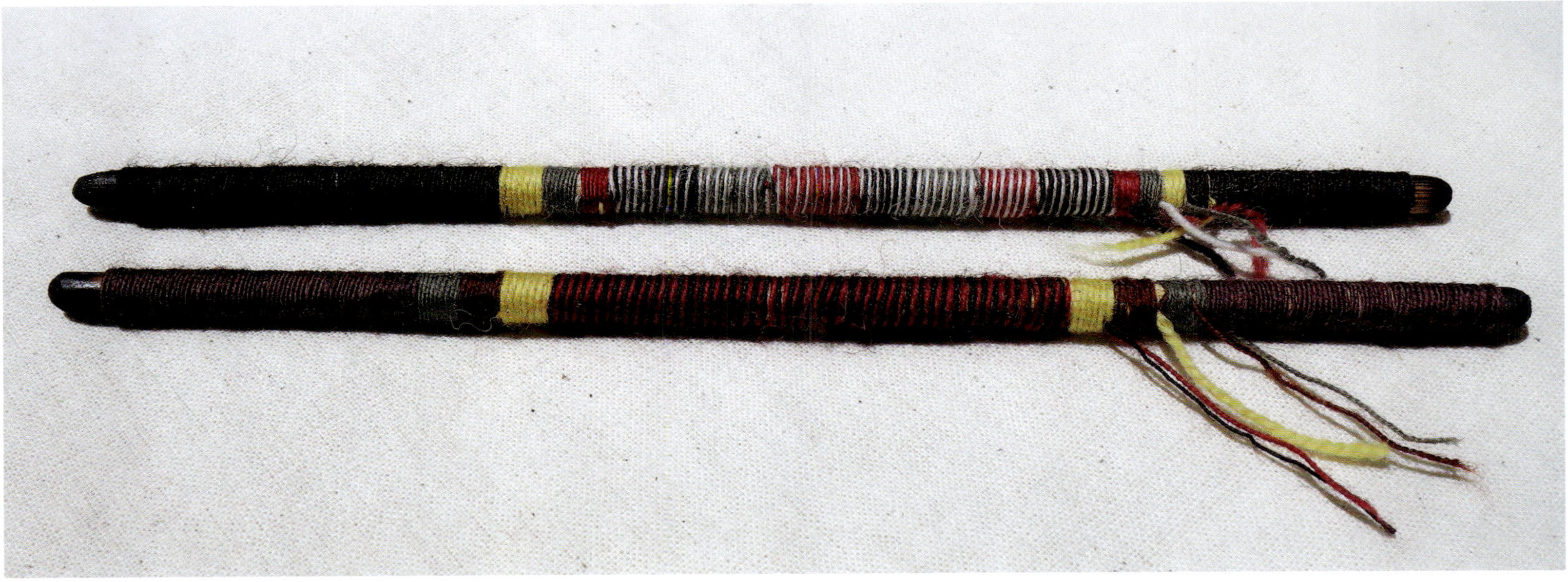

The Bauhaus and Indigenous Cultural Production

Ailton Krenak and Bené Fonteles

For decades, the craftwork and art of the indigenous peoples of Brazil has been the focus of exhibitions in cultural institutions. But these presentations have placed a stronger emphasis on crafts and considerations about use in daily life, which has meant that the great potential of the work's mythopoesis, its magical and spiritual aspects, its amalgamated relation to nature and the non-separation between life and art, have rarely been presented.

All those exhibitions were an immense inspiration for Brazilian culture and art, after the work of the ethnic groups from the Xingu was exhibited with care and respect in the Bienal de São Paulo in the 1970s,[1] and the work of other indigenous peoples was part of exhibitions in important institutions such as the Museu de Arte Moderna de São Paulo (MAM-SP) and the Museu de Arte de São Paulo (MASP) in the 1980s,[2] and also subsequently – and the more recent exhibitions are as relevant as those early ones.

The artists that are part of the art system were not only charmed by work of such high aesthetic and poetic rigour. Some, for decades, recreated or translated this rich universe in their works, as the modernist artists did when the Modern Art Week was launched in São Paulo in 1922. Their anthropophagic and autogenous proposal was to 'eat' international art, chewed together with the native indigenous and Afro-Brazilian art and the popular, *mestizo* and *caboclo*[3] arts. The modernism of that decade was anchored in Mário de Andrade's writings, especially his book *Macunaíma* (1928); in Tarsila do Amaral's paintings; and in Oswald de Andrade's poetry, theatre and novels, made explicit in his two manifestos, the 'Anthropophagic' and the 'Pau-Brasil': 'Tupi or not Tupi / That is the question', or, paraphrasing him, 'Before the Portuguese discovered Brazil / The indigenous had already discovered happiness'.[4]

Such 'happiness of the warrior', of creating on the grounds of thousands of years of heritage that began with rock and cave art, founded with its extraordinary imaginary a whole set of patterns based on movement or in the typologies of the skin and fur of animals present in the indigenous mythopoesis; indigenous graphic designs that move to the skin of the indigenous peoples, to their basketry, and to their ceramics. A sort of Constructivism with a sophisticated geometry of the highest aesthetic value is thus born – a style that would have not only impressed the Bauhaus artists, but also, perhaps, influenced them to create a new aesthetics. Perhaps a less rationalist and functionalist one, closer to the organic character of the natural systems and the bodily nature of what is human.

It could perhaps have been an even more humanist Bauhaus than the one shaped by the great artists who recreated the world and gave it the potential for a spiritual art, such as Piet Mondrian, Wassily Kandinsky and Paul Klee. The Bauhaus professors were persecuted (as have been our indigenous peoples for more than five hundred years) by National Socialism, forced to migrate when the school was shut down in Berlin.

In order to know more about what could be called indigenous design, we can look at anthropologist Lux Vidal's book *Grafismo indígena* (Indigenous Graphic Design, 1992),[5] which shows the enormous aesthetic contributions that the art of the indigenous people made to Brazil and to art history, be it in the mastery of body painting or in the manufacture of any of the objects of use that always go beyond mere usability. Bordering the sacred.

What remains, as the indigenous peoples' legacy for Brazilian and universal culture, is a reflection on how the contemporary production of indigenous artists may preserve its original essence and transform its mythopoesis, full of potential and imagination, as a strong reference that inspires art in the world. This is art that is already in dialogue, sometimes even in confrontation when it comes to its insertion in the market, in the media or in ideological circles.

Fragile is the world that marginalizes a production anchored in the need for spiritual and magical expression, which tries to understand our presence in the world and is made by societies that are conscious of the 'continuum' among collective subjects, a continuum that forms a constellation of people. Even in indigenous society, beyond its use function in the activities in indigenous villages, the production of objects is the result of a taste for transcendence. The same should be the case in the history of white artists, who, in addition to the pressure of the market and the media, also need to deal with dangerous ego affirmations. In indigenous artistic production, individual work melts within the collective purpose to produce together the beauty of function for the function of this beauty, and for the enjoyment of the community as a whole.

Therefore, one of our burning questions is how to escape the anonymity inherited from ethnocentric prejudices in relation to indigenous art, which placed it in the scientific void of museology or of the exotic, and labelled it as the production of simple artefacts that express collectivity. These concepts kept indigenous art outside of art history for centuries. It must escape this so that it may be admired and loved in its true expressive potential of nature and culture, transcendence and spirituality, which in the indigenous universe are inseparable.

Be they white or indigenous, artists have a vital need to place themselves at the service of their people in the forest or their city, as an imaginary collective vector that intends to turn visible what is invisible, as Klee once said when attempting to define art.

The question is how the image production of the indigenous peoples has reached cultural institutions and the art market without losing its aura, and how it will continue to do so. This has to do not only with its spontaneous authenticity, but also with the magical aspect that reveals the spiritual world by embodying the invisible inhabited by the beings that guide and maintain the universe so that the sky doesn't collapse over our heads.

Everything that was constructed through trance and dream in so many ethnic groups during thousands of years of indigenous civilization – and that is for us a legacy of utmost importance, not only for Brazil's art and culture but also for the world – is present in the words of the Yanomami shaman and leader Davi Kopenawa, published in his essential book *The Falling Sky*, which was written in collaboration with anthropologist Bruce Albert.[6] The title refers to the sky that must exist to sustain the Yanomami home, with its four pillars from a tree, which are a metaphor not only for an *oca*[7] in the middle of the forest, but also for the symbolic pillars that preserve the creative, primordial and ancestral dream that sustains the world and the universe.

These are questions that go beyond the mythopoesis that anthropologists have been trying to understand since the beginning of the twentieth century. They cannot succeed, because it is not just the result of an expressive need to live and to *have* a world, but rather the exemplary and singular warp of a transcendent art that weaves and is the world.

A world, indeed, that has shown intolerance towards the persistent presence of these native peoples – the 'indians' – within the West's narrative. Even when instigated by what indigenous art reveals about the war of worlds caused by a society dominated by consumption and merchandise, it tends to see that production as one more thing to be appropriated by capital. A Mother Earth for the native peoples, seen by capital as 'resources' to be appropriated – this has created incommensurable distances. Dialogue is therefore limited to those who inhabit the transcendent world of creation, far from what we call the system of art that feeds the spaces of the galleries and museums throughout the world, privileging the big centres that extract the wealth from the periphery in a planet devastated by ambition. Few are the artists or *artivists* who, in different regions of the world, especially the American and African continents, manage to establish a dialogue with what we call contemporary artistic production.

The emphasis on the western notion of art, in which the exercise of creation is confined within a specific activity, separated from other spheres of life, contrasts with the cultural practices of the indigenous peoples. The mechanisms of production and dissemination of the art system – with its insistence on the predominance of the object – tend to instrumentalize artistic production, neutralizing its political potential and its power to contaminate. Such a perspective is not concerned by issues of agency and collectivity, by languages and urgencies, or by rhythms and conditions of production that are different from those it is used to, marked by the separation between social life – as was outlined in the text describing the seminar 'Indigenous Cultural Production and the Art System: Approximations and Tensions',[8] in which indigenous artivists from different regions and ethnic groups in Brazil presented their ideas about the growing interest from galleries and museums in our country in the formation of 'indigenous art collections'.

Whatever might be the understanding of 'indigenous art' in this process, what we see is a mercantilization of any expression of such production made in our villages. This regards both what is made for ritual practices – such 'ritual objects' as masks, sceptres, feather work or wooden, ceramic artefacts that carry representations proper to each cultural context – and the creation motivated by other endeavours of indigenous individuals and collectives, who already have some insight into the exchanges and today are included in exhibitions and shows in the large urban centres.

The Brazilian south-east, with São Paulo and Rio de Janeiro at the forefront, has become the privileged corridor of the exhibitions that gain stronger attention from the market. This acritical approximation could promote the idea that indigenous cultural production is being accepted into another world – a world that clearly invests against the fundaments of the cosmological order and ontologies that sustain the originary worlds of the indigenous collectives, and which impregnate their lives, forests and rivers, the source of their existences, the expression of their creations and the cause of estrangement for the West.

This estrangement has its origins in the fact that such expression is not the result of egocentric demands, organized around the production of objects of value within an aesthetic and artistic canon that contemporary art has constructed. Rather, it is born from a magical world that unveils the unconscious and reveals the 'third bank' of a river that can't be reached with an actual canoe. In order to cross it, what we need is the technology of a mind with imagination, but also an invisible canoe that may take us to that bank without expecting goals or outcomes. Everything requires more than a mystical and magical trance, a free transit between visible and invisible worlds that are not separated. As the Toltec shaman Miguel Ruiz says, 'you are both the dream and the dreamer'.[9]

In order to be that primordial dream and to compose it, indigenous peoples need to be left in peace in the forest, unaffected by the barbarism of 'civilization', continuing to create an art that can navigate the different banks with interdisciplinary independence, with solidarity and interaction, involved with everything rather than developed, without losing its creative body and its cultural and spiritual essence, which persists from cave and rock painting to the plural and instigating contemporary art forms.

Paulo Tavares

Des-Habitat

DES-HABITAT

revista das artes no Brasil

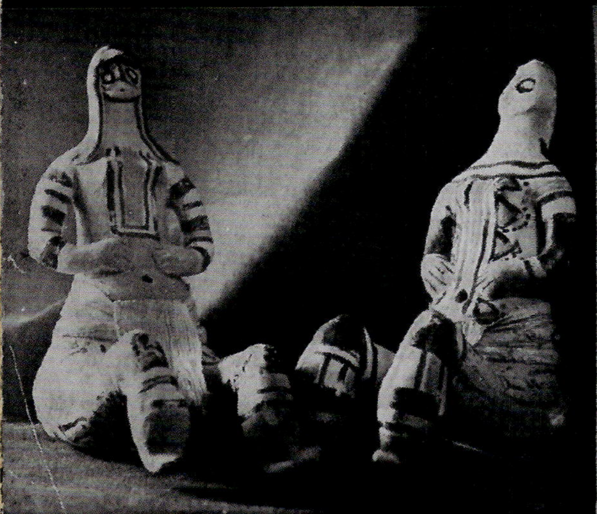

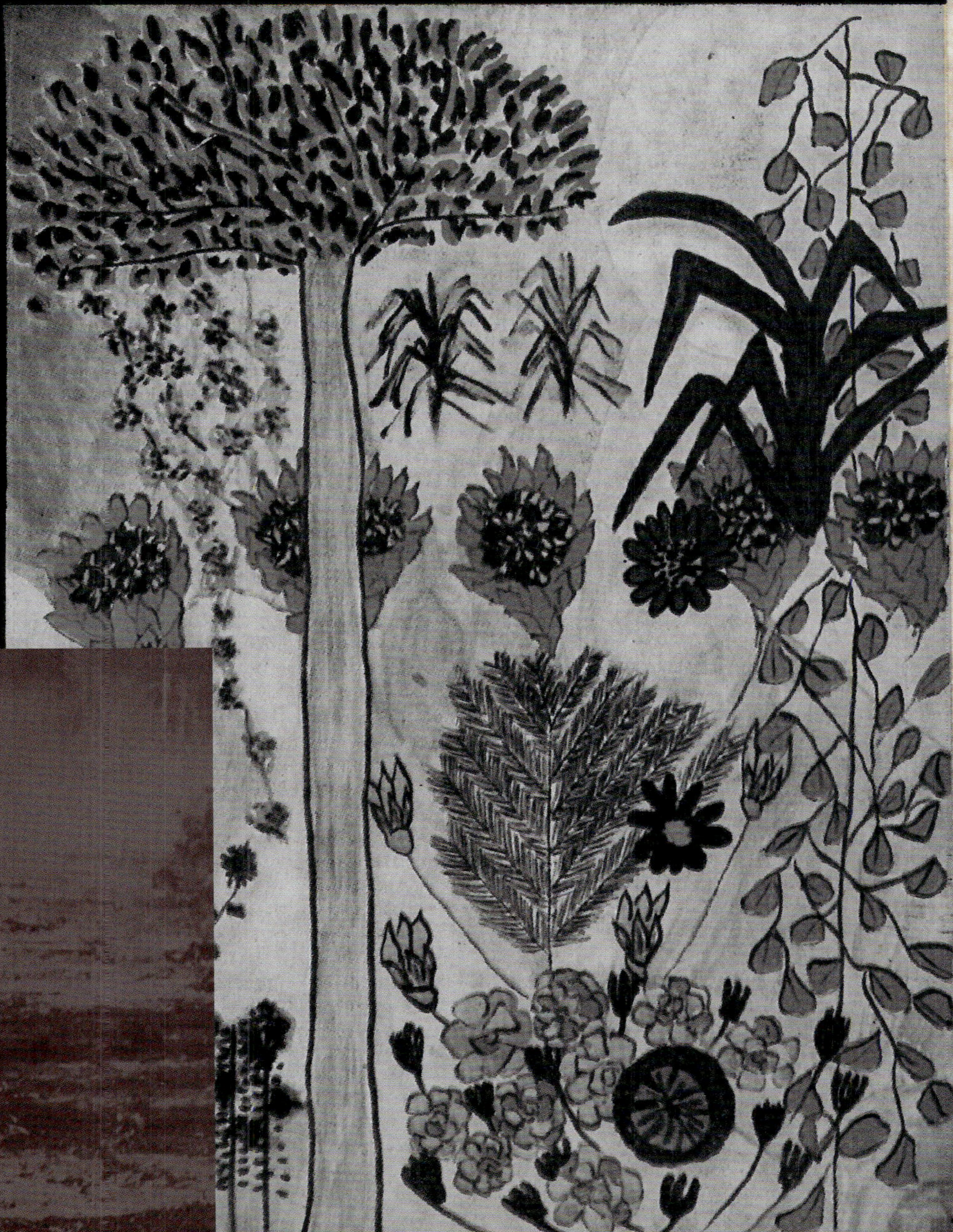

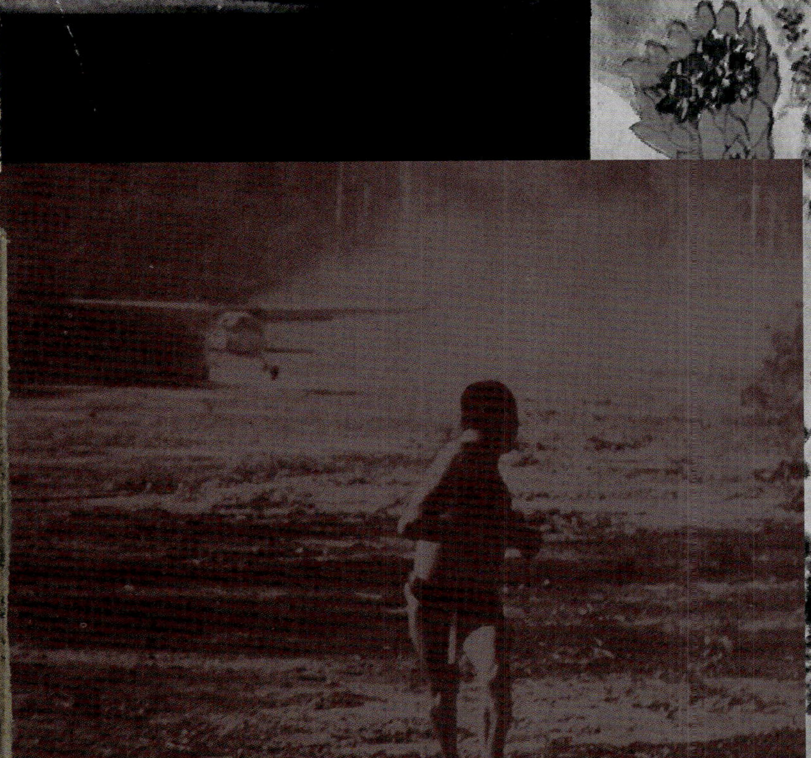

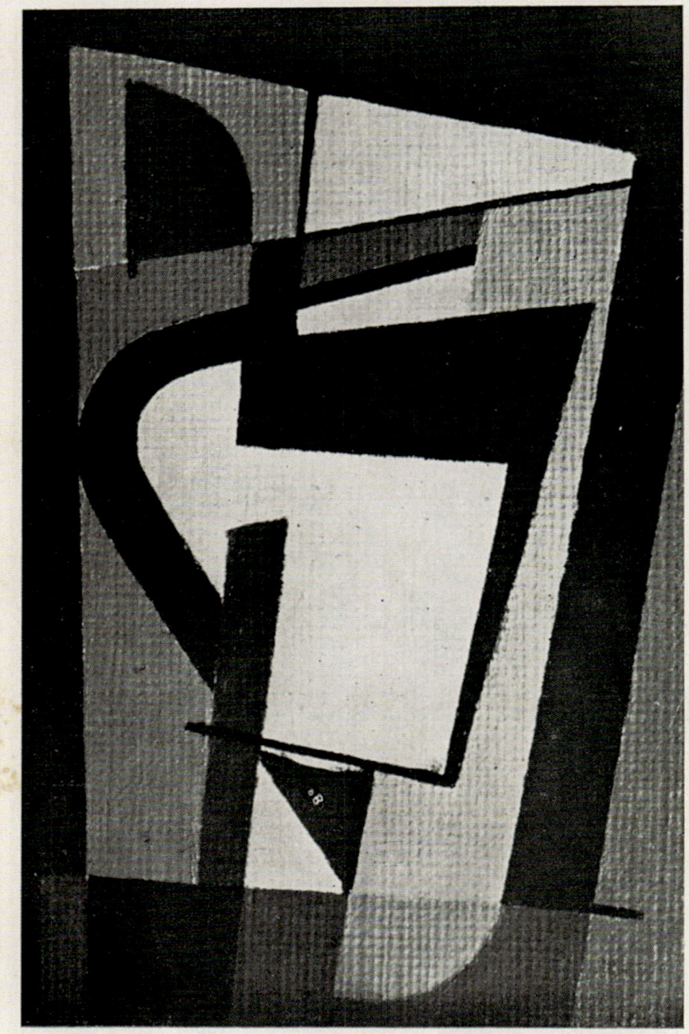

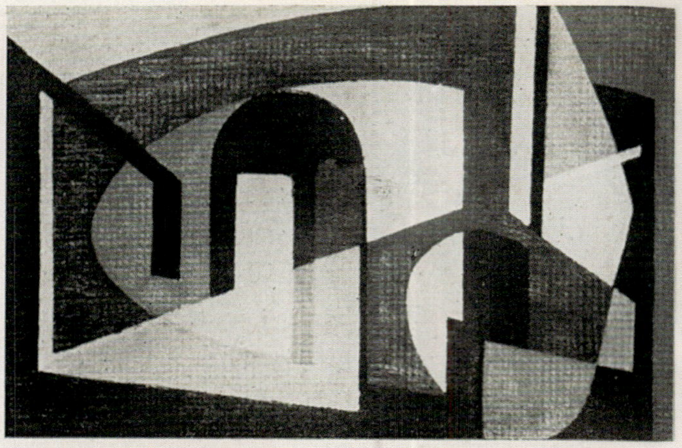

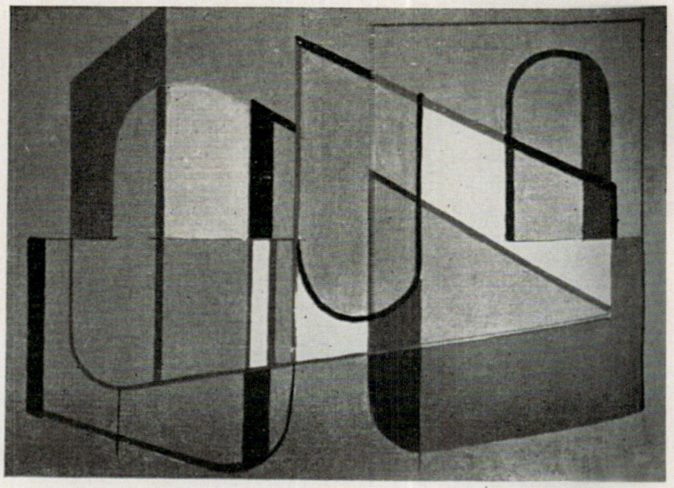

Created in 1950 by Italo-Brazilian architect Lina Bo Bardi, the arts and architecture magazine *Habitat – revista das artes no Brasil* (magazine of the arts in Brazil) was one of the most important vehicles by which modernism was debated and diffused in Brazil after the Second World War. *Habitat* was part of a larger project gestated at the São Paulo Museum of Art (MASP) under the guidance of curator Pietro Maria Bardi, Bo Bardi's collaborator and partner and the founding director of the museum, which opened in 1947. In its heroic years MASP pioneered a unique 'pedagogic program', establishing a series of outreaching initiatives with the aim of forming a public constituency around modern art, architecture and design. Besides showing consecrated European modernists, this program included the realization of so-called 'didactic exhibitions' on art history; the creation of the Institute of Contemporary Art, a Bauhaus-inspired design school; and *Habitat*, its own printed medium, which was published until 1965.

Similar to other militant modernist architectural magazines that flourished at that time in Brazil, *Habitat* not only propagated images of modern art and design, but also images of popular and indigenous cultures, introducing its audience, the urban elites of São Paulo and Rio de Janeiro, to the vocabulary of modernism and vernacular and native forms of cultural expression at the same time. Images of Amerindian ceramics, ornaments and paintings were placed in relation to a constellation of images of contemporary art, architecture and design, performing a pivotal function in defining the modern sensibility that the magazine sought to impress upon its public-in-the-making.

The articulation between the indigenous and the modern was often didactically conveyed through the texts that accompanied the images, explaining to the reader how indigenous drawings were comparable to the 'most sophisticated contemporary painter', their ornaments with the designs of a 'European stylist',[1] their ceramics aesthetically equivalent to avant-garde sculptures: 'some Picassos in thongs, silently modelling their anonymous oeuvre'.[2] Further, the magazine's constructivist, neat graphic design often displayed images in such a way as to emphasize this relation on the visual plane.

To be modern, *Habitat* pedagogically communicates, is to be connected both to the language of modernism as well as to popular, indigenous, 'primitive' forms of art. Figurations of the primitive, the

Des-Habitat

Carajás

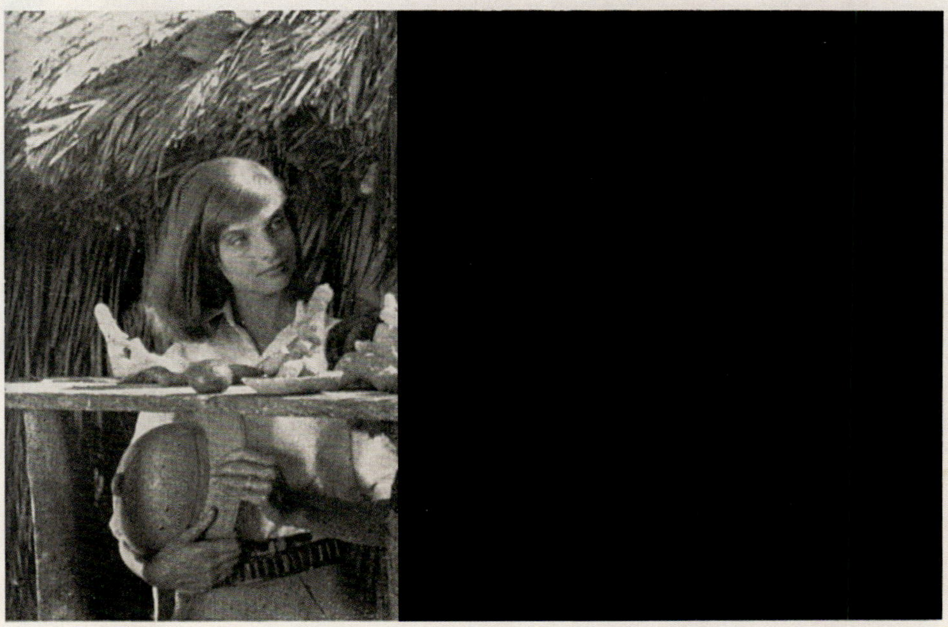

indigenous and the wild played a central role in shaping the modern movement in Brazil, and for that matter of modernism *tout court*. Different from the European context, however, where the avant-gardes sought a radical break from past and tradition, the encounter of Brazilian modernists with the primitive was associated with the fabrication of a sense of national culture and identity. Images of indigenous objects appeared in *Habitat* under this codification, serving as references to a particular type of modern language which, despite its affiliation to internationalism, was grounded in vernacular and native forms of expression, the aesthetic resources of a truly authentic national-modern culture.

***

By virtue of its pedagogic design and language, *Habitat* framed the images of indigenous bodies, arts and crafts as if they were displayed in a space between the ethnographic museum and the museum of modern art, objects detached from their social and territorial milieu, which should be contemplated as autonomous works of art. Likewise, such framing bracketed out the social processes by which these images were produced. The crucial question they ask is far from anything related to the 'ethnographic art' they show; it rather concerns that which is outside the frame. For what was the historical and social context that allowed such images of indigenous bodies and objects to be produced, reproduced and circulate in sophisticated mass media publications as formal references to the 'new language'?

After the 1930 Revolution, which initiated the fifteen-year rule of Getúlio Vargas, the Brazilian state embarked on aggressive project of hinterland colonization. This was operationalized by government policies such as the 'March to the West', which prompted a series of expeditions with the aim of establishing outposts and towns across the unexplored territories of central Brazil. By the late 1950s, under the democratic presidency of Juscelino Kubitschek, this frontier ideology was being pursued through ambitious projects of territorial and regional modernization, the most expressive of which was Brasília, the modernist capital city built

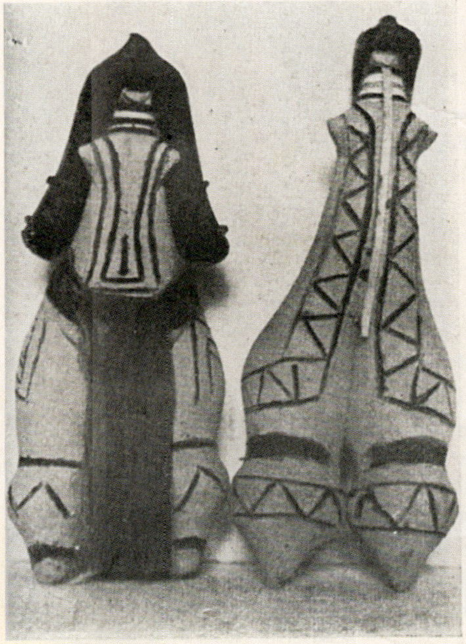

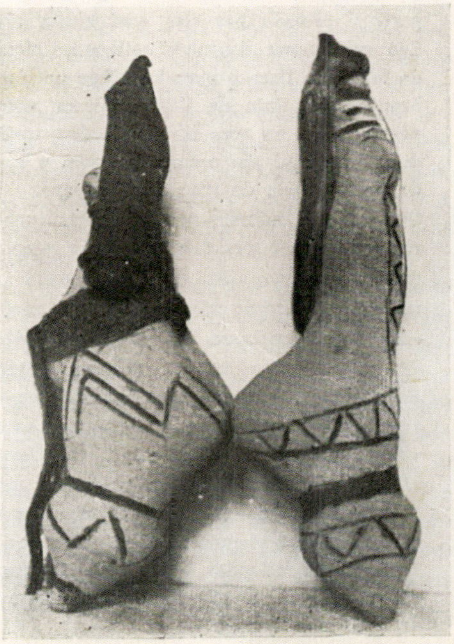

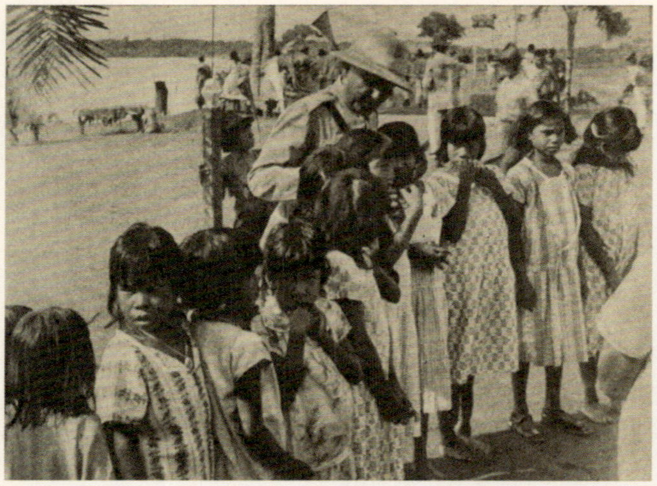

SPI documentation of the Indigenous Post Bananal in the Bananal Island, Karajá Territory, photo by Luis Thomaz Reis, circa 1907-1909.

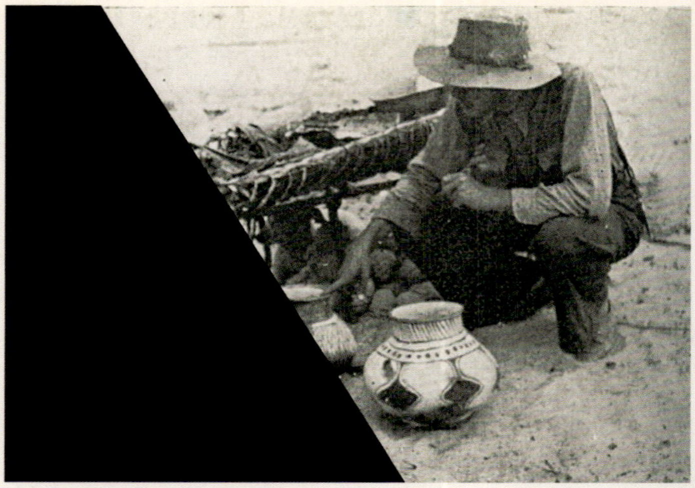

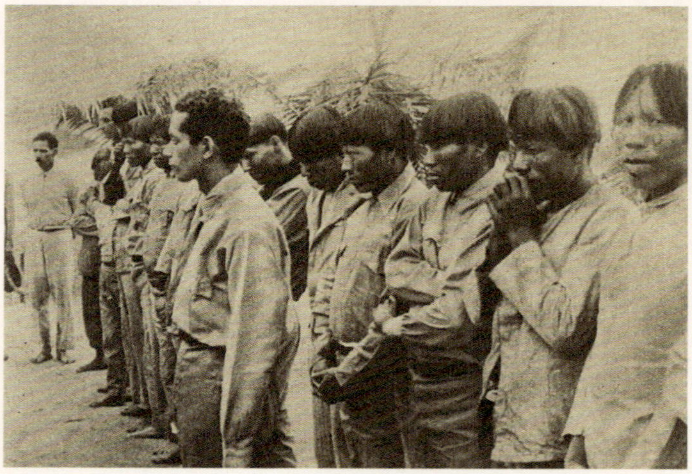

SPI documentation of the Indigenous Post Bananal in the Bananal Island, Karajá Territory, photo by Luis Thomaz Reis, circa 1907-1909.

from scratch at the centre of the country. As urban planner Lucio Costa wrote, Brasília was conceived as 'a deliberate act of possession, a gesture similar to that of explorers, in the mode of the colonial tradition'.

In order to accomplish this project, the Brazilian state counted on an agency dedicated to govern indigenous affairs called Indian Protection Service or SPI. The SPI was responsible for executing what was then officially known as the 'pacification' of indigenous groups whose territories were designated to development projects. Founded in 1910 and originally named SPILTN – which adds the phrase 'and Localization of the National Worker' – SPI's ideology and practice of protection was integrationist and expansionist, aimed at transforming indigenous populations into national citizens while at the same time opening their lands for colonization. The agency actualized forms of territorial and social control developed by colonial administrators and missionaries, employing a similar strategy to the *descimentos* or *reducciones*. This consisted in displacing and concentrating communities in centralized villages, thereby containing their movements and depopulating vast territories in order to appropriate their lands.

By 1950, when *Habitat* was first published, the SPI counted on more than a hundred outposts distributed across the Brazilian territory, forming a geographical network organized according to stages of acculturation of native groups: 'frontier posts'; 'posts of attraction'; 'posts of medical treatment and alphabetization'; 'posts of nationalization'. Initially serving as 'advanced bases' where indigenous groups were coerced to move, encampments gradually developed into farming colonies governed by SPI officers where communities were indoctrinated into the habits of western civilization, agricultural labour and the ideologies of nationalism.

The activities of the SPI were extensively documented in texts, photographs and films, especially after the creation of the Section of Studies in 1942, an associated bureau dedicated to register the culture of the indigenous groups that were being 'pacified' by the agency. Under the leadership of anthropologist

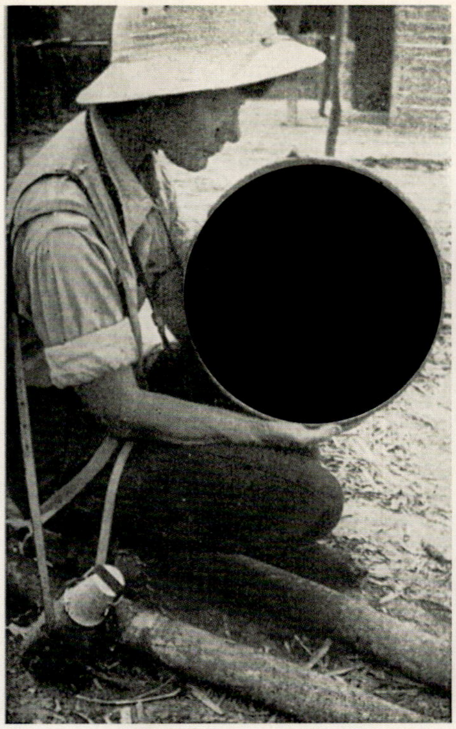

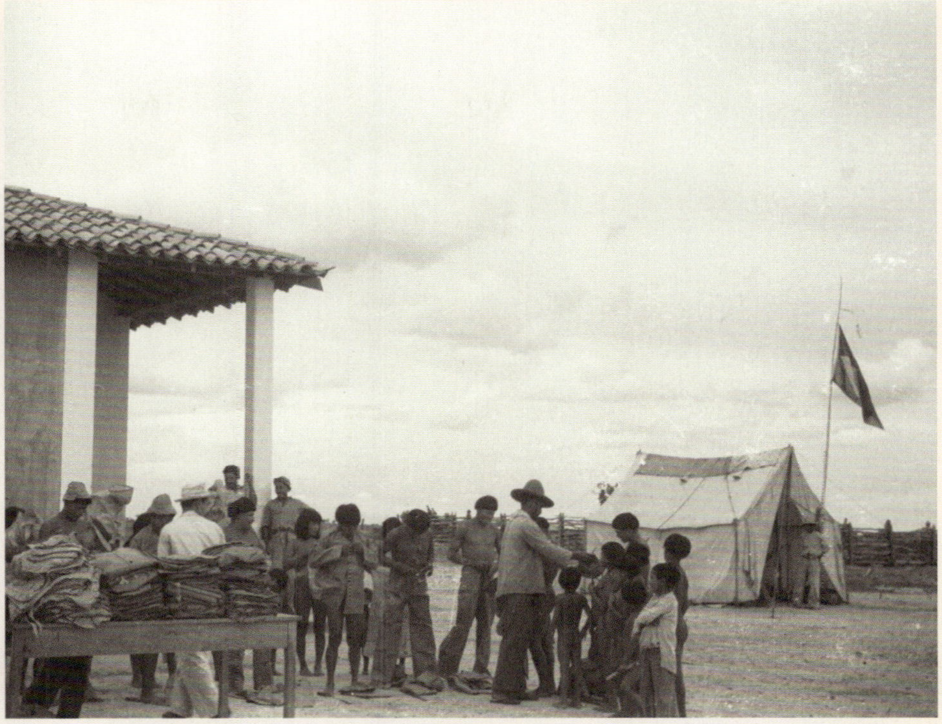

SPI – Section of Studies, "Distribution of clothes and gifts to the indians", Indigenous Post of Attraction Curisevo, Scientific and Documentary Exploration of the Curisevo River, photography by Heinz Foerthmann, 1945. Gift-giving was a widely-used tactic in contacting indigenous groups (courtesy of the Museum of the Indian-FUNAI).

Darcy Ribeiro, a prominent intellectual of this generation, and counting on pioneering modernist filmmakers and photographers, the Section of Studies was responsible for producing an impressive audio-visual archive that latter acquired the status of a museum, the Museum of the Indian, today headquartered in Rio de Janeiro.

The images and imaginaries of the indigenous, the primitive and the wild that informed the modern movements in the metropolitan areas were furnished by the circulation of photos, films and artefacts that were captured and collected during the pacification missions conducted by the SPI, as well as a series of other exploratory incursions that with increasing frequency penetrated the Brazilian hinterlands during the twentieth century. Moreover, in the 1940s and 1950s these exploratory missions became connected to burgeoning practices of photojournalism whose images were diffused not only by the general interest illustrated magazines of that time, but also by architectural publications such as *Habitat*.

***

The Karajá people, an indigenous nation that for centuries has inhabited the banks of the Araguaia River in central Brazil, was one of the groups who most prominently featured in the pages of *Habitat*. Not only was their sculptural ceramic work easily comparable to modernist art, thus serving as an excellent 'pedagogic device', but by that time it was also easy to get access to these objects and their images.

Since the 18th century the Karajá villages were targeted by countless missionary and colonizing fronts. From the 1930s onwards, as a result of the expansionist policies of the Vargas regime, their territory was subjected to a series of state interventions, including the instalment of SPI outposts and a base of the Brazilian Air Force. Journalists and photographers came alongside the pacifiers, and the Karajá land turned into a highly mediatized space from where images of nature, primitiveness and national identity were produced, diffused and manipulated.

The Karajá appeared for the first time in *Habitat* No. 7 (1952), which dedicated several pages to display their ceramics. In 1956 *Habitat* No. 33, 34 and 37

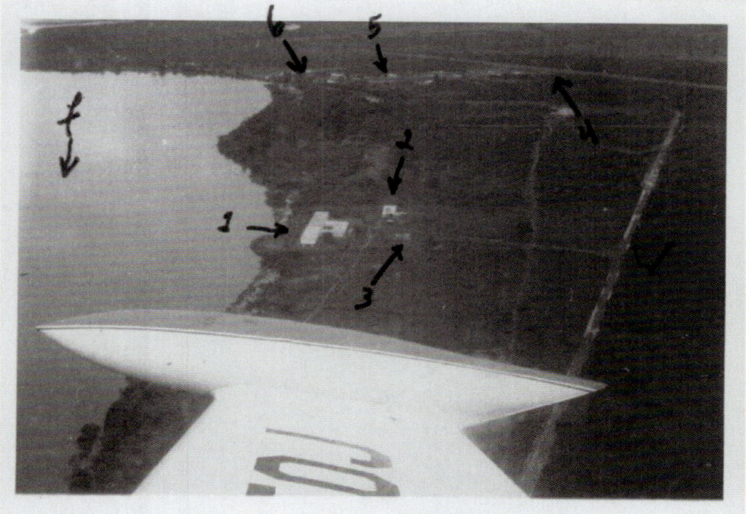

Image from the archive of the Brasil Central Foundation, one of the state-led expeditions realized in the 1940s–1960s, showing an aerial view of the complex Hotel JK on Bananal Island. [1 – Hotel; 2, 3 – Annexes; 4 – Airport / Military Base; 5, 6 – Indigenous Village; 7 – Araguaia River]. (courtesy of Brazil National Archive).

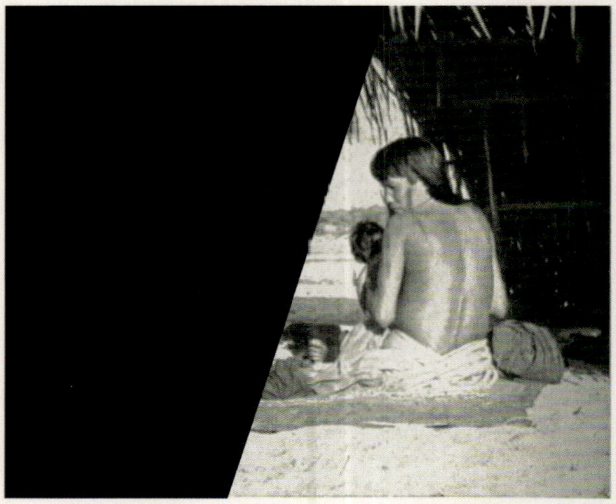

published a sequence of long essays on the Karajá by photojournalist Mario Baldi, who often accompanied the expeditions of the SPI. Baldi's ethnographically-informed narrative portrays the Karajá as an isolated cultural entity and erases much of the context that made it possible for him to construct such a narrative. The only traces of it are registered in a short comment by Baldi: 'Before they used to live dispersed in many villages. In 1936, I visited twenty-seven of them... today, however, all of them, or at least the great majority, live on the Bananal Island where they have been concentrated by the SPI.'[3]

By the time these images were published in *Habitat* the Karajá territory was undergoing another intense process of territorial and social transformations due to new state-led colonial initiatives. Together with Brasília the Kubitschek administration envisioned the creation of a luxurious tourism complex on the Bananal Island, in the heart of the Karajá ancestral territory, for which architect Oscar Niemeyer was commissioned. Conceived as tropical resort for the political and bureaucratic elites of the new capital, Hotel JK was built next to the Karajá village of Santa Isabel do Morro, or *Hawaló*. Niemeyer's project, with its panoramic view over the river island, translated the articulation between modernism, the primitive and the wild into a lived experience mediated by means of an architectural panoptic display. From the hotel windows the indians could be observed in the same fashion as their images appeared in the pages of *Habitat*, suspended in between a modern and a colonial gaze. Modern design functioned as a tool to block out the social violence implied in that gaze, fabricating a modern experience of primitiveness and wilderness whose foundations were essentially colonial.

***

The images published in *Habitat* are representative of a paradoxical preservationist impulse of collecting and archiving the 'heritage' of indigenous populations at a moment when their

Karajá sculptures displayed in a vitrine in the reception lobby of Hotel JK. Archive of the Brasil Central Foundation, undated (courtesy of Brazil National Archive).

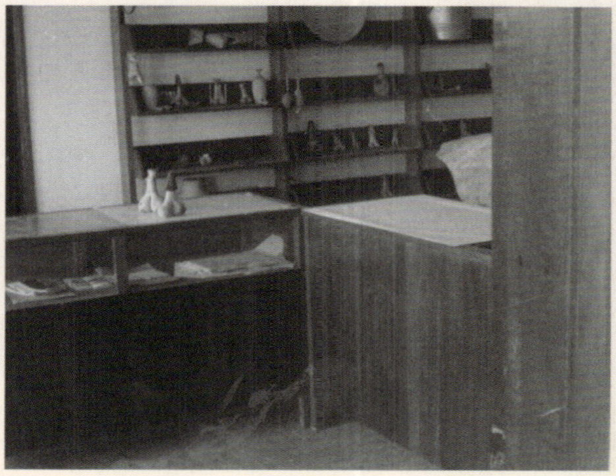

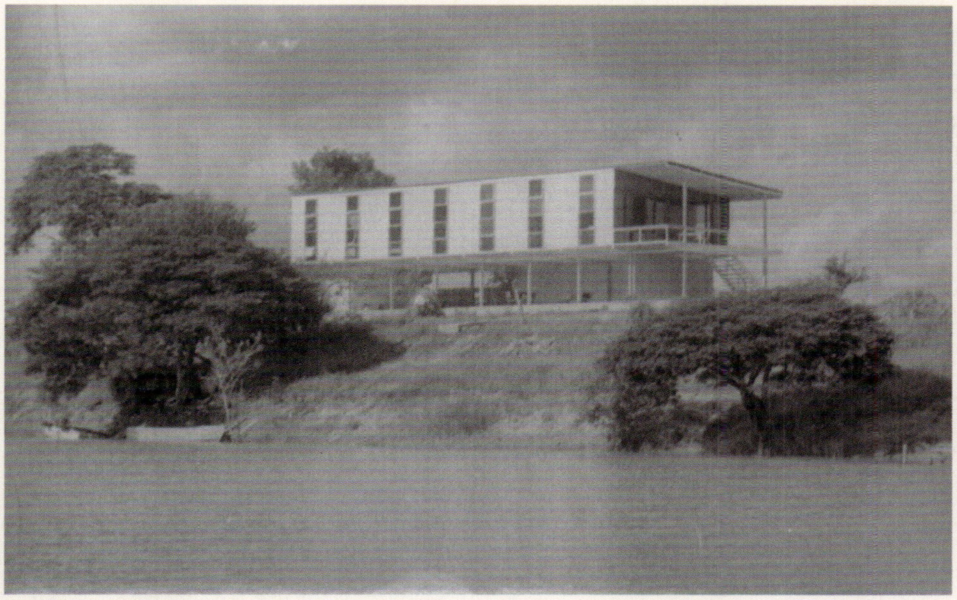

One of the buildings in the tourism complex Hotel JK. Archive of the Brasil Central Foundation, undated (courtesy of Brazil National Archive).

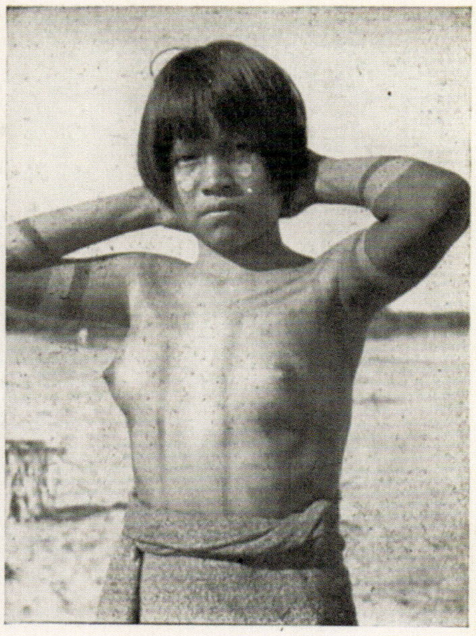

lands were being rapidly encroached and their modes of life were increasingly threatened. In 1957, one year after the publication of Baldi's photo-essays in *Habitat*, Ribeiro published an appalling report demonstrating that most of the 230 indigenous groups known in Brazil in the early 1900s were on the verge of total disintegration due to the violence of colonial contact. In less than sixty years the indigenous population of Brazil had diminished by over 80%, and those who survived were living in wretched conditions.[4]

The Karajá were amongst the most affected nations. Observing the images of *Habitat* carefully, but also carefully looking to what they do not show, we realize they are close-ups of one of the most dramatic periods in the history of the people they portray, taken at a time when the Karajá population had reached a demographic historic low. They say nothing about 'the primitive', but reveal much of the colonial violence inherent to the moderns. Outside the frame we see episodes of dis-possession, des-territorialization, des-habitat.

1. *Habitat*, No. 1, 1950, 66–67. **2**. *Habitat*, No. 7, 1952, 65. **3**. *Habitat*, No. 34 1956, 24. Darcy Ribeiro, 'Culturas e Línguas Indígenas do Brasil', in *Educação e Ciências Sociais*, Vol. 2, 1957.

Des-Habitat
a project by Paulo Tavares / autonoma; research and design by Ana Tranchesi, Isabella Beneduci and Paulo Tavares; text by Paulo Tavares

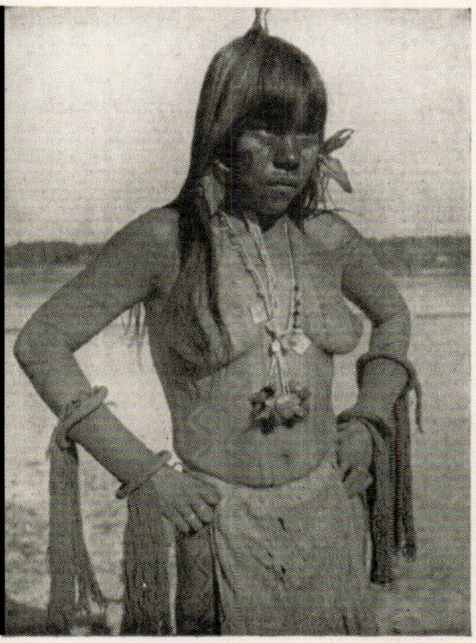

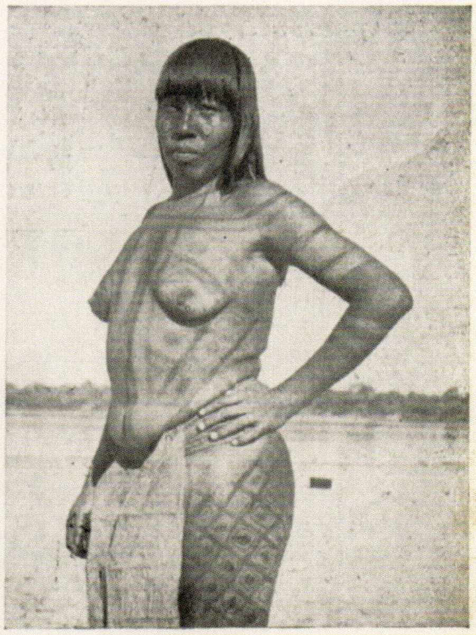

Chapter 3

Moving Away

► Marcel Breuer, *ein bauhaus-film. fünf jahre lang* (A Bauhaus Film: Five Years Long), 1926, from *Bauhaus*, Vol. 1, 1926, offset litho print, 42 × 29.7 cm

ein bauhaus-film

fünf jahre lang

autor:
das leben, das seine rechte fordert

operateur:
marcel breuer, der diese rechte anerkennt

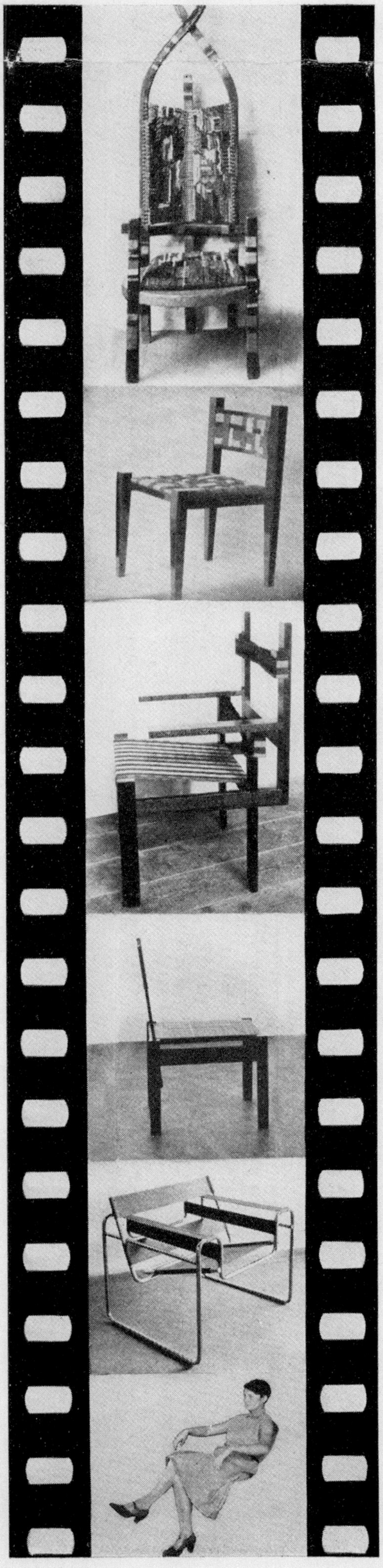

1921

1921½

1924

1925

19??

es geht mit jedem jahr besser und besser.
am ende sitzt man auf einer elastischen luftsäule →

A small collage by Marcel Breuer, secreted within the fold-out pages of the first issue of the Bauhaus journal, *bauhaus. zeitschrift für gestaltung*, presents a filmstrip with each frame depicting a chair designed by Breuer during the first years of the Bauhaus. The sequence visualizes a series of rapid style changes in an avant-garde manner, from Expressionist to De Stijl-inspired to functionalist, and, in the final frame, next to the date '19??', a woman seated on air. This vacuum where a chair should be, and its accompanying question marks, might suggest a future technology, but equally signify the future of design, of subjects and societies unforeseen by Breuer in 1926, the year this collage, titled *ein bauhaus-film*, was published.

The collage itself already conveys a moving away from the original Bauhaus concept of the 'unity of art and craft' and the subsequent phases at the school, which in 1926 had already moved to Dessau. These struggles were influenced by external pressures – financial, political, ideological – but also reflected internal debates among directors, teachers and students and their clashing opinions about the social and commercial orientation of the school and its artistic and polytechnical education. The rise of National Socialism and subsequent political attacks that finally resulted in the closure of the school by the SA produced waves of migration, with Bauhaus émigrés fanning out across the globe. This force of migration, the effects of living precarious lives, the need to survive financially, entanglements with shifting state policies towards design and architecture, and the interface with other cultures – all meant that Bauhaus ideas were made to adapt further.

Already in 1930 Hannes Meyer, who, following pressure from conservative circles in Dessau, had been dismissed as Bauhaus director for supporting the communist student union, applied to the Soviet embassy for passage to Moscow; in 1931 seven of his former students and staff followed. Like many other modernist architects at that time, they were driven by political convictions but also by the promise of large contracts in a new socialist and rapidly industrializing state, where they hoped to realize modernist cities on a previously unimaginable scale. Applying the functional analysis taught by Meyer at the Bauhaus, including the study of climate, topography, transport and demographics, he was asked to propose large-scale urban schemes for Moscow and the regional Soviet Republics. But this labour migration was not without its complications. By the end of the first Five-Year Plan, the tide had turned against the avant-garde, and under the official doctrine of Socialist Realism in a newly repressive climate, Meyer, together with the few members of his group who were still able to, left the USSR. Others died in Stalin's Gulag system. The ideological conflict between *neues bauen* (New Building) and socialist realist architecture that reflected a wider geopolitics was played out during the 4th CIAM Congress in 1933, with architects including Walter Gropius and Le Corbusier refusing to hold the congress in Moscow; it ultimately took place on a passenger ship journeying in the Mediterranean. Hannes Meyer, Lena Bergner, Tibor Weiner, Bela Scheffler, Lotte Stam Beese and Konrad Püschel later worked in Mexico, Chile, Hungary, the German Democratic Republic, North Korea and Switzerland, respectively.

Through the passage of Bauhaus émigrés to the United States, such as Gropius, Breuer, Herbert Bayer and Ludwig Mies van der Rohe, a 'Bauhaus idea' was reframed to signify in particular concepts of freedom and democracy. It was canonized in American museums such as the Museum of Modern Art (MoMA) in the 1930s, and propagated through academic institutions including the Institute of Design (IIT) in Chicago and the Harvard Graduate School of Design in Cambridge, Massachusetts. This regrouping of the Gropius-led Bauhaus across the Atlantic transferred cultural capital to the US but also helped propagate Bauhaus influences in Asia. In 1946 Gropius established The Architects Collaborative (TAC) in Harvard in close collaboration with Chen Chi-kwan. There, he also trained Henry Huang and Ieoh Ming Pei, who later became influential in China and Taiwan, which seemingly had few connections to the Bauhaus, designing architectural projects that proposed a new form of regional modernism, combining rationalist principles and modern engineering with vernacular elements.

In post-independence India Jawaharlal Nehru negotiated Cold War politics by maintaining a policy of nonalignment, something that constituted an international movement in 1961, the year India's preeminent design school the National Institute of Design (NID) was inaugurated in Ahmedabad, Gujarat. The history of this school and the Indian government's focus on design as a development tool reflect the geopolitics of the postcolonial period. While design was part of a Soviet-style Five-Year Plan, it was also propagated in India as US cultural diplomacy, in an effort to promote a capitalist way of life and resist the spread of communism, which by 1949 had been adopted by other great Asian powers such as China. At NID, aspects of Bauhaus design pedagogy detoured largely via what many consider to be the Bauhaus's post-war successor school, the Hochschule für Gestaltung (HfG) Ulm (Ulm School of Design), with the understanding that design must be harnessed to meet the needs of a newly independent nation. This could be done by improving the quality of its products, reaching a largely rural, non-affluent population and taking into account the existing diversity of techniques and skills developed over centuries on the subcontinent. Later, at the United Nations Industrial Development Organization (UNIDO)'s conference on design and development in 1979, academics and designers from India along with international counterparts debated the notion of a standard of living, questions of sustainability and the applicability of western design to local problems.[1]

Conflicts and debates about design, architect, urbanism and ruralism typify the case studies which have been outlined above. In a 1928 article 'Metal Furniture and Modern Spatiality', Breuer states that constantly evolving forms of life will always demand a new response from the designer – an argument against a universalist principle of design. Unforeseen events, including the Second World War, the rise of dictatorships, the return of democracy, independence movements and new globalized markets, have produced situations in which specific design practices have emerged. Through all of this, former Bauhaus teachers and their students had to hold open their approach to design, while the broader reception of the Bauhaus has remained both tenacious and incredibly diversified.

Marion von Osten and Grant Watson

From the estate of Philipp Tolziner, *Expelled Bauhäusler Departing from the Dessau Station*, 1930, gelatin silver print, mounted on paper, image 8.3 × 10.9 cm, paper 29.6 × 20.9 cm

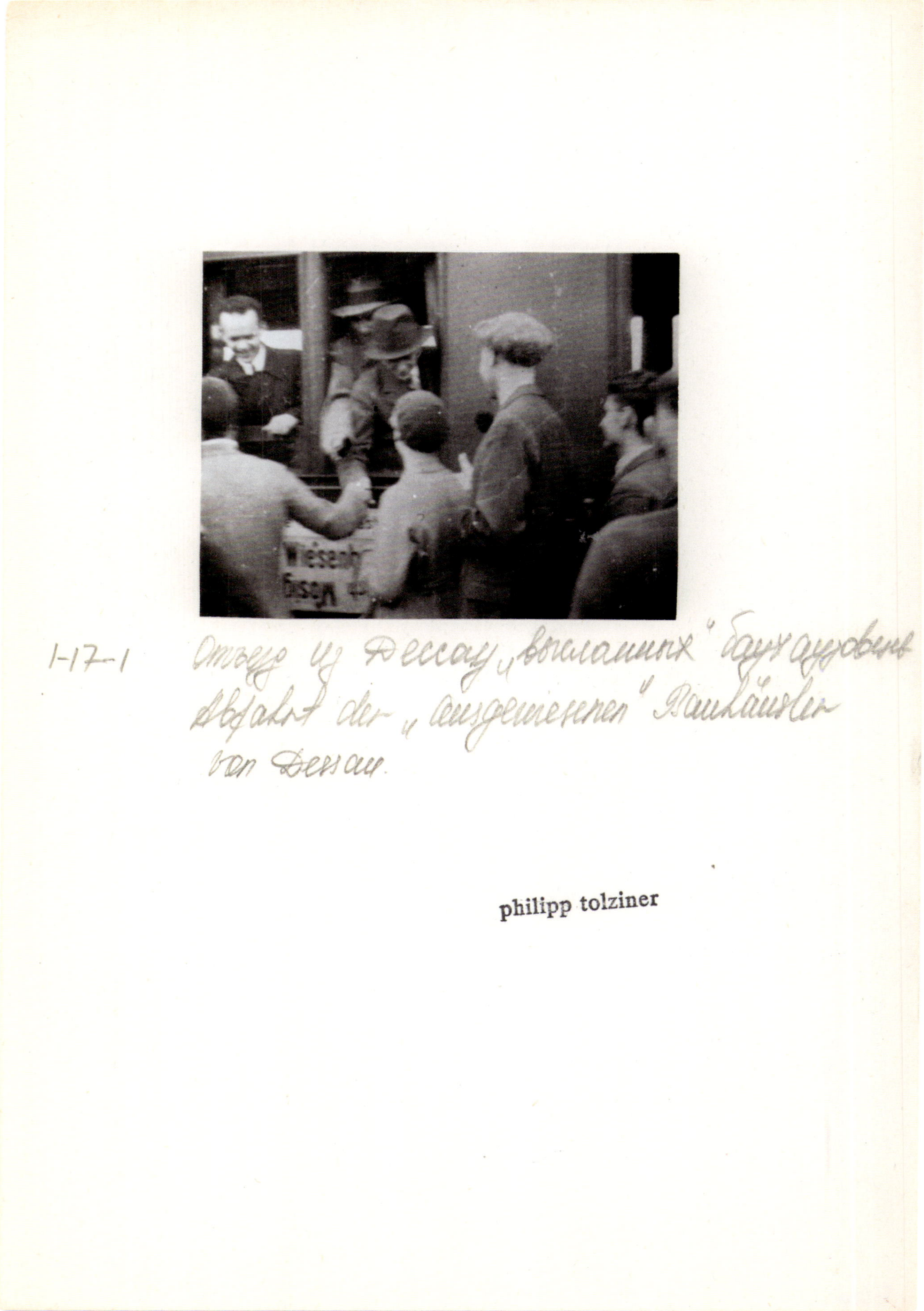

Philipp Tolziner, *Studie zur Periodizität des Lebensraum* (Study of the Periodicity of the Habitat), *c.* 1929, work from Hannes Meyer's Bauhaus class, photograph of original drawing, gelatin silver print mounted on paper, 15.9 × 24.1 cm

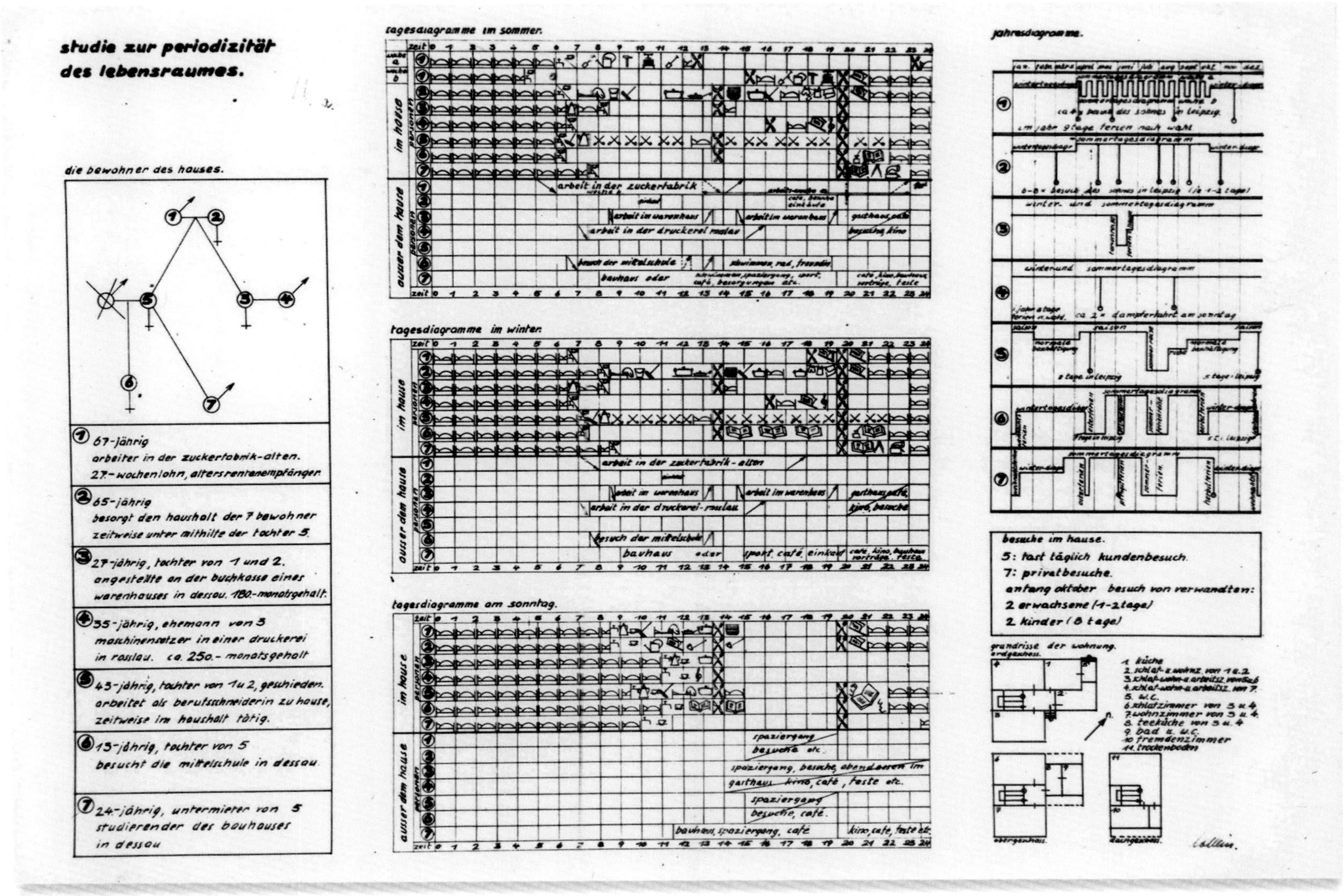

Hinnerk Scheper, colour design for the hallways of the Narkomfin Building, Moscow, 1929, tempera, print on paper, 29.2 × 21.5 cm

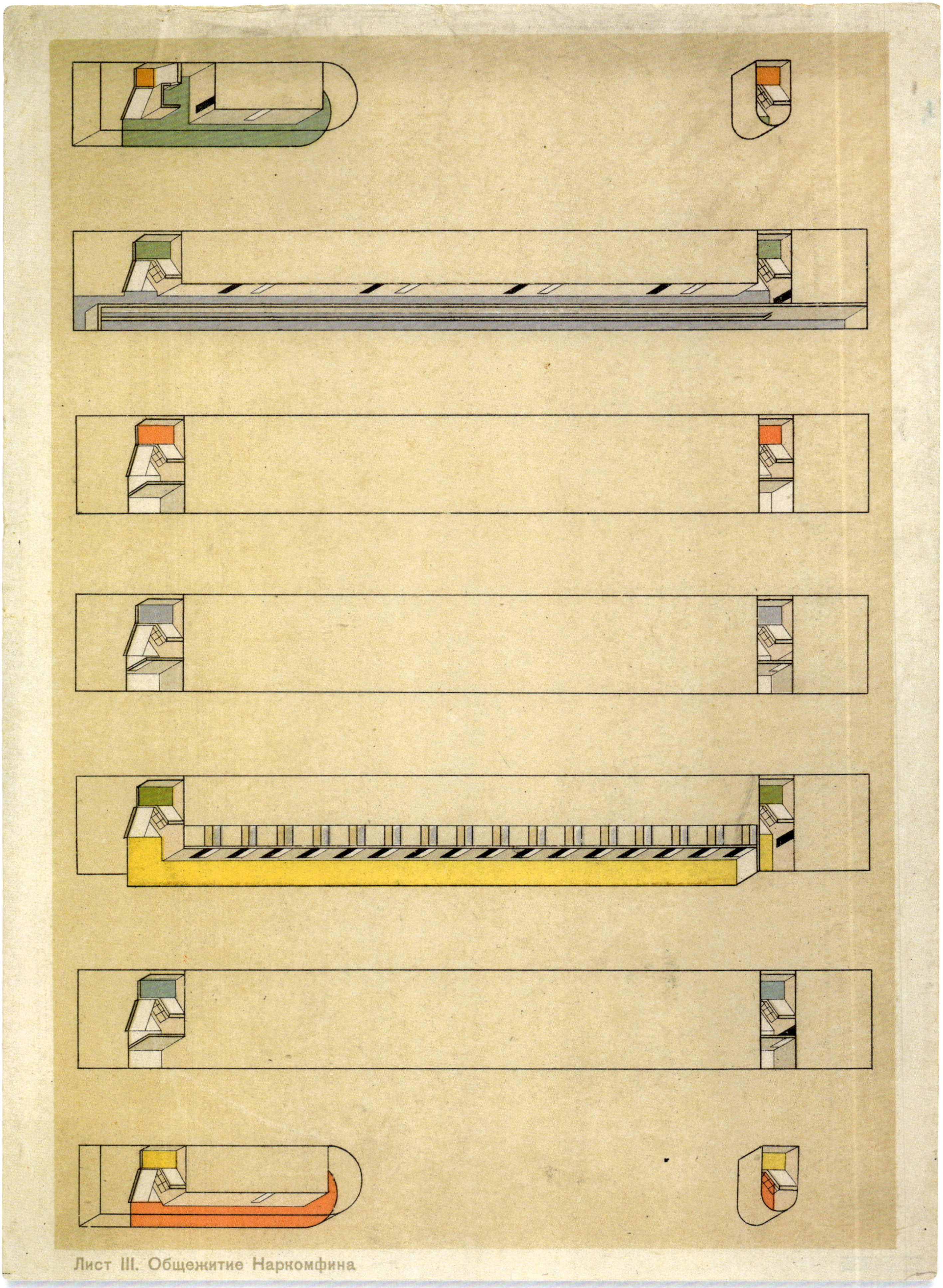

Hinnerk Scheper, colour design for apartment 'Type K' of the Narkomfin Building, Moscow, 1929, tempera, print on paper, 29.2 × 21.5 cm

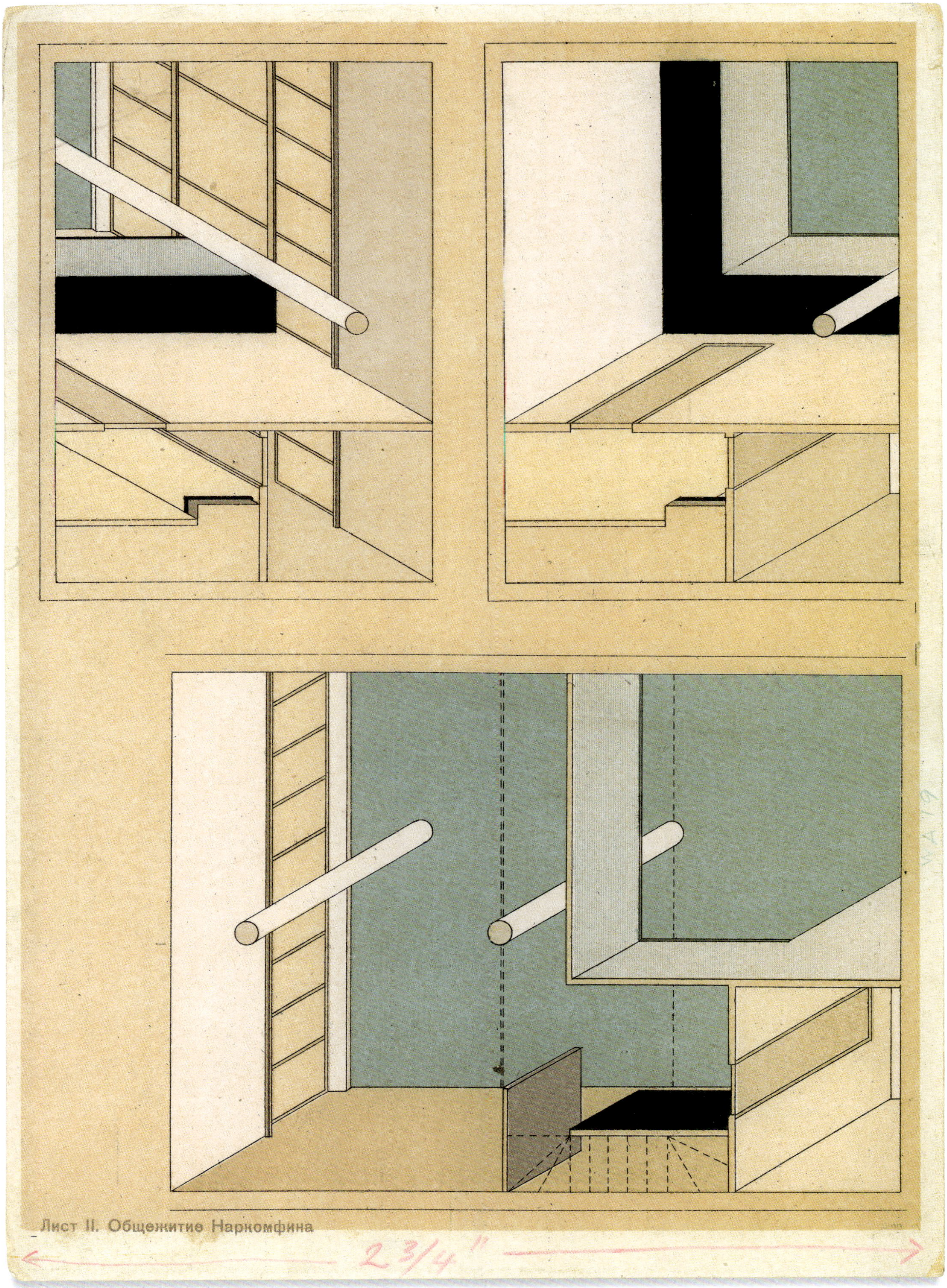

Konrad Püschel, page from a photograph album of North Korea, reconstruction of Hamhŭng, 1956–59, gelatin silver print on cardboard, 30.6 × 22.7 cm

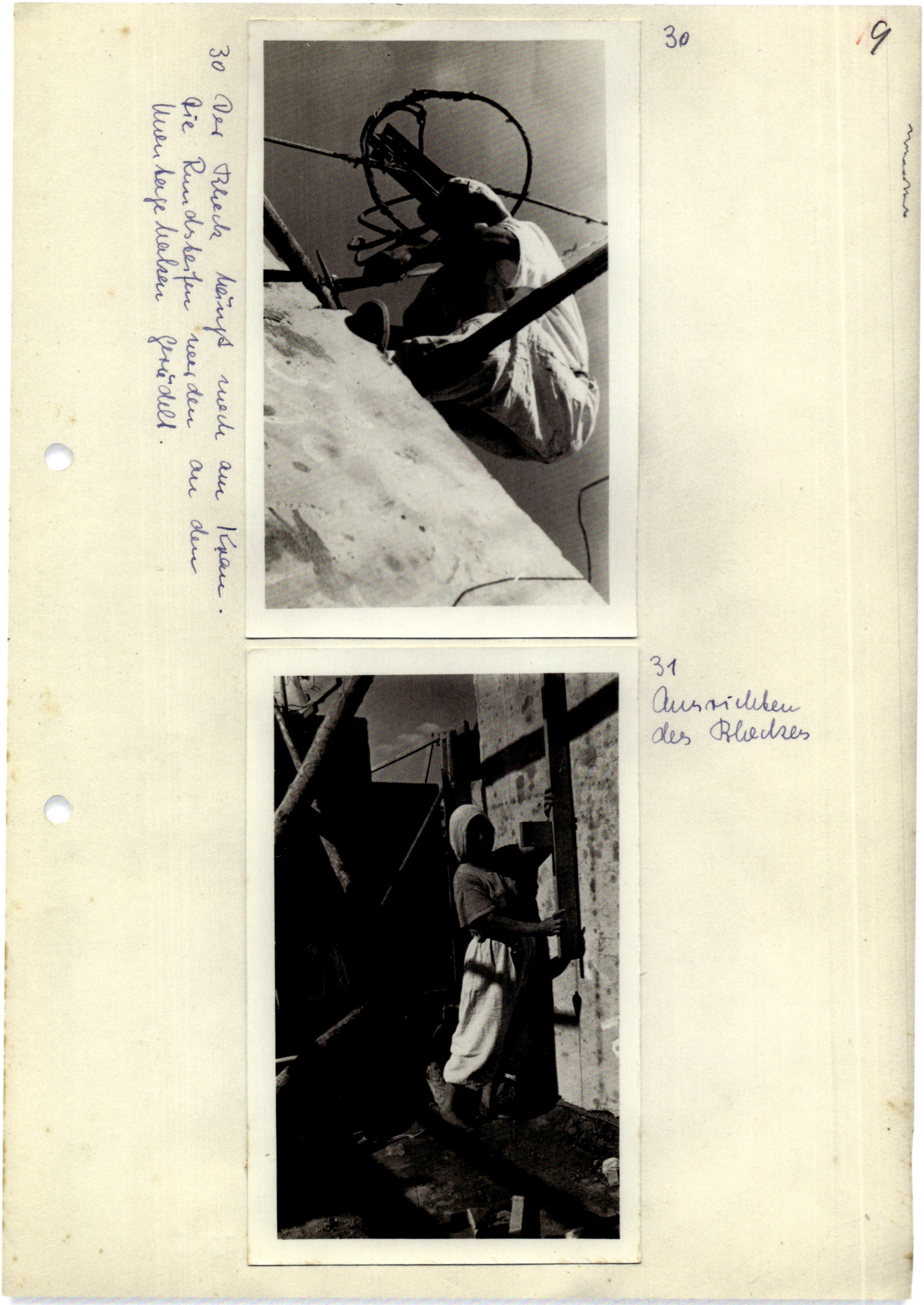

Shanghai Urban Planning and Design Institute, first-draft drawings of the Greater Shanghai Plan, 1946, print on paper, original size unknown

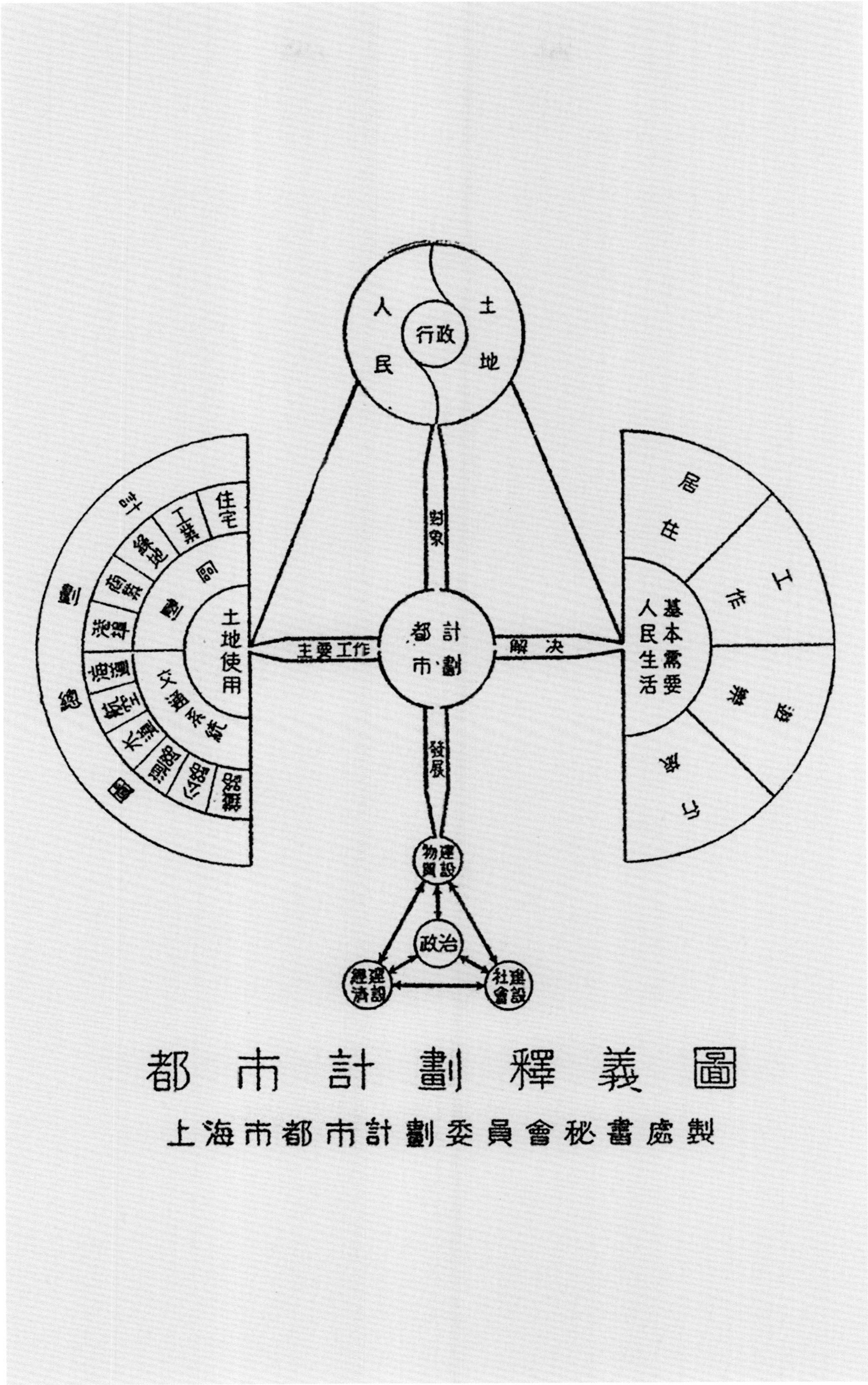

Photograph of a Chinese woman with a tubular steel chair, n.d. [between 1912 and 1951]

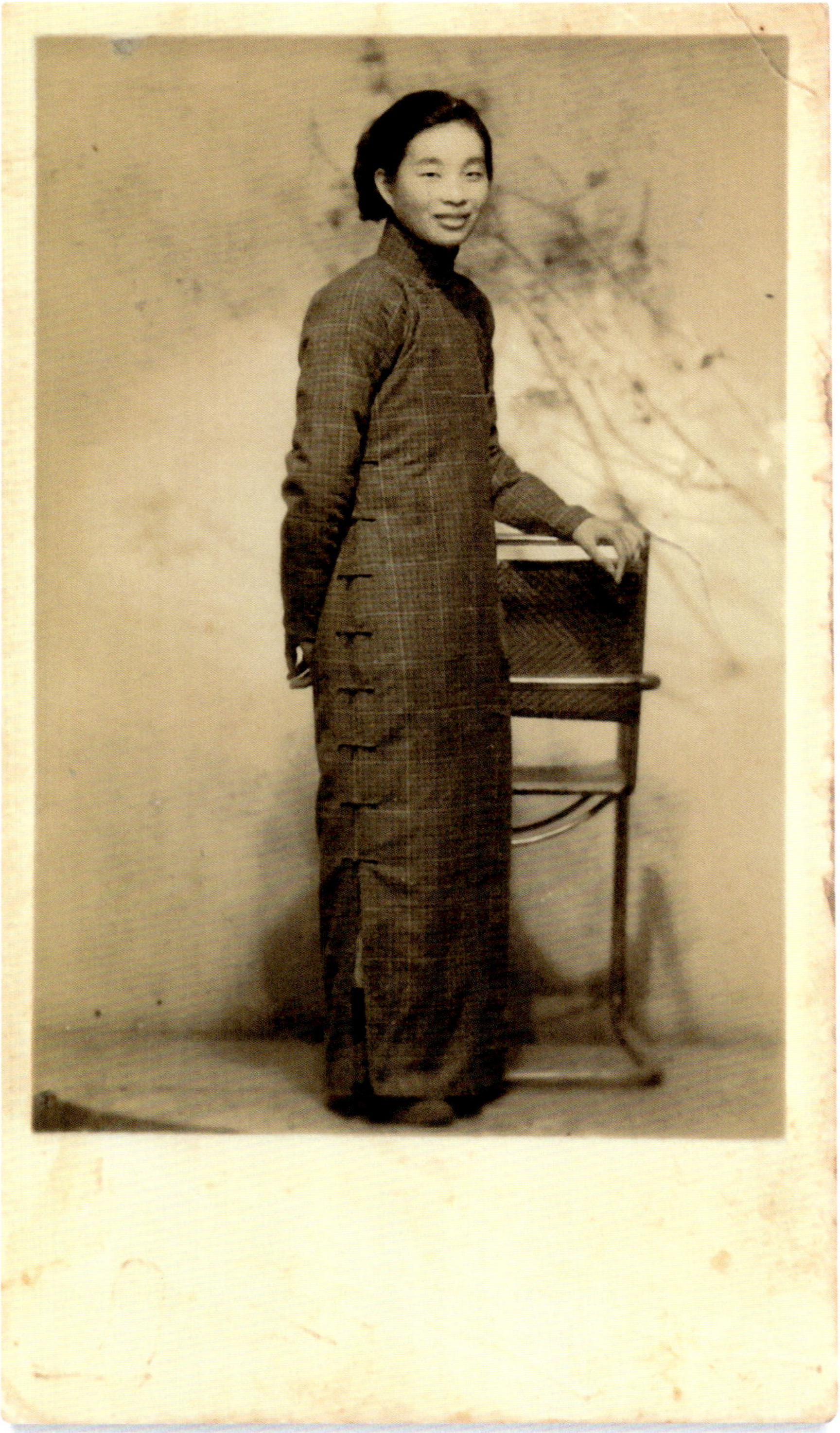

M. P. Ranjan, Bamboo Cube Stools, n.d., bamboo, top stool 43 × 43 × 43 cm, bottom stool 36 × 52 × 52 cm

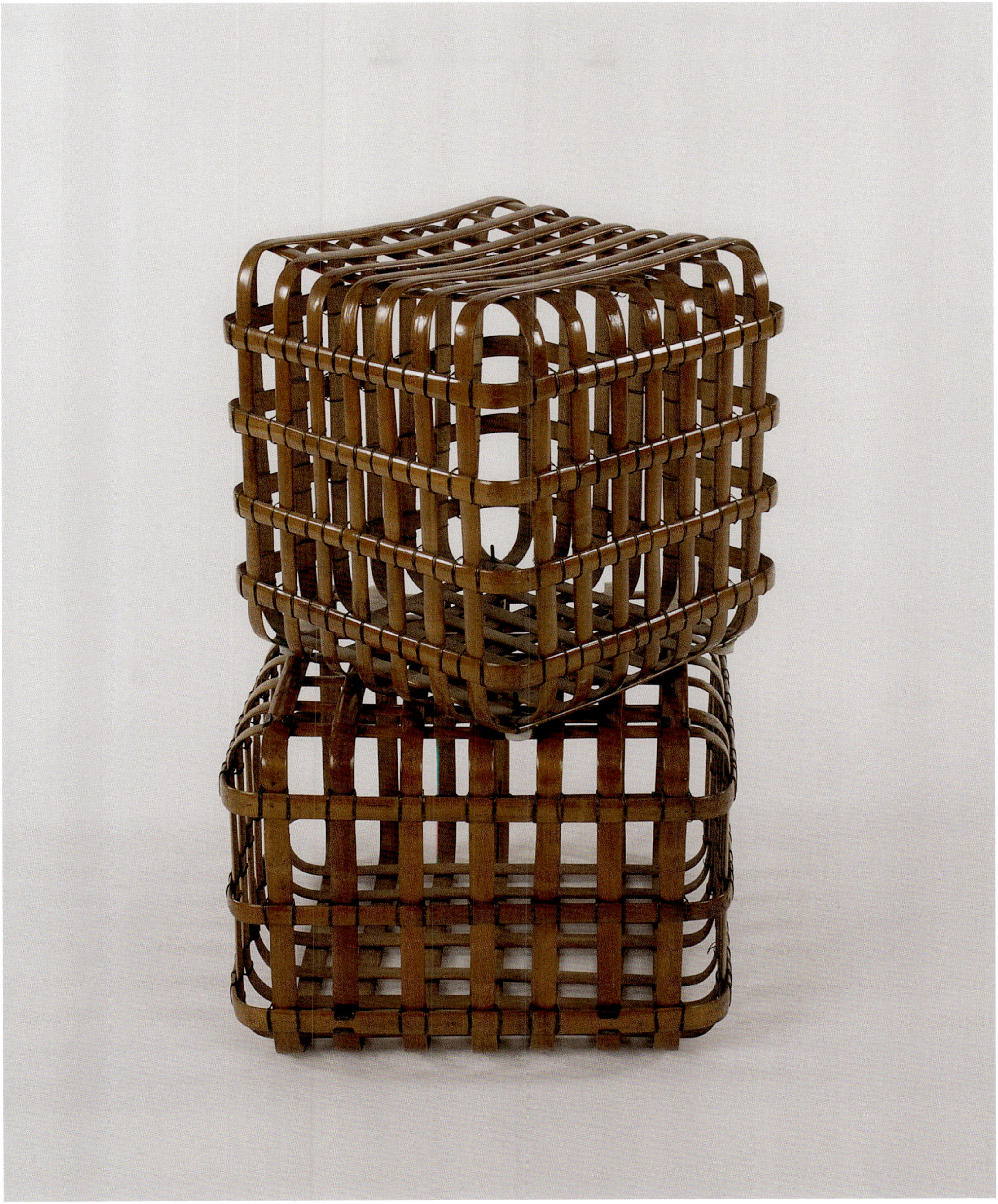

Otl Aicher, drawings of cars from the 'Indien 1960' (India 1960) report, 1960, drawing on paper

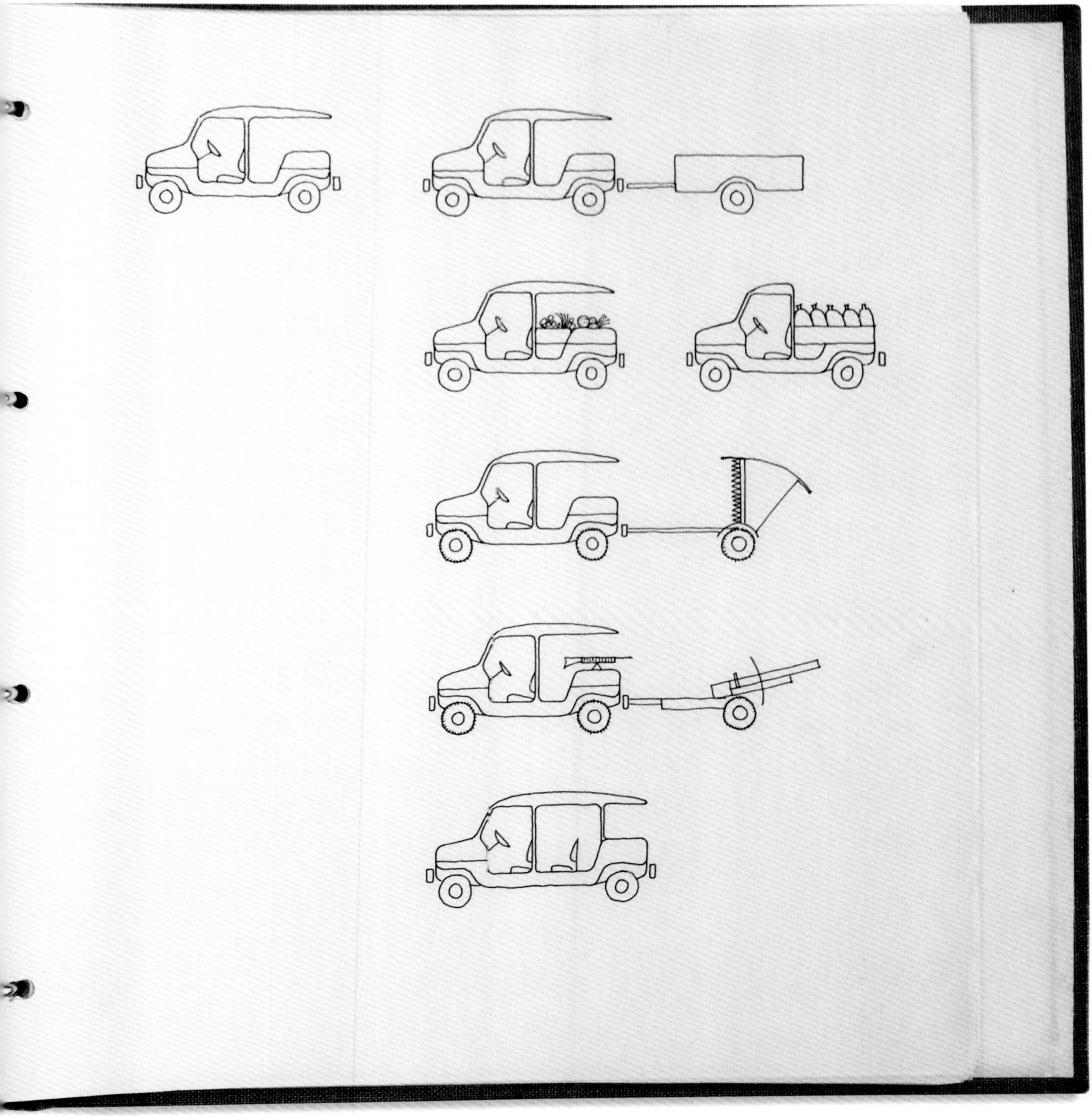

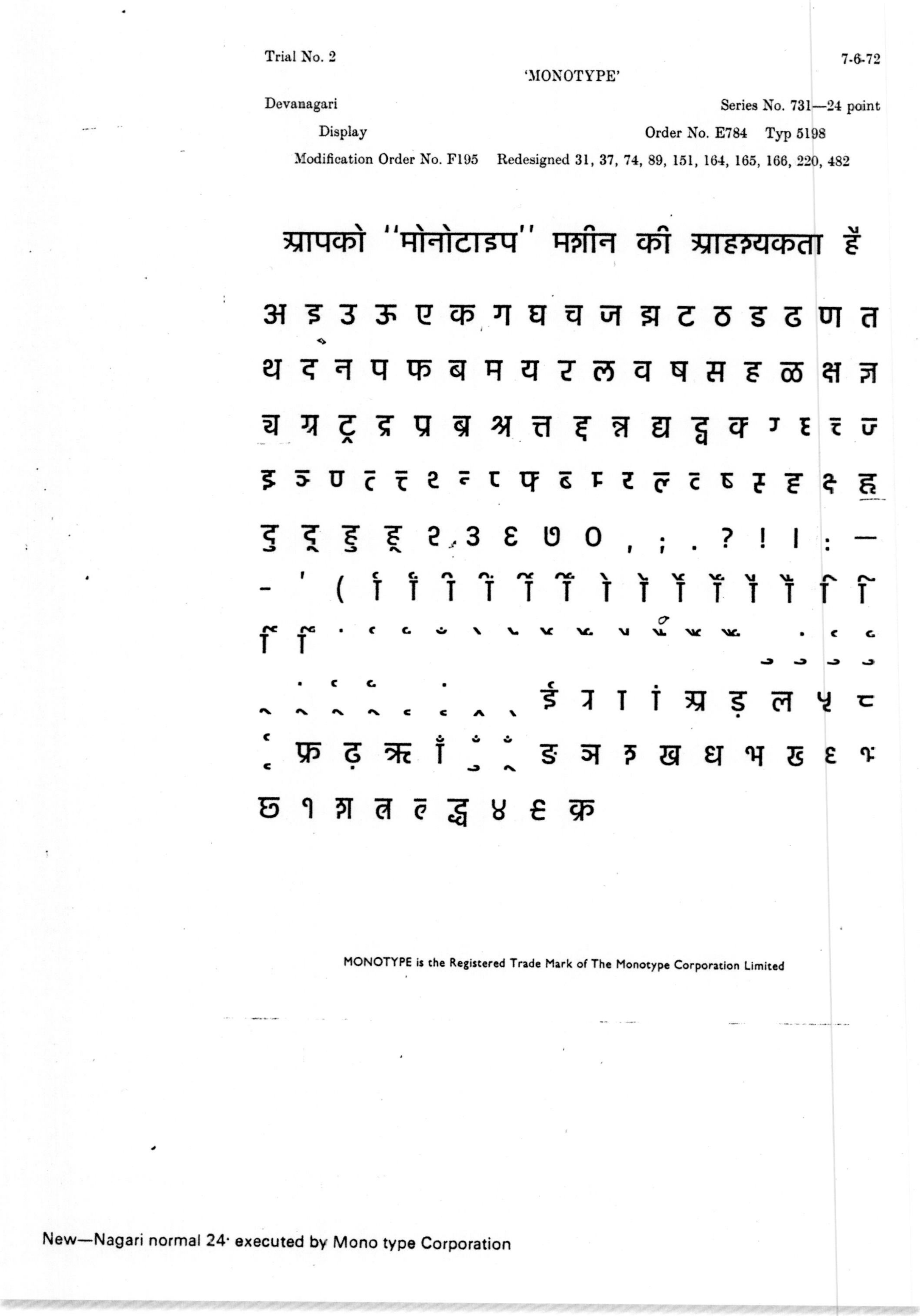
Trial No. 2 7-6-72

'MONOTYPE'

Devanagari Series No. 731—24 point

Display Order No. E784 Typ 5198

Modification Order No. F195 Redesigned 31, 37, 74, 89, 151, 164, 165, 166, 220, 482

आपको ''मोनोटाइप'' मशीन की आवश्यकता है

अ इ उ ऊ ए क ग घ च ज झ ट ठ ड ढ ण त

थ द न प फ ब म य र ल व ष स ह ळ क्ष ज्ञ

MONOTYPE is the Registered Trade Mark of The Monotype Corporation Limited

New—Nagari normal 24· executed by Mono type Corporation

David Abraham, fashion images for diploma project at the National Institute of Design, Ahmedabad, India, 1980, gelatin silver prints mounted on paper, each 21 × 29.7 cm

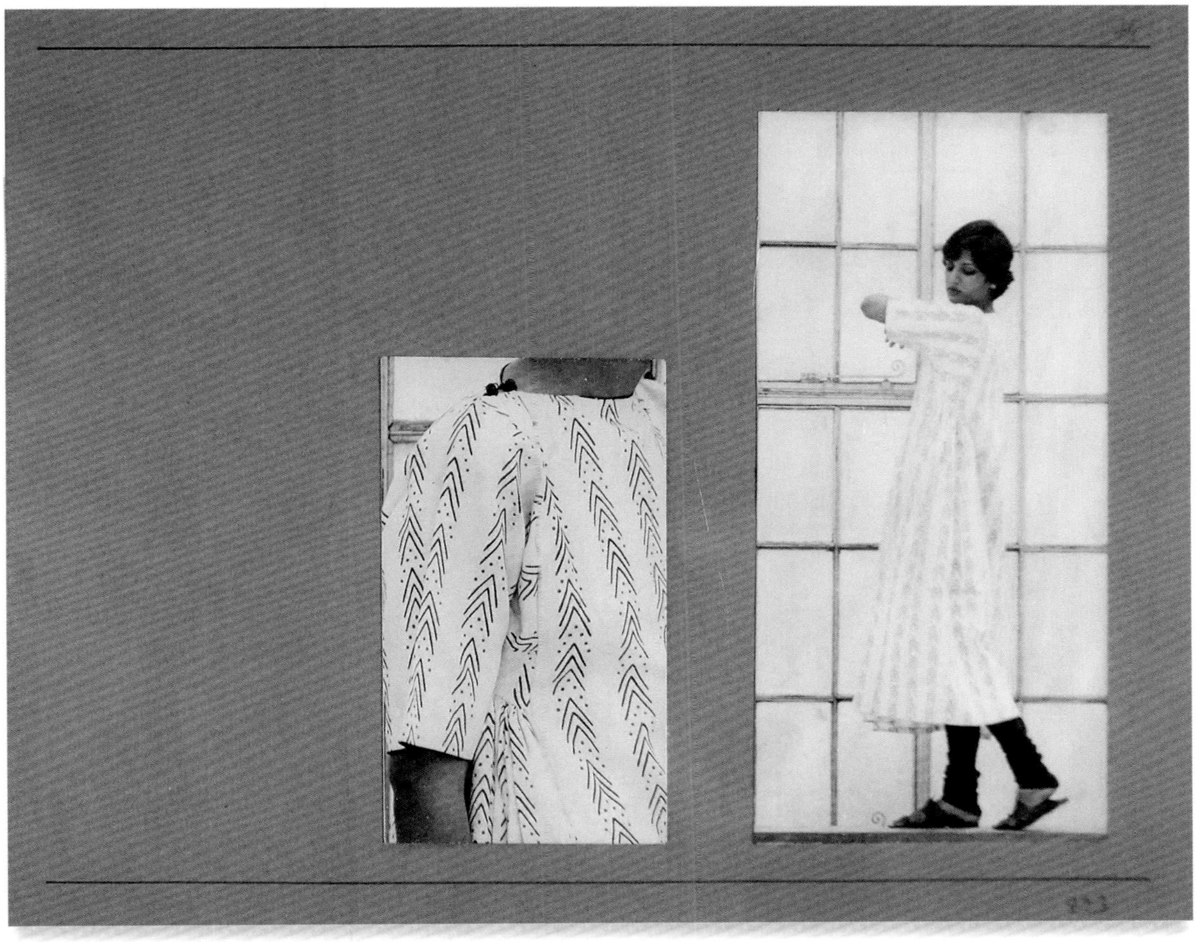

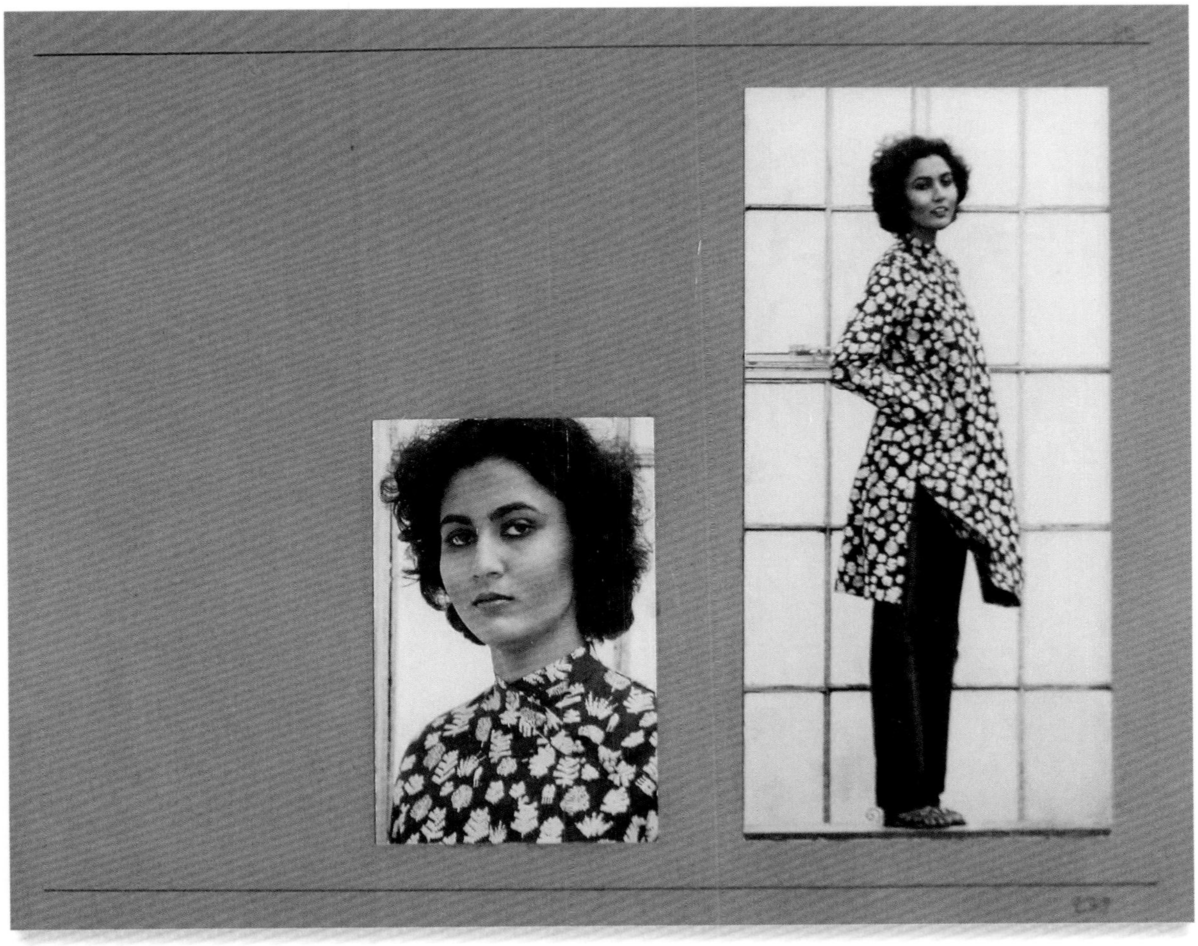

Anticipating the Future: Three Lines of Development

Hilde Heynen

Marcel Breuer's 1926 filmic collage *ein bauhaus-film*, featuring a series of his chairs designed between 1921 and 1925, provides an almost uncanny depiction of modernism's tendency towards nothingness. Umberto Eco famously described this ambition of the avant-garde:

> The avant-garde destroys, defaces the past: *Les Demoiselles d'Avignon* is a typical avant-garde act. Then the avant-garde goes further, destroys the figure, cancels it, arrives at the abstract, the informal, the white canvas, the slashed canvas, the charred canvas. In architecture and the visual arts, it will be the curtain wall, the building as stele, pure parallelepiped, minimal art; in literature, the destruction of the flow of discourse, the Burroughs-like collage, silence, the white page; in music, the passage from atonality to noise to absolute silence.[1]

In furniture, as Breuer so aptly demonstrated, the sequence moved from crafted, highly ornamental and symbolically significant thrones to geometrically simple chairs with straight lines, then to industrialized tubular steel ones and ultimately towards imaginary 'resilient air columns'. The surprising thing is that this sequence, which summarized the whole development cycle of the avant-garde in one collated image, apparently took only five years to reach completion – five years, moreover, that covered Breuer's maturation from adolescent student to Bauhaus master (he was only twenty-three when he was given the title of 'Junior Master' in 1925).

Four of the six seating supports depicted in the film have reached iconic status by now. The first one is the so-called African chair, a 1921 student work of Marcel Breuer and Gunta Stölzl, which is now part of the collection of the Bauhaus-Archiv in Berlin. Inspired by folk art and a 'primitivist' fascination for African motifs, it is the result of rough woodworking combined with skilled weaving. The second chair, designed and realized only half a year later, also is a collaborative piece between the same students. The 'chair with belt cover' is more simplified, using sturdy pear wood as legs, which are emphasized by being slightly raised above the seating and the back panel. The bright colours of the woven upholstery are typical for the products of the weaving workshop at that time: abstract patterns that double the interaction of warp and weft of the textile by interlacing woolen straps of different hues. Chair number three is known as the 'slatted chair', clearly inspired by the De Stijl furniture of Gerrit Rietveld (De Stijl founder Theo van Doesburg had visited Weimar and the Bauhaus in 1922, hence its students were well aware of the experiments going on in the Netherlands). This prototype decomposed the basic constituents of a chair into a series of orthogonally combined slats with clearly articulated interconnections, suggesting a momentarily halted movement of linear elements in space. The strategically positioned pieces of textile allow for a seating position that is

Below and pages 176–78: Hannes Meyer, sketches in a dummy for a Bauhaus book, 1947–49

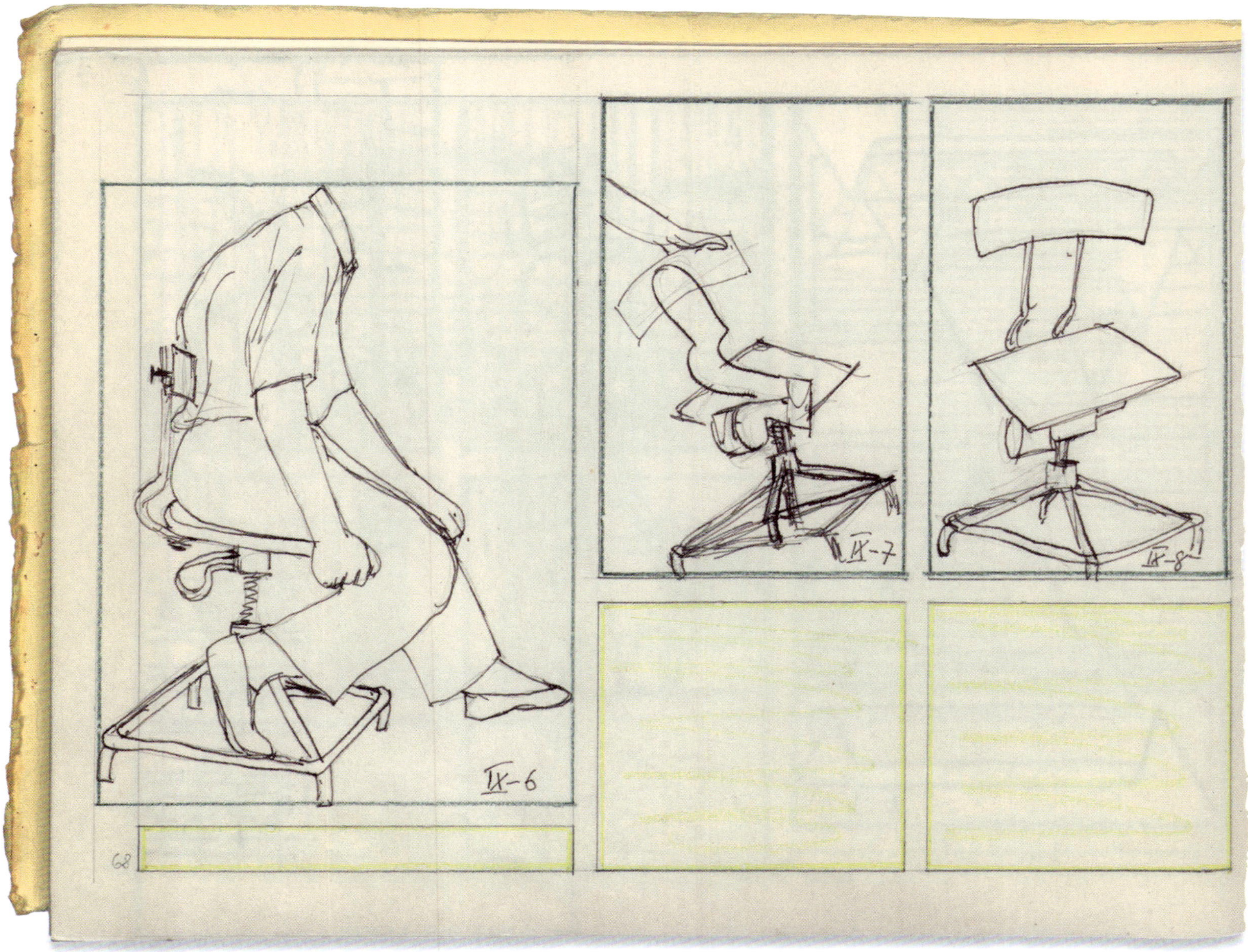

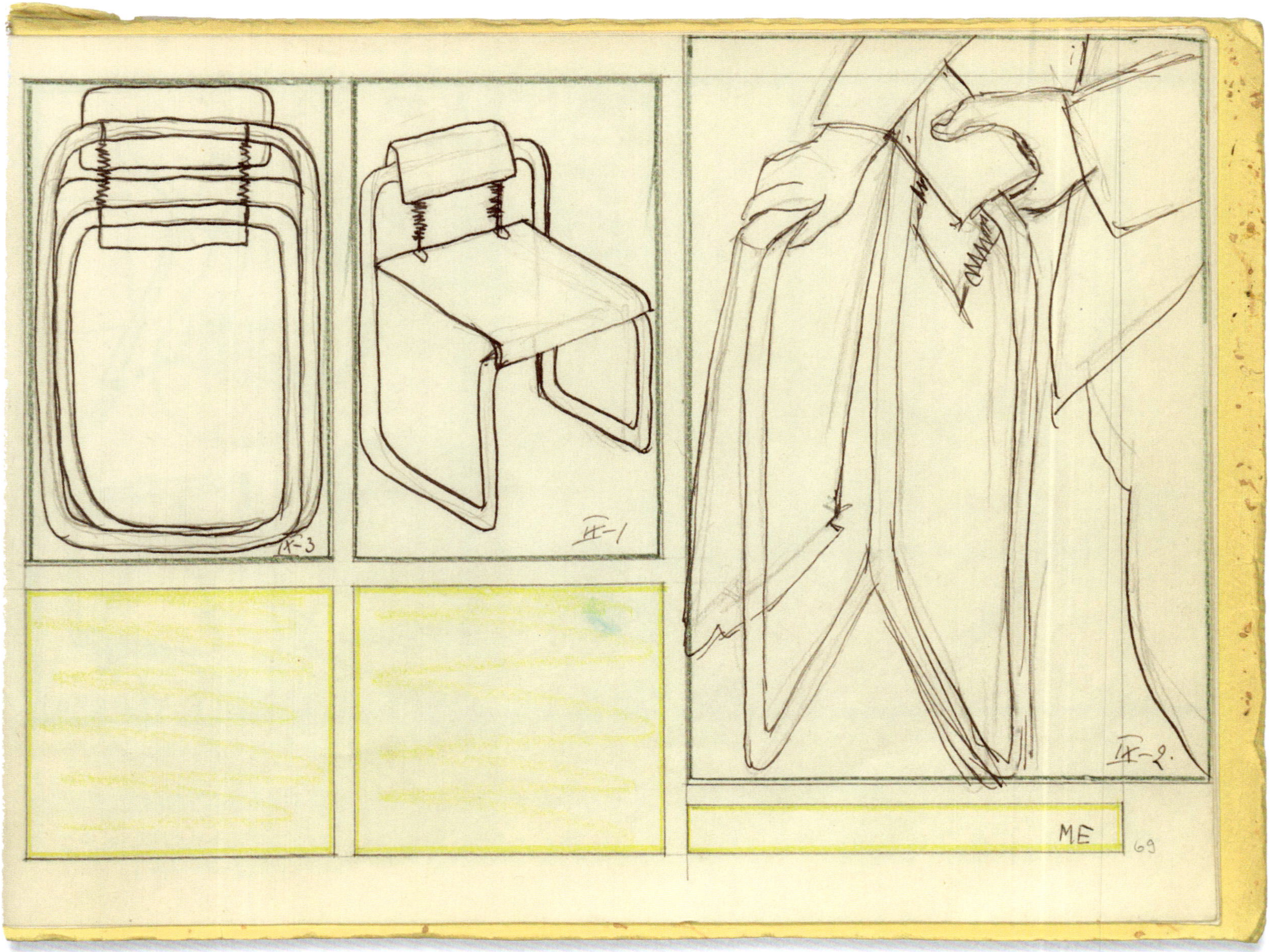
IX-3
II-1
IX-2.
ME
69

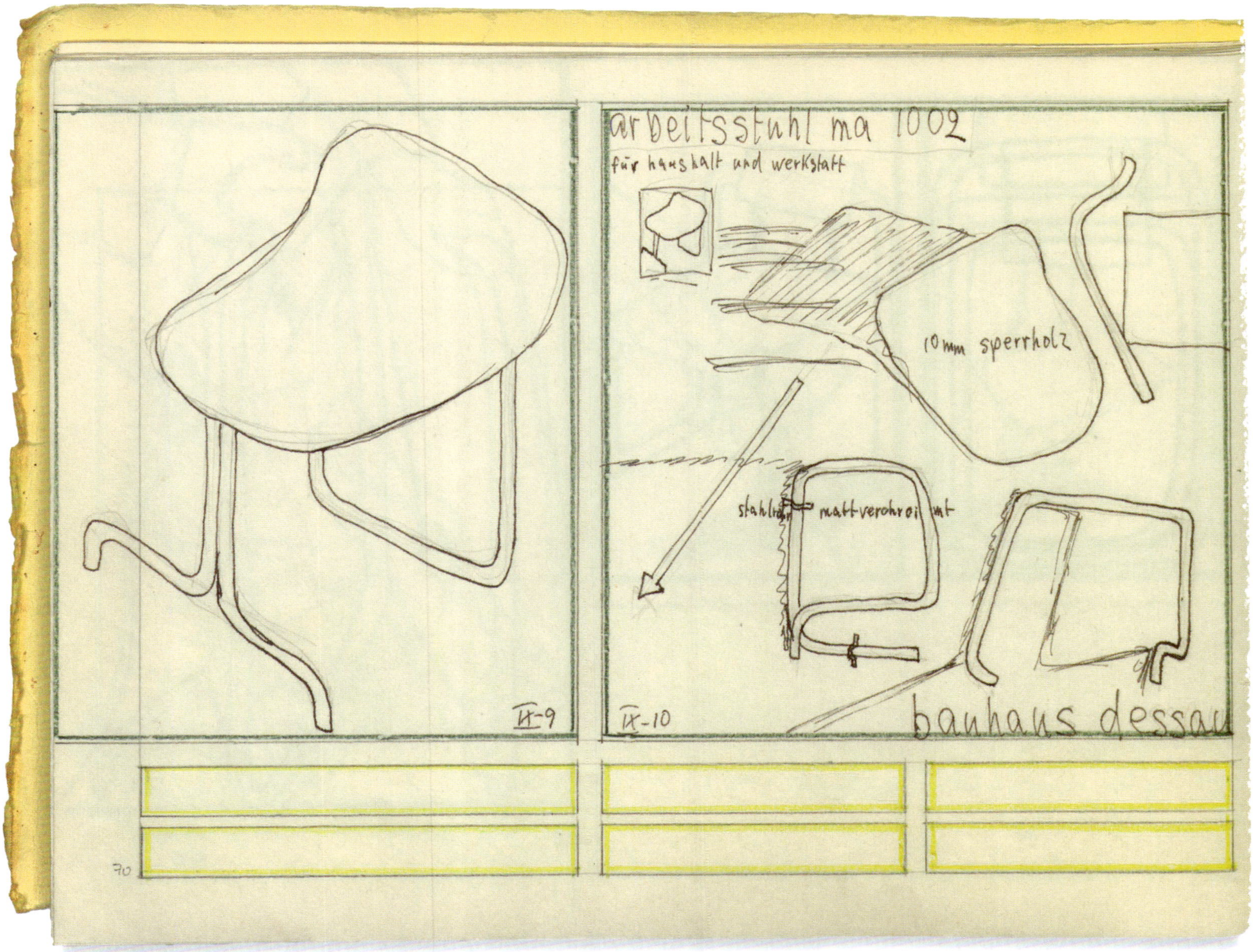
arbeitsstuhl ma 1002
für haushalt und werkstatt
10mm sperrholz
stahlrohr mattverchromt
IX-9
IX-10
bauhaus dessau
70

►► Pages 180–81: Erich Consemüller, *Untitled (Woman [Lis Beyer or Ise Gropius] in B3 Club chair by Marcel Breuer Wearing a Mask by Oskar Schlemmer and a Dress Made out of Fabric Designed by Beyer)*, c. 1926, negative film, 9 × 12 cm

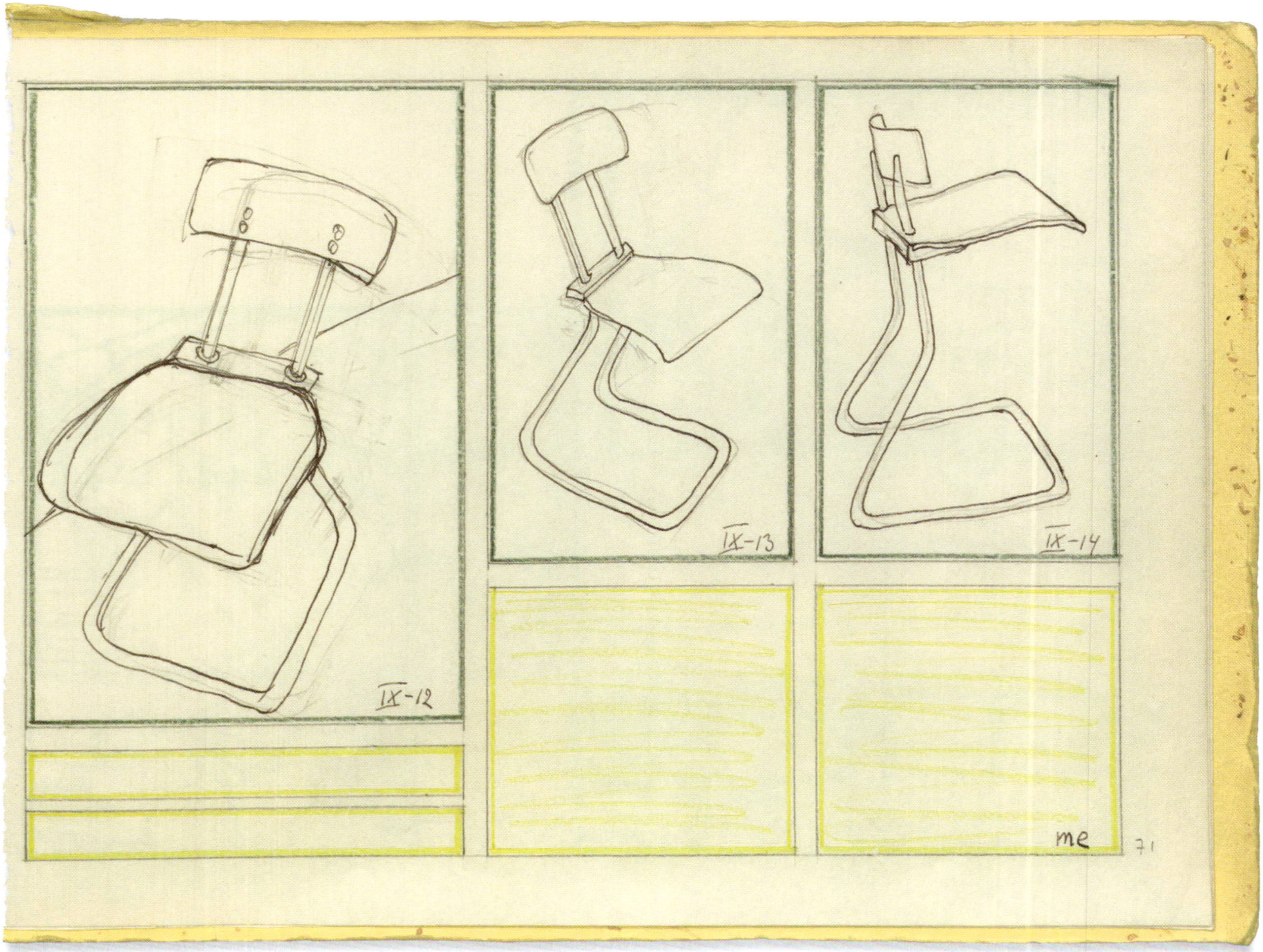

not exactly ergonomic yet strives at being comfortable. A real level of comfort is however only reached in chair number five – the famous 'Wassily' armchair, designed by Breuer, which in later editions would be equipped with a canvas upholstery consisting of so-called *Eisengarn* (steel yarn), a new type of thread developed by Bauhaus student Grete Reichardt (the first prototype depicted here was made before Reichardt was at the Bauhaus). Chair number four lacks the iconic status of the others. It is not as easily identifiable by a simple search on the internet. That is, I assume, because this chair rather belongs to the anonymous production of the Bauhaus carpentry workshop. The non-existent chair number six is evoked by a woman in a seating position whose seat is cut away in the montage.

This series of six images can be understood, in retrospect, to represent different lines of development departing from the Bauhaus. The first leads to IKEA, the second to Knoll and Vitra and the third to cyborgs. If one only looks at chairs one to four, the line 'modern furniture for the masses' comes to the fore. One sees a development which goes from intricately crafted, very individualistic pieces towards more geometrically simple designs that are fit to be produced on an industrial basis. Chair number four seems to anticipate later IKEA designs, which combine simple straight legs with flat planes for seating and back rest. IKEA would tweak the design to adjust the construction for flat-pack distribution, and made the chairs somewhat more comfortable. Its design philosophy nevertheless follows the basic principles set out by Walter Gropius, whose ambition to reconcile arts and crafts, and afterwards arts and industry, was originally meant to produce consumer goods for the masses. This ambition was certainly not always realized – it was only in the Hannes Meyer years that the Bauhaus did real business in this manner.[2] It took the commercially inclined spirit of IKEA to realize this ambition, and to make furniture that was indeed affordable (unlike Breuer's own designs).

The second line unfolds by looking at chairs number one to five. It is often said that Breuer bought his first bicycle in 1925 and that this gave him the idea for his tubular steel furniture. In experimenting with that material, he developed the design for his 'Wassily' chair – named after fellow Bauhaus master Wassily Kandinsky, who apparently was a fan of the chair. The Bauhauslers favoured this material because it really looked cool and industrial. The lightness of the chair also allowed for its mobility and the suggestion of transparency and porosity was much stronger than in the heavier wooden exemplars. The Wassily chair created a lineage that was very different from the anonymous chair number four. This tubular steel chair became part of the production of up-market signature design furniture and is still part of the collection of Knoll International (these days, one can buy a 'real' one for around 2,500 euros). Vitra, which does not have the rights to the full-scale version, has a miniature on offer at a scale of 1:6 – and this for around 280 euros.

The suggestive image number six, of the woman sitting on air, evoked for me a third line of development leading to cyborgs. Very often images depicting women on chairs or in cars are used to highlight the desirability of the chair or the car as consumption objects; the sexual attractiveness of the woman is somehow expected to be transferred to the object she is posing on. This kind of logic certainly was at work in many Bauhaus images displaying women on chairs – most famously the one in which Ise Gropius (or Lis Beyer?) was posing, equipped with a Schlemmer mask, in a Wassily chair for a photograph taken by Erich Consemüller. What happens however when the chair (or the car) is removed from the image, and the woman remains, strangely hovering in mid-air? Her sexual appeal now cannot be transferred to the nothingness that supports her, but is becoming imminent. The image seems to suggest that the woman now incorporates her own supporting devices – she is becoming a cyborg-like creature that is upheld by an invisible kind of exoskeleton. Is this the anticipation of the posthumanist vision articulated sixty years later by theorist Donna Haraway?[3] Is this the announcement of a new future in which boundaries between nature, human and machine are transgressed? Perhaps without consciously realizing it, Breuer might have left us here with a promise of a future in which the discriminatory gender policies of the Bauhaus somehow made way for the emergence of hybrid, contradictory and fractured entities that realize the original Bauhaus ambitions in unexpected, and feminist, ways.

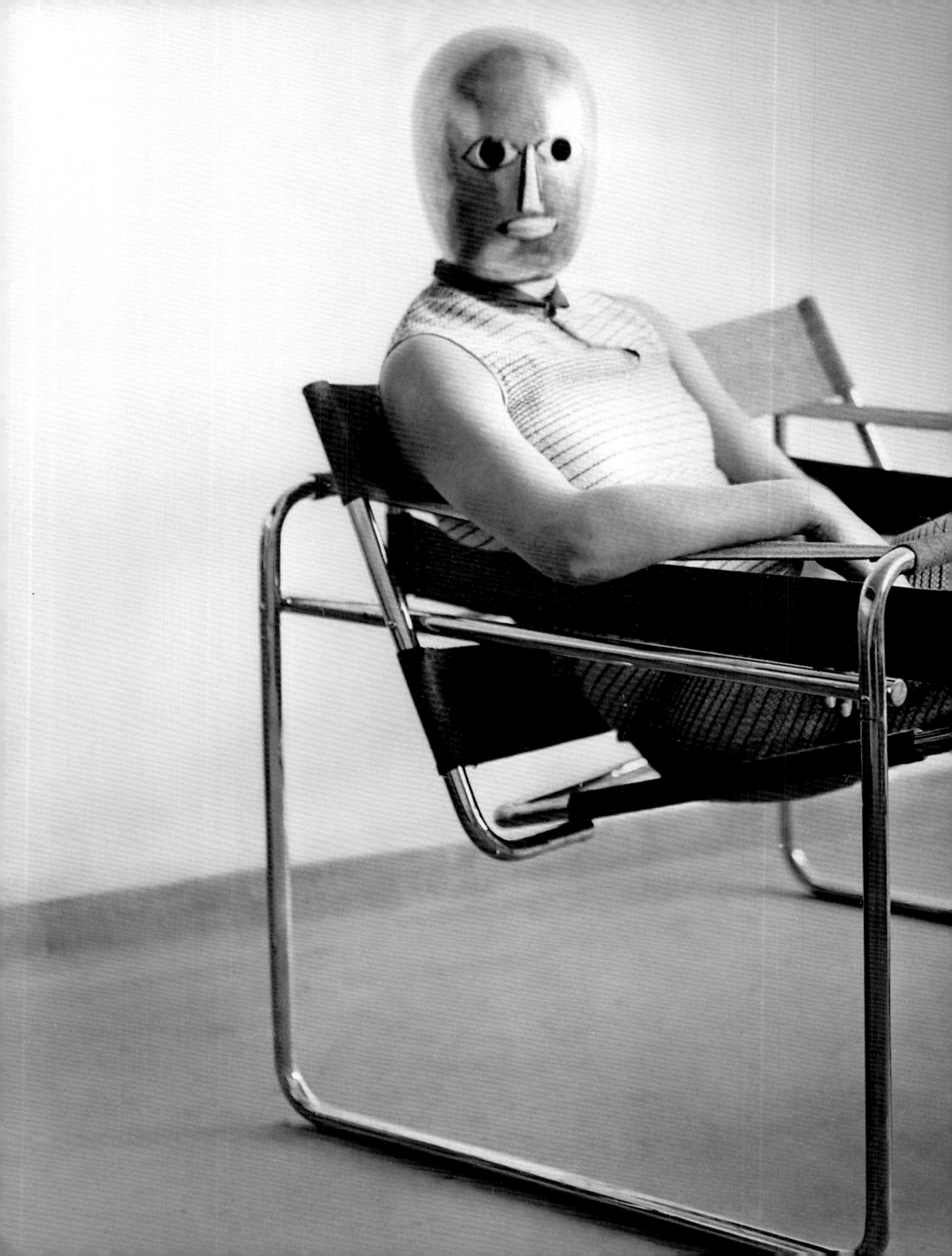

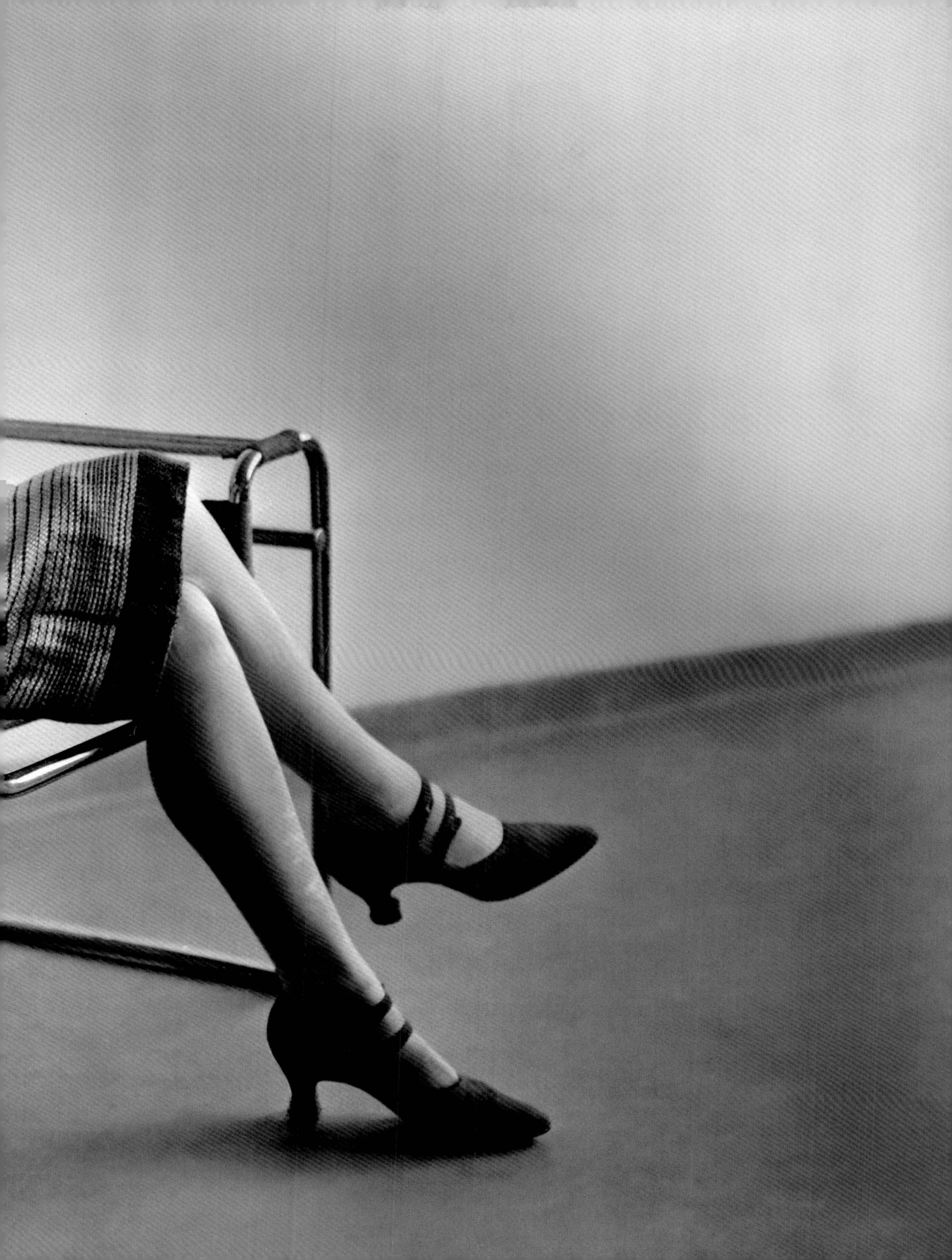

Designing Life

Beatriz Colomina and Mark Wigley

Walter Gropius orchestrated a sustained attempt to design the 'new human' as director of the Bauhaus, the school that did the most to consolidate the modern concept of industrial design and is still emblematic of the concept of design today. His founding manifesto of the Bauhaus in 1919 centred its experimental work on the damaged, traumatized and obsolete human figure immediately after the First World War: 'The old forms are in ruins, the benumbed world is shaken up, the old human spirit is invalidated and in flux toward a new form.'[1] Having been seriously wounded in 1918, Gropius repeatedly tried to counter any perception that the school was abandoning the human in favour of the standardizing logic of the machine. His 1925 *The New Architecture and the Bauhaus*, for example, insisted that his thinking, like that of most fellow architects, was galvanized by the 'violent interruption' of the war that called for 'an intellectual change of front'.[2] The dehumanizing effects of unrestrained mechanization are condemned: 'were mechanization an end in itself it would be an unmitigated calamity...stunting men and women into sub-human, robot-like automatons'.[3] Gropius's *Internationale Architektur* survey of the same year, based on the exhibition he had curated two years before at the Bauhaus, identified 'humanity' (*Menschheit*) as the most important, all-encompassing guiding principle.[4]

Yet Bauhaus design is ambiguously suspended between preserving and transforming the human, with the ultimate argument being that the human can only be preserved by being transformed. The well-designed object is a hybrid of human and machine. It is both an interface to the vast, rapidly evolving industrial machine world and a way of industrializing the human – or reindustrializing the human species that had already been turned into a machine-like servant of mechanization. The Bauhaus was a belated response to the nineteenth-century debates that machines such as those in the big factories were now being treated as a new form of life and humans were increasingly only valued inasmuch as they could act like machines, performing repetitive movements that keep the new mechanical species alive.

Unknown photographer, Walter Gropius on the Western Front, August 1916

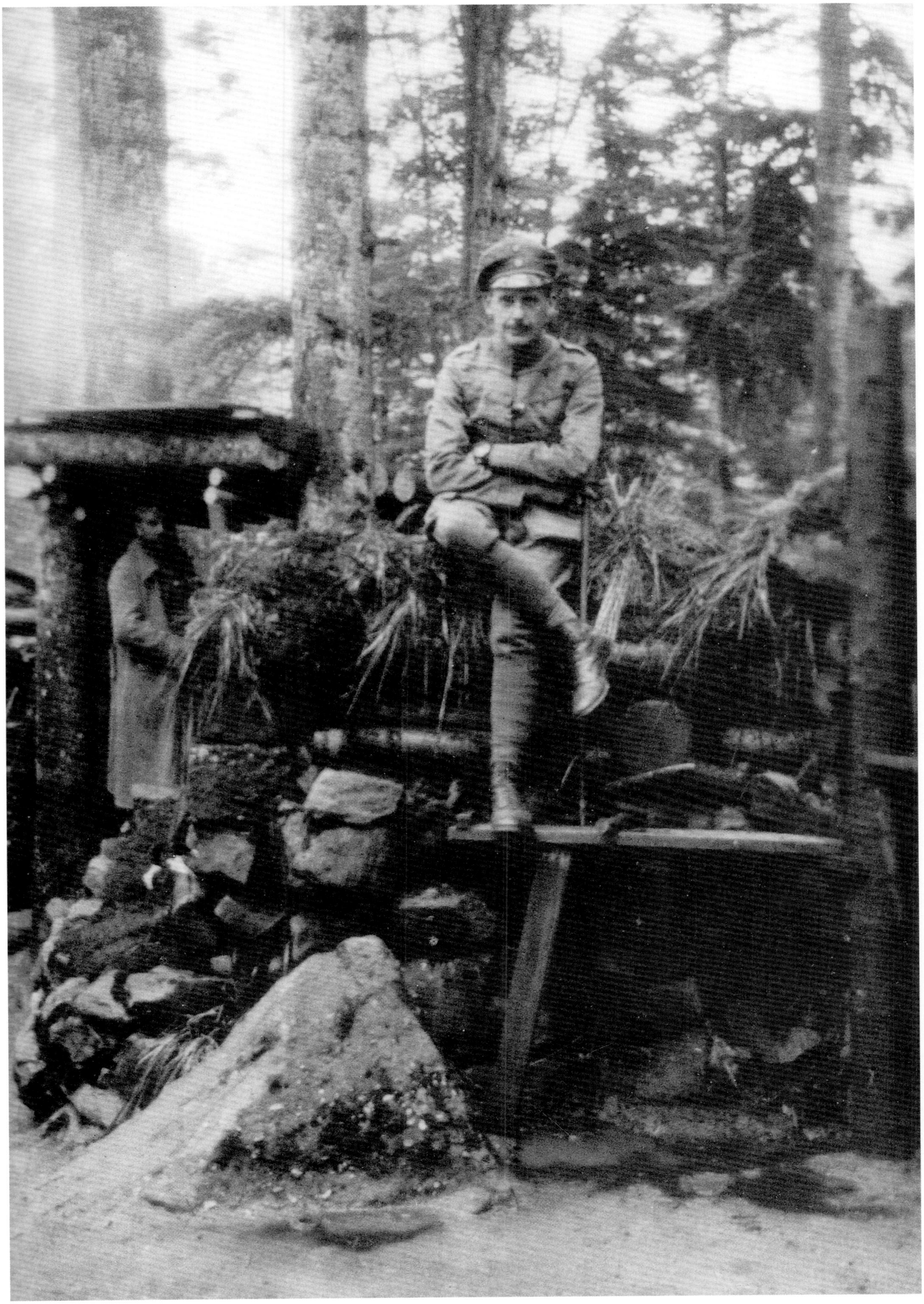

Oskar Schlemmer, costume design for *Das Triadische Ballett* (The Triadic Ballet), in Oskar Schlemmer *et al.*, *Die Bühne im Bauhaus* (The Stage at Bauhaus), Bauhausbücher 4, Munich: Albrecht Langen Verlag, 1925, p. 35

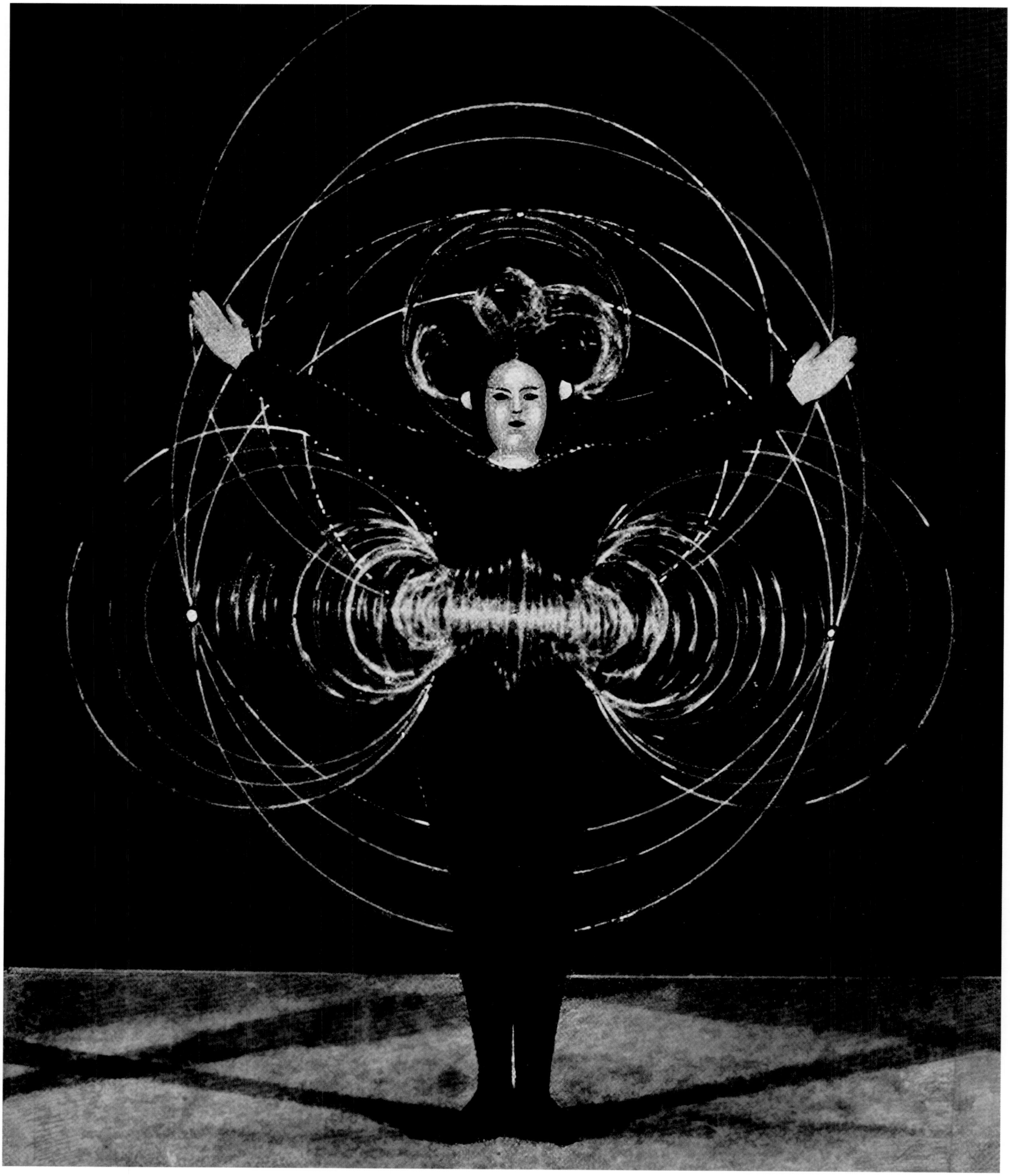

Central to the Bauhaus experiment was the explicit project of designing a 'new human' adapted to the demands of modern industrialization. The species traumatized by mechanization and its apotheosis in the war machine was to be itself turned into a more refined industrial product. All the different phases of the Bauhaus rethought the body and brain of the individual. Bauhaus design was directly understood as a form of bio-technical engineering. But it was never simply a matter of modernizing the species and equipping it for modern life with a set of efficient industrial objects. Bauhaus design gave modern equipment its own life. The aim was not to design a more modern life as a kind of performance for citizens to act out, with the assistance of Bauhaus objects acting as useful and loyal props. Rather, the objects themselves were seen to act out the new life. The objects became surrogates or avatars of the new human. Simply purchasing the objects would give access to modernity, even to the new sense of human biology. A couple of chairs or a lamp or two are sufficient. This freed up the consumer to live whatever version of life they could. Despite the counter efforts during Hannes Meyer's short tenure as director (1928–30), a huge part of the viral success of Bauhaus design over the past hundred years was its successful attempt to seemingly depoliticize the designed object, allowing almost any personal or collective ideology to be supported by the visual and tactile aesthetic of smooth surfaces and simple geometry. The deep legacy of the Bauhaus is simultaneously aesthetic and economic. The Bauhaus object serves no particular lifestyle other than the global marketplace itself.

The ubiquitous iPhone of today, for example, faithfully embodies the Bauhaus logic of smooth simplicity and wants to appear to take no position and therefore be appropriate for use by anyone, anywhere, any time. It offers itself as the ultimate lightweight smooth servant while actively sustaining the project of turning every second of everyone's lives on the planet into full-time work. Mobile phone users are used by mobile phones. They are seemingly in charge of unprecedented amounts of connectivity and interactivity, but are in fact permanently attached to a vast machine that is now bigger than the planet and treats them as a useful, well-trained but ultimately disposable resource.

It was not by chance that Apple co-founder Steve Jobs absorbed the logic of the Bauhaus in 1981 when first visiting the Aspen International Design Conference with its campus, furniture and typography designed by Herbert Bayer, and he would declare in a 1983 speech at the conference that 'new design should take Bauhaus as its starting point and relate more to the functionality and true character'.[5] But this rhetoric of the smooth, simple object is never more than rhetoric. In fact, the mobile phone reveals almost nothing of its operation or effects. Indeed, Bauhaus and Bauhaus-inspired objects are rarely more efficient or produced more efficiently. They tend to be paradoxically more expensive representations of utilitarian efficiency. They insert a certain gloss as a kind of anaesthetic right at the acupuncture points where the human species is least certain of itself.[6] The Bauhaus object speaks neither of the human nor of the vast ever-expanding technological world that is paradoxically both the most human thing about humans and seemingly the greatest threat to them.

Humans only became human in transforming themselves with technology a few hundred thousand years ago. The human is the species that redesigns itself. But if design is uniquely human in this sense, and always redesigns the human, the human is also unique in designing life itself – crafting new forms of mechanical, electronic and biological life. The ancient search for a thinking machine that would be indistinguishable from a human may have already been accomplished. Humans are increasingly asked by machines to prove that they are human. Whole new forms of life are now produced in laboratories with genetic editing techniques. With bio-design, the sense of the human redesigning itself and every element of the living environment is direct and palpable. It is as if the human brain has touched and transformed everything it encounters. New organisms are constantly invented and chimeric hybrids of humans and other animals are already here. This fusion of machines, organisms, computation and genetics that is moving from the laboratory into everyday life – and into the land, air and the oceans – poses urgent ethical questions that call for a public conversation about design.

In these terms, Bauhaus design is not simply a specific phase in design history. The Bauhaus aesthetic is an anaesthetic – a way for our species to remain insensitive to the shocking scale and effect of design, to the rapidly evolving life of objects and the ongoing redesign of life itself. This redesign is not carried out by a set of 'designers' but by a vast interactive ecology in which no simple distinction between human and machine is possible. Humans, other animals, plants, technologies, bacteria, data and software form a dense plastic ecology that is unaffected by a perfect looking and unchanging chair or table lamp. The ever-expanding legacy of the Bauhaus experiment simply reflects the deep fear of our species: to simply look at ourselves and ask, 'Are we human?'

Unknown photographer (Bauhaus student), *Disappearing Figure Seated on Marcel Breuer Chair*, *c*. 1932, photograph

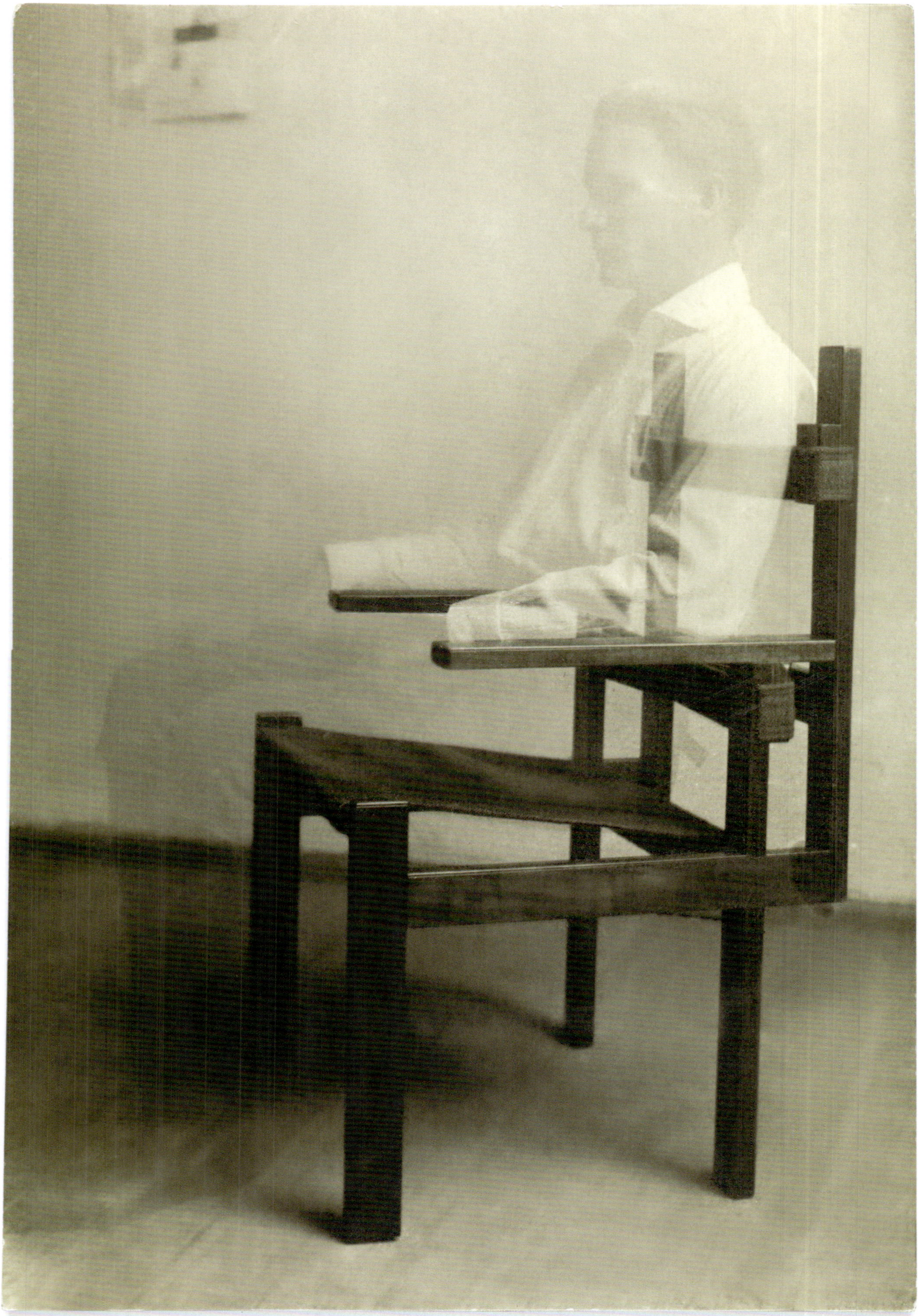

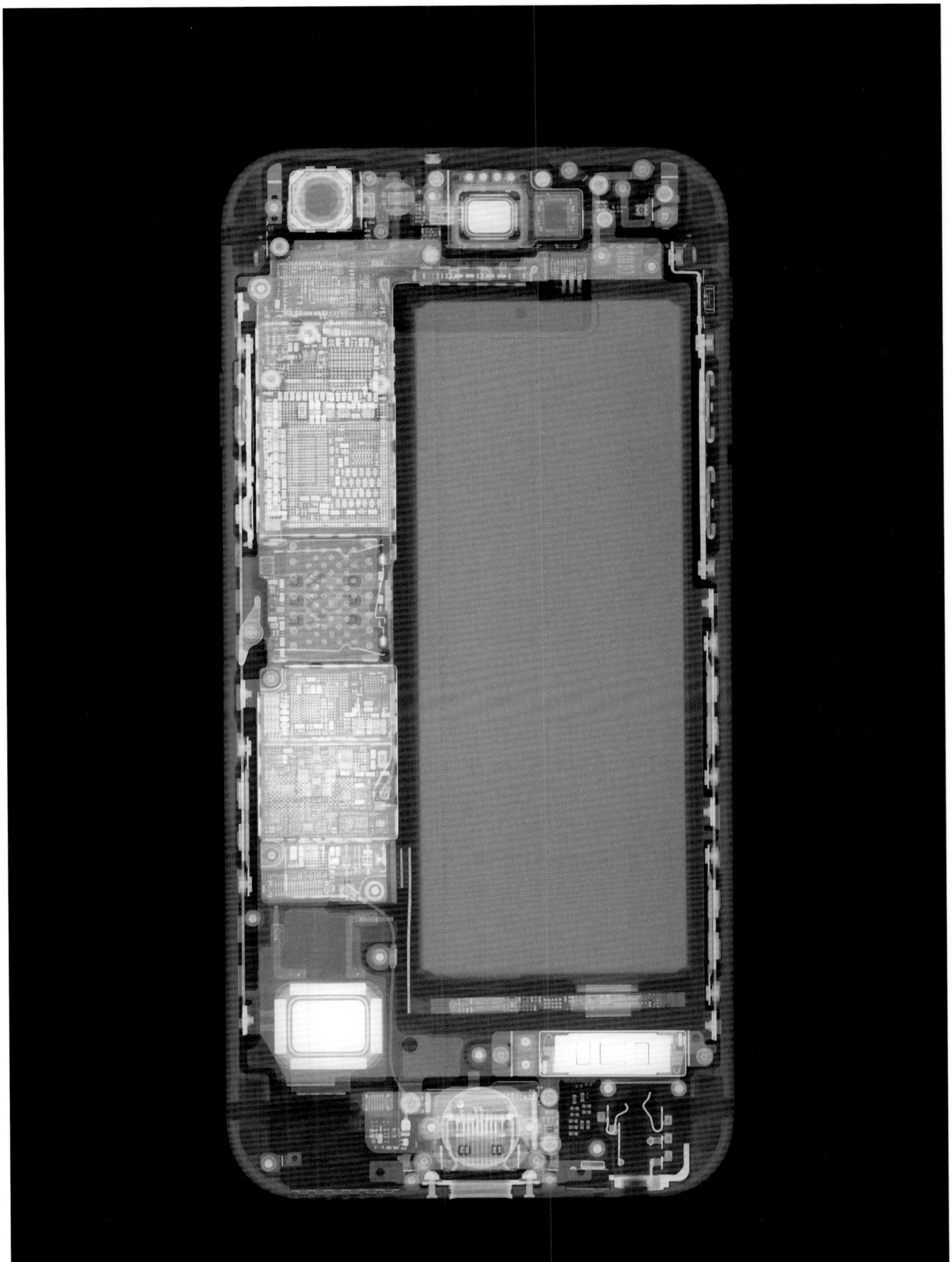

The Red Itinerary

Daniel Talesnik

Vilified for his politics and for the politics of some students, Hannes Meyer was expelled from the Bauhaus directorship on 1 August 1930 by the Dessau city council. The declared reasons were that he was a Marxist and that he had not been transparent about his beliefs when he was hired. After his expulsion, Meyer personally organized his next job by contacting the Soviet embassy and the Soviet trade representative in Germany.[1] Before the end of 1930 Meyer had moved to the Soviet Union, first with one student, and by the beginning of 1931 there were a total of seven Bauhaus graduates working with him.

The seven students were René Mensch, Klaus Meumann, Konrad Püschel, Philipp Tolziner, Béla Scheffler, Antonin Urban and Tibor Weiner, all of whom had studied architecture under Meyer at the Bauhaus. This short-lived 'brigade' was part of a larger Bauhaus scene in the Soviet Union during the 1930s that included both architecture and non-architecture Bauhaus students.[2] German architect Bruno Taut also had a brief Soviet stint, as did Werner Schneidratus (who worked in the Moscow office of Albert Kahn), and Ernst May and his Brigade in its two iterations (that included some architects with Bauhaus connections). Kurt Liebknecht, who was part of May's Brigade, estimated in his memoir that between 1933 and 1936 the Soviet Association of Architects had a thousand members who were foreigners, and half of those were German.[3] Considering that not every foreign architect was enrolled in the association, the actual number of foreign architects in the Soviet Union was likely much larger. Although from the standpoint of 1930, the Soviet Union was a haven – particularly for those on the left and far left – these numbers do not imply that all of these foreigners were politically aligned with communist ideas (in hindsight some were not even anti-fascists). Nevertheless, they were working for the Soviet cause and, at a minimum, did not actively disapprove of it at the time.

From the estate of Philipp Tolziner, Tibor Weiner, Margarete Mengel, Philipp Tolziner, Antonin Urban, Frau Urban (bottom photograph only), Konrad Püschel and unknown marcher (top photograph only), 1 May 1931, Moscow, gelatin silver prints mounted on paper, images 8.6 × 11.7 cm, 12.6 × 8.3 cm, paper 29.5 × 20.9 cm

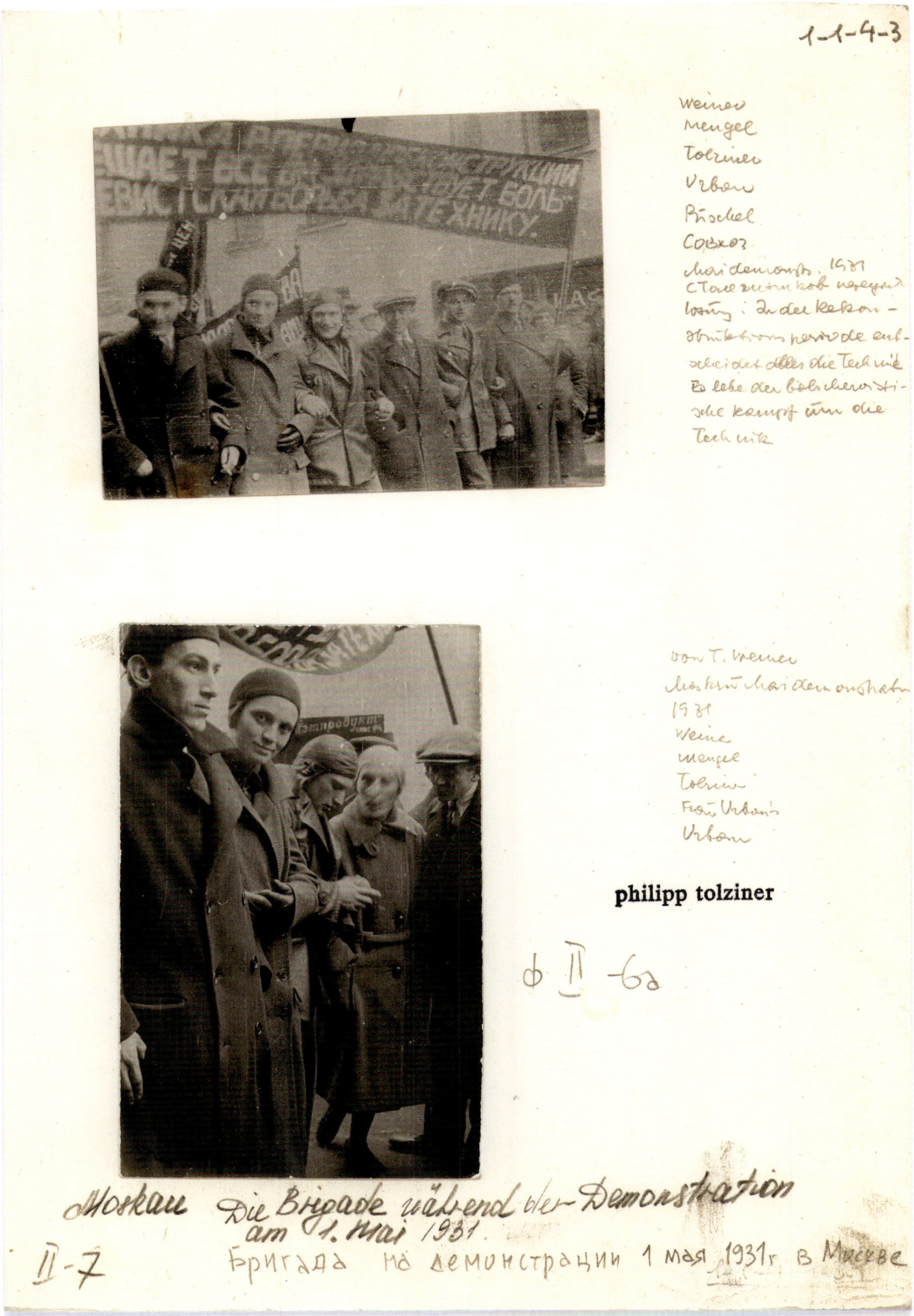

Why did so many foreign architects, especially Germans, work in the Soviet Union during this period? A variety of factors played a role here. Europe at large was submerged in an economic crisis after the stock market crash of 1929, and high unemployment rates were helping the National Socialists rise to power. In the early 1930s, when the Soviet Union was pushing for an unprecedented transformation, the government repressed the architecture of its avant-gardes from the 1920s, and instead invited foreign experts to collaborate with a normalization (standardization) of architectural solutions to speed up the process. Industrialization had been decreed a national objective in 1925, and the efforts related to this goal had been systematized through the First Five-Year Plan for the Development of the National Economy. The development targets were extremely ambitious, and there was a huge demand for infrastructure of all sorts, hence the Soviet Union welcomed foreign architects, urban planners and construction-related professionals to design and build industrial, educational, residential and urban infrastructure. Meyer and his students, as well as other brigades of foreign architects, were brought to the Soviet Union as building technicians to help keep up with the new demands.

Of course, Meyer's architectural teachings at the Bauhaus had focused on searching for objective inputs; he had envisioned the architect as a technician who could interpret evidence and turn it into designs that served society. This rationality was affected by what Meyer and his former students encountered in the Soviet Union. Perhaps not at first, but as the 1930s advanced, several of their projects exemplify both a moving away from their Bauhaus origins and the shifts in the Soviet discourse. This is visible for example in the design of buildings, and is already evident in some aspects of the 1931 Palace of the Soviets competition entry by Tolziner, Urban and Weiner (with Meyer allegedly acting as a consultant, but evidently involved in the design), such as the use of statuary in public space, the inclusion of a frieze in the main building with the phrase 'Workers of the World Unite' and a mural on the façade of the secondary building. It is also clear in the 1935 Kolkhoz club prototype Urban made with his wife Ludmila Konstantinova-Urban, in the squared columns with decorated capitals in the interior, the double-pitched roofs with roof tiles, arched windows, the pergolas in the exterior and a grand column with what appears to be a statue of Lenin on top at the entrance.[4]

The first show trials in 1936 prompted the beginning of the exodus of all of the foreigners who could leave. Those who stayed past the end of 1937 usually had no choice, and many ended up in the Gulag, accused of espionage. Meyer had the option of exiting in June 1936 and went back to his native Switzerland, where he worked on the Mümliswil Children's Home. In 1938 he travelled to Mexico to participate in XVIth International Housing and Town Planning Congress, where he established the contacts that eventually led him in 1939 to move to Mexico, where he stayed for a decade. Mexico, a country that had its own revolutionary experience throughout the 1910s, offered Meyer another opportunity to participate in post-revolutionary efforts through the development of a pedagogical project that could influence the urban development of a country. However, Meyer's involvement in the Mexican Institute for Planning and Urbanism only lasted for the first couple of years he lived there.

Konrad Püschel, general plan of Hamhŭng, North Korea,
1956, gelatin silver print mounted on paper, 29.7 × 21 cm

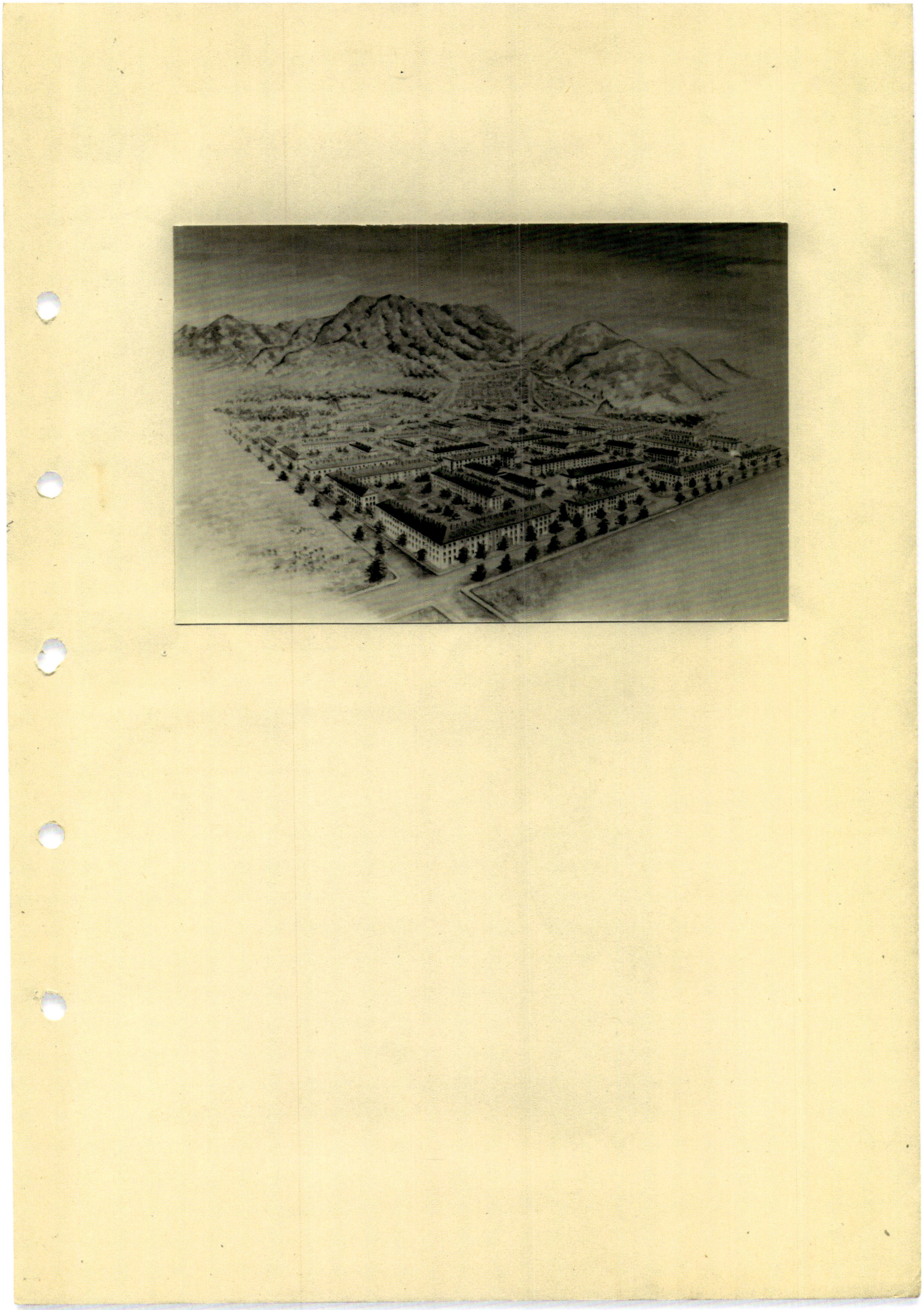

‘Der Mann der eine Stadt erbaute’ (The Man who Built a City), article about Tibor Weiner, 1962, offset print, 31.5 × 23.8 cm

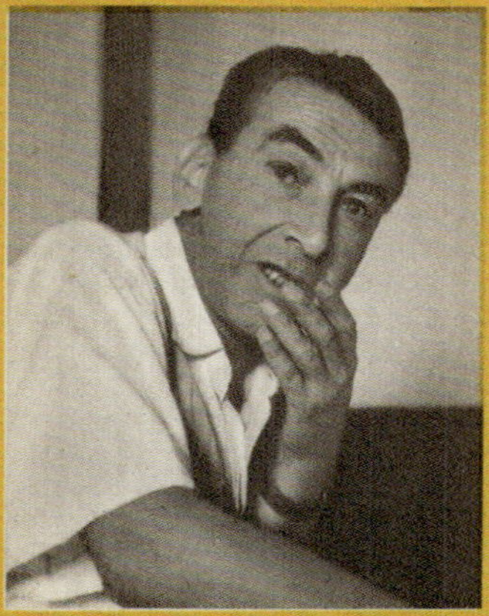

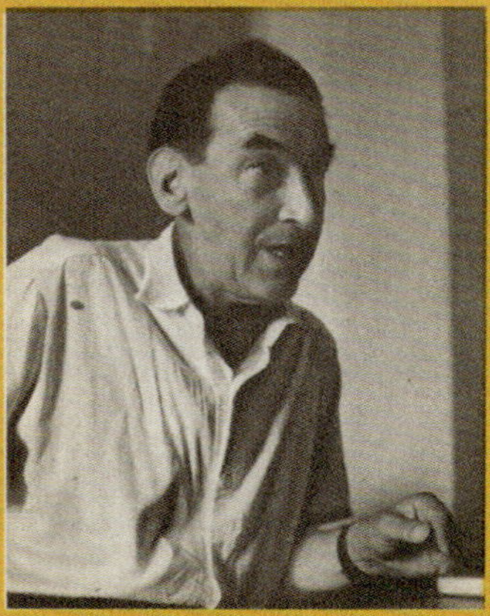

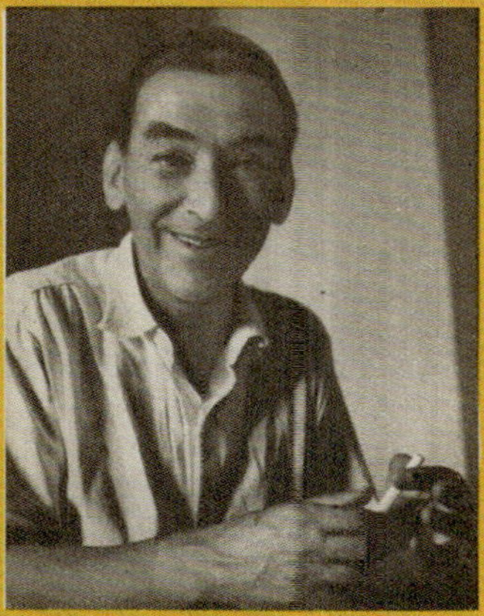

DER MANN der eine Stadt erbaute

Es ist eine merkwürdige Laune des Schicksals, daß ich mit ihm erst jetzt bekannt geworden bin, obwohl ich seit etwa zwölf Jahren jährlich mehrere Reportagen über Dunaújváros schreibe. Beim Durchblättern der alten Aufsätze sehe ich, daß ich fast alle interessanten Ereignisse und Menschen der Stadt kennengelernt habe.

Aber diesem leicht ergrauten Mann mit den markanten Zügen, dem Hauptarchitekten der Stadt, Tibor Weiner, bin ich erst jetzt begegnet, und nicht einmal am Reißbrett oder während er die Bauarbeiten inspizierte. Im Gebäude des städtischen Rates — Weiner ist Stellvertreter des Vorsitzenden des Rates — diktierte er gerade seiner Sekretärin einen Text in Verbindung mit der Verkehrsregelung. Das Fenster seines Zimmers geht auf einen Park, in dem dunkeläugige Stiefmütterchen ihre Blüten auf unzähligen Beeten entfalten. Vor knapp einer Minute hat sich der Leiter der städtischen Buchhandlung gebrüstet, daß in Dunaújváros dreißig Personen die Bücher vertreiben und der Umsatz sich von Jahr zu Jahr um zwanzig Prozent erhöht.

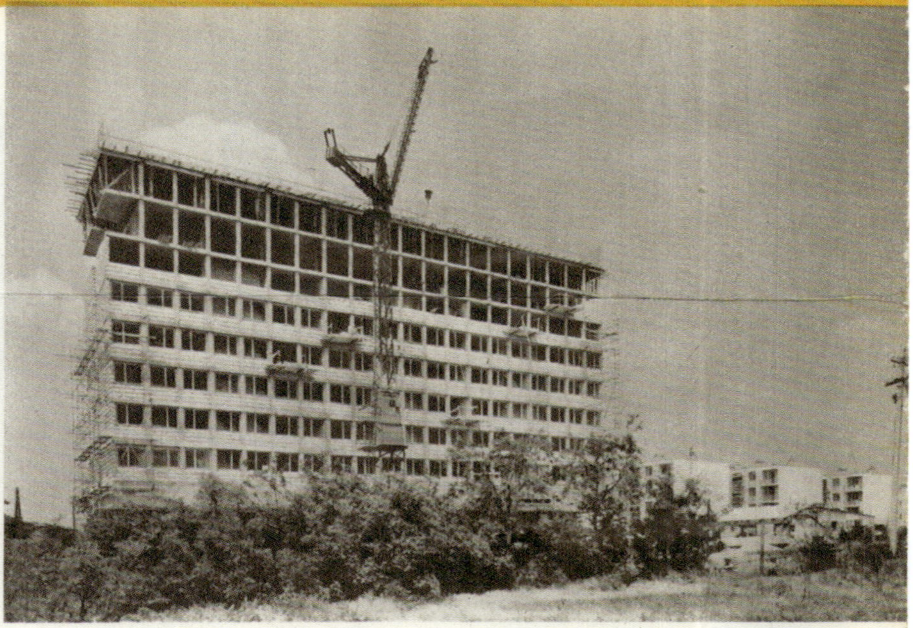

In diesem Haus werden 80 Junggesellen ein komfortables Heim finden

Im Foyer des Arbeiterheims

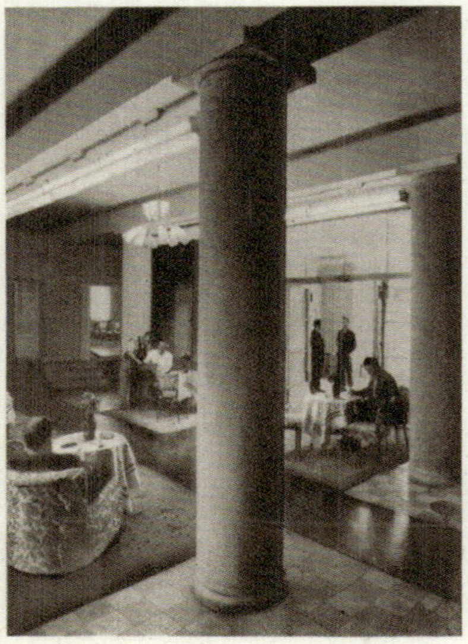

Der Hauptarchitekt fragte mich:

„Sie interessieren sich für die Stadt?“

„Besonders Ihr Leben interessiert mich jetzt.“

Zunächst versuchte er, mich zu überzeugen, wie uninteressant sein Leben ist im Vergleich mit jenem Wunder, daß hier in kurzer Zeit eine Stadt entstand. Währenddessen wickelte er vier Telefongespräche ab, diskutierte heftig mit irgend jemandem über irgendwelche Baupläne, unterzeichnete Urkunden und dann, nachdem er wohl vergessen hatte, worüber wir zu sprechen begonnen haben, beantwortete er geduldig meine Fragen.

„Seit wann leben Sie hier?“

„Seit fünf Jahren.“

„Und seit wann arbeiten Sie in der Stadt?“

„Seit zwölf Jahren.“

Er machte noch einen Versuch, das Gespräch in eine andere Richtung zu lenken. Er warf ein, daß das Durchschnittsalter der Bevölkerung der Stadt siebenundzwanzig Jahre ist, aber ich lachte nur und leierte herunter: „Die Stadtfläche beträgt eintausendeinhundert Katastraljoch, die Zahl ihrer Gebäude . . .“

Er winkte resigniert ab und ergab sich. So sprachen wir denn über ihn, den Erbauer der Stadt.

Sein Leben gleicht einem Roman, der

6

Regarding the students, the careers of Weiner, Püschel, Tolziner and Mensch extended well beyond the period they spent together in the Soviet Union and took divergent paths. Some moved beyond Europe to Latin America or the Middle East, while others lived out the war years either as soldiers or imprisoned. Weiner went to Chile for several years and later returned to his native Hungary in 1948, where he subsequently worked as an urban planner and teacher. After leaving the Soviet Union, Püschel returned to Germany, fought in the Second World War and later dedicated his life to a professorship in Weimar – save for an intense work assignment in North Korea in the 1950s, for which he headed an East German delegation that was sent to help with reconstruction after the Korean War. Weiner and Püschel's work as urban planners in a Cold War context could be read as a continuation of what they had attempted in the Soviet Union in the 1930s, but under very different circumstances. Tolziner, by contrast, never left the Soviet Union. He survived the Gulag and became a specialist in the restoration of historic buildings in the Urals, only to return to Moscow after he was rehabilitated to work once again on the design of collective housing types. Mensch worked as an architect in Iran, Chile and his native Switzerland, under circumstances removed from a red itinerary, but still by and large determined by Cold War variables. Of the remaining members of the original Meyer group, Scheffler and Urban died in the Soviet Gulag and there is no trace of Meumann after the 1930s, which probably means he shared the same tragic fate.

The tendency of architects such as Meyer, Püschel, Mensch and Weiner to jump from one country to another was often the product of changes in the political tides as well as personal circumstances. After leaving the Soviet Union, Meyer was looking for work opportunities and a place from which to continue developing his ideas, but for Weiner, a left-wing architect of Jewish descent, it was a matter of life and death. Returning to Hungary, where Admiral Horthy was ruling over his so-called 'kingdom' of Hungary, was a particularly bleak prospect, and South Africa, Ceylon, England, Turkey and Australia – all places where he thought about or attempted to emigrate to – trace his search for a safe haven. Eventually, Weiner managed to secure papers for Chile, and it is possible to assume that this emigration saved his life.[5]

Although Weiner's building designs in Chile, just like Meyer's building drawings in Mexico, show no apparent connection to the type of architecture that had taken over in the Soviet Union, when Weiner later returned to Hungary and worked on the planning for Sztálinváros (renamed Dunaújváros), he effectively engaged with ideas related to post-war socialist city planning, visible in the monumental main avenue or the Communist Party headquarters on the main square. Also exemplary of a red itinerary is Püschel's work in North Korea. These examples speak to a phenomenon that several of these architects share: their distinct professional approaches can be read against their Bauhaus origins and Soviet experience, but are not reducible to them.[6]

The CIAM Protest: From Moscow to the Patris II (1932)

Thomas Flierl

Against all international expectations – after all, Walter Gropius, Le Corbusier, Erich Mendelsohn and others had been invited – there was no modern architect among the main award-winners (Ivan Žoltovsky, Boris Iofan and Hector Hamilton) of the first competition round for the Palace of the Soviets in Moscow announced on 29 February 1932. So even before the assembly of delegates (CIRPAC) of the International Congresses of Modern Architecture (CIAM) in Barcelona (29 to 31 March), Le Corbusier, who had participated in the competition, met with the former People's Commissioner for Education, Anatoly Lunacharsky, in Geneva on 5 March, and again voiced his indignation in a letter to him dated 13 March. The CIRPAC assembly in Barcelona then voted 'to resolutely take a stand against this decision of the competition and make the responsible authorities in Soviet Russia aware of the mistakes that were made'. Turning down Moscow's invitation to the 4th CIAM Congress was even considered. Finally, the president, vice-president and general secretary of CIAM sent a letter of protest to Stalin personally on 20 April: 'The Palace of the Soviets, which was presented to the modern world as the spiritual crowning of the rational work of the five-year plan, will demonstrate the subservience of modern technology to reactionary intellectual forces: The Palace of Soviets, in the shape that the committee apparently wants to lend it, will embody the old regimes and demonstrate the total contempt for the gigantic cultural efforts of modernity. What a dramatic betrayal!' Iofan's design expresses 'in the most bourgeois way the most academic thinking'; that of Žoltovsky is 'a copy of the architecture of the Italian Renaissance', and the form of the architecture 'opposes the mass of the people with the inherited power of feudal rulers. The undisputable perfection of these architectural forms can, of course, not claim to satisfy needs and problems, which can only be solved by applying the achievements of modern technology.' And Hamilton's design is 'only a grandiloquent transcription of pompous methods from the era of monarchies under a modern guise'.

Below and page 196: Protest letter (in French) to Joseph Stalin, signed by Sigfried Giedion, Victor Bourgeois and Cornelis van Eesteren, 20 April 1932, type on paper, 29.7 × 21 cm

4-1-51F

Les Congrès Internationaux d'Architecture Moderne.

Secrétariat: Zurich, 7, Doldertal 7. 20. avril 1932.

Monsieur Staline,
Président du Conseil des commissaires du peuple,
M o s c o u .

Monsieur le Président,

Nous avons l'honneur de vous faire part d'une situation nouvelle intervenue entre l'autorité suprême de l'URSS et l'opinion mondiales. Il s'agit de faits qui ont provoqué subitement dans les milieux professionnels la plus grande émotion. Mais ces faits d'ordre professionel risquent d'avoir sur l'opinion publique une réaction dont nous avons pensé devoir vous entretenir.

Il s'agit des décisions récentes prises à l'occasion de la construction du palais des soviets.

En 1931 le gouvernement de l'URSS, par l'entremise d'un comité pour la construction du palais des soviets, faisait appel à la collaboration mondiale en ouvrant un concours international destiné à fournir les plans de construction du palais. Aucun jury n'était designé mais il apparaissait, comme évident que le verdict qui serait porté,serait inspiré de la ligne générale qui conduit le plan quinquenal et représenterait la plus éclatante manifestation de la pensée contemporaine. Le palais des soviets parle le langage infalsifiable de l'architecture exprimerait la révolution accomplie par la civilisation neuve des temps modernes.

L'appel du comité aux architectes précisait que: "le plan quinquenal ayant réussi avec éclat, le gouvernement de l'URSS, dans le désir de couronner l'oeuvre entreprise décide de réaliser l'oeuvre adoptée en 1922 par la réunion plenière de la IIIème internationale, la construction du palais de soviets. C'est dans ces conditions que des architectes et des penseurs du monde entier offrirent au gouvernement de l'URSS le fruit de leur travail.
En date du 29 février l'agence Tass communiquait : " le conseil de construction du palais des soviets vient de terminer l'examen des projets présentés au concours.
Les projets des architectes Joltovsky et Jofan, ainsi que celui de l'architecte américain G.O. Hamilton ont été considérés comme les meilleurs.....
...... le conseil a décidé de prolonger le concours en indiquant que lesprojets ultérieurs doivent être composés de manière à pouvoir adapter les meilleures méthodes de l'architecture classique à l'aboutissement de la technique architecturale moderne.

La " Bauwelt" (Heft 12.1932) publie ces trois sus mentionnés: celui de Jofan exprime sous la forme la plus bourgeoise la pensée la plus académique.
Celui de Joltovsky est une copie de l'architecture de la renaissance italienne cette fomme d'architecture opposait aux masses populaires la puissance héréditaire des princes féodaux, la perfection

▶▶ Pages 198–99: Sigfried Giedion, *Protest Collage*, sent by CIAM to Joseph Stalin, 1931, collage, 24.4 × 18.2 cm

- 2 -

incontestable de ses formes d'architecture ne peut, bien entendu, prétendre à satisfaire les besoins et les problèmes, dont la solution n'est possible qu'avec l'application des conquêtes de la technique moderne.

Celui de Hamilton n'est qu'une transcription présomptueuse sous forme d'apparence moderne des procédés pompeux de l'époque des rois, sans aucun rapport avec les fonctions organiques du programme du palais.

Le verdict du comité du palais des soviets est une insulte directe à l'esprit de la révolution russe et à la réalisation du plan quinquenal.

Tournant le dos aux inspirations de la société moderne qui a trouvé sa première expression en Russie soviétique ce verdict consacre l'architecture d'apparat des anciens régimes monarchiques, Le palais des soviets proposé au monde moderne comme le couronnement spirituel l'immense oeuvre rationnelle du plan quinquenal montera l'asservissement des techniquesmodernes au bénéfice de la réaction spirituelle: le palais des soviets incarnera dans la forme que prétend lui donner le comité les régimes anciens et manifestera le dédain total du gigantesque effort cultural des temps modernes. Dramatique trahison !

Le monde qui a lex yeux fixés sur le développement de l'oeuvre soviétique en sera stupéfait.

Dans sa réunion du 29 mars 1932 à Barcelone, le cirpac (Comité international pour la réalisation des problèmes architecturaux contemporains) représentant le Congrès international d'architecture moderne fondé à La Sarraz en 1928, a examiné la situation ainsi créée à Moscou, étant précisément réuni à Barcelone pour fixer les dernières modalités du IV-e congrès qui doit se tenir sur le thème " la ville fonctionnelle ", il a décidé de s'adresser à l'autorité suprème de l'Urss pour lui signaler la gravité desfaits dont il est parlé ci-dessus et de considérer que l'esprit qui a dicté la décision du comité constitue une erreur qui ne saurait subsister, il lui demande de bien vouloir par une intervention opportune apporter au verdict du comité la modifiation qu'attendent les élites. Car s'il devait être suivi à la décision du comité pour la construction du palais. des soviets il deviendrait douteux que le cirpac engagé devant l'opinion publique par ses travaux antérieurs et sa destination même puisse continuer à considérer que l'Urss soit un pays désigné pour abriter un congrès fructueux sur le thème qui ne prête à aucun compromis: " la ville fonctionnelle".-

C'est en soumettant cette question capitale à votre sagesse que nous vousprions, Monsieur le Président, d'agréer l'expression de notre considération la plus grande.

Signé: le Président:c.van Eesteren
Vice-Président: Victor Bourgeois
Secrétaire général : Giedion

When information spread that the design of Hamilton, a New York-based architect, was to be realized, since he had been invited to Moscow, a second letter was sent to Stalin on 28 April 1932, accompanied by a collage with the inscription: 'Proposed plan for the Palace of the Soviets compared to the pseudo-modernist architecture of supermarkets and churches.' The examples shown were from Berlin (Karstadt Department Store on Hermannplatz, 1927–29, architect Philipp Schaefer, church at Hohenzollernplatz, 1930–33, architect Ossip Klarwein). But in Moscow, the decision was made to continue the competition procedure. Hamilton and other foreign contributors no longer played a role. In 1934 the revised design by Iofan was chosen for realization, but it was never built.

The protest of the CIAM against the result of the competition for the Palace of the Soviets led to the later cancellation of the 4th CIAM Congress planned to be held in Moscow in 1933. It was instead held in Greece, and would go down in the history of urban construction as the 'Athens Congress'. CIAM members, including Gropius, Sigfried Giedion and Le Corbusier, had briefly explored Warsaw, Milan and Algiers as alternative congress locations. As if the modernist avant-garde had no homeland, it finally decided to debate its principles on the passenger ship *Patris II*, travelling from Marseilles to Athens. Under the illuminated Acropolis, the opening of the exhibition 'The Functional City' took place in the Technical University. On the return trip, working sessions were held with lectures and discussions of city analysis prepared by groups from diverse countries. Le Corbusier's influential publication the 'Charter of Athens' (1943) on urban planning came out ten years after the statements and guidelines for new buildings were formulated in 'The Functional City' by CIAM 4 members.

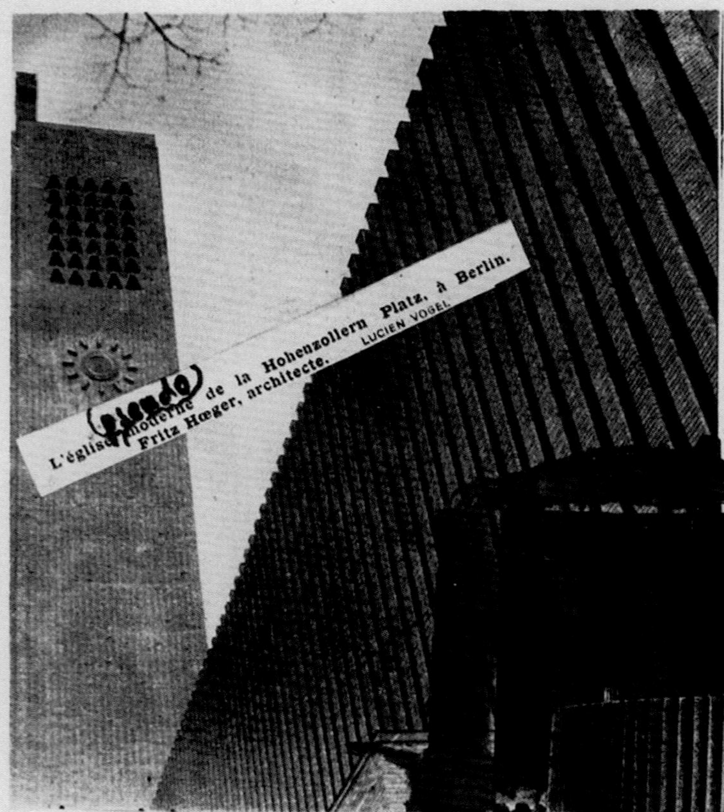

(pseudo) L'église moderne de la Hohenzollern Platz, à Berlin. Fritz Hœger, architecte. LUCIEN VOGEL

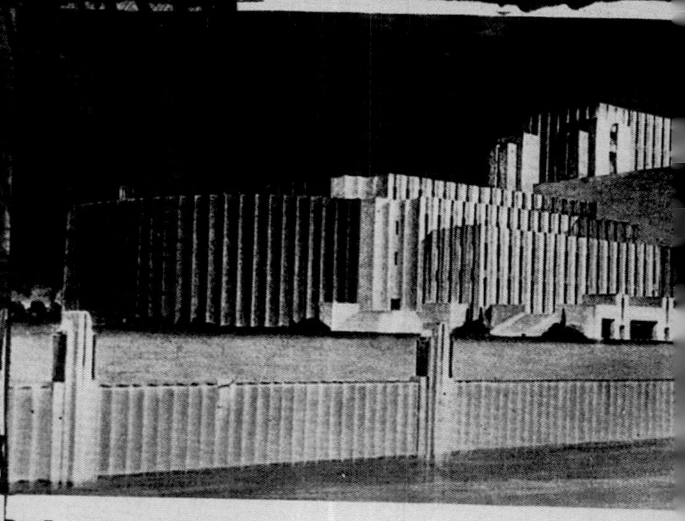

Der Entwurf des Amerikaners Hamilton (ein weiterer Preis von 12000 Ru

DER PALAST DER SOWJETS, der zur Ausführung gelangen soll, im Vergleich mit pseudo-moderner Warenhaus- und Kirchenarchitektur.

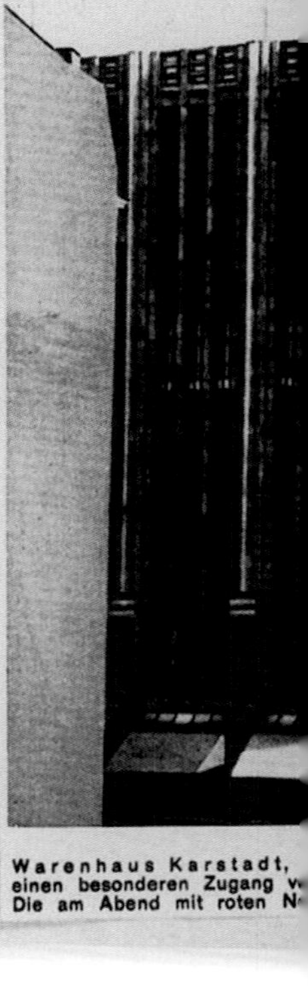

Warenhaus Karstadt,
einen besonderen Zugang v
Die am Abend mit roten N

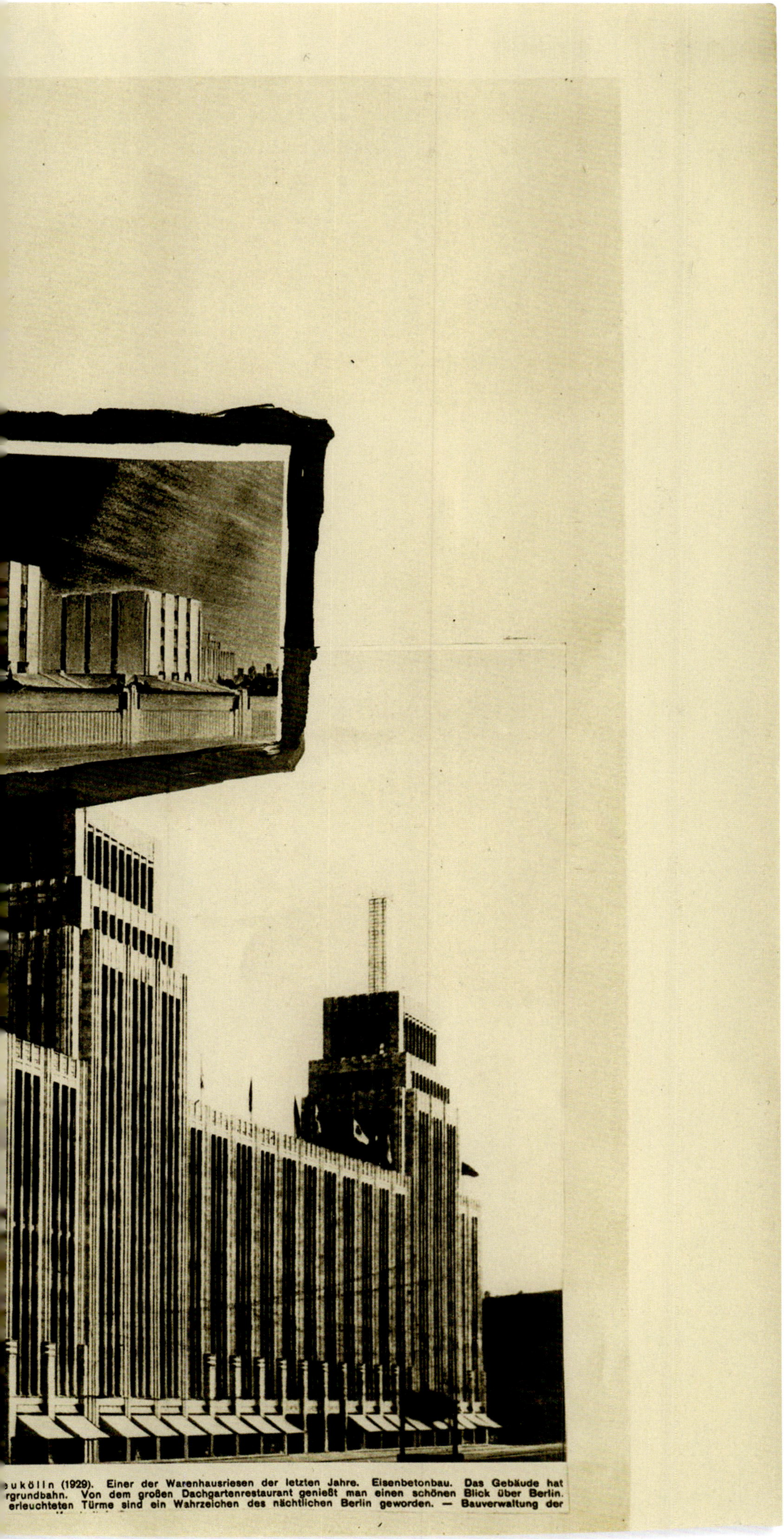
eukölln (1929). Einer der Warenhausriesen der letzten Jahre. Eisenbetonbau. Das Gebäude hat
rgrundbahn. Von dem großen Dachgartenrestaurant genießt man einen schönen Blick über Berlin.
erleuchteten Türme sind ein Wahrzeichen des nächtlichen Berlin geworden. — Bauverwaltung der

Walter Gropius, sketch for 'The Functional City', 4th CIAM Congress, 1932

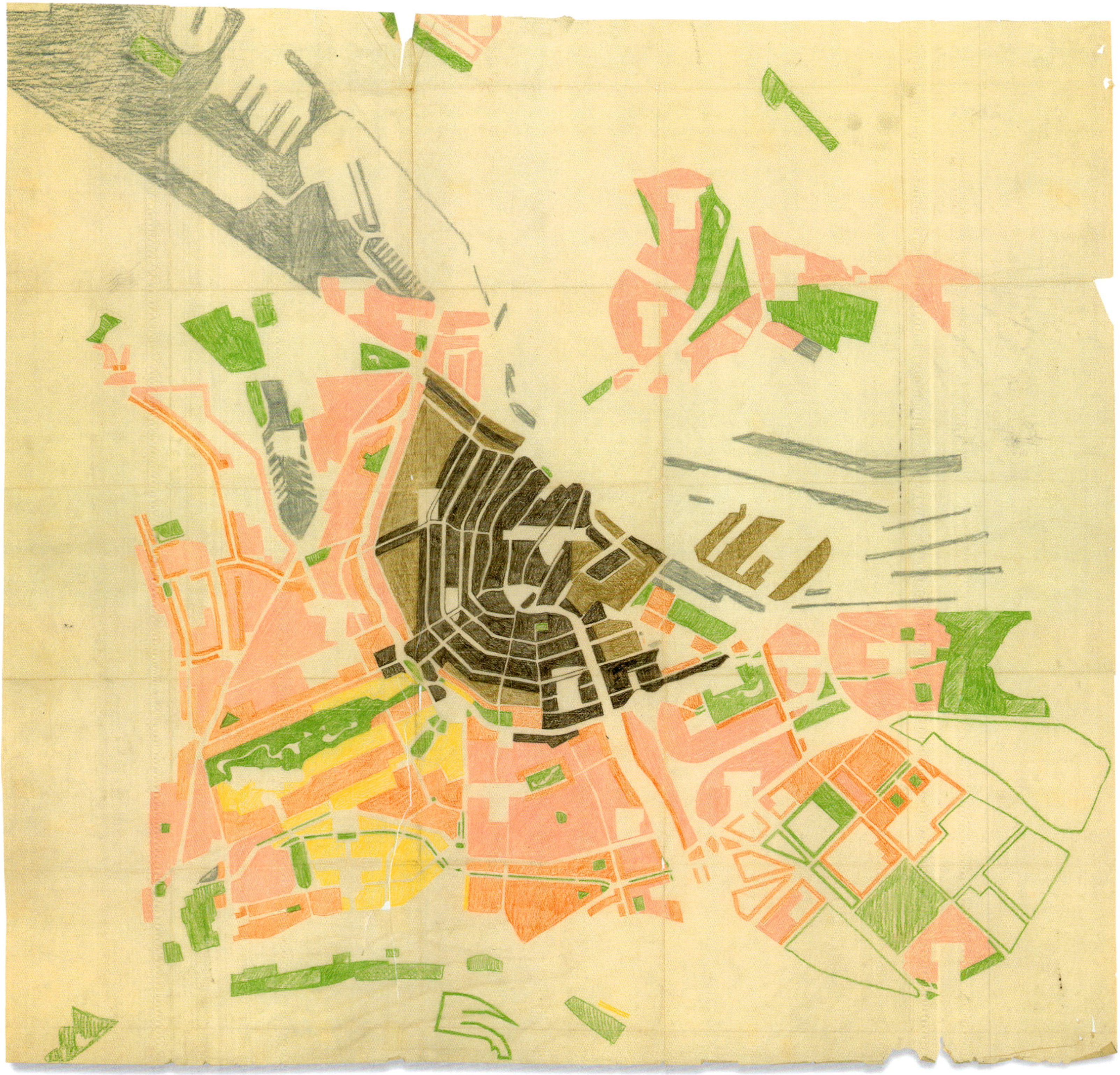

László Moholy-Nágy, stills from *Architects' Congress*, 1933, 16-mm black-and-white film, silent, 29 minutes

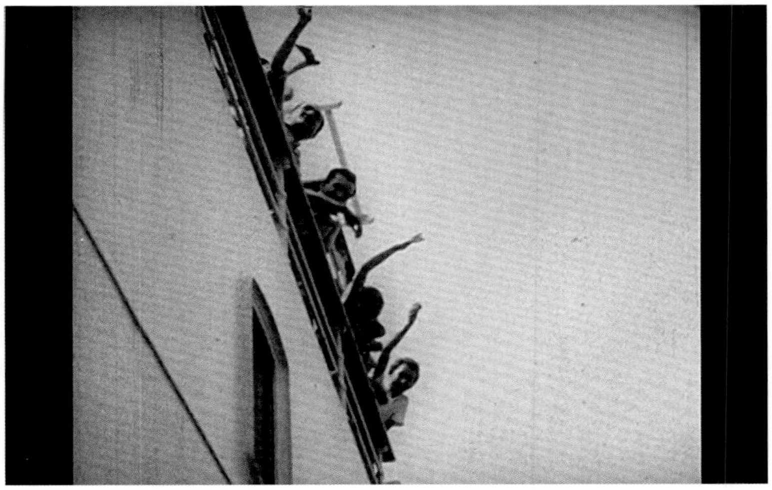

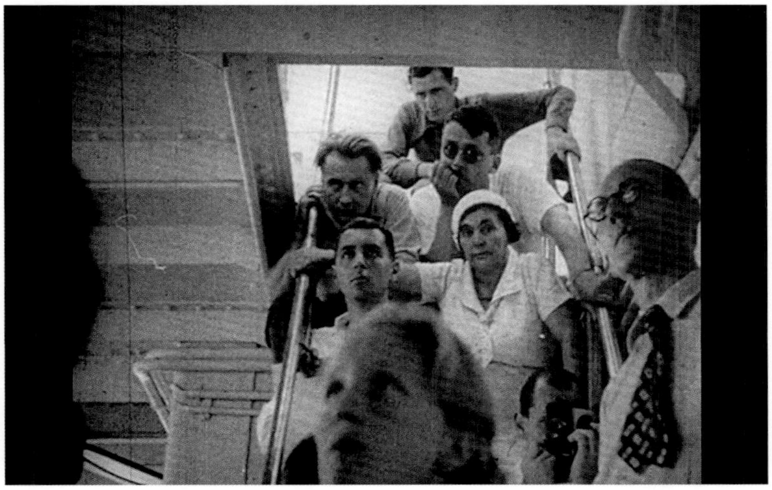

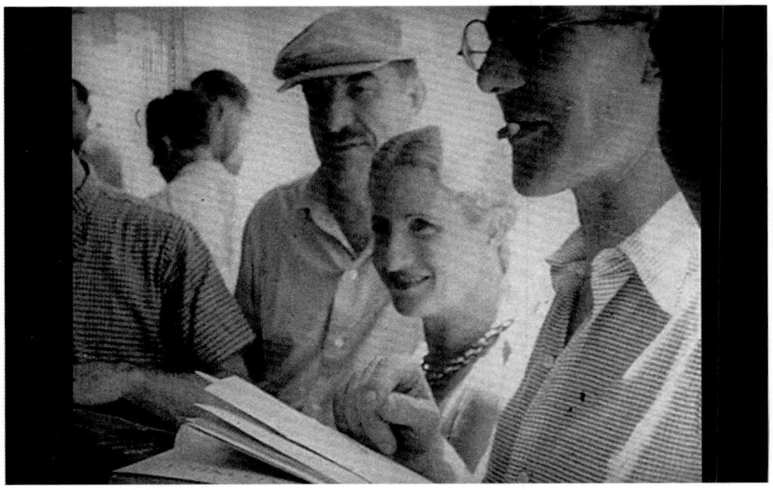

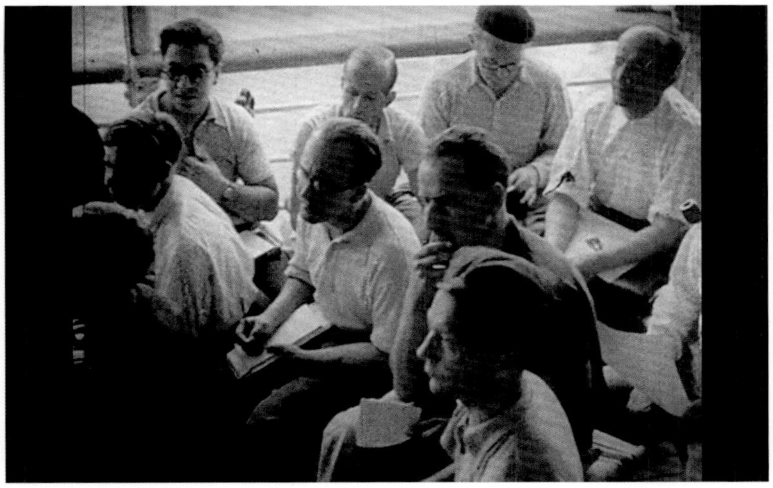

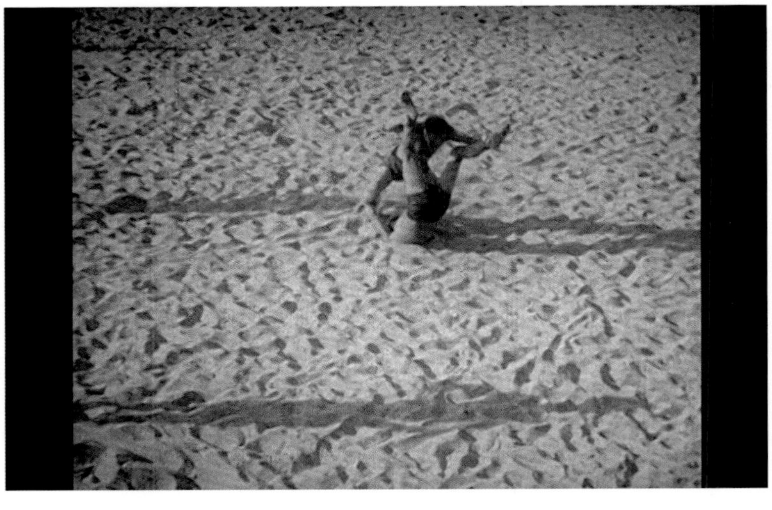

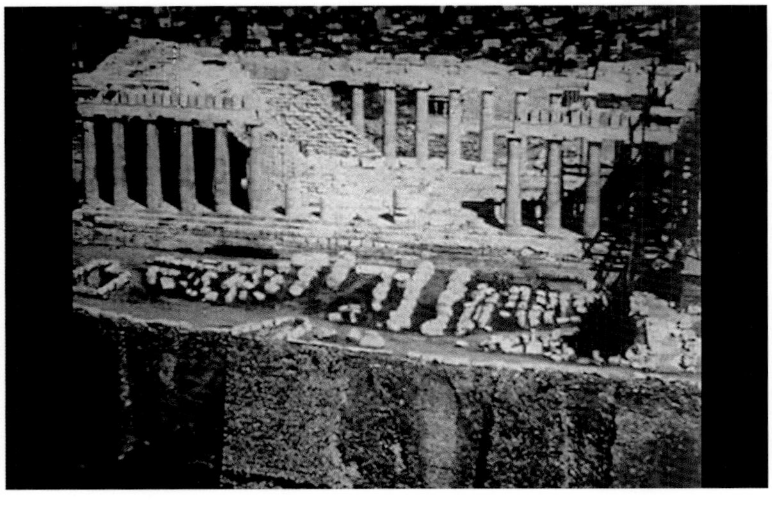

Modern Craft and Art (1932): An Introduction

Zoe Zhang

近代工艺美术 (Modern Craft and Art) by Zhang Guangyu was published in 1932. Zhang had been engaged in commercial art design in Shanghai in his early years. The book was the first theory publication on design in China that systematically introduced and reflected on western modern design. Just 192 pages long, it includes 9 sections: modern architecture, interior design, crafts, textile design, commercial painting, sculpture and advertisement, book design, commercial photography and stage design. Within its pages, photographs of Walter Gropius's Bauhaus building in Dessau and other new architecture in Germany can be found. In addition, the Bauhaus was addressed as a school of craft and art.

In China in the early 1930s, there was not any clear or unified definition of design in a modern sense. But clearly Zhang understood modern design, which is what makes his book so interesting. For example, he emphasized the simple and austere forms of plywood furniture in the section on interior design and indicated the advantages and technological aspects of the new material. He also included his own highly abstract design of an office after the introduction on plywood. Two articles in the book also feature other modern materials, steel tube and plate glass, and explain functional design with works by Gropius and Marcel Breuer.

As a designer, Zhang is a very good example of the kind of trajectory that some Chinese designers in first half of the twentieth century followed. He started from Chinese traditional art and was then impacted and influenced by western modern design. Finally he combined the Chinese methods and western abstract form into his work, such as in his design draft for the animation movie *Monkey Makes Havoc in the Heaven* (1964).

The preface of the book is called a 'Chinese manifesto of modern design in the early part of the twentieth century'.[1] Zhang wrote: 'Art is what is always attached to the life world and, in turn, separated from reality. In other words, art would not be restrained by any bounds in the universe.... The human being will cultivate a perfect view of life not only through progress at the material level, but also through the nature of Art.'[2] The pioneer of Chinese modern design interpreted the combination of material and art in the term of 'material art'. According to his theory, the 'Being' is a world consisting of material art, which is integrated in country, nation, society, culture, education and so on. Thus, there are no essential differences between art, architecture and craft. Further he thought that the progress of material art would be a way to bring the next renaissance to a weak China. These ideas of the early Chinese modern designers and artists share a similar approach and aims with the Bauhaus approach.

Zhang Guangyu (ed.), *Modern Craft and Art*, Shanghai, 1932

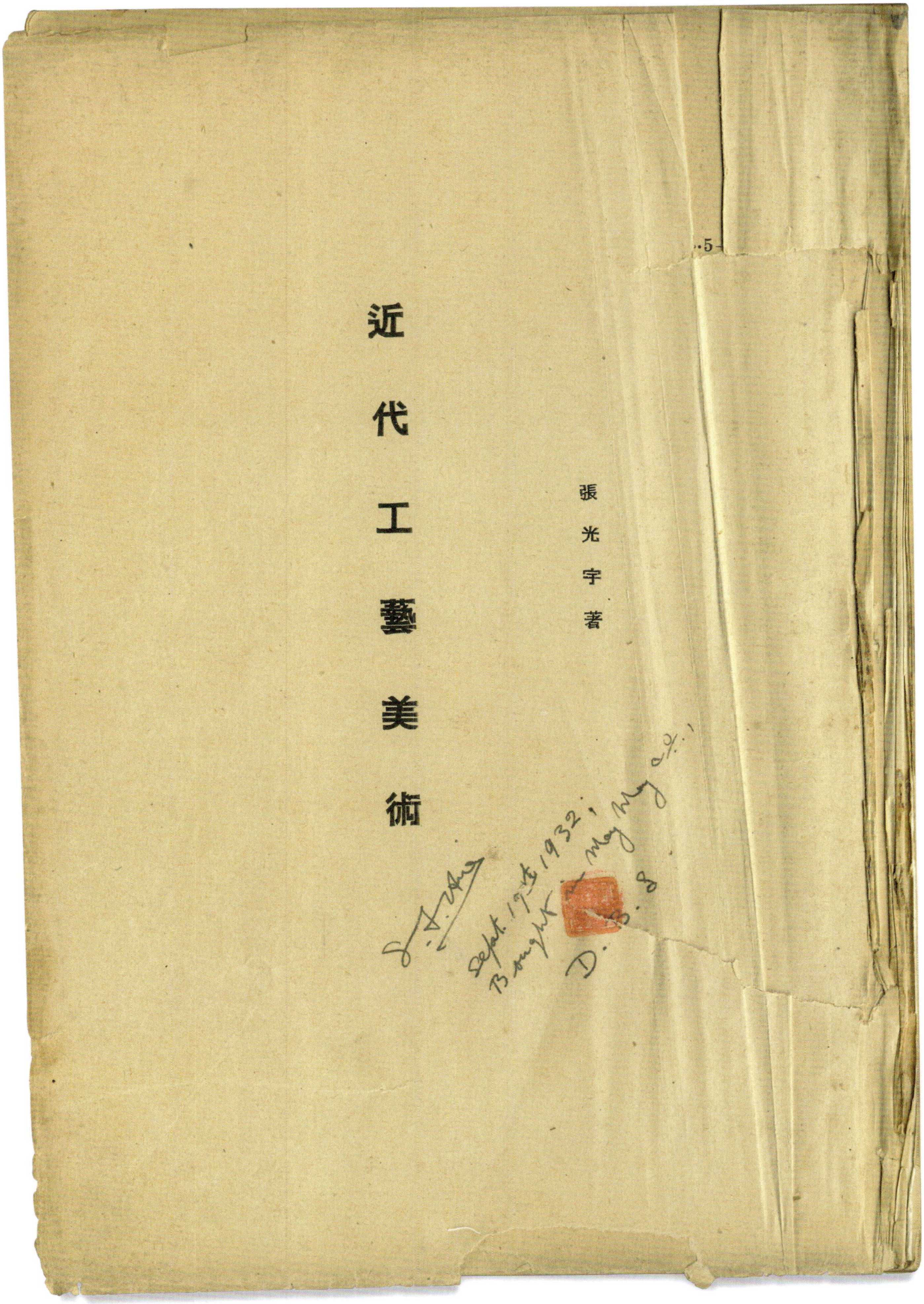

Zhang Guangyu (ed.), *Modern Craft and Art*, Shanghai, 1932, p. 37

Zhang Guangyu (ed.), *Modern Craft and Art*, Shanghai, 1932, p. 56

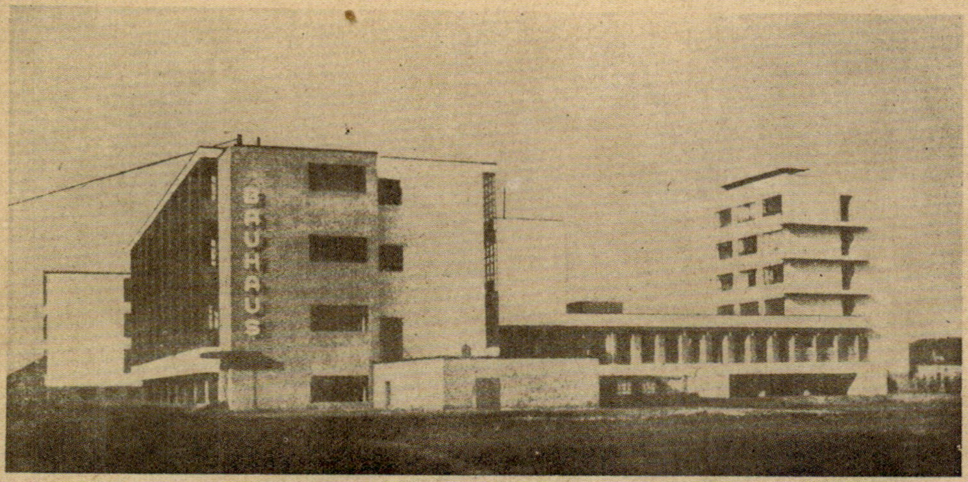

德國伯綏司(Bauhaus)工藝美術學校之校舍建築，廣大的範圍，立體味的藝術的強烈，予人以快覺；式樣的高低有序，簡直沒有一處不調和的。

37

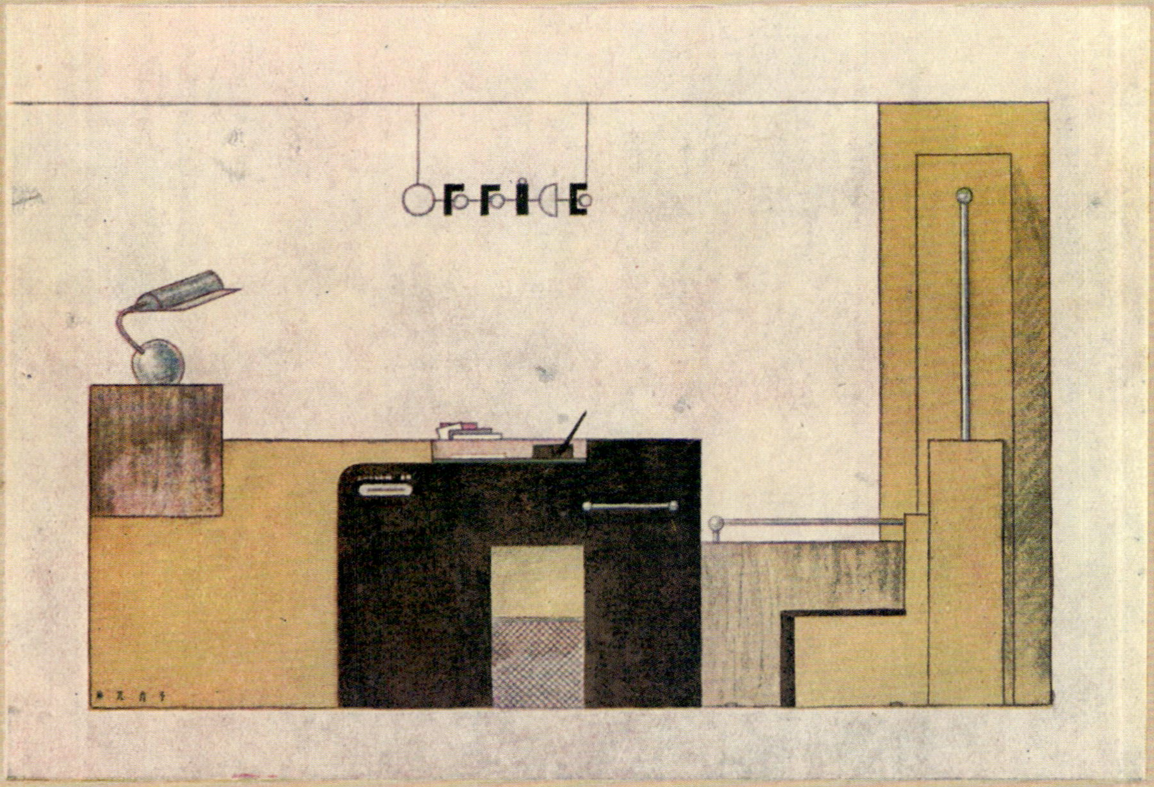

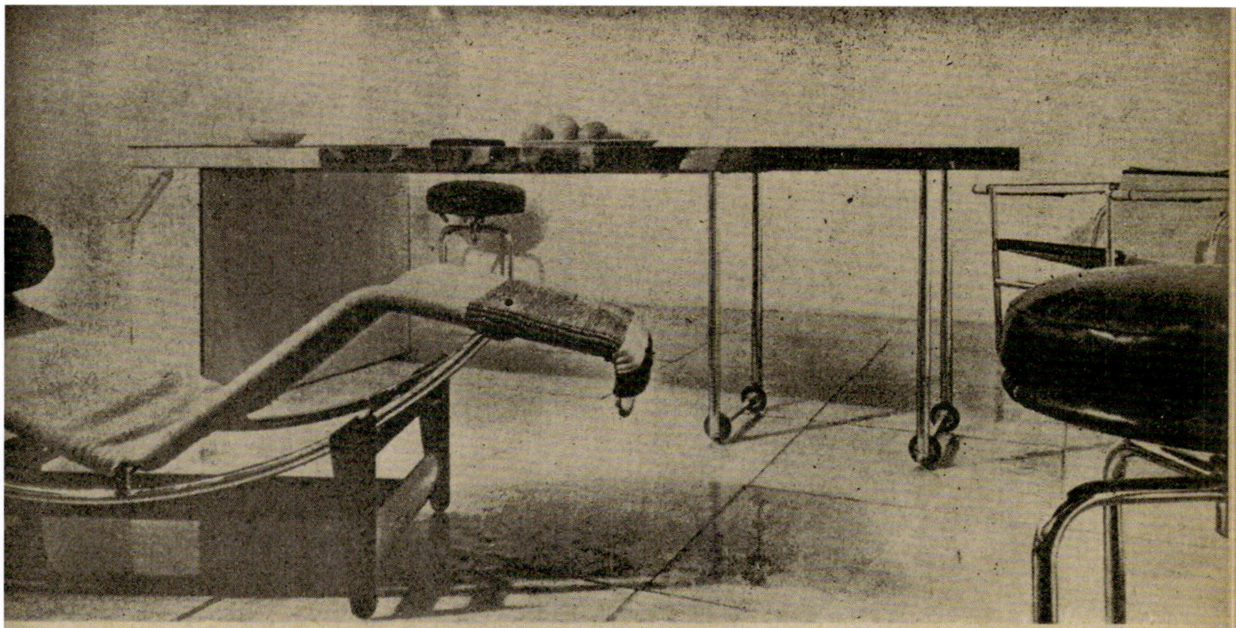

鋼骨製之睡椅，新的式樣擱脚向上，背脊骨貼服得穩定異常，可以移動的食桌，輕靈小巧，係巴黎潘利安的作品，(Charlotte perriand)

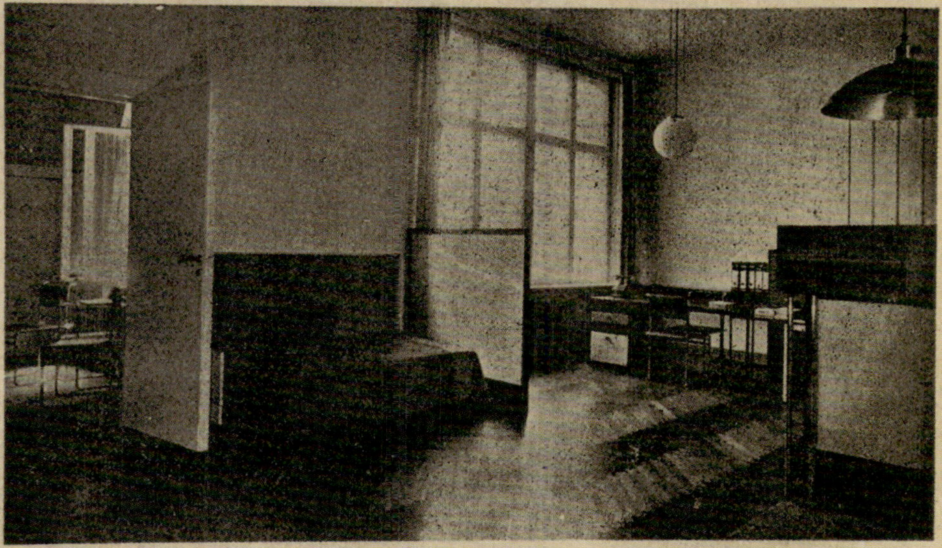

較廣闊的起居間，立方體的屏障，球形的燈，光滑的門，上下左右清靜簡樸，爲勃柳歐(Marcel Breuer)之設計

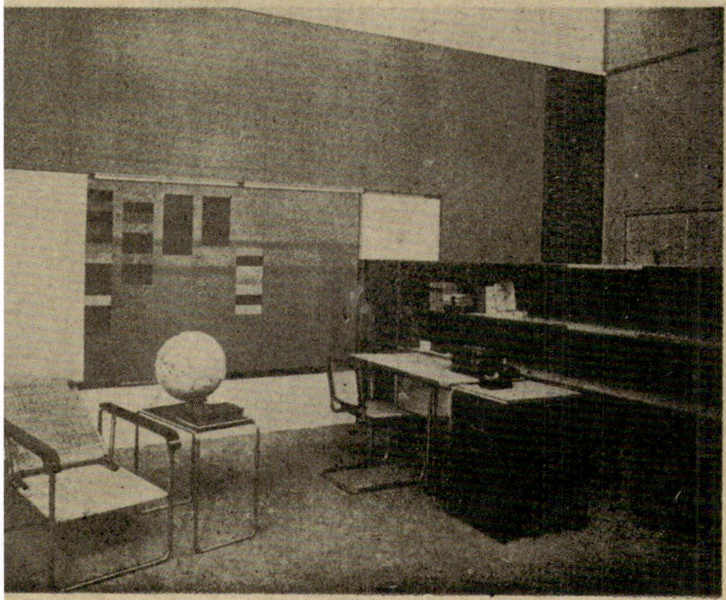

柏林葛洛潑司 (Walter Gropius)之設計，寫字房的一角，鋼骨穿藤的椅子，裝置在壁內的暗櫥上，更懸掛着可以伸縮的捲軸，取用極便利！

Useful Tradition? Walter Gropius meets China (or I. M. Pei)

Eduard Kögel

Walter Gropius never made it to Shanghai, but after the Second World War he was awarded a commission from the US-based United Board of Christian Colleges in China to design a new campus university there. In 1946 Gropius founded The Architects Collaborative (TAC) and the university became one of the first projects for the group.[1] Alongside Gropius, the project supervisor was Norman Fletcher, joined by former Gropius student I. M. Pei as an associate. In the layout of the overall concept for the university campus in Shanghai, the traditional features of Chinese gardens – such as a pond in the centre, connecting walkways and an open composition of rectangular courtyards – are clearly reflected.[2]

In describing the design process for the university, Gropius wrote: 'The gap from the traditional master crafts to the present methods of design and building in our period of industrial civilization has not yet been filled.'[3] He argued for the combination of economically efficient contemporary building techniques with basic Chinese design elements:

> balancing volumes and space, land and water, building and trees…. The basic architectural pattern chosen, therefore, is a combination of two or three-storied tile roofed buildings around patios and court-yards of varying sizes interwoven with intimate landscaping, with ponds, pools and streams, and with open pergolas connecting the individual buildings…. Such an approach with its intimate relation of buildings and landscape should help to resume a genuine thread of tradition. Avoiding outright imitation of the old style, it tends to express an ancient philosophy of the Chinese people and their love for nature.[4]

Gropius's arguments sound simple. But besides the economic aspects, he argues for a reflection of traditional values, which indeed appear here for the first time in his oeuvre.

The Hua Tung University was planned tentatively to be built on the airfield of Hongqiao in the western suburbs of Shanghai. The urban layout of the complex for 2,100 male and 900 female students was subdivided into four parts around an artificial lake with the campus to the south and the three residential compounds, each for 1,000 students and staff, to the east, west and north. Pei designed the residential units, each with its own chapel for the Methodists, the Presbyterians and the Episcopalians. Sketches show the architectural approach, with a covered walkway as the basic structural element framing the space. The pavilions in the sketches are almost of Miesian character, reduced to a skeleton construction with some slightly sloped and some flat roofs. Pei's sketches of the architectural character of the housing area are particularly reminiscent of skeleton buildings designed by Mies van der Rohe, whereas the urban layout in the landscape refers to abstracted examples of traditional Chinese groupings around courtyards. One of Pei's

Perspective of residential area, Hua Tung University, Shanghai, China, drawing by I. M. Pei

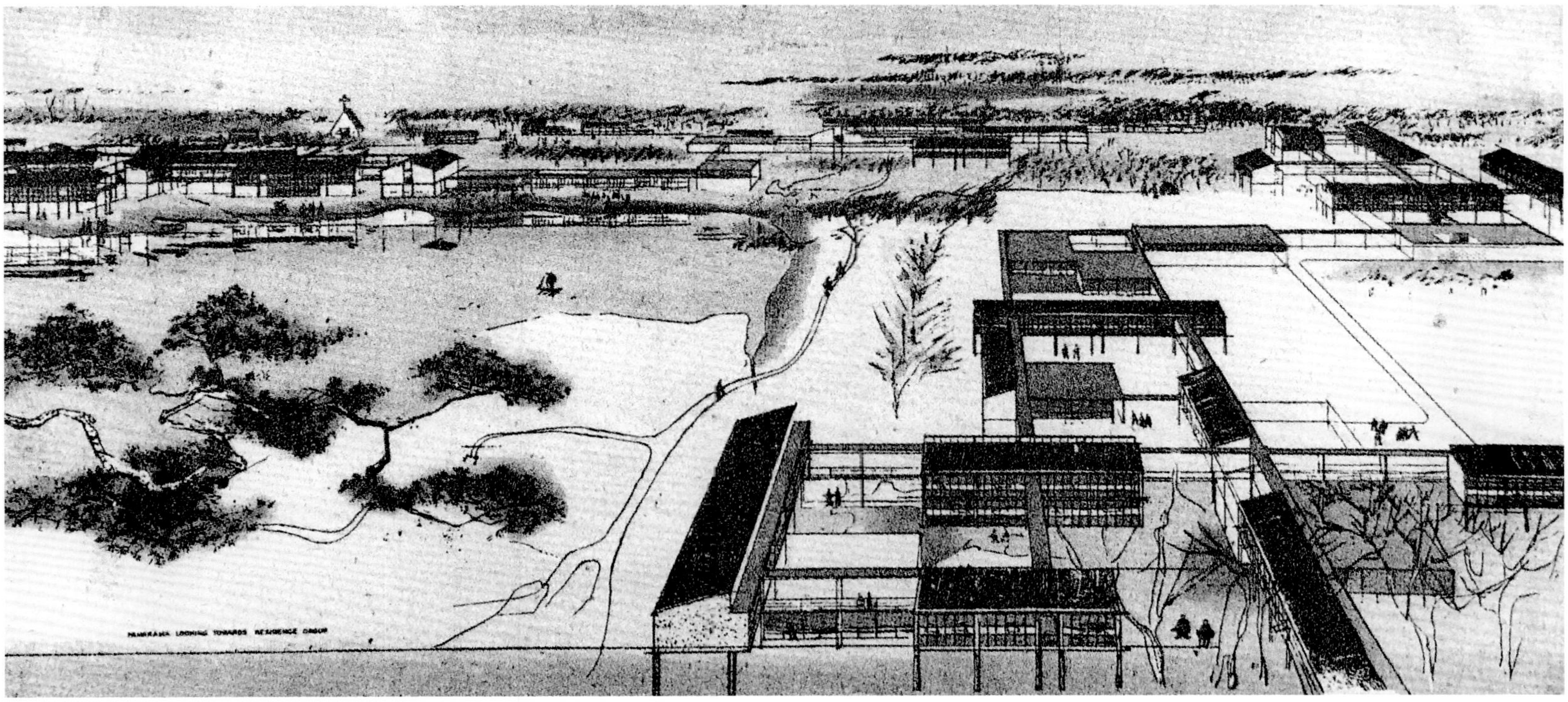

Looking under classroom building towards the library, Hua Tung University, Shanghai, China, drawing by N. Fletcher

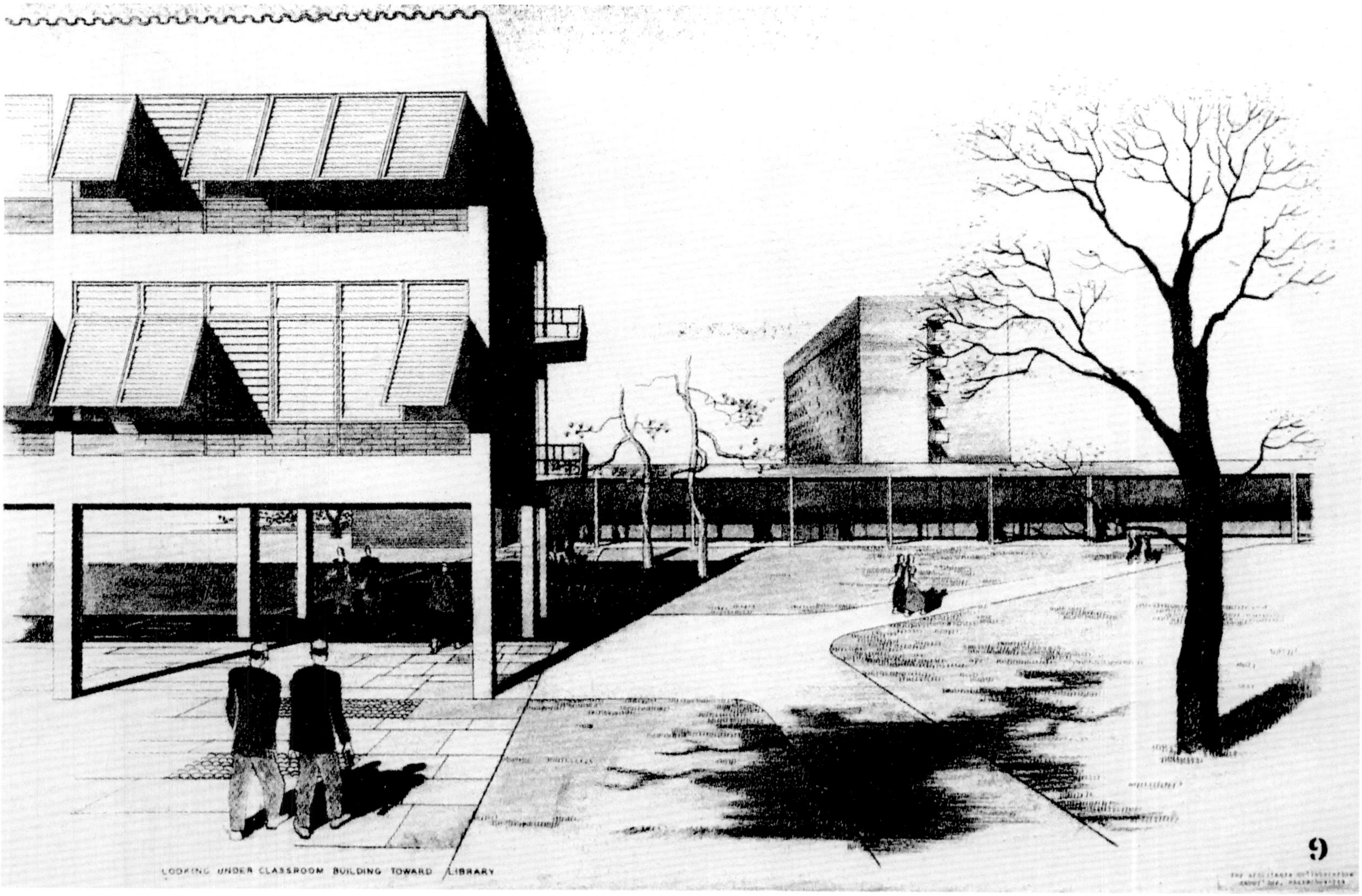

Interior view looking through into courtyard dormitories,
Hua Tung University, Shanghai, China

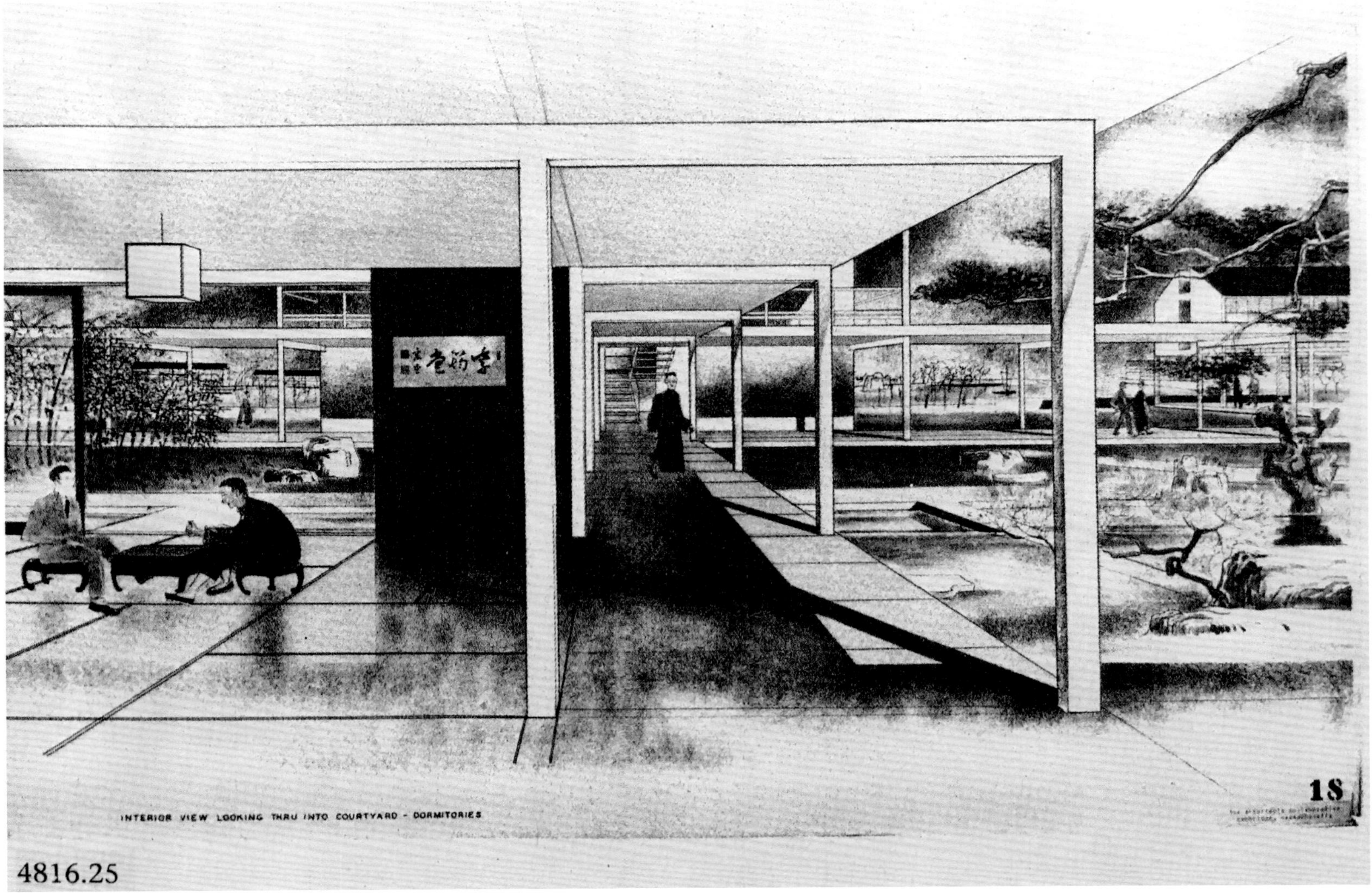

The campus of Tunghai University in Taiwan in a drawing by Chen Chi-kwan, with the Luce Memorial Chapel by I. M. Pei in the foreground and the various faculties behind it, each organized around a courtyard and connected by covered walkways

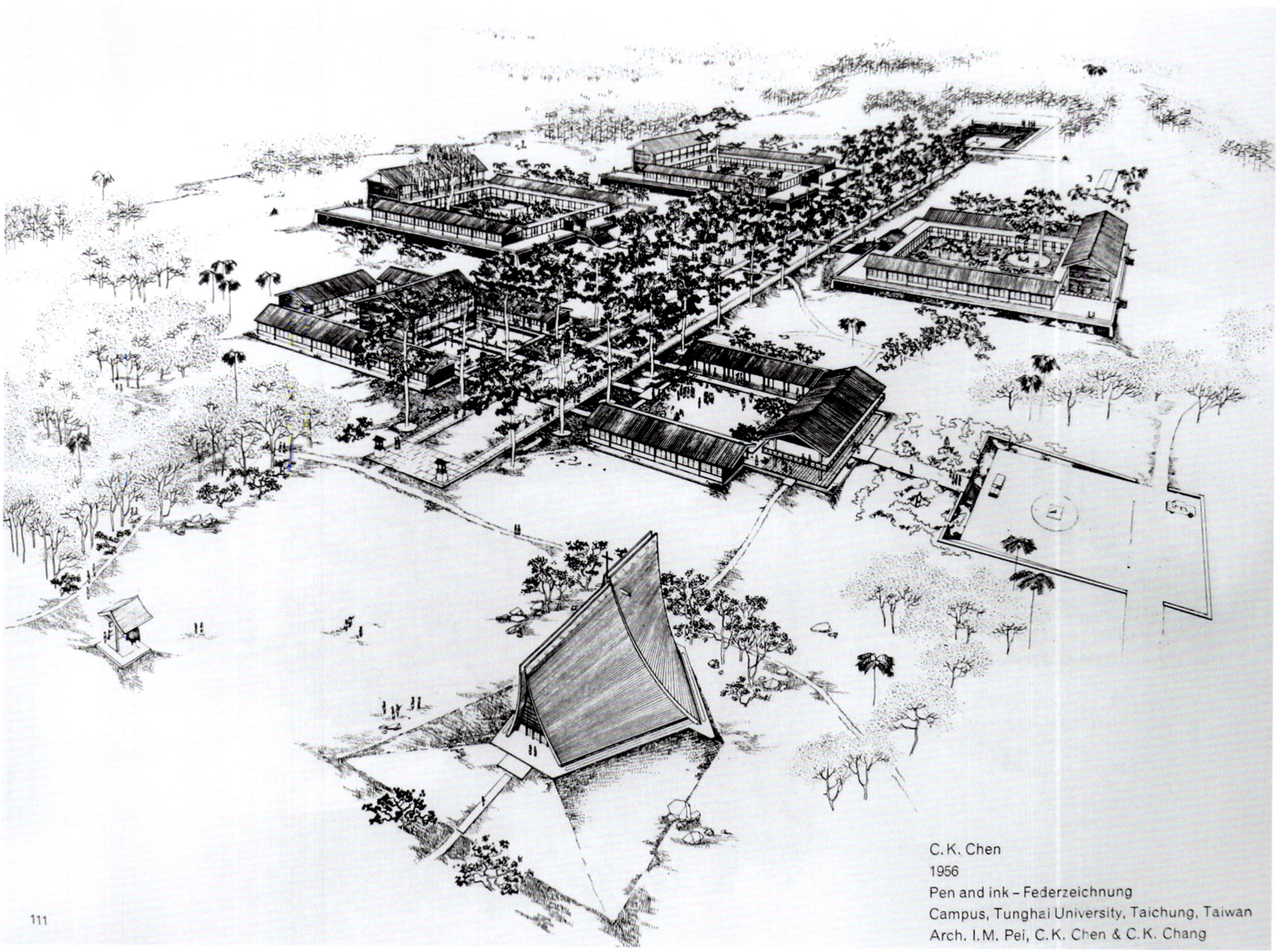

statements – that he admired the aesthetic of Mies more than of Gropius – is clearly reflected here.[5] Later, Pei belittled his influence in the project by saying: 'I merely helped them [TAC] with a few of the drawings.'[6] However, the outstanding spatial arrangement and the strong skeleton structure of the buildings tell another story.

In 1948 Pei joined the firm of William Zeckendorf in New York and worked freelance for the Hua Tung project. In the early 1950s, foreign missionary institutions in China were forced to close after the establishment of the People's Republic in October 1949. A contemporary western critic recognized the significant character of the scheme and expressed regret that it was not built: 'The site plan is magnificently worked out in terms of shape and space relations. There is a lightness and airiness about the whole that has a Chinese flavour, and this is achieved without resorting to ancient material or form.'[7]

This project was clearly a turning point in Gropius's approach and it would have been impossible without Pei. Gropius used his new knowledge and later argued for local references, such as in a 1954 letter for his projects in Baghdad: 'the Hua Tung University, which I think is good evidence for our capability to adapt to the conditions of foreign countries. My own line is particularly to go really after the actual conditions in a region and derive the design expression from the acquired knowledge.'[8]

In 1955, Pei received a commission from the same client to design the Tunghai campus in Taiwan, which he did in cooperation with Chen Chi-kwan and Chang Chao-kang (the former was a collaborator in TAC and the latter had studied with Gropius). The Tunghai campus is clearly a result of the exploration of tradition and modernity in the context of the planning for Shanghai he undertook with Gropius.

Designing Life in India

Suchitra Balasubrahmanyan

The aesthetics and values of the Bauhaus and its successor school, the Hochschule für Gestaltung (HfG) Ulm (Ulm School of Design), were refracted in India through a particular set of historical circumstances: decolonization and the processes of nation-building; the United States of America's post-war cultural diplomacy efforts in India; and the discourse on design initiated by the English-speaking elite through two influential journals, which led to the establishment of institutions for design education that adapted Euro-American design pedagogy. The leitmotif of all these efforts was the urgency of bringing a certain 'standard of living' to the majority of Indians.

India became independent in 1947, and embarked on a programme of nation-building through a series of Soviet-style Five-Year Plans 'to initiate a process of development which will raise living standards and open out to the people new opportunities for a richer and more varied life'.[1] Presiding over the effort was the first Prime Minister, Jawaharlal Nehru, who wanted to create 'the temples of modern India' – hydroelectric dams, steel plants and heavy industries – while also promoting small-scale and cottage industries, public housing, education, health and the welfare of women, youth and children. In 1950, his government invited Le Corbusier to build Chandigarh, a new town that he hoped would be 'symbolic of the freedom of India, unfettered by traditions of the past…an expression of the nation's faith in the future'.[2] Thus, the postcolonial state played a powerful role in shaping the lives of its citizens to give them what Nehru called 'the garb of modernity'.

Faith in modern industrial development was accompanied by the anxiety of losing sight of cultural anchors from the past. Nehru was concerned 'that when India puts on her new garment, as she must, for the old one is torn and tattered, she will have it cut in this fashion, so as to conform both to present conditions and her old thought'.[3] Accordingly, the new government's official crest was adapted from ancient Mauryan sculpture, the Indian Constitution was illustrated with images drawn from art and sculpture from the Indus Valley civilization onwards and the national flag bore emperor Ashoka's wheel of righteousness.

Concurrently, the cultural presence of the United States became more pronounced. In 1952, the Ford Foundation established its first office outside the US in New Delhi, believing that its support would be 'for the good of the future of India and the good of the free world'.[4] In the early years the foundation provided technical assistance and a major proportion of grants were 'spent on bringing foreign experts to show the Indians the way'. In 1955, supported by the Rockefeller Brothers Fund, the Museum of Modern Art (MoMA) organized the 'Textiles and Ornamental Arts of India' exhibition showcasing India's craft traditions in New York. An accompanying publication noted that independence had brought India 'to life' and that a 'renaissance' was underway

Jawaharlal Nehru signing the Third Five-Year Plan, 1961

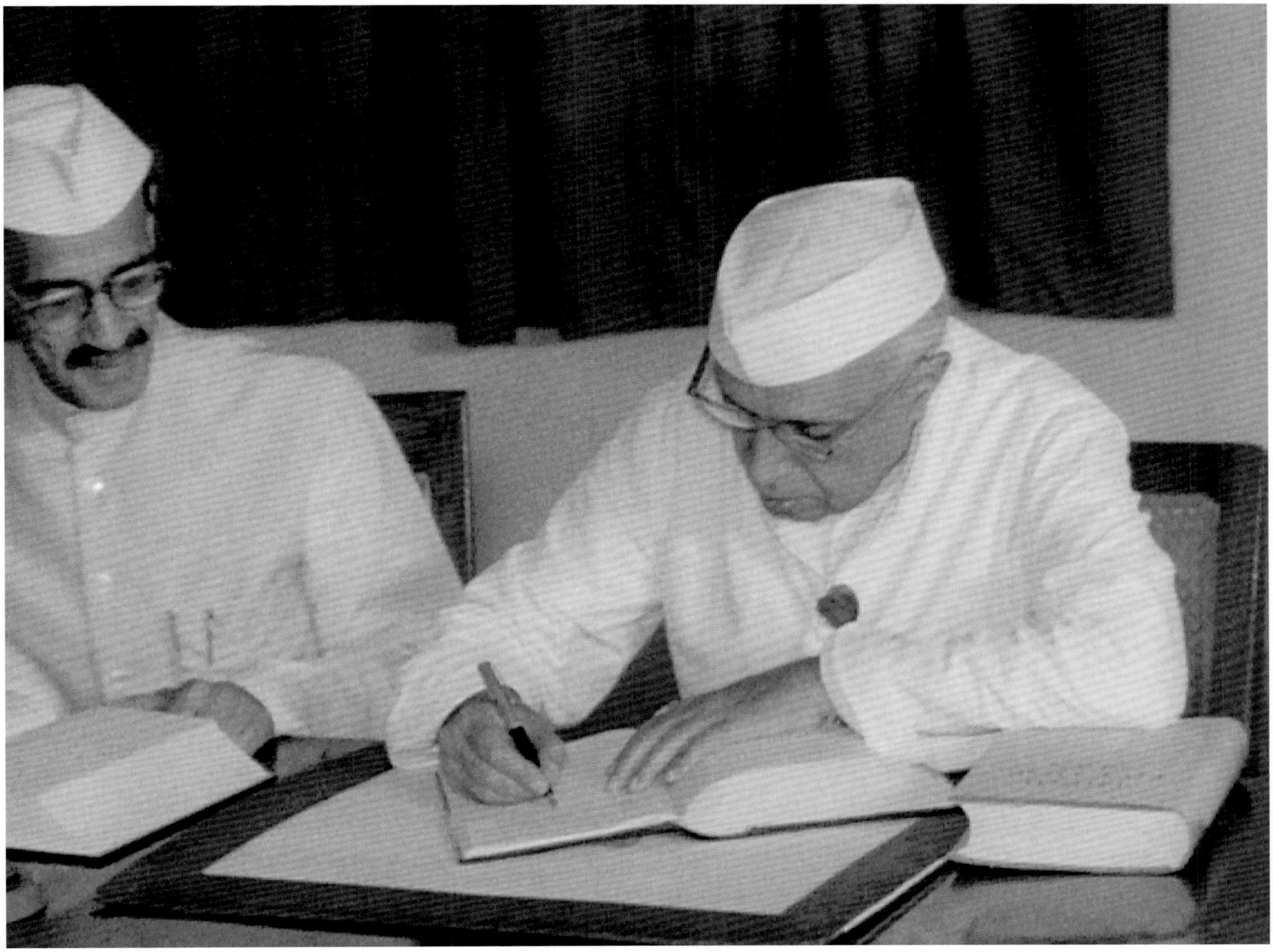

View of the exhibition 'Textiles and Ornamental Arts of India' at the Museum of Modern Art, New York, 1955

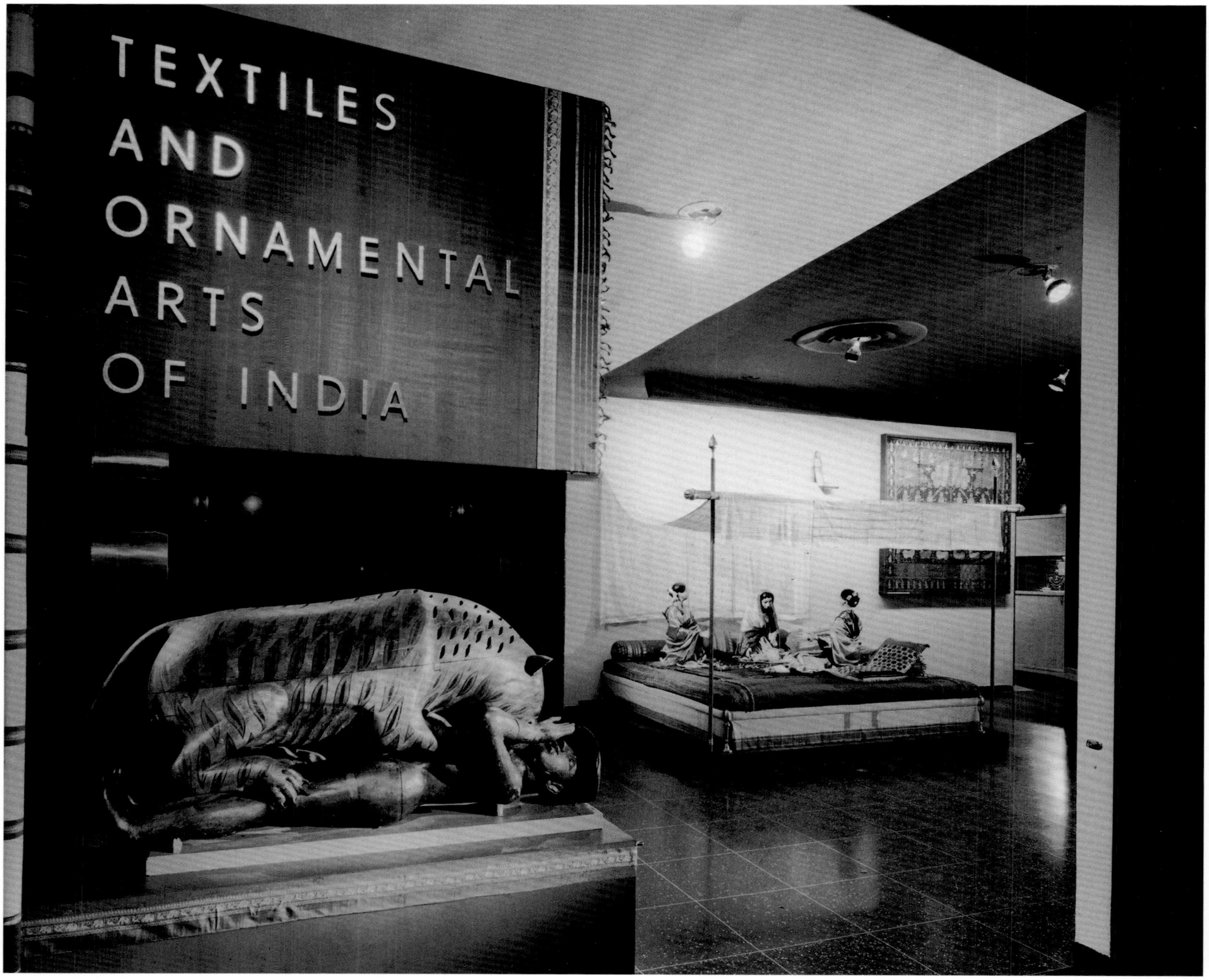

Charles Eames, *Lotas, India*, 1958, photograph

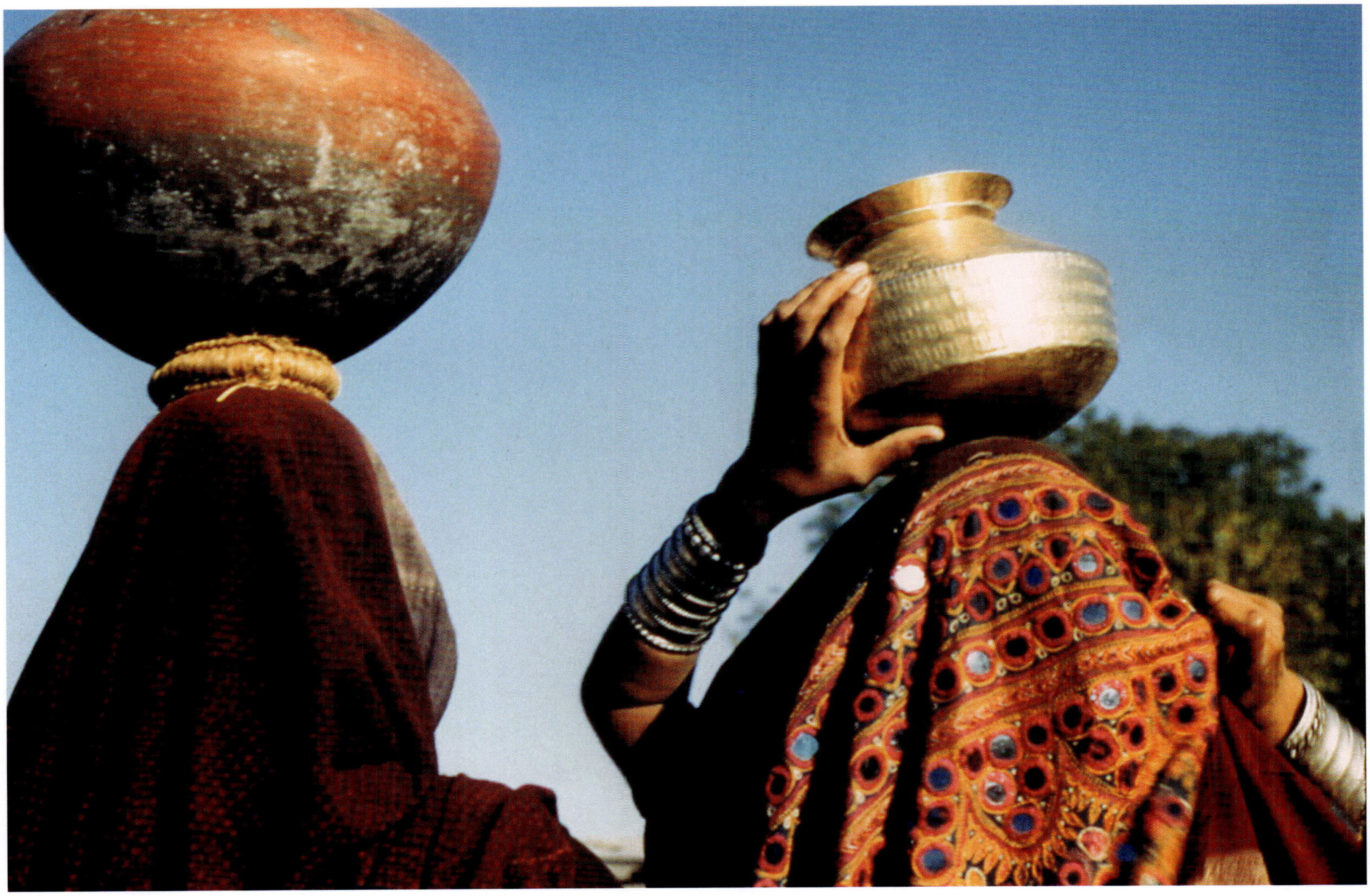

with 'enthusiastic expressions of the desire to improve living standards, to provide better education, and at the same time to revive the esthetic traditions and techniques of the great past'.[5] Also included in the volume was the essay 'Indian Fabrics in Indian Life' by Pupul Jayakar of the All India Handicrafts Board. Jayakar pointed to the challenges posed by industrialization and urbanization and wondered if modern design would destroy crafts and craftspeople by introducing 'incomprehensible forms' from the West, further underlining the tension of reconciling past and present through modernization.

At the MoMA exhibition Jayakar met Charles Eames who, along with his wife Ray, later visited India on the invitation of the government and with the sponsorship of the Ford Foundation 'to recommend a programme of training in the area of design', which would play a catalytic role in the development of small-scale industry in the country, and 'to state what India can do to resist the rapid deterioration of consumer goods within the country'. Drawing design values from an analysis of the form and function of the *lota* (pot), their *India Report* (1958) outlined the transformative role that traditional craft and contemporary design approaches could play at that particular juncture and context in India. Significantly, they posed two questions about 'those things that constitute a "Standard of Living" in India: "What does India ultimately desire? What do Indians desire for themselves and for India?"'[6]

Answers to these questions can be glimpsed in two journals, *Marg* (1946–present) and *Design* (1957–88), through which Euro-American ideas about architecture and design circulated among an English-reading elite in India. Both were designed to be far-reaching, non-technical and generously illustrated, reflecting an all-India character with material covering architecture, planning, art, crafts, industrial design and the performing arts. Self-consciously in conversation with European and American architects and designers, and with contributions from them, *Marg* and *Design* were conduits for modernist ideas of living. Their editors and contributors campaigned to transplant modern materials, industrial manufacturing and aesthetics to the Indian context, while presenting them as necessary ways to think about nation-building and securing a 'standard of living' for the majority of Indians. The inaugural issue of *Marg* voiced the hope that the magazine would clear the 'cobwebs out of the minds of our intelligentsia and the middle sections of our population' and that constructive ideas realized at the moment 'only by a very few' may 'percolate among the vast majority of our countrymen'.[7] Similarly, an advertisement announcing the publication of *Design* declared that it was for people who want to know about 'new vistas of thought and expression' to 'make a life well spent and well lived, a design for living'.[8] Walter Gropius and Marcel Breuer were on *Design*'s editorial board and the journal included articles on the activities and approaches of the Bauhaus and HfG Ulm as well as Charles Eames's view on Indian handicrafts. Each month's issue brought the reader news of new products and graphic design from around the world as well as regular updates on furniture, ceramics and textiles produced under the aegis of the All India Handicrafts Board and its regional design centres. For almost two decades after independence, 'Design for Living' was a popular slogan, used to popularize tubular furniture in *Marg* in 1952 and advertise handicrafts in *Design* in 1959. It even appeared as the title of a project in the UNESCO round table on Nehru in 1966.

While both journals presented an overwhelmingly urban emphasis, at times the editorial spotlight shone on rural settings and, occasionally, on working-class neighbourhoods. Though they campaigned to transplant modern materials, industrial manufacturing and a western aesthetic to the Indian context, *Marg* and *Design* also vigorously promoted Indian handicrafts contemporized by design, valorizing the vernacular as a source of essential cultural anchors in the rapidly modernizing postcolonial society.

Barely a year after the *India Report* was submitted, MoMA organized another exhibition entitled 'Design Today in America and Europe'. It consisted of furniture and consumer products selected 'to bring to the attention of the Indian public the aesthetic values of the west' and to 'provide an inspiration to Indian manufacturers and craftsmen for a solution to the many new problems that confront them'.[9] The MoMA collection of well-designed objects arrived in India in 1959 and toured major cities all over the country.

Following the *India Report*, funds were allocated in the Third Five-Year Plan to set up an industrial design institute and, accordingly, the National Institute of Design (NID) was established in Ahmedabad in 1961 and, later, the Industrial Design Centre (IDC) at the campus of the Indian Institute of Technology, Bombay (now Mumbai) in 1969. Their objective was to train students and to provide design services to Indian industry and the Indian government and, through them, to the Indian people as they strove to create a new life as an independent nation. The Ford Foundation made further grants for equipment and faculty development through exchanges with HfG Ulm and the Ulm Foundation Programme was adapted at both institutions to inculcate a functional approach to design. The MoMA objects of 'good design' were installed as a teaching collection at the National Institute of Design and generations of students imbibed their aesthetic ideals.

Marg: A Magazine of Architecture & Art, Vol. 1, No. 1, October 1946

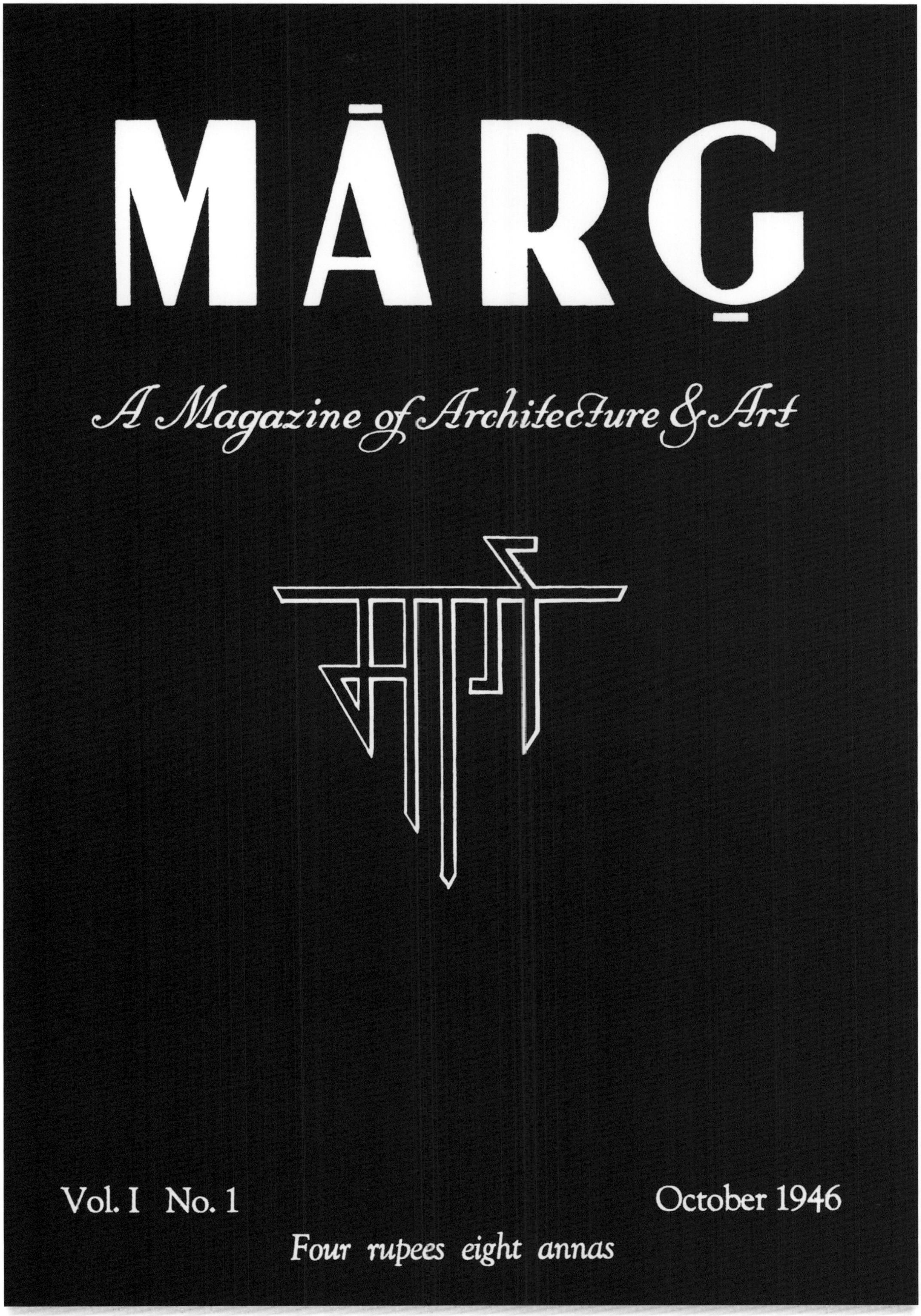

Benoy Sarkar, visual identity for Ind an Airlines, 1973, brochure, print on paper

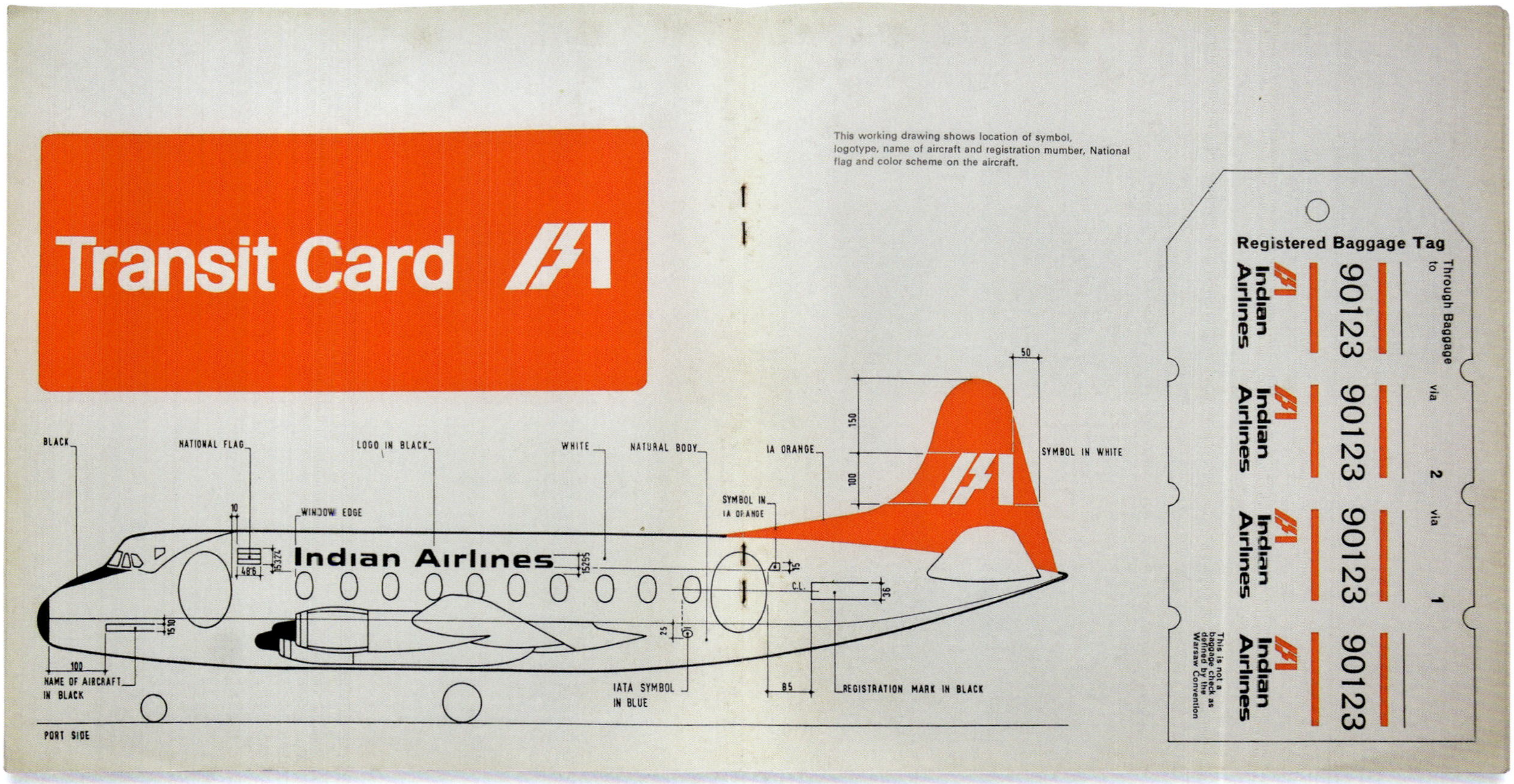

Student exercises from the foundation programme at the National Institute of Design, Ahmedabad, India, in National Institute of Design (ed.), *Documentation 1964–69*, Ahmedabad: NID, 1969

Elements of product design

8 Design of a container from point of view of ease of storage and readability of information.

9 Design of simple office objects from ergonomics point of view.

10 Two solutions for a simple need of weighing letters.

Workshop tasks

11 Design of a construction element from different materials based on the initial investigation into the scope of tools and nature of materials. This forms the 'Brick' to build a growth structure of various dimensions and shapes. (A) Sheet metal (B) Solid metal (C) Wood

12 Use of plaster as material to demonstrate the exercises in constructive geometry.

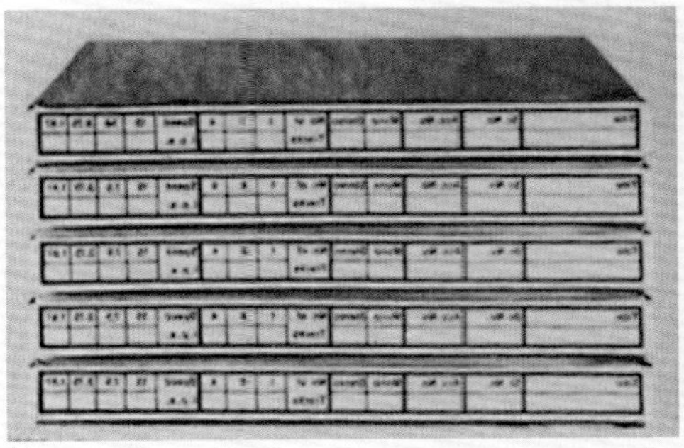
8A

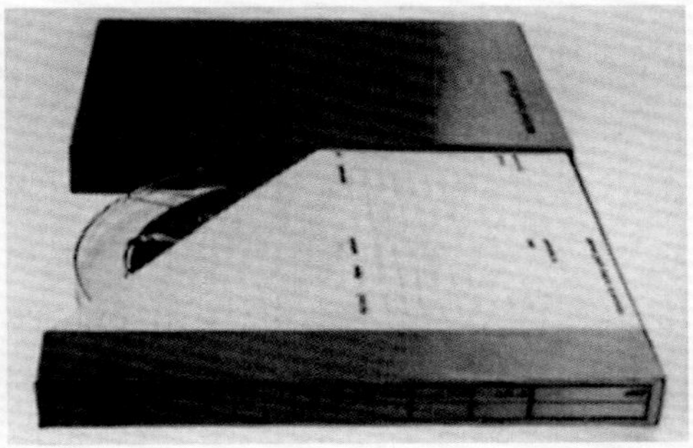
8B

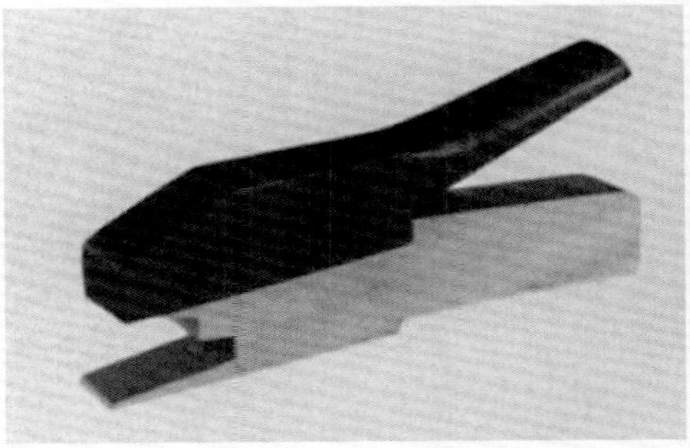
9A

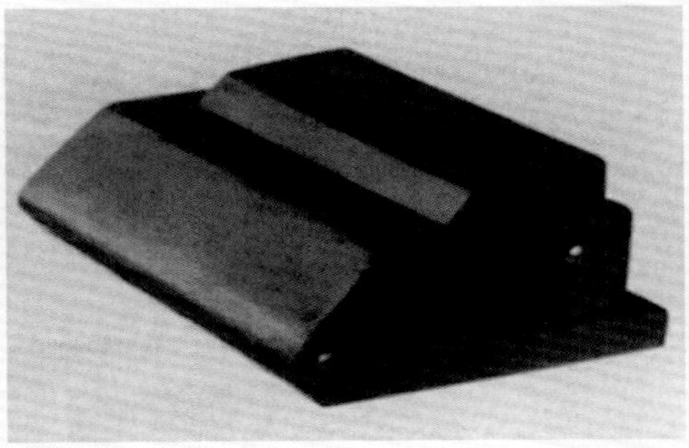
9B

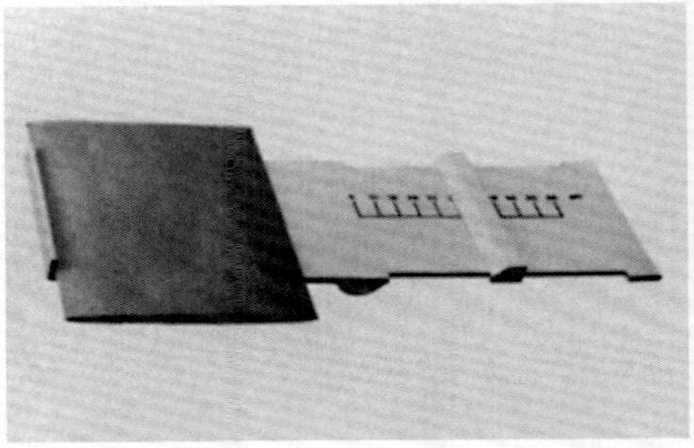
10

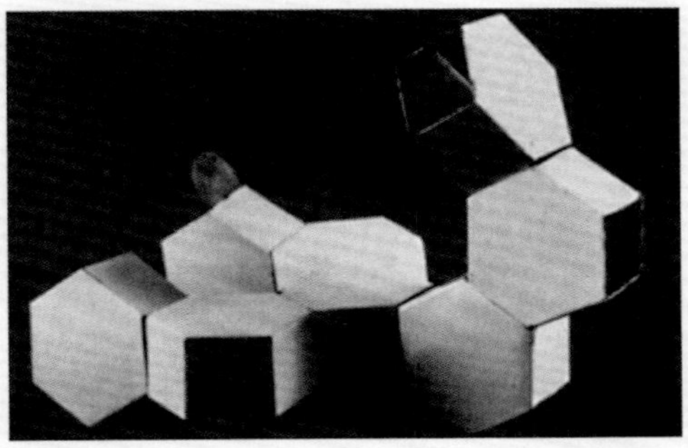
11A

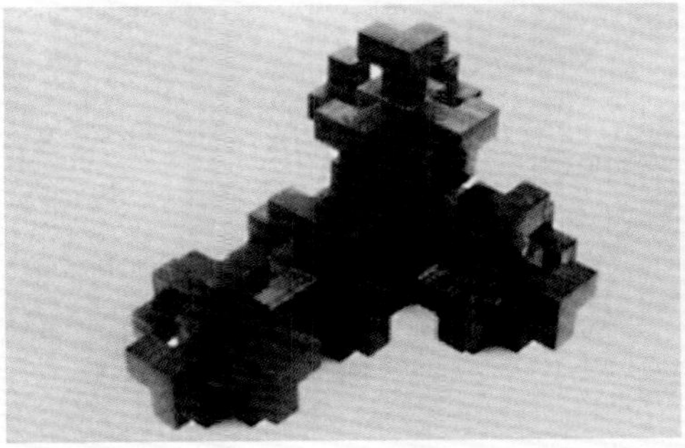
11B

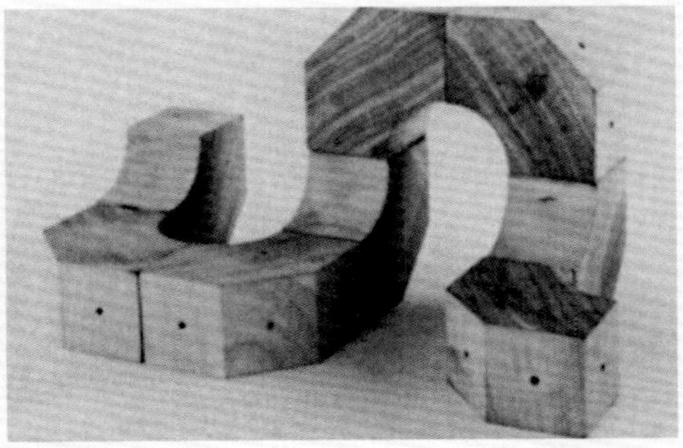
11C

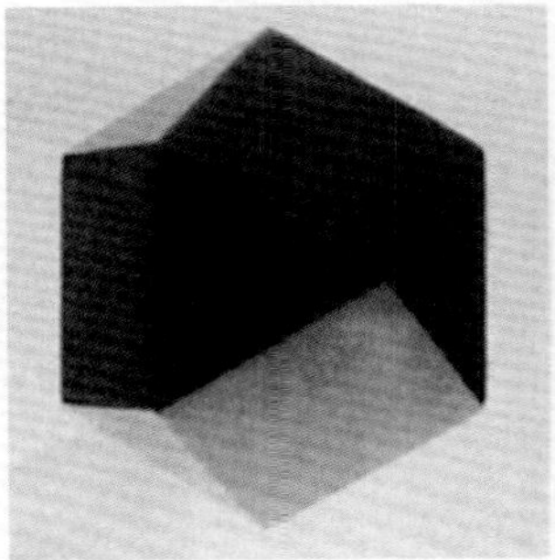
12A

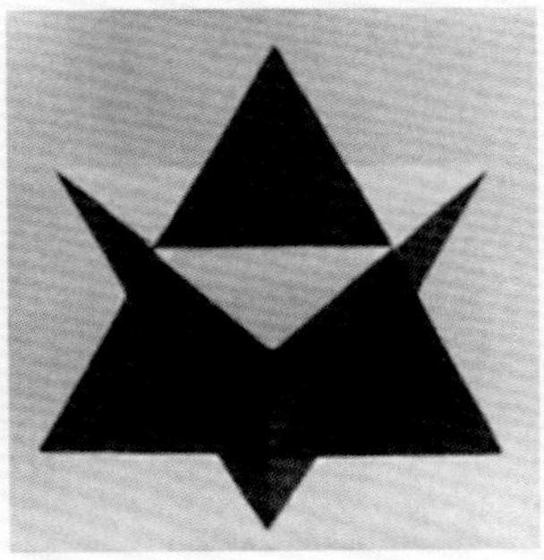
12B

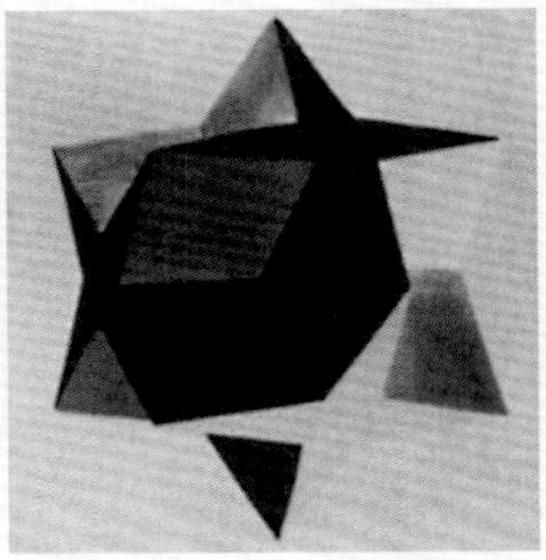
12C

Ahmedabad Declaration on Industrial Design for Development, adopted at the UNIDO-ICSID conference at the National Institute of Design, Ahmedabad, India, 1979

Ahmedabad Declaration on Industrial Design for Development

UNIDO-ICSID INDIA 79

Design for Development
January 14-24

A. Ahmedabad Declaration

1 The Meeting for the Promotion of Industrial Design in Developing Countries convened by the United Nations Industrial Development Organization (UNIDO) in close cooperation with the International Council of Societies of Industrial Design (ICSID) and the Indian National Institute of Design in January 1979, in line with the Lima Declaration and Plan of Action and in pursuance of the Memorandum of Understanding signed between UNIDO and ICSID on April 26,1977 to accelerate jointly industrial design activities in developing countries in order to satisfy the urgent needs in this field, and to carry out as extensively as possible the promotional activities necessary to alert developing countries to the advantage of including industrial design in their planning processes,

Adopts

The Ahmedabad Declaration on Industrial Design for Development.

2 **Having reviewed** the situation with respect to industrial design in a number of developing countries,

3 **Bearing in mind** that design improves function, enhances communication, simplifies manufacture, use and maintenance,

4 **Recognising** that the problem faced in most developing countries is that although design is a real need, it is not yet a sufficiently felt need,

5 **Noting** that design methodology is inadequately known and insufficiently used as an economic resource,

6 **Aware** that few countries have the organisational, financial and personnel resources which can enable industrial design to assume its proper role,

7 **Convinced** that design can help raise the quality of life within economic planning and that the designer can become an agent of progress,

8 **Recognising** that through design, relevant cultural traditions can be preserved and utilised to current advantage,

9 **Recognising** that cooperation between UNIDO and ICSID should not only further the transfer of technology, know-how and information in the field of industrial design, but should help to stimulate self-reliance,

10 **Noting** that UNIDO and ICSID have agreed to carry out as extensively as possible the promotional activities necessary to alert developing countries to the advantages of including industrial design in their planning processes,

11 **Bearing in mind** that as a first step towards achieving these objectives, this Meeting was convened to help initiate meaningful cooperation and exchange between institutions and designers concerned with problems of the developing world,

12 **Having decided** to adopt a common position and a line of action, the Meeting

Solemnly declares

13 Its firm conviction that design can be a powerful force for the improvement of the quality of life in the developing world;

14 Its firm belief that designers must have a clear understanding of the values of their own societies and of what constitutes a standard of life for their own people;

15 That design in the developing world must be committed to a search for local answers to local needs, utilising indigenous skills, materials and traditions while absorbing the extraordinary power that science and technology can make available to it;

16 That designers in every part of the world must work to evolve a new value system which dissolves the disastrous divisions between the worlds of waste and want, preserves the identity of peoples and attends the priority areas of need for the vast majority of mankind;

17 That in view of the foregoing, the Meeting adopts the various measures set forth in the following Plan of Action.

B. Plan of Action

Measures

1 Developing countries are encouraged to consider the establishment of design institutions, design centres and/or other design-practising and promotional institutions to spread design methodology, awareness and consciousness.

2 These institutions should develop close and sustained links with industrial activity in government and in the private sector, at every level including heavy industries, medium-scale industries, small-scale, rural and craft industries, as well as with educational and research institutions, and with people who are the ultimate users of design.

3 In developing countries, the establishment of professional design associations which can function parallel to the design promotional institutions should be seriously considered, and such efforts assisted.

4 Design institutions are worthy of financial and other support by their governments, which must be their prime source of succour at this early stage of development.

5 These institutions must work to establish a priority for industrial design through the creation of a national design consciousness. They must hasten the awareness that in all areas of public expenditure, the integration of design in the planning process can ensure optimum quality and utilisation of resources. They must communicate that industrial design is concerned with the improvement of our environment through the appropriate use of raw materials, increased productivity, with the protection of health, human safety, natural and cultural resources, with the enhancement of working environments, and with expanding work opportunities and earnings at all levels, including exports. Therefore design considerations should be incorporated in plans for national development.

6 To achieve these purposes, such institutions in developing countries may consider the importance of articulating a statement on the importance of design which can serve as a national consensus on the need for creating design awareness and for utilising design as a discipline for better planning.

7 Such institutions must stress the importance of establishing and improving facilities for design education and training, upgrading design experience, as well as assisting designers to act as trainers and as catalysts for design awareness wherever they work, so that design skills can be disseminated at several levels simultaneously, and thus influence industrial activity on a broad scale in the developing world.

8 The establishment of national design awards, exhibitions, documentation and publication programmes should be encouraged as aids to a wider understanding of industrial design and of design traditions and resources.

9 Systems of active cooperation should be established and promoted between design institutions in the developed and less developed countries, and between these institutions in the less developed world.

10 These cooperative arrangements could be bilateral as well as multilateral. International organisations including ICSID, UNIDO, UNESCO, UNCTAD, WHO, UNEP, IBRD, the Asian Development Bank and the African Development Bank, IADB and others should be encouraged to provide active support to such cooperative arrangements.

Yet, both NID and IDC were keenly aware that Bauhaus values and the Ulm pedagogy had little to offer in linking design to development issues and the reality that Indian industry was not ready for the Ulm approach. It was through projects that they explored how design might become relevant in the Indian context – revitalizing traditional craft practices in contemporary settings, designing typefaces for Indian languages for digital applications, exhibitions, energy-efficient cooking stoves, corporate identities for national institutions, the electronic voting machine and contemporizing handspun and handwoven *khadi* popularized by Gandhi.

The impulse to design life in India continued over the next decades exemplified by the meeting for the 'Promotion of Industrial Design in Developing Countries' convened by United Nations Industrial Development Organization (UNIDO) and the International Council of Societies of Industrial Design (ICSID) in 1979 at NID. Participants adopted the 'Ahmedabad Declaration on Industrial Design for Development' which underlined that 'design can be a powerful force for improving the quality of life in the developing world' and must be committed to 'finding local answers for local needs, utilising indigenous skills, material and traditions while absorbing the extraordinary power that science and technology can make available to it'.[10]

The life of the postcolonial Indian citizen was thus designed through a discourse generated by a state which gave itself the mandate to prescribe and implement a 'standard of living', by international actors, each with their own conception of world development and a globalized Indian elite who saw themselves as interlocutors and mediators between the two. The discourse was served by a design pedagogy innovated as a response to post-war conditions at two historical moments in Germany, sometimes with the participation of the creators, in ways that were perhaps not anticipated in Weimar, Dessau and Ulm.

Page from A. G. Rao (ed.), *Industrial Design Centre: A Decade of Design Experience*, Bombay: Indian Institute of Technology, 1979

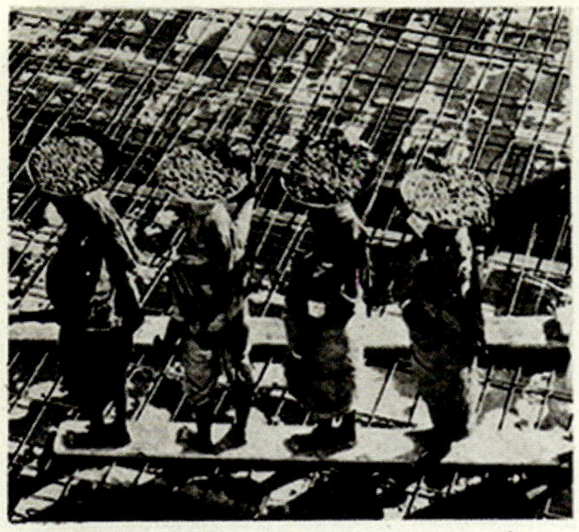

Gamela

Gamela, a pan shaped container, is widely used in carrying various types of materials like concrete, mortar and bricks. Detailed studies revealed problems in handling, stacking, carrying and transfering material. The new shape with elliptical contour facilitates stackability with or without material, gives better hand grip and guides the material for transfer in addition to making the gamela more comfortabl to carry on heads.

Design : S. K. Dastoor
Guide : S. Nadkarni

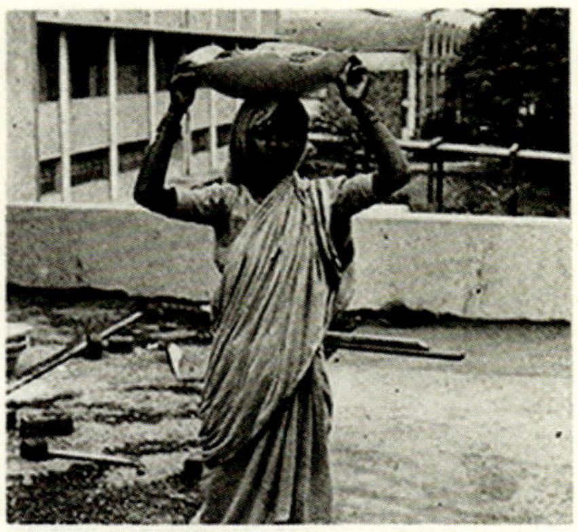

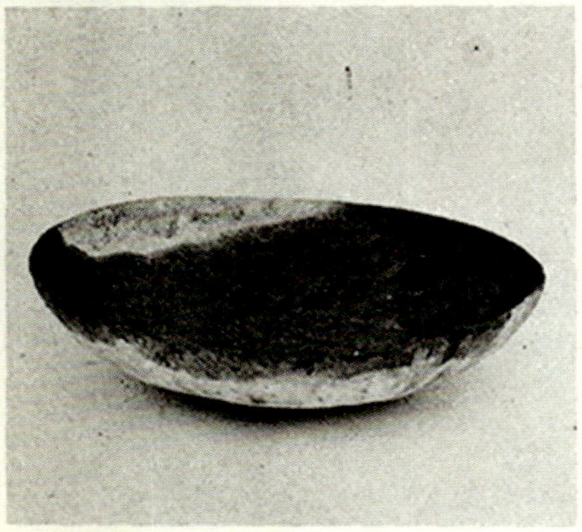

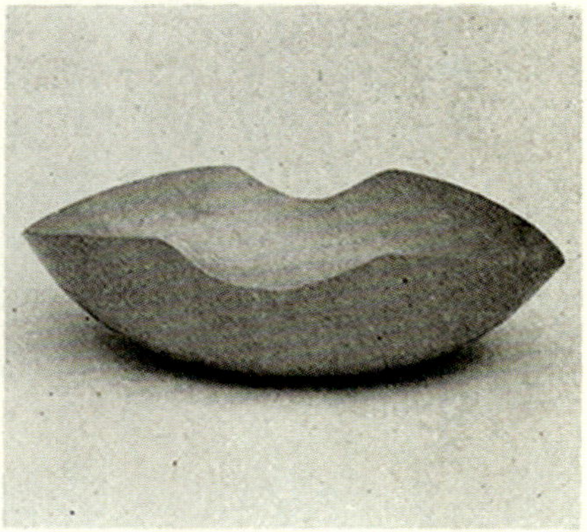

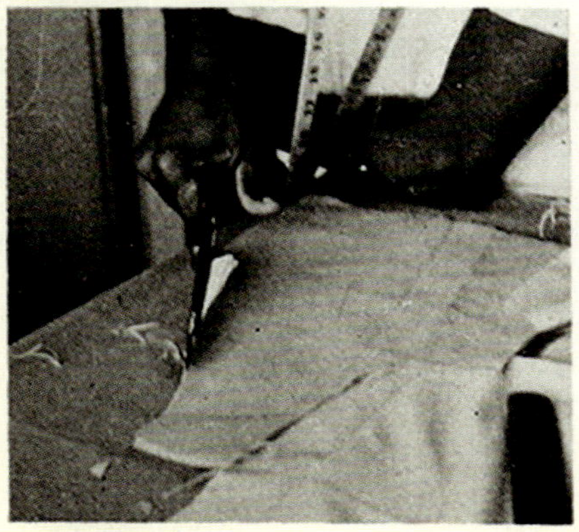

Scissors

Tailors prefer heavy scissors and rest them on the table while cutting. With the new design scissors can be used without lifting it from table as only one part is moved for cutting.

Design : S. K. Menon
Guide : A. G. Rao

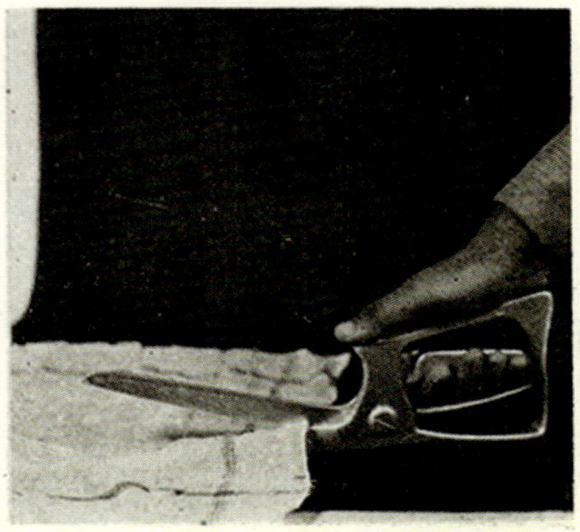

16 Industrial Design Centre- a decade of design experience

Design for Need: Sudhakar Nadkarni's Milk Kiosk

Regina Bittner

Events in the summer of 1965 may have coincided: while the design student Sudhakar Nadkarni was at the Hochschule für Gestaltung (HfG) Ulm (Ulm School of Design), working on his diploma dedicated to the design of a milk kiosk for the megapolis of Mumbai, his home city, the German architect and designer Hans Gugelot travelled to the National Institute of Design (NID) Ahmedabad (founded in 1961) to teach a summer course. The latter belonged to a circle of experts on product design at the institute who were in charge of developing a series of ventilators for domestic use as well as an affordable line of furniture. The 'tangential fan' developed that summer together with Indian students was part of his assignment. The NID had engaged a number of international experts alongside Gugelot to support the establishment of the first modern design school in India: Charles and Ray Eames, Alexander Girard, Louis Kahn, George Nakashima, Claude Stoller and others. Their consulting work was generously sponsored by the American Ford Foundation, which had already financed the assessment on developing a modern design school commissioned by Jawaharlal Nehru – the *India Report* (1958), a document that today belongs to the foundation narrative of the NID. Nadkarni was from a middle-class Indian family and studied applied art at the Sir J. J. Institute of Applied Art Bombay. At that time, the profession of industrial designer was just emerging in India. In his memoirs, Nadkarni recalls how the occupational field of industrial design was first brought to his attention through a lecture by James Gardner, a distinguished expert on modern design in post-war Britain. Nadkarni learned about HfG Ulm from the Indian designer Yeshwant Chaudhary, a fellow graduate of the Sir J. J. Institute of Applied Art and the Central School of Arts and Crafts, London, who then also wrote him a letter of recommendation for the HfG Ulm.[1]

The reason why the design of modern consumer goods was such a fascinating profession for the young generation of the Indian middle class can only be understood against the backdrop of the enormous cultural and economic changes that took place in the wake of the modernization agenda of Jawaharlal Nehru, the president of the young, independent state of India. Massive infrastructure projects, the expansion of big industry, the promotion of modern educational facilities – they all belonged to the state's Five-Year Plans with which modern India sought to leave its colonial past behind. Modern architecture and design not only symbolized this change but were themselves agents for practising a modern way of life.

Sudhakar Nadkarni, model of a milk kiosk, diploma thesis, Hochschule für Gestaltung Ulm, 1964/65

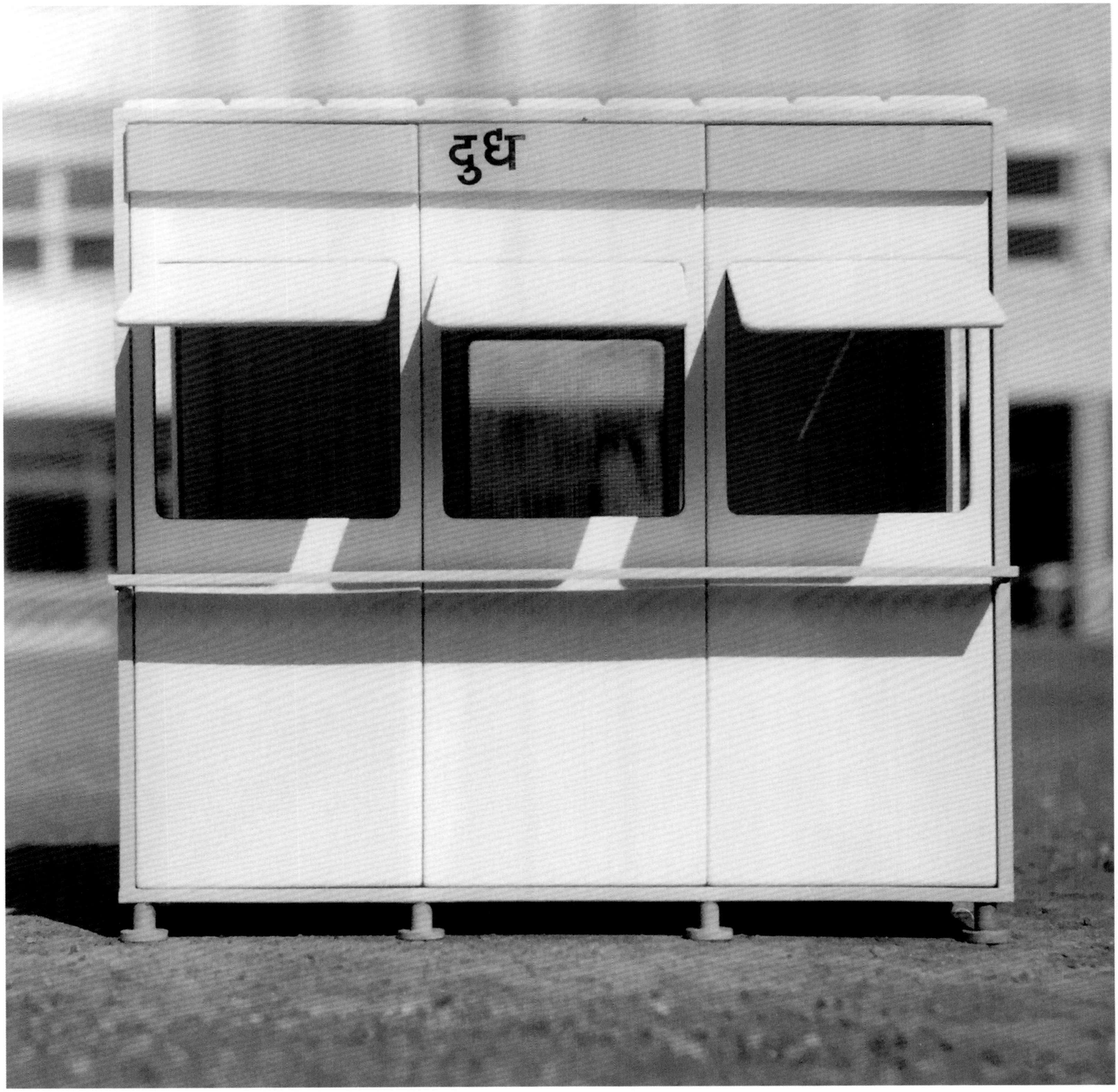

In 1962 Nadkarni travelled to Ulm to study product design under Gugelot, among others. During his studies there, he met Kumar Vyas from the Central School of Arts and Crafts, who was in Ulm for six months. Both went on to form the faculty for teaching product design at the NID. The Indian student experienced the HfG Ulm in a phase in which the teaching of design was consistently oriented towards the cooperation between science, engineering and industry.

From the onset, the HfG Ulm was an exemplary platform facilitating the networking and international exchange of post-war modernism. The list of teachers reads like a who's who of the international architecture and design scene: Bruce Archer, Reyner Banham, Charles and Ray Eames, Buckminster Fuller, Abraham Moles, Norbert Wiener and many others.

Although the HfG Ulm is regarded as a legitimate successor institution of the Bauhaus, the Argentine Tomás Maldonado, who was the director of the school when Nadkarni studied there, distanced himself from his predecessor, the Swiss architect and former Bauhaus student Max Bill. Bill had invited Maldonado, a proponent of geometric abstraction and founder of the Asociación Arte Concreto-Invención in Buenos Aires (1944), to Ulm. The relation of the HfG Ulm to the historical Bauhaus indeed reflected the cultural and political diversity in post-war Germany. As an initially non-governmental educational facility supported by the US's re-education fund, the HfG Ulm and its founding members – including Inge Scholl, the sister of Hans and Sophie Scholl, who had been murdered in Nazi Germany – resolutely advocated an explicitly political, democratic form of education. The legacy of National Socialism, on the one hand, and the critique of post-war Germany's fascination with American consumer society on the other (Inge Scholl spoke of the 'nightmare of the kidney-shaped table'), marked the field of tension in which the extraordinary school on the Kuhberg wrestled for a stance towards modern design. Although Bill opined that genuine social and cultural reforms must start with a change in the way the social environment is shaped, in the architecture of the design of everyday objects, the debate on the extent to which designed products are 'cultural assets' or scientifically founded commodities revealing varying degrees of complexity remained an ongoing issue on the campus.[2] While former Bauhaus members, such as Josef Albers, Walter Peterhans and Helene Nonné-Schmidt still taught during the formative years, it appeared as if the pedagogical principles of the historical Bauhaus, anchored in the arts and crafts, could not provide the knowledge required to deal with the complicated conditions of industrial development in the post-war period. Maldonado vehemently rejected Bill's Bauhaus and *Werkbund* idealism, with concepts of the 'good form' belonging to this set of values. He distanced himself from the narrative favoured in post-war Germany, according to which the Expressionist Bauhaus was the legacy of humanistic, bourgeois culture that remained uncontaminated by National Socialism. His 1963 polemic 'Ist das Bauhaus noch aktuell?' (Is the Bauhaus Still Up-to-Date?), published in the in-house periodical, underscored which Bauhaus legacy was to be relevant in Ulm: the Bauhaus under the direction of Hannes Meyer, which was oriented towards scientific rationality.[3] He aimed for a secularized design method rooted in the principles of rational production and freed from the Expressionist artist's ethos.[4] The post-war debates on the Bauhaus were ultimately about a redefinition of the relationship between design and society. Nadkarni, who wanted to contribute to the modernization processes of his country, was also convinced of this eminently social role of the designer.

Hence the task Nadkarni selected for his diploma, 'Die Gestaltung eines Milchkiosk' (The Design of a Milk Kiosk), was already an indication of the designer's social awareness, of his wish to make a contribution to the direct needs of the Indian population. The diploma consisted of two parts – a scientific analysis and the design section. The first part provided an introduction to the task: why is the improvement of the system of distributing milk in India's large metropolises so important? Five years after independence, the first state-run dairy plant was built in Mumbai, meeting modern hygienic requirements to secure the supply of milk as a building block of healthy nutrition for 1.5 million people. It was a large-scale project internationally supported by UNICEF. The milk was delivered from the modern dairy plant to smaller distribution centres that organized its sale. Nadkarni designed a kiosk for this system aimed at improving the supply and distribution. For his endeavour of developing a modular structure, he first drew upon international examples of prefabricated kiosks, bus stops and pavilions. A comprehensive diagram visualized the individual steps of the analysis necessary to comprehend the complex system of milk distribution. He started with a detailed study of the surroundings of the milk kiosk, its location in urban space with regard to traffic, residential areas and the urban infrastructure. In the next step, he described the social composition of the consumers and the procedures and activities of such a distribution centre, underpinned by a questionnaire-based survey of more than forty milk kiosk operators and users in Mumbai. This was followed by research conducted on the climatic conditions and movement sequences in the kiosk.[5] This systematically gained knowledge formed the basis for the design of the milk kiosk. The proposed material was cost-effective because it consisted of standardized and durable modules that were available in India; the size was sufficient for two people to work the kiosk. Functional, ergonomic and also climatic aspects were taken into account in regard to the users. Its white colour responded to climactic conditions and hygienic requirements, while the simple lettering 'Milk' visually communicated the object's function in a sufficient way.

Even though the kiosk remained a prototype, the diploma thesis is not only an interesting document of the method taught in Ulm – of the systematic approach to a design task in which scientific analysis provides the grounds for the respective design phases.[6] Nadkarni's diploma also provides direct insights into the social circumstances and material conditions of young, independent India in the 1960s, when the infrastructure of daily milk supply was indeed the foundation for fulfilling the basic needs of the megapolis. The thesis is underpinned by a conviction shared in Ulm and in Ahmedabad that only a rationally founded design that addresses the basic systems of society – infrastructure, health care and food supply – can take people's immediate needs seriously. It is an outstanding document of an attitude grasping design as a tool to enhance the everyday life of the majority of the population.

Arieh Sharon's Nigerian Campus Project: Ife University (1960–85)

Zvi Efrat

In his autobiography, *Kibbutz + Bauhaus: An Architect's Way in a New Land* (Stuttgart: Krämer, 1976), Arieh Sharon dedicates a chapter to the topic of planning in developing countries. This chapter contains impressions of encounters with exotic cultures, comments about tropical architecture and descriptions of several schemes for hospitals and one fairly elaborate built project, recounted as his 'most important challenge' in foreign territory – the Ife University in Western Nigeria, a project done in several stages on which the Sharon office worked for about two and a half decades (1960–85). What makes the story of this campus epic is Sharon's full engagement with the preliminary geographic, demographic, cultural and infrastructural considerations of the Nigerian government. He was first commissioned to advise on the choice of site for the future university, surveyed sixteen medium-sized towns and compiled data on their socio-economic structures and their services, amenities and communication networks.

Following Sharon's report, the Nigerian government decided to send a delegation, consisting of 'the ministers of Culture and Labor, the leader of the Opposition, several professors of the future university and the advising architect and town planner', to study the plans of some British, American and South American universities. The last visit was to Israel, where the campus of the Hebrew University in Givat Ram, Jerusalem, had just been completed and the delegation's impression of it was positive. 'It was obviously the result of the simple character of the buildings, courtyards and gardens and the modest scale of teaching programs and goals', Sharon recounts in *Kibbutz + Bauhaus*.[1]

The Hebrew University campus in Givat Ram, one of the most prolific modernist projects in Israel of the 1950s and a prime initiation site of the post-war generation of local architects, may therefore be considered as the ur-form of the Ife University campus. Its rational master-plan, locally adapted 'international style' architecture, elaborate landscape of open gardens and pocket patios and circulation system of covered walkways feeding perpendicular serial buildings would be exported to the Nigerian wooded countryside and re-interpreted accordingly. Sharon writes that the very compactness of the Hebrew University campus was considered an advantage both practically and culturally: 'We agreed with the professors that, in view of the local conditions and customs...the layout of the campus...should be as compact as possible', he recalled.[2]

Arieh Sharon and Eldar Sharon, University of Ife (Obafemi Awolowo University), Ile-Ife, Osun, Nigeria, late 1960s

► Pages 230–31: Arieh Sharon and Eldar Sharon, University of Ife (Obafemi Awolowo University), Ile-Ife, Osun, Nigeria, late 1960s

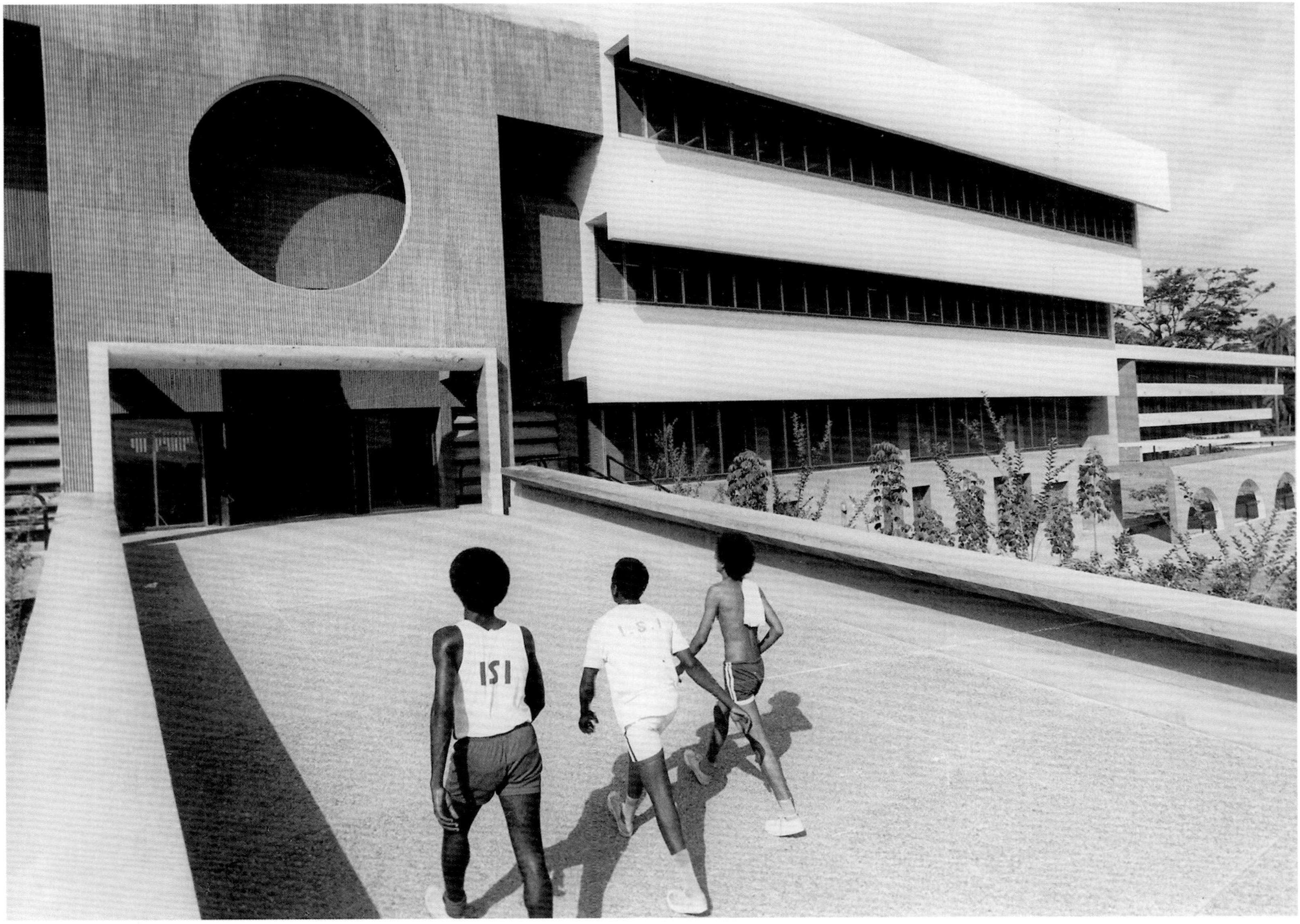

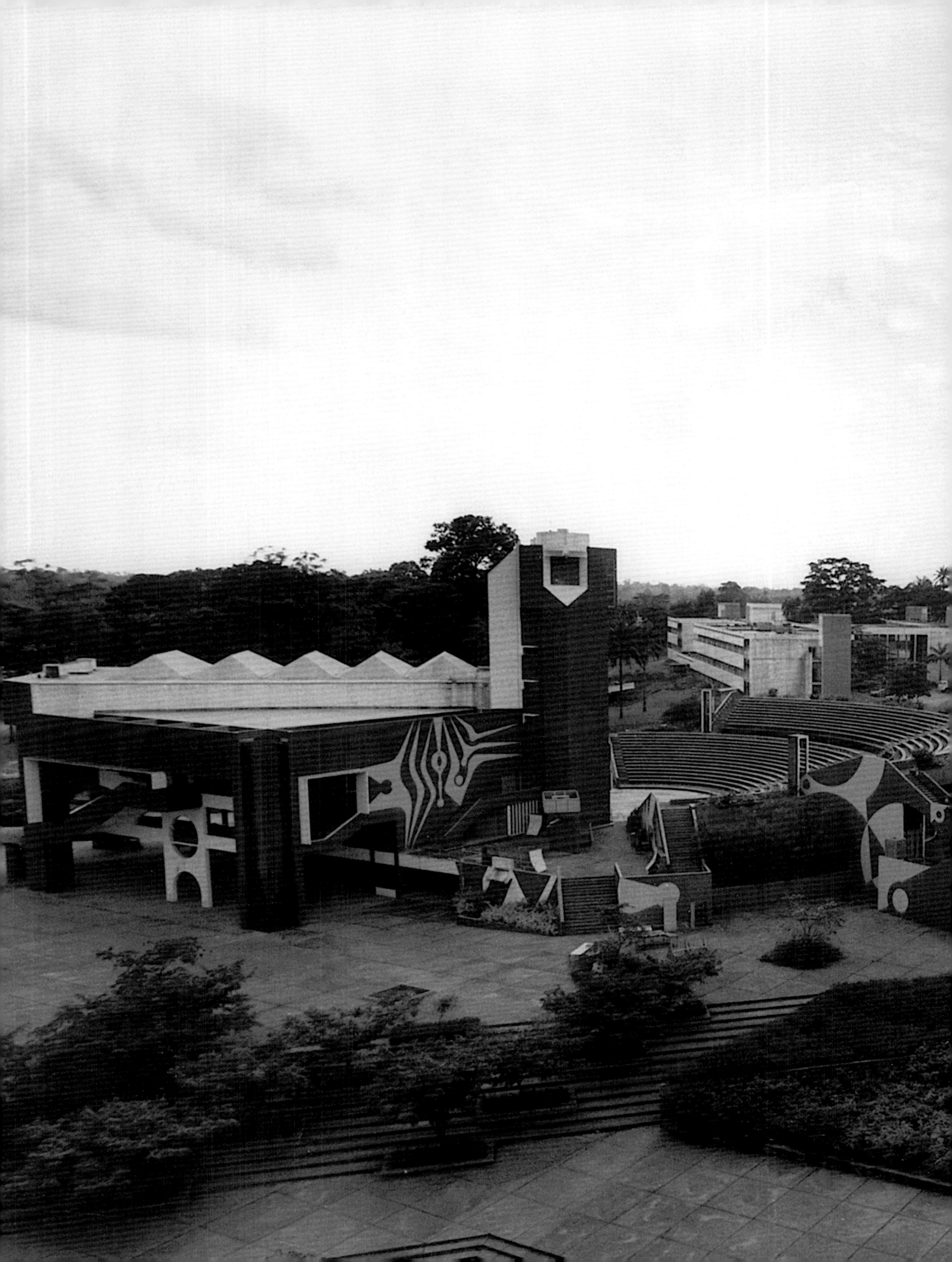

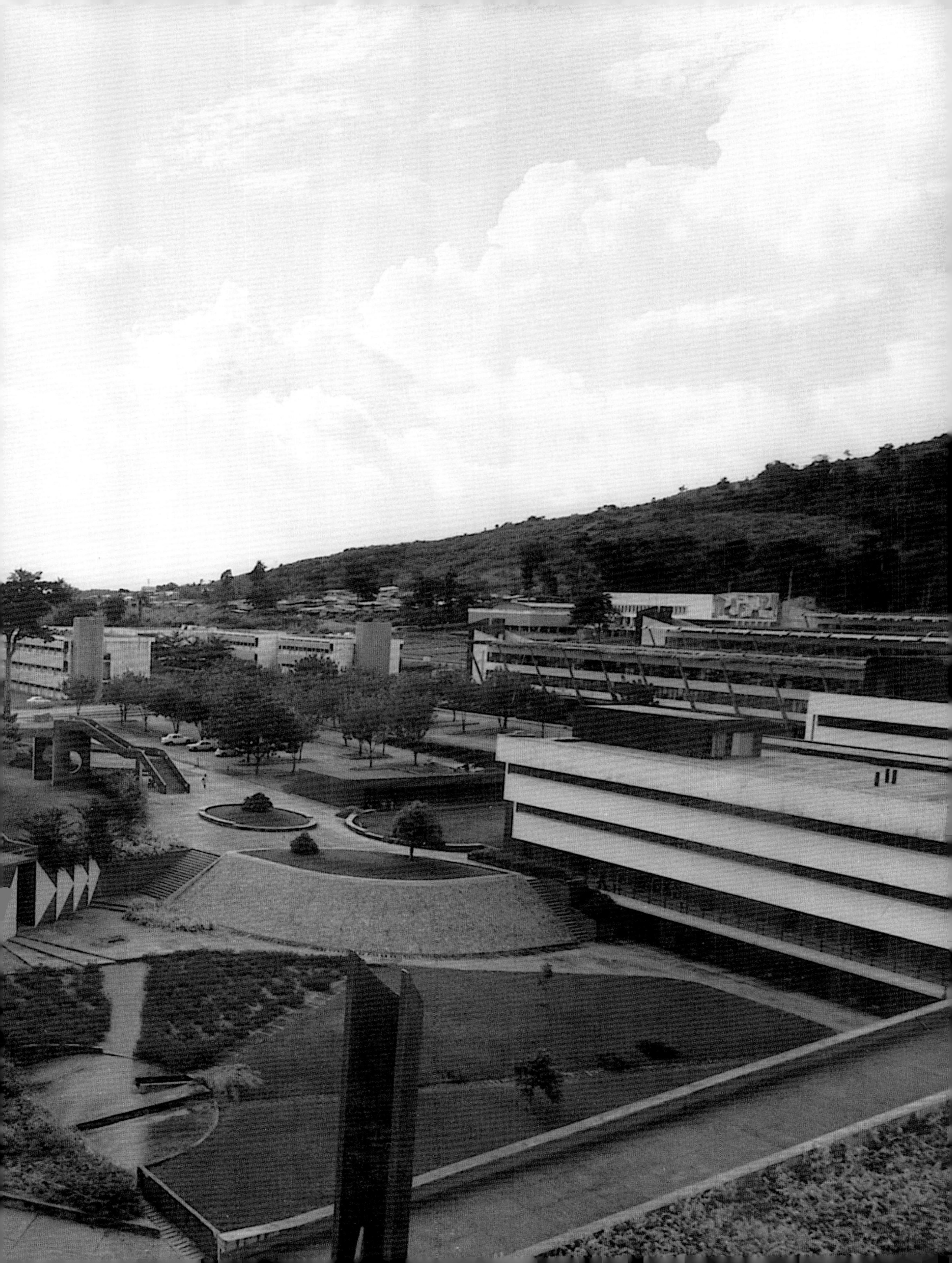

However, the Ife University campus holds such a seminal place in Sharon's portfolio (and occupies more pages in the book than any other project) not so much because Sharon regarded it an offshoot of Israeli institutional architecture, or indeed yet another offhand export of 'international style', but rather because he genuinely considered it a paradigm shift in his own oeuvre, a shift from a strict *Sachlichkeit* without distinctive identity marks, towards an environmentally sensitive planning and a culturally inquisitive design. It seems that in Ife, Sharon's fascination with the native cultures of Africa, expressed in his memoirs and manifested in the Yoruba art objects he accumulated in his house in Tel Aviv, merged naturally as it were with his quasi-scientific methodology for adapting to local climatic conditions, in the hard-line functionalist spirit of his Bauhaus mentor Hannes Meyer.

Indeed, drawings and photographs of the built campus – showing self-shading inverted ziggurats as well as an elaborate system of internal ventilated passages and public spaces framed by the buildings' skeletons and enveloped by the shells – support Sharon's claims for a structural climate-responsive approach. This in contrast to what he criticized as a mere applicative approach, common in so-called 'tropical architecture' as well as in Israeli doctrinaire architecture of the 1950s and 1960s, of which he himself was one of the main articulators. In the Ife campus project, Sharon writes, the design does not rely anymore on climate protection elements and fixtures, such as 'concrete canopies and frames around the windows, or louvers and precast ornamental elements around the terraces'.[3] Instead, it offers a newfound plasticity, porosity, resilience and artistry to temper the African environment and folklore according to postcolonial propriety.

Arieh Sharon and Eldar Sharon, University of Ife (Obafemi Awolowo University), Ile-Ife, Osun, Nigeria, 1960s

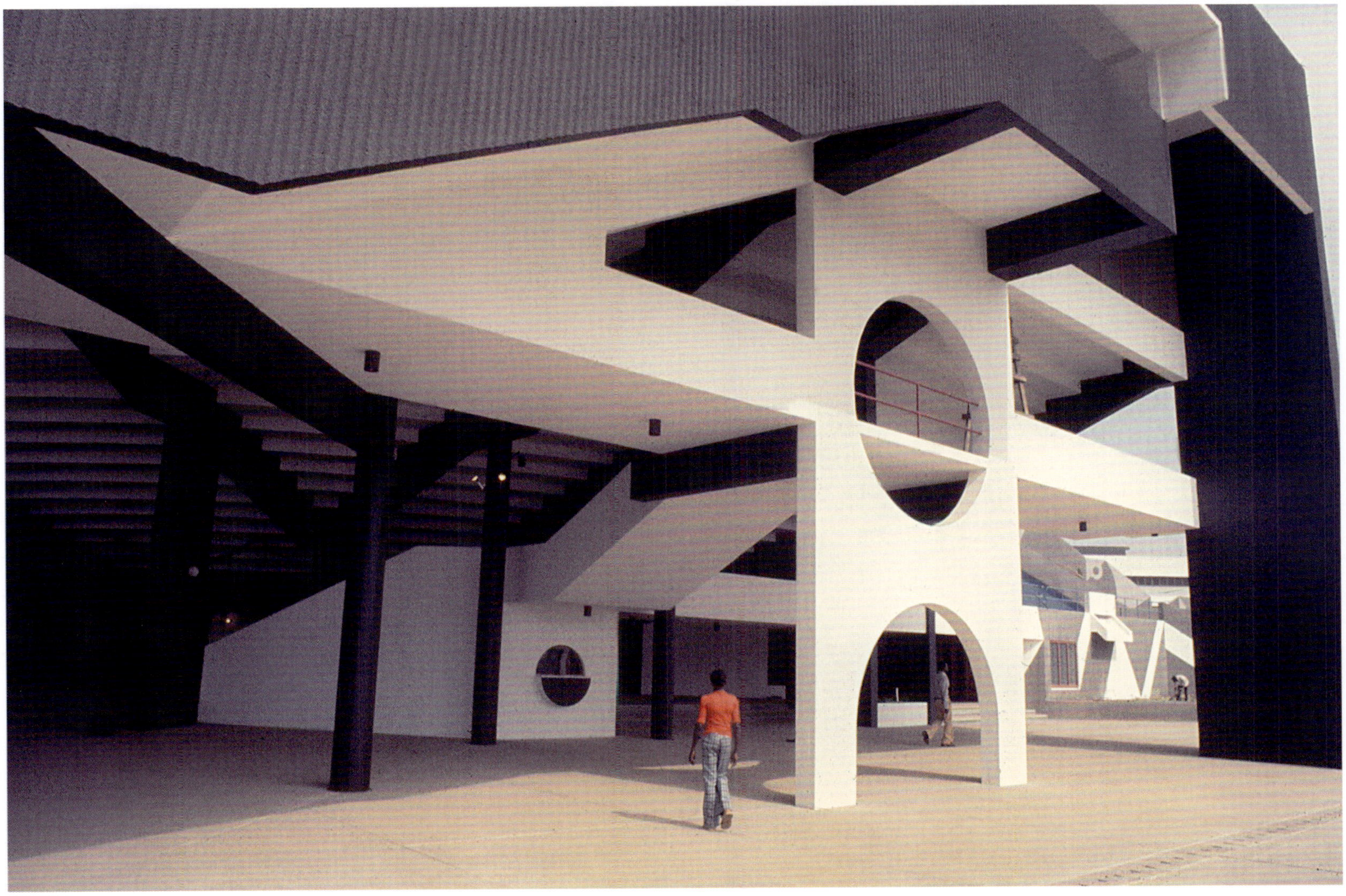

Arieh Sharon and Eldar Sharon, University of Ife (Obafemi Awolowo University), Ile-Ife, Osun, Nigeria, model, 1960

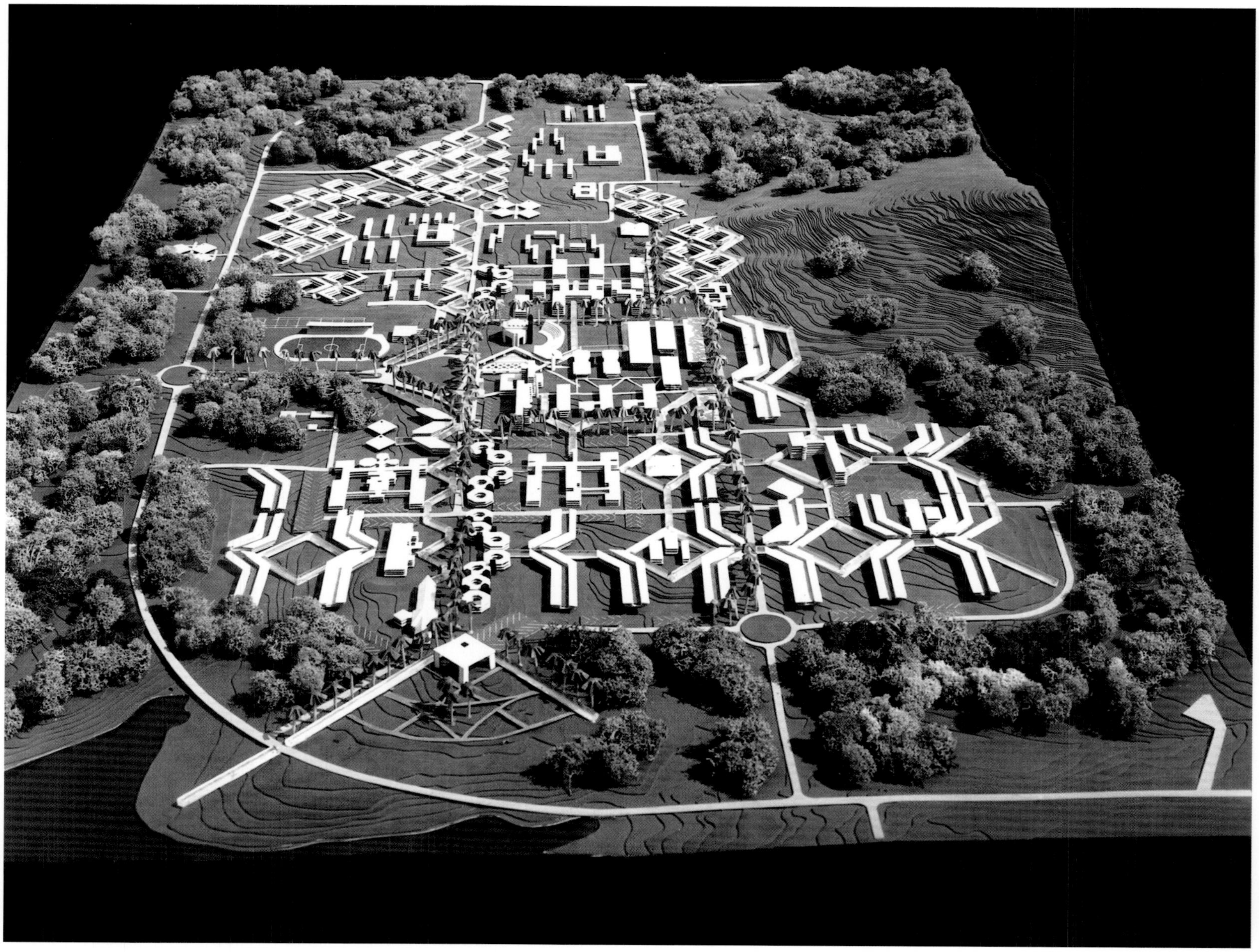

Wendelien van Oldenborgh

Housing with Shadows and Mirrors: Notes towards a Work

Questions about the way we live together today appear when the ideals of post-war Dutch housing intersect with the reality of colonial-modernist trauma; when designing for equality collides with management and policy with biased intent; and when daily liveability meets the aesthetic and moral standards of a dominant culture.

▶▶ Page 238: Hélène Damen and Anne-Mie Devolder (eds), *Lotte Stam-Beese, 1903–1988: Dessau, Brno, Charkow, Moskou, Amsterdam, Rotterdam*. Rotterdam: Uitgeverij Hef, 1993, p. 12

▶▶ Page 239: From the Lotte Stam-Beese archive at Het Nieuwe Instituut, Rotterdam

▶▶▶ Pages 240–41: Plan for Pendrecht district, Rotterdam, as presented at the CIAM conference, Bergamo, 1949. Insert: Lotte Stam-Beese, design for the section of the KhTZ Settlement, Kharkov, *c*. 1932. Both from the Lotte Stam-Beese archive at Het Nieuwe Instituut, Rotterdam

1930s

Around the same time that the Bauhaus-educated architect Lotte Beese – who had been the lover of Hannes Meyer, became a single mother and was fired from her design job with the modernist architect Bohuslav Fuchs in Brno, Czechoslovakia – decided to go to the Ukraine to practise her profession and pursue her ideals, the politically active Hermina Huiswoud left the United States to live and work in the Soviet Union to contribute to the struggles against inequalities in race and class, and to fight for the sovereignty of all colonies, together with her husband Otto Huiswoud.

In the Soviet city of Kharkov, Lotte Beese worked in a collective towards the design of children's homes and a housing complex for the workers of the Kharkov Tractor factory, KhTZ. Hermina and Otto Huiswoud worked for the Profintern from Moscow and eventually published and distributed the magazine the *Negro Worker* from the headquarters of the International Trade Union Committee for Negro Workers (ITUC-NW) in Hamburg and elsewhere.

1950s

Around the same time that Lotte Stam-Beese – by then divorced from the functionalist Mart Stam, with whom she had lived and worked in the Soviet Union – became the Chief Architect for Urban Planning for the Rotterdam Department for Urban Development and Reconstruction, Hermina and Otto Huiswoud settled in Amsterdam to continue their struggles for equality and against imperialism through culture and other means of organization beyond party politics.

Hermina and Otto Huiswoud were leading figures in the association 'Ons Suriname' and whilst relating to artists and literary figures worldwide, large parts of the Caribbean-Dutch community in the Netherlands were politicized under their influence. Lotte Stam-Beese earned her reputation by designing various post-war districts, notably the neighbourhood Pendrecht in the southern part of Rotterdam, which were introduced internationally through her participation in the Congrès Internationaux d'Architecture Moderne (CIAM). This decade also saw a large immigration to the Netherlands from the former Dutch Indies, as well as from the still-existing colonies in the Caribbean. Many settled in post-war neighbourhoods all over the country. A substantial number of these neigbourhoods, which reflected a national image of what modern housing looked like, were modelled on Pendrecht.

2000s

Around the same time that Pendrecht was called one of the 'worst neighbourhoods in the Netherlands', housing had changed from being a right to being a privilege. By then, Pendrecht was inhabited in large part by a non-white Dutch population or recent immigrants. Over decades, neighbourhoods once designed based on socialist principles, like the right to a proper place to live and towards equality of living conditions, had been afflicted by housing policy and management reflecting continuous patterns of structural racism and classism.

Both Lotte Stam-Beese and Hermina Huiswoud passed away at the end of the twentieth century. For the regions that she designed during her almost three decades at the Rotterdam Department for Urban Development and Reconstruction, Lotte Stam-Beese had carefully thought of diverse ways of living and the needs of differentiated spaces for that but had not taken racial difference or colonial-modernist trauma into account as urgent issues central to development. Hermina and Otto Huiswoud continuously adhered to communist ideals as the way to fight against ongoing injustice and inequality, expressed through direct political struggle and through alliances in art and culture.

The Bauhaus had a few fundamental principles. First: don't limit yourself to your own views; have a look into your neighbour's garden. And second: we were not allowed to draw in perspective.

Lotte Stam-Beese

Perspective is about your position in relation to the world, and once you know it, you can mess with it.

Paul Klee's rule four

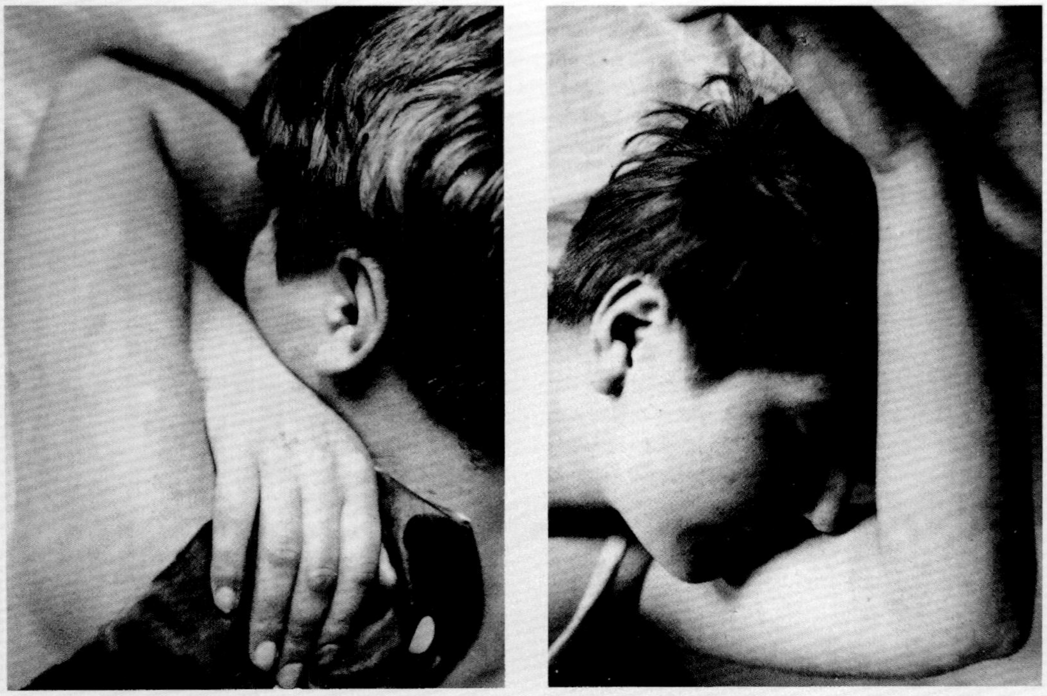

Portretten van Lotte Beese.
Foto: Hannes Meyer, ca. 1928.

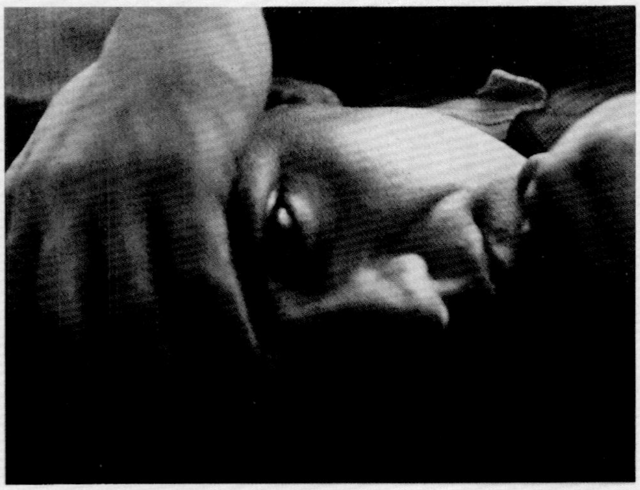

Portret van Hannes Meyer.
Foto: Lotte Beese, ca. 1928.

12

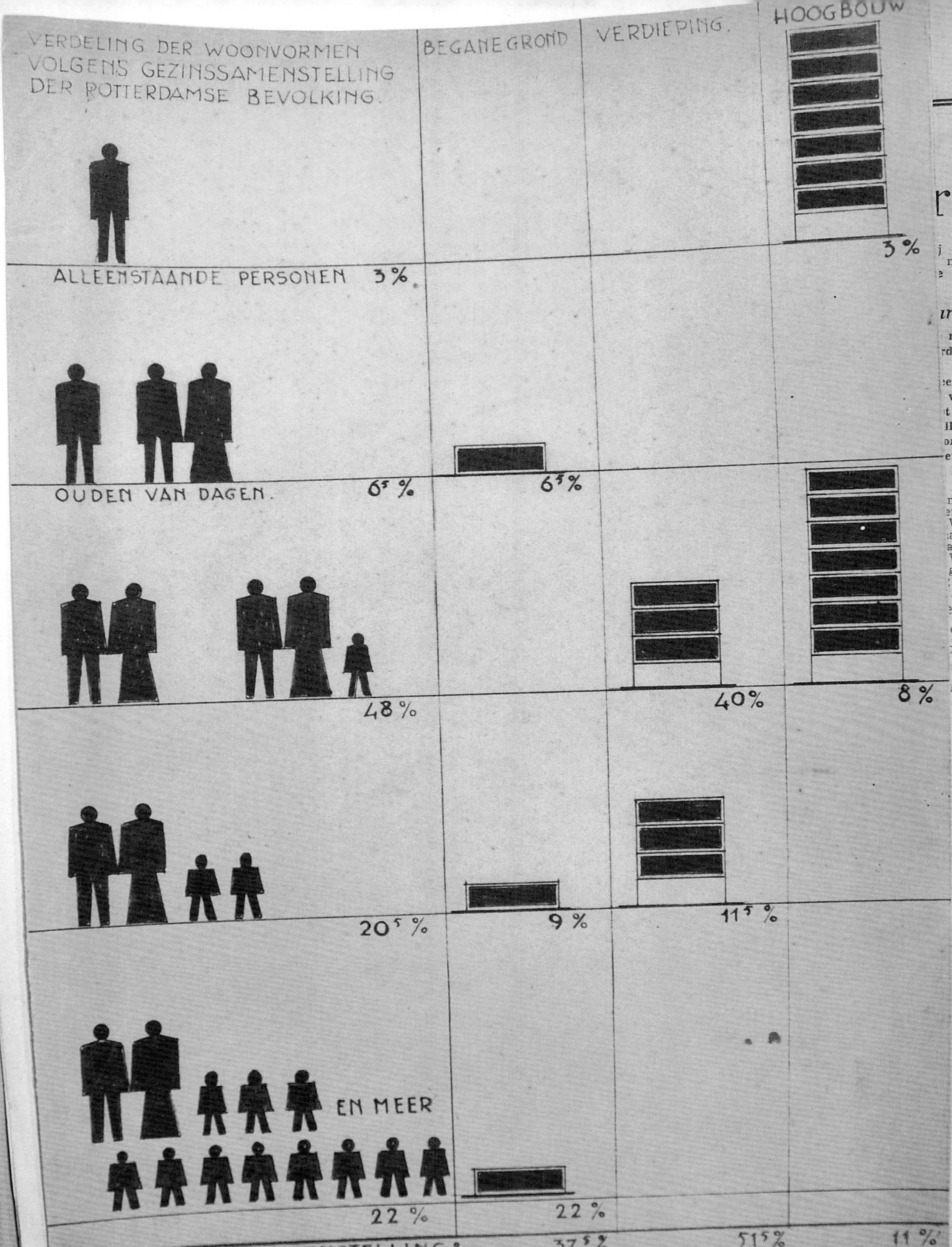

Over het ... ouden van dagen, ... groenvoorziening geprojecteerd is. De groenvoorziening is afwisselend uitge- ... bouwen gedeelte, een geografisch afgerond geheel is en gescheiden door hoofdwegen van de andere onderdelen.

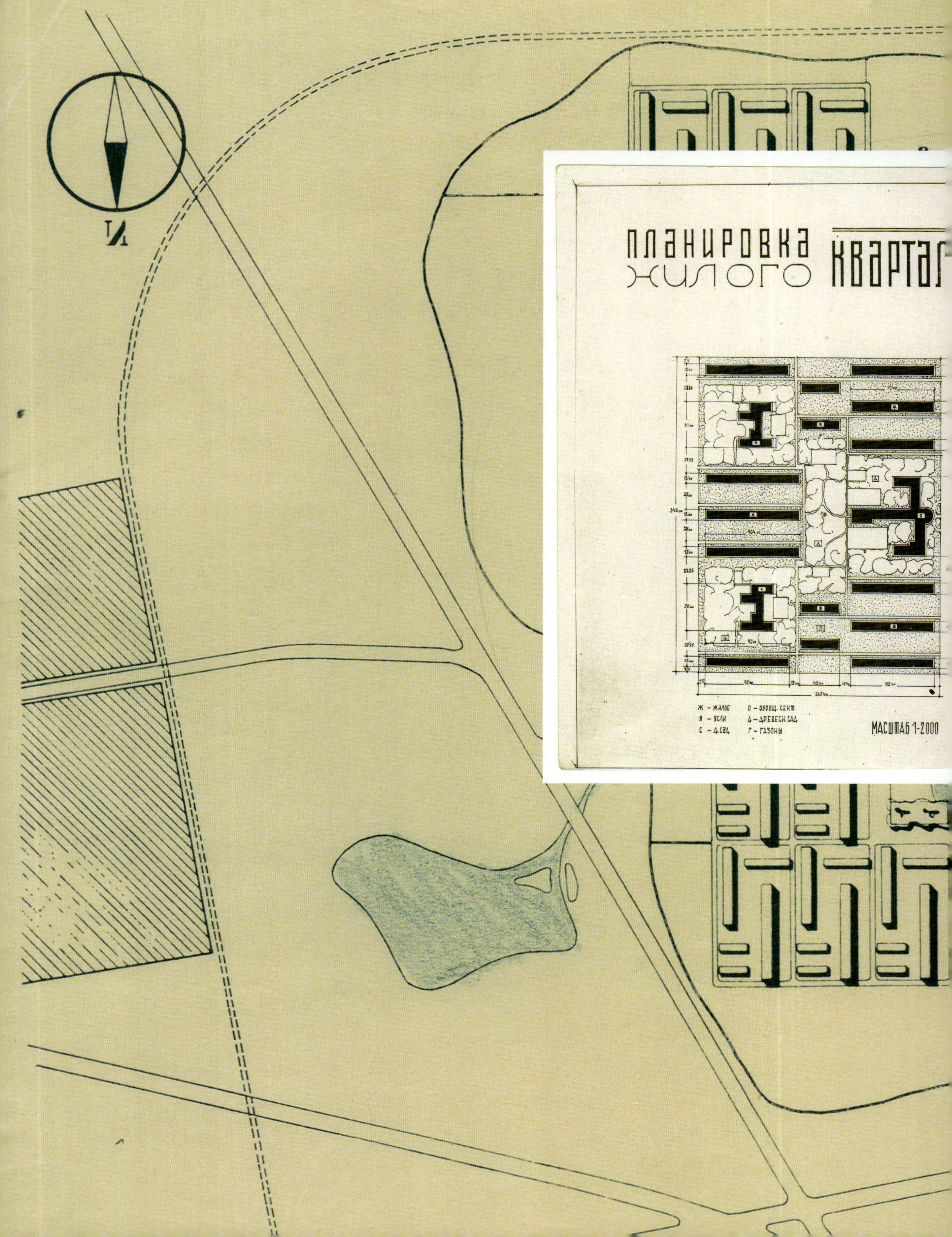
Ю
ПЛАНИРОВКА
ЖИЛОГО
КВАРТАЛ
Ж – ЖИЛЬЕ
Я – ЯСЛИ
С – Д.САД
О – ОБОБЩ. СЕКТ.
Д – ДРЕВЕСН. САД
Г – ГАЗОНЫ
МАСШТАБ 1-2000

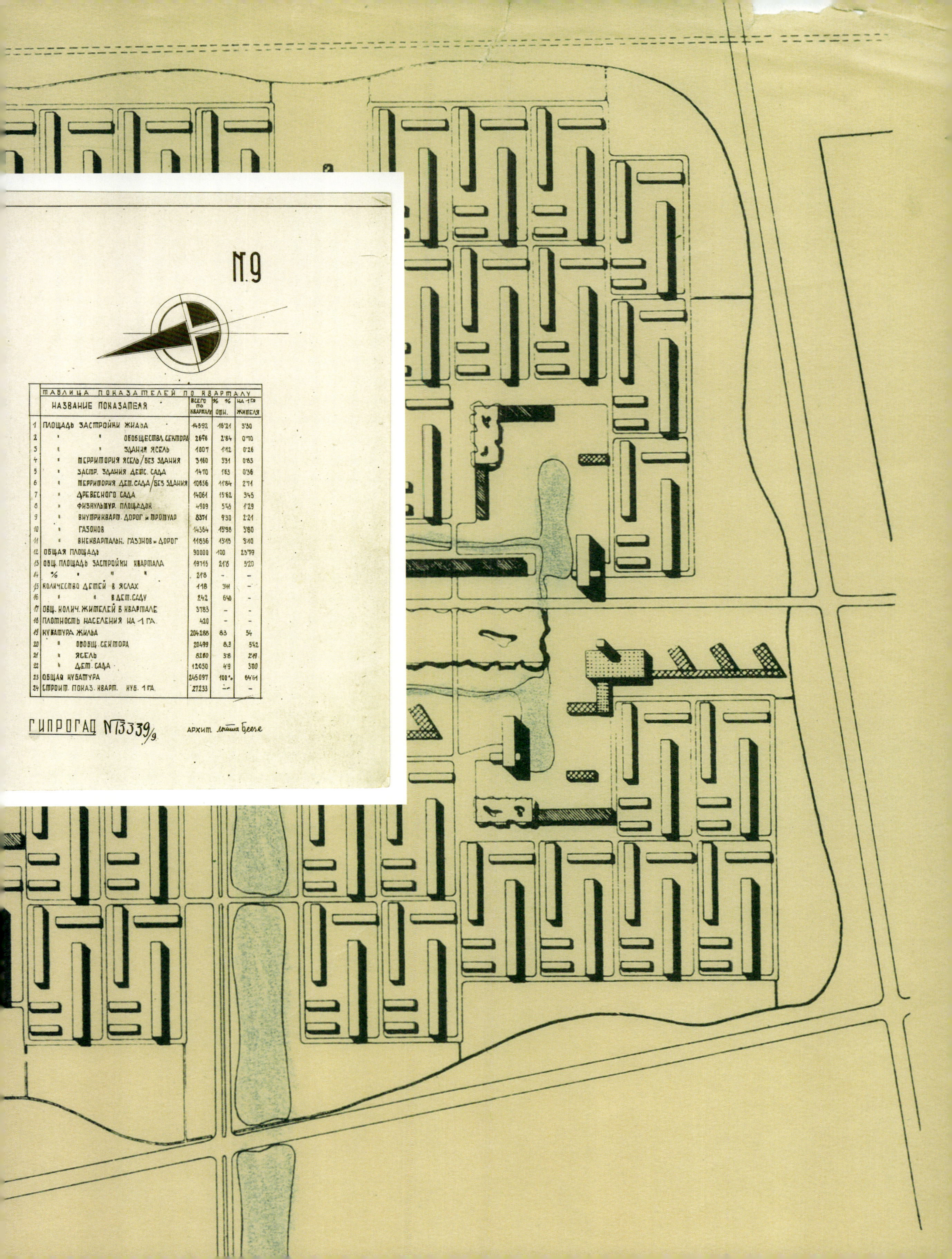

№ 9

	ТАБЛИЦА ПОКАЗАТЕЛЕЙ ПО КВАРТАЛУ			
	НАЗВАНИЕ ПОКАЗАТЕЛЯ	ВСЕГО ПО КВАРТАЛУ	% % ОТН.	НА 1-ГО ЖИТЕЛЯ
1	ПЛОЩАДЬ ЗАСТРОЙКИ ЖИЛЬЯ	14592	16'21	3'30
2	" " ОБОБЩЕСТВЛ. СЕКТОРА	2646	2'84	0'70
3	" " ЗДАНИЯ ЯСЕЛЬ	1007	1'12	0'26
4	" ТЕРРИТОРИЯ ЯСЕЛЬ/БЕЗ ЗДАНИЯ	3160	3'51	0'83
5	" ЗАСТР. ЗДАНИЯ ДЕТС. САДА	1470	1'63	0'36
6	" ТЕРРИТОРИЯ ДЕТ. САДА/БЕЗ ЗДАНИЯ	10656	11'84	2'71
7	" ДРЕВЕСНОГО САДА	14061	15'62	3'45
8	" ФИЗКУЛЬТУР. ПЛОЩАДОК	4909	5'45	1'29
9	" ВНУТРИКВАРТ. ДОРОГ и ТРОТУАР	8371	9'30	2'21
10	" ГАЗОНОВ	14384	15'98	3'80
11	" ВНЕКВАРТАЛЬН. ГАЗОНОВ и ДОРОГ	11836	13'15	3'10
12	ОБЩАЯ ПЛОЩАДЬ	90000	100	23'79
13	ОБЩ. ПЛОЩАДЬ ЗАСТРОЙКИ КВАРТАЛА	19715	21'8	5'20
14	% " " "	21'8	-	-
15	КОЛИЧЕСТВО ДЕТЕЙ В ЯСЛАХ	118	3'11	-
16	" " В ДЕТ. САДУ	242	6'40	-
17	ОБЩ. КОЛИЧ. ЖИТЕЛЕЙ В КВАРТАЛЕ	3783	-	-
18	ПЛОТНОСТЬ НАСЕЛЕНИЯ НА 1 ГА.	420	-	-
19	КУБАТУРА ЖИЛЬЯ	204288	83	54
20	" ОБОБЩ. СЕКТОРА	20499	8,3	5'42
21	" ЯСЕЛЬ	8260	3'8	2'19
22	" ДЕТ. САДА	12050	4'9	3'00
23	ОБЩАЯ КУБАТУРА	245097	100%	64'61
24	СТРОИТ. ПОКАЗ. КВАРТ. КУБ. 1 ГА.	27233	-"-	-

ГИПРОГАЦ №13339/9

АРХИТ. Лотта Беезе

Chapter 4

Still Undead

▶ Kurt Schwerdtfeger, *Reflektorische Farblichtspiele* (Reflecting Colour-Light-Play), 1922, light performance, apparatus reconstructed 2016

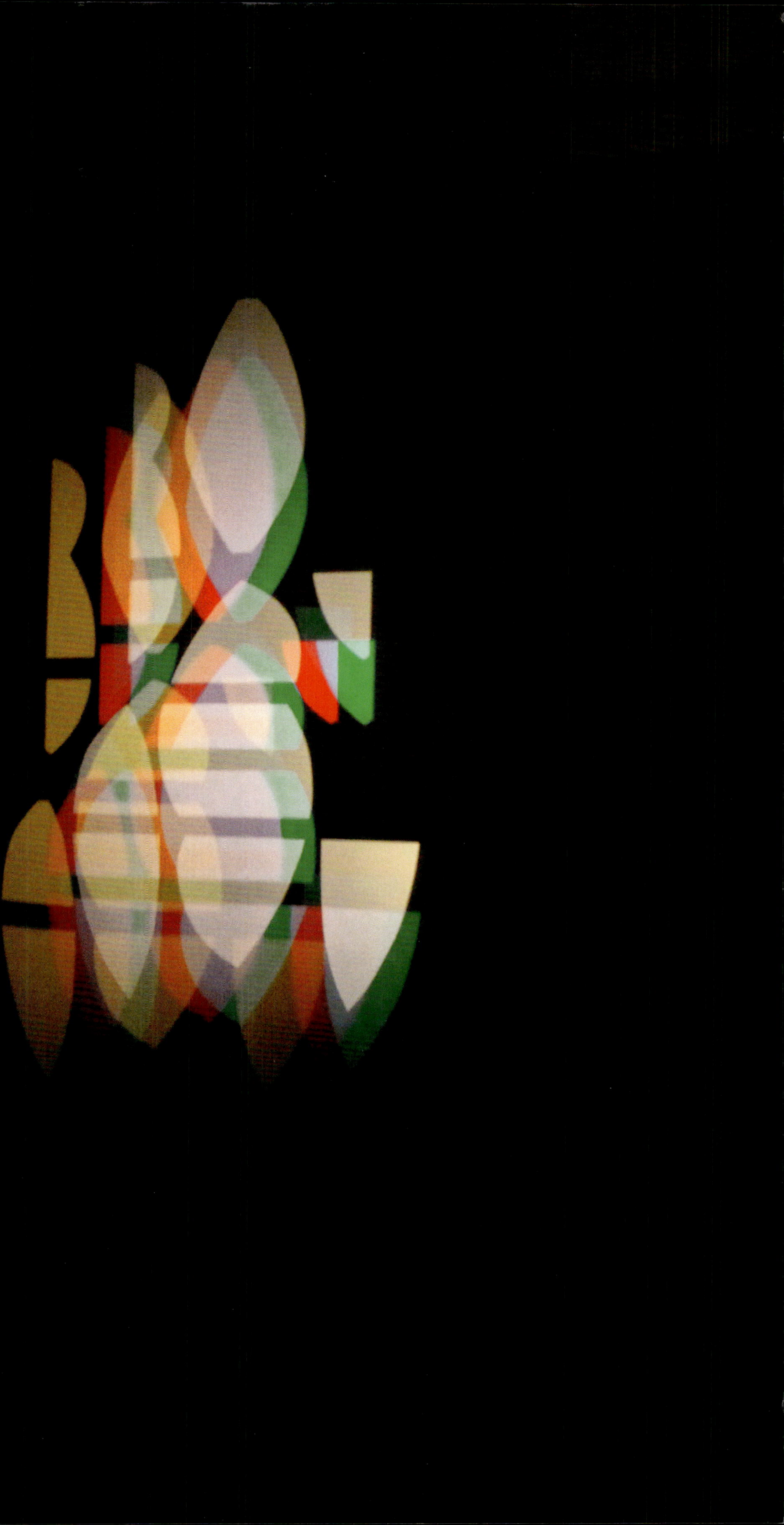

In 1922, Bauhaus student Kurt Schwerdtfeger invented an experimental device to project shadow and light for a Bauhaus party. The 'reflecting light plays' generated by this novel apparatus and a group of performers was first demonstrated in the apartment of Wassily Kandinsky to the accompaniment of specially arranged music. The intelligence and ingenuity that went into making this device – its arrangement of lights, shutters and coloured filters, the effects produced by its abstract shapes in their different combinations – were given over to the stimulation of the sensory perception of the modern human. With his reflecting light plays, Schwerdtfeger created an innovative audio-visual environment outside the curriculum, within the free-flowing atmosphere of a party. The artistry of the legendary Bauhaus parties, such as the one that took place in Kandinsky's apartment, and their varied creative expressions represent a surplus at the Bauhaus, where aesthetic work was predominantly geared towards function. Nevertheless, the apparatus that generated Schwerdtfeger's reflecting light plays was developed further through Ludwig Hirschfeld-Mack's 'colour light play' (1923) and subsequently this approach was integrated into the Bauhaus theatre workshop. Here, Bauhaus master Lászlό Moholy-Nagy's *Light Prop for an Electric Stage* (1930) further explores the relationship between technology and sensory perception. Moholy-Nagy did this in other works as well, by proposing forms of immersion such as a poly-cinematic multi-projection and the synthesis of form, movement, sound, colour, light and even smell.

This concept of a 'media surround', as developed at the Bauhaus, found its place in academia in the United States largely through the work of Bauhauslers, including Moholy-Nagy as director of the New Bauhaus (later named the Institute of Design, IIT) in Chicago from 1937, as well as fellow Hungarian artist György Kepes, who taught film and photography, or rather light design. An optimism about new image technologies and the idea of them being harnessed by artists and designers to create multi-perspectival experiences and expand the perceptual horizons of the viewer was seen in the US to mirror the diversity of an open society. Experimentation with light and new media became a defined element of the curriculum under Kepes at the IIT, and later at the Massachusetts Institute of Technology (MIT), where he was the first artist on its staff. Kepes went on to found the MIT Center for Advanced Visual Studies (CAVS) in 1967 to produce an interface between art, science and technology. Kepes built a bridge between the New Bauhaus and the ideas of Moholy-Nagy in the context of contemporaneous discussions about visual perception, and heralded a subsequent generation of artistic practice that utilized new technologies as a medium. CAVS merged with the MIT Media Lab in 1980 and, in this context, Kepes's experimentation and group work was developed further under the guidance of designer Muriel Cooper and was applied to the emergent computer technologies. Cooper, who had designed the standard US reference work on the Bauhaus, also directed pioneering efforts in the field of data visualization together with her students at the MIT. Beyond academia and industrial use, as Tom Holert points out in his text, experiments with light and sound also found their way into cinema subcultures, as seen in Stan VanDerBeek's expanded cinematic works, and into pop culture (for example, beat poet Brion Gysin's Dreamachine), as well as ultimately into the strobe lighting in nightclubs.

Prior to their arrival in the United States, Bauhaus émigrés such as Moholy-Nagy and Hirschfeld-Mack, along with Walter Gropius and Marcel Breuer, spent time in the United Kingdom but were unable to establish a foothold in academia and influence its development as they would do in the US. Instead, the integration of Bauhaus ideas into UK art schools was filtered through such British artists as Richard Hamilton, Victor Pasmore and Harry Thubron, mainly via the introduction of 'Basic Design', a foundation course in the principles of art and design. A book on this subject published in 1964 pays tribute to the Bauhaus, to Johannes Itten, Wassily Kandinsky and Paul Klee, but also signals a link to Kepes's pedagogical exercises at MIT. Yet the interdisciplinary approach that this helped foster at, for example, Leeds School of Art in the 1980s – unlike the elite and corporately funded MIT – took place in a cultural atmosphere shaped by punk and New Wave, which favoured gestures of disaffection. Light, sound and performance became key components in the output of New Wave bands developed in the crucible of the Leeds school. In a meeting of extracurricular activities and the assigned syllabi, students argued that performing in a band was art and should be assessed as such. Having imbibed the experimental legacy of the Bauhaus in the classroom, they referred to it obliquely via a fascination with early twentieth-century avant-garde aesthetics and Weimar-era decadence. A similar reading but with a different emphasis can be found in West German bands such as Kraftwerk, which embraced the ambivalence of the artist-engineer concept of the Bauhaus to develop new electronic music technologies, sounds and performances.

Schwerdtfeger's performance of his reflecting light plays at a party in 1922, and how this is traced through a genealogy of both academic and extra-institutional settings, points to the way creativity exceeds and transgresses institutional structures, as well as how it is incorporated by them. It mirrors the circulation of new ideas and aesthetics from art and the counterculture in such western post-war economies as the US, the UK and West Germany. This circulation signifies not only resistance but also innovation within commodity culture, and the blurring of the lines between experimentation, curriculum and commercialization at the Bauhaus, which has become the norm today.

Marion von Osten and Grant Watson

Ludwig Hirschfeld-Mack, colour chord 21-stringed flat sound box, n.d. [c. mid-20th century]

► Pages 246–47: Still from László Moholy-Nagy, *Ein Lichtspiel: Schwarz Weiss Grau* (A Light-Play: Black White Grey), 1930, 35-mm film, black and white, no sound, 5 min. 30 sec.

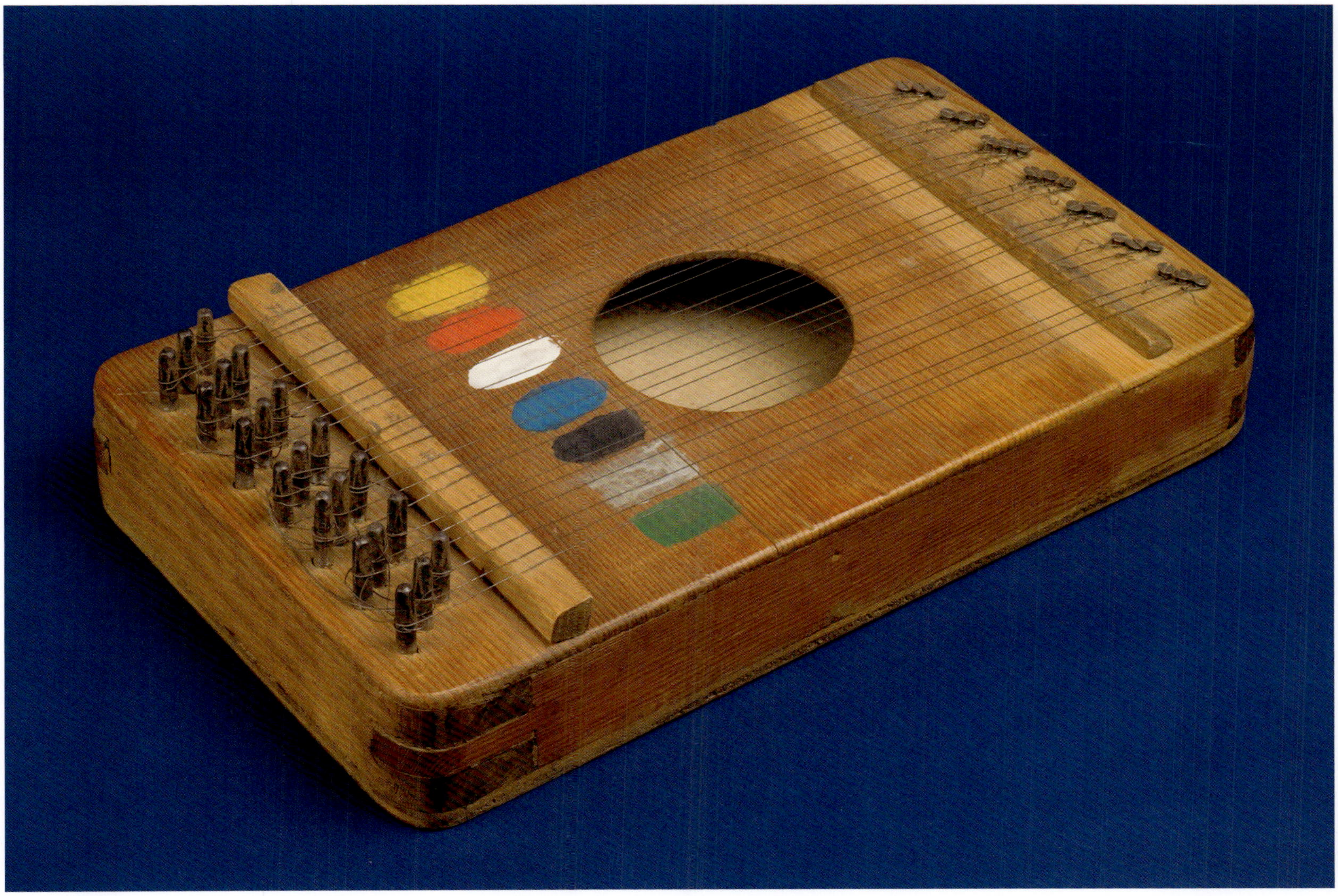

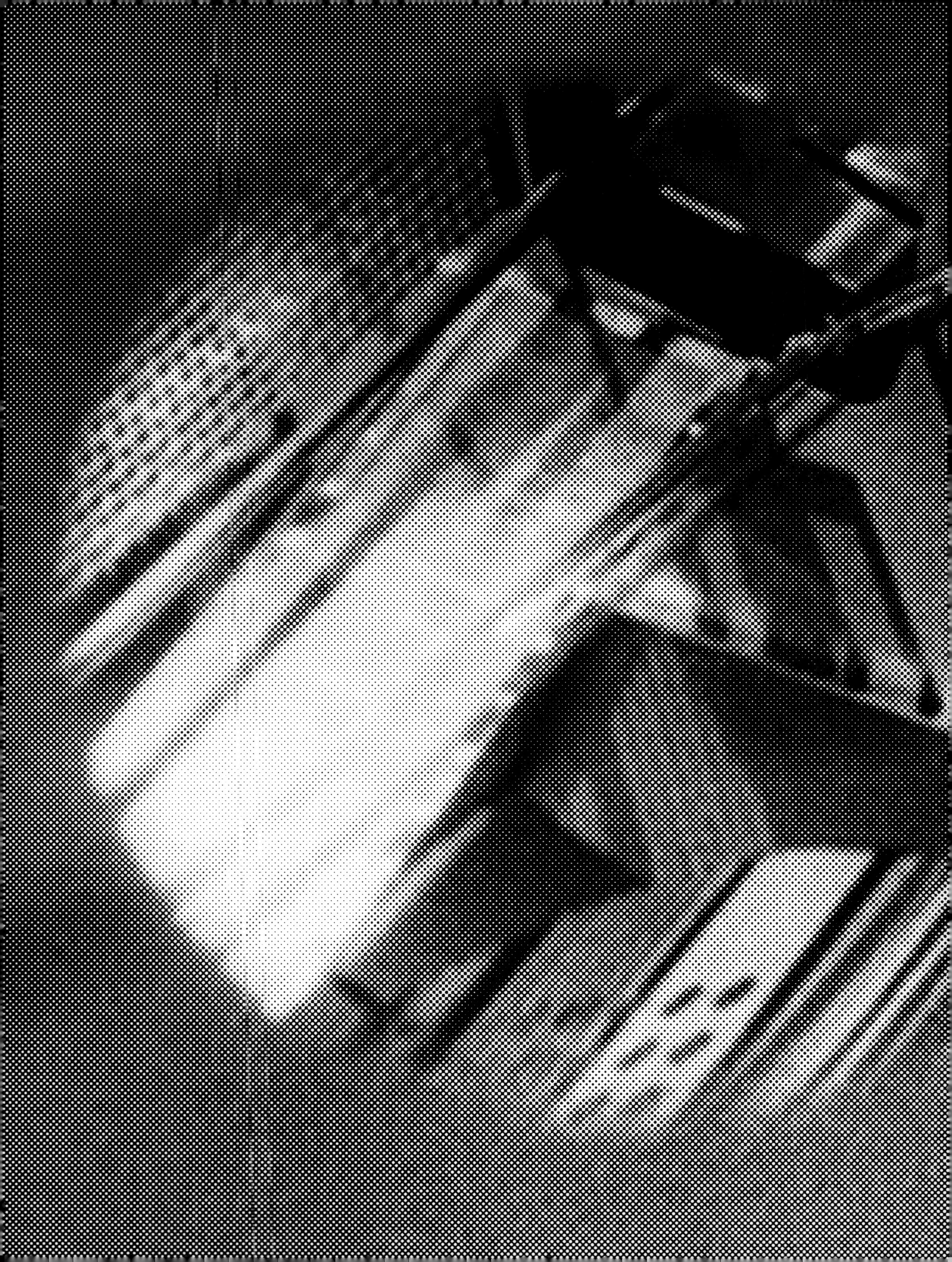

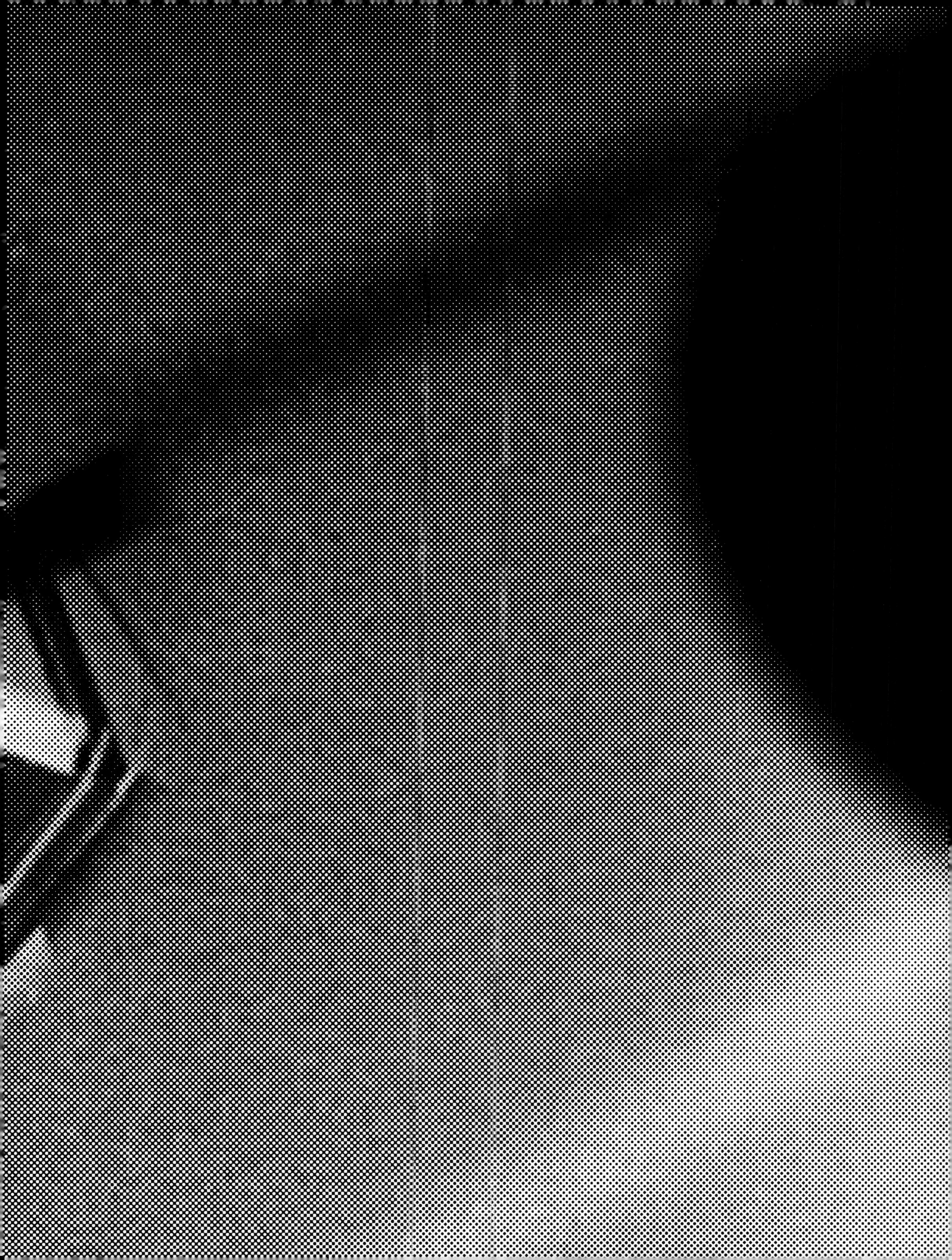

Simpsons of Piccadilly in London during its opening week, with window displays by László Moholy-Nagy, 8 May 1936

▶ György Kepes, programmed kinetic light mural for the KLM offices in New York, 1959

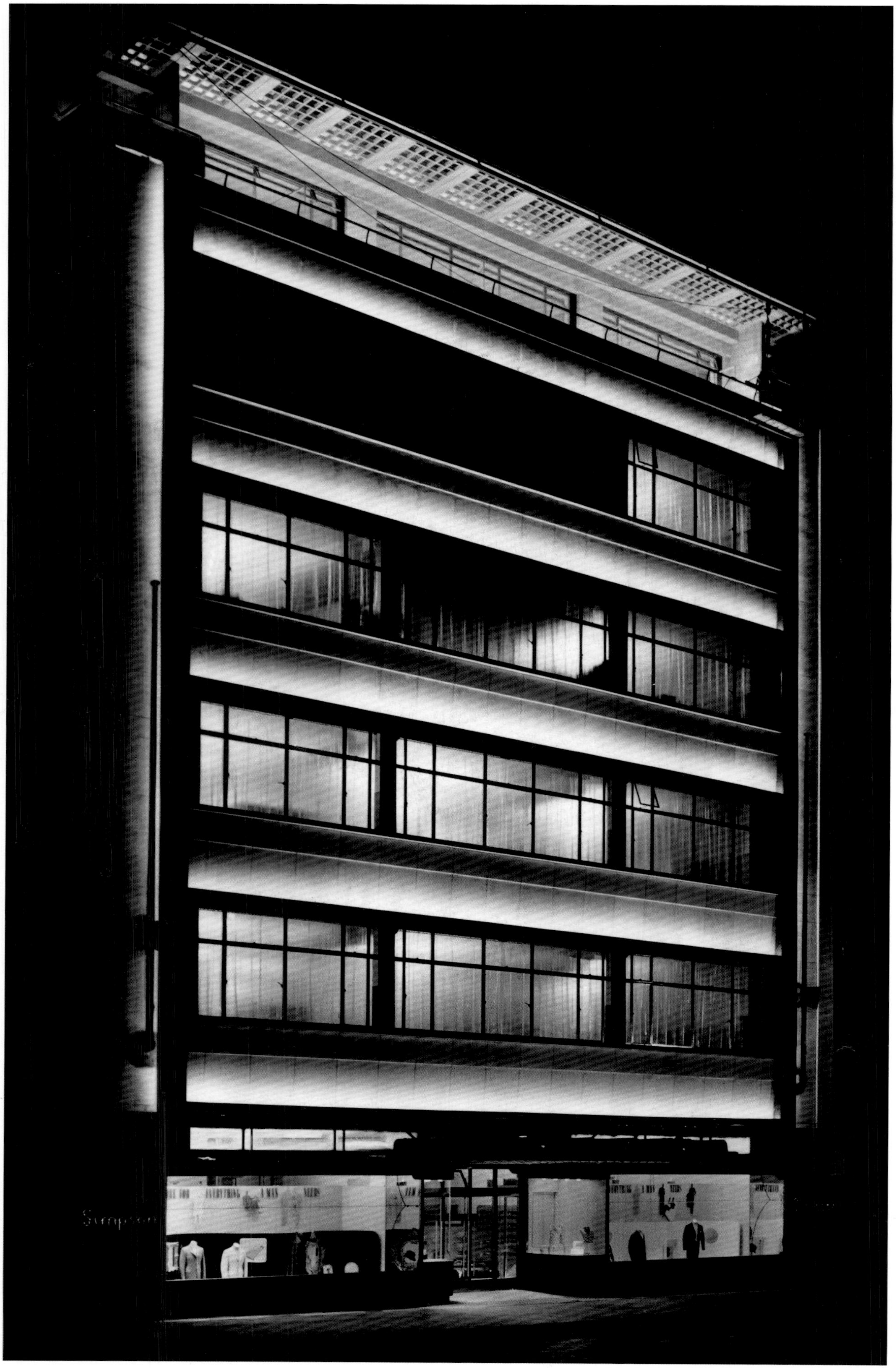

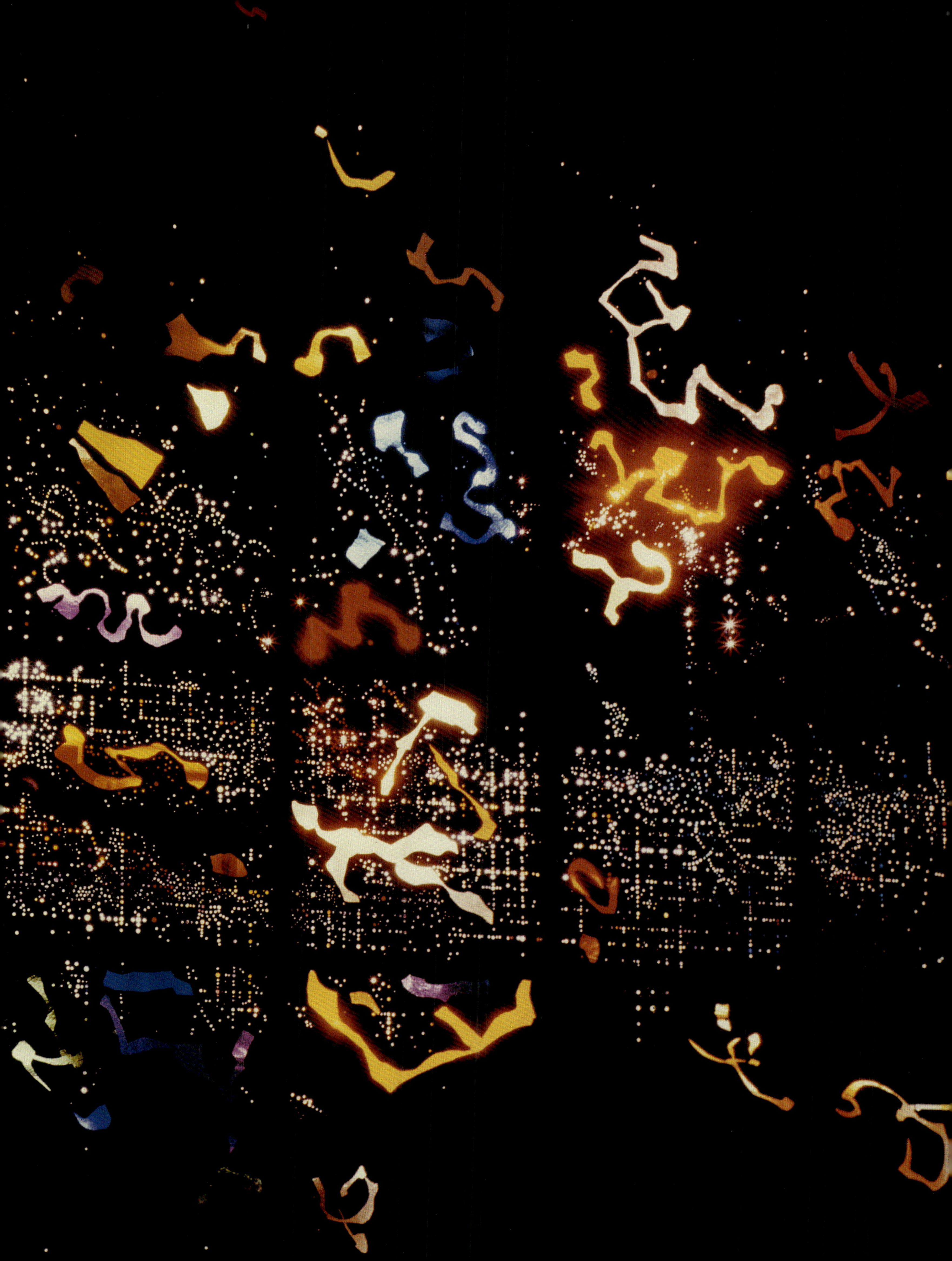

Student of Black Mountain College, North Carolina, in costume for Valentine's Day Ball, 1940, Kodachrome slide by Josef Albers

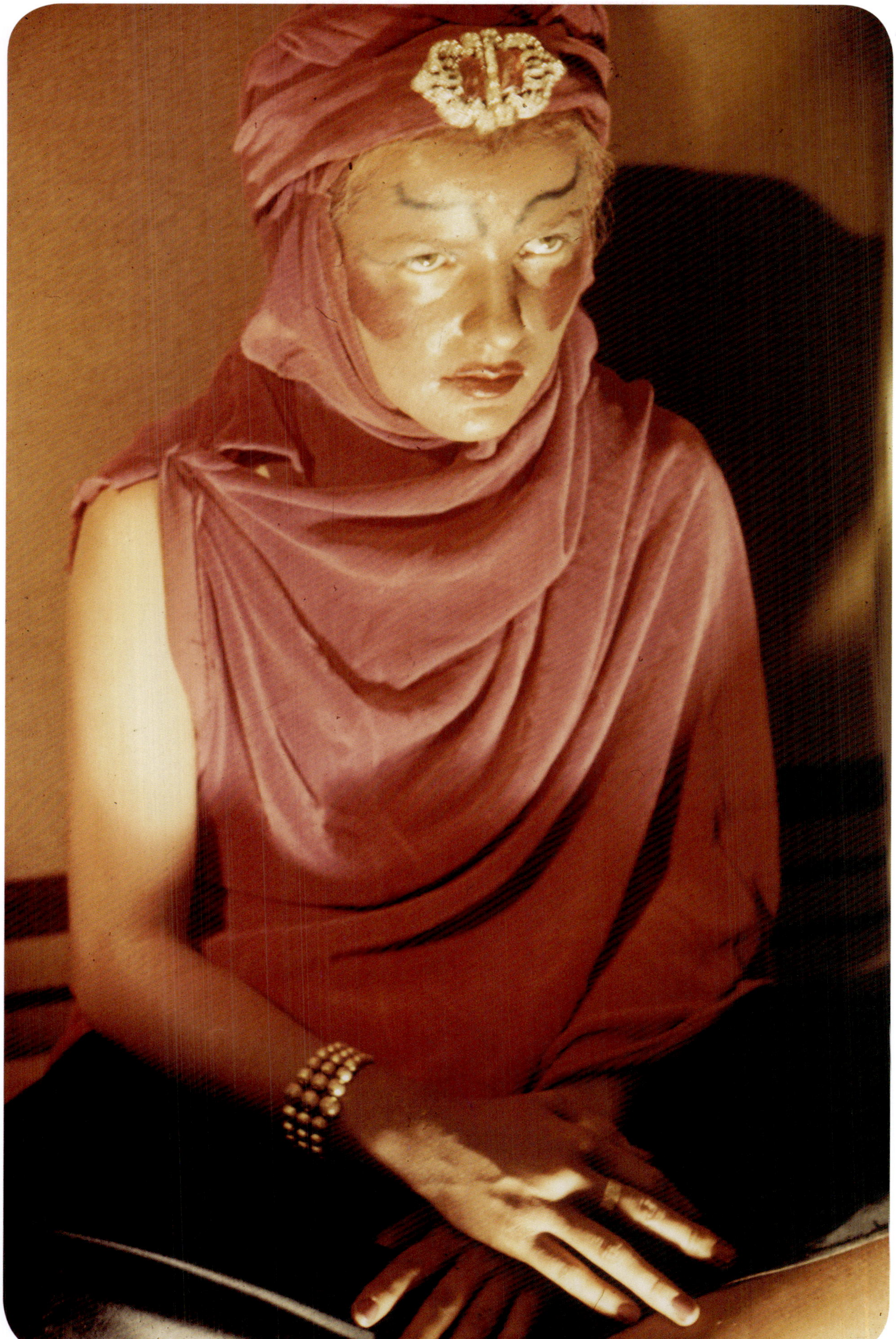

Josef Albers in costume for Valentine's Day Ball, Black Mountain College, North Carolina, 1940, Kodachrome slide by Josef Albers

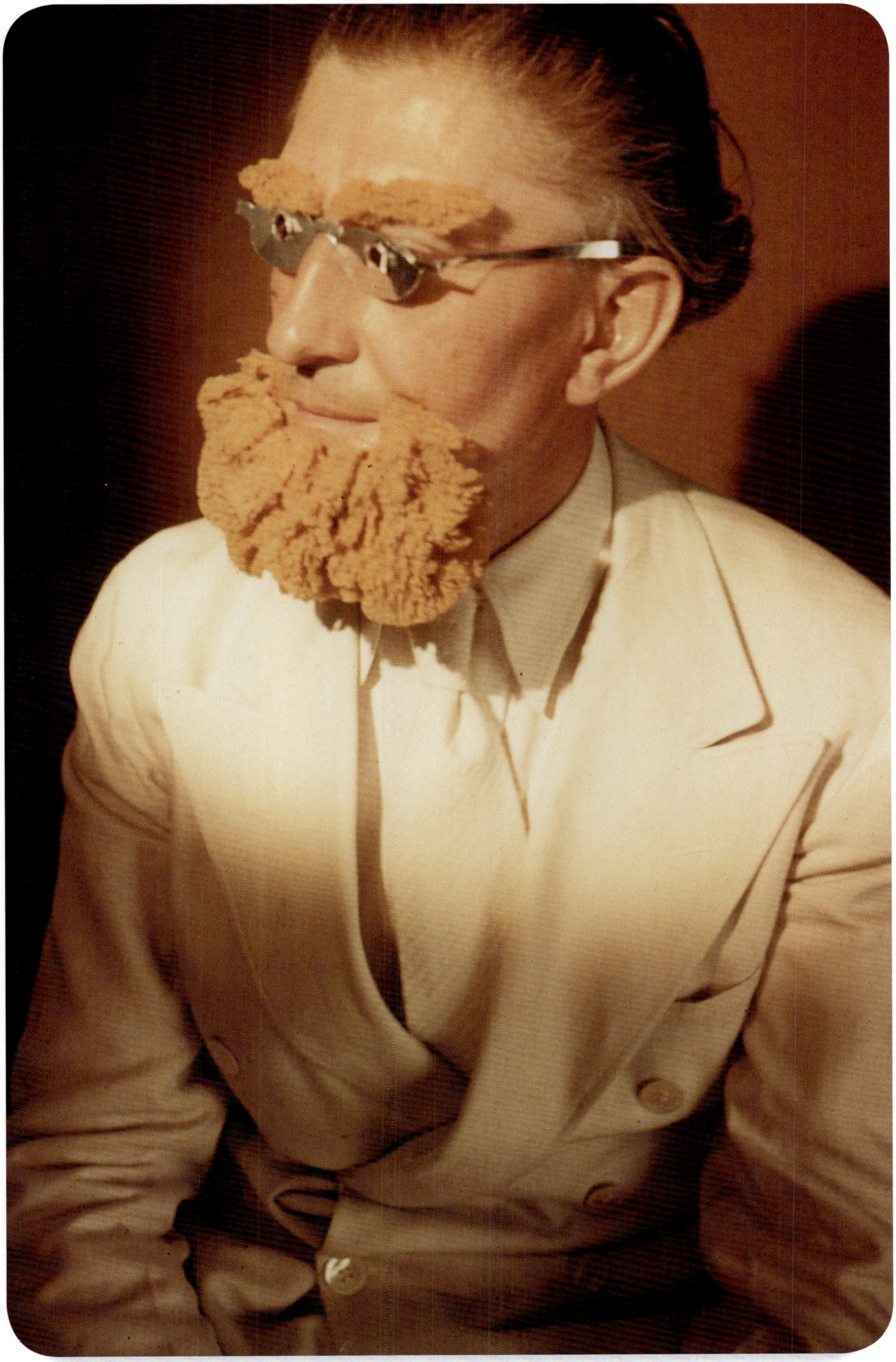

Peter Moore, *Untitled (Stan VanDerBeek's Movie-Drome)*, 4 November 1968, colour photographic print, 22.7 × 33.8 cm

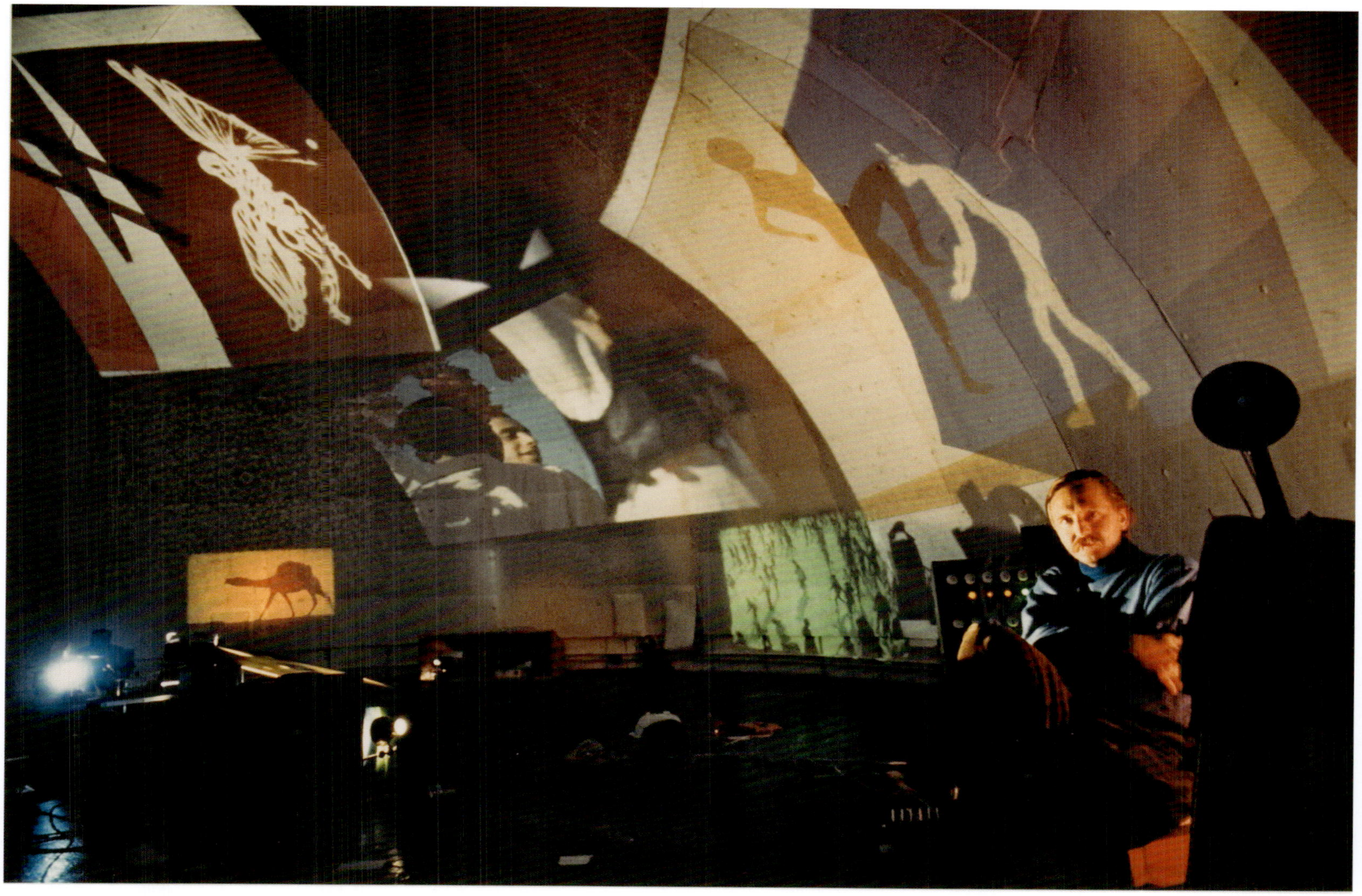

Nam June Paik, *Video Synthesizer*, 1969/92, installation, original synthesizer in 2 mobile racks, 12 screens of different sizes, 2 video-disc players, 305 × 155 × 150 cm

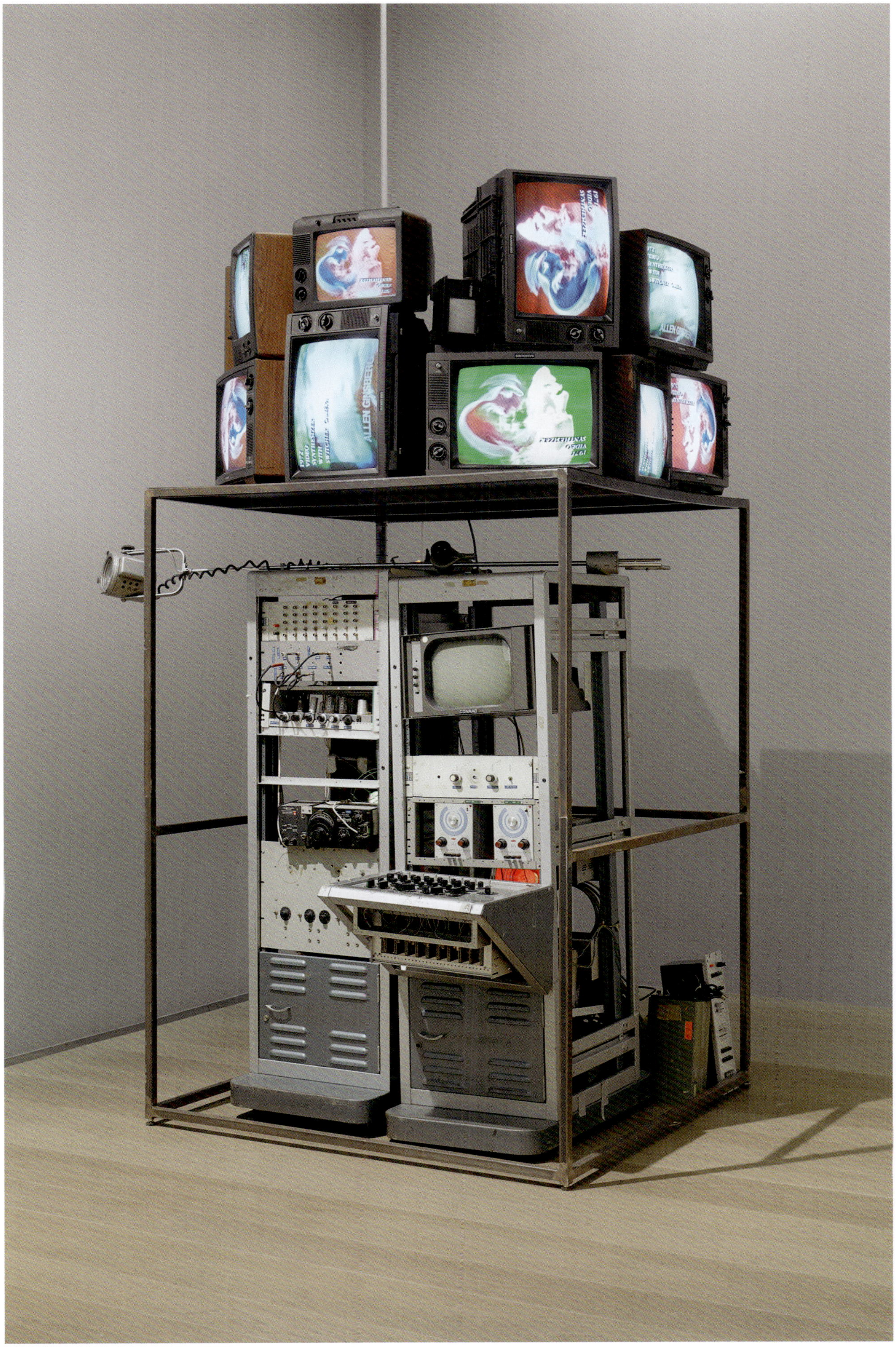

Richard Hamilton, *Diab DS-101 Computer*, 1985–89, minicomputer, 70 × 50 × 50 cm

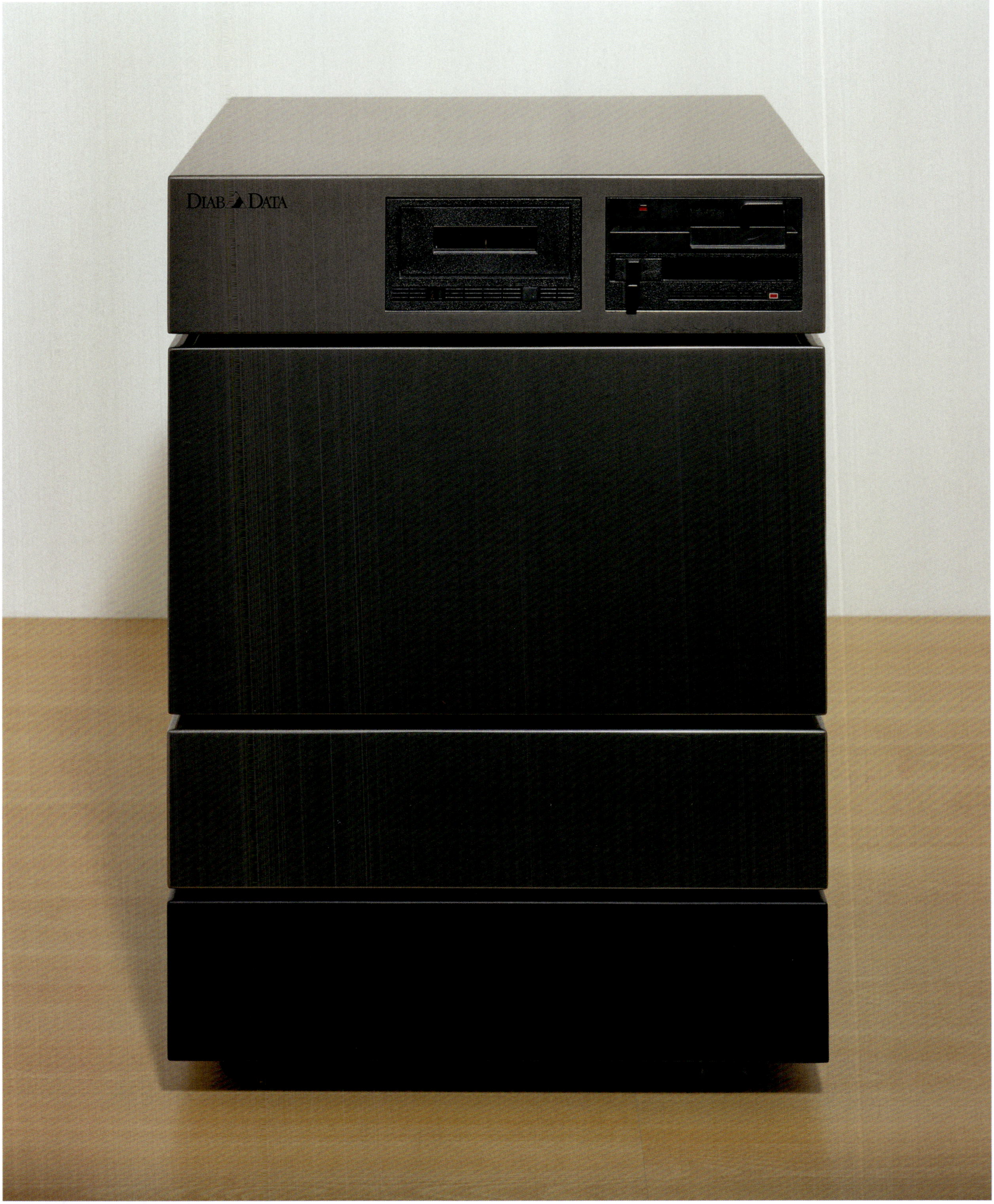

'Bauhaus', in *New Sounds New Styles*, October 1981, p. 29

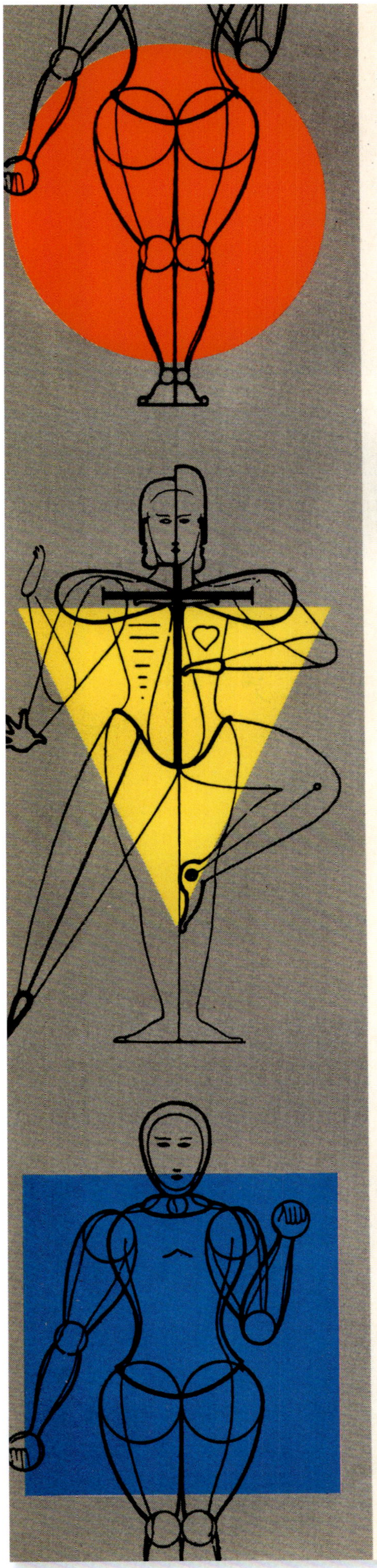

Take it or leave it, but no compromise. Bauhaus make no concessions to fashion, musical trends, audience, press — perhaps not even to each other.

Daniel Ash, David Jay, Kevin Haskins and Peter Murphy (who wasn't there to defend himself) all maintain different angles on their music, a practice illustrated in their forthcoming 'Consequences' video, in which each member of the band contributes a separate section to make up the whole.

"The same process was used on the B side of 'The Passion Of Lovers'. We didn't refer on any point, but it's interesting to see if there are any natural or unconscious links."

This diversity of ideas tends to make their collective music stronger and unpredictable; there is no 'typical' sound, from

two pieces unaccompanied — I decided to superimpose the sounds, resulting in the double tracking of all the instruments on the record. The melody and counter-melody on 'Nothing' is played on a pocket calculator, recorded at a higher level."

René, now an avid Bauhaus fan, is an artist living in Cornwall with his own retrospective exhibition currently running in Bristol.

"Any other connections with the original movement are natural rather than studied," says David. But they do seem to exist — especially in the theatrical/visual elements. There is a stage similarity, a confrontation between performer and spectator, presented by stark lighting contrasts, Peter's dynamic use of space and the band's synchronisation.

BAUHAUS

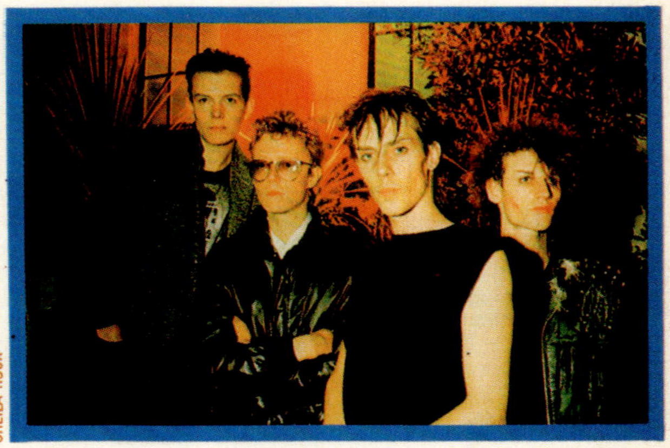

SHEILA ROCK

Bauhaus are, left to right, Kevin Haskins (drums), David Jay (bass), Peter Murphy (vocals) and Daniel Ash (guitar).

their classic debut single, 'Bela Lugosi's Dead', right through to 'Mask', the new album.

"The whole band is very spontaneous," says Daniel, "there's no preconceived strategy or specific influence as far as the creation of our music is concerned — in fact there's a lack of it."

"Obviously there are certain issues where we cross," adds David, "But sparks are often ignited by our conflict in ideas."

Bauhaus do not associate their motives with those of the original Weimar movement. In fact, some aspects of their music (for example the Gothic/romantic element) are directly contradictory to that school of thought.

"At first we called the band Bauhaus 1919. The implications seemed right at the time, but even then they were very tenuous; the only real link being that we wanted to strip everything down and just include the most essential components: straight, functional and stark, though we are a bit more elaborate now."

David retains an interest in the Bauhaus approach, which he is separately pursuing in a one-off single: 'Nothing'/'Armour', made with René Halkett, one of the original members of the Bauhaus movement. "He was intrigued when he heard that there was a group going by the name of Bauhaus and contacted us; so I visited him and had the idea of combining some of his poetry with my music.

"Originally I just wanted to use soft drums as a background, but after working with the tape — a recording of René reciting

But live on stage, Bauhaus are in a different world: visually stunning, and they have an untouchable method of delivery — almost a barrier — which makes the impact much more powerful.

"That's how it is — we like it like that and so do the audience, but it's not a conscious barrier.

"When we play live it is an honest portrayal of how we feel — we're not posing or pretending. We don't try to be 'one of the lads', if you like, but neither do we maintain that we're superior to the audience — we're not alienated to that extent. And if that comes across it's a misconception.

"It's sincerity to yourself. A live gig isn't going to last very long, and people will see through it in the end if it's not sincere. Audiences are very receptive to that, but the press are not."

Bauhaus are probably justified in feeling that they've been misinterpreted by the music papers, but whether this is a criticism of press understanding/honesty, or an inability on the part of the band to put themselves across in their own terms, depends on how you look at it.

Whichever way, it does not unduly upset them ("we used to burst into tears," says Danny) for, as David points out: "If you are successful at what you're doing, then it's enough that you present your ideas through whatever's your chosen medium. So why should you need the often superficial press coverage?"

This is the essence. The Bauhaus playground is a relatively inaccessible one, which makes it all the more attractive.

JESSAMY CALKIN

29

Kurt Schwerdtfeger's Reflektorische Lichtspiele (Reflecting Light Plays, 1922)

Melissa Venator

In 1922, Kurt Schwerdtfeger joined a small group of Bauhaus students and teachers working on one of the elaborate party spectacles for which the school was already famous. They decided to stage a shadow play at that year's Lantern Festival, which was held every 18 May to celebrate Walter Gropius's birthday.[1] The night-time festival's motif of artificial light played out in handmade paper lanterns carried by partygoers through Weimar's streets and in the shadow play's modern electric lighting. Its mock-serious subject of the Old Testament's creation story from the Book of Genesis also reinforced the festival theme, from the biblical command 'let there be light' to the less spiritual 'genesis' of Gropius's birth.[2] In hindsight, the shadow play's subject was prophetic: it provided the creative spark for Schwerdtfeger's *reflektorische Lichtspiele* (reflecting light plays).

During rehearsals, Schwerdtfeger discovered he could achieve striking visual effects using lamps of different colours. He developed this idea into the reflecting light plays, a new genre of performance-based kinetic light art in which abstract geometric shapes of coloured light moved in a pre-set pattern on a projection screen accompanied by music. Schwerdtfeger first performed his reflecting light plays in February 1922 at a private viewing hosted by Wassily Kandinsky, and still photographs of his light art were reproduced in the catalogue for the seminal 1923 Bauhaus exhibition in Weimar, which showcased art, design and architecture from the school's first five years of operation.[3] The following year, Schwerdtfeger organized what would be the only public performance of his reflecting light plays in the interwar years at Berlin's Galerie Der Sturm on 2 April 1924.[4] He left the Bauhaus soon after for a long and distinguished teaching career, first at Werkkunstschule Stettin (Stettin School of Applied Arts) and later at the Pädagogische Hochschule Alfeld (College of Education Alfeld), where he reinstituted the reflecting light plays as a classroom exercise for his students.[5]

Despite Schwerdtfeger's sophisticated reincarnation of the shadow play as light art and pedagogical exercise, he did little to update its primitive technology. The reflecting light plays began with a room-sized assembly of coloured lamps, stencils and filters operated by trained performers who followed a score to project choreographed compositions of moving coloured shapes on to a screen. A lamp array at the back of the assembly pointed at a large wooden framework holding cardboard stencils from which abstract or figurative shapes were cut. A single lamp pointed at the stencil produced one shape; by adding more lamps to the array, overlapping coloured shapes repeated across the screen to produce an uncanny optical illusion of depth. Adjustable lamps and stencil tracks allowed the shapes to move back and forth or change to a new motif.[6] The audience, who watched from a darkened room on the other side of the projection screen, saw nothing of this complicated apparatus. Instead, coloured shapes moved slowly across the screen, shrinking and growing, multiplying and disappearing, accompanied by a simple musical score to coordinate the performers' actions.

When Schwerdtfeger performed the reflecting light plays in the early 1920s, he placed the Bauhaus at the forefront of film and film-adjacent experiments with the moving image. Abstract films, such as Hans Richter's *Rhythmus 21* (Rhythm 21, 1921) and Walter Ruttmann's *Lichtspiel Opus I–IV* (Light Play Opus I–IV, 1921–25), among others, established film as the most technologically and artistically advanced medium of its day.[7] The reflecting light plays, with their cinematic viewing experience and moving geometric shapes, emulated key features of abstract film while obscuring its primitive technologies. But Schwerdtfeger's rudimentary shadow play also freed his invention from film's limitations. Chief among these was colour, which had to be added by hand before the advent of commercial colour film in the 1930s.[8] When Schwerdtfeger performed his reflecting light plays, his audiences enjoyed the rare sight of moving vibrant colours totally unlike anything they experienced in a movie theatre.

As a pseudo-cinematic experiment, the reflecting light plays had a brief life. In the mid-1920s, dwindling public interest caused Schwerdtfeger to abandon them as a viable art form; however, he recognized their great potential in the realm of art education. The reflecting light plays' composite nature required students to create harmony from the disparate compositional elements of coloured light, shapes, movement and music. Done well, it produced an immersive and holistic artistic experience in which both the performers and audience members learned how to interpret artistic ideas analogically between different modes of expression to create a unified work of art.[9]

The reflecting light plays' qualities of sensory immersion and intermediality prompted their reappraisal in the 1960s. Photographs and texts in Bauhaus publications, including László Moholy-Nagy's popular 1925 book *Malerei, Photografie, Film* (Painting, Photography, Film), attracted the attention of a new generation of artists interested in media-, time- and performance-based practices.[10] Exhibitions were not far behind, and curators looked for opportunities to include historical forerunners from the interwar period in their presentations of post-war light and space arts. This impulse led the Hannover Kunstverein to commission a performance of Schwerdtfeger's reflecting light plays in conjunction with the exhibition 'Musische Geometrie' (1966).[11] Schwerdtfeger passed away shortly before the performance, but it renewed critical interest in his reflecting light plays, which continue to be staged today.

▶ Pages 258–59: Kurt Schwerdtfeger, *Reflektorische Farblichtspiele* (Reflecting Colour-Light-Play), 1922, light performance, apparatus reconstructed 2016

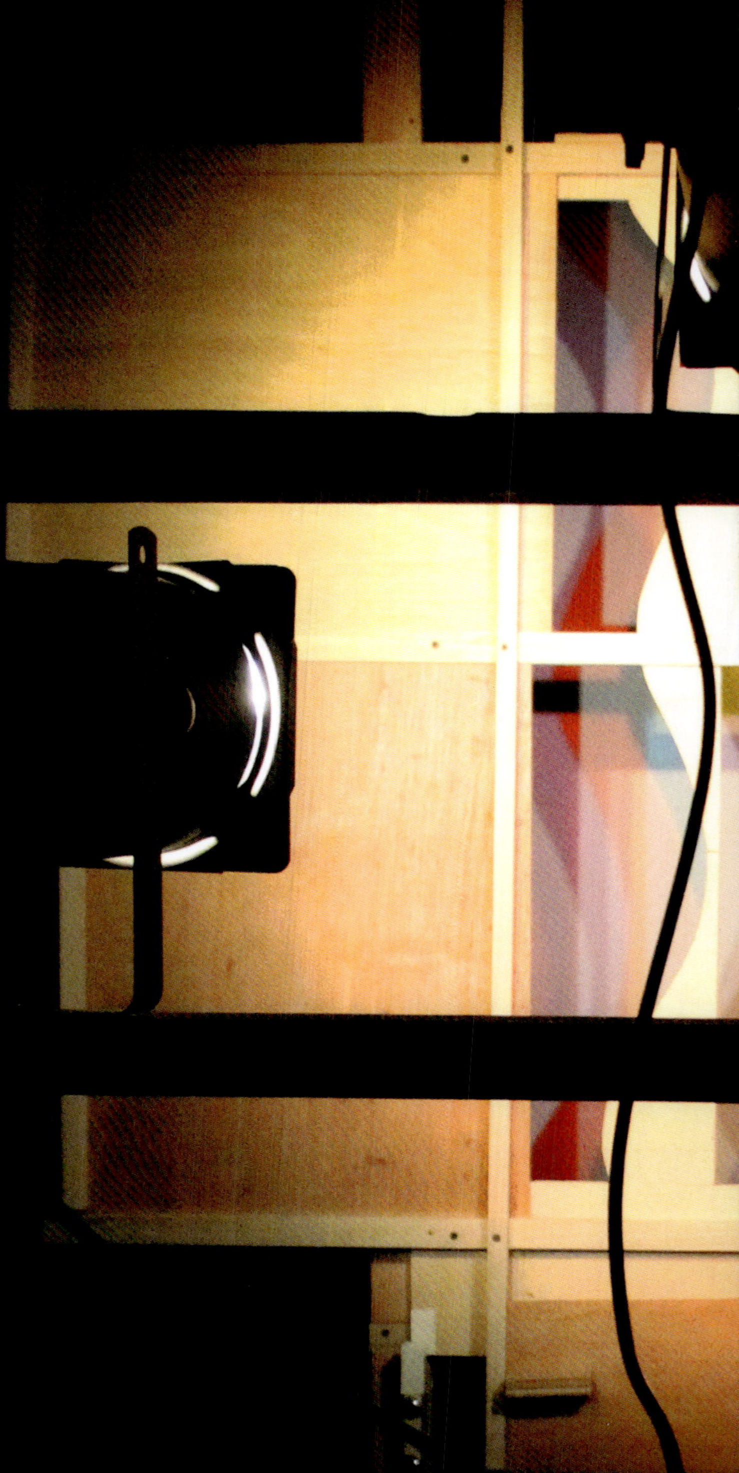

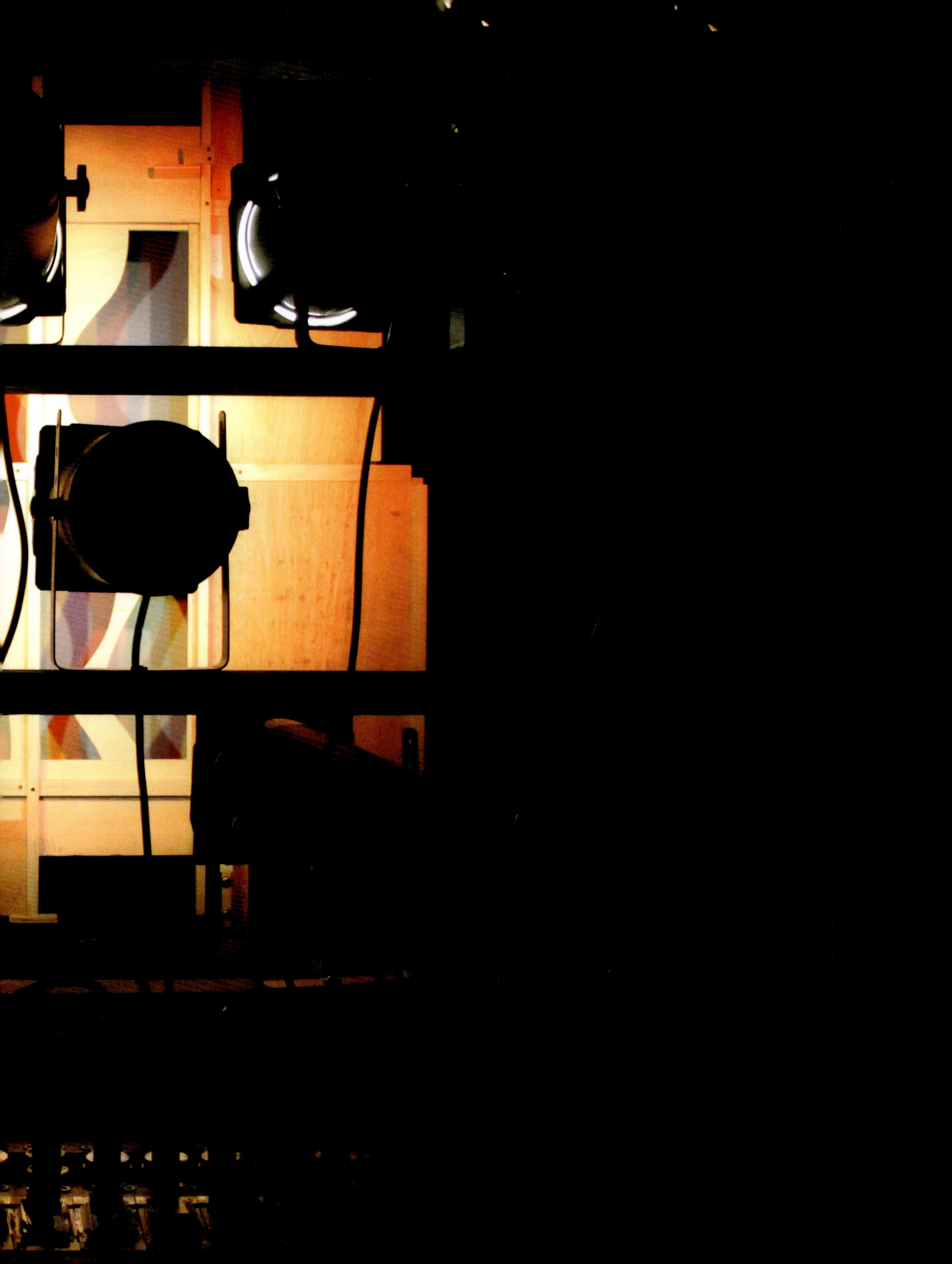

bauhaus past forward

Christian Hiller

Play >

658 pages dedicated to the Bauhaus in one minute.[1] *Bauhaus* by Muriel Cooper tells the story of the institution and its protagonists in time-lapse. The filmic experiment is based on the book *Bauhaus: Weimar, Dessau, Berlin, Chicago*; it features hundreds of illustrations and documents and thousands of words that pass by the eye of the viewer at high speed. Each double page can be seen for just a split second – much too briefly to actually recognize an individual page. It's like watching a film in fast-forward mode that visualizes and dissipates the history of the Bauhaus: Weimar–Dessau–Berlin–Chicago.

Rewind << Weimar Dessau Berlin Chicago Cambridge

The film is based on a reference book on the history of the Bauhaus. *Das Bauhaus 1919–1933. Weimar, Dessau, Berlin* was published in 1962; the second and expanded edition, *Das Bauhaus 1919–1933. Weimar, Dessau, Berlin und die Nachfolge in Chicago seit 1937*, in 1968. For the first time, the New Bauhaus, the School of Design and the Institute of Design were incorporated in the Bauhaus historiography, and the developments in Chicago were reflected back to the German-speaking public. The publication was edited by Hans Maria Wingler, who founded the Bauhaus Archive in Darmstadt in 1960. Wingler played a key role in reconnecting Bauhaus émigrés to Germany, making contact with numerous Bauhaus members who had fled from the National Socialists, and establishing an international network.

On the occasion of the fiftieth anniversary of the Bauhaus in 1969, MIT Press published the English edition: *Bauhaus: Weimar, Dessau, Berlin, Chicago.* It is no coincidence that the book was produced at the Massachusetts Institute of Technology (MIT) in Cambridge. Alongside Chicago with the New Bauhaus, the MoMA in New York and Black Mountain College in North Carolina, the metropolitan area of Boston had become a centre for Bauhaus émigrés in the United States. Walter Gropius had arrived in Cambridge in 1937, where he was appointed professor of architecture at the Graduate School of Design of Harvard University. Marcel Breuer and T. Lux Feininger, but also other modernists, such as Sigfried Giedion and Martin Wagner, followed.

Muriel Cooper, promotional poster for *Bauhaus: Weimar, Dessau, Berlin, Chicago*, 1969

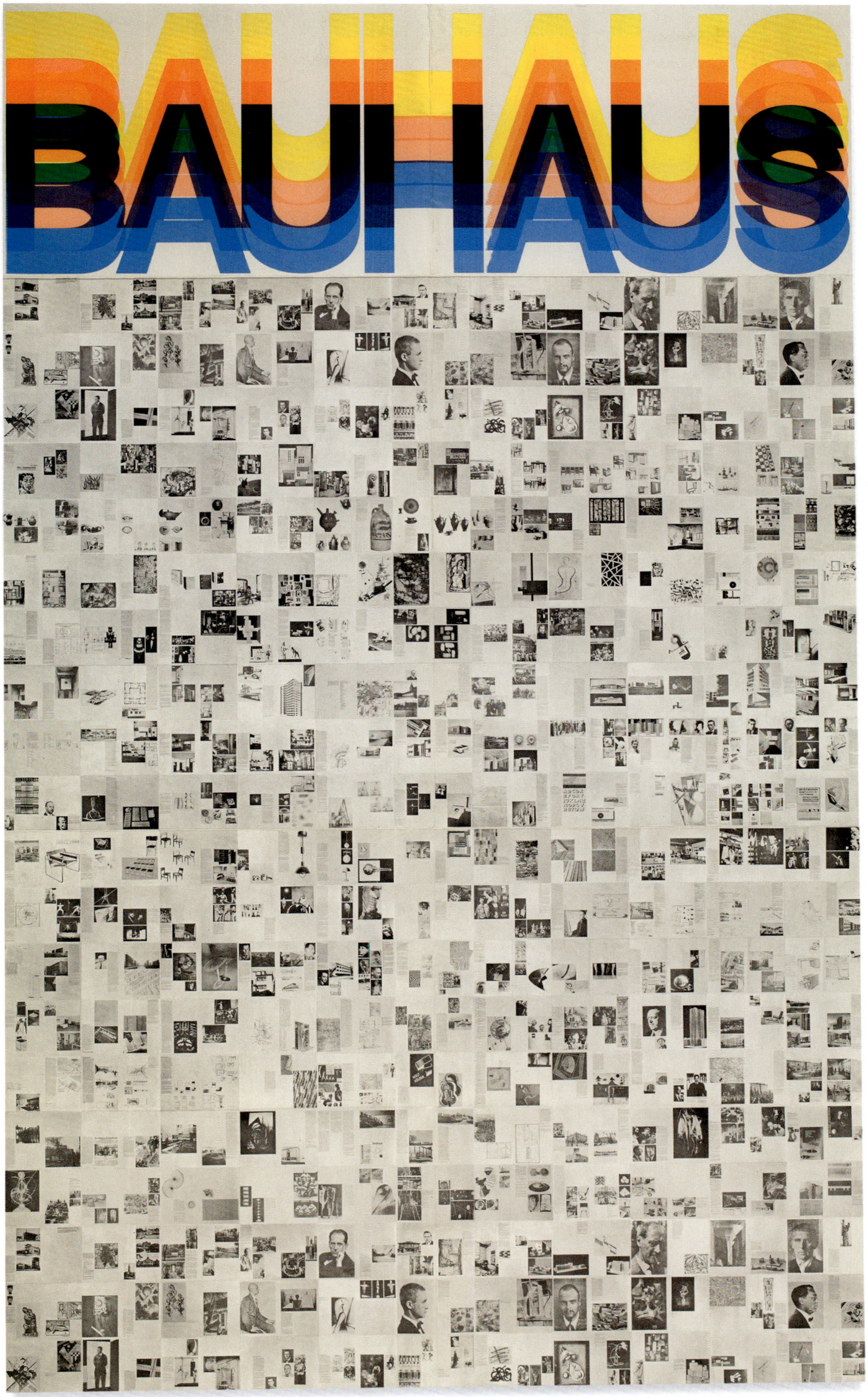

Rewind << György Kepes

György Kepes, who was never a teacher at the historical Bauhaus but had worked closely with László Moholy-Nagy for many years, taught at MIT. They knew each other from Hungary and had collaborated in Berlin and London. Moholy-Nagy brought Kepes to the New Bauhaus, Chicago, in 1937 and appointed him head of the Light and Color Department. With books such as *Language of Vision* (1944), *The New Landscape in Art and Science* (1956) and the publication series 'Vision + Value', he developed path-breaking approaches to the relationship between art, science and society. In *The New Landscape* Kepes wrote: 'Science has opened up resources for new sights and sounds, new tastes and textures. If we are to understand the new landscape, we need to touch it with our senses and build the images that will make it ours. For this we must remake our vision.'

In 1945 Kepes went to MIT, where he introduced visual design courses at the School of Architecture and Planning. In 1967 he founded the Center for Advanced Visual Studies (CAVS), which for the first time brought artists to MIT in a systematic way and established an intensive exchange between art, architecture and science. This approach is still flourishing today at the MIT Media Lab and in the MIT Program in Art, Culture and Technology (ACT).

Fast Forward >> Muriel Cooper

The English edition of *Bauhaus: Weimar, Dessau, Berlin, Chicago* was designed by Muriel Cooper, who had already worked with Kepes at MIT in the 1950s. Cooper developed the world-famous logo of MIT Press, became its design director in 1967 and designed a large number of seminal publications during her career (e.g. *Learning from Las Vegas*). Taking the Bauhaus workshops as her model, she founded the Visible Language Workshop at MIT with the following programme: 'a unique interdisciplinary graphics laboratory... to explore verbal and visual communication as information and as art on both personal and public levels. The synthesis of concept and processes is informed by tradition and technology.' Cooper combined modernist design approaches with cybernetic graphic principles and was one of the first to explore the potential of digital technologies and computer graphics. She died unexpectedly in 1994, shortly after the presentation of Information Landscapes, a spatially structured, virtual information system.

Cooper had worked for two years on the Bauhaus book, which became a key source of inspiration for her further activities. In addition to establishing the use of such modern sans serif fonts as Helvetica, she developed graphic principles that were based on standardization and grids, systematization and cybernetics, among other things. Even after its publication, she still felt attached to the Bauhaus book. Inspired by the film and media experiments of Kepes, Moholy-Nagy and Ludwig Hirschfeld-Mack, she transferred the book to other forms of presentation employing various narrative principles and temporal logics. This resulted in the production of a series of posters, an installation of the manuscript, an exhibition and the aforementioned film.

Past Forward <<>>

The 16-mm film, whose original is lost and which is today only available as a reconstruction, is probably the most radical media transfer. The printed object becomes a moving image. With the film, Cooper adds a new time factor to the book's retrospective view of the Bauhaus: one minute. The monumental impression of the book dissipates in the film. The history of the Bauhaus is made dynamic by the rapid flow of information and becomes 'vision in motion', in Moholy-Nagy's sense.

The printed book, meanwhile, became standard literature for architecture and design students in the United States. With its publication on the occasion of the Bauhaus's fiftieth anniversary and the foundation of the CAVS, which coincided not by chance, a new era commenced. The ideas of the Bauhaus and Cooper's design concepts inspired a future generation: the designers, architects and programmers of the information age.

György Kepes in the Center for Advanced Visual Studies (CAVS) at MIT, Cambridge, Massachusetts, 1967

► Pages 264–65: Muriel Cooper at a three-screen workstation, Visible Language Workshop, MIT, 1989

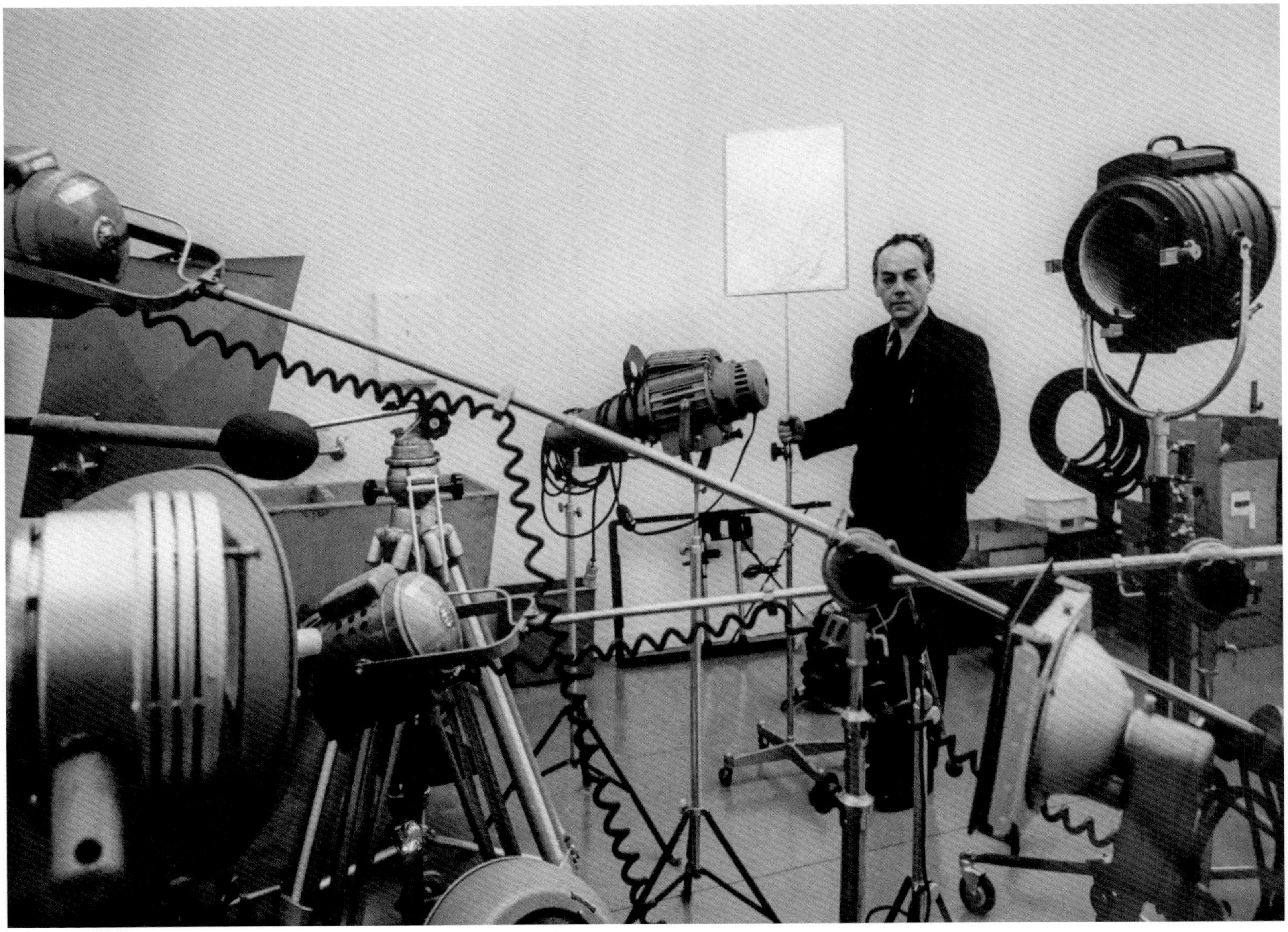

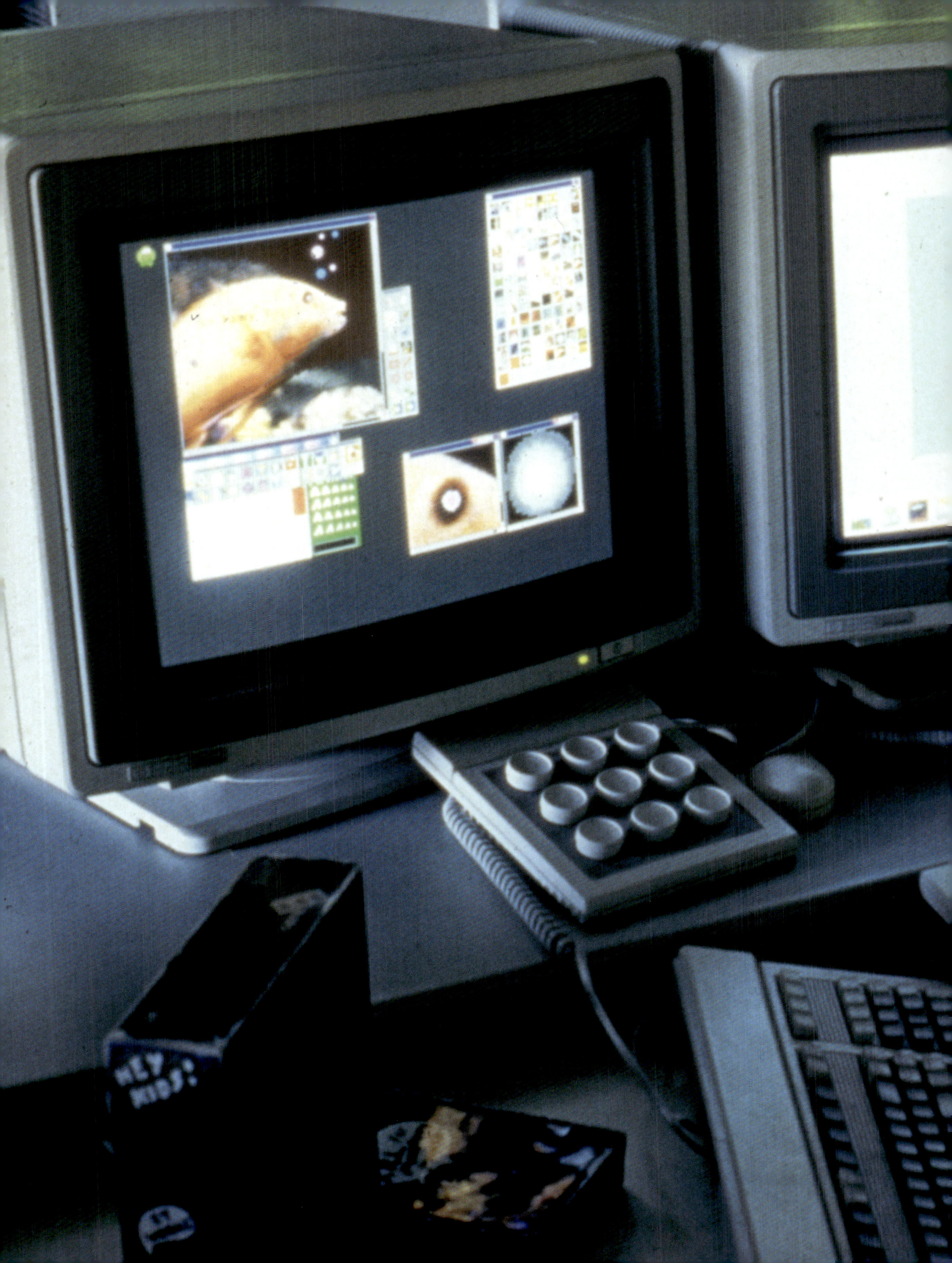
HEY KIDS!

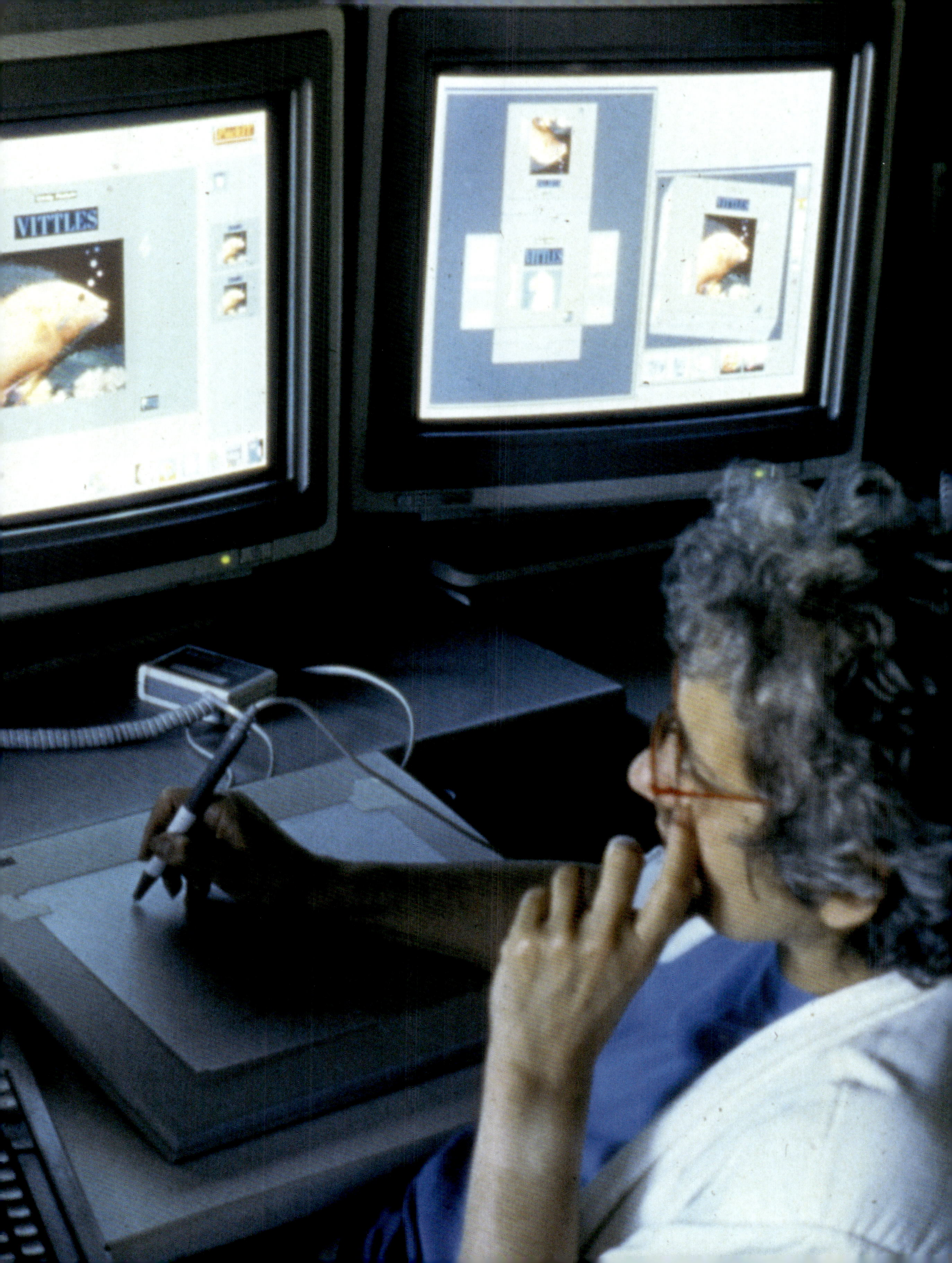
VITTLES

Muriel Cooper in front of running sheets for the MIT Press book *Bauhaus*, *c*. 1976

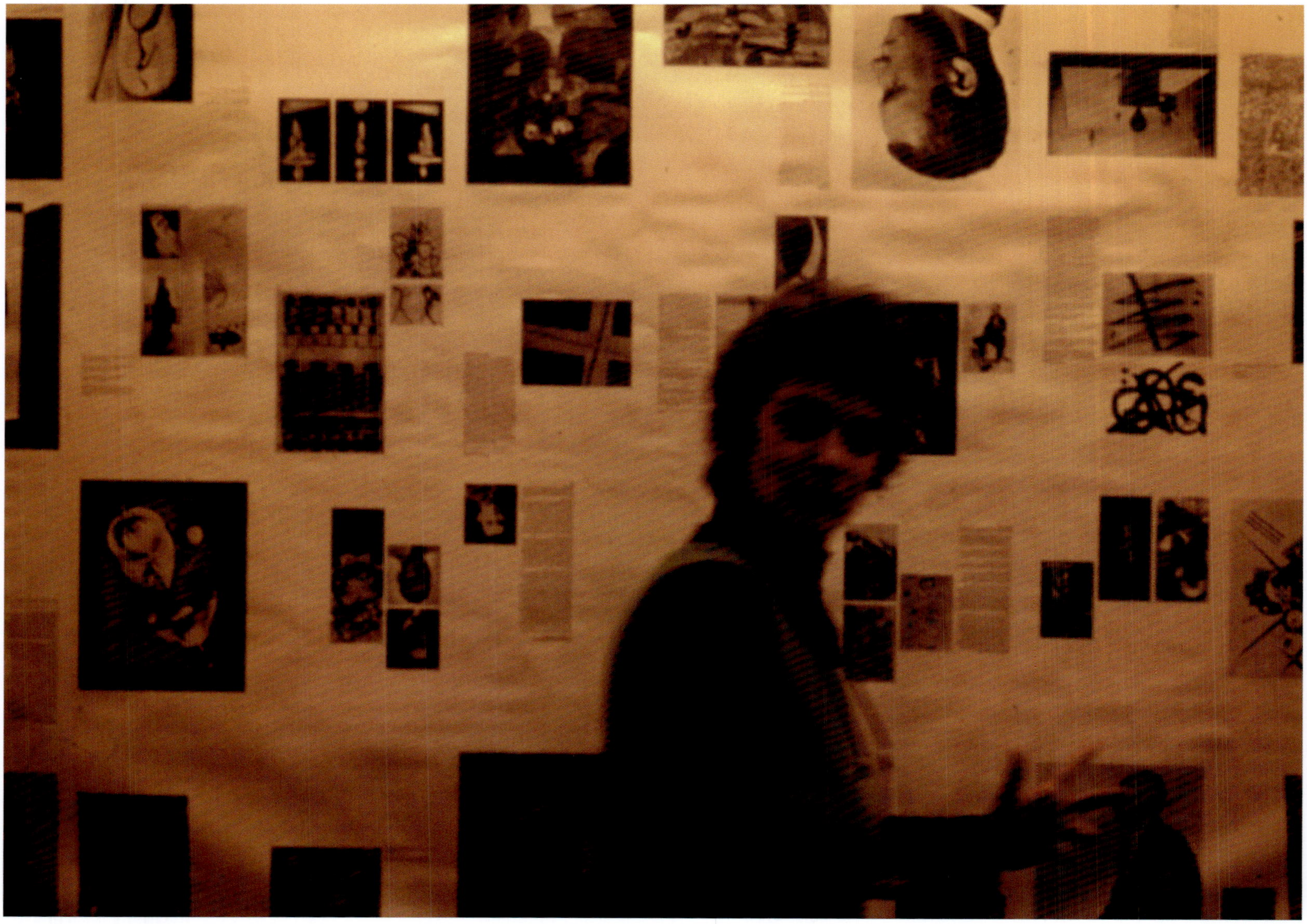

Still from Information Landscapes presentation, Muriel Cooper *et al.*,
Visible Language Workshop, MIT, Cambridge, Massuchetts, 1994

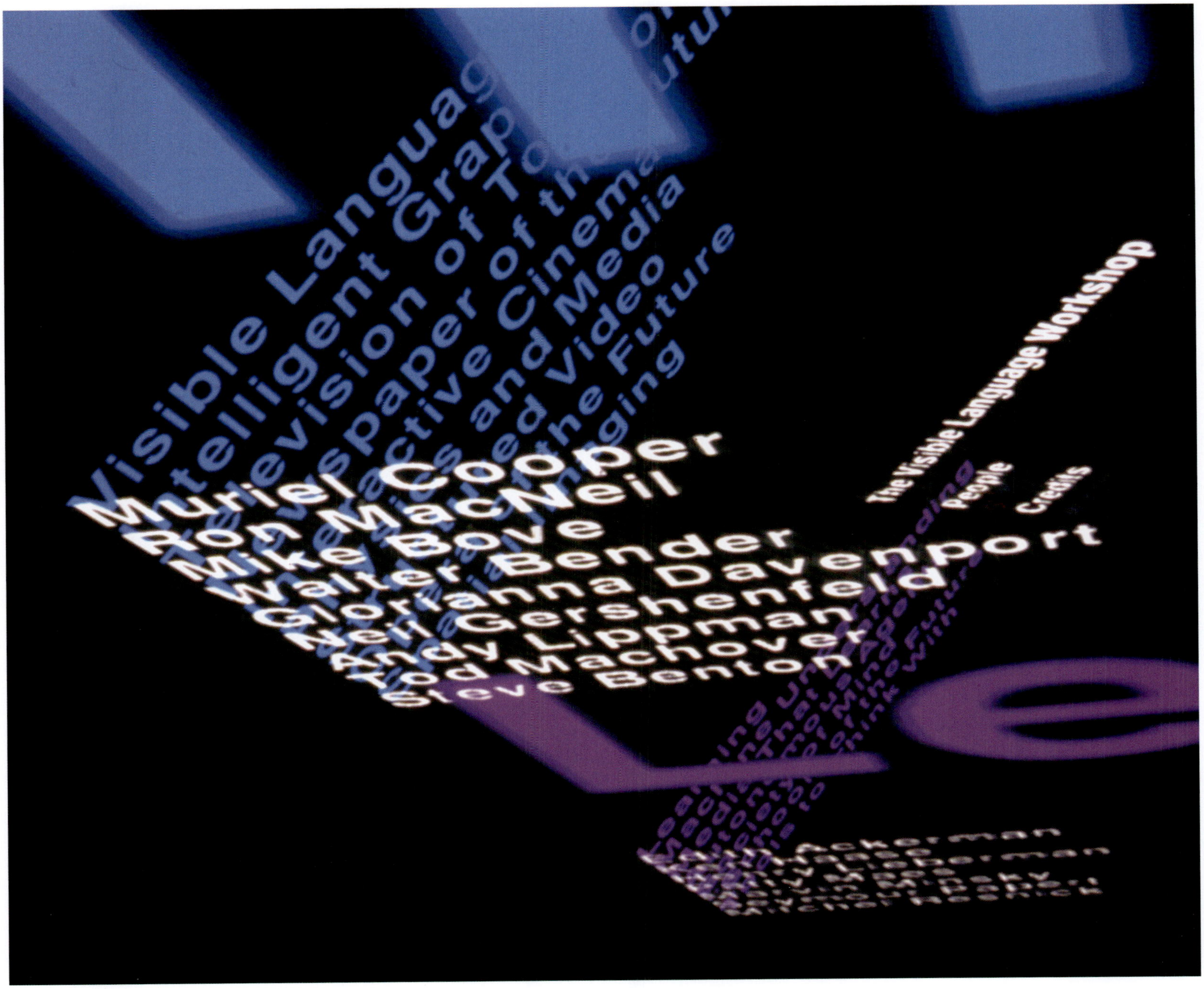

From Giving to Unforgiving Light: Remarks on the Kaleidoscopic and the Stroboscopic

Tom Holert

In January 1964, Kurt Schwerdtfeger, then a professor at the Pädagogische Hochschule Alfeld (College of Education Alfeld), wrote a letter from Hildesheim to Hans Haffenrichter, a fellow student from Schwerdtfeger's time at the Bauhaus in Weimar in the early 1920s.[1] Haffenrichter had turned to Schwerdtfeger to learn more about the historical origins of the *reflektorische Lichtspiele* (reflecting light plays) from 1922 – probably in conjunction with research for a lecture on the Bauhaus years. Schwerdtfeger then sent him excerpts of a letter he had written shortly beforehand to Lothar Schreyer (director of the Bauhaus theatre from 1921 to 1923); Schreyer was preoccupied with similar questions of a retrospective appraisal. On the one hand, the letter addresses the behaviour of Ludwig Hirschfeld-Mack, with whom Schwerdtfeger had developed the first version of the reflecting light plays – the product of an experimental mechanism consisting of moving lights, adjustable colour templates and transparent projection screens – for the Bauhaus Lantern Festival in 1922. The origin of the device owes not a small amount to several coincidences while handling carbide lamps.

Schwerdtfeger and Hirschfeld-Mack's working relationship did not last long, with the exact circumstances of their parting remaining somewhat unclear. At any rate, Schwerdtfeger and Hirschfeld-Mack each appeared with their own performances during the Bauhaus Week held in 1923 at the theatre in Jena (Schwerdtfeger in the official theatre programme, Hirschfeld-Mack in the party section). In his letter from 1964, Schwerdtfeger wrote about how he felt deceived by Hirschfeld-Mack and others and subsequently left the Bauhaus.

This break highlights how seriously research and development were taken by the Bauhaus students and what outsized dimensions competition among them could take. While Schwerdtfeger, presumably because he was disappointed by the experiences he had had at the Bauhaus, continued his work on the reflecting light plays in a pedagogical context – for example, at the Werkkunstschule Stettin (Stettin School of Applied Arts) and, after the war, at the College of Education Alfeld, as well as in advanced training courses for teachers in Lower Saxony[2] – Hirschfeld-Mack turned his reflecting light plays into a downright, albeit hardly profitable, avant-garde, multimedia entertainment business that he praised in advertising letters to potentially interested parties. Following a performance at the Berliner Volksbühne in May 1924 and engagements in Vienna, Leipzig, Greiz, Celle and Hamburg, Hirschfeld-Mack participated in the legendary matinee 'Der absolute Film' (The Absolute Film) at the UFA-Theater on Berlin's Kurfürstendamm on 3 May 1925 (as well as in Hanover on 22 May 1925, upon the invitation of the Kestner-Gesellschaft).

Ludwig Hirschfeld-Mack (on the piano), F. W. Bogler and Marli Heimann during a performance of Hirschfeld-Mack's *Farbenlichtspiele* (Colour Light Plays), 1924, gelatin silver print, 18 × 24 cm

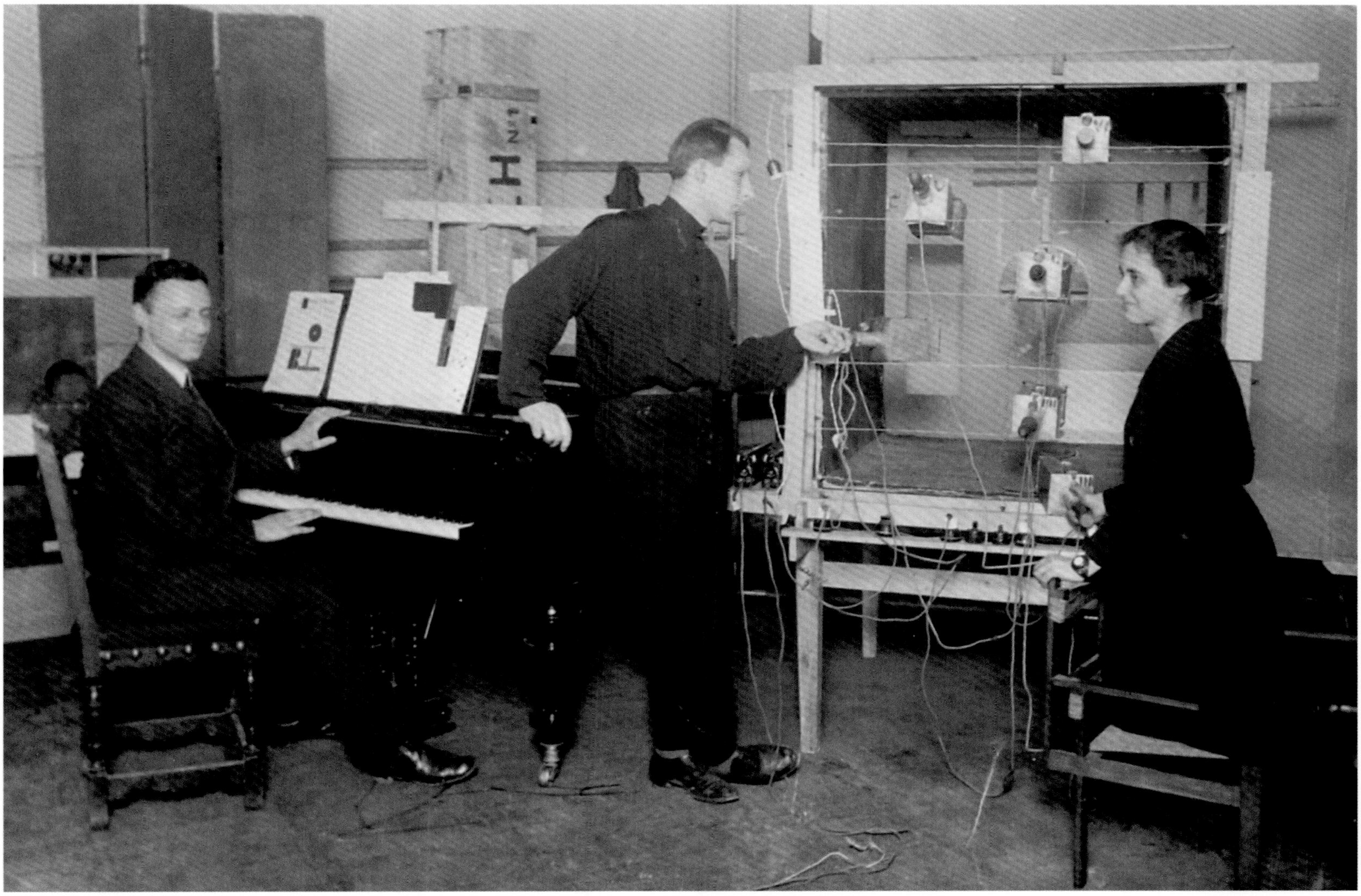

Brion Gysin (left) and William S. Burroughs with Gysin's Dreamachine, *c.* 1950s

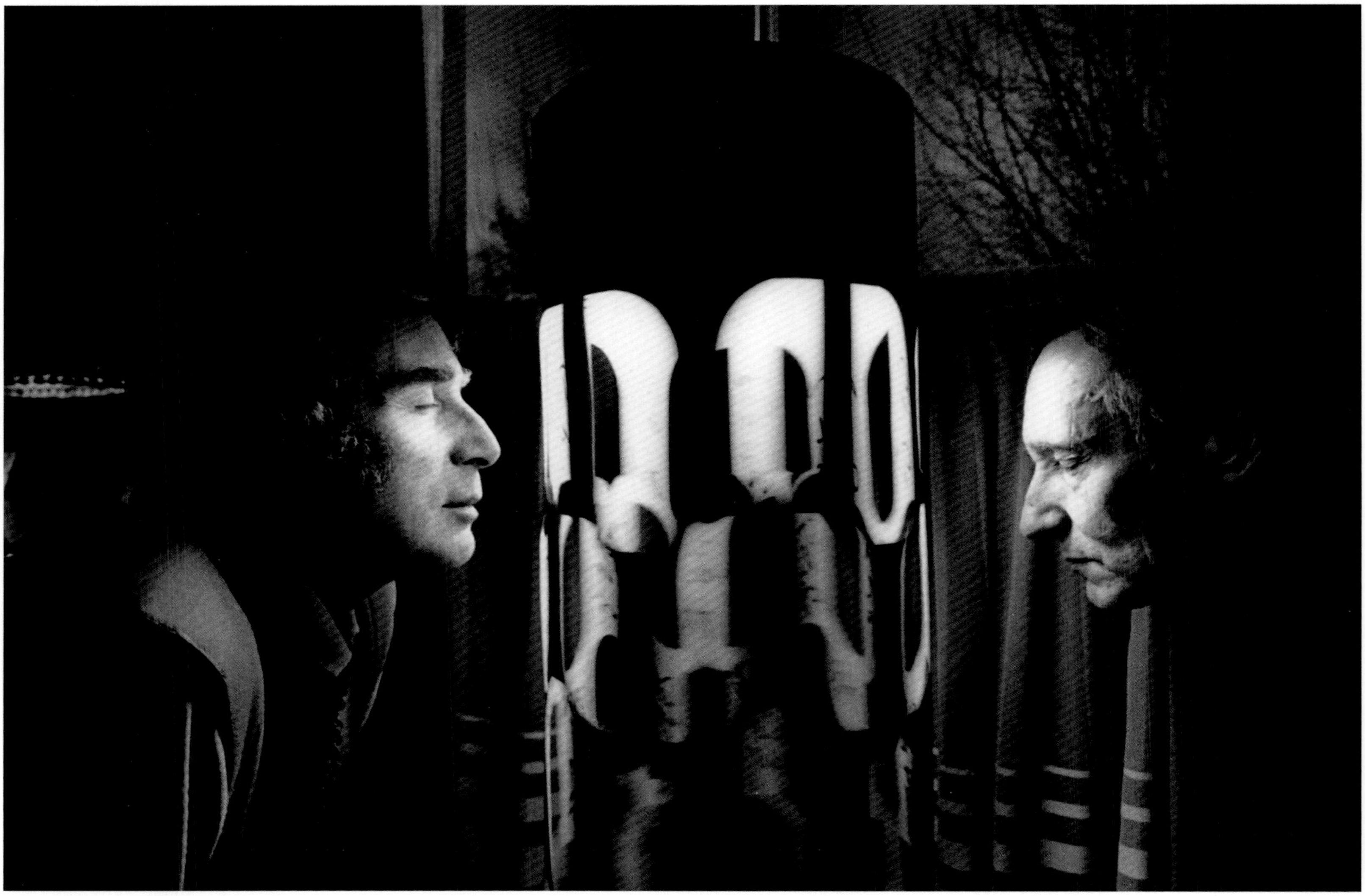

Given that he performed with a self-designed device that had to be operated by three people and did not use filmstrips running through a projector, Hirschfeld-Mack's contribution can only be conditionally attributed to the category of film. Nevertheless, he did maintain a certain relation to cinema (more so than Schwerdtfeger), specifically to silent film accompanied by music. Unlike Schwerdtfeger, Hirschfeld-Mack sought an intermedial, audio-visual dimension. His reflecting light plays were perhaps more compatible with the 1920s entertainment culture informed by the avant-garde due to the synesthetic, multisensory effects stimulating rhythmic body movements. They were also useful for the 'establishment of a joyous ceremony' that the Bauhaus guidelines laid out for the 'friendly contact between masters and students outside of work'.[3] One of the reviews of his performances, which Hirschfeld-Mack printed in a self-published brochure in 1925, drew comparisons with the feelings one has 'during cosmic events': 'The rigidity of mathematical structures is suspended by movement – brought into play and thus closer to sensibility.'[4]

In the critical late phase of the Bauhaus in Weimar, the reflecting light plays were an important means to disseminate and promote the idea of the Bauhaus. With their transdisciplinary psychophysic offerings of synthesis, mediating between music, dance, painting, film and engineering, they integrated a large part of the artistic-methodical and programmatic-ideological concerns of the university. Moreover, they were conceived as a technical apparatus to form and activate a collectivity that indeed had *völkisch* traits. Clearly following Richard Wagner, Wassily Kandinsky, Paul Klee and László Moholy-Nagy, Hirschfeld-Mack wrote in his brochure about the 'unrelatedness to his Volk (people)' that characterizes 'today's painter', and of the 'strong binding and expressive essentiality' that the 'moving photograph' – replacing painting – could pose for the 'community'.[5] The development of electric light in the early twentieth century promised the realization of the Wagnerian visions of atmospheres that had already existed under the conditions of gaslight in the nineteenth century, seeking in light the counterpart of musicality in the visible world – something that could lead all the way to the light mysticism of the Nazis.[6]

When at around 1965, Schwerdtfeger and Hirschfeld-Mack – the former in Hildesheim, the latter in Australia – began reactivating their reflecting light plays, the memory of their interweaving of avant-garde experimentation and (at least potential) ideological function couldn't and oughtn't have played a predominant role. The forging of a community of the people or use in the 'joyous ceremony' of the Bauhaus community was less on their minds than recalling their own historical achievements. In his letter to Haffenrichter/Schreyer, Schwerdtfeger wrote about his plans for a performance with his Alfeld students at the Bauhaus Archive in Darmstadt in August 1964, which actually took place with musical-rhythmic accompaniment a bit later in 1965 and is documented on colour film. Beforehand, Hirschfeld-Mack had also been invited by the Bauhaus Archive to reconstruct and present his reflecting light plays in Darmstadt during his travels to Europe in 1964, an event that was also recorded on film.

The moment of these reconstructions is highly revealing, for it coincides with a time in which the filmic and light-kaleidoscopic avant-garde of the 1920s was rediscovered by a new generation of experimental film-makers and theorists who pursued other agendas, ones in which the engagement with technological media was shaped less by the notion of collectivism than by individualistic self-experience and psychotropic self-transgression. When reading 'Movie Journal', the underground film column that Jonas Mekas wrote for New York's *Village Voice* in the 1960s, for example, one can find signs precisely around 1964 of a radically new understanding of cinema expressed, on the one hand, by an expansion of cinematography to stages, music clubs and discos, and, on the other, by the individual confrontation with light stimuli under the influence of drugs. The year 1964 saw Andy Warhol reach an early culmination point of his film productions with *Eat*, *Empire*, *Sleep*, *Haircut* and other movies that prompted Mekas to speak of the 'most revolutionary of all film-makers working today', 'opening to film-makers a completely new and inexhaustible field of cinema reality'.[7] Mekas celebrated the return of fades and superimpositions of photographic and filmic images as they hadn't been seen since the early works of Man Ray, in movies by Ron Rice, Barbara Rubin or Carl Linder – 'people whose perception – by whatever process – has been expanded, intensified'.[8] The images of these novel types of film-makers reveal a new speed, a new constitution, new conditions of perception, a reprogrammed sensorium: 'Things must happen fast, many things. Lines, colours, figures, one on top of another, combinations and possibilities, to keep the eye working.'[9]

It was also in 1964 that Mekas discovered for New York's underground scene a new optical device, developed by the beat poet Brion Gysin in collaboration with the mathematically minded Ian Sommerville and writer William S. Burroughs. Already patented in 1961, the machine was something like the equivalent of Schwerdtfeger's and Hirschfeld-Mack's reflecting light plays, albeit under the conditions of a post-war culture characterized equally by experiments with mind-expanding drugs and by pop culture along with neuroscientific and cybernetic developments. On 21 December 1958, Gysin penned the following experience in his diary: 'Had a transcendental storm of colour visions today in the bus going to Marseilles. We ran through a long avenue of trees and I closed my eyes against the setting sun. An overwhelming flood of intensely bright colours exploded behind my eyelids: a multidimensional kaleidoscope whirling out through space. I was swept out of time. I was out in a world of infinite number.' To reproduce these sensations with closed eyes at any time, Gysin and Sommerville built the Dreamachine; a sort of zoetrope, a cylinder with a lightbulb inside that rotated on a record player with 45 or 75 rpm, the outer wall of which was perforated with slits.[10] Mekas cited Sommerville in February 1964, a few weeks after Schwerdtfeger's letter to Haffenrichter, with the words: 'Visions start with a kaleidoscope of colours on a plane in front of the eyes and gradually become more complex and beautiful, breaking like the surf in a shore until whole patterns of colour are pounding to get in.'[11] The strobe effect of the Dreamachine produced those vision-expanding superimpositions that Mekas soon discovered everywhere in the new films, not on the screen (or on the transparent foils of the Bauhaus reflecting light plays), but behind the eyelids of the individual in a kind of hypnosis or trance, mostly, if not necessarily, induced by drugs.

'What are all these lights doing?', Mekas asked in 1966, when stroboscopic light had become common in the kinetic lightshows of the Expanded Cinema movement. Tony Conrad's *The Flicker* (1965) had already unsettled the audience, Andy Warhol's Factory and the 'Exploding Plastic Inevitable' shows with the Velvet Underground set about making the hard, bright-as-lightning, no longer multicoloured-kaleidoscopic use of the stroboscope into an underground routine that manipulated the brainwaves and overtaxed the senses in general. In an interview with Steve Durkee from the multimedia group USCO, Mekas speaks of his fundamental ontological experiences on a dance floor flooded with stroboscopic light: 'On the dance floor, under the strobes, very often you lose the sense of the musical rhythm, you pick up the strobe rhythm instead – you can't even hear the sound, you lose the sense of sound.... We are cut by strobe light into single frames, to eight frames per second or whatever the strobe frequency is, on and off', and in the end he asks: 'What's the meaning of our becoming single frames?'[12]

Around two years later, in 1968/69 in Düsseldorf, two journalism students make the deal of their lives with a strobe system – a business model based on this radical fragmentation of movement into single frames: 'The audience seemed to have been waiting only for the stroboscope', writes Bernd Cailloux in his autobiographic novel on this era. 'It already loved the effect, its rebellious flashing, its electrifying, liberating essence. It destroyed the old dance styles, made them impossible. The extremely rapid change from darkness to over-brightness appeared to hit the centre of everyone's double nature, the flash awakened dormant powers, freeing energies, desires and dispositions, and chasing inhibitions away.'[13]

In the 1920s, Schwerdtfeger and Hirschfeld-Mack, ideologically in line with aesthetic programmes such as the *Gesamtkunstwerk* (total work of art), 'absolute theatre' (Oskar Schlemmer) and 'absolute cinema' (Oskar Fischinger, Viking Eggeling, Hans Richter, and others), regarded themselves as the liberators of light from the constraints of traditional art media and as forgers of long-lasting communities. In the 1960s, they were engaged with the self-historicization of their inventions as fundamental elements of a synaesthetic pedagogy. The fact that the new communities of the single-frame dancers of the 1960s beat and pop generation radicalized light – i.e. made it stroboscopic, to unleash it directly, without taking the possible detour via pedagogy, at the brainwaves and bodily sensations – was also a sign of a new technology of the subject, which had shifted from the cosmic whole to the chaosmic singular, from eudaemonic synthesis to hedonistic dispersion, the repercussions of which continue up to the present in stroboscopic and at times kaleidoscopic nightlife.

The Velvet Underground performs at the Trip, Los Angeles, California, as part of Andy Warhol's 'Exploding Plastic Inevitable' series of staged, multimedia events, early May 1966

▶ Pages 274–75: Andy Warhol (centre, behind the spotlights) observes a performance of his 'Exploding Plastic Inevitable' at the Dom, New York, 31 March 1966

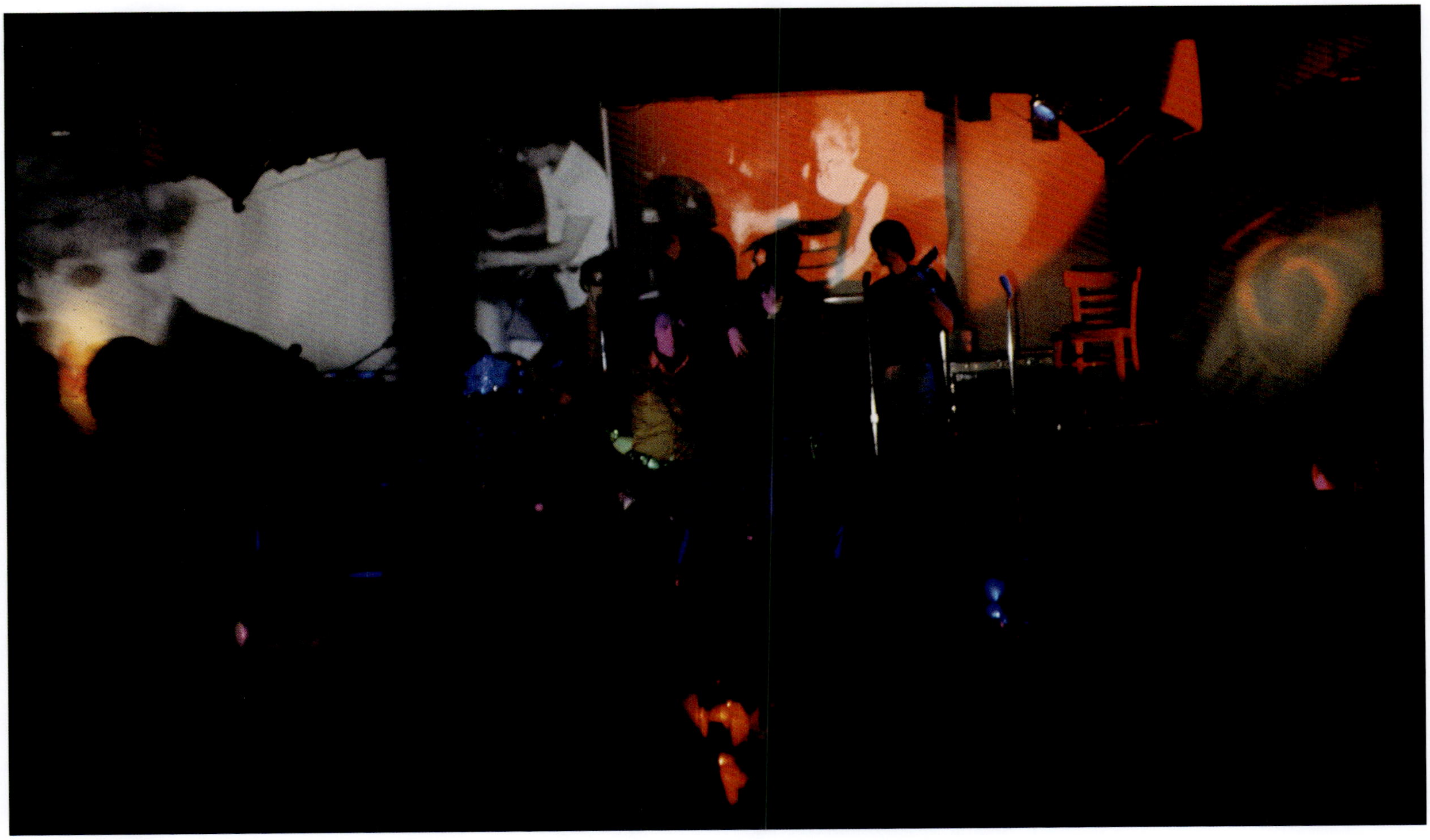

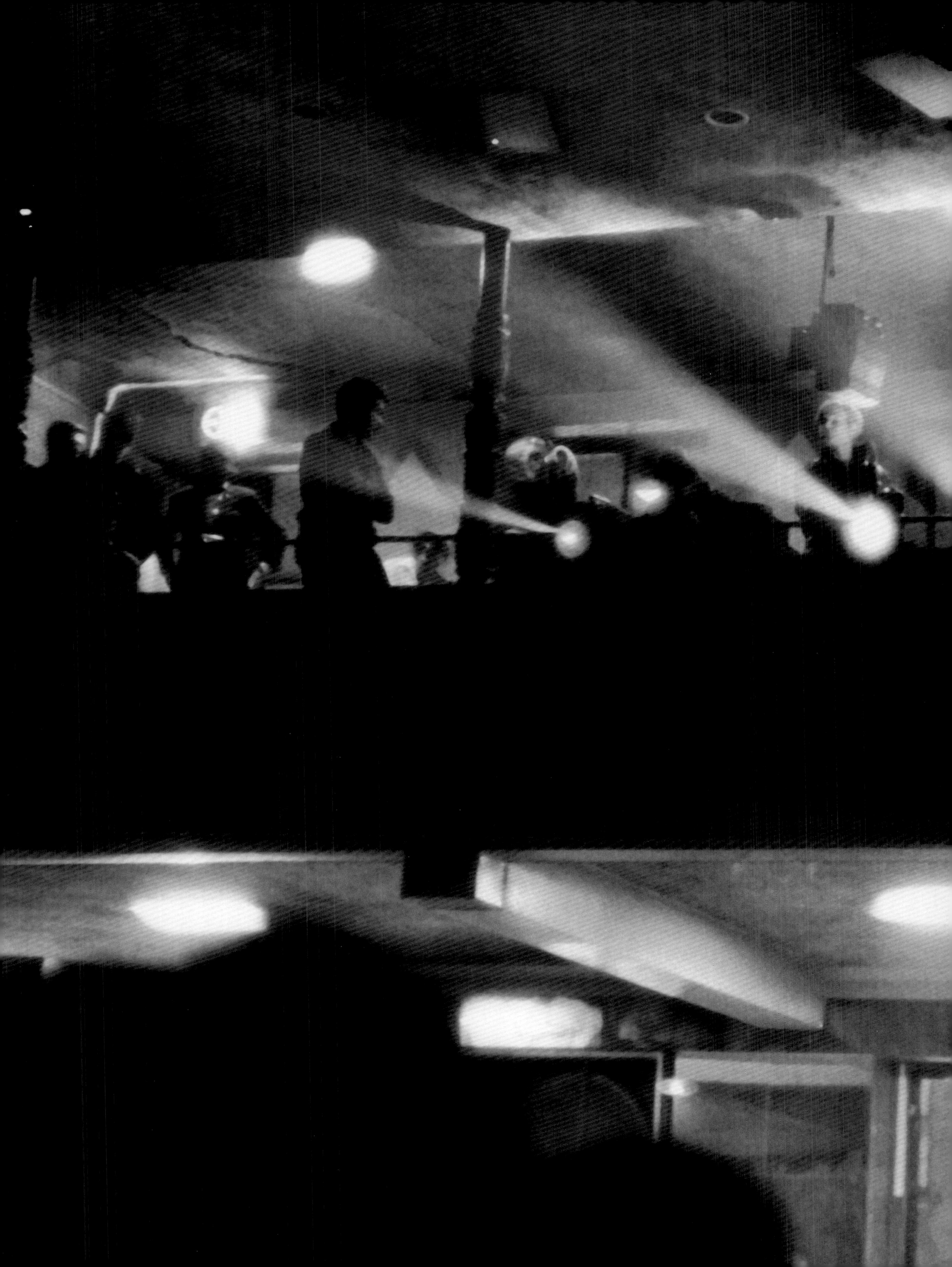

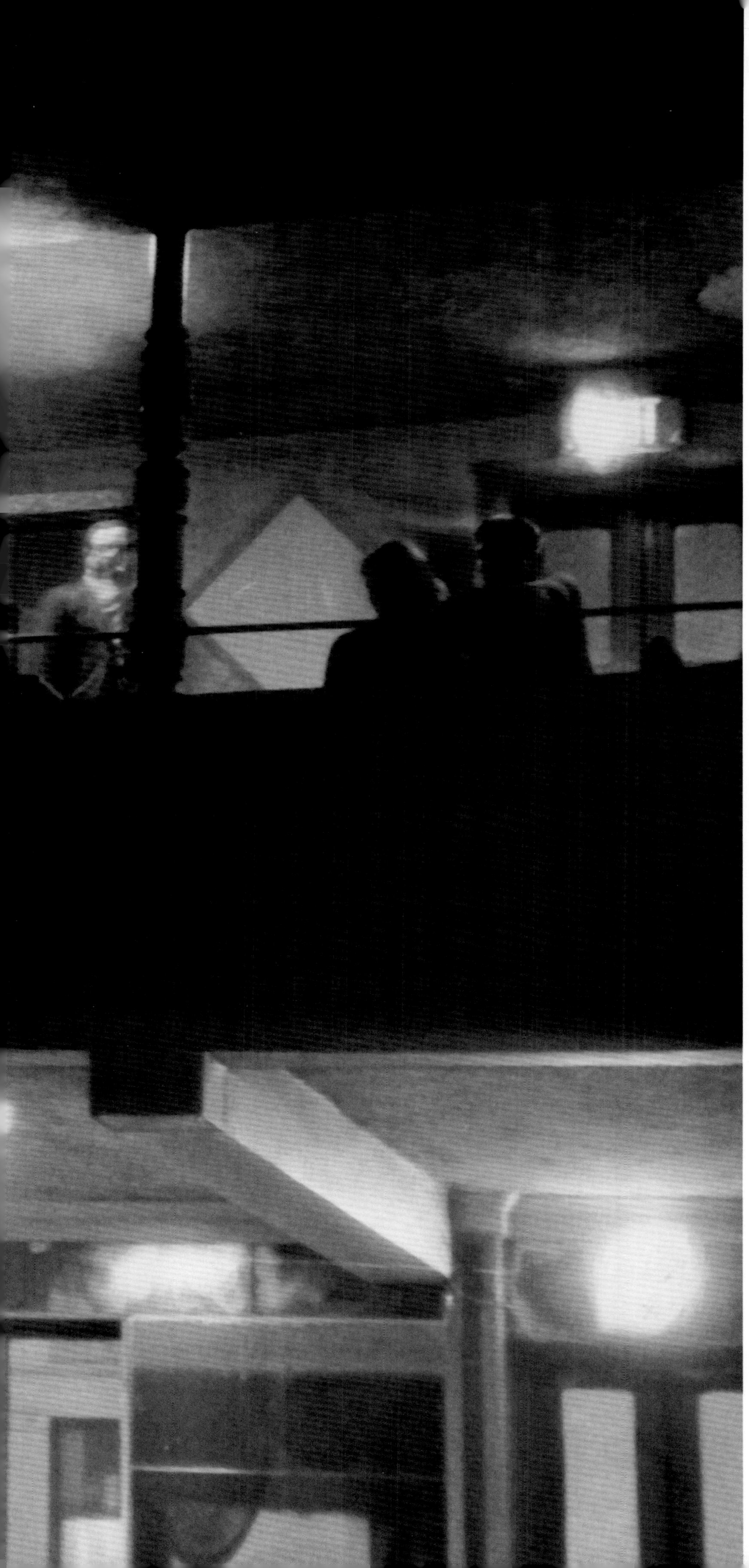

Untimely lessons, or how we could no longer learn from the Bauhaus

Adrian Rifkin

Around 2002 – this is a personal memoir concerning the relation of art-school/Bauhaus in recent decades – I found myself in a tussle with colleagues at a well-known London university over what looked like its legacy, which I wanted to let drop; I was pretty much alone. The theory programme for the first-year undergraduates was common to all disciplines and crafts, and was thus the distant bearer of a kind of 'interdisciplinarity' once widely attributed to the Bauhaus, and often defended and fought for.

Fine art, in its diverse practices, graphics, fashion, interior design and textiles, though not the performing arts, were thought of has having a need for a common grounding. This was to be at the level of an understanding of critique or 'reflexivity' that I would characterize as a kind of post-Barthesian suspicion of the sign coupled with a normative account of heroic modernity as a history of abstraction on the one hand and political engagement on the other. If all the students were to grasp this model, which can only become a model at the expense of also becoming a liturgy, then whatever the differences between the stuff that they made, they would belong to a common enlightenment.

I disagreed. I said this: 'These days, such as they are, you can and should set out to make a comfortable chair, however radical its design and materials, but if you set out to make a comfortable art work then you would never be an artist.'

If this perhaps put too much emphasis on intention, one could reply that, in its basic design courses, the Bauhaus paid too little, or rather too much to purity. Or that the intention to be commercial and other intentions do work out with *dissimilar* kinds of stress in art and design, stress in the subjectivation of the artist/maker as well as in unsettled notions of and criteria for beauty.

Thirty years prior I had taught a course on the Bauhaus together with the Constructivist artist Jeffrey Steele, who himself and whose circles (including Gillian Wise, Malcolm Hughes and many others) implicated aspects of Bauhaus-like procedures into their work – something that is hard to specify as a general relation, given the already disturbed relation of system and singularity, of syntax and enunciation. We all read and some wrote for *Leonardo*, a journal that bore the self-importance of art education's becoming science-like. So you can see that this, imprecisely, demarcates possibilities of being at once in your enunciation from those of being in a system as such. Or, the Bauhaus was a fine idea but it was also a burden. Why else should we, an art historian and an artist, combine our ideas to teach it?

The course got off to a difficult start; not one of the students knew much more than the name 'Bauhaus', though all of them must have been on foundation courses in different provincial art schools.

Weimar – none at all knew where it was.

The First World War, or 'first imperialist world war' as we ultras called it, was likewise a blank.

So Jeffrey and I took out a large coloured map of Europe in our own time, showing clearly the national boundaries, and we tracked out from Weimar to what had been which country before 1914, so the map took on different colours. And back from the war to the Revolution in Russia and the Treaty of Versailles and the colours of the map began to actualize themselves again. And again then back to what was happening in these geographical spaces before the war, in something we used to call the avant-gardes, and so in and out, and spirally, not contextually in any determining or even explanatory manner, but spirally up to the point that a certain possibility emerges of a subject called the Bauhaus. In our terms – perhaps – a syntactical structure in which something such as the Bauhaus could become one enunciatory practice.

It was a process, I would now want to say, of subjectivation, in which the Bauhaus, as it was dispersed, then became a small part of a new set of processes, at once a critical element within the mainstream of art languages and practices and a liturgy, or dogma, or certitude of a Lessing-like correspondence between the arts of a kind that I so roundly refused in the early 2000s. But the notion of subjectivation is crucial now, nowadays, because even in looking at the Bauhaus as a kind of ideal, the more it becomes flawed for us – one might say in the optic so elegantly constructed by Philip Hensher in his novel *The Emperor Waltz*. The passage from the scenes of chilly geometric sodomy between two Bauhaus students and the chaotic couplings of 1980s and 1990s London could not be more telling in terms of realizing what the Bauhaus can signify as a limit, and even as Jeffrey and I were teaching our course the clamour of identities threw its vitality into question:

> Women's body art (Judy Clark, a student; Judy Chicago, a 'mistress') and the death of an abstract beauty, which is a trope in processes of art making as forms of renewal.
>
> Gay students being gay. Black students being black.
>
> Scottish students being Scottish.
>
> Class anger and political critique – Walter Gropius's contribution to the Playboy Club on Park Lane in 1966 may have shifted our leftish attention to Hannes Meyer, but that too was split by left political tendencies; after all he worked for Stalin.

And on and on and on. There is no centenary for all of this. The Bauhaus, over the years, becomes nothing more than a glimmer: a glitter of hope for high-end consumerism as for its mainstreaming; for rules that will hold in place the explosion of forms of subjectivization in making art. And if our syllabus back then was broken by the students' coming to find out about the subject in such a way as to occlude it as anything other than an accessory for study, then its own ideal either melts or explodes into newly useful forms of accessorizing.

Polytechnics and Punks: The 1970s After-life of the Bauhaus

Gavin Butt

In 1971, the painter Patrick Heron wrote luminously about the 'murder' of progressive art education in Britain.[1] Speaking on behalf of a sizable proportion of the United Kingdom fine art establishment, Heron bemoaned how independent art schools were being 'dismembered and swallowed piecemeal' by the UK government's creation of larger, multidisciplinary institutions – polytechnics. The teaching of so-called Basic Design, a post-war and idiosyncratic English pedagogy developed variously by experimental art educators in Newcastle, Leeds, Reading, Ipswich and London, was taken to be mortally imperilled by such developments. The centrality and autonomy enjoyed by fine art media in Basic Design teaching – perpetuating the importance given to open-ended explorations in drawing and painting by Paul Klee and Wassily Kandinsky at the Bauhaus – risked being usurped by the priorities of industry and commerce supposedly guiding the activities of newly appointed polytechnic administrators.

Polytechnic officials themselves, however, publicly demurred from this point of view. Rather than destroying the Bauhaus legacy in British education, polytechnic-ization was instead touted as a state-level, even logical, development of it. 'What Walter Gropius insisted on – "The fundamental unity underlying all branches of design" – may now be capable of being realised', wrote Patrick Nuttgens, then Director of Leeds Polytechnic, and 'on a scale he could not envisage'.[2] Others still looked forward to the opportunity to 'desegregate' art and design teaching by more closely allying it with that of business and technology (the fruitfulness of which is, arguably, borne out in the work of late seventies Manchester Polytechnic Graphic Design graduates Linder Sterling and Peter Saville).[3]

Such divergent perspectives on the desired futures of art and design education, fiercely played out within a largely progressivist elite governing early 1970s UK institutions, became quickly moot however, by around 1974, when faith in progressivism itself began to wane – especially among the young. The optimism of the long 1960s faded, as did belief in the social democratic futures envisaged by modernism and the 'dematerialized' forms of avant-garde art which went with it. The 1973 oil crisis hit the UK's economic fortunes hard and reductions in public expenditure soon became a reality, despite the election of a Labour government in 1974 – thus beginning the shift to neoliberalism well before Margaret Thatcher's victory at the polls in 1979.

Linder, *Untitled*, 1978, photomontage, 29.5 × 20.8 cm

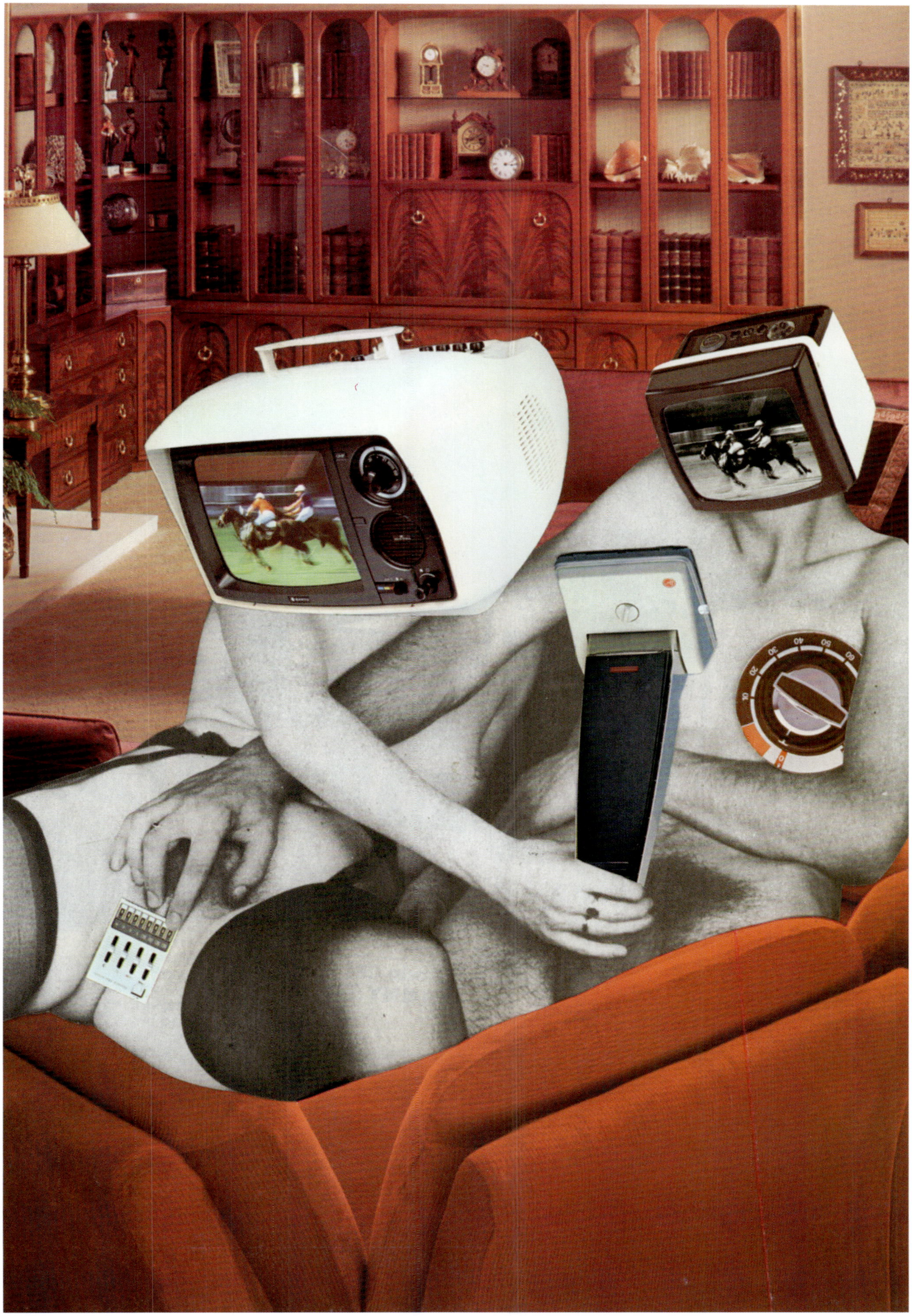

Chris Neate, poster for performance by Marc Almond, Leeds, 1980

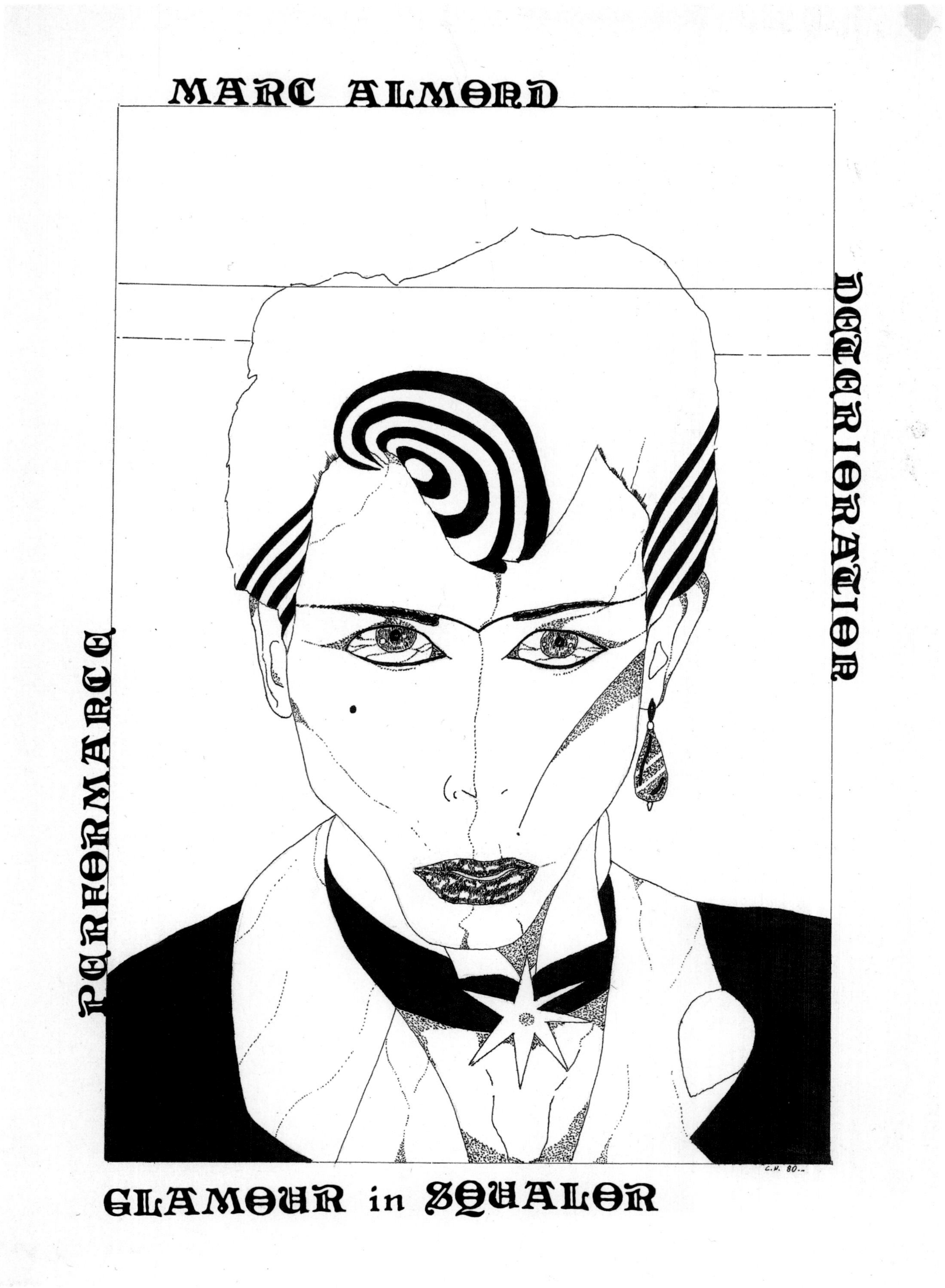

In Leeds, home to 'the most influential art school in Europe since the Bauhaus' according to Heron, fresher art students in the mid-seventies recall the crumbling edifice of Quarry Hill flats as an icon of technocratic failure. Once a beacon for modernist hopes for social housing, in its later run-down state it appeared as ugly reality, staining the rhetorical gleam of Harold Wilson's 'white heat' of economic modernization. If the Bauhaus was relevant at all at this point, it was as filtered through David Bowie's invocations of Berlin, of cabaret and dystopian electronic soundscapes, rather than as the standard bearer of future utopias. If a lingering utopianism did still surround art school provision of film, performance and sound studio facilities, such as at Leeds Polytechnic, alongside those of traditional fine art media, student use of such facilities was often driven by very different concerns. Whether in Frank Tovey's performance theatre productions, or in Marc Almond and Dave Ball's creation of electronic music, narratives and images of pathological agency prevail – of delusion, familicide, autophobia, consumer obsessions – all speaking to subjective forms of *dis*function in the planner's would-be functional city of the 1970s.

By 1976 punk rock's cry of 'no future' became the favoured antithesis to a discredited avant-gardism. Inspired by punk's DIY example, many art students started up bands and transferred their art-making from the gallery and its bourgeois social world to the alternative habitat of popular music culture and working-class audiences. In doing so, bands such as Gang of Four, Scritti Politti, Delta 5 and the Mekons – all art school bands from Leeds – became world-making machines that continued the work of the avant-garde but only by sublating, and transcending, it within the common culture. Informed variously by Marxism, feminism, anti-racism and anti-fascism, such bands sought to create new musical forms to further political awareness and help create an opposing social bloc to the growing right-wing forces of late-seventies British society. The importance of being in a band meant artists were readily disposed to turn to each other in forging such novel aesthetico-political forms, perhaps more than they were to artistic forebears and prior authorities. In doing so, one might argue, they belatedly fulfilled Bauhaus ideals: both of collective working, and of harnessing the fruits of specialized aesthetic experiment for the benefit of everyday living. But, by the time of punk, the Bauhaus had ceased to be a key reference point for young artists: the urgencies of creating counter-hegemonic forces and of creating anew the arts of a common culture favoured Gramsci, not Gropius, as an indispensable guide for making the next step.

Frank Tovey, *Berg*, 1978

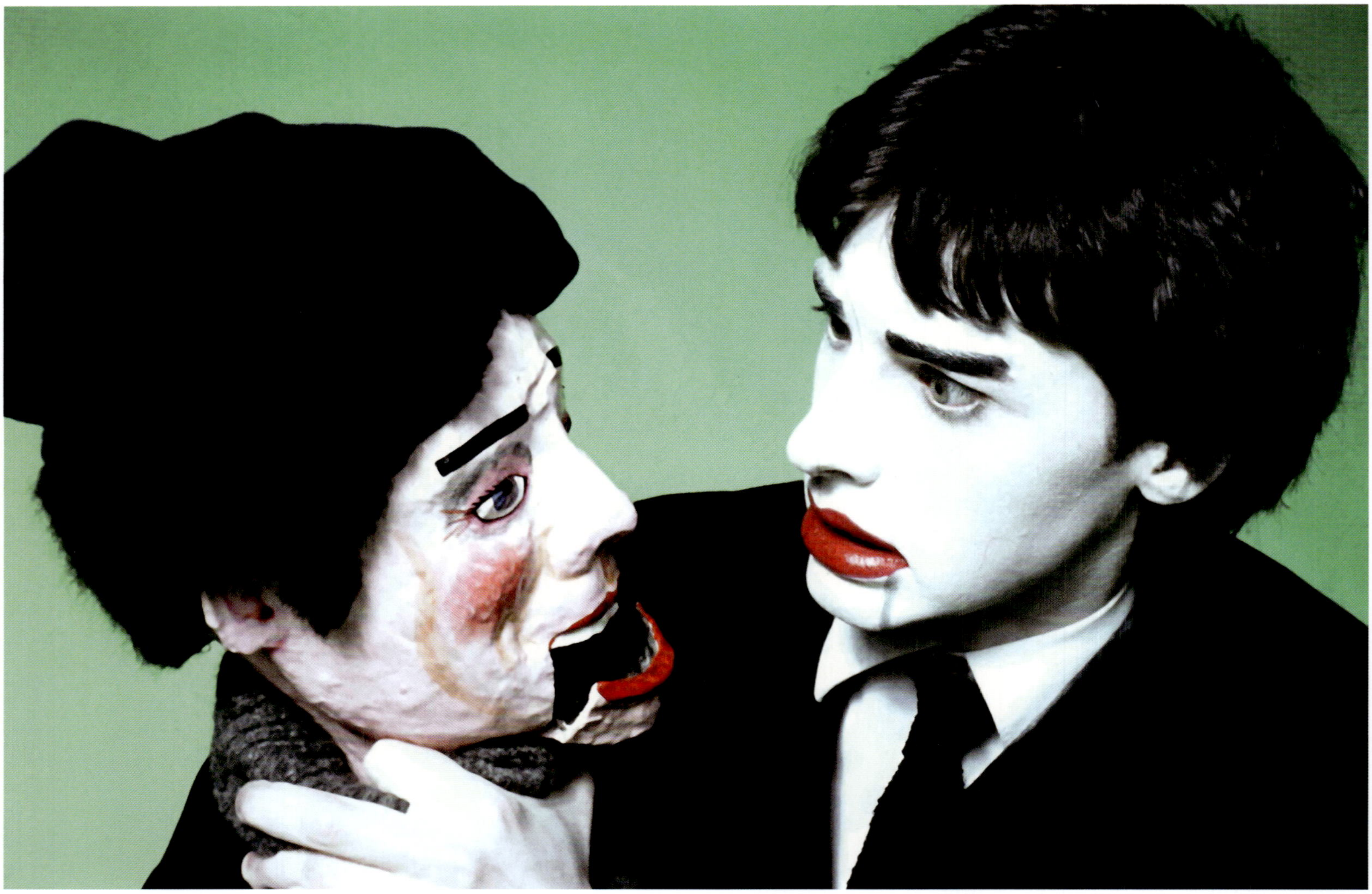

László Moholy-Nagy

Sketch for a Score for a Mechanized Eccentric

▶ Pages 285–87: László Moholy-Nagy, *Partiturskizze zu einer mechanischen Exzentrik* (Sketch for a Score for a Mechanized Eccentric), 1923, collage, ink, watercolour and pencil on cardboard, 17.8 × 140 cm

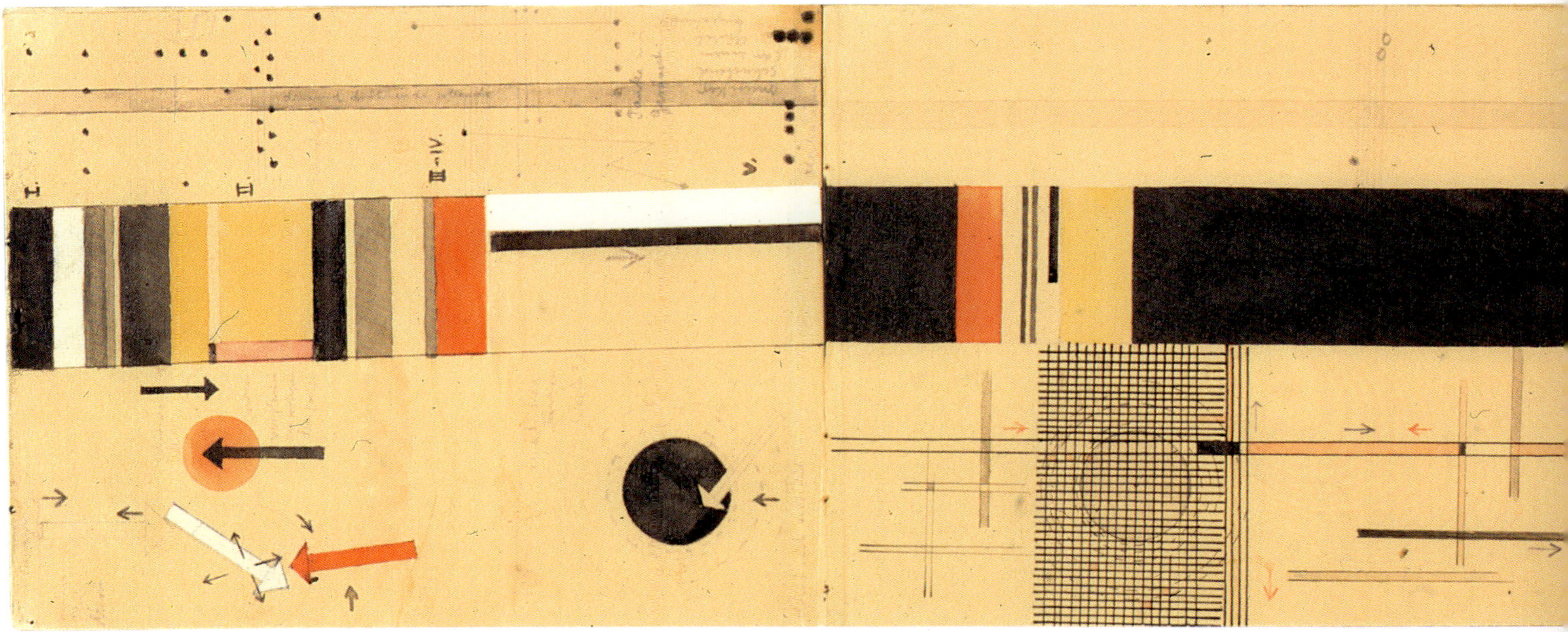

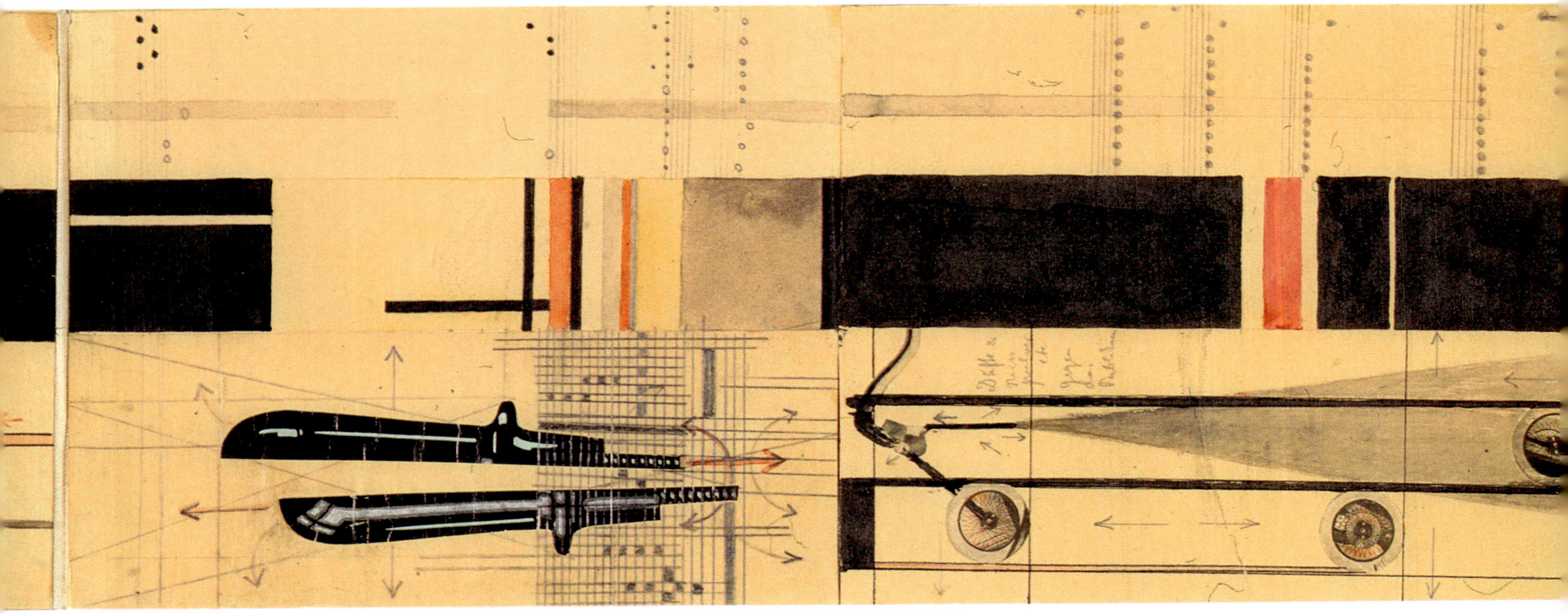

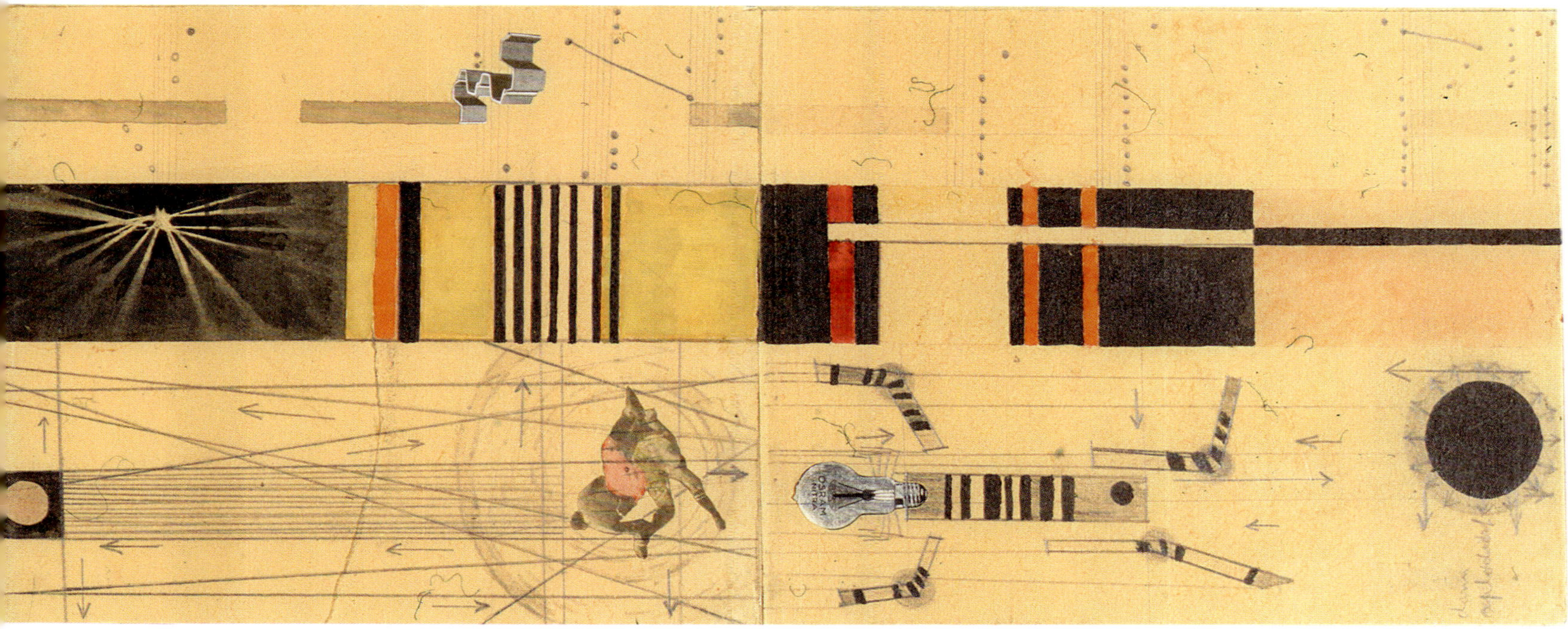

Notes

Pages 12–13
bauhaus imaginista
Marion von Osten and Grant Watson

1 In the spirit of decentring the hegemonic West, which permeates many of the contributions in this book, as well as the overall undertaking of the bauhaus imaginista project, we have consciously chosen not to capitalize 'western' throughout the publication.
2 Further information about the scope and various iterations of the overall bauhaus imaginista project, as well as a list of researchers and other partner institutions, can be found on pages 296–97.

Page 16
Corresponding With: Introduction
Marion von Osten and Grant Watson

1 Its official name was Staatliches Bauhaus in Weimar (Weimar State Bauhaus). Over the course of its existence, the Bauhaus had three directors: Walter Gropius (1919–28), Hannes Meyer (1928–30) and Ludwig Mies van der Rohe (1930–33). It was located first in Weimar (1919–25), then in Dessau (1925–31) and finally in Berlin (1932–33).
2 See Regina Bittner and Kathrin Rhomberg (eds), *The Bauhaus in Calcutta: An Encounter of the Cosmopolitan Avant-Garde*. Ostfildern: Hatje Cantz, 2013.
3 The exhibition included works by Gaganendranath Tagore, Kshistindranath Mazumdar, Asit Halder and R. N. Chakravarty, among others.

Pages 26–28
Walter Gropius's Bauhaus Manifesto
Magdalena Droste

1 *Arbeitsrat für Kunst 1918–1921* [Workers' Council for Art 1918–1921] (exhibition catalogue). Berlin: Akademie der Künste, 1980.
2 On the foundation history, see Volker Wahl, 'Wie Walter Gropius nach Weimar kam. Zur Gründungsgeschichte des Staatlichen Bauhauses in Weimar 1919' [How Walter Gropius Came to Weimar: On the Foundation History of the Staatliches Bauhaus in Weimar 1919], in *Weimar-Jena: Die Große Stadt. Das kulturhistorische Archiv* [Weimar-Jena: The Big City – The Cultural-Historical Archive], Vol. 1, No. 3, 2008, 167–211.
3 On the origin and history of the Manifesto, see Karen Koehler, 'The Bauhaus Manifesto Postwar to Postwar: From the Street to the Radio to the Memoir', in Jeffrey Saletnik and Robin Schuldenfrei (eds), *Bauhaus Construct: Fashioning Identity, Discourse and Modernism*. London: Routledge, 2009, 13–36; Charles Haxthausen, 'Walter Gropius and Lyonel Feininger: Bauhaus Manifesto. 1919', in Barry Bergdoll and Leah Dickerman, *Bauhaus 1919–1933: Workshops for Modernity*. New York: Museum of Modern Art, 2009, 64–67; and Magdalena Bushart, 'Am Anfang ein Missverständnis. Feiningers Kathedrale und das Bauhaus-Manifest' [At the Beginning of a Misunderstanding: Feininger's Cathedral and the Bauhaus Manifesto], in Bauhaus-Archiv/Museum für Gestaltung, Berlin and Stiftung Bauhaus Dessau/Klassik Stiftung Weimar (eds), *Modell Bauhaus* [Model Bauhaus]. Ostfildern: Hatje Cantz, 2009, 29–32.
4 Letter from Gropius to Richard Engelmann dated 16 April 1919, cited in Wahl, *Weimar-Jena*, 2008, footnote 139.
5 Walter Gropius, 'Ansprache an die Studierenden des Staatlichen Bauhauses, gehalten aus Anlaß der Jahresausstellung von Schülerarbeiten im Juli 1919' [Discussions with Students of the Bauhaus on the Occasion of the Annual Exhibition of Student Work in July 1919], in Hans Maria Wingler, *Das Bauhaus 1919–1933 Weimar Dessau Berlin* [The Bauhaus 1919–1933 Weimar Dessau Berlin], 3rd edition. Cologne: Verlag Gebr. Rasch & Co./DuMont, 1975, 45–46, here 46.
6 Annemarie Jaeggi, 'Ein geheimnisvolles Mysterium: Bauhütten-Romantik und Freimaurerei am frühen Bauhaus' [A Secret Mystery: Mason's Guild Romanticism and Free Masonry at the Early Bauhaus], in Christoph Wagner (ed.), *Das Bauhaus und die Esoterik: Johannes Itten, Wassily Kandinsky, Paul Klee* [The Bauhaus and Esotericism: Johannes Itten, Wassily Kandinsky, Paul Klee] (exhibition catalogue). Bielefeld/Leipzig: Kerber, 2005, 37–45.
7 Regina Bittner and Kathrin Rhomberg (eds), *The Bauhaus in Calcutta: An Encounter of the Cosmopolitan Avant-Garde*. Ostfildern: Hatje Cantz, 2013.
8 Johannes Itten, *Die Tagebücher. Stuttgart 1913–1916. Wien 1916–1919* [Diaries: Stuttgart 1913–1916, Vienna 1916–1919], edited and annotated by Eva Badura-Triska. Vienna: Löcker, 1990, annotation, 97. One version of Itten's lecture can be found in Rainer Wick (ed.), *Johannes Itten. Bildanalysen* [Johannes Itten: Picture Analyses]. Ravensburg: Otto Maier, 1988, 91–101. Itten also mentions the Indian Vedas.
9 Boris Friedwald, 'The Bauhaus and India: A Look Back to the Future – "Building! Design! Gothic – India!"', in Bittner and Rhomberg (eds), *The Bauhaus in Calcutta*, 2013, 117–33, here 117.
10 Robin Rehm, *Das Bauhausgebäude in Dessau. Die ästhetischen Kategorien Zweck, Form, Inhalt* [The Bauhaus Building in Dessau: The Aesthetic Categories of Purpose, Form, Content]. Berlin: Gebr. Mann, 2005, 127–34.
11 Katerina Rüedi Ray, *Bauhaus Dream-house: Modernity and globalization*. London: Routledge, 2010, 146–49.
12 Helena Čapková, 'Transnational Networkers – Iwao and Michiko Yamawaki and the Formation of Japanese Modernist Design', *Journal of Design History*, Vol. 27, No. 4, 2014, 370–85.
13 Cf. Karl Lagerfeld (ed.), *Iwao Yamawaki*. Göttingen: Steidl, 1999.
14 Cf. Čapková, 'Transnational Networkers', 2014.

Thanks to Ute Ackermann and Anke Blümm.

Pages 36–41
Teaching Art at Santiniketan and Weimar: Some Unexpected Meeting Points
Partha Mitter

1 Thus Ferdinand Tönnies's famous distinction between two social groups, one bound by togetherness and other as marking indidividualism (Ferdinand Tönnies, *Gemeinschaft und Gesellschaft*. Leipzig: Fues's Verlag (R. Reisland), 1887).
2 Rabindranath Tagore, 'Tapoban', in *Rabindra Rachanabali* [Rabindranath's Complete Works], XI (Centenary Edition). Kalikata [Kolkata]: West Bengal Government, 1368 [c. 1961], 589.
3 See theoria.art-zoo.com/the-theory-and-organization-of-the-bauhaus (28 April 2018).
4 See Partha Mitter, 'Bauhaus in Kalkutta', in Bauhaus-Archiv Berlin (ed.), *bauhaus global*. Berlin: Gebr. Mann Verlag, 2010, 149–58, and Regina Bittner and Kathrin Rhomberg (eds), *The Bauhaus in Calcutta: An Encounter of the Cosmopolitan Avant-Garde*. Ostfildern: Hatje Cantz, 2013.
5 On Cižek see Ratan Parimoo, *The Paintings of the Three Tagores*. Baroda: Maharaja Sayajirao University, 1973, 118.
6 Nandalal Basu [Bose], 'Art, Patronage

and Institution', *Visvabharati Quarterly*, Nandalal Number, XXXIV, Nos 1–4, January 1971, 70–76. For a detailed discussion of Nandalal's contribution to art teaching at Santiniketan, see Partha Mitter, *The Triumph of Modernism: India's Artists and the Avant-garde*. London: Reaktion Books, 2007, 78–81.

7 Partha Mitter in 'Rabindranath Tagore, Okakura Tenshin and the Creation of a Regional Modernist Art in Asia', unpublished paper delivered at the conference 'Concrete Media', held at MUMOK and Academy of Fine Arts, Vienna, 2011.

8 Nandalal Basu [Bose], 'Manush, Poshu, Pakhir Rup-ankan' [Drawing Humans and Animals], in *Drishti o Srishti*. Kalikata [Kolkata]: Visva-Bharati Granthan Bibhag, 1392 [1985], 161.

9 Benodebehari Mukhopadhyay (Mukherjee), *Adhunik Shilpashiksha* [Modern Art Education]. Kalikata [Kolkata]: Visva-Bharati Granthan Bibhag, n.d. [1972], 53–55.

10 Basu, *Drishti o Srishti*, 1985, 14.

11 Benodebehari Mukhopadhyay (Mukherjee), 'Baratiya murti or bimurtabad', in *Chitra Katha*. Kolkata: Aruna Prakashani, 1390 [1983], 39–52.

12 I have been developing the concept of the 'virtual cosmopolis' as a means of virtual communication by the transmission of print culture across the globe in negotiating global modernity, see Mitter, *Triumph of Modernism*, 2007, 11–20, 100. On the dialogic generation of cross-cultural ideas, see Partha Mitter, 'Frameworks for Considering Cultural Exchange: The Case of India and America', in Cynthia Mills *et al.* (eds), *East-West Interchanges in American Art: A Long and Tumultuous Relationship*. Washington, DC: Smithsonian Institution Scholarly Press, 2012, 20–37. On the crisis of style in German art and responses of modernist critics in the early twentieth century, see Charles Mark Haxthausen, 'Paul Klee, Wilhelm Hausenstein and the "Problem of Style"', lecture delivered at the Institute for Advanced Study, Princeton and posted online on 21 August 2014. https://www.ias.edu/ideas/2014/haxthausen-klee-video (28 April 2018).

Pages 56–64
Framing Renshichirō Kawakita's Transcultural Legacy and His Pedagogy
Helena Čapková,

1 Sadanosuke Nakada, 'Kokuritsu Bauhaus' [The State Bauhaus], *Mizue*, Vol. 244, Nos 6 & 7, 1925, 4–5.

2 Hiromitsu Umemiya, 'Kawakita Renshichirō no Jiseki; Ukuraina gekijō-an kokusai sekkei kyōgi saikō' [A study of the Arch. Renshichirō Kawakita; A Re-examination of the International Competition of Ukrainian Theatre], *Research Reports: Architectural Institute of Japan,* 1994, 1371–72.

3 One more example of education practice that accommodated an array of diverse modernist art and design practices was the approach to education found at the Jiyū Gakuen (Free College), which had applied innovative methods to teaching arts to educate and emancipate young Japanese Christian women since 1921. The initial method, *jiyūga* (free drawing), was formulated by the school's leading art teacher Kanae Yamada (1882–1946), prolific artist, printmaker and progressive educator with transnational experience, who studied in France prior to his distinguished career in Japan and at the school. In the early 1920s, artists, musicians and esoteric practitioners, Zina and Stefan Lubienski (1893–1976) were invited to teach classes on art and music. Zina trained in a Duncan-style of modern dance and tutored the students in Greek dancing. See Stefan Lubienski, *Vor Der Schwelle, Lebenserzahlung eine polnischen Künstlers und Suchers* [At the Threshold, Memories of a Polish Artist and Seeker]. Driebergen: Selbstverlag, 1974, 108. The quest for a new teaching method continued in Jiyū Gakuen Arts and Crafts Institute in 1932, which became a hub for applying the Bauhaus and Johannes Itten's methods to the school's curriculum. See Tami Murakami, 'Art and Craft Education of Jiyu Gakuen in 1921–1932: Collaboration between Mr and Mrs Hani and Kanae Yamamoto', *Seikatsu Daigaku Kenkyu*, Vol. 1, 2015, 26–44. For broader context consult Yoko Yamasaki and Hiroyuki Kuno (eds), *Educational Progressivism, Cultural Encounters and Reform in Japan* (London: Routledge, 2017).

4 Takehiko Mizutani, 'Kōsei kiso kyōiku' [The Basic Kōsei Education], *Kenchiku gahō*, Vol. 22, no. 10, 1931, 1–4.

5 The prolific impact is analysed, for example, in Keisuke Takayasu, 'The Development of Design Education for Children in Japan', in Haruhiko Fujita and Keiko Hashimoto (eds), 'Theme III: Design Education after the Bauhaus', *The ACDHT Journal*, No. 1, 2016, 95–103.

6 For more details see Helena Čapková, 'Transnational Networkers – Iwao and Michiko Yamawaki and the Formation of Japanese Modernist Design', *Journal of Design History*, Vol. 27, No. 4, 2014, 370–85.

7 In German, *Spannung* can be literally translated as 'tension', 'friction' or 'pressure', but the term was advanced by Wassily Kandinsky to describe an approach to art practice. Kawakita used this term transcribed to Japanese *katakana* script and explained it as follows: 'There are two "Shupannunku." One is "passive Shupannunku", which occurs when all human senses receive and perceive something from the outer world. The other is "technical Shupannunku", which generates positive tension in every creation and criticism. *Kosei Kyoiku* refers to "Shupannunku" as follows: to receive all "Shupannunku" generated by nature or in daily life, process them, and transform them into the "technical Shupannunku"', translation in Hidehiro Ikegami, 'Kosei and Zokei Education: Bauhaus and the Formation of Kuwasawa Design School', in Haruhiko Fujita and Keiko Hashimoto (eds), 'Theme III: Design Education after the Bauhaus', *The ACDHT Journal*, No. 1, 2016, 85–94, 89; original in Renshichirō Kawakita and Katsuo Takei, *Kōsei Kyōiku Taikei* [Manual for Teaching Thinking through Construction]. Tokyo: Gakkō Bijutsu Kyōkai Press, 1934, 16.

8 Ikegami, 'Kōsei and Zokei Education: Bauhaus and the Formation of Kuwasawa Design School', 2016, 89. The struggle is analysed in detail in Hiromitsu Umemiya, 'Kawakita Renshichirō no Kōsei Kyōiku ni taisuru Seinen Kenchikuka Club no hihan ni tsuite' [Renshichirō Kawakita: the criticism against the idea of his design education], *Research Reports: Architectural Institute of Japan*, 1992, 1057–58.

9 See Yasuko Suga, 'Modernism, Commercialism and Display Design in Britain: The Reimann School and Studios of Industrial and Commercial Art', *Journal of Design History*, Vol. 19, 2006, 137–54, here 137; Yuko Kikuchi, 'Visualising Oriental Crafts: Contested Notions of "Japaneseness" and the Crafts of the Japanese Empire', in *The 38th International Research Symposium, Questioning Oriental Aesthetics and Thinking: Conflicting Visions of 'Asia' under the Colonial Empires*, International Research Center for Japanese Studies, Kyoto, 2011, 211–35, here 214–15, 225.

10 Renshichirō Kawakita, *Kōsaku Gijutsu Taikei* [A General Guide to Industrial Techniques]. Tokyo: Zuga Kōsaku, 1942, in Takayasu, 'The Development

of Design Education for Children in Japan', 2016, 98–9.
11 Ikegami, 'Kōsei and Zokei Education: Bauhaus and the Formation of Kuwasawa Design School', 2016, 91. Quote from: Message by Walter Gropius to Yoko Kuwasawa, translated by Masaru Katsumi, in Taro Takamatsu, *Kuwasawa: So-so no Tsui-oku* [Memory of the early days in Kuwasawa. Tokyo: Kuwasawa Gakuen, 2004 (back cover). Ikegami demonstrated the impact of art critic and educator Masaru Katsumi and the shift from the German Bauhaus model to the New Bauhaus model from the US. The Japanese 'Bauhaus'/Kuwasawa Design School still exists and keeps on promoting Bauhaus educational principles. Gropius's presence fuelled the interest in Bauhaus ideas of a younger generation of designers, such as Gropius's Harvard student Kiyoshi Seike (1918–2005), who transferred the teaching to his own students at the Tokyo National University and Tokyo Institute of Technology.

Pages 66–67
On the Reception of Johannes Itten's Art Education in Japan
Yoshimasa Kaneko

1 Yoshimasa Kaneko, 'A Study on the Educational Relationship between Johannes Itten and some Japanese People – With a Special Reference to the Activities of Shounan Mizukoshi and Kuniyoshi Obara' (in Japanese with English summary), *Daigaku Bijutsukyoiku Gakkaishi*, No. 32, 2000, 133–40.
2 Yoshimasa Kaneko, 'A Study on the Lessons of "Japanese Picture" at the Ittenschule' (in Japanese with English summary), *Daigaku Bijutsukyoiku Gakkaishi*, No. 25, 1993, 247–56; Yoshimasa Kaneko, 'A Study on the Art Education of Yumeji Takehisa at the Ittenschule' (in Japanese with English summary), *The Journal for Society of Art Education in University*, No. 33, 2001, 143–50.
3 Yoshimasa Kaneko, 'A study on the accepting process of the formative education from the Ittenschule to Japan – Based on the achievements of Mrs Mitsuko Yamamuro and Mrs Kazuko Sasagawa' (in Japanese), *Bijutsukyoikugaku*, No. 16, 1995, 85–99. See also Yoshimasa Kaneko, 'Jiyū -Gakuen school students who studied at the Itten-Schule', in Yasuaki Okamoto (ed.), *Johannes Itten Wege zur Kunst Ronbun-Shū* (Academic Articles Collections) (in Japanese). Utsunomiya: Utsunomiya Museum, 2005, 53–80.
4 *Kenchiku Kōgei I See All* (Architecture Design I See All), January 1933, 83.
5 Kaneko, 'A study on the accepting process of the formative education from the Ittenschule to Japan', 1995.
6 Renshichirō Kawakita and Katsuo Takei, *Kōsei Kyōiku Taikei* [Manual for Teaching Thinking through Construction]. Tokyo: Gakkō Bijutsu Kyōkai Press, 1934, 169.
7 *Gakuen Shinbun* [School Paper], Jiyū-Gakuen, Tokyo, 25 September 1958, 3.
8 Yoshimasa Kaneko, 'Johannes Itten's Philosophy of Human-Centered Art Education – Content Analysis of *Tagebuch von Johannes Itten*, based on a Conversation with Eva Plaut' (in Japanese with English summary), *Bijutsukyoikugaku*, No. 28, 2007, 143–55, 444.
9 Kaneko, 'A Study on the Educational Relationship between Johannes Itten and some Japanese People', 2000.
10 Shūzō Takiguchi, *Paul Klee Ron-Shū*. Tokyo: Satani Gallery, 1990, 126–42; Yoshimasa Kaneko, 'Johannes Itten and Zen', in Christoph Wagner (ed.), *Esoterik am Bauhaus. Eine Revision der Moderne?* [Esoterism at the Bauhaus: Revising the Modern?], Regensburger Studien zur Kunstgeschichte, Vol. 1. Regensburg: Verlag Schnell & Steiner, 2009, 150–72.

Pages 92–102
Paul Klee's Pictures of Architectural Tapestries
Fabienne Eggelhöfer

1 Jürgen Glaesemer, *Paul Klee. Handzeichnungen II. 1921–1936* [Paul Klee. Drawings II. 1921–1936]. Bern: Kunstmuseum, 1984, 99. See the drawings by Klee *1927, 39* to *1927, 62*.
2 On the 'decorative' Klee see Jenny Anger, *Paul Klee and the Decorative in Modern Art*. Cambridge: Cambridge University Press, 2004.
3 *bauhaus. junge menschen kommt ans bauhaus!* [bauhaus. young people come to the bauhaus!]. Bauhaus Dessau (ed.). Dessau, 1929, 3. The same brochure features a reprint of Klee's essay 'exacte versuche im bereich der kunst' [Exact Experiments in the Realm of Art], first published in 1928 in *bauhaus zeitschrift*, Vol. 2, Nos 2/3. English translation in Jürg Spiller (ed.), *Paul Klee: The Thinking Eye – The Notebooks of Paul Klee*. London/New York: Lund Humphries/George Wittenborn, 1961, 69–70.
4 Lesson plan in the pocket calendar WS 1927/28, in Felix Klee (ed.), *Paul Klee, Briefe an die Familie 1893–1940. Band 2: 1907–1940* [Paul Klee, Letters to the Family 1893–1940. Volume 2: 1907–1940]. Cologne: DuMont, 1979, 1093.
5 Cited in Wulf Herzogenrath and Werner Poschel (eds), *Benita Koch-Otte: Farblehre und Weberei: Bauhaus Weimar und Dessau, Burg Giebichenstein, Weberei Bethel* [Benita Koch-Otte: Colour Studies and Weaving: Bauhaus Weimar and Dessau, Giebichenstein Castle, Bethel Weaving Mill] (exhibition catalogue). Bielefeld: Graphischer Betrieb Ernst Gieseking, 1976, 21. First printed in Gunta Stölzl, 'In der Textilwerkstatt des Bauhauses 1919–1931' [In the Bauhaus Textile Workshop 1919–1931], in *Das Werk*, Vol. 55, No. 11, 1968, 744–48. The lesson plans and minutes of the committee of Bauhaus masters do not substantiate this, since for the period between 1921 and 1925 Georg Muche is named as the form master of the weaving workshop.
6 Jenny Anger, 'Klees Unterricht in der Webereiwerkstatt des Bauhauses' [Klee's Classes in the Bauhaus Weaving Workshop], in Anger, Magdalena Droste and Michael Siebenbrot (eds), *Das Bauhaus Webt. Die Textilwerkstatt am Bauhaus* [Bauhaus Weaves: The Bauhaus Weaving Workshop] (exhibition catalogue). Berlin: G & H Verlag, 1998, 33–41.
7 Pocket calendar 1928: '04/16. Weaving workshop: more recent course. Teaching of structure according to measurements. Older course: more-several centres', in Felix Klee, *Paul Klee, Briefe an die Familie 1893–1940*, 1979, 1078. In the winter semester of 1928/29, Klee even taught the third, fourth and fifth semesters of the weaving workshop; see the pocket calendar in *Briefe*, 1979, 1079. For a detailed list of Klee's teaching activities at the Bauhaus, see Fabienne Eggelhöfer, 'Paul Klees Lehre vom Schöpferischen' [Paul Klee's Creative Doctrine], doctoral thesis, University of Bern, 2012, 18–21 and 230–32, http://biblio.unibe.ch/download/eldiss/12eggelhoefer_f.pdf (9 April 2018).
8 Lena Bergner married Hannes Meyer in 1936, although she continued to use her maiden name as an artist.
9 Hamid Sadighi Neiriz, 'Paul Klee und die Kelims der Nomaden' [Paul Klee and the Kilims of Nomads], in Anger, Droste and Siebenbrot (eds), *Das Bauhaus Webt*, 1998, 120–43. See also Alain Nadaud, 'La couleur me possède' [Colour Possesses Me], in Sadika Keskes, Alain Nadaud and Jean Lancri

(eds), *Paul Klee et le tapis tunisien. Aux portes de l'abstraction* [Paul Klee and the Tunisian Carpet: At the Gates of Abstraction] (exhibition catalogue). Tunis: Sa'Al Editions, 2014, 11–98.

10 For more on the watercolours, see Roger Benjamin, '"Schöne Aquarelle": Paul Klee und indigene Kunst aus Kairouan' ['Pretty Watercolours': Paul Klee and Indigenous Art from the Kairouan], in *Die Tunisreise 1914. Paul Klee, August Macke, Louis Moilliet* [Travel to Tunis 1914: Paul Klee, August Macke, Louis Moilliet] (exhibition catalogue). Ostfildern: Hatje Cantz, 2014, 233–39.

11 In his diary, Klee wrote: 'Began the synthesis of urban architecture and pictorial architecture. Not yet pure, but quite attractive, somewhat too much of the mood, of the enthusiasm of traveling in it – the Self, in a word. Things will no doubt get more objective later, once the intoxication has worn off a bit.' Felix Klee (ed.), *The Diaries of Paul Klee, 1898–1918*. Berkeley: University of California Press, 1964, 287.

12 Klee's wife, Lily, gave him the first edition of Carl Einstein's path-breaking 1915 book *Negerplastik* [Negro Sculpture] with a dedication from Einstein to Klee. Furthermore, Einstein personally gave Klee his book *Afrikanische Plastik* [African Sculpture] published in 1921. Klee's estate library includes further publications by Leo Frobenius and Ernst Fuhrmann on African art as well as books on Asian art. Magazines such as *Cahiers d'art* or *Omnibus* probably also served as sources.

13 See the illustrations in Eckart von Sydow, *Die Kunst der Naturvölker und der Vorzeit* [The Art of Indigenous Peoples and of Prehistory], 2nd edition. Berlin: Propyläen, 1927, 173, 198, 221, 332, 410ff. On the library at the Bauhaus in Weimar, see Michael Siebenbrodt and Frank Simon-Ritz (eds), *Die Bauhaus-Bibliothek. Versuch einer Rekonstruktion* [The Bauhaus Library: Attempt at a Reconstruction]. Weimar: Verlag der Bauhaus-Universität Weimar, 2009; on the ethnological material, see 31–33 and 65–72.

14 For more on Klee's teachings, see the introductions to each chapter at www.kleegestaltungslehre.zpk.org or Fabienne Eggelhöfer and Marianne Keller Tschirren (eds), *Paul Klee. Bauhaus Master* (exhibition catalogue). Madrid: La Fábrica/Fundación Juan March, 2013.

15 Klee did not use the same teaching notes in the years 1923–24 and 1927–28, as Jenny Anger has previously assumed. Cf. Anger, *Paul Klee and the Decorative in Modern Art*, 2004, 179, note 2. The notes by Gunta Stölzl in Mappe 2 at the Bauhaus-Archiv Berlin are transcripts of Klee's classes in the summer semester of 1922 and winter semester of 1922–23, and therefore correspond with the lectures from the *Beiträge zur bildnerischen Formlehre* [Contributions to a Pictorial Theory of Form]. The transcripts in Mappe 4 are identical to the transcripts by Otti Berger and Gertrud Arndt. They correspond with Klee's teaching notes that he later used for his design classes for weaving in Dessau.

16 Paul Klee, *Beiträge zur bildnerischen Formlehre*, BF/49–50.

17 As revealed by a comparison between Klee's notes on the teachings of design and the surviving transcripts of his students in the Bauhaus archives in Weimar, Dessau and Berlin, Klee indeed created all geometric drawings for his courses.

18 For more on this topic, see Magdalena Droste, 'Anpassung und Eigensinn. Die Webereitwerkstatt des Bauhauses' [Adaptation and Obstinancy: The Bauhaus Weaving Workshop], in Anger, Droste and Siebenbrot (eds), *Das Bauhaus Webt*, 1998, 11–20.

19 Gunta Stölzl, 'Weberei am Bauhaus' [Weaving at the Bauhaus], *Offset. Buch- und Werbekunst*, No. 7, 1926, 405ff, reprinted in Anger, Droste and Siebenbrot (eds), *Das Bauhaus Webt*, 1998, 190.

Pages 106–10
Books on World Art from the 1920s: On the Ambivalence of a Discursive Awakening
Susanne Leeb

1 On the Bauhaus library, see Michael Siebenbrodt and Frank Simon-Ritz (eds), *Die Bauhaus-Bibliothek. Versuch einer Rekonstruktion* [The Bauhaus Library: Attempt at a Reconstruction]. Weimar: Verlag der Bauhaus-Universität Weimar, 2009.

2 Published by Folkwang-Auriga Verlag between 1919 and 1923, initiated by Karl Ernst Osthaus, museum founder in Hagen, headed by Ernst Fuhrmann. In the early 1920s, the Folkwang-Archive possessed the largest picture collection on non-European arts.

3 Here the geographical spectrum also includes China, East Gotland, Mexico, Indonesia and Persia.

4 The series consists of the following volumes: 1) Indian Architecture, 2) Old Russian Art, 3) Archaic Sculpture of the Greeks, 4) Chinese Landscape Painting, 5) Asian Monumental Sculpture, 6) Indian Miniatures from Islamic Times, 7) African Sculpture, 8) Old Mexican Art History, 9) Hittite Art, 10) Oldest German Painting, 11) Medieval Ivory Works, 12) Chinese Small Sculptures, 13) Masks, 14) Islamic Architecture, 15) Classicism in France, 16) Early Japanese Woodcuts, 17) North-west American Indian Art, 18) Old French Tapestry, 19) Assyrian Sculpture and 20) Early German Stone Sculptures.

5 Christian Kravagna, 'Für eine postkoloniale Kunstgeschichte des Kontakts' [For a Postcolonial Art History of Contact], *Texte zur Kunst*, No. 91, September 2013, 111–32, here 117.

6 For example, the captions for objects referenced in the series prioritize current location (i.e. to which collection an object now belongs) over place of origin. The following museums, among others, are named: Berlin, Museum für Völkerkunde; Museum Folkwang Essen; Leipzig, Museum für Völkerkunde; Vienna, Naturhistorisches Museum; Darmstadt, Museum für Völkerkunde; Frankfurt, Völkermuseum; Lübeck, Museum für Völkerkunde; Bremen, Städtisches Museum.

7 Otto Weber, 'Einleitung' [Introduction], in *Die Kunst der Hethiter* [Hittite Art] (*Orbis Pictus/Weltkunst-Bücherei*), Vol. 9. Berlin: Verlag Ernst Wasmuth, undated, 5–19, here 5.

8 Carl Einstein, *Afrikanische Plastik* [African Sculpture] (*Orbis Pictus/ Weltkunst-Bücherei*), Vol. 7. Leipzig: Verlag Ernst Wasmuth, undated, 5.

9 Cf. in more detail Susanne Leeb, *Die Kunst der Anderen. 'Weltkunst' und die Konfiguration der anthropologischen Moderne* [The Art of the Others: 'World Art' and the Configuration of Anthropological Modernity]. Berlin: b_books, 2015.

10 Cf. Sylvester Ogbechie, 'Transcultural Interpretation and the Production of Alterity: Photography, Materiality, and Mediation in the Making of "African Art"', in Gabriele Genge and Angela Stercken (eds), *Art History and Fetishism Abroad: Global Shiftings in Media and Methods*. Bielefeld: transcript, 2014, 113–28, here 113.

11 *Ibid.*

12 Carl Einstein, 'Handbuch der Kunst', 1930s, typescript (beginning of the remarks on Vol. V, 'Die gesamte Kunstgeschichte in einem Band von 300 Seiten Text' [The Entire History of Art in One Volume with 300 Pages of Text]), Akademie der Künste, Berlin, Carl-Einstein-Archiv, No. 219.

13 Cf. T'ai Smith, *Bauhaus Weaving Theory: From Feminine Craft to Mode of Design*. Minneapolis: University of Minessota Press, 2014, especially Chapter 3: 'The Haptics of Optics: Weaving and Photography'.
14 The critique of ethnographic museums is extensive and endless. For a more specific analysis of the Humboldt-Forum from a decolonial perspective see http://www.africavenir.org/de/projekte/projekte-deutschland/dekoloniale-einwaende-gegen-das-humboldt-forum.html. For a more general critique of ethnographic museums, especially in the German-speaking context, see https://blog.uni-koeln.de/gssc-humboldt (12 May 2018).

Pages 118–22
The Bauhaus as a Catalyst
Mohamed Melehi

1 See Bert Flint, *Forme et symbole dans les arts du Maroc* (Forms and Symbols in Moroccan Art), Vols 1 & 2. Tangier: EMI, 1973.
2 See Mohamed Melehi, 'Notes sur les peintures des mosquées et les zaouias du Souss' [Notes on the Paintings within the Mosques and Zawiyas of Souss], *Maghreb Art*, No. 3, 1969 (published by the School of Fine Arts, Casablanca).
3 The course in Arabic calligraphy was taught by Mohamed Chabâa while that in architectural drawing was led by Mohamed Bensalem.

Pages 128–30
The Andean Textile Paradigm at the Bauhaus
Virginia Gardner Troy

1 Texts dealing with primitivism in pre-First World War Germany include Donald Gordon, 'German Expressionism', in William Rubin (ed.), *'Primitivism' in Twentieth Century Art*. New York: Museum of Modern Art, 1984; Jill Lloyd, *German Expressionism: Primitivism and Modernity*. New Haven: Yale University Press, 1992; Gill Perry, 'Primitivism and the Modern', in Francis Frascina, Gill Perry and Charles Harrison (eds), *Primitivism, Cubism, Abstraction*. New Haven: Yale University Press, 1993; Colin Rhodes, *Primitivism and Modern Art*. London: Thames & Hudson, 1994. For educational theories relevant to Bauhaus pedagogy see J. Abbott Miller, 'Elementary School', in Ellen Lupton and J. Abbott Miller (eds), *The ABC's of Circle, Square, Triangle: The Bauhaus and Design Theory*. New York: Cooper Union, 1991.
2 Immina von Schuler-Schömig, 'The Central Andean Collections at the Museum für Völkerkunde, Berlin, Their Origin and Present Organization', in Anne-Marie Hocquenghem (ed.), *Pre-Columbian Collections in European Museums*. Budapest: Akademiai Kiado, 1987, 169–75. Major donations of Andean art to the museum include the Baessler donation of 11,690 items in 1899 and the Reiss and Stübel donation of 2,000 items in 1879. The museum acquired 2,400 items in 1882 from Dr José Mariano Macedo of Lima, and subsequently the large Centeno collection, from Cuzco, in 1888, and the Bolivar collection in 1904. Wilhelm Gretzer sold 27,254 ancient American pieces to the museum in 1907; Corinna Raddatz, 'Christian Theodor Wilhelm Gretzer and his Pre-Columbian Collection in the Niedersächsisches Landesmuseum of Hannover,' in Hocquenghem, op. cit., 163–65.
3 These factors were discussed in two important pre-First World War German publications: W. Reiss and A. Stübel, *Das Totenfeld von Ancon*, Berlin, 1880–87 (English translation, *The Necropolis at Ancon in Peru*. London and Berlin: Asher & Co., 1906); and Max Schmidt, 'Über Altperuanische Gewebe mit Szenenhaften Darstellungen' [On Ancient Peruvian Textiles Depicting Scenes], in P. Ehrenreich (ed.), *Baessler-Archiv Beitrage Zur Völkerkunde* [Baessler Archive Articles on Ethnography], Vol. 1. Leipzig and Berlin: Teubner Verlag, 1910. Reprint by Johnson Reprint Corp., 1968. During the Weimar Bauhaus period, these factors were discussed in Ernest Fuhrmann, *Reich der Inka* [Inca Empire]. Hagen and Darmstadt: Folkwang Museum, 1922; Wilhelm Hausenstein, *Barbaren und Klassiker: ein Buch von der Bildnerei exotischer Volker* [Barbarians and Classics: A Book on the Imagery of Exotic Peoples]. Munich: Piper Verlag, 1922; Herbert Kühn, *Die Kunst der Primitiven* [The Art of the Primitives]. Munich: Delphin-Verlag, 1923; Eckart von Sydow, *Die Kunst der Naturvolker und der Vorzeit* [The Art of the Primitive People and Prehistoric Times]. Berlin: Propyläen-Kunstgeschichte, 1923. These were books that Albers and other members of the Bauhaus were most likely familiar with.
4 Anni Albers and Sevim Fesci, interview for the Archives of American Art, 5 July 1968, transcript at the Josef and Anni Albers Foundation, Orange, CT, 6.

Pages 132–37
The Appropriation of the Ancient Past in Modern Fibre Art
Elissa Auther

1 Clément Dirié (ed.), *Sheila Hicks. Apprentissages* [Sheila Hicks: Apprenticeships]. Zurich: JRP/Ringier, 2017, 30. On the subject of Andean influence in Hicks's work see also *Sheila Hicks: 50 Years*. New Haven: Yale University Press/Addison Gallery of American Art, 2010.
2 Dirié (ed.), *Apprentissages*, 2017, 31.
3 *Ibid.*, 30.
4 *Hicks: 50 Years*, 2010.
5 Rebecca Klassen, 'Constructions: US Fiber Artists and Pre-Columbian Peruvian Textiles', MA thesis, Bard Graduate Center, 2011, 113.
6 See Paul J. Smith, *Woven Forms*. New York: Museum of Contemporary Craft, 1963, n.p.
7 Mildred Constantine and Jack Lenor Larsen, *Beyond Craft: The Art Fabric*. New York: Van Nostrand, 1973, 267.
8 Jack Lenor Larsen, 'Lenore Tawney: Inspiration to Those Who Want to Develop Their Artistic Potential', *House Beautiful*, March 1962, 177.

Pages 142–44
Watch and Learn: Local Instructions from My Community
Elvira Espejo

1 A spool or reel around which thread is wound for weaving. Eds.
2 A *quipus* is a device used by the ancient Peruvians to record information, consisting of an arrangement of variously coloured and knotted cords attached to a base cord. Eds.

Pages 146–48
The Bauhaus and Indigenous Cultural Production
Ailton Krenak and Bené Fonteles

1 The presentation referred to here was in a section organized by Maureen Bisilliat as part of the 12th Bienal de São Paulo (São Paulo Biennial) in 1973.
2 The exhibitions organized by the MASP include 'Arte karajá' (Karajá Art, 1984), 'Índios Yanomami' (Yanomami Indians, 1985) and 'Arte indígena kaxinawá' (Indigenous Kaxinawá Art, 1987). At the MAM-SP, the 1980 exhibition 'Arte Plumária do Brasil' (Feather Art from Brazil), organized by Norberto Nicola, was expanded for the 17th Bienal de São Paulo in 1983.

3 *Caboclo* refers to a person of mixed indigenous and European descent. *Mestizo* is the Spanish equivalent.

4 The actual manifesto says: 'Brazil had already discovered happiness', but this can only refer to the inhabitants of the territory that was to be designated as Brazil. See Oswald de Andrade, 'Anthropofagite Manifesto', in *24ª Bienal de São Paulo – Núcleo Histórico – Antropofagia e histórias do Canibalismo* [24th São Paulo Biennial – Historical Centre – Anthropology and Stories of Cannibalism] (exhibition catalogue). São Paulo: Fundação Bienal São Paulo, 1998, 532.

5 Lux Vidal, *Grafismo indígena: estudos de antropologia estética* (Indigenous Graphic Design: Studies of Aesthetic Anthropology) (2nd edition). São Paulo: Studio Nobel/FAPESP/Editora da Universidade de São Paulo, 2000.

6 Davi Kopenawa and Bruce Albert, *The Falling Sky: Words of a Yanomami Shaman*. Cambridge, MA: Belknap Press, 2013.

7 An *oca* is an indigenous construction made with wood and fibres with a circular shape, used as a home for one or more families.

8 The seminar 'Indigenous Cultural Production and the Art System: Approximations and Tensions' took place at the Goethe Institut São Paulo on 1–2 December 2017 and brought together indigenous and non-indigenous artists, activists, thinkers and agents.

9 Don Miguel Ruiz, *The Four Agreements: A Practical Guide to Personal Freedom* (A Toltec Wisdom Book). San Rafael, CA: Amber-Allen Publishing, 1997.

Pages 160–61
Moving Away: Introduction
Marion von Osten & Grant Watson

1 For example, in his papers from the conference Sudhir Nadkarni notes that western technology and consumption buttress inequality in India, thus it is important to consider Gandhi's emphasis on investing in 'low technology' items that cover minimum needs. Meeting Papers, UNIDO, ICSID INDIA 79. Design for Development, National Institute of Design Ahmedabad, 1979.

Pages 174–79
Anticipating the Future: Three Lines of Development
Hilde Heynen

1 Umberto Eco, 'Reflections on "The Name of the Rose"', *Encounter*, April 1985, 15–16.

2 Magdalena Droste, 'The Bauhaus Object between Authorship and Anonymity', in Jeffrey Saletnik and Robin Schuldenfrei (eds), *Bauhaus Construct: Fashioning Identity, Discourse and Modernism*. New York: Routledge, 2009, 205–25; Fredric J. Schwartz, 'Utopia for Sale: The Bauhaus and Weimar Germany's Consumer Culture', in Kathleen James-Chakraborty (ed.), *Bauhaus Culture: From Weimar to the Cold War*. Minneapolis: University of Minnesota Press, 2006, 115–38.

3 Donna J. Haraway, 'A Cyborg Manifesto: Science, Technology, and Socialist-Feminism in the Late Twentieth Century,' in *Simians, Cyborgs, and Women – The Reinvention of Nature*. New York: Routledge, 1991, 149–81.

Pages 182–85
Designing Life
Beatriz Colomina and Mark Wigley

1 *Ja! Stimmen des Arbeitsrates für Kunst* [Yes! Voices of the Workers' Council for Art]. Berlin: Arbeitstrat für Kunst, 1919, 32.

2 Walter Gropius, *The New Architecture and the Bauhaus*. Cambridge, MA: MIT Press, 1965, 48.

3 *Ibid.*, 33.

4 Walter Gropius, *Internationale Architektur*. Munich: A. Langen, 1925, 7.

5 Steve Jobs, 'The Future Isn't What it Used to Be', talk at the 1983 International Design Conference in Aspen, cited in Evgeny Morozov, 'Form and Fortune', *The New Republic*, 22 February 2012.

6 Beatriz Colomina and Mark Wigley, *Are We Human? Notes on An Archeology of Design*. Zurich: Lars Müller, 2016, 89.

Pages 188–93
The Red Itinerary
Daniel Talesnik

1 Letter from Hannes Meyer (Berlin) to Heinrich Ludwig (Moscow), 24 August 1930, Hannes Meyer Papers, Deutsches Architekturmuseum-Archiv, Frankfurt am Main.

2 A brigade, if taken in its non-military definition, is 'a company or crew of people', or simply, 'a disciplined band of workers'. As an organizational system, the word 'brigade' had currency in the Soviet Union and was used to identify labour units. This terminology was taken up by some of the foreign architects mentioned here, particularly by Ernst May. Today Meyer and his group of seven students are sometimes referred to as the 'Red Bauhaus Brigade', and although Meyer did describe this group at the time as a 'brigade' or *Rotfront* (Red Front), this precise label was applied retroactively by some members of the group, particularly Püschel.

3 Kurt Liebknecht, *Mein bewegtes Leben* [My Eventful Life]. Berlin: Verlag für Bauwesen, 1986, 49.

4 The original drawings of both the 1931 entry to the second competition for the Palace of the Soviets by Tolziner, Urban, Weiner (and Meyer), and of the 1935 Kolkhoz club prototype by Urban and Konstantinova-Urban are held in the archive of the Schusev State Museum of Architecture, Moscow.

5 The welcoming attitude of countries like Mexico, Chile and the Dominican Republic towards Spanish political refugees after the Spanish Civil War, or the foreign policy of Turkey before the start of the Second World War, are examples of countries that welcomed intellectuals, scientists, university professors, technicians and others as part of an effort to develop education, culture and science to higher levels. However, this 'welcoming attitude' was nuanced. At first foreigners were accepted, but in countries such as Mexico and Chile, the changes of government and political shifts at large in the 1940s complicated the lives of Meyer and Weiner, and they returned to Europe.

6 See Daniel Talesnik, 'The Itinerant Red Bauhaus, or The Third Emigration', PhD dissertation, Columbia University, New York, 2016.

Page 202
Modern Craft and Art (1932): An Introduction
Zoe Zhang

1 Tang Wei, 'Zhang Guangyu and the Modern Craft and Art', *Decoration*, Vol. 205, May 2010, 67.

2 Guangyu Zhang, 近代工艺美术 [Modern Craft and Art]. Shanghai: China Art Publisher, 1932, 5. The original quotation reads: '艺术，我们认为永远追随人间也永远隔离现实！或者说：艺术不为宇宙间一切束缚所束缚…人类企求生存不单单凭借物质的改进，还得要有艺术的修养的情心，才得有完美的人生的观念.'

Pages 206–11
Useful Tradition? Walter Gropius meets China (or I. M. Pei)
Eduard Kögel

1 For a full documentation see John C. Harkness (ed.), *The Walter Gropius Archive. Volume 4: 1945–1969. The Work of The Architects Collaborative*. New York/London: Garland Publishing Inc., 1991.
2 It is striking that in late 1946 and early 1947, several experts on Chinese garden art gave lectures in the Department of Landscape Architecture at Harvard. In December 1946 George N. Kates gave three lectures on the 'Palaces and Gardens of Peking' and Grace M. Boynton gave a lecture about 'Gardens in Peking'. In April 1947 the Swedish art historian Osvald Sirén also spoke about Chinese gardens. For some time after, there were no further lectures on Chinese topics in that department at Harvard.
3 Walter Gropius, 'Université de Hua-Tung' [University of Hua-Tung], *L'Architecture d'aujourd'hui*, February 1950, 28.
4 *Ibid*.
5 Ulf Meyer, 'I. M. Pei, architect (Interview)', in Kai Vöckler and Dirk Luckow (eds), *Peking, Shanghai, Shenzhen*. Frankfurt/New York: Campus Verlag, 2000, 127.
6 *Ibid*., 487.
7 Winston Weisman, 'Group practice', *The Architectural Review*, September 1953, 150.
8 Letter from Gropius to Ellen and Nazwar Jawdat, 9 September 1954, cited in Regina Göckede, *Spätkoloniale Moderne: Le Corbusier, Ernst May, Frank Lloyd Wright, The Architects Collaborative und die Globalisierung der Architekturmoderne* [Late-Colonial Modern: Le Corbusier, Ernst May, Frank Lloyd Wright, The Architects Collaborative and the Globalization of Modern Architecture]. Basel: Birkhäuser, 2016, 392.

Pages 212–22
Designing Life in India
Suchitra Balasubrahmanyan

1 See the First Five-Year Plan, Chapter 1, http://planningcommission.nic.in/plans/planrel/fiveyr/1st/1planch1.html (4 April 2018).
2 Quoted in Ravi Kalia, *Chandigarh: The Making of an Indian City* (1987). New Delhi: Oxford University Press, 1999, 21.
3 Jawaharlal Nehru, *An Autobiography*. New Delhi: Oxford University Press, 1985, 432.
4 B. G. Verghese, *Project India – Human Resource Development and Capacity Building: The Ford Foundation in India 1952–2002*. New Delhi: Centre for Policy Research, 2006, 12–13.
5 Monroe Wheeler (ed.), *Textiles and Ornaments of India: A Selection of Designs*. New York: Museum of Modern Art, 1956, 9.
6 Charles and Ray Eames, *The India Report*. Ahmedabad: National Institute of Design, 1997, 10.
7 Mulk Raj Anand, 'Planning and Dreaming', *Marg*, Vol. 1, No. 1, October 1946, 3–6, here 5.
8 Advertisement in *The Indian Builder*, Vol. 5, No. 1, January 1957, 65.
9 *Design Today in America and Europe* (exhibition catalogue). New York: Museum of Modern Art, 1958, 4.
10 'Ahmedabad Declaration on Industrial Design for Development'. Ahmedabad: National Institute of Design, 1979, 1.

Pages 224–27
Design for Need: Sudhakar Nadkarni's Milk Kiosk
Regina Bittner

1 See dossier on the work of Professor Sudhakar Nakarni: http://www.dsource.in/sites/default/files/resource/history-product-design-india/design-mentors/prof-s.nadkarni/file/Prof_Sudhakar_Nadkarni.pdf (4 April 2018).
2 Paul Betts, *The Authority of Everyday Objects: A Cultural History of West German Industrial Design*. Berkeley: University of California Press, 2004, 153.
3 Tomás Maldonado, 'Ist das Bauhaus noch aktuell?' [Is the Bauhaus Still Up-to-Date?], *ulm: Zeitschrift der Hochschule für Gestaltung*, 8/9, 1963, 5–13.
4 Betts, *The Authority of Everyday Objects*, 2004, 170.
5 Nadkarni Sudhakar, 'Gestaltung eines Milchkiosk' [The Design of a Milk Kiosk], diploma thesis, 1966, HfG Archiv Ulm K_68_1_1.
6 Research on the milk kiosk was part of the Bauhaus Lab 2017, *Between Chairs: Design Pedagogies in Transcultural Dialogue*. Leipzig: Spector Books, 2018.

Pages 228–32
Arieh Sharon's Nigerian Campus Project: Ife University (1960–85)
Zvi Efrat

1 Arieh Sharon, *Kibbutz + Bauhaus*, p. 127.
2 *Ibid*.
3 *Ibid*., p. 128

Pages 256–57
Kurt Schwerdtfeger's Reflektorische Lichtspiele (Reflecting Light Plays, 1922)
Melissa Venator

1 Ute Ackermann, 'Bauhaus Parties – Histrionics between Eccentric Dancing and Animal Drama', in Jeannine Fiedler and Peter Feierabend (eds), *Bauhaus*. Cologne: Könemann, 2000, 126.
2 Felix Klee, '"Actually They're All Crazy at the Bauhaus": An Anthology of Quotations', in Fiedler and Feierabend (eds), *Bauhaus*, 2000, 172.
3 Stefan Schwerdtfeger, 'Talking Backgrounds', interview by Michael Stoeber, 2009, in *Kurt Schwerdtfeger (Bauhaus Weimar): Reflektorische Farblichtspiele (1922/1968)* [Kurt Schwerdtfeger (Bauhaus Weimar): Reflecting Colour-Light-Play (1922/1968)], Red Avocado Film, 2010.
4 Kurt Schwerdtfeger, 'Reflektorisches Lichtspiel', *Der Sturm*, 15 March 1924, 46.
5 Kurt Schwerdtfeger, *Bildende Kunst und Schule* [Fine Art and School], 7th edition, Pädagogische Bücherei 24. Hannover: Hermann Schroedel Verlag KG, 1970, 195.
6 For more technical information about the apparatus, see Schwerdtfeger, *Bildende Kunst und Schule*, 1970, 195–96; Rudolf Jüdes, *Reflektorisches Farblichtspiele von Kurt Schwerdtfeger* [Kurt Schwerdtfeger's Reflecting Colour-Light-Plays], documentary, 1968, in *Kurt Schwerdtfeger (Bauhaus Weimar)*, 2010.
7 See Christian Kiening and Heinrich Adolf, *Der absolute Film: Dokumente der Medienavantgarde (1912–1936)* [Absolute Film: Documents of the Media Avant-Garde (1912–1936)]. Zurich: Chronos, 2012.
8 In Germany, Agfacolor colour film appeared in 1936.
9 Schwerdtfeger, *Bildende Kunst und Schule*, 1970, 196–99.

10 *Staatliches Bauhaus Weimar 1919–1923* [Weimar State Bauhaus 1919–1923]. Weimar/Munich: Bauhausverlag, 1923, 155; László Moholy-Nagy, *Malerei, Fotografie, Film* [Painting, Photography, Film], Bauhausbücher 8. Munich: Bauhaus, 1925, 77.
11 S. Schwerdtfeger, 'Talking Backgrounds', 2009.

Pages 260–62
bauhaus past forward
Christian Hiller

1 The following sources were consulted in the writing of this essay: *Bauhaus*, a film by Muriel Cooper, *c.* 1970, recreated by David Small; 'Computers and Design', *Design Quarterly*, No. 142, 1989; György Kepes, *The MIT Years 1945–77.* Cambridge, MA/London: MIT Press, 1978; David Reinfurt and Robert Wiesenberger, *Muriel Cooper.* Cambridge, MA/London: MIT Press, 2017; Robert Wiesenberger, 'Latter-day Bauhaus? Muriel Cooper and the Digital Imaginary', in Nanni Baltzer and Martino Stierli (eds), *Before Publication: Montage in Art, Architecture and Book Design*. Zurich: Park Books, 2016; Hans Maria Wingler, *Bauhaus: Weimar, Dessau, Berlin, Chicago*. Cambridge, MA/London: MIT Press, 1969 (design by Muriel Cooper).

Pages 268–72
From Giving to Unforgiving Light: Remarks on the Kaleidoscopic and the Stroboscopic
Tom Holert

1 See Kurt Schwerdtfeger to Hans Haffenrichter, 11 January 1964, cited in Sonja Breuker and Alexandra Wolf, 'Ludwig Hirschfeld-Mack, Spiel und Kampf mit dem reflektorischen Licht', in '"Pupillenrausch" und "optischer Lärm". Der absolute Film – eine Berliner Matinee, 1925'; exhibition of students of the Faculty of Art History of the Technische Universität Berlin, 28–31 May 2011, headed by Lars Blunck, https://www.kunstwissenschaft.tu-berlin.de/fileadmin/i2/Forschung/Hirschfeld-Mack.pdf (24 April 2018).
2 See Kurt Schwerdtfeger, *Bildende Kunst und Schule* [Fine Art and School], 6th edition. Hannover: Hermann Schroedel Verlag KG, 1965, 195.
3 [Walter Gropius], 'Manifest und Programm des Staatlichen Bauhauses Weimar in der gedruckten Programmschrift vom April 1919', in Volker Wahl (ed.), *Das staatliche Bauhaus in Weimar. Dokumente zur Geschichte des Instituts 1919–1926* [The State Bauhaus in Weimar: Documents on the History of the Institute 1919–1926]. Cologne and Weimar: Böhlau, 2009, 98.
4 Ludwig Hirschfeld-Mack, *Farbenlicht-Spiele – Wesen, Ziele, Kritiken* [Colour-Light-Plays – Nature, Aims, Reviews]. Weimar: self-published, 1925, 4; cf. Peter Stasny, 'Die Farbenlichtspiele' [The Colour-Light-Plays], in Andreas Hapkemeyer and Peter Stasny (eds), *Ludwig Hirschfeld-Mack. Bauhäusler und Visionär* [Ludwig Hirschfeld-Mack: Bauhäusler and Visionary] (exhibition catalogue). Ostfildern: Hatje Cantz, 2000, 94–112.
5 Ibid., 2; cf. Anne Hoormann, *Lichtspiele. Zur Medienreflexion der Avantgarde in der Weimarer Republik* [Light Plays: On the Avant-garde's Reflection on Media in the Weimar Republic]. Munich: Fink, 2003, 92ff.
6 Cf. Wolfgang Schivelbusch, *Licht, Schein und Wahn. Auftritte der elektrischen Beleuchtung im 20. Jahrhundert* [Light, Shine and Delusion: Scenes of Electric Illumination in the Twentieth Century]. Berlin: Ernst & Sohn, 1992, 20ff., 39ff.
7 Jonas Mekas, 'On Cinéma vérité, Ricky Leacock, and Warhol' (*Village Voice*, 13 August 1964), in Mekas, *Movie Journal: The Rise of the New American Cinema, 1959–1971*, 2nd edition, ed. Gregory Smulewicz-Zucker. New York: Columbia University Press, 2016, 161.
8 Mekas, 'On Laterna Magica, Superimpositions, and Movies under Drugs' (*Village Voice*, 27 August 1964) in Mekas, *Movie Journal*, 2016, 65.
9 *Ibid.*
10 Cf. Branden W. Joseph, *Beyond the Dream Syndicate: Tony Conrad and the Arts after Cage*. New York: Zone, 2008, 305ff.
11 Jonas Mekas, 'On the Expanding Eye' (*Village Voice*, 6 February 1964), in Mekas, *Movie Journal*, 2016, 126.
12 Mekas, 'Movie Journal: More on Strobe Light and Intermedia' (*Village Voice*, 16 June 1966), in Mekas, *Movie Journal*, 2016, 253.
13 Bernd Cailloux, *Das Geschäftsjahr 1968/69* [The Business Year 1968/69]. Frankfurt am Main: Suhrkamp, 2005, 60.

Pages 278–81
Polytechnics and Punks: The 1970s After-life of the Bauhaus
Gavin Butt

1 Patrick Heron, 'Murder of the Art Schools', *Guardian*, 12 October 1971, 8.
2 Patrick Nuttgens, 'No Murder in the Art Schools', *Guardian*, 2 November 1971, 8.
3 Ben C. Hirst, 'Desegregating Art', *Guardian*, 29 January 1971, 15.

Contributors

Kader Attia is an artist who grew up between Algeria and the suburbs of Paris. In his work he takes a poetic and symbolic approach to exploring the wide-ranging repercussions of western modern cultural hegemony and colonialism on non-western cultures, investigating identity politics from tradition to modernity in light of our globalized world. In 2016, Attia founded La Colonie, a space for discussion and ideas in Paris that focuses on decolonization not just of peoples, but also of knowledge, attitudes and practices. He is a commissioned artist for bauhaus imaginista's 'Learning From' section, whose project investigates the complex (mis-) interpretations and translations of premodern handicrafts.

Elissa Auther is the Windgate Research and Collections Curator at the Museum of Arts and Design (MAD) and Visiting Associate Professor at the Bard Graduate Center, New York. Her research focuses on hierarchies and boundaries in the art world, the women's art movement of the 1970s, feminist art and theory in general and the history of fibre in art. Her book *String, Felt, Thread: The Hierarchy of Art and Craft in American Art* was published by the University of Minnesota Press in 2009. Auther is also active as a curator; her most recent exhibition at the Museum of Arts and Design was 'Surface/Depth: The Decorative After Miriam Schapiro' (2018). Auther is a curatorial researcher for bauhaus imaginista's 'Learning From' section.

Suchitra Balasubrahmanyan is Professor at the School of Design, Ambedkar University, Delhi in India. Her research interests centre on nineteenth- and twentieth-century craft and design from the Indian subcontinent from historical and sociological perspectives, as well as the evolution of modern design education in India against the backdrop of decolonization and Cold War diplomacy. She is author or co-author of numerous publications including *The Shaping of Modern Gujarat: Plurality, Hindutva and Beyond* (2005) and *Ahmedabad: From Royal City to Megacity* (2011). Her most recent publication *Craft and Design in the Hindu Way of Life* is forthcoming from Bloomsbury Academic. She is a research advisor for bauhaus imaginista's 'Moving Away' section.

Regina Bittner is an art historian, cultural theorist and curator who has been Deputy Director of the Bauhaus Dessau Foundation since 2009. Her research focuses on transcultural modernism in architecture and design and heritage studies. She has curated numerous exhibitions on the architectural, design and cultural history of modernism and the Bauhaus. Recent publications include: *Craft becomes Modern: The Bauhaus in the Making* (with Renée Padt, 2017); *In Reserve: The Household! Historic Models and Contemporary Positions from the Bauhaus* (with Elke Krasny, 2016); and *The Bauhaus in Calcutta: An Encounter of the Cosmopolitan Avant-Garde* (with Kathrin Rhomberg, 2013). Bittner is curatorial advisor for the bauhaus imaginista project 2018–19.

Gavin Butt is Attenborough Chair in Drama, Theatre and Performance at the University of Sussex. He is author of *Between You and Me: Queer Disclosures in the New York Art World 1948–1963, Visual Cultures as Seriousness* (with Irit Rogoff, 2005), and co-editor of *Post-Punk Then and Now* (2016). Between 2009 and 2014 he was co-director of 'Performance Matters', a creative research project exploring the cultural value of performance, during which he made his first feature-length documentary film with Ben Walters, *This Is Not a Dream*. He is currently completing a book on post-punk bands and the UK art school. Butt is a research fellow for bauhaus imaginista's 'Still Undead' section.

Helena Čapková is a Czech-born, Tokyo-based curator, researcher and art history professor at Waseda University, Tokyo. She studied transnational visual culture and Japanese studies in Prague and London. Her writings on the Bauhaus include 'Transnational Networkers – Iwao and Michiko Yamawaki and the Formation of Japanese Modernist Design' (2014) and 'Bauhaus and tea ceremony: a study of mutual impact in design education between Germany and Japan in the interwar period' (2017). For the past two years she has curated events together with the Czech Centre in Tokyo, ranging from exhibitions to talks and screenings. Čapková is a curatorial researcher for bauhaus imaginista's 'Corresponding With' section.

Beatriz Colomina is Professor of Architecture and Director of the Media and Modernity programme at Princeton University. She has written extensively on questions of architecture, art, sexuality and media. Her books include *The Century of the Bed* (2014), *Manifesto Architecture: The Ghost of Mies* (2014), *Clip, Stamp, Fold: The Radical Architecture of Little Magazines 196X–197X* (2010), *Domesticity at War* (2007), *Privacy and Publicity: Modern Architecture as Mass Media* (1994) and *Sexuality and Space* (1992). She has curated the exhibitions 'Clip/Stamp/Fold' (2006), 'Playboy Architecture' (2012) and 'Radical Pedagogies' (2014). In 2016, she co-curated the third Istanbul Design Biennial with Mark Wigley and published *Are We Human? Notes on an Archeology of Design*.

Anshuman Dasgupta is an art historian and curator teaching at Visva-Bharati University, Santiniketan since 1997. He holds a PhD in Curatorial/Knowledge from the Department of Visual Cultures, Goldsmiths College, University of London. He was elected chief curator for Kala Bhavan in its 100 years (a school founded by Rabindranath Tagore in the year 1919, the same year as the Bauhaus). Dasgupta's texts appear in edited volumes including *The Curatorial: A Philosophy of Curating* (2013) and *Curating Subjects* (2007) and journals such as *Marg* and *Art-India*. He was co-editor (with Monica Szewczyk and Grant Watson) of *Santhal Family: Positions around an Indian Sculpture* (2009). Dasgupta is a curatorial researcher for bauhaus imaginista's 'Corresponding With' section.

Magdalena Droste is a professor of art history and a former chair of art history at Brandenburg University of Technology Cottbus Senftenberg, a post she held from 1997 to 2017. She studied art history and German studies at the Rheinisch-Westfälische Technische Hochschule Aachen (RWTH Aachen) and the Philipps University of Marburg, where she completed her PhD. From 1980 to 1997, she was curator at the Bauhaus Archive, Berlin. Droste has authored and edited numerous publications on the subject of the Bauhaus and the history of nineteenth- and twentieth-century design, among them *bauhaus 1919–1933* (1990), considered a definitive volume in the field, and the exhibition catalogue *Das Bauhaus Webt. Die Textilwerkstatt am Bauhaus* (Bauhaus Weaves: The Bauhaus Weaving Workshop, with Jenny Anger and Michael Siebenbrot, 1998).

Zvi Efrat is an architect and architectural historian and a partner in Efrat-Kowalsky Architects (EKA). Previously he was head of the Department of Architecture at the Bezalel Academy of Arts and Design, Jerusalem from 2002 until 2010. His book, *The Israeli Project: Building and Architecture 1948–1973*, was published in Hebrew in 2004. As a commissioned architect for bauhaus imaginista's 'Moving Away' exhibition, Efrat produced a short film that critically illuminates Israeli architect and former Bauhaus student Arieh Sharon's design for Ife University campus in Nigeria, which was built in 1962 as part of an Israeli development programme in West Africa.

Fabienne Eggelhöfer has been chief curator and head of collections, exhibitions and research at the Zentrum Paul Klee, Bern, since 2017. Previously she was curator for modern and contemporary art at Zentrum Paul Klee since 2007. In 2012 Eggelhöfer completed a research project on Paul Klee's teaching at the Bauhaus that culminated in an online database of Klee's teaching notes and an exhibition. In addition, she also analysed the meaning of nature in Klee's teaching in a dissertation leading to a PhD. In several exhibitions, she focused her interest on the continuities and discontinuities in the development of art since the beginning of the twentieth century.

Elvira Espejo is Director of the Museum of Ethnography and Folklore in La Paz, Bolivia. She is also a weaver, storyteller, poet, artist and curator. Espejo is co-author (with Denise Y. Arnold) of *The Andean Science of Weaving Structures and Techniques for Warp-Faced Weaves*, a groundbreaking volume that used as its point of departure the technical terms employed by Andean weavers in their native Aymara and Quechua languages. The result of extensive field and archival research, the volume was published by Thames & Hudson in 2015.

Thomas Flierl studied philosophy and aesthetics and is active as a cultural researcher, architectural historian and writer. He is a fellow of the Institute for History and Theory of Architecture and Planning at Bauhaus University in Weimar. Flierl has also been working in the political field; from 2001 to 2006, he was the senator for science, research, and culture in Berlin. His most recent publication *Der Architekt, die Macht und die Baukunst* (The Architect, Power and the Art of Building) is a profile of influential East German architect Hermann Henselmann's work in Berlin in the period 1949–95. Flierl is a research advisor for bauhaus imaginista's 'Moving Away' section.

Bené Fonteles is a Brazilian artist, journalist, publisher, poet and composer whose diversified production often goes beyond traditional boundaries of art. Fonteles, one of the founders of the Movimento Artistas pela Natureza (Movement of Artists for Nature), considers himself an 'artivist', creating installations, sculptures and manifestos that express his interest in exploring the relationship between notions of being, popular knowledge and environmental concerns. His work has been shown at several exhibitions, including five editions of the São Paulo Biennial, most recently in 2016.

Luca Frei is an artist whose work, which includes a wide range of media such as drawing, collage, painting, installation, performance, video and photography, often develops in response to a specific context in the form of architectural interventions, narrative environments or exhibition structures that invite public participation and dialogue. As a commissioned artist for bauhaus imaginista's 'Corresponding With' section, Frei created an artist's impression of the Bauhaus-related exhibition produced by Renshichirō Kawakita in collaboration with Takehiko Mizutani at the Tokyo Academy of Arts in 1931. This new work includes a sculptural installation with photographic documentation and a sound element.

Hilde Heynen is Professor of Architectural Theory at the Department of Architecture at the University of Leuven. Her research focuses on issues of modernity, modernism and gender in architecture. She is the author of *Architecture and Modernity: A Critique* (1999), and the co-editor of *Back from Utopia: The Challenge of the Modern Movement* (with Hubert-Jan Henket, 2002), *Negotiating Domesticity: Spatial Productions of Gender in Modern Architecture* (with Gülsüm Baydar, 2005) and *The SAGE Handbook of Architectural Theory* (with Greig Crysler and Stephen Cairns, 2012). She is currently writing a biography of Sibyl Moholy-Nagy (forthcoming from Bloomsbury).

Christian Hiller is a media scientist, curator and editor at *ARCH+ Zeitschrift für Architektur und Stadtdiskurs* (ARCH+ Journal for Architecture and Urban Discourse). As guest curator for the Bauhaus Dessau Foundation he realized exhibitions including 'bauhaus.film' (SESC, São Paulo, 2013; Museo Nacional de Bellas Artes, Santiago de Chile, 2014) and 'Human-Space-Machine: Stage Experiments at the Bauhaus' (Bauhaus Dessau, 2013; Henie Onstad Kunstsenter, Oslo, 2014; National Museum of Modern and Contemporary Art, Seoul, 2014). From 2014 to 2016 he was head of research for the exhibition project 'Wohnungsfrage' at Haus der Kulturen der Welt, Berlin and edited the publication series under the same title. Hiller is a curatorial researcher for bauhaus imaginista's 'Still Undead' section.

Tom Holert is a Berlin-based independent scholar. In 2015 Holert co-founded the Harun Farocki Institut in Berlin (harun-farocki-institut.org). In 2018 he co-curated 'Neolithic Childhood: Art in a False Present, *c.* 1930' at Haus der Kulturen der Welt, Berlin (the accompanying book, co-edited with Anselm Franke was published in summer 2018). Holert's current research focuses on interwar avant-garde art and theory as well as on post-war configurations of art, architecture and knowledge production. An upcoming book attends to the interlacing of contemporary art and politics of knowledge.

Yoshimasa Kaneko is Professor of Art Pedagogy at Kochi University, Japan. His research focuses on art education at the Bauhaus and the Itten-Schule (Itten School), based on the original documents of Johannes Itten with a particular emphasis on art education through the activities of his German students and some Japanese people (students, teachers, visitors) related to the Itten School. His published texts include: 'Johannes Itten's Philosophy of Human-Centered Art Education – Content Analysis of *Tagebuch von Johannes Itten*, based on a Conversation with Eva Plaut' (in Japanese), *Bijutsukyoikugaku*, No. 28 (2007), and 'Johannes Itten and Zen', in Christoph Wagner (ed.), *Esoterik am Bauhaus. Eine Revision der Moderne?* (Esotericism at the Bauhaus: A Revision of the Modern?, 2009).

Eduard Kögel studied architecture, urban and landscape planning. He has contributed to journals such as *Archis*, *archithese* and *Bauwelt*, served as guest editor on special editions of *Arch+*, *Bauwelt* and the *Journal of World Architecture*, and published books on Chinese cities and architecture. Since 2006 he has maintained the internet platform chinese-architects.com. Kögel currently works as an independent advisor and researcher focusing on histories of exchange between Europe and Asia in the fields of architecture and urban development. He is a curatorial researcher for bauhaus imaginista's 'Moving Away' section.

Ailton Krenak is an indigenous journalist, writer, graphic producer and activist. He founded and directs the Festival of Dances and Indigenous Cultures at the Indigenous Culture Centre, Serra do Cipó, Brazil. He received the prestigious Onassis Award – Man and Society, from the Alexander S. Onassis Foundation, Greece, 1990; the National Human Rights Award, Brazil, 2005; and the Commendation of the Order of Cultural Merit of Brazil, 2008. He was presenter of the series *Índios no Brazil*, TV Educativa in 1998 and the series *Tarú Andé*, Futura in 2007. In 2015, Krenak published the book *Encontros com Ailton Krenak*. In 2016, he received an honorary professorship from the Federal University of Juiz de Fora-UFJF, Brazil.

Susanne Leeb is Professor for Contemporary Art at Leuphana Universität Lüneburg with a focus on post- and decolonial questions. She is part of the advisory board of the journal *Texte zur Kunst* and has co-conceptualized the issues 'Globalism' (2013), 'They are us' (2017) and 'Idiom' (2017). Leeb also co-edits the book-series Polypen at b_books, Berlin. Recent publications include *The Art of the Others: 'World Art' and the Anthropological Configuration of Modernity* (2015); 'Asynchronic Objects', *Texte zur Kunst*, No. 91 (2013); 'Local Time, Or the Presence of an Ancient Past', *Texte zur Kunst*, No. 105 (2017); and 'Idioms', *Texte zur Kunst*, No. 108 (2017).

Mohamed Melehi is an artist who was born in Asilah in 1936 and was one of the first Moroccan students to graduate from the National Institute of Fine Arts of Tétouan in 1956. He continued his studies abroad, and after returning to Morocco in 1962 became head of the Painting and Photography departments at the School of Fine Art in Casablanca. Under his leadership, these became veritable laboratories in which artistic experimentation went hand in hand with the development of a new body of knowledge on art in relation to associated disciplines (sociology, anthropology, philosophy); the School thus formed a new thought-community based on the need to create a public space for artistic practices that broke with established academic institutions.

Partha Mitter is Emeritus Professor in Art History, University of Sussex, Member of Wolfson College, Oxford and Honorary Fellow, Victoria and Albert Museum, London. As writer and historian of art and culture, he specializes in the reception of Indian art in the West, as well as in modernity, art and identity in India, and more recently in global modernism. His many publications include: *The Triumph of Modernism: India's Artists and the Avant-Garde – 1922–1947* (2007) and *Art and Nationalism in Colonial India, 1850–1922: Occidental Orientations* (1994). Mitter's groundbreaking book *Much Maligned Monsters: History of European Reactions to Indian Art* (1977; new edition, 2013) was one of the first comprehensive accounts of the western reception of Indian art. He is a curatorial advisor for bauhaus imaginista's 'Corresponding With' section.

Wendelien van Oldenborgh is an artist who utilizes film, and in particular the format of a public film shoot, as a form of social production. Among concerns such as the transmission of history, slippages in language and hybrid identities, van Oldenborgh regularly examines aspects of Dutch colonial history and its reverberations and consequences in contemporary Dutch society. Van Oldenborgh's work has been exhibited widely; her project *Cinema Olanda* was recently shown in the Dutch Pavilion in the 57th Venice Biennale (2017). She is a commissioned artist for bauhaus imaginista's 'Moving Away' section, where she presents a work based on her research examining the life and work of Bauhaus architect Lotte Stam-Beese and her legacy in the modern-day Netherlands.

Marion von Osten is a curator, researcher and writer, and artistic director, curator and researcher of bauhaus imaginista (2018–19) since 2014. Previous research and exhibition projects include 'Viet Nam Discourse', Württembergischer Kunstverein, Stuttgart, and Tensta Konsthall, Stockholm (2016–18); 'In the Desert of Modernity – Colonial Planning and After', Les Abattoirs de Casablanca (2009) and Haus der Kulturen der Welt, Berlin (2008); and 'Projekt Migration' (with Kathrin Rhomberg), Kölnischer Kunstverein (2003–06). Von Osten's publications include: (as co-editor) *Transcultural Modernisms* (2013), *Das Erziehungsbild. Zur visuellen Kultur des Pädagogischen* (2010) and *Colonial Modern: Aesthetics of the Past, Rebellions for the Future* (2010).

The Otolith Group, founded in 2002 by London-based artists Anjalika Sagar and Kodwo Eshun, draws from a wide range of resources and materials, exploring the moving image, the archive, the sonic and the aural in the gallery context. Its work is research-based and focuses in particular on the essay film as a form. The Otolith Group has presented its artwork, research, installations and publications nationally and internationally. In 2010, The Otolith Group was nominated for the Turner Prize. As commissioned artists for bauhaus imaginista's 'Corresponding With' section, The Otolith Group presents a new film, shot on the university campus at Santiniketan, India, which explores founder Rabindranath Tagore's utopian community and pedagogical experiment there.

Adrian Rifkin is Visiting Professor at Central Saint Martins, University of the Arts, London. His collected essays, *Communards and Other Cultural Histories*, edited by Steve Edwards, were published by Haymarket Press in 2017. Rifkin has worked with various institutions in workshops and performances including Haus der Kunst, Munich; Van Abbemuseum, Eindhoven; CASCO, Utrecht; Dutch Art Institute, Amsterdam; LUX, London and others since leaving full-time work.

Daniel Talesnik is a trained architect specializing in modern and contemporary architecture and urbanism, with a particular focus on architectural pedagogy and relationships between architecture and political ideologies. He was awarded a PhD by Columbia University in 2016 with the dissertation 'The Itinerant Red Bauhaus, or the Third Emigration', which describes a group of Bauhaus students that followed Hannes Meyer to the Soviet Union in 1930. Since September 2017 he has taught at the Technical University of Munich, where he is also a researcher at its Architekturmuseum, located in the Pinakothek der Moderne, Munich. Talesnik is a curatorial researcher for bauhaus imaginista's 'Moving Away' section.

Paulo Tavares is a Brazilian architect, artist and urbanist whose projects, emerging from research-based practices and active field work, address the spatial and aesthetic politics of territorial conflicts in urban space and diverse ecologies. His project on colonial violence and the politics of climate change and decolonial resistance in Amazonia was undertaken in the PhD Programme of the Centre for Research Architecture, Goldsmiths, University of London. Parallel to his activities as a researcher/architect, Tavares has been involved with many autonomous media practices since the late 1990s. He was recently named co-curator (with Yesomi Umolu and Sepake Angiama) of the 2019 Chicago Architecture Biennial.

Virginia Gardner Troy is an art historian who examines twentieth-century textiles in terms of their visual, technical and contextual significance. She is Associate Professor of Art History at Berry College in Georgia, USA. Troy is interested in twentieth-century designers who collected and admired non-western and ancient textiles. She has authored two books, *The Modernist Textile: Europe and America 1890–1940* (2006) and *Anni Albers and Ancient American Textiles: From Bauhaus to Black Mountain* (2002), as well as articles on Appalachian weaving, weaving during the Cold War, Bauhaus textiles, Marie Cuttoli and pictorial tapestry, and the textile work of Futurist artist Fortunato Depero.

Hiromitsu Umemiya is Professor at the Graduate School of Human Development and Environment, Kobe University. From 2006 to 2008 he was on the Editorial Board of the *Journal of Architecture and Planning*, Architectural Institute of Japan. Umemiya's research focuses on the Bauhaus's influence on Japanese design. Recent publications include the articles 'Renshichirō Kawakita: Reciprocating Motion between Real Life and Utopia' in *Modernist Reconsidered Japan* (2017) and 'Sadanosuke Nakada and Modernist Architects: From the Context of Acceptance of Bauhaus in Japan' in *Selected Literary Works of Art Critic Sadanosuke Nakada* (2016). Umemiya is a curatorial advisor for bauhaus imaginista's 'Corresponding With' section.

Melissa Venator is the Stefan Engelhorn Curatorial Fellow in the Busch-Reisinger Museum at Harvard Art Museums, Cambridge, Massachusetts, home of the largest collection of Bauhaus art outside of Germany. Her research focuses on the art of interwar Germany with a special interest in avant-garde engagement with technology, industry and science. Current projects examine artistic experiments with electric light in the 1920s, heavy industry in the art of critical realist Carl Grossberg, and colour science at the Weimar Bauhaus. Venator earned her PhD from Rice University in 2017 with a thesis on the light-based work of Raoul Hausmann, Nikolaus Braun, Ludwig Hirschfeld-Mack und László Moholy-Nagy.

Grant Watson is a curator based in London, and is artistic director and curator of bauhaus imaginista (2018–19). Recent projects include 'How We Behave', long-term research exploring questions of life practice and politics through filmed interviews with If I Can't Dance Amsterdam (2014–present). Previously Watson was Senior Curator at the Institute of International Visual Arts, London (2010–14), and Curator at the Museum of Contemporary Art (M HKA), Antwerp (2006–10). Other projects include 'Keywords', Tate Liverpool (2014); 'Practice International' with Iniva, Iaspis and CASCO (2013); 'Tagore, Pedagogy and Contemporary Visual Cultures', Iniva, Goldsmiths College (2013); 'Textiles: Open Letter', Abteiberg Museum, Generali Foundation (2013); 'Social Fabric', Iniva (2013) and *Nasreen Mohamedi: Notes*, OCA (2012).

Mark Wigley is Professor of Architecture at Columbia University, New York who explores the intersection of architecture, art, philosophy, culture and technology. His books include: *Derrida's Haunt: The Architecture of Deconstruction* (1993); *White Walls, Designer Dresses: The Fashioning of Modern Architecture* (1995); *Constant's New Babylon: The Hyper-Architecture of Desire* (1998); and *Buckminster Fuller Inc.: Architecture in the Age of Radio* (2014). Wigley is co-author of *Are We Human? Notes on an Archeology of Design* (2016) with Beatriz Colomina in association with their curation of the 3rd Istanbul Design Biennial. His latest book is *Cutting Matta-Clark: The Anarchitecture Investigation* (2018).

Zoe Zhang is the Assistant Director of China Design Museum (CDM) at the China Academy of Art (CAA), Hangzhou. She has also been a guest lecturer on art and design history at CAA. Her own research focuses on the dissemination and acceptance of Bauhaus ideas in China. She has edited the book *Bauhaus: Design as Enlightenment* (2014) and several papers on Bauhaus. Zhang was curator of the Chinese installation of the bauhaus imaginista exhibition 'Moving Away' at CDM (2018). She also recently curated the exhibition 'World Life: the Collection of Western Modern Design' at CDM (2018).

bauhaus imaginista: The Project

The Bauhaus was founded in 1919 as a manifestation of the ambition shared by artists, designers, architects and intellectuals throughout Europe, Asia, Latin America and the United States to reinvent society. The radical premise of the Bauhaus was to understand design as a social project, and to undertake a reform of art and design education as a step towards this new society. Through exhibitions, publications, symposia, workshops and long-term research, bauhaus imaginista tracks the international reception of the Bauhaus and how this was transformed through contact with other cultures worldwide. bauhaus imaginista is realized with partners in eight countries and at the Haus der Kulturen der Welt in Berlin. It was developed by the curators and artistic directors Marion von Osten and Grant Watson with the help of an international team of researchers, artists and designers, as well as with institutional partners in Morocco, China, the United States, Japan, Russia, Brazil, Nigeria, India, Germany and the UK.

bauhaus imaginista:
Chronological Overview

23 & 24 March 2018
Panel discussion and workshop
bauhaus imaginista: Learning From
Le Cube – Independent Art Room, Rabat, and Goethe-Institut Rabat, Morocco

8 April – 26 August 2018
Exhibition
bauhaus imaginista: Moving Away
China Design Museum/China Academy of Art, Hangzhou, China

9 April 2018
Workshop and symposium
bauhaus imaginista: Moving Away
China Design Museum/China Academy of Art, Hangzhou, China, and Goethe-Institut China

7, 8 & 9 June 2018
Workshop and symposium
bauhaus imaginista: Learning From
Metropolitan Museum of Art, the National Museum of the American Indian, the American Museum of Natural History, the Lenore Tawney Foundation and Goethe-Institut New York, USA

4 August – 8 October 2018
Exhibition
bauhaus imaginista: Corresponding With
The National Museum of Modern Art, Kyoto, Japan

4 & 5 August 2018
Symposium
bauhaus imaginista: Corresponding With
Goethe-Institut Tokyo, Japan

12 September – 30 November 2018
Exhibition and symposium
bauhaus imaginista: Moving Away
The Internationalist Architect
Garage Museum of Contemporary Art and Goethe-Institut Moscow, Russia

24 October – 6 January 2018
Exhibition
bauhaus imaginista: Learning From
SESC Pompéia São Paulo, Brazil

25 October 2018
Symposium
Goethe-Institut São Paulo, Brazil

23 & 24 November 2018
Symposium
bauhaus imaginista: Moving Away
Decolonizing the Campus
Goethe-Institut Lagos, Nigeria

2–18 December 2018
Exhibition
bauhaus imaginista: Moving Away
Kiran Nadar Museum of Art, New Delhi, India

2 December 2018
Symposium
bauhaus imaginista: Moving Away
India International Centre, New Delhi, India, and Goethe-Institut India

15 March – 10 June 2019
Exhibition
bauhaus imaginista
Haus der Kulturen der Welt, Berlin, Germany

20 September 2019 – 12 January 2020
Exhibition
bauhaus imaginista
Zentrum Paul Klee, Bern, Switzerland

21 September – 24 November 2019
Exhibition
bauhaus imaginista: Still Undead
Nottingham Contemporary, Nottingham, United Kingdom

bauhaus imaginista

Team
Artistic Directors and Curators:
Marion von Osten, Grant Watson
Project Manager: Julia Jung
Project Administrator: Philipp Krüger
Curatorial Assistant: Franziska Zahl (Bureau Konkret)
Registrar: Annette Schryen
Student Assistant and Media Production:
Jonas von Lenthe
Image Editor: Iris Ströbel
Editors, Online Journal: Anja Guttenberger, Michael Baers
Copy-Editors: Martin Hager, Karl Hoffmann, Clemens Krümmel, Robert Schlicht, Rebecca Williams
Catalogue Editor: Jill Winder
Graphic Designers: Studio Matthias Görlich (labels and brochure), Julie Peeters with a typeface by Dinamo (logo)
Exhibition Designers: Kooperative für Darstellungspolitik
Public Relations: Hendrik von Boxberg

Researchers
Elissa Auther
Suchitra Balasubrahmanyan
Regina Bittner
Gavin Butt
Helena Čapková
Anshuman Dasgupta
Tatiana Efrussi
Thomas Flierl
Erin Alexa Freedman
Anja Guttenberger
Christian Hiller
Maud Houssais
Eduard Kögel
Mariana Meneses
Partha Mitter
Luiza Proença
Adrian Rifkin
Daniel Talesnik

Artists
Kader Attia
Alice Creischer
Zvi Efrat
Luca Frei
Doreen Mende
Paulo Tavares
The Otolith Group
Wendelien van Oldenborgh

bauhaus100
Head of Bauhaus Verbund 2019 Office:
Christian Bodach
Programme Coordination: Doreen Reinhold
Communications: Andrea Brandis
Administration: Andreas Oelsner
Finance: Nicole Dunkel
Office Management: Linda Schmidt
Assistance/Events Database:
Maximilian Netter, Dominique Wollniok

Executive Directors, Bauhaus Kooperation Berlin Dessau Weimar GmbH
Head of Administration, Bauhaus Archiv e.V./Museum für Gestaltung, Berlin:
Dagmar Seydell
Head of Administration, Klassik Stiftung Weimar: Thomas Leßmann
Director of Bauhaus Dessau Foundation:
Claudia Perren

Goethe-Institut
Secretary General: Johannes Ebert
Head of Visual Arts: Rainer Hauswirth
Advisor/Curator of Visual Arts, Project Manager bauhaus imaginista:
Mathilde Weh
Head of Press: Jessica Kraatz Magri
Head of Press, Goethe-Institut Berlin:
Viola Noll
Press Officer, Berlin: Hannah Cuvalo

Haus der Kulturen der Welt (HKW), Berlin, Germany
Director: Bernd Scherer
Head of Project: Annette Bhagwati
Project Coordination: Jessica Páez
Project Assistance: Laura Mattes

Communications Department
Head: Daniel Neugebauer
Press Office: Anne Maier, Laura Mühlbauer
Editorial Office: Franziska Wegener, Sabine Willig, Anna Etteldorf
Cultural Education, Programme Coordination: Eva Stein

Acknowledgments

The organizers of the bauhaus imaginista project would like to thank the following individuals, companies and institutions for their invaluable help and cooperation:

Ute Ackermann
Kunlé Adeyemi
Ariel Aloni
Bayo Amole
Peter Anders
Makoto Aoyama
Artothek
Abimbola Asojo
Nassim Azarzar
Erika Babatz
Astrid Bähr
Subir Banarjee
Farah Batool
Silke Baumann
Susanne Baumgart
Daniel Beginsky
Kerstin Bittner
Regina Bittner
Georg M. Blochmann
Rüdiger Bolz
Supratik Bose
Juliana Braga
Silke Briel
Jana Buhl
Juliana Okuda Campaneli
Helena Casas
Ira Chaudhuri
Nouredine Cherkaoui
Beth Citron
Maria Inigo Clavo
Esther Cleven
Brenda Danilowitz
Stefanie Dathe
Davis Museum
Sebastian De Line
Pauline De Mazieres
Kaj Delugan
Detlef Diedrichsen
Diedrich Diedrichsen
Amanda Diez
Kai-Inga Dost
Eames Office LLC USA
Ecole Parque
Nicolas Ehler
Kate Elliott
Leonhard Emmerling
Familia Aniceto
Gudrun Föttinger
Kate Fowle
Anselm Franke
Heidi Frautschi
Barbara Frost
Camuset Gabrielle
Isa Gebara
Natascha Ginwala
Petra Goertz
Anastasia Golovanova
Grainger Museum
GV Sreekumar
Markus Hannes
Alexandra Jacopetti Hart
Sabine Hartmann
Ulrike Hennecke
Sheila Hicks
Sibylle Hoiman
Ellen J. Holdorf
Candice Hopkins
Amber Husain
Helga Huskamp
Yuko Ikeda
Instituto Lina Bo e P.M. Bardi
J. Paul Getty Museum
Annemarie Jaeggi
Karin Jaenecke
E. Babatunde Jaiyeoba
Tanishka Kachru
Bouchaib Kenza
Keren Kinberg
Martin Komuschiewitz
Ulrike Krautheim
Miriam Krautwurst
Grit Kurth
Kanika Kuthiala
Kyoka
Lina Larraki
Hannah Le Roux
Céline Lebret
Frida Lee Frei
Luciana Lehfeld
Carine Lemouneau
Ethel Leon
Thomas Leßmann
Aurea Leszczynski Vieira
Maria Lind
Tatjana Lorenz
Sarat Maharaj
Anne Maier
Chinatsu Makiguch
Katharine Maller
Martin Mäntele
Toni Maraini
Marg Foundation Mumbai India
Bruno Maurer
Metropolitan Museum
Anastasia Mityushina
Barbara Moore
Wanderley Moreira dos Santos
Friederike Möschel
Jin Motohashi
Museum of Modern Art Rio de Janeiro
Chris Neate
Adele Nelson
Johanna Neurath
Kathleen Nugent Mangan
Chika Okele
Yukimasa Okumura
Kenji Okuyama
Márton Orosz
Ayako Otsu
Katarzyna Pieprzak
Heloisa Pisano
Elisabeth Piskernik
Irina Posrednikowa
Kate Pourshariati
Fábio Prata
Patrícia Queiroz
Luiz Rangel
Judith Reddy
Krishna Reddy
Rachel Riddell
Malte Roloff
Suely Rolnik
Margot Rumler
Natalia Sabrodskaja
Satoko Saeki
Lahlou Salma
Kahena Sanaa
Roberta Saraiva
John Saunders-Griffiths
Scala Group SpA Italia
Laura Scemama
Anke Schmidt
Anna Schüller
Felicity Scott
M. Jennifer Sellar
Sabujcoli Sen
Hiroko Shikida
Tsuyoshi Shira
Frank Simon-Ritz
Hans Snoeck
Kaho Somada
Irina Sopina
Thomas Soraperra
Peter Spillmann
Monika Stadler
Claire Louise Staunton
Stedelijk Museum
Mariko Takagi
Cristine Takuá
Wolfgang Thöner
Sam Thorne
Roger Thorp
Clare Tillyer
Clemens Treter
Hiromitsu Umemiya
Cecilia Vicuña
Aurea Vieira
Ekaterina Vladimirtseva
Katharina von Ruckteschell-Katte
Olga von Schubert
Pradyumna Vyas
Christoph Wagner
Astrid Wege
Daniel Weiss
Lisa Welitschko
Wolfgang Welker
Lesley Whitworth
Anne Wilson
Christiane Wolf
Olaf Wünsch
Kaijin Xie
Teruhi Yamano
Masaki Yanagihara
Katsuhiko Yashiro
Yuan Youmin
Gao Yuan
Zeitkratzer
Sylvia Ziegner
Nina Zimmer
David Zwirner Gallery

Picture Credits

l = left; r = right; t = top; b = bottom

Back cover (clockwise from top left): see credits for pp. 200, 165, 111, 138–39, 125, 99, 217, 225, 253, 255, 279

4 Bauhaus-Archiv Berlin, photo: Hermann Kiessling

8 The Josef and Anni Albers Foundation, 1976.4.106, © The Josef and Anni Albers Foundation/VG Bild-Kunst, Bonn 2018, photo: Tim Nighswander/ Imaging4Art

15 Bauhaus-Archiv Berlin, © VG Bild-Kunst, Bonn 2018, photo: Markus Hawlik

17 Bauhaus-Archiv Berlin, photo: Markus Hawlik

18 Bauhaus-Universität Weimar, Archiv der Moderne/Bauhaus-Archiv Berlin, © (Alfred Arndt) VG Bild-Kunst, Bonn 2018

19t Kala Bhavan, Visva-Bharati, Santiniketan

19b Photo: Grant Watson

20 Courtesy of the artist

21 Bauhaus-Archiv Berlin, photo: Markus Hawlik

22 Zentrum Paul Klee, Bern, © Heirs to Lena Bergner

23t Musashino Art University Museum & Library, Tokyo, © Yamawaki Iwao & Michiko Archives

23b Bauhaus-Archiv Berlin

27 Bauhaus-Archiv Berlin, photo: Markus Hawlik

29 Landesarchiv Thüringen – Hauptstaatsarchiv Weimar, Generalintendanz des Deutschen Nationaltheaters und der Staatskapelle Weimar Nr. 1891, Bl. 279r

30–31 Private collection, © VG Bild-Kunst, Bonn 2018, photo: Martin Richi

32–33 Landesarchiv Thüringen – Hauptstaatsarchiv Weimar, Staatliches Bauhaus Weimar Nr. 57, Bl. 64r/v

34 The J. Paul Getty Museum, Los Angeles, © Ursula Kirsten-Collein, Berlin

35 Universitätsbibliothek Heidelberg, http://digi.ub.uni-heidelberg.de/diglit/ moholy_nagy1929, CC BY-SA 3.0 DE

37 Museum Kala Bhavan, Santiniketan

39 Photo: © 2013 Christie's Images Limited

40 Photo: © 2013 Christie's Images Limited

42–43 Still from The Otolith Group, *The O Horizon*, 2018, HD video, colour, sound, 81 min., courtesy of the artist

45 Akar Prakar Gallery, Kolkata

46t Akar Prakar Gallery, Kolkata

46b Akar Prakar Gallery, Kolkata

47t Courtesy of the Gauri Bhanja Centenary Catalogue, Kala Bhavan

47b Museum Rabindra Bhavan, Santiniketan

48tl Courtesy of the Gauri Bhanja Centenary Catalogue, Kala Bhavan

48tr Courtesy of the Gauri Bhanja Centenary Catalogue, Kala Bhavan

48b Museum Rabindra Bhavan, Santiniketan

49t Subir Banarjee, Prabhatmohan Bandyopadhyay Collection, West Bengal

49bl Subir Banarjee, Prabhatmohan Bandyopadhyay Collection, West Bengal

49br Museum Rabindra Bhavan, Santiniketan

50t Courtesy of the author

50bl Museum Rabindra Bhavan, Santiniketan

50br Museum Rabindra Bhavan, Santiniketan

51tr Courtesy of Visva-Bharati Publications and Rabindra Bhavana

51bl Courtesy of Visva-Bharati Publications

51br Courtesy of Visva-Bharati Publications

52t Museum Kala Bhavan, Santiniketan

52bl Museum Rabindra Bhavan, Santiniketan

52br Museum Kala Bhavan, Santiniketan

54–55 Courtesy of the artists

57 Private collection (Prof. Dr Hiromitsu Umemiya)

58 Private collection (Prof. Dr Hiromitsu Umemiya)

60 Kyoto University, Graduate School and Faculty of Engineering, Library of Architecture (Yoshica), Kyoto, © Yamawaki Iwao & Michiko Archives

61 Private collection (Prof. Dr Hiromitsu Umemiya)

62–63 Musashino Art University Museum & Library, Tokyo, © Yamawaki Iwao & Michiko Archives

65 Image courtesy of MoMAK

69 Bauhaus-Archiv Berlin

70 Bauhaus-Archiv Berlin

73 Courtesy of the artist, photo: Karl Isakson

73 (inset) Private collection (Prof. Dr Hiromitsu Umemiya)

74 Private collection (Prof. Dr Hiromitsu Umemiya)

75 Courtesy of the artist, photo: Karl Isakson

75 (inset) Private collection (Prof. Dr Hiromitsu Umemiya)

76 Private collection (Prof. Dr Hiromitsu Umemiya)

77 Courtesy of the artist, photo: Karl Isakson

79 Hans Snoeck Private Collection, New York, photo: © 2017 Christie's Images Limited

81 The Metropolitan Museum of Art/ Purchase, Fletcher Fund, Claudia Quentin Gift, and Harris Brisbane Dick Fund, 2017/CC0 1.0 Public Domain Dedication

82 The Josef and Anni Albers Foundation, 1976.40.481, © The Josef and Anni Albers Foundation/VG Bild-Kunst, Bonn 2018, photo: RIT Public Relations Department

83 Stiftung Bauhaus Dessau (I 15598 G), © Heirs to Lena Bergner

84–85 Bauhaus-Universität Weimar, Archiv der Moderne, © VG Bild-Kunst, Bonn 2018

86 Courtesy of Penn Museum Archive

87 Courtesy of Penn Museum Archive

88t Luther College Fine Arts Collection, Decorah, Iowa

88b © Instituto Bardi/Casa de Vidro, São Paulo, Brazil, photo: Armin Guthman

89 Courtesy of Cinemateca Brasileira

90–91 Courtesy of Toni Maraini

93 Zentrum Paul Klee, Bern

94 E. W. K., Bern

95 Zentrum Paul Klee, Bern, © Heirs to Lena Bergner

96–97 Bauhaus-Archiv Berlin, © VG Bild-Kunst, Bonn 2018, photo: Markus Hawlik

99 Location unknown, image courtesy of Zentrum Paul Klee, Bern

100 From a private collection in Switzerland, deposited in the Zentrum Paul Klee, Bern

101 From a private collection in Switzerland, deposited in the Zentrum Paul Klee, Bern, Inv. Nr. Lg AKM Ko PK 565

103 Zentrum Paul Klee, Bern, Inv. Nr. GBI.3/93

104 Zentrum Paul Klee, Bern, © Heirs to Lena Bergner

105 Zentrum Paul Klee, Bern

113–17 Courtesy of the artist, © VG Bild-Kunst, Bonn 2018, photos: Kader Attia

119 Private archive, © Mohamed Melehi

120tl Private archive, © Mohamed Melehi

120tr Private archive, © Mohamed Melehi

120bl Private archive, © Mohamed Melehi

120br Private archive, © Mohamed Melehi

121 Private archive, © Mohamed Melehi

123 Private archive, © Mohamed Melehi

124 Private archive, © Mohamed Melehi

125 Courtesy of Toni Maraini, © Mohamed Melehi

126–27 Private archive, © Mohamed Melehi

129 Bauhaus-Archiv Berlin

131 Museum of Modern Art, New York (MoMA). Gift of the designer in memory of Greta Daniel. 246.1965, © The Josef and Anni Albers Foundation/VG Bild-Kunst, Bonn 2018, DIGITAL IMAGE © (2018) The Museum of Modern Art/ Scala, Florence

133 Smithsonian American Art Museum, Gift of S. C. Johnson & Son, Inc., © VG Bild-Kunst, Bonn 2018

135 Museum of Modern Art, New York (MoMA). Gift of Knoll Associates 430.1964, © VG Bild-Kunst, Bonn 2018, DIGITAL IMAGE © (2018) The Museum of Modern Art/Scala, Florence

136 Courtesy of the Lenore G. Tawney Foundation, photo: George Erml

138–39 Courtesy of the Lenore G. Tawney Foundation, photos: Adam Reich
140–41 Museum of Arts and Design, New York, gift of the Dreyfus Corporation, through the American Craft Council, 1989/courtesy of the Lenore G. Tawney Foundation, photo: Ed Watkins, 2007
143 Photo: Elvira Espejo
145t Photo: Elvira Espejo
145b Photo: Elvira Espejo
151–57 Courtesy of Paulo Tavares
159 Bauhaus-Archiv Berlin
162 Bauhaus-Archiv Berlin
163 Bauhaus-Archiv Berlin
164 Bauhaus-Archiv Berlin, © Nachlass Scheper, Berlin,
165 Bauhaus-Archiv Berlin, © Nachlass Scheper, Berlin,
166 Stiftung Bauhaus Dessau (I 018378/52 F), © (Konrad Püschel) Erbengemeinschaft nach Konrad Püschel
167 Shanghai Urban Planning & Design Research Institute
168 Courtesy of China Design Museum
169 National Institute of Design, Knowledge Management Center, Archive Collection
170–71 Otl Aicher-Archiv, HfG-Archiv, Museum Ulm, © Florian Aicher
172 National Institute of Design, Knowledge Management Center, Archive Collection
173t National Institute of Design, Knowledge Management Center, Archive Collection
173b National Institute of Design, Knowledge Management Center, Archive Collection
175–78 gta Archiv/ETH Zürich, © Heirs of Hannes Meyer
180–81 Bauhaus-Archiv Berlin, © (Consemüller) Dr Stephan Consemüller, (Breuer) unknown
186 Getty Research Institute, Los Angeles (850514)
187 Getty Images/Untitled X-Ray, photo: Nick Veasey
189 Bauhaus-Archiv Berlin
191 Stiftung Bauhaus Dessau (I 10015/79 D), © (Konrad Püschel) Erbengemeinschaft nach Konrad Püschel
192 Bauhaus-Archiv Berlin
195–96 gta Archiv/ETH Zürich
198–99 gta Archiv/ETH Zürich
200 Het Nieuwe Instituut/on loan from collection EFL Foundation, Amsterdam/ archive (code): EEST/inv. nr.: 4.316-1, © VG Bild-Kunst, Bonn 2018
203 Courtesy of China Design Museum
204t Courtesy of China Design Museum
204b Courtesy of China Design Museum
205 Courtesy of China Design Museum
207 Image from John C. Harkness (ed.), *The Walter Gropius Archive. Volume 4: 1945–1969. The Work of The Architects Collaborative*, Garland Publishing, Inc., New York, London, 1991, p. 11
208 Image from John C. Harkness (ed.), *The Walter Gropius Archive. Volume 4: 1945–1969. The Work of The Architects Collaborative*, Garland Publishing, Inc., New York, London, 1991, p. 8
209 Image from John C. Harkness (ed.), *The Walter Gropius Archive. Volume 4: 1945–1969. The Work of The Architects Collaborative*, Garland Publishing, Inc., New York, London, 1991, p. 15
210 Image from Helmut Jacoby, *Architectural Drawings*, Gert Hatje, Stuttgart, 1965
213 Getty Images/Archive Films: Editorial
214 Museum of Modern Art, New York (MoMA). Photographic Archive. The Museum of Modern Art Archives, New York. Cat. no.: IN 576.1, photo: Alexandre Georges. DIGITAL IMAGE © (2018) The Museum of Modern Art/ Scala, Florence
215 © 2018 Eames Office, LLC (eamesoffice.com)
217 Reproduced with the permission of The Marg Foundation, Mumbai, India
218 National Institute of Design, Knowledge Management Center, Archive Collection
219 National Institute of Design, Knowledge Management Center, Archive Collection
220–21 National Institute of Design, Knowledge Management Center, Archive Collection
223 Industrial Design Centre, Indian Institute for Technology, Bombay
225 HfG-Archiv, Museum Ulm, © Sudhakar Nadkarni
229 Arieh Sharon Digital Archive, the Yael Aloni Collection
230–31 Arieh Sharon Digital Archive, the Yael Aloni Collection
233 Arieh Sharon Digital Archive, the Yael Aloni Collection
234 Arieh Sharon Digital Archive, the Yael Aloni Collection
238 Photo: Wendelien van Oldenborgh
239 Collection Het Nieuwe Instituut/STAB, d18, photo: Wendelien van Oldenborgh
240–41 Collection Het Nieuwe Instituut/ STAB, d10
240–41 (inset) Collection Het Nieuwe Instituut/STAB, ph174
243 Courtesy of Microscope Gallery and Kurt Schwerdtfeger Estate © 2016
245 Grainger Museum Collection, University of Melbourne. Gift of Olive Hirschfeld, 1980. 01.0017, © Chris Bell
248 Joseph Emberton Archive, University of Brighton Design Archives/EMB/2/7/1, photo: Sasha
249 Kepes Institute, Eger, Hungary, © Kepes Estate
250 The Josef and Anni Albers Foundation, 1976.35.1001, © The Josef and Anni Albers Foundation/VG Bild-Kunst, Bonn 2018
251 The Josef and Anni Albers Foundation, 1976.35.1001, © The Josef and Anni Albers Foundation/VG Bild-Kunst, Bonn 2018
252 Courtesy of the Paula Cooper Gallery, New York, © 2018 Barbara Moore/ Licensed by VAGA, New York, NY
253 Kunsthalle Bremen, © Nam June Paik Estate, photo: Tobias Hübel – ARTOTHEK
254 © Tate, London 2018, © R. Hamilton. All Rights Reserved/VG Bild-Kunst, Bonn 2018
255 From *New Sounds New Styles*, October 1981, edited by Kasper de Graaf, designed by Malcolm Garrett
258–59 Courtesy of Microscope Gallery and Kurt Schwerdtfeger Estate © 2016
261 Image courtesy of the Muriel R. Cooper Collection, Morton R. Godine Library, Archive, Massachusetts College of Art and Design, reprinted by permission of the MIT Press
263 Courtesy of the MIT Museum, Ivan Massar Photographer
264–65 Courtesy of the Visible Language Workshop Archive, MIT Program in Art, Culture and Technology (ACT), © Massachusetts Institute of Technology
266 Photograph courtesy of the MIT Press, © 2017 Massachusetts Institute of Technology, by permission of the MIT Press
267 Courtesy of the Visible Language Workshop Archive, MIT Program in Art, Culture and Technology (ACT), © Massachusetts Institute of Technology
269 Bauhaus-Archiv Berlin, © Kaj Delugan, photo: A. & E. Frankl, Berlin
270 The Image Works, photo: Charles Gatewood
273 Getty Images/Corbis Premium Historical, photo: Steve Schapiro
274–75 Getty Images/Premium Archive, photo: Fred W. McDarrah
279 Courtesy of Stuart Shave/Modern Art, London, © Linder
280 Courtesy of the artist
285–87 Theaterwissenschaftliche Sammlung, Universität zu Köln

Index

Page numbers in *italic* refer to the illustrations.

A
Abraham, David
fashion images for diploma project at the National Institute of Design, Ahmedabad, India *173*
'Der absolute Film' (The Absolute Film) 268
African art 80, 174
Ahmedabad, Gujurat, India 161, 216, 227
Ahmedabad Declaration on Industrial Design for Development *220–21*, 222
Aicher, Otl
drawings of cars from the 'Indien 1960' (India 1960) report *170–71*
Ajanta caves 41
Al Tatawi 112
Albers, Anni 80, 128–30, 132, 134
Black-White-Gray 131
On Weaving 80
Albers, Josef 28, 80, 122, 134, 226
Detail of Loggia Wall 82
Valentine's Day Ball, Black Mountain College *250–51*
Albert, Bruce
The Falling Sky 147
Alfeld 256, 268, 271
Algeria 112
Algiers 112–14, 197
All India Handicrafts Board 216
Almond, Marc *280*, 281
Amaral, Tarsila do 80, 146
American Museum of Natural History, New York 134
Amsterdam 237
Andean textiles 80, 128–30, 132–37
Andrade, Mário de
Macunaíma 146
Andrade, Oswald de 146
'Anthropophagic' manifesto 146
'Cultural Anthropophagi' 114
'Pau-Brasil' manifesto 146
Anger, Jenny 98
Apple 185
Arbeitsrat für Kunst 26
Archer, Bruce 226
The Architects Collaborative (TAC) 206–11
Argentina *81*
Arndt, Alfred *18*
Arndt, Gertrud (née Hantschk) 102
work sheet 92, *96–97*
Arts and Crafts movement 12, 16
Asawa, Ruth 132
Ashoka, Emperor 212
Asociación Arte Concreto-Invención, Buenos Aires 226
Aspen International Design Conference (1981) 185
Atlas Mountains 118
Australia 193, 271
Aymara peoples 142–44

B
Bagh caves 41
Baghdad 211
Baij, Ramkinkar 38
Ball, Dave 281
Bandopadhyay, Prabhatmohan 49
Banham, Reyner 226
Barcelona 194
Bardi, Pietro Maria 80
Basic Design 244, 278
Bauhaus
closure 12, 28, 80, 146, 160, *162*
Dessau building 202
émigrés 160, 188–93, 260
exhibition in Weimar (1923) 256
foundation of 16, 26
Indian exhibition 16, 28, 36
and indigenous cultural production 146–48
and industrial design 179, 182–85
influence in India 16, 28, 212–22
influence in Japan 56–68
influence in Morocco 118–22
interest in other cultures 80
international students 12, 28, 56, 59
Lantern Festival 268
legacy 276–81
library 80, 98, 106
light plays 244, 256–57, 268–72
'media surround' 244
Meyer expelled from 188
Mural Workshop *18*
and the 'new human' 182–85
parties 244, 256
theatre workshop 244, 268
'unity of art and craft' 160
Weaving Workshop 98, 102, 128–34, *129*
Bauhaus: Weimar, Dessau, Berlin, Chicago (MIT Press) 260, *261*, 262, *266*
Das Bauhaus 1919–1933. Weimar, Dessau, Berlin 260
Das Bauhaus 1919–1933. Weimar, Dessau, Berlin und die Nachfolge in Chicago seit 1937 260
Bauhaus-Archiv, Berlin 174
Bauhaus Archive, Darmstadt 260, 271
Bauhaus Manifesto *14–15*, 16, *17*, 26–28, *27*, 41, 182
Bauhaus Week, Jena (1923) 268
bauhaus. zeitschrift für gestaltung 160
Bayer, Herbert 122, 160
Aspen International Design Conference 185
Beese, Lotte *see* Stam-Beese, Lotte
Belkahia, Farid 118, *125*
'Bengal School' 16
Berbers 80, *113*, *115–17*
Berger, Otti 102
Bergner, Lena 80, 102
Detail of a Medieval Knotted Carpet from the Orient 95, 98
Reinschrift von Paul Klees Unterricht (Clean Copy of Paul Klee's Teaching) *104*
studies from the Paul Klee course *22*
Untitled (Draft of a Hand-Loom) 83
Berlin 26, 80, 197, 281
Berliner Volksbühne 268
Beyer, Lis 179, *180–81*
Beyer, Oskar
Welt-Kunst (World Art) 109
Bhanja, Gauri 48
design for *alpana* (flat design on ground) *48*
design on board for batik *48*
Studies from Nature 47
Bienal de São Paulo 146
Bill, Max 80, 226
bio-design 185
Bird, Junius 134
Black Mountain College, North Carolina 80, *250–51*, 260
Bo Bardi, Lina 80
Bogler, F. W. *269*
Bolivia *81*
Bombay (Mumbai) 216, 224, 226
Bose, Nandalal 38, 48–49, 51
Carpenters 46
Drishti O Srishti (Vision and Creation) *51*
Fishing Line Maker 45
Instructions for Mural Painting 19
postcards *45–46*, 49, *49*, *52*
Sahaj Path 51
Untitled (mural) *50*
Untitled (Santal Woman Welcomes Her Father-in-Law) 40
Untitled (Temple on Hill Top) 39
Boston 260
Bowie, David 278
Brazil 80, 112, 114, 146–48
Breuer, Marcel 202
ein bauhaus-film. fünf jahre lang (A Bauhaus Film: Five Years Long) *159*, 160, 174
chairs *159*, 160, 174–79, *180–81*, *186*
and *Design* journal 216
'Metal Furniture and Modern Spatiality' 161
in UK 244
in US 160, 260
Britain 193
art schools 244, 278–81
Brno, Czechoslovakia 237
Bunka Gakuin (School of Culture), Tokyo 72
Burroughs, William S. *270*, 272

C
Cailloux, Bernd 272
Cairo 112
Calcutta (Kolkata) 16, 28, 36, 38, 41
Cambridge, Massachusetts 260
Caribbean 237
Casablanca, Morocco 80, 118
cave art 146
Celle, Germany 268
Center for Advanced Visual Studies (CAVS) 244, 262, *263*
Central America 80, 132
Central School of Arts and Crafts, London 224
Centre for Weaving and Fashion Design, Tokyo 59
Ceylon 193
Chabâa, Mohamed 118, 120, 123, 124, *125*, 126

chairs
in Breuer's film *159*, 160, 174–79
tubular steel *168*, 179
Chalfen, Richard
film-makers Johnny Nelson and Alta Kahn while shooting *Navajo Film Themselves 86–7*
Chandigarh, India 212
Chang Chao-kang 211
Chaudhary, Yeshwant 224
Chen Chi-kwan 160
Tunghai University, Taiwan *210*, 211
Chicago 137, 160, 244, 260
Chicago, Judy 277
Chile 160, 193
China 160, 161, 202, 206–11
China Bhavan, Santiniketan, India 50
Chinese woman with Tubular Steel Chair *168*
CIAM (Congrès Internationaux d'Architecture Moderne) 194–97, *195–96*, *198–201*, 237
CIAM Congress, 4th, Athens (1933) 160, 197, *200–01*
CIAM Congress, 7th, Bergamo (1949) *240–41*
CIRPAC 194
'Civilização do Nordeste', Salvador, Brazil (1963) *88*
Cižek, Franz 38
Clark, Judy 277
Cold War 161, 193
Collein, Edmund 28
Photoplastik, Japanese Student at Bauhaus Holding Circle of Shadows 34
colonialism, and tradition 112–14
colour
light plays 257
planning in textiles 142–44, *143*, *145*
Comenius, Johann Amos
Orbis sensualium pictus 106
communism 161
Communist Party (Hungary) 193
computer technology 244
Congrès Internationaux d'Architecture Moderne *see* CIAM
Conrad, Tony
The Flicker 272
Consemüller, Erich
Untitled (Woman in B3 Club chair by Marcel Breuer Wearing a Mask by Oskar Schlemmer and a Dress Made out of Fabric Designed by Beyer) 179, *180–81*
Constructivism 12, 130
Coomaraswamy, Ananda 51
Cooper, Muriel 244, 262, 264–67
promotional poster for *Bauhaus: Weimar, Dessau, Berlin, Chicago 261*, 262
counterculture 244
Cubism 98
cyborgs 179

D
Damen, Hélène
Lotte Stam-Beese, 1903–1988: Dessau, Brno, Charkow, Moskou, Amsterdam, Rotterdam 238
Darmstadt 260, 271
Delta 5 281
Descartes, René 112
Design (journal) 216
'Design Today in America and Europe', India (1959) 216
Dessau, Germany 28, 56, 59, 130, 188, 202
see also Bauhaus
Deutsches Nationaltheater, Weimar *29*
Devi, Protima *49*
Devolder, Anne-Mie
Lotte Stam-Beese, 1903–1988: Dessau, Brno, Charkow, Moskou, Amsterdam, Rotterdam 238
digital technology 244
Disappearing Figure Seated on Marcel Breuer Chair 186
Doesburg, Theo van 174
The Dom, New York *274–75*
Duarte, Rogério
film poster, *Deus e o Diabo na Terra do Sol 89*
Duchamp, Marcel 114
Dunaújváros, Hungary 193
Durkee, Steve 272
Düsseldorf 272
Dutch Indies 237

E
Eames, Charles 216, 224, 226
Lotas, India 215
Eames, Ray 216, 224, 226
Eco, Umberto 174
École des Beaux-Arts de Casablanca (School of Fine Arts) 80, *90–91*, 118–22, *119–21*, *123–24*, *126–27*
Eesteren, Cornelis van *195–96*
Eggeling, Viking 272
Egypt 102, 112–14
Ehrman, Marli 137
Einstein, Carl 109
Afrikanische Plastik (African Sculpture) 109
El-Ariss, Tarek
Trials of Arab Modernity 112, 114
Ellora cave paintings 16
Expanded Cinema movement 272
'Exploding Plastic Inevitable' 272, *273–75*
Expressionism 16, 28, 130, 160

F
Factory 272
Faizpur Congress, India 46, 49, *52*
FEA-Congress, Basel (1958) 67
Feininger, Lyonel 10
exhibition in Calcutta 32–33
Kathedrale (Cathedral) *15*, 16, 28
Feininger, T. Lux 260
feminism 281
Fibre Art Movement 132, 137
film 257, 271
First World War 28, 182, 277
Fischinger, Oskar 272
Five-Year Plans (India) 212, *213*, 216, 224
Five-Year Plans (Soviet Union) 160, 161, 190
Fletcher, Norman
Hua Tung University, Shanghai, China 206, *208*
Flint, Bert 118
Fonteles, Bené 80
Ford Foundation 212, 216, 224
France 114
Frei, Luca
Design for Pillows 73–75
Model for a Pedagogical Vehicle 72, *77*
Frick, Louise *101*
Fuchs, Bohuslav 237
Fuhrmann, Ernst 106, 110
Mexiko III (Mexico III) *111*
Peru II 108
Reich der Inka (The Inca Empire) *107*
Fujin gahō magazine 59
Fujin-no-Tomo (Women's Friend) magazine 66
Fuller, Buckminster 226
'The Functional City', Athens (1933) 197, *200*
functionalism 160
furniture *see* chairs

G
Galerie Der Sturm, Berlin 256
Gandhi, Mahatma 38, 46, 222
Gang of Four 281
Gardner, James 224
Geddes, Patrick 41
Genesis, Book of 256
Geneva 194
German Democratic Republic (GDR) 160
Gesamtkunstwerk (total work of art) 272
Giedion, Sigfried *195–96*, 197, 260
Protest Collage 198–99
Girard, Alexander 224
Glaesemer, Jürgen 92
Good Design Selection System (Japan) 64
Gothicism 28
Gramsci, Antonio 281
Greece 109, 197
Greiz, Germany 268
Gropius, Ise 179, *180–81*
Gropius, Walter 80, 122, 277
Arbeitsrat für Kunst 26
Bauhaus Dessau building 202
Bauhaus Manifesto *15*, 16, *17*, 26–28, *27*, 41, 182
and CIAM 160, 194, 197
and *Design* journal 216
exhibition in Weimar (1923) 130
in First World War 182, *183*
founds Bauhaus 10, 12, 26
Hua Tung University, Shanghai, China 206–11
interest in India 28
Internationale Architektur 182
in Japan 64
Lantern Festival 256
The New Architecture and the Bauhaus 182
and the 'new human' 182

'Programm des Staatlichen Bauhauses in Weimar' (Programme of the Weimar State Bauhaus) 16, 26
reconciling art and industry 56, 179, 278
sketch for 'The Functional City' *200*
The Architects Collaborative (TAC) 206–11
'The Theory and Organization of the Bauhaus' 36
trains Asian architects 160
in UK 244
in US 160, 260
Gugelot, Hans 224
guilds, medieval 16, 28
Gulag 190, 193
Gysin, Brion 244, 271–72
Dreamachine *270*, 272

H
Habitat magazine *151–57*
Haffenrichter, Hans 268, 271, 272
Hamburg 80, 237, 268
Hamhüng, North Korea *191*
Hamilton, Hector 194–97
Hamilton, Richard 244
Diab DS-101 Computer 254
Hannover Kunstverein 257
Hanover 268
Haouz 118
Haraway, Donna 179
Harcourt, Raoul d'
Les textiles anciens de Pérou et leur techniques (The Ancient Textiles of Peru and Their Techniques) 134
Haripura Congress, India 46, 49
Harvard Graduate School of Design, Cambridge, Massachusetts 160, 260
Hausenstein, Wilhelm 109
Barbaren und Klassiker (Barbarians and Classics) 109
Bild und Gemeinschaft (Image and Community) 109
Hebrew University, Givat Ram, Jerusalem 228
Heimann, Marli 269
Helvetica font 262
Hensher, Philip
The Emperor Waltz 277
Heron, Patrick 278
Hicks, Sheila 132–34
Ancient Writing 134
Blue Letter 134
The Evolving Tapestry 134
The Principal Wife Goes On 133, 134
White Letter 135
Hildesheim 271
Hindi Bhavan, Santiniketan, India 50
Hirschfeld-Mack, Ludwig 244, 262, 268, *269*, 271, 272
colour chord 21-stringed flat sound box *245*
Farbenlichtspiele (Colour Light Plays) 268–71, *269*
Hochschule für Gestaltung (HfG) Ulm (Ulm School of Design) 161, 212, 216–22, 224–27
Hohenzollernplatz church, Berlin 197
Horthy, Admiral 193
Hua Tung University, Shanghai, China 206–11, *207–09*
Huang, Henry 160
Hughes, Malcolm 277
Huiswoud, Hermina 237
Huiswoud, Otto 237
humans, redesigning 182–85
Humboldt-Forum, Berlin 110
Hungary 160, 193, 262

I
Ife University, Nigeria 228–32, *229–31*, *233–34*
IKEA 179
Imai, Kazuko 66, 67
India
independence 212–16
Kala Bhavan 16, *19*, 28, 38, 41, 44–52, *48*
links with Bauhaus 16, 28, 36–41
modernization of design 161, 212–22, 224–27
temple architecture 80
India Report 216, 224
Indian Airlines *218*
Indian Institute of Technology, Bombay 216
Indian National Congress 46, 49
Indian Society of Oriental Art, Calcutta 16
indigenous art 146–48
Indus Valley civilization 212
industrial design 36, 182–85, 216, 222, 224
Industrial Design Centre (IDC), Bombay 216–22
Institute of Contemporary Art (IAC), Brazil 80
Institute of Design (IIT), Chicago 137, 160, 244, 260
International Congresses of Modern Architecture *see* CIAM
International Constructivism 130
International Council of Societies of Industrial Design (ICSID) 222
International Housing and Town Planning Congress, XVIth, Mexico 190
International Trade Union Committee for Negro Workers 237
Iofan, Boris 194, 197
iPhones 185, *187*
Ipswich 278
Iran 193
Israel 228–32
Italy 194
Itten, Johannes 16, 28, 36, 244
influence in Japan 28, 66–7
interest in India 28
Kunst der Farbe (The Art of Colour) 67
Mein Vorkurs am Bauhaus (Design and Form: The Basic Course at the Bauhaus) 67
'On Composition' 28
Porträt Tagore (Portrait of Tagore) *30–31*
and the Weaving Workshop 130
Itten-Schule (Itten School), Berlin 66

J
Japan
Bauhaus exhibition 16
influence of Bauhaus 56–68
Itten's art education and 66–67
Renshichirō Kawakita's legacy and pedagogy 56–64, 68
Java 16
Jayakar, Pupul
'Indian Fabrics in Indian Life' 216
Jena 268
Jerusalem 228
jewelry, Berber *113*, *115–17*
Jikken Kōbō (Experimental Workshop) 72
Jiyū Gakuen Arts and Crafts Institute (Laboratory), Tokyo 66
Jiyū Gakuen School, Tokyo 59, 66, 67
jiyūga (free drawing) 68
Jobs, Steve 185
Jones, Owen
The Grammar of Ornament 109

K
Kageyama, Shizuko 59
Kahn, Albert 188
Kahn, Alta *86–87*
Kahn, Louis 224
Kala Bhavan, Santiniketan, India 16, *19*, 28, 38, 41, 44–52, *48*
Kamekura, Yūsaku 64, 66
Kandinsky, Wassily 10, 28, 36, 122, 146, 244, 271, 278
Bauhaus parties 244
light plays 256
and the 'Wassily' armchair 179
Kant, Immanuel 112
Karstadt Department Store, Hermannplatz, Berlin 197
Kawakita, Renshichirō 16, *24–25*, 28, 56–64, 66, 72
Kenchiku Shincho (New Wave of Architecture) *65*
Kōsaku Gijutsu Taikei (A General Guide to Industrial Techniques) 64
Kōsei Kyōiku Taikei (Manual for Teaching Thinking through Construction) 16, *23*, 56, 64, 66–67, 68, *69–70*
Kenchiku Kōgei I See All (Architecture Design I See All) 56, *57–58*
Kepes, György 244, 262, *263*
Language of Vision 262
The New Landscape in Art and Science 262
programmed kinetic light mural for KLM offices in New York *249*
'Vision + Value' 262
Kestner-Gesellschaft 268
Kharkov, Ukraine 56, 237
Kharkov Tractor factory (KhTZ) 237
kinetic light art *249*, 256–57, 271–72
Klarwein, Ossip 197
Klassen, Rebecca 137
Klee, Paul 28, 36, 146, 147, 244, 271, 278
I.2 Principiellen Ordnung (I.2 Principle Order) 102
II. Planimetrische Gestaltung

(II. Planimetric Configuration) 102
II.21 Mechanik (II.21 Mechanics) 102
Beiträge zur bildnerischen Formlehre (Contributions to the Pictorial Theory of Form) 102
Beride, 1927, 41 92, *94*
Beride (Wasserstadt) (Beride (Water Town)) 92, 93
Bildnerische Gestaltungslehre: I.3 Specielle Ordnung (Theory of Pictorial Configuration: I.3 Special Order) 102, *103*
Monument in Fruchtland (Monument in the Fertile Country) 102, *105*
pictures of architectural tapestries 92–102
rule four 238
Teppich (Carpet), *1914, 19* 98, *99*
Teppich (Carpet), *1927, 48* *79*, 92, 102
in Tunisia 98, *100–01*, 102, 122
Unterricht, I. Allgemeiner Teil, I.4 Gliederung (Teachings, I. General Part, I.4 Structure) 102
weaving classes 98, 102, 130
KLM offices, New York *249*
Knoll International 179
Kōgei Shidōsho (Design Research Institute) 64
Kokusai Kenchiku (International Architecture) *60*
Kolkhoz clubs 190
Konstantinova-Urban, Ludmila 190
Kopenawa, Davi
The Falling Sky 147
Korea, North 160, *166*, 193
Korean War (1950–53) 64, 193
kōsei, Japanese education 16, *24–25*, 59, 64
'Kōsei Kyōiku Sakuhin-ten' (Exhibition of Study Works of Education about Construction), Wakayama, Japan (1934) *61*
Kraftwerk 244
Kramrisch, Stella 16, 28, 38
Krenak, Ailton 80
Kubler, George 134
Kulturen der Erde (Cultures of the World) 106, *107–08*, 109, 110, *111*
Die Kunst der Hethither (Hittite Art) 109
Kuwasawa, Yōko 64
Kuwasawa Design School 64

L
Lacan, Jacques 114
Lantern Festival, Weimar 256, 268
Larsen, Jack Lenor
Beyond Craft: The Art Fabric 137
Le Corbusier 194, 197, 212
'Charter of Athens' 197
Leeds 278, 281
Leeds Polytechnic 278, 281
Leeds School of Art 244
Leipzig 268
Lenin 190
Leonardo (journal) 277
Liebknecht, Kurt 188
light plays 244, 256–57, 268–72
Linder, Carl 271
Untitled 279
London 277, 278
Los Angeles *273*
Lower Saxony 268
Lunacharsky, Anatoly 194

M
Maghreb Art 119–21, 123–24, 126–27
Maldonado, Tomás 226
'Ist das Bauhaus noch aktuell?' (Is the Bauhaus Still Up-to-Date?) 226
Maltan, Josef *18*
Mamani, Doña Lucía 144
Maraini, Toni *90–91*, 118, *121*
Marg: A Magazine of Architecture & Art 216, *217*
Marrakesh 118
Marseilles 197, 272
Marx, Karl 109
Marxism 281
Massachusetts Institute of Technology *see* MIT
Mauryan sculpture 212
May, Ernst 188
Maya 134
Mediterranean 160, 197
Mekas, Jonas
'Movie Journal' 271, 272
The Mekons 281
Melehi, Mohamed 80, 118
Maghreb Art 120–21, 123
poster *125*
Mendelsohn, Erich 194
Méndez, Leopoldo *84–85*
Mengel, Margarete *189*
Mensch, René 188, 193
Meso-America 134
Meumann, Klaus 188, 193
Mexican Institute for Planning and Urbanism 190
Mexico 132, 134, 160, 190, 193
Meyer, Hannes 12, 80, *163*, 226, 277
and Arieh Sharon 232
expelled from Bauhaus 188
and Lotte Beese 237
in Mexico 190, 193
reconciling art and industry 179, 185
sketches in a dummy for a Bauhaus book *175–78*
in Soviet Union 160, 188, 190, 193
in Switzerland 190
TGP Mexico, el taller de gráfica popular, doces años de obra artistica colectiva (The Workshop for Popular Graphic Art: A Record of Twelve Years of Collective Work) *84–85*
and the Weaving Workshop 130
Middle East 112, 193
Mies van der Rohe, Ludwig 12, 122, 130, 160, 206, 211
Milan 197
Ministry of Education (Japan) 64
Ministry of Trade and Industry (Japan) 64
MIT (Massachusetts Institute of Technology) 244, 260, 262
Center for Advanced Visual Studies (CAVS) 244, 262, *263*
Media Lab 244, 262
Program in Art, Culture and Technology (ACT) 262
Visible Language Workshop 262, *267*
MIT Press 260, 262, *266*
Mizue art journal 56
Mizukoshi, Shōnan 66, 67
Mizutani, Takehiko 16, 28, 56, 59, 66, 68
Studie zum Simultankontrast (Unterricht Josef Albers) (Study on Simultaneous Contrast (Class of Josef Albers) *21*
mobile phones 185, *187*
Modern Art Week, São Paulo 146
Mohamed Ali, Sultan 112
Moholy-Nagy, László 28, 36, 122, 137, 244, 262, 271
Ein Lichtspiel: Schwarz Weiss Grau 246–47
Light Prop for an Electric Stage 244
Malerei, Photografie, Film (Painting, Photography, Film) 257
Partiturskizze zu einer mechanischen Exzentrik (Sketch for a Score for a Mechanized Eccentric) *284–87*
Simpsons of Piccadilly *248*
stills from *Architects' Congress 201*
Von Material zu Architektur (From Material to Architecture) *35*
Moles, Abraham 226
Mondrian, Piet 146
Moore, Peter
Untitled (Stan VanDerBeek's Movie-Drome) 252
Morocco 80, 118–22
Moscow 160, 193, 194–97
Narkomfin Building *164–65*
Muche, Georg 98
Mukherjee, Benodebehari (Mukhopadhyay) 38–41, 46, 51
Adhunik Shilpashiksha (Modern Art Education) *51*, 52
Life of Medieval Saints 42–43
Mumbai (Bombay) 216, 224, 226
Mümliswil Children's Home, Switzerland 190
Munich 80
musa waraña (colour planning) 142–44, *143*, *145*
Museu de Arte Moderna de São Paulo (MAM-SP) 146
Museu de Arte de São Paulo (MASP) 80, 146

Museum of Contemporary Craft, New York 137
Museum of Modern Art (MAM), Salvador, Brazil *88*
Museum of Modern Art (MoMA), New York 160, 212–16, *214*, 260
Museum für Völkerkunde, Berlin 128
music 13, 16, 244, 256
'Musische Geometrie', Hannover (1966) 257

N
Nadkarni, Sudhakar 224–27
'Die Gestaltung eines Milchkiosk' (The Design of a Milk Kiosk) 224, *225*, 226–27
Nakada, Sadanosuke 56
'The State Bauhaus' 56
Nakashima, George 224
Napoleon III, Emperor 114
Narkomfin Building, Moscow *164–65*
National Institute of Design (NID), Ahmedabad, India 161, *173*, 216–22, *219*, 224
National Socialism (Nazis) 80, 226, 260
art history 109
closure of Bauhaus 12, 146, 160
light mysticism 271
rise to power 190
Native Americans 132, 137
Navajo Film Themselves 86–87
Navajo weaving 132
Neate, Chris
poster for performance by Marc Almond *280*
Negro Worker magazine 237
Nehru, Jawaharlal 161, 212, *213*, 216, 224
Nelson, Johnny *86–87*
Netherlands 174, 236, 237
neues bauen (New Building) movement 12, 160
New Architecture and Industrial Arts Research Institute, Ginza 66
New Bauhaus, Chicago 244, 260, 262
New Building movement *see neues bauen*
New Delhi 212
New Objectivity 110
New Sounds New Styles 255
New York 212, 271
Newcastle 278
Nigeria 228–32
Non-Cooperation movement (India) 38
Nonné-Schmidt, Helene 102, 226
North Africa 98, 112–14, 118–22
North Korea 160, *166*, 193
Nuttgens, Patrick 278

O
Obara, Kuniyoshi 67
Ōchi, Hiroshi 67
Shin-Seikatsu-Bi-no-Houkou (The Direction of New Beauty in Life) 67
Ogbechie, Sylvester Okwunodu 109
Old Testament 256
Oldenborgh, Wendelion van 235–37
Olympic Games, Tokyo (1964) 64
Ōno, Tamae *23*, 66
'Ons Suriname' 237
Orbis Pictus/Weltkunst-Bücherei (Orbis Pictus/World Art Library) 106
Otolith Group *54–55*

P
Pädagogische Hochschule Alfeld (College of Education Alfeld) 256, 268, 271
Paik, Nam June
Video Synthesizer 253
Palace of the Soviets, Moscow 190, 194–97
Pan-Asianism 38
Paris 112
Parrott, Alice Kagawa 132
Pasmore, Victor 244
Patel, Mahendra C.
Devanagari typeface *172*
Patha Bhavan, Santiniketan, India 50, *50*
Patris II (passenger ship) 197
Pei, I. M. 160
Hua Tung University, Shanghai, China 206–11, *207*
Tunghai University, Taiwan *210*, 211
Pendrecht district, Rotterdam 237, *240–41*
Peru 80, *81*, 128, 132, 134, 137
Peterhans, Walter 226
phones, mobile 185, *187*
photography 109, 110
Picasso, Pablo
Les Demoiselles d'Avignon 174
Platonism 36
Plaut, Eva 67
Playboy Club, London 277
pre-Columbian art and architecture 134, 137
'primitive' art 128
Profintern 237
'Promotion of Industrial Design in Developing Countries' (1979) 222
punk rock 281
Püschel, Konrad 188, *189*, 193
general plan of Hamhŭng, North Korea *191*
page from a photograph album of North Korea *166*

R
Ranjan, M. P.
Bamboo Cube Stools *169*
Rao, A. G.
Industrial Design Centre: A Decade of Design Experience 223
Ray, Man 271
Reading, England 278
Reddy, Krishna
Untitled 20
Reichardt, Grete 179
Renaissance 38, 194
Research Institute of Life Construction, Tokyo 16
Rice, Ron 271
Richter, Hans 272
Rhythmus 21 (Rhythm 21) 257
Rietveld, Gerrit 174
Rio de Janeiro 148
Rocha, Glauber *89*
rock art 146
Rockefeller Brothers Fund 212
Rockefeller Foundation 64
Romanticism 28
Rossbach, Ed 132
Rotterdam 237
Pendrecht district 237, *240–41*
Rotterdam Department for Urban Development and Reconstruction 237
Rubin, Barbara 271
Ruchti, Jacob 80
Ruiz, Miguel 148
Russian Constructivism 130
Russian Revolution 277
Ruttmann, Walter
Lichtspiel Opus I–IV (Light Play Opus I–IV) 257

S
Santa Rosa Junior College Art Gallery *88*
Santiniketan, India 16, *19*, 36–52
São Paulo 146, 148
São Paulo Biennial 80
Sarkar, Benoy
visual identity for Indian Airlines *218*
Saville, Peter 278
Schaefer, Philipp 197
Scheffler, Béla 188, 193
Scheper, Hinnerk
colour designs for the Narkomfin Building, Moscow *164–65*
Schlemmer, Oskar 36, 179, *180–81*, 272
Die Bühne im Bauhaus (The Stage at Bauhaus) *184*
costume design for *Das Triadische Ballett* (The Triadic Ballet) *184*
Schneidratus, Werner 188
Scholl, Hans 226
Scholl, Inge 226
Scholl, Sophie 226
School of Design, Chicago 260
School of Fine Arts, Casablanca *see* École des Beaux-Arts de Casablanca
School of New Architecture and Design, Tokyo 16
Schreyer, Lothar 268, 271

Schwerdtfeger, Kurt 256, 268, 271, 272
Reflektorische Farblichtspiele (Reflecting Colour-Light-Play) *243*, 244, *258–59*
Reflektorische Lichtspiele (reflecting light plays) 256–57, 268
Scritti Politti 281
Second World War 64, 161, 193
'Seikatsu Kōsei Exhibition', Tokyo (1931) 72
Seikatsu Kōsei Kenkyūsho (Research Institute of Life Construction), Tokyo 16
Seinen Kenchiku-ka Club (Young Architects' Club) 64
Sekimachi, Kay 132
Sen, Jamuna 48
shadow plays 256–57
Shanghai 202, 206–11
Shanghai Urban Planning and Design Institute
Greater Shanghai Plan *167*
Sharon, Arieh 228–32
Kibbutz + Bauhaus: An Architect's Way in a New Land 228
University of Ife 228–32, *229–31*, *233–34*
Sharon, Eldar
University of Ife *229–31*, *233–4*
Shin Kenchiku Kōgei Gakuin (School of New Architecture and Design), Tokyo 16, 56, 59, 64, 66
Shiseidō gallery, Tokyo 59
Simpsons of Piccadilly, London *248*
Sir J. J. Institute of Applied Art, Bombay 224
Smith, Paul J. 137
Socialist Realism 160
Sommerville, Ian 272
Souss 118
South Africa 193
South America 80, 134, 193, 228
Soviet Association of Architects 188
Soviet Union 237
Bauhaus émigrés in 160, 188–93
Five-Year Plans 160, 161, 190
industrialization 190
Palace of the Soviets competition 190, 194–97
show trials 190
Spengler, Oswald 109
Sriniketan, India 52
Stalin, Joseph 194–97, *195–96*, *198–99*, **277**
Stam, Mart 237
Stam-Beese, Lotte, 237, *238–41*
Steele, Jeffrey 277
Sterling, Linder 278
Stettin 256, 268
De Stijl 28, 130, 160, 174
Stoller, Claude 224
Stölzl, Gunta 98, 102, 174
stroboscopic light 13, 244, 272
Strzygowski, Josef 109
sumi-ink drawing 66, 67
Switzerland 160, 190, 193
Sydow, Eckart von
Die Kunst der Naturvölker und der Vorzeit (The Art of Indigenous Peoples and of Prehistory) 98
'synthetic art' 56
Sztálinváros, Hungary 193

T
Tagore, Abanindranath 38
Tagore, Rabindranath 16, 28, *29–31*, 36–38, 41, 44, 51
'The Hermitage' 36
Sahaj Path 51
Tagore, Rathindranath 49, *49*
Taiwan 160
Takehisa, Yumeji 66
Takei, Katsuo
Kōsei Kyōiku Taikei (Manual for Teaching Thinking through Construction) 16, *23*, 56, 64, 66–67, 68, *69–70*
Takiguchi, Shūzō 67
Tamagawa Gakuen school 67
Taut, Bruno 64, 188
Tavares, Paulo
Des-Habitat. Revista das artes no Brasil 150, *151–57*
Tawney, Lenore 132, 137
Orinoco 136, 137
Peruvian 137, *138–39*
Shield II 140–41
Shield IV 137
Woven Forms 137
Teinosuke, Nakata 28
Tel Aviv 232
Tenshin, Okakura 38
Teshigahara, Sōfū 66
textiles
Andean 128–30, 132–37
planning colour 142–44, *143*, *145*
weaving workshops 98, 102, 128–34, *129*
'Textiles and Ornamental Arts of India', New York (1955) 212–16, *214*
Tezuka, Matashirō 67
Thatcher, Margaret 278
The Architects Collaborative (TAC) 206–11
Thubron, Harry 244
Tiwanaku peoples 130
Tokyo 16, 56
Toltec people 148
Tolziner, Philipp 188, *189*, 190, 193
Expelled Bauhäusler on Their Way to the Station 162
Studie zur Periodizität des Lebensraum (Study of the Periodicity of the Habitat) *163*
Tovey, Frank 281
Berg 282
Das Triadische Ballett (The Triadic Ballet) *184*
The Trip, Los Angeles *273*
Tunghai University, Taiwan *210*, 211
Tunisia 98, *100–01*, 102, 122
Turkey 193

U
UFA-Theater, Berlin 268
Ukraine 237
Ulm Foundation Programme 216
UNESCO 216
UNICEF 226
UNIDO-ICSID conference, Ahmedabad, India (1979) *220–21*
United Board of Christian Colleges in China 206
United Nations Industrial Development Organization (UNIDO) 161, 222
United States of America 228
Bauhaus émigrés 160, 260
and the Bauhaus's 'media surround' 244
and India 212
Untitled (Fantasy Architecture with Three-gated Propylons) 100
Urals 193
Urban, Antonin 188, *189*, 190, 193
USCO 272
Ushiyama, Genichirō
Shin-Seikatsu-Bi-no-Houkou (The Direction of New Beauty in Life) 67

V
VanDerBeek, Stan 244, *252*
Velvet Underground 272, *273*
Versailles, Treaty of (1919) 277
Vidal, Lux
Grafismo indígena (Indigenous Graphic Design) 147
Vienna 80, 268
Village Voice 271
Visva-Bharati (Indian universe), Santiniketan, India 38
Visva-Bharati News 37
Vitra 179
Vyas, Kumar 224

W
Wagner, Martin 260
Wagner, Richard 271
Wakayama, Japan *24–25*
Warhol, Andy 272, *273–75*
Eat 271
Empire 271
Haircut 271
Sleep 271
Wari peoples 130
Warsaw 197
weaving *see* textiles
Weber, Otto 106
Weimar, Germany
Bauhaus exhibition 256
Lantern Festival 256
see also Bauhaus
Weiner, Tibor 188, *189*, 190, *192*, 193
Werkbund 36, 41, 226
Werkkunstschule Stettin (Stettin School of Applied Arts) 256, 268
West Germany 244
Westheim, Paul 106
Wiener, Norbert 226
Wildenhain, Marguerite 80
pamphlet for exhibition *88*

Wilson, Harold 281
Wingler, Hans Maria 260
Wise, Gillian 277
Woermann, Karl
Geschichte der Kunst aller Zeiten und Völker (Art History of All Times and Peoples) 106
world art, books on 106–10
'Woven Forms', New York (1963) 137
Wright, Frank Lloyd 28

X
Xingu 146

Y
Yale University 132–34
Yamamuro, Mitsuko 66, 67
Yamawaki, Iwao 28, 59, 64, 66
'About the Tendency of Tubular Furniture in Germany' *60*
Bauhaus und Bäuhausler, dessau – berlin 62–63
Der Schlag gegen das Bauhaus (The Attack on the Bauhaus) 28
'Tamae Ōno and Michiko Yamawaki in Berlin' *23*
Yamawaki, Michiko *23*, 28, 64, 66
Bauhaus und Bäuhausler, dessau – berlin 62–63
Yanomani people 147
Yoruba art 232

Z
Zeckendorf, William 211
Zeisler, Claire 132
Zen Buddhism 67
Zhang Guangyu
Modern Craft and Art 202, *203–05*
Monkey Makes Havoc in the Heaven 202
Žoltovsky, Ivan 194

Page 4
László Moholy-Nagy (design), Stefan Sebök (drawing), *Die Mechanik des Lichtrequisits* (Mechanics of the Light Prop), 1930, watercolour, black ink and pencil, mounted on masonite, diameter: 52 cm

Page 8
Josef Albers, *Shrine*, from the series 'Graphic Tectonic', 1942, lithograph, 61 × 48.3 cm

This book documents the international research project bauhaus imaginista, curated by Marion von Osten and Grant Watson, a common project of the Bauhaus Kooperation Berlin Dessau Weimar, Goethe-Institut and Haus der Kulturen der Welt, funded by the German Ministry of Foreign Affairs and Federal Cultural Foundation, on the occasion of the centenary '100 years of bauhaus'.

First published in the United Kingdom in 2019 by Thames & Hudson Ltd, 181A High Holborn, London WC1V 7QX

Editors: Marion von Osten and Grant Watson
Associate editor: Jill Winder
Picture research: Iris Ströbel
Design: Daly & Lyon

Translations: French to English (Melehi), Maria Vlotides; German to English (Bittner, Droste, Eggelhöfer, Hiller, Holert, Leeb), Karl Hoffmann; Japanese to English (Umemiya), Helena Čapková, (Kaneko) Yoshimasa Kaneko; Portuguese to English (Krenak/Fonteles), Pablo Lafuente; Spanish to English (Espejo), Pablo Lafuente

British Library Cataloguing-in-Publication Data
A catalogue record for this book is available from the British Library

ISBN 978-0-500-02193-4

Printed and bound in China by C&C Offset Printing Co. Ltd

bauhaus imaginista

Project partners

Goethe Institut · bauhaus kooperation berlin dessau weimar · HKW Haus der Kulturen der Welt

Funded by

Federal Government Commissioner for Culture and the Media · Federal Foreign Office · Kulturstiftung des Bundes

Media partners

3sat · Deutschlandfunk Kultur

On the occasion of

100 jahre bauhaus

Institutional partners

Le Cube – Independent Art Room, Rabat, and Goethe-Institut Rabat, Morocco

China Design Museum/China Academy of Art, Hangzhou, China

The Independent Administrative Institution of National Museum of Art/National Museum of Modern Art Kyoto, Japan

Garage Museum of Contemporary Art, Moscow, Russia

SESC Pompéia São Paulo, Brazil

Haus der Kulturen der Welt, Berlin, Germany

Zentrum Paul Klee, Bern, Switzerland,

Nottingham Contemporary, Nottingham, United Kingdom

Kiran Nadar Museum of Art, New Delhi, India